# A Brief History of Chinese and Japanese Civilizations

## Third Edition

**Conrad Schirokauer**
*Senior Scholar, Columbia University*

**Miranda Brown**
*University of Michigan*

**David Lurie**
*Columbia University*

**Suzanne Gay**
*Oberlin College*

Australia • Brazil • Canada • Mexico • Singapore
Spain • United Kingdom • United States

**THOMSON**

**WADSWORTH**

*A Brief History of Chinese and Japanese Civilizations,*
**Third Edition**
Conrad Schirokauer, Senior Scholar, Columbia University
Miranda Brown, University of Michigan
David Lurie, Columbia University
Suzanne Gay, Oberlin College

Publisher: *Clark Baxter*
Assistant Editor: *Paul Massicotte*
Editorial Assistant: *Lucinda Bingham*
Technology Project Manager: *David Lionetti*
Marketing Manager: *Lori Grebe Cook*
Marketing Assistant: *Teresa Jessen*
Project Manager, Editorial Production: *Katy German*
Creative Director: *Rob Hugel*
Art Director: *Maria Epes*

Print Buyer: *Judy Inouye*
Permissions Editor: *Stephanie Lee*
Production Service: *Graphic World Inc.*
Text & Cover Designer: *Andrew Ogus*
Photo Researcher: *Terri Wright*
Copy Editor: *Graphic World Inc.*
Cover Image: *Tsutsugaki Dye Work: Celebratory Indigo. Japan Folk Crafts Museum, Tokyo, Japan.*
Printer: *Quebecor World-Taunton*

For more information about our products, contact us at:
**Thomson Learning Academic Resource Center**
**1-800-423-0563**
For permisson to use material from this text or product, submit a request online at **http://www.thomsonrights.com**
Any additional questions about permissions can be submitted by email to **thomsonrights@thomson.com**.

Library of Congress Control Number: 2005925208

ISBN 0-534-64307-8

*Dedicated to our spouses: Lore, David Burke, Hikari Hori, and James Dobbins*
*our children:*
*David & Oliver, Emily & Jeffrey*
*and representing the next generation:*
*Leo Kipton and Somiya*

# Contents

# Part Three: A New and Crucial Phase  203

# Preface

A revised edition such as this demands a new preface, because there is much about this book that is new. Most significantly, what was a solo has become a quartet, extending our range and enriching our sound.

Before saying something about our collaboration, we need to affirm that some things said in earlier editions still apply. Certainly, the reasons for studying China and Japan are as urgent as ever and still can be subsumed under three broad headings: the richness of their long historical record, which forms such an important part of the total history of the human race and illuminates the nature of the human condition; the enduring value of their cultural achievements; and the contemporary importance of the world's most populated country and the second strongest economy. Setting aside China and Japan's contemporary importance, surely some acquaintance with their civilizations is required of one who would be educated, because to be educated means to be able to see beyond the narrow geographic, temporal, and cultural bounds of one's immediate neighborhood. Indeed, it entails the ability to see oneself in a broader perspective, including that of history. In this day and age, that means not only the history of one's own tribe, state, or even civilization but also, ideally, the history of all humans—because it is all our history.

That history is woven of many strands, so we have economic and political history and the study of social structure, thought, and art. This text is based on the belief that an introduction to the history of a civilization requires consideration of all these facets of human activity, a general mapping out of the terrain so that the beginner may find his or her bearings and learn enough to consider in which direction to explore further, with some idea of the rewards to be gained for the effort. An introduction, then, is not a catalog (although it should contain basic data) or a personal synthesis or summation, nor is it the proper vehicle for extending the expanding frontiers of present knowledge. Instead, it should, among other things, introduce the reader to the conventions of a field of study and attempt to convey the state of our present understanding. The basic aim of this text, then, is to provide orientation. Thus where applicable, the standard dynastic framework provides the basic historical chronology. We have further decided to replace the B.C. and A.D. of previous editions with B.C.E. and C.E. (before and in the common era) because that seemed most appropriate for a twenty-first-century (C.E.!) book. It also appears to have become standard—especially, but not exclusively—among students of the history of religion.

History is the study of change and continuity, and both elements are always present. Neither the people we study nor we ourselves begin with a blank slate, and our task is not to choose between change and continuity but the more challenging one of weighing the change within the continuity and the continuity within the change. Such a determination requires, in the final analysis, as much art as science, and no assessment is ever final. This is so not only because of the continual discovery of new evidence and new techniques (for example, in the dating of materials) but also because scholars' intellectual frameworks and analytic concepts change, and we all learn to ask new questions. Even if that was not the case, history would have to be rewritten at intervals, inasmuch as the ultimate significance of any individual historical episode depends, in the final analysis, on the whole story: as long as history is unfinished, so is its writing.

If this is true of all history, it seems especially so with the history of East Asia, about which we know a great deal more now than we did just a generation ago. Nevertheless, the areas of our ignorance continue to be enormous. Etienne Balazs (1905–1963) once compared students of China with Lilliputians clambering over the Gulliver that is Chinese history, and his words are still apt. Indeed, one of the continuing attractions of the field is that it offers great opportunities to the intellectually adventurous and hardy to work on major problems. Our hope is that the very inadequacies of a text such as this will spur some readers on to these endeavors. Thus, for this text to succeed, it must fail: readers must come away hungry, their appetites whetted but not satiated.

A broad survey such as this is by necessity based on the studies of many scholars (indeed, our pleasure in wide reading is matched only by our fear of inadvertent plagiarism). No attempt has been made to list all the works consulted. The suggested readings in the Appendix have been drawn up in the hope of meeting some readers' needs, not of acknowledging our indebtedness, although there is considerable overlap. It is also impossible to list all the individuals who contributed to this textbook by offering suggestions, criticism, and encouragement, or who helped by suggesting references, supplying a date or a translation for a term, and so forth. Similarly, we are unable to acknowledge individually the teachers, students, and colleagues who have influenced our thoughts about the broader problems of history, about Japan and China, and about the teaching of these subjects. As in previous editions, however, the senior author, Conrad Schirokauer, wants to single out Professor Arthur F. Wright (1913–1976), scholar and humanist, whom he had the privilege of knowing as both teacher and friend. Similarly, we want to express our admiration and thanks for David Keightley, although only Miranda Brown had the pleasure of taking his History 116A, which brimmed with good illustrations, colorful anecdotes, and scholarly controversy, and among other things, laid the foundations for her contributions to this textbook. If it were not for that course, her career would have taken a different shape. Similarly, David Lurie is grateful to Wayne Farris and Joan Piggott for the inspiration provided by their work and for the generosity with which they encouraged his explorations of early

Japanese history. Suzanne Gay looks regularly to Japanese historians of the medieval period but also credits scholars in the West, such as Mary Elizabeth Berry, Hitomi Tonomura, and Andrew Goble, for extending the foundational work of John W. Hall.

In recent years scholarship has been so productive, as well as specialized, that it has become impossible for one person to keep up with it all, but we owe a debt to the membership of the University Seminars at Columbia and the Michigan Center for Chinese Studies' brown bag series. Their role in keeping us informed on scholarly trends has been indispensable. Furthermore, at Michigan, Bill Baxter has been an exceptionally helpful colleague and a reliable source of good cheer and of stimulating, almost daily, early China talk. At Columbia, Schirokauer also wants to thank the members of the Department of East Asian Languages and Cultures, including fellow senior scholars Pei-yi Wu and Arthur Tiedemann, as well as Wm. Theodore de Bary, whose contributions and accomplishments are far too numerous to list here, but include founding the Society for Senior Scholars. Also at Columbia, Lurie would like to thank his friends and comrades in teaching the Japanese history survey, Max Moerman and Greg Pflugfelder, for their advice, encouragement, and flexibility.

Although our interests remain broad, in the present edition there is a clear temporal division of responsibility, with Brown responsible for the first three chapters. Lurie was primarily responsible for Chapter 6, with an occasional assist from Schirokauer. Lurie also made revisions to Chapter 7 and suggested a few improvements to Chapter 11, which Gay helped to bring up to date; she also made a major contribution to Chapter 12. Schirokauer is responsible for the remainder of the book but wants to point out that the "modern" (post-1600) chapters already appeared in *Modern East Asia: A Brief History*.

That we are different people is obvious at first sight: two of us are at the beginning of our careers, charging up the tenure hill at full steam; another as a department chair may be said to be perched at the top of the hill; and the remaining author unabashedly claims senior discounts on trains and planes but not in his scholarly endeavors and hopes to demonstrate, to some at least, that he is not yet "over the hill." That we enjoyed our collaboration augurs well for the future. We have maintained our own voices and views even as we encourage our readers to develop their own.

Miranda Brown
Suzanne Gay
David Lurie
Conrad Schirokauer

# Acknowledgments

We need to acknowledge those who contributed so much to the previous edition of this book and its precursors but will limit ourselves here to naming those directly involved in the present edition. These include Clark Baxter, Paul Massicotte, and the entire Wadsworth team as listed on the copyright page.

Foremost among the people specifically involved in making this book possible is Michael Nylan, who brought Schirokauer and Brown together and remains a major force shaping our understanding of early China. We want to thank the scholars whose critical reading of parts of the manuscript saved us from many an error of commission or omission, even though we did not always follow their advice. Several prefer to remain anonymous, but we can and do acknowledge Mark Csikszentmihalyi, Robert Hymes, Jeffrey Barlow, Suzanne Cahill, Craig Canning, Wayne Farris, W. Dean Kinzley, Fred G. Notehelfer, Margaret J. Pearson, and Marcia Yonemoto.

Among those at Columbia, Li Feng merits special mention, as do the young scholars with whom Schirokauer has cotaught East Asian courses during the past few years, listed in chronological order: Jaret Weisfogel, Letty Chen, Naomi Fukumori, Katherine Rupp, Suzanne O'Brien, Nicole Cohen, Yasu Makimura, and Kerry Ross.

Also at Columbia, Lurie is grateful to the students in his Japan Civ. classes of Spring and Fall 2003 and especially to his teaching assistants: Adam Clulow, Michael Emmerich, Eric Han, Federico Marcon, and Leila Wice. He also thanks Adam Clulow and Steve Wills for reading parts of the manuscript and providing invaluable suggestions for their improvement. We all want to thank our students for fresh perspectives and ideas, with very special thanks to the Winter 2004 Asian 455 class at Michigan, good-humored guinea pigs on a test drive through all material presented in Chapters 1 through 3.

Also deserving special mention are the staff of the Starr East Asian Library at Columbia for their help with books. For help in manuscript production and reproduction, we wish to thank Lenore Szekely, a graduate student of Chinese literature at Michigan, and Diana Nobile-Hernandez of the Heyman Center at Columbia.

Our greatest debt is to our families who have lived with this book and to whom it is dedicated. Lore, also known as Mrs. Schirokauer, not only helped in innumerable direct and indirect ways but also contributed greatly to the artwork, which includes several of her own photographs.

Miranda Brown
Suzanne Gay
David Lurie
Conrad Schirokauer

# *About the Authors*

Conrad Schirokauer currently serves as Senior Scholar and Adjunct Professor at Columbia University as well as Professor Emeritus at the City University of New York. In addition to *A Brief History of Chinese and Japanese Civilizations* (and its separate volumes on China and Japan), he has published articles on Song intellectual history and served as co-editor (with Robert Hymes) of *Ordering the World: Approaches to State and Society in Sung Dynasty China* and as translator of *China's Examination Hell,* by Miyazaki Ichisada.

Miranda Brown is a Professor in the Department of Asian Languages and Cultures at the University of Michigan in Ann Arbor. Her published work has dealt with the history of the family in pre-modern China, as well as elite burial practices.

David Lurie is an Assistant Professor in the Department of East Asian Languages and Cultures at Columbia University. His research concerns writing systems in Japan and, more broadly, in pre-modern East Asia; he also works on the cultural, intellectual, and literary history of Japan through the Heian Period. He is currently completing a manuscript titled *Realms of Literacy: Early Japan and the History of Writing.*

Suzanne Gay is a Professor of East Asian Studies at Oberlin College. Her research interests include the social and economic history of medieval Japan, with a particular emphasis on the role of commoners in history. Her monograph, *The Moneylenders of Late Medieval Kyoto,* was published by University of Hawaii Press in 2001.

The master map shows both the agricultural regions that comprise what most scholars call China proper. It also shows the vast areas of Inner Asia and other lands beyond the Great Wall, which have only recently become incorporated into China today. Whereas the former were largely inhabited by the ancestors of the modern Chinese, who were settled agricultural peoples, the latter were inhabited by generally nomadic peoples.

With the area that now comprises China proper, the basic geographical division is between North and South. This division gave rise to two different agricultural traditions from around 5000 B.C.E. The outstanding geographical feature of the North is the Yellow River, which flows from the highlands of the West, through the alluvial lowlands of the Central Plain to empty into the sea near the Shandong Peninsula. At present, the Yellow River valley is a region of temperate climate, cold winters and warm summers, but rainfall is scarce. This is particularly true in the arid west, but in the moister areas as well, the annual rainfall is extremely variable. Although the area is subject to drought, the soil is fertile. It is a region suitable for growing millet and, in moister parts, wheat and beans.

At present, very different conditions prevail south of a line that runs roughly along the 33rd parallel, following the Qinling Mountains and the Huai River. Here, rain is abundant, the climate is subtropical, and the soils are leached. The dominant river is the Yangzi, which is about 3,200 miles long. (Hence, the Yangzi is also called the Chang jiang or "Long River"). Once the necessary technology was developed and the land was laboriously drained over several centuries, this region proved ideal for intensive rice culture.

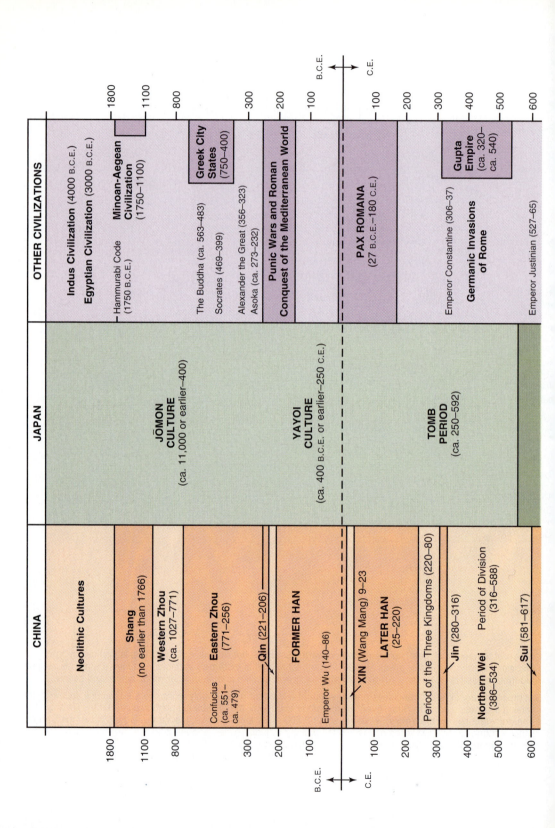

| CHINA | JAPAN | OTHER CIVILIZATIONS |
|---|---|---|
| | | Indus Civilization (4000 B.C.E.) |
| | | Egyptian Civilization (3000 B.C.E.) |
| Neolithic Cultures | | Minoan-Aegean Civilization (1750–1100) |
| Shang (no earlier than 1766) | JŌMON CULTURE (ca. 11,000 or earlier–400) | Hammurabi Code (1750 B.C.E.) |
| Western Zhou (ca. 1027–771) | | Greek City States (750–400) |
| Eastern Zhou (771–256) | | The Buddha (ca. 563–483) Socrates (469–399) |
| Confucius (ca. 551– ca. 479) | | Alexander the Great (356–323) Asoka (ca. 273–232) |
| Qin (221–206) | YAYOI CULTURE (ca. 400 B.C.E. or earlier–250 C.E.) | Punic Wars and Roman Conquest of the Mediterranean World |
| FORMER HAN | | |
| Emperor Wu (140–86) | | PAX ROMANA (27 B.C.E.–180 C.E.) |
| XIN (Wang Mang) 9–23 | | |
| LATER HAN (25–220) | | |
| Period of the Three Kingdoms (220–80) | TOMB PERIOD (ca. 250–592) | Emperor Constantine (306–37) |
| Jin (280–316) Period of Division (316–588) | | Germanic Invasions of Rome |
| Northern Wei (386–534) | | Gupta Empire (ca. 320– ca. 540) |
| Sui (581–617) | | Emperor Justinian (527–65) |

B.C.E. 1800 1100 800 300 200 100
C.E. 100 200 300 400 500 600

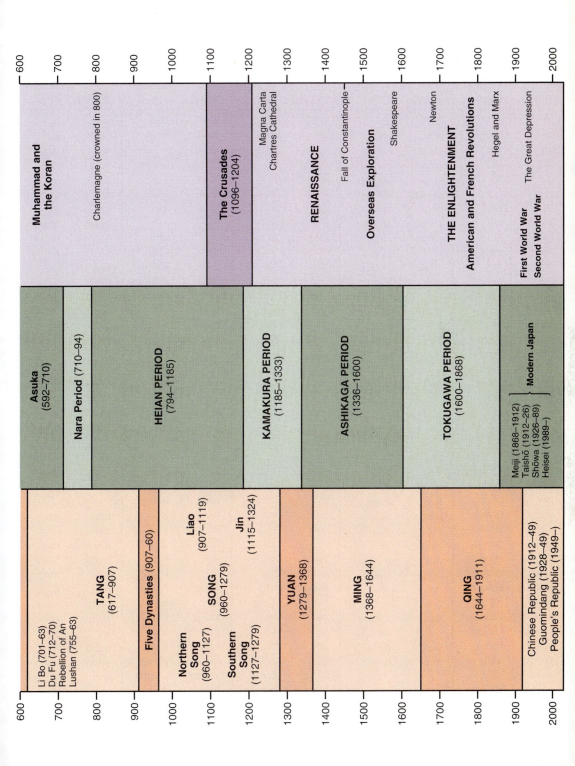

600 700 800 900 1000 1100 1200 1300 1400 1500 1600 1700 1800 1900 2000

**Muhammad and the Koran**

Charlemagne (crowned in 800)

**The Crusades (1096–1204)**

Magna Carta
Chartres Cathedral

Fall of Constantinople

**RENAISSANCE**

**Overseas Exploration**

Shakespeare

Newton

**THE ENLIGHTENMENT**

**American and French Revolutions**

Hegel and Marx

The Great Depression

**First World War**
**Second World War**

Asuka (592–710)

Nara Period (710–94)

**HEIAN PERIOD (794–1185)**

**KAMAKURA PERIOD (1185–1333)**

**ASHIKAGA PERIOD (1336–1600)**

**TOKUGAWA PERIOD (1600–1868)**

Meiji (1868–1912)
Taishō (1912–26)
Shōwa (1926–89)
Heisei (1989–)

**Modern Japan**

Li Bo (701–63)
Du Fu (712–70)
Rebellion of An Lushan (755–63)

**TANG (617–907)**

**Five Dynasties (907–60)**

Liao (907–1119)

**Northern Song (960–1127)**

**SONG (960–1279)**

Jin (1115–1324)

**Southern Song (1127–1279)**

**YUAN (1279–1368)**

**MING (1368–1644)**

**QING (1644–1911)**

Chinese Republic (1912–49)
Guomindang (1928–49)
People's Republic (1949–)

600 700 800 900 1000 1100 1200 1300 1400 1500 1600 1700 1800 1900 2000

# Hanyu Pinyin to Wade-Giles Conversion Table

| Pinyin | Wade-Giles |
|---|---|
| a | a |
| ai | ai |
| an | an |
| ang | ang |
| ao | ao |
| ba | pa |
| bai | pai |
| ban | pan |
| hang | pang |
| bao | pao |
| bei | pei |
| hen | pen |
| beng | peng |
| bi | pi |
| bian | pien |
| biao | piao |
| bie | pieh |
| bin | pin |
| bing | ping |
| bo | po |
| bou | pou |
| bu | pu |
| ca | ts'a |
| cai | ts'ai |
| can | ts'an |
| cang | ts'ang |
| cao | ts'ao |
| ce | ts'e |
| cen | ts'en |
| ceng | ts'eng |
| cha | ch'a |
| chai | ch'ai |
| chan | ch'an |
| chang | ch'ang |
| chao | ch'ao |
| che | ch'e |
| chen | ch'en |
| cheng | ch'eng |
| chi | ch'ih |
| chong | ch'ung |

| Pinyin | Wade-Giles |
|---|---|
| chou | ch'ou |
| chu | ch'u |
| chua | ch'ua |
| chuai | ch'uai |
| chuan | ch'uan |
| chuang | ch'uang |
| chui | ch'ui |
| chun | ch'un |
| chuo | ch'o |
| ci | tz'u |
| cong | ts'ung |
| cou | ts'ou |
| cu | ts'u |
| cuan | ts'uan |
| cui | ts'ui |
| cun | ts'un |
| cuo | ts'o |
| da | ta |
| dai | tai |
| dan | tan |
| dang | tang |
| dao | tao |
| de | te |
| deng | teng |
| di | ti |
| than | then |
| diao | tiao |
| die | tieh |
| ding | ting |
| diu | tiu |
| dong | tung |
| dou | tou |
| du | tu |
| duan | tuan |
| dui | tui |
| dun | tun |
| duo | to |
| e | o |
| en | en |
| er | erh |

| Pinyin | Wade-Giles |
|---|---|
| fa | fa |
| fan | fan |
| fang | fang |
| fei | fei |
| fen | fen |
| feng | feng |
| fo | fo |
| fou | fou |
| fu | fu |
| ga | ka |
| gai | kai |
| gan | kan |
| gang | kang |
| gao | kao |
| ge | ko |
| gei | kei |
| gen | ken |
| geng | keng |
| gong | kung |
| gou | kou |
| gu | ku |
| gua | kua |
| guai | kuai |
| guan | kuan |
| guang | kuang |
| gui | kuei |
| gun | kun |
| guo | kuo |
| ha | ha |
| hai | hai |
| han | han |
| hang | hang |
| hao | hao |
| he | ho |
| hei | hei |
| hen | hen |
| heng | heng |
| hong | hung |
| hou | hou |
| hu | hu |

| Pinyin | Wade-Giles |
|---|---|
| hua | hua |
| huai | huai |
| huan | huan |
| huang | huang |
| hui | hui |
| hun | hun |
| huo | huo |
| ji | chi |
| jia | chia |
| jian | chien |
| jiang | chiang |
| jiao | chiao |
| jie | chieh |
| jin | chin |
| jing | ching |
| jiong | chiung |
| jiu | chiu |
| ju | chü |
| juan | chüan |
| jue | chüeh |
| jun | chün |
| ka | k'a |
| kai | k'ai |
| kan | k'an |
| kang | k'ang |
| kao | k'ao |
| ke | k'o |
| kei | k'ei |
| ken | k'en |
| keng | k'eng |
| kong | k'ung |
| kou | k'ou |
| ku | k'u |
| kua | k'ua |
| kuai | k'uai |
| kuan | k'uan |
| kuang | k'uang |
| kui | k'uei |
| kun | k'un |
| kuo | k'uo |

| Pinyin | Wade-Giles |
|---|---|
| la | la |
| lai | lai |
| lan | lan |
| lang | lang |
| lao | lao |
| le | le |
| lei | lei |
| leng | leng |
| li | li |
| lia | lia |
| lian | lien |
| liang | liang |
| liao | liao |
| lie | lieh |
| lin | lin |
| ling | ling |
| liu | liu |
| long | lung |
| lou | lou |
| lu | lu |
| lü | lü |
| luan | luan |
| lüan | lüan |
| lue | lüeh |
| lun | lun |
| luo | lo |
| ma | ma |
| mai | mai |
| man | man |
| mang | mang |
| mao | mao |
| mei | mei |
| men | men |
| meng | meng |
| mi | mi |
| mian | mien |
| miao | miao |
| mie | mieh |
| min | min |
| ming | ming |
| miu | miu |
| mo | mo |
| mou | mou |
| mu | mu |

| Pinyin | Wade-Giles | Pinyin | Wade-Giles | Pinyin | Wade-Giles | Pinyin | Wade-Giles | Pinyin | Wade-Giles |
|---|---|---|---|---|---|---|---|---|---|
| na | na | | | shao | shao | wa | wa | zan | tsan |
| nai | nai | qi | ch'i | she | she | wai | wai | zang | tsang |
| nan | nan | qia | ch'ia | shen | shen | wan | wan | zao | tsao |
| nang | nang | qian | ch'ien | sheng | sheng | wang | wang | ze | tse |
| nao | nao | qiang | ch'iang | shi | shih | wei | wei | zei | tsei |
| nei | nei | qiao | ch'iao | shou | shou | wen | wen | zen | tsen |
| nen | nen | qie | ch'ieh | shu | shu | weng | weng | zeng | tseng |
| neng | neng | qin | ch'in | shua | shua | wo | wo | zha | cha |
| ni | ni | qing | ch'ing | shuai | shuai | wu | wu | zhai | chai |
| nian | nien | qiong | ch'iung | shuan | shuan | | | zhan | chan |
| niang | niang | qiu | ch'iu | shuang | shuang | xi | hsi | zhang | chang |
| niao | niao | qu | ch'ü | shui | shui | xia | hsia | zhao | chao |
| nie | nieh | quan | ch'üan | shun | shun | xian | hsien | zhe | che |
| nin | nin | que | ch'üeh | shuo | shuo | xiang | hsiang | zhen | chen |
| ning | ning | qun | ch'ün | si | ssu | xiao | hsiao | zheng | cheng |
| niu | niu | | | song | sung | xie | hsieh | zhi | chih |
| nong | nung | ran | jan | sou | sou | xin | hsin | zhong | chung |
| nou | nou | rang | jang | su | su | xing | hsing | zhou | chou |
| nu | nu | rao | jao | suan | suan | xiong | hsiung | zhu | chu |
| nü | nü | re | je | sui | sui | xiu | hsiu | zhua | chua |
| nuan | nuan | ren | jen | sun | sun | xu | hsü | zhuai | chuai |
| nüe | nüeh | reng | jeng | suo | so | xuan | hsüan | zhuan | chuan |
| nuo | no | ri | jih | | | xue | hsüeh | zhuang | chuang |
| | | rong | jung | ta | t'a | xun | hsün | zhui | chui |
| ou | ou | rou | jou | tai | t'ai | | | zhun | chun |
| | | ru | ju | tan | Van | ya | ya | zhuo | cho |
| pa | p'a | ruan | juan | tang | t'ang | yai | yai | zi | tzu |
| pai | p'ai | rui | jui | tao | t'ao | yan | yen | zong | tsung |
| pan | p'an | run | jun | te | t'e | yang | yang | zou | tsou |
| pang | p'ang | ruo | jo | teng | t'eng | yao | yao | zu | tsu |
| pao | p'ao | | | ti | t'i | ye | yeh | zuan | tsuan |
| pei | p'ei | sa | sa | tian | t'ien | yi | i | zui | tsui |
| pen | p'en | sai | sai | tiao | t'iao | yin | yin | zun | tsun |
| peng | p'eng | san | san | tie | t'ieh | ying | ying | zuo | tso |
| pi | p'i | sang | sang | ting | t'ing | yong | yung | | |
| pian | p'ien | sao | sao | tong | t'ung | you | yu | | |
| piao | p'iao | se | se | tou | t'ou | yu | yü | | |
| pie | p'ieh | sen | sen | tu | t'u | yuan | yüan | | |
| pin | p'in | seng | seng | tuan | t'uan | yue | yüeh | | |
| ping | p'ing | sha | sha | tui | t'ui | yun | yün | | |
| po | p'o | shai | shai | tun | tun | | | | |
| pou | p'ou | shan | shan | tuo | t'o | za | tsa | | |
| pu | p'u | shang | shang | | | zai | tsai | | |

Source: *People's Republic of China: Administrative Atlas* (Washington, D.C.: Central Intelligence Agency, 1975), 46–47.

# Wade-Giles to Pinyin Conversion Table

Each entry in the Wade-Giles column represents the initial letter or letter pair of a syllable or word. Unless otherwise indicated, conversion is accomplished simply by changing that initial letter. Where other changes are necessary or the conversion is irregular, the entire word or syllable is listed.

| Wade-Giles | Pinyin | Wade-Giles | Pinyin | Wade-Giles | Pinyin | Wade-Giles | Pinyin |
|---|---|---|---|---|---|---|---|
| a | a | ch'en | chen | i | yi | p'ien | pian |
| | | ch'eng | cheng | | | | |
| cha | zha | ch'i | qi | j | r | s | s |
| chai | zhai | ch'ia | qia | jih | ri | shih | shi |
| chan | zhan | ch'iang | qiang | jo | ruo | so | suo |
| chang | zhang | ch'iao | qiao | jung | rong | sung | song |
| chao | zhao | ch'ieh | qie | | | ssu, szu | si |
| che | zhe | ch'ien | qian | k | g | | |
| chen | zhen | ch'i | chi | ko | ge | t | d |
| cheng | zheng | ch'in | qin | kuei | gui | tieh | dieh |
| chi | ji | ch'ing | qing | kung | gong | tien | dian |
| chia | jia | ch'iu | qiu | | | to | duo |
| chiao | jiao | ch'iung | qiong | k' | k | tung | dong |
| chieh | jie | ch'o | chuo | k'o | ke | | |
| chien | jian | ch'ou | chou | k'ung | kong | t' | t |
| chih | zhi | ch'u | chu | | | t'ieh | tie |
| chin | jin | ch'ü | qu | l | l | t'ien | tian |
| ching | jing | ch'uai | chuai | lieh | lie | t'o | tuo |
| chiu | jiu | ch'uan | chuan | lien | han | t'ung | tong |
| chiung | jiong | ch'üan | quan | lo | luo | | |
| cho | zhuo | ch'uang | chuang | lüeh | lüe | ts, tz | z |
| chou | zhou | ch'üeh | que | lung | long | tso | zuo |
| chu | zhu | ch'ui | chui | | | tsung | zong |
| chü | ju | ch'un | chun | m | m | tzu | zi |
| chua | zhua | ch'ün | qun | mieh | mie | | |
| chuai | zhuai | ch'ung | chong | mien | mian | ts', tz' | c |
| chuan | zhuan | | | | | ts'o | cuo |
| chüan | juan | f | f | n | n | ts'ung | cong |
| chuang | zhuang | | | nieh | nie | tz'u | ci |
| chüeh | jue | h | h | nien | nian | | |
| chui | zhui | ho | he | no | nuo | w | w |
| chun | zhun | hung | hong | nüeh | ne | | |
| chün | jun | | | | | y | y |
| chung | zhong | hs | x | o | o | yeh | ye |
| | | hsieh | xie | | | yen | yan |
| ch'a | cha | hsien | xian | p | b | yu | you |
| ch'ai | chai | hsiung | xiong | pieh | bie | yü | yu |
| ch'an | chan | hsü | xu | pien | bian | yüan | yuan |
| ch'ang | chang | hsüan | xuan | | | yüeh | yue |
| ch'ao | chao | hsüeh | xue | p' | p | yün | yun |
| ch'e | che | hsün | xun | p'ieh | pie | yung | yong |

# Part One

# The Classical Civilization of China

The first part of our book examines the beginnings of Chinese civilization and takes the story through the Han dynasty. It was a classical age in that it produced books later venerated as authoritative not only in China but also in Japan and elsewhere in East Asia. It was also during this period that many institutional, intellectual, and political traditions achieved the form in which they profoundly influenced the future of the East Asian mainland and the Japanese archipelago.

By the second century C.E. horses and bronze had a long and prominent history going back to the first dynasty. In this figure the horse is balanced on a swallow as it flies off into the air and very likely off the page.

# "China" in Antiquity

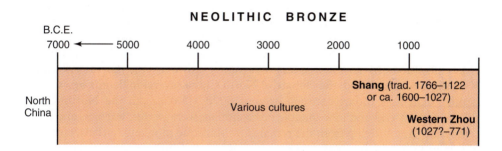

**NEOLITHIC    BRONZE**

B.C.E.

7000 ←——— 5000          4000          3000          2000          1000

North
China                                    Various cultures

**Shang** (trad. 1766–1122
or ca. 1600–1027)

**Western Zhou**
(1027?–771)

When and where did "Chinese" civilization begin? Forty years ago, scholars in China and elsewhere agreed that it emerged from an area now known as the North China Plains (see Master Map) five millennia ago and subsequently spread from there. Thirty years ago, however, archeologists in the People's Republic of China began to challenge this picture, and today archeological discoveries and scholarly debates provide a complicated, if not conflicting, picture of origins.

## The Neolithic Age

Most accounts of the origins of civilization on any part of the globe begin with the Neolithic, while acknowledging that human origins and societies go back much earlier. In what is now China, the first trace of humanoid remains was discovered by archeologists in 1965 in Yunnan Province. (Unless specifically indicated, all geographical designations are contemporary.) Based on this evidence, archeologists have surmised that humanoids lived as long as one million years ago in Southwest China and had the use of fire. Judging from fossil remains earlier discovered near Beijing, archeologists inferred that another kind of humanoid, the Peking man (or the *Homo erectus pekinensis*) lived about half a million years ago in North China. However, the Peking man was not an anatomically modern human, but a proto-human who used fire and worked with primitive flaked or pebble tools. Unfortunately, little else is known about the most ancient inhabitants of what became China, and scholars can only speculate about the connection between anatomically modern humans and their precursors.

Similarly, we know little about the humans who lived in East Asia during the Paleolithic but can only speculate that like elsewhere they were foragers employing crude stone tools. It is with the Neolithic that we begin to have more solid evidence. The Neolithic Age (or new stone age) began in China about 10,000 years ago. *Neolithic* is a term used by archeologists to describe cultures that use polished stone implements, as distinguished from the cruder implements of earlier ages. Neolithic cultures are also distinguished by their pottery and are often associated with agriculture and fixed human settlements. As in a number of other places on the globe, agriculture arose in China some 10,000 years ago, apparently more or less simultaneously in South and North China. In the South, archeologists found evidence of rice cultivation as well as the raising of dogs and pigs in Jiangxi Province. Then, as now, the South provided a warm, wet climate well suited for rice cultivation. Meanwhile, millet cultivation arose in the north. As David Keightley recently noted, the climate of North China several millennia ago was far gentler than it is today: between around 6000–1000 B.C.E., the North China plains, now an arid and inhospitable environment, were wetter, warmer, and more temperate. And judging from the remains of Macaque monkeys, jackals, and even alligators found in the fossil record, parts of North China may have been a sub-tropical region with abundant water.[1]

Because our understanding of the early period is still very much in flux as new archeological data is discovered and analytical frameworks change, it is appropriate to introduce two accounts of "Chinese" origins.

The *nuclear area* thesis is arguably the oldest modern narrative of the origins of Chinese civilization. It received its classical formulation in the 1960s by the American-trained archeologist, Kwang-chih Chang (1931–2001), who later changed his mind. It held that Chinese civilization originated from a single culture of millet farmers, the Yangshao culture, in the North China Plains. Around 5000 B.C.E., this culture radiated outwards, extending from the Northeast coast all the way to present-day Qinghai in the distant Northwest.[2] Scholars have been able to track the diffusion of Yangshao culture based on the movement of Yangshao material culture, in particular, its colorful painted red or brown pottery (see Figure 1.1).

A second account of the origins of Chinese civilization is called the *interactive spheres* thesis. In many ways a revision of the nuclear area thesis, it argues that the Yangshao was one culture among many in the Neolithic Age and takes into account discoveries of other cultures in various parts of China, each with its own phases. Examples of these cultures include the Daxi (5000–3000

**FIGURE 1.1** Painted pottery *gang* urn (bird eating fish) from North Central China, c. 3500–3000 B.C.E. This is from the Yangshao culture. In later pottery the fish design becomes increasingly abstract. (© National Museum of China.)

**FIGURE 1.2** Map of Neolithic Age cultural sites.

B.C.E.), the Hemudu and Majiabang (5000–3000 B.C.E.), the Dalongtan, the Dapenkeng (5000–2500 B.C.E.), and the Xinle (7000–5000 B.C.E.) (see Figure 1.2). Each of these, as Chang pointed out in one of his last articles, had distinct styles of pottery. Thus, a site located in the Yangzi River valley has yielded pottery that is black in color with dark brown bands, sometimes with dragon designs painted on. In contrast, ceramic artifacts from sites in Northern Zhejiang and Jiangsu on the Eastern coast, yield pottery that was brown and black. There, archeologists have also found bone and ivory ritual artifacts decorated with or shaped in bird motifs. Unlike the millet found in Yangshao, the other sites show the presence of rice farmers. In many ways, the presence of different cultures in various locations in China should come as little surprise, given its size and geographic diversity.

According to the interactive spheres thesis, around 4000 B.C.E., a number of Neolithic cultures in the North China Plains began to trade and share technology with each other. According to Chang, many of these interacting cultures converged about a millennium later, around 3000 B.C.E. The convergence of these cultures, Chang emphasized, was to give rise to the civilization now called *China*.[3]

Although the second narrative, that of interactive spheres, has numerous merits, many scholars have challenged it. More recent accounts by archeologists and even historians studying much later texts have questioned whether China as a single, coherent civilization did emerge as early as 3000 B.C.E. Some critics, working from the material record, point out that although it is true that there was a great deal of coherence and unity to the cultures of the North China Plains, a great deal of cultural variation persisted after the Neolithic Age. And indeed, judging from the material record, there were important, but distinctive, material cultures right through the Bronze and Iron Ages up until the present day. (See the discussion of the Xingan and Sanxingdui sites later in this chapter.[4])

Meanwhile, textual scholars point out that the notion of Chinese civilization itself is a relatively recent invention. They point to the absence of a single word in *Chinese* up until the nineteenth century for *China*. Before the twentieth century, the territory that would become China was known by the name of successive dynasties, such as the *Qin*, the *Han*—or much later, as the *Great Qing state* (*da Qing guo*).[5]

In ancient times, the place now known as China was inhabited by ethnically diverse speakers of many languages belonging to different linguistic families, ten of which have been identified by linguists. Arguably the most important language family was Sino-Tibetan, a language family that later gave rise to both modern Chinese and Tibetan. A second cluster of languages still found in present-day China was Austroasiatic, probably spoken in South China in preimperial times and later giving rise to modern languages such as Vietnamese and Khmer.* A third language family was Indo-European, a language family that, among others, gave rise to modern French, English, and Hindi. Scholars know that some Indo-European speakers lived in parts of what is now Northwest China because of the discovery of manuscripts written in an Indo-European language called Tocharian and dating from around 600 C.E. Apart from these manuscripts, evidence for the presence of Indo-European speakers comes in the form of loanwords from Tocharian. Thus, the modern Chinese term for honey (*mi*) was taken from the Tocharian word for honey.[7] In addition to Sino-Tibetan, Austroasiatic, and Indo-European, the boundaries of present-day China also included Tai-Kadai (which gave rise to modern-day Zhuang), Hmong-Mien (which gave rise to Miao-Yao), Austronesian (the ancestor to the language still spoken by the original people of Taiwan), Altaic (which gave rise to Turkic languages and Mongol, as well as possibly to Korean and Japanese), and Xiongnu (which gave rise to the Yeniseian languages now spoken in Siberia).[8]

---

*The influence of Austroasiatic can still be detected through loanwords used in modern Chinese such as *Yue*, a Chinese place name (e.g., Yuenan for Vietnam), *jiang*, a term for river, and *hu*, meaning tiger.[6]

# The Rise of the Bronze Age

The late Neolithic Era was not only a period of considerable cultural diversity but also was one of great social changes. For example, in the North China Plains, archeologists have been struck by the differences between Longshan (3000–2000 B.C.E.) and the earlier Yangshao cultural sites. One major difference is the discovery of town enclosures built with rammed earth at Longshan sites, implying the need of communities to defend themselves against hostile "others." Another major difference is the concentration of wealth in the graves of Longshan elites, suggesting that the distribution of wealth in Longshan society, unlike that of Yangshao society, was highly unequal.[9]

Increased social stratification is one of a number of Late Neolithic trends that foreshadowed developments of the Chinese Bronze Age beginning around the second millennium B.C.E. Before we continue, a word about how archeologists define the Bronze Age in China and elsewhere is in order. As the term implies, Bronze Age cultures are characterized by the use of bronze and the rise of metallurgical technologies. They are also associated with sharp social and economic differentiation; the rise of urban centers; and occupational specialization. Two dynasties, the Shang (c. 1500–1045 B.C.E.) and the Western Zhou (1055–771 B.C.E.), fall into the category of Bronze Age civilizations.

# The Shang

Despite the fact that the Shang was the first civilization within present-day China known to leave written records, its origins are nevertheless murky. This is because the first surviving written records are from the latter part of the dynasty, that is, the twelfth and eleventh centuries B.C.E. Traditional Chinese accounts, based on much later records, fix the date of the Shang founding several centuries earlier, to 1766 B.C.E. Yet most archeologists now think that the Shang emerged from the Longshan and other late Neolithic cultures in North and Northeast China somewhat later, by around 1500 B.C.E.[10]

The earliest evidence of the Shang comes from a site in North Central China called Erlitou, which is near modern-day Luoyang. There, archeologists discovered foundations of large buildings, an extensive foundry, pottery, and cast bronze vessels. From these kinds of artifacts, archeologists have inferred that the Erlitou—or early Shang—civilization already had a great deal of occupational differentiation. Later Shang sites found at Erligang in Northwest China, however, hint at an even more complex state and society by the fifteenth and fourteenth centuries B.C.E. There, archeologists found evidence that bronze vessels were even more numerous and sophisticated in design, which suggests that bronze production had by then become a large-scale enterprise. More strikingly, Erligang vessels were found outside of the Yellow River valley, which suggests that Erligang technology had disseminated widely.[11]

By the late Shang (c. twelfth century B.C.E.) written sources became available. The invention of writing was to be one of the period's lasting legacies.

# The Origins of Chinese Writing

The origins of the Chinese script are difficult to trace. Some Chinese scholars have speculated that the earliest traces of writing predate the Shang and can be found on Neolithic pottery fragments dating to the fifth millennium B.C.E. True, archeologists have occasionally found pieces of pottery bearing incised or painted marks, but it is difficult to verify whether or not these marks are in fact parts of a script, because none of the marks match any of the characters found in the Shang oracle bones. There has also been speculation that the Chinese writing system was imported from outside of China. Although this is a distinct possibility, there is little evidence to date for this hypothesis. Given the paucity of evidence about the pre-Shang origins of writing, most scholars now agree that the emergence of a Chinese script probably occurred not long before 1200 B.C.E. and that it was of indigenous origin.[12]

A common myth about the Chinese script is that it, unlike our alphabet, consists of pictographs and ideograms. Pictographs are stylized pictorial representations of things, whereas ideograms are visual representations of a thing or concept through association. People who say that the Chinese language is pictographic often point to characters, such as sun, which might be construed as a visual representation of the sun (see Figure 1.3). Yet few characters, ancient or modern, are true pictographs.[13] As Figure 1.4 demonstrates, one could not tell that the early graphs represent *dragon* by merely looking at them. Early Chinese graphs, like our own alphabetic words, represent words.

Another common myth is that the Chinese script is entirely unphonetic. Although it is true that it is not as phonetic as our own, most characters have some phonetic component. Even in early China, most Chinese characters had two graphic components. One of these components represented the sounds of a word. The other component, the signifier or radical, which was used with little consistency before the first or second century B.C.E., differentiated the meaning of the graph from its homophones. As an example, consider the following characters:

1. *mu* 幕 "tent" (cloth radical)
2. *mu* 慕 "to long for" (heart radical)
3. *mu* 墓 "grave" (earth radical)
4. *mu* 募 "to summon" (strength radical)

In Modern Chinese, all four of these characters have the same pronunciation, because they are all read with a falling tone or pitch. In addition, they all share in common one graphic component, located at the top of the character. However, each of the four characters is distinguished by its radical, which here is located at the bottom half of the character. These basic principles are already present in the earliest known examples of writing.[14]

Although it is true that the basic principles of the Chinese script are already present in the oracle bones, the Chinese language was far from impervious to change. For one thing, the sounds of words have changed dramatically. The graph for humans, now pronounced *ren*, was pronounced as *\*nin* in the early Western Zhou (eleventh–tenth centuries B.C.E.). The script, furthermore, was far from standardized in the early period. Radicals were used inconsistently up through the Han dynasty (206 B.C.E.–220 C.E.). Graphs were also subject to regional variations and looked very different from each other (see Figures 1.5 and 1.6).

**FIGURE 1.3** The character for sun, *ri*, as found in the Shang oracle bone inscriptions.

DRAGON

**FIGURE 1.4** Early Chinese writing: inscriptions on bronze (heavy ink) and bone (lighter ink). (Calligraphy by Dr. Léon L. Y. Chang.)

## Oracle Bones

One of the most, if not the most, important sources for our understanding of the Shang are the oracle bone inscriptions, divinatory records of the Shang kings inscribed on the backs of cattle scapulas and turtle shells. Scholars first became aware of oracle bone inscriptions in 1898 and quickly realized that they were the lost records of the Shang kings. Over time, archeologists have collected and excavated the fragments of around 200,000 oracle bones from the area near modern-day Anyang, the site of the late Shang capital. The discovery of the oracle bones has not only greatly enhanced our knowledge of the Shang, but it has also provided independent confirmation that later accounts had some basis in historical evidence actually dating from the Shang.

The oracle bone shown in Figure 1.7 records several divinations from the reign of King Wuding (1200–1180 B.C.E.). As interpreted and translated by David Keightley, the inscription confirms the king's forecast of disaster. It reads:

> [*Preface:*] Crack-making on *guisi* day [day 40], Que divined: "In the next ten days there will be no disasters." [*Prognostication:*] "There will be calamities; there may be someone bringing alarming news." [*Verification:*] When it came to the fifth day, *dingyou* [day 34], there really was someone bringing alarming news from the west. Guo of Zhi [a

FIGURE 1.5 A bronze inscription dating to the fourth century B.C.E. from the state of Zhongshan, in North China near present-day Beijing. As a casual glance confirms, the script from the Zhongshan area tended to be elongated. (© Berkeley, Society for the Study of Early China, 1997.)

Shang general] reported and said: "The Tufang [an enemy country] have attacked in our eastern borders and have seized two settlements." The Gongfang [another enemy country] likewise invaded the fields of our western borders.[15]

Along with thousands of Shang ritual bronzes, the oracle bones provided valuable clues about the lives of the Shang rulers. They reveal the degree to which ancestral worship pervaded Shang state religion and political culture. Shang kings believed that their ancestors played an active role in their daily lives and fortunes.

**FIGURE 1.6** The image above is an example of Chu writing from South China (modern-day Hubei) on bamboo, fourth century B.C.E. Unlike the graphs from the image in Figure 1.5, the graphs here, excavated from a Southern tomb in present-day Hubei, are relatively wide and stout. (© Cultural Relics Publishing House.)

On behalf of the Shang kings, the ancestors could intercede with the Shang deity, Di (the Lord on High), to ensure good harvests to fuel the military campaigns and displays of wealth by which he asserted his power and to bring victory in war. The latter also depended on superior bronze weapons. Unsurprisingly, the legitimacy of the Shang kings was rooted in the power and influence of their ancestors. The ancestors also punish the mortal kings (sometimes with toothaches), as well as provide clues about the future.[16] For example, in one case, the King Wuding divined about the pregnancy of one of his consorts. This inscription reads:

> Crack-making on *jiashen* [day 21], Que divined: [*Charge:*] "Lady Hao's childbearing will be good." [*Prognostication:*] The king read the cracks and said: "If it be a *ding*-day childbearing, it will be good; if it be a *geng*-[day] childbearing, there will be prolonged luck." [*Verification:*] [After] thirty-one days, on *jiayin* [day 51], she gave birth; it was not good; it was a girl."[17]

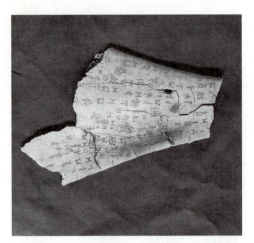

**FIGURE 1.7** Oracle bone from the reign of King Wuding (twelfth century B.C.E.). According to David Keightley, the Shang created the oracle bones by gathering cattle scapulas and turtle shells. The cattle and turtles would be killed, and the bones would be cleaned before being ritually cracked by application of heat. The cracks would subsequently be interpreted as an auspicious or inauspicious answer from the ancestors to a query. Lastly, the scapulas and shells would be inscribed with a record of the divination. (© C.V. Starr East Asian Library, Columbia University.)

Given the importance of ancestors, it is not surprising that the Shang paid "assiduous attention" to the treatment of the special dead.[18] The Shang elite dead, which included petty elites as well as members of the royal lineage, were buried in style: the higher the rank of the individual, the larger the tomb. Even tombs of lesser elites were costly to construct and often had one ramp. Sitting at the top of the political and social hierarchy, the Shang kings were buried in massive burial chapters, dug deep in the ground and connected to the surface with four ramps.[19] In addition to being large, the tombs of elites were often filled with lavish grave goods. The tomb of Wuding's consort, Lady Hao, provides a good example. In the larger scheme of things, her tomb was probably relatively modest. But when excavated in 1976, archeologists discovered 468 bronzes, weighing together more than 1.5 metric tons; 755 jades; and 6880 cowry shells.[20] If Lady Hao's tomb was only modest, one wonders what treasures once lay in the tombs of the Shang kings, which were long ago looted by grave robbers.

There is still further evidence that the Shang elites paid assiduous attention to their special dead: human sacrifice. Longshan elites had also sacrificed humans to accompany their special dead—the large scale of human sacrifice was something new and perhaps unique to the Shang. A relatively modest elite burial site, like that of Lady Hao, only had about a dozen or so victims. A particularly lavish burial site, however, could hold as many as 400 victims. Most of these were low-status young males—probably foreign prisoners of war. But there were also women and children among the victims in some tombs. In other cases, the dead included high-status victims: royal relatives or personal dependents of the deceased, in turn accompanied by *their own* human sacrifices (see Figure 1.8).[21]

The lavish burials of the Shang elite suggest that they commanded the lion's share of wealth and human resources. They controlled a large army of labor conscripts, conscripts who represented the basis of state power: "They served in armies, built temple-palaces, excavated tombs, hauled supplies, cleared land and farmed it, and worked at the sundry tasks of production and manufacture required by the elites."[22]

**FIGURE 1.8** Photograph displaying sacrificial victims found in a Shang tomb. Humans being sacrificed were decapitated and dismembered before being buried in the pits and ramps of the tomb. (From Loewe and Shaughnessy, *The Cambridge History of Ancient China.*)

# Bronze Vessels

The wealth of the Shang is perhaps most clearly demonstrated by the large-scale use of costly bronzes. The bronze vessels that the elites used to drink, for banquets, and to make ancestral sacrifices required large-scale and well-organized mining and smelting industries with a forced labor pool, as well as a high degree of professional specialization. Such professional specialization is evident in the quality of Shang bronzes, which were noted for their clarity of detail and perfection of craftsmanship (see Figures 1.9 and 1.10). Bronze was worked in foundries outside Shang cities by artisans who had quarters beyond the city walls, with floors of stamped earth. Although hardly luxurious, these houses were nevertheless superior to those of peasants, who lived in semi-subterranean dwellings. Bronze was a material almost exclusively reserved for the elite, as peasants continued to use stone tools and Neolithic agricultural methods.

The bronze vessels of the ruling elite were cast in many forms. Some bronze forms derived from older pottery traditions. In contrast, other forms were based on containers made of more perishable materials. Still other bronze forms appear to have been new to the Shang, and these were receptacles for storing or serving various solids and liquids used in ritual ceremonies.

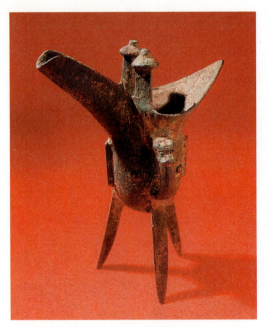

**FIGURE 1.9** This is a bronze *jue* or wine vessel, dating to the late Shang, c. 1200 B.C.E. It is 14.69 in tall and weighs 9.70 lbs. This is a common kind of ritual vessel from the Shang, one used by the political elites. (© HIP/Scala/Art Resource, NY.)

Characteristically, all available space on Shang bronzes is covered by decorations. One popular decoration was the forms of real and imaginary animals. Figure 1.10 provides some examples. The pieces in this set of collected bronzes date from the late Shang or perhaps early Zhou dynasty. The set includes vessels in various styles. Most clearly visible in the illustration of the set are the heads, perhaps of rams, on the handles of the two ritual vessels at the top and the single-legged creature resembling a dragon. Some abstract forms also derive from animals. For instance, the *gu* vessel on the far right is decorated with what looks like a flower petal but is actually a stylized cicada. Other forms, such as the *taotie*, the most common motif on early bronzes, are still more abstract (see Figure 1.11). The *taotie*, which some scholars believe depicts a mythological being, is also presented frontally as though squashed onto a horizontal plane to form a symmetrical design. Over the centuries, various explanations of the *taotie* have arisen. In the late Zhou dynasty, some commentators described it as a covetous man banished by the Shang to guard a corner of heaven against evil monsters or, more fancifully, as a monster equipped with only a head, who tries to devour men but hurts only itself. Yet there is uncertainty about how seriously to take these explanations. One problem is that only much later, that is, during the Song dynasty (960–1279 C.E.), was the form appearing on the bronzes identified as a *taotie* at all.

## Other Bronze Age Civilizations

Despite the impressiveness of the Shang written and material record, it is important to bear in mind that theirs was not the only advanced bronze culture within the borders of present-day China. By the thirteenth century B.C.E., bronze-casting technologies and styles from the Yellow River area spread elsewhere, prompting

**FIGURE 1.10** Bronze set (© Metropolitan Museum of Art, Munsey Fund, 1931. [24.72.1-14]. Photogtraph by Schecter Lee. © 1986 The Metropolitan Museum of Art.)

**FIGURE 1.11** *Taotie* design. (From William Willets, *Chinese Art, Vol. 1* [Hamondworth, England, 1958] by permission Penguin Books Ltd. and courtesy of William Willets.)

the development of other, very distinctive Bronze Age cultures with many of the marks of civilization, even though we have no evidence of writing. Two of these were discovered in the last 30 years, one centered in the Lower Yangzi River area and another centered in Southwest China.

In 1972 archeologists discovered a new civilization when they excavated a rich tomb from Xingan in Jiangxi Province dated to around 1200 B.C.E., making it roughly contemporaneous with the late Shang kings. It is the richest Bronze Age tomb ever found in present-day China. Although many of the artifacts found there revealed the diffusion of Erligang or middle Shang bronze casting technologies, they were clearly not made by Shang artisans, nor were they mere copies of Shang bronzes (see Figure 1.12). As Bagley argues, the bronzes were of "an undeniable local character" and thus suggest that local craftsmen had adapted the technologies and styles from the North China Plains to create products to suit local tastes.

The second civilization is that of Sanxingdui in Southwest China, which was discovered by archeologists in 1980. Chinese archeologists excavated there the remains of a city wall and two sacrificial deposits, which, like the Xingan site, also date to around 1200 B.C.E. The pits yielded a wealth of material culture, including several hundred bronze, jade, and gold artifacts, cowry shells, and thirteen elephant tusks. Like the artifacts found at the Xingan site, some of the material remains from the Sanxingdui site point to early contacts with the late Neolithic precursors to the Shang—and to *other* non-Shang Bronze Age civilizations from the middle Yangzi region. More interestingly, there is no evidence that the Sanxingdui artisans, unlike their Xingan contemporaries, had much contact with Shang culture.[23] In fact, much of what was found at Sanxingdui strongly suggests the presence of a tradition distinct from those found in the North China Plains. For example, in one of the sacrificial pits, archeologists discovered a life-size statue on a pedestal, forty-one heads, and twenty or so mask-like items (see Figure 1.13). These masks have caught the attention of

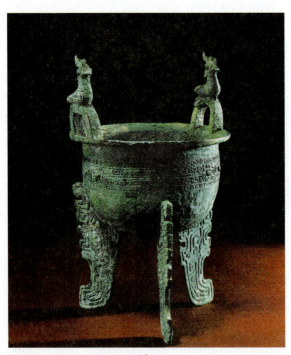

**FIGURE 1.12** Bronze tripod from Xingan site, Jiangxi Province (c. 1400–1200 B.C.E.). It is 24.57 in tall with a diameter of 6.10 in and weighs 62.83 lbs. (© Asian Art & Archaeology, Inc./CORBIS.)

scholars because they are so different from anything found in the North China Plains, where craftsmen showed little interest making human representations.[24]

# The Western Zhou Dynasty

Led by King Wu (r. 1049/ 45–1043 B.C.E.), Zhou armies from the West invaded the Central Plains and defeated the last Shang king in battle at Muye around 1045 B.C.E. For several millennia thereafter, this was seen not as a simple coup d'état, but as a momentous event expressing the will of Heaven itself. Later, it was commemorated in the *Odes* (*Shi*), the classic anthology of poetry:

> The Yin-Shang legions,
> Their battle flags like a forest,
> Were arrayed on the field of Muye.
> "Arise, my lords,
> The Lord on High looks down on you;
> Have no second thoughts."
> The field of Muye was so broad.
> The sandalwood chariots were so gleaming.
> The teams of four were so pounding.
> There was the general Shangfu.
> He rose as an eagle.
> Aiding that King Wu,
> And attacked the great Shang,
> Meeting in the morning, clear and bright.[25]

**FIGURE 1.13** Bronze standing figure from Sanxingdui, Sichuan, c. 1300–1100 B.C.E. The figure stands 103.15 in. (© Cultural Relics Publishing House.)

According to later Chinese historians, the Shang house lost its mandate because their rulers had failed to serve the people. As a result, Heaven (*tian*)—the Zhou's highest deity—revoked the mandate and gave it to the Zhou house, which had a healthy supply of virtuous men. But the Zhou mandate did not last. Less than 300 years later, the dynastic cycle had come full circle. Like their Shang predecessors, the last of the Western Zhou kings had neglected their responsibilities as guardians of the people. As a legend recounted by historian Sima Qian (c. 140–c. 90 B.C.E.) notes, the last of the Western Zhou kings, King You (r. 781–771 B.C.E.) had been the epitome of a bad last ruler of a dynasty. Smitten with a royal concubine of purported supernatural origin, King You spared no effort or expense in seeking to please his beloved, but all for naught. One day, however, a beacon was lit mistakenly to warn of an invasion of an alien group, and, as was customary, all the lords sworn to protect the king came to the capital, ready to fight the invaders. This spectacle caught the beloved's fancy, so the king had the beacon lit again so that the lords would come to the capital. This occurred repeatedly, but each time the beacon was lit, fewer of the king's lords came into the capital. Finally, in 771 B.C.E., the enemy did invade. The beacon was lit, but none of the lords came to assist the king. The king was killed, the capital was sacked, and the Western Zhou came to a rather inglorious end.[26]

Before we plunge into the details of the origins and development of the Western Zhou, a few words about our sources are in order. One set of sources are texts, which are most likely later in date and of unknown provenance. These include the *Odes* (*Shi*), the *History* (*Shangshu*), and the *Changes* (*Yi*). A second source for historians is the tens of thousands of inscriptions that were cast into ritual bronze vessels. Although generally more reliable than much later accounts, the bronze inscriptions too have their limitations as sources, as they tend to focus exclusively on events that brought glory to the owners. These vessels were commemorative and were often cast for individuals by the royal court in recognition of past achievements or future charges.[27] The following inscription dates to around 825 B.C.E. and begins by setting the stage for a solemn ceremony and continues by quoting the king himself:

> The king said: "Song, [I] command you to officiate over and to su-
> pervise the Chengzhou warehouse, and to oversee and supervise the
> newly constructed warehouses, using palace attendants. [I] award you
> a black jacket with embroidered hem, red kneepads, a scarlet demi-
> circle, a chime pennant, and a bridle with bit and cheekpieces; use
> [them] to serve."[28]

Inscriptions such as this tell us something of the time but leave many questions unanswered. Thus, the origins of the Zhou remain murky. The Zhou float in and out of the Shang oracle bones, as foreign enemies, as embittered allies, and then as a powerful enemy before dropping out of the record altogether. Later legends offer conflicting accounts. Thus, according to the *Odes,* the Zhou were of divine parentage. A woman known as Jiang Yuan was supposed to have become pregnant by stepping into the footprint of the Lord on High (*di*), the same deity from the Shang. Subsequently, Jiang Yuan gave birth to Hou Ji or the "Lord of Millet," who was not only the Zhou founder but also was reputed to have invented agriculture.

Traditional Chinese scholars, often in disagreement with each other, provide more mundane accounts of the origins of the Zhou. Some scholars state that the Zhou were from the East, in the Fen River valley of Shanxi. Others, however, insist that the Zhou were originally from a place called Bin, which is believed to have been in the West, in Shaanxi. If the latter is correct, then the Zhou would have been of Western and, hence, alien origins. Along these lines, art historian Jessica Rawson has argued that the Zhou emerged from the consolidation of a group of loosely connected tribes in the Northwest. These peoples, she notes, were culturally distinct from the Shang and other peoples from the Central Plains. Judging from their emphasis on military rituals and material culture, the Zhou were part of a larger cultural milieu common to other peoples from the Northwest.[30]

The Western Zhou king, known as the "son of Heaven" (*t*
rectly rule over all of the conquered territory, which increased ἁ
the early years of the dynasty. Instead, he or his advisors initi
bers of the royal family with territory to rule more or less v
from the Zhou king. Later, the dynasty also sought alliances wiш ᷤᷤ
These alliances were cemented—or more accurately, tenuously held together—
with fictive kinship ties.

Also included, but to a much lesser degree, among the ranks of subordinate
rulers were the descendants of the Shang royal house, who would reemerge, if only
briefly, as a threat to the Zhou house. Given territory, the Shang descendants continued to perform sacrifices to their ancestors, perhaps to relieve the Zhou from
the threat of supernatural retribution.

During the early years of the dynasty, the Zhou king managed the core territory
in the Zhou homeland, in the Wei River valley, while the brothers and nephews of
King Wu, the Zhou founder, were sent to defend and govern important territories
in North and Northeast China. This arrangement set the pattern for subsequent
generations. Later Zhou kings continued to charge their relatives with governing and
defending a large number of territories for the Zhou house. Often, each time they
charged their relatives, they would order a bronze inscription to commemorate the
event.[31] As time went on, however, the bond between the main line of the Zhou
house and the descendants of their kin and allies grew increasingly thin.

The relationship between the Zhou kings and the subordinate territorial au-
thorities resembles, to a certain extent, that between lords and vassals in medieval
Europe. As a result, the Zhou political system has often been identified as feudal.
Nevertheless, there are major differences, such as the absence in the Zhou of subin-
feudation (the phenomenon of vassals having their own vassals). Unlike their
European counterparts, the Zhou appealed to bonds of kinship rather than to contractual agreements. Furthermore, the contrasts between the history of postfeudal
Europe and post-Zhou make it very difficult to apply the term *feudalism* to both in
the sense of a stage of development in a universal historical process. Awareness of
the differences between them further serves to restrain the temptation to overin-
terpret the Zhou evidence, which is much more meager than that available for the
student of Europe almost 2000 years later. The difficulties are further compounded
by disagreements over the definition of feudalism itself. This is not the place for a
study of comparative feudalism, but, in any case, post-Heian Japan presents a much
richer and more fruitful field for such a study than does Western Zhou because the
parallels between Japan and Europe are far more numerous.

From the start, the early Western Zhou rulers and their allies discovered that
governing the realm was difficult. For one, political loyalty tends to weaken as
blood ties thin. One hundred years after the Zhou conquest, the Zhou King Mu
was faced with rather weak ties with relatives, who at best were second or third
cousins, administering distant territories and vice versa.[32] For another, even close
kinsmen could not always be counted on to be either loyal or cooperative. Not
long after the Shang conquest, the virtuous King Wu died, leaving an heir, King
Cheng (r. 1042/35–1006 B.C.E.), who was too young to rule. One of the younger
brothers of King Wu declared himself the regent for the king, an action that proved

ontroversial—and politically disastrous. Three of King Wu's brothers rebelled against the young king from the East, aligning themselves with the descendants of the vanquished Shang.[33]

Finally, there was the threat of emerging regional powers. In the West, the Quan Rong, an alien group, invaded the capital at Chengzhou, in the East were the Xu Rong, and in the South were the Yi, who lived in the Yangzi River area. Not only were they hostile to the Zhou ruling house, but at least one of these groups was able to form a block against the Zhou, thereby uniting for a time peoples in *thirty-six* states in the Northeast, as well as Central and South China.[34]

# The Odes

One of the greatest works of world literature, the *Odes,* also known as the *Classic of Poetry* or the *Book of Odes,* was begun in the Western Zhou dynasty. According to Eastern Zhou lore, Confucius (see Chapter 2) selected some 300 of the odes and edited them into their present form. Later, the *Odes* became part of what many scholars came to refer to as the *Five Classics* (*Wu jing*), which included the *Changes* (*Yi*), the *Documents* (*Shangshu*), the *Spring and Autumn Annals* (*Chunqiu*), and the *Ceremonials* (*Yili*). Although there is much in the *Odes* that appeals to people of all places and times, it is important not to forget that most people did not read the odes to themselves in silence, but recited them out loud and learned them by heart. They were also probably sung in public performances or communal gatherings, not just read or recited in silence.

The *Odes* was not unique in that it was memorized and orally transmitted, but what is extraordinary about the *Odes* is that it represents a wide range of human experience for people from all walks of life. As seen earlier, it contains commemorative odes that recount the victory of the Zhou king against the Shang. There are religious hymns and the stately songs that accompanied royal, festive, and ceremonial occasions. There are prayers evoking Lord Millet (Hou Ji), the reputed ancestor of the Zhou.

In addition to these perspectives, the *Odes* represents those of peasants—perspectives unseen in Zhou inscriptions. Some songs show ordinary people at work: the men clearing weeds from the fields, plowing, planting, and harvesting; and the girls and women gathering mulberry leaves for the silkworms, making thread, carrying food hampers out to the fields for their men to have lunch. There is much about millet—both the eating variety and that used for brewing wine for use in rites. There are joyful references to granaries full of grain and to the men gathering thatch for their roofs in the off-season. Mention is made of lords' fields and private fields, and a bailiff is referred to, but the details of the system are not provided. There are also, more strikingly, odes of political protest. One compares tax collectors to big rats:

> Big rat, big rat,
> Do not gobble our millet!

Three years we have slaved for you,
Yet you take no notice of us.
At last we are going to leave you
And go to that happy land;
Happy land, happy land,
Where we shall have our place.[35]

Another tells of the hardships of military service: men constantly on the march, living in the wilds like rhinoceroses and tigers, day and night without rest. Sometimes a soldier survives the hardships and dangers of war and returns home only to find that his wife has given him up for dead and remarried. Consider the following:

We plucked the bracken, plucked the bracken;
While the shoots were soft
Oh, to go back, go back!
Our hearts are sad,
Our sad hearts burn,
We are hungry and thirsty,
But our campaign is not over,
Nor is any of us sent home with news.[36]

Still other odes give us glimpses of the day-to-day hardships of Zhou peasants, who lived at the mercy of what was becoming an increasingly inhospitable environment:

The drought is long and deep,
Parched and barren in the landscape.
The drought demon is vicious
Like a burn, like a blaze.
Our hearts are tormented by the heat,
Our grieved hearts as if aflame.
The former ministers and their lords,
Even they do not hear our plea.
Mighty Heaven,
God on High
Why do you force us to flee?[37]

In addition to royal and peasant perspectives, the *Odes* is also famous for its love poetry, which often employs the feminine perspective:

In the wilds, there is a dead doe.
With white rushes we cover her.
There was a lady longing for the spring;
A fair knight seduced her.
In the woods there is a clump of oaks.
And in the wilds a dead deer
With white rushes well bound;
There was a lady fair as jade.

> "Heigh, not so hasty, not so rough;
> Heigh, do not touch my handkerchief.
> Take care, or the dog will bark." [38]

The feminine perspective in ancient China could be quite erotic or even ribald, as this ode reveals:

> That the mere glimpse of a plain cap
> Could harry me with such longing,
> Cause pain so dire!
> That the mere glimpse of a plain coat
> Could stab my heart with grief!
> Enough! Take me with you to your home.
> That a mere glimpse of plain leggings
> Could tie my heart in tangles!
> Enough! Let us two be one. [39]

To be sure, with these odes, as with all poetry, much depends on the vision of the translator and interpreter. For Liu Wu-chi, the ode tells of "the tragedy of love." In the mind of another contemporary scholar, Wai-lim Yip, the first ode cited in the last paragraph is an "animated pastiche of a lovely rural seducement song." [40]

It is a truism that to translate is to interpret, and much is inevitably lost in the process. But to read is also to interpret, and in reading these odes, later literary and scholarly elites from Han times on "translated" them to conform to their own ideas of what a classic should be, namely a repository of lessons in social and political morality. And commentators worked hard to show how this should be done. For example, the ribald ode (second in the last paragraph) was transformed into a lament for the decline in ritual propriety, an indication of the decay of filial piety, because white is the color of mourning in China. Thus, in a nineteenth-century English translation by James Legge, following Chinese commentators, the ode begins:

> If I could but see the white cap,
> And the earnest mourner worn to leaness!
> My toiled heart is torn with grief. [41]

Given the fact that Victorian elites by and large frowned upon expressions of female desire, it is not surprising that the translator would have preferred to interpret the ode in staid terms. But no matter which translation of the ode about the dead doe one selects, it is not the traditional interpretation: the *Odes* we read today is not the same as that read by traditional scholars, for *all* modern readers bring a different vision to the text. But the study of civilization cannot even begin without an attempt to understand traditional views and images. This is true of all periods, but it is especially pertinent to a consideration of antiquity, because the gap between the classical understanding of the odes and the modern is not any wider than that between the account of origins presented in this chapter and the traditional view once held by educated persons in what is now China.

# *Notes*

1. David N. Keightley, "The Environment of Ancient China," in Edward Shaughnessy and Michael Loewe, eds., *The Cambridge History of Ancient China: From the Origins of Civilization to 221 BC* (Cambridge: Cambridge Univ. Press, 1999), pp. 35–36.

2. K.C. Chang, "China on the Eve of the Historical Period," in *Cambridge History of Ancient China*, pp. 49–52.

3. Chang, p. 59.

4. Robert Bagley, "Shang Archaeology," in *Cambridge History of Ancient China*, pp. 124–25.

5. For this view, see Lydia Liu, *The Clash of Empires: The Invention of China in Modern World Making* (Cambridge: Harvard Univ. Press, 2004); Laura Hostetler, *Qing Colonial Enterprise: Ethnography and Cartography in Early Modern China* (Chicago: Univ. of Chicago Press, 2001), p. 27.

6. William G. Boltz, "Language and Writing," *Cambridge History of Ancient China*, pp. 81–83.

7. Boltz, pp. 83–87.

8. William Baxter, Private communication, 2 February 2004.

9. Chang, pp. 59–65.

10. Keightley, "The Shang: China's First Historical Dynasty," in *Cambridge History of Ancient China*, p. 232.

11. Bagley, "Shang Archaeology," p. 157.

12. Boltz, p. 108.

13. Boltz, pp. 109–12.

14. Boltz, pp. 118–23.

15. Keightley, "The Shang," p. 242.

16. Keightley, "The Shang," pp. 236–37.

17. Keightley, "The Shang," pp. 236–37.

18. Keightley, "The Shang," p. 263.

19. Keightley, "The Shang," p. 268.

20. Bagley, "Shang Archaeology," pp. 194–95.

21. Keightley, "The Shang," pp. 266–67; Bagley, "Shang Archaeology" pp. 195–96.

22. Keightley, "The Shang," p. 282.

23. Bagley, "Shang Archaeology," pp. 121–213.

24. Xiaoneng Yang, ed., *Golden Age of Chinese Archaeology: Celebrated Discoveries from the People's Republic of China*, (Washington, D.C.: National Gallery of Art, 1999), p. 209.

25. Edward Shaughnessy, "Western Zhou History," in *Cambridge History of Ancient China*, p. 310.

26. Shaughnessy, "Western Zhou History," p. 350.

27. Shaughnessy, "Western Zhou History," p. 298.

28. Shaughnessy, "Western Zhou History," pp. 298–99.

29. Shaughnessy, "Western Zhou History," p. 299–305.

30. Jessica Rawson, "Western Zhou Archaeology," in *Cambridge History of Ancient China*, pp. 383–85.

31. Shaughnessy, pp. 317–19.

32. Shaughnessy, p. 323.

33. Shaughnessy, pp. 310–13.

34. Shaughnessy, pp. 323–25.

35. *The Book of Songs*, trans. Arthur Waley (New York, Grove Press, 1996), pp. 88–89.

36. *The Book of Songs*, p. 140.

37. *The Book of Songs*, p. 271.

38. *The Book of Songs*, p. 114.

39. *The Book of Songs*, p. 114.

40. Wai-lin Yip, *Chinese Poetry* (Berkeley: Univ. of California Press, 1975), p. 53.

41. James Legge, *The Chinese Classics, IV: The She King* (Reprinted Hong Kong: Hong Kong Univ. Press, 1960), p. 216.

# 2

# Turbulent Times and Classical Thought

The Spring and Autumn Period

The Warring States Period

"The Hundred Schools"

Confucius

Mozi

Mencius

Xunzi

Laozi and Zhuangzi

Han Feizi

B.C.E.

| 800 | 700 | 600 | 500 | 400 | 300 | 200 |

Eastern Zhou (771–256)

Spring and Autumn Period (772–453)

Warring States Period (453–221)

Qin Unification ⟶ 221

The 550 years from 771 to 221 B.C.E., a time of major social change and political upheaval, were regarded by traditional scholars as a period of decline from the heights of the early Zhou dynasty. In this they followed the great majority of articulate, elite men who lived through these turbulent centuries and did not consider themselves fortunate to have been born in an age when great changes were underway, changes that were to lead to a stronger, more extensive, and more prosperous civilization. They could not know what the future would bring, and for them, it was a bewildering and disturbing age. Old beliefs and assumptions were challenged, prompting questions never before raised and stimulating intellectual exploration in many directions. Some of these new concepts were later abandoned; others became the guidelines for Chinese and Japanese thought for centuries.

The period from 771 to 221 B.C.E. is known as the Eastern Zhou Period because the dynastic capital was in the Eastern city of Chengzhou. It is further divided into two periods: the Spring and Autumn Period (771–453 B.C.E.) and the Warring States Period (453–221 B.C.E.). The former derives from the *Spring and Autumn Annals,* a terse and opaque chronicle that covers the years after the fall of the Western Zhou capital to the beginning of the Warring States Period. The latter gets its name from the long and protracted nature of its wars.

# The Spring and Autumn Period

During this period, the Zhou kingship continued to experience a decline of prestige and power. Not only were Zhou kings unable to defend themselves, but they were also increasingly at the mercy (or under the protection) of the powerful lords of "vassal" states. The last Western Zhou king (781–771 B.C.E.) had been removed

**FIGURE 2.1** States of the Spring and Autumn Period.

and killed by a joint force led by vassal states, and his successor, King Ping, survived only after being rescued by the rulers of two powerful states, Jin and Qi, and removed from the Wei River valley in the West to Chengzhou. In many ways, these two incidents exemplify what became the dominant trends of the Spring and Autumn Period: the decline of Zhou kingship accompanied by the rise of vassal states. The most prominent of these new states included Qi in Shandong and Jin in Shanxi, as well as two powerful but culturally distinct states, Chu (in the Yangzi River area) and Qin (in Shaanxi) (see Figure 2.1).

In 667 B.C.E., a new interstate political system headed by hegemons (*ba*) filled the power vacuum left by the decline of the Zhou kingship. The hegemons were the lords of the most powerful states. They were not only the custodians or caretakers of the Zhou king but were also heads of leagues of smaller and less powerful states. The hegemon would occasionally convene the rulers of allied states and make everyone take blood oaths, swearing loyalty to each other. In theory, the alliances were guaranteed by the spirit world, but, in fact, they proved to be unstable. As later records show, states that were supposed to be allied often went to war. The failure of these alliances led to an increase in tensions among the states and created a general aura of suspicion and betrayal in the sixth century B.C.E.

The best-known hegemon is Duke Wen (r. 636–628 B.C.E.), also known as Chong'er or Double Ears. Lord Wen's life story in many ways exemplifies the moral and political decline depicted by most traditional scholars, a situation in which fathers and sons were alienated while concubines and unscrupulous ministers usurped the role of proper consorts and heirs. Lord Wen, along with his elder brother, was a son of Lord Xian of Jin (r. 676–651 B.C.E.) by his proper consort. In early China, elite men often practiced polygamy but were allowed only one proper wife or consort. His other women were considered concubines. Only the children of the wife qualified as proper heirs.

Lord Xian happened in old age to be given a beautiful concubine, even though he already had two able and virtuous grown sons. Although the new concubine knew that they should succeed Lord Xian, she hoped that her own son would instead become the next lord of Qi. With this in mind she convinced her infatuated husband to order his two eldest sons killed. Although the eldest was killed, the younger, the future Duke Wen, escaped. He then spent many years wandering in foreign lands before returning to Qi and exacting revenge upon his stepmother and half-brother. Assuming the lordship of Jin, he consolidated his rule by annexing smaller states next to Jin, seizing major trade routes and salt flats, and absorbing the semi-assimilated Rong, Di, and Yi tribes. Having in his possession a large and powerful state, Duke Wen was poised to become a hegemon.

Despite political uncertainties, some important economic developments took place. One such development was the introduction of soybean cultivation, which had originated northwest in Manchuria. In the second half of the seventh century B.C.E., soybean cultivation spread to what is now China proper. In addition to being a rich source of protein and an important addition to the Chinese diet, this new crop plant also contains nitrogen-fixing bacteria that helped augment the fertility of the soil in which it was grown.

Another important development affecting the land and pointing to the future involved the taxation system. In Lu, a small state in Shandong, the ruling house enacted a reform in 594 B.C.E. that required peasants to pay land rents directly to them rather than to landlords. This represents the first example of a system of direct taxation that was indispensable to the rise of increasingly centralized states independent of the Zhou. Also noteworthy as a harbinger of change was the appearance of iron.

# The Warring States Period

During the Warring States Period (453–221 B.C.E.), the trends already visible in the late Spring and Autumn Period accelerated. Some states, such as Chu and Qin, became increasingly powerful and annexed their neighbors, whereas other states, even formerly strong states such as Jin and Qi, were destroyed.

Neither Chu nor Qin was located in the Central Plains, the old heartland. Qin was located in Shaanxi in the Northwest, the same region from which the Zhou had emerged. Its location in the area of the Wei River provided Qin with an economic basis on which to build a strong political and military apparatus. Its location was also strategically advantageous, because the area was protected from attack by mountains whose passes were easy to defend and yet provided avenues for offensives to the east. The Qin considered their neighbors in the Central Plains less civilized than they were, merely "semicivilized," and the archeological record confirms that the Qin were in some ways culturally distinct. For example, the dead of the Central Plains were buried in graves dug into vertical shafts in a supine position. In contrast, the Qin dead were often buried in cave-like structures and in a retroflex position. Nevertheless, it is also clear that the Qin ruling class adopted many aspects of Zhou culture, including the script and aspects of its ritual system.[1]

Like Qin, Chu had many natural advantages that favored its rise. Located in the semitropical regions of the Huai and Yangzi Rivers, Chu territory provided ideal conditions for rice cultivation. Rice and fish were staples in the Chu diet. Their technological level was on a par with that of the North: they had iron as well as bronze, made fine ceramics, and used bronze coins. Like Qin, Chu was on the fringes of Zhou culture, but also like those in Qin, the Chu elites had borrowed and adapted many practices from other elites living in the Central Plains.[2] Some notable differences between the Chu elites and their Northern counterparts included language. The language of the Chu was said to be incomprehensible to the people of the Central Plains: one source compared it to the language of birds. Another difference lay in the style of the burials of the Chu elite, which were distinctive in their use of lacquer and bright colors (see Figures 2.2 and 2.3).

One artifact of Chu culture worth mention is the *Chuci,* an anthology of poems. Although it is impossible to date the poems precisely, the earliest may have been written as early as the fourth century B.C.E. A number of the poems, in particular, the "Li Sao" (Encountering Sorrow) have traditionally been attributed to Qu Yuan. Contrasts between the "Li Sao" and the *Odes* are striking. As David Hawkes points out, in the (presumably northern) *Odes,* the persona of the poet is not prominent. Out of the 305 odes, there are exactly three in which the bard identifies himself or herself by name. By contrast, in the "Li Sao," Qu Yuan stands very much at the forefront of the poem: he "bares his breast to us, examines his motives, admits his doubts, reveals his aspirations, argues, cites historical precedents in defense of his opinions. . . ."[3] And indeed, by traditional accounts, the "Li Sao"

**FIGURE 2.2** Painted lacquer coffin, c. 316 B.C.E. This comes from a tomb found in Hubei (Chu territory). It is specifically from the Baoshan tomb, and it is one of three nested coffins. The privilege of having many coffins was reserved for the elite. This was probably necessary because the bodies of the elite lay in state for relatively long periods of time—anywhere from several weeks to years—before they were buried. When one considers the heat and humidity, as well as the lack of interest in any rudimentary embalming practices, it is understandable why people would have wanted to put some distance between themselves and the dead. Commoners, on the other hand, were buried as soon as they died. (© Cultural Relics Publishing House.)

is autobiographical. According to the Han dynasty historian Sima Qian, the "Li Sao" relates Qu Yuan's own personal disappointments. Though loyal to his lord, Qu Yuan fell victim to slander, causing him great pain. The "Li Sao" reads:

> How well I know that loyalty brings disaster;
> Yet I will endure: I cannot give it up.
> I called on the ninefold heaven to be my witness,
> And all for the sake of the Fair One [for example, his lord], and
>     no other.
> There once was a time when he spoke with me in frankness;
> But then he repented and was of another mind.
> I do not care, on my own count, about this divorcement,
> But it grieves me to find the Fair One so inconstant.[4]

**FIGURE 2.3** Lacquer cabinet and vessels. This is also from the Baoshan tomb (c. 316 B.C.E.). These contain an animal motif, although art historians are not sure whether the artists had any particular animal, or a general zoomorphic design, in mind. This is probably something that was used in everyday life. (From Xiaoneng Yang, *The Golden Age of Archaeology* [New Haven: Yale University Press, 1999], p. 334).

Banished from court, Qu Yuan committed suicide in despair ("The world is impure and envious of the able/Eager to hide men's good and make much of their ills").[5] Clasping a large stone, he jumped into the Miluo River.

Along with the emergence of new major powers, the Warring States Period witnessed major political, economic, and military changes including changes in warfare. During the Spring and Autumn Period armies comprising chariots and infantry amounting to no more than 30,000 men fought pitched battles staged on flat terrain. All this changed during the Warring States Period when armies composed of massed infantry may have included as many as 600,000 men, although more skeptical historians say no more than 100,000. Although more frequent than those in the Warring States Period, Spring and Autumn Period campaigns might have lasted a season but no more than one year, whereas during the Warring States Period military conflicts often lasted more than one year and sometimes as long as five.[6] Military technology also changed as new and deadlier weaponry was developed. In addition to iron weapons from around 600 B.C.E., Warring States Period armies were equipped with new tools, such as the crossbow and lamellar armor. Finally, whereas Spring and Autumn Period armies consisted mainly of members of the ruling elite, Warring States Period infantry comprised all segments of society.[7]

The new modes of warfare that emerged in the Warring States Period have been interpreted as reflecting social change. Spring and Autumn Period society, like that of the Western Zhou, was highly stratified. Not only were commoners (*min*) distinguished from members of the ruling elite, but within the ruling elite there were stark differences of status. Beneath the Zhou king were the nobles (*qing*), usually lords or members of a lord's immediate family. Below the nobles were the lesser aristocrats (*shi*). *Shi* is a term also later used for elites who could identify with their predecessors even though they lived in very different societies. Spring and Autumn Period *shi*, far above commoners, were usually distant descendants of and lesser relatives of lords. Many were individuals of culture, learning, and even wealth. Yet ministerial positions, like military commands, were reserved for the nobles.

In the Warring States Period, the old social hierarchies began to break down. With some luck and ability, a man of *shi* or even occasionally of humble birth could become a powerful minister or general. A famous man of humble birth who rose to spectacular heights was Lü Buwei (d. 235 B.C.E.), a merchant who profited from the growth of interstate trade facilitated by the building of new roads and better communication systems (see Figure 2.4). For many years, Lü was the chief counselor of the Qin ruler and was even rumored to have been the actual father of the future First Emperor of the Qin dynasty.

Despite the possibilities for social mobility, political life in the Warring States Period was not without its dangers. According to historians, Lü was murdered by the future First Emperor of Qin. The reasons are not clear, although legend has it that he was displeased by

**FIGURE 2.4** These bronze tallies date to the late fourth century B.C.E., and this set was discovered in what was Chu territory. Bronze tallies exempted the bearers, in this case, a merchant, from tolls along Chu roads. Not all tallies were made of bronze; those used by lower-status individuals came in different varieties, and many of them used cheaper materials, such as bamboo. (© National Museum of China.)

the liberties that the minister had taken with his mother. By some accounts, the First Emperor was the illegitimate son of Lü, and by killing Lü, he unwittingly killed his own father. Most likely, however, the young ruler felt that Lü had gotten too powerful. Lü was not alone in this regard. A similar fate met another eminent Qin statesmen, Shang Yang (d. 338 B.C.E.), originally from Chu and famous for spearheading the reforms that brought Qin to power and for instituting harsh laws. As minister, Shang Yang reportedly had insisted that the laws apply equally to all regardless of status and followed this dictum when he punished the crown prince for an infraction of the law and had the prince's teacher branded. Later when the prince became king, he had his revenge: Lord Shang reportedly suffered dismemberment, his body torn apart by chariots pulling in opposite directions.

Qin best exemplifies the consolidation and centralization of states with Shang Yang taking the lead in advising the ruler to undertake important political and economic reforms. First, the Qin rulers instituted universal military service, thereby no doubt increasing the number of men in the Qin army. Second, in 350 B.C.E., they abolished estates maintained by nobles and divided Qin territory into *xian* or counties, which they governed directly rather than through nobles as before. This increased the amount of territory under their effective control while limiting the ability of nobles to rebel. Third, they established the individual household, as opposed to the estate, as the basis for taxation and military service. In addition, they prohibited more than one adult male from living in the same household. This augmented tax revenues because it increased the number of households that could be taxed and at the same time broke down large estates, the economic and military backbone of potentially rebellious nobles.

Qin accomplishments are certainly impressive, but they were neither unique nor original, for it borrowed freely from others. For example, the *xian* or county system originated in Chu, Shang Yang's original home state, which was traditionally more centralized than the others and without strong noble clans. The Qin rulers were also not alone in their attempts to limit the power and influence of noble lineages. Lord Wen of Jin also took steps to suppress members of the nobility. He also prohibited members of the nobility from occupying high government posts and had adopted the *xian* system in 534 B.C.E.

However, by the end of the fourth century, Qin was poised to conquer all the other states. By 316 B.C.E., Qin increased its resources without adding to its vulnerability when it conquered the state of Shu in present-day Sichuan. The conquest of Shu gave the Qin rulers two advantages. It was a region that was easy to defend, being well protected by mountains, and it was a fertile area, all the more so after the Qin rulers built the Zhengguo canal, one of the most impressive waterworks projects in the ancient world. In 312 B.C.E., Qin managed to defeat the powerful southern state of Chu at the battle of Danyang, but it had to wait until the next century for its complete triumph.

# "The Hundred Schools"

The traditional designation of the Eastern Zhou as the period of a hundred schools reflects the importance later accorded to the age as the formative period of Chinese intellectual history, as well as to the profusion of ideas that accompanied social and political upheaval of the times. This section will examine seven well-known texts: the *Analects, Mozi, Mencius, Xunzi, Laozi, Zhuangzi,* and *Han Feizi.*

The reasons for selecting these texts rather than others are twofold. First is the importance scholars have placed on these thinkers in the formation of what they thought were four distinct schools: the *Ru* (as termed in the Chinese classical tradition) or Confucian (the traditional European designation), Mohist, Daoist, and Legalists. (See Chapter 3 for more recent views that challenge the analytical usefulness of grouping thinkers into "schools.") Second, the authors of these texts grappled at length with major problems of their day such as: What are the roots of present political chaos? How can it be remedied—through a return to the traditions of a golden age or by radical cultural and political change? What is the ideal man like, and what does it mean to be human?

# Confucius

Kong Qiu or Confucius is arguably the best-known Chinese thinker. Yet surprisingly little is known about his life other than the fact that he probably lived from c. 551 to 479 B.C.E., that he was a man from the state of Lu and was of good birth, and that he unsuccessfully attempted to play an important role in government. However, many contrasting legends and traditions are associated with Confucius, starting from the late Warring States Period. By most accounts, he was famous as a teacher and moral exemplar, a mentor surrounded by a retinue of disciples, some sagacious and some not, following him in his search for official employment. By other accounts, Confucius was author of the *Spring and Autumn Annals,* the political chronicle from which the period he lived in derives its name. Confucius was also credited by some thinkers for editing and arranging the *Odes* (see p. 20), containing poems intoned for millennia by the educated elite.

Besides crediting him with more orthodox scholarly achievements, some accounts depict Confucius as a prophet and "uncrowned king," the author of the apocrypha, a set of Han prophetic texts. Still other images left behind by later commentators represent Confucius as a fatherless child and man unaware of his own illustrious birth. By this account, Confucius was the result of a fleeting sexual encounter between two strangers in the wild.

Modern images of Confucius also diverge. Some modern scholars regard Confucius as an egalitarian, a teacher who would accept students without regard to their class or birth. Other scholars regard him as a conservative figure clinging to old feudal institutions on the eve of radical social and political change.

One reason why images of Confucius contrast so sharply is that none of his own writing survives. Most accounts of Confucius's life, furthermore, date from long after his death. The main source on Confucius's life and thought is the *Analects,* a collection that purports to record the words and deeds of Confucius and his disciples. The authorship of the *Analects* is difficult to determine. Some portions of the text date as early as Confucius's own time whereas other portions of the text appear to have been later additions. The content of the text does not provide, as one might expect, a systematic philosophy. Rather, it is a hodgepodge of conversations between Confucius and his disciples, ethical pronouncements, and anecdotes. Many of the passages in the *Analects* are terse, cryptic, and open to multiple interpretations. Nevertheless, scholars have managed to imagine what Confucius might have been like and what sorts of beliefs he might have held.

The *Analects* depicts Confucius as a man frustrated by his lack of recognition from rulers and by his inability to reform a world he sees descending into chaos.

Despite his frustration, the *Analects* represents Confucius as anything but an unpleasant person. We know that he enjoyed singing. His manner is described as "easygoing," and on a few occasions, Confucius is represented as having a wry sense of humor. For example, in one case, Confucius dryly notes that he has discovered that few men have a desire to learn as strong as their desire for women! Confucius is also described as a person who had strong emotional attachments. When his favorite pupil died, Confucius is reported to have been shattered and to have wailed without restraint.

The *Analects* devotes much space to describing the ethical ideal of a man, particularly the *junzi,* a term that can be translated as "gentleman" or "princely man" to reflect its class connotations. In other texts, it refers to men of noble birth, and the use of the term in the *Analects* reflects this history. The *junzi* is not only a man who is an ethical ideal, but he is also a cultural ideal—a man who has mastered all of the *Odes* and who speaks in a refined manner. Most likely, when Confucius reportedly spoke of the *junzi,* he was referring to other men like him—men of learning, culture, and noble birth. In addition to being a master of tradition and cultural refinement, Confucius claimed that the *junzi* (gentleman or princely man) is *ren* (humane, benevolent), *yi* (dutiful, righteous), and *xiao* (filial). The *junzi,* furthermore, has the power to influence positively those around him.

Confucius is famous for declaring in the *Analects* that he is merely a "transmitter" not an "innovator." Many scholars interpret that statement as proof that Confucius was "past-logged"—that he believed the only hope for the future lay with restoring past traditions. True, Confucius's reported admiration of Zhou traditions and moral exemplars is undeniable. And Confucius even claimed that the sagely Duke of Zhou, dead for more than five centuries, came to visit him in his dreams! But to say that Confucius was merely a conservative does little justice to what it means to transmit traditions. For Confucius, the gentleman was more than a passive custodian of the tradition. He was to have an active role in reinventing and updating traditions. For example, in one place Confucius observed that it was appropriate for a person of limited economic means to substitute caps made of black silk for more expensive linen on occasions when ritual propriety required their use. A gentleman could modify existing traditions because he understood the basic principles of the tradition. By doing so, he demonstrated not only active mastery of the tradition but also ensured that the tradition had continued relevance and value.

The *Analects* further depicts Confucius as an advocate of *li,* a term whose meaning encompasses ritual, ceremony, propriety, and good etiquette. *Li* governed all aspects of elite life in early China. It prescribed not only the way one dressed, ate, or spoke, but it also dictated the manner in which a person offered sacrifices to ancestors, how he mourned, and the way in which he was buried. For Confucius, adherence to *li,* in particular the *li* of the Zhou, was the basis of good social order.

According to Confucius, a man or woman was not only supposed to perform the *li* properly but to do so with the right attitude. For example, in mourning, a son should not only mourn and bury his father or mother according to the rules of *li,* but he was also supposed to mourn them with the utmost sincerity.

Another important aspect of Confucius's thinking about *li* has to do with his view that the *li* were invaluable for inculcating people with a respect for hierarchy. In one place in the *Analects,* he complained about a family who offered sacrifices in a manner befitting only the king of Zhou. Such an act, he felt, was symptomatic of a larger problem of his time: people were not fulfilling their proper social roles. Lords should act as lords, whereas subjects should act just as subjects and thus should *not* usurp the privileges or power of the lord. In this sense, Confucius was apparently resisting the incredible social upheavals of his own time, when high official positions were no longer reserved for men of high birth but were increasingly given to men with ability, regardless of family background.

# Mozi

Mo Di, later known as Mozi ("Master Mo"), was probably of obscure origins and humble birth. He lived from approximately 470 to 391 B.C.E. According to some accounts, he was from the state of Song; by other accounts, he was, like Confucius, a native of the state of Lu. Very little else is known about him, although scholars have made interesting guesses about his background. Some think Mozi had a criminal past because of his surname, which also means tattoo, as criminals in ancient China were often tattooed as punishment.[8] Others believe that Mozi had been a low-status artisan or carpenter, which might explain his apparent interest in the practical utility of traditions.[9] By one Han account, Mozi was once a follower of Confucius or one of his disciples.[10] And judging from his impressive grasp of ritual protocol and the virulence of his attacks on Confucius's followers, this seems quite plausible. What is known about Mozi mainly comes down to us in the form of the text called the *Mozi,* which purports to record his treatises or speeches. The *Mozi* lacks subtlety or adornment. Its language hammers at a point repetitively with a kind of relentless logic. Despite its lack of aesthetic appeal, the *Mozi* was highly influential, not only as a challenge to traditional ways of thinking, but also in the development of logic and rhetoric in early China.

Mozi's frustrations with the present age are clearly voiced in the text. And one might go so far as to argue that Mozi was the earliest thinker to provide a systematic explanation for the chaos of his age. According to Mozi, the basic reason why governance so often failed and why there was incessant warfare had to do with the human tendency to be partial. Men tended to be partial to their own kin or to their own states, and because of this, they sought benefit for their own families and states at the expense of others. Not surprisingly, strife and warfare often resulted. Rulers also suffered from partiality—partiality to their own relatives and especially to sexually attractive men. Because of their partiality, many rulers only elevated such men for powerful positions. The problem, then, is that, because all important government posts are filled with close relatives and sexually attractive men, there are few capable men in office. "If a government is rich in worthy men," Mozi observed, "then the administration will be characterized by weight and substance; but if it is paltry in such men, then the administration will be a paltry affair."[11]

Mozi's diagnosis begged the question of what was to be done. Whereas it was relatively easy for him to suggest that rulers needed to employ more men of real merit, the problem of encouraging the population to transcend the altogether human tendency to favor one's own family or state remained. In a characteristically strident tone, Mozi replied that the latter problem was not difficult to resolve. All that had to be done was to make men and women understand that the interests of others ultimately coincided with their own. "If a man were to regard the states of others as they regarded their own, then who would raise up his state to attack the state of another? It would be like attacking his own. . . . If men were to regard the families of others as they regard their own, then who would raise up his family to overthrow that of another? It would be like overthrowing his own. Now when states and cities do not attack or injure one another, is this harm or a benefit to the world? Surely it is a benefit."[12]

In relation to the *Analects*, the *Mozi* seems quite iconoclastic. For instance, whereas the Confucius of the *Analects* also urged rulers to employ capable individuals such as him, there is no indication that it would never have occurred to authors of the *Analects* to disregard considerations of social status and birth entirely. Mozi, however, insisted that rulers ought to employ the "worthy," regardless of origin or birth. Mozi's suggestion that all men and women should transcend their particular affinities to their own families probably would have raised the eyebrows of the *Analects* authors, as portions of that text emphasize obligations to kin over all others.

What the *Analects* authors would have perhaps objected to most was Mozi's position on the Zhou mourning and burial customs. For them, as well as for the many later self-proclaimed followers of Confucius, prolonged mourning and generous burials were an expression of children's devotion to their parents and subjects' loyalty to their lords. But Mozi took issue with these traditional mortuary practices. To understand his objections, we need to consider what they entailed. Prolonged mourning or three years of mourning was a *li* (ritual, etiquette) practiced by sons of noble houses when their fathers, mothers, and lords died. When practicing three years of mourning, a son was to forego the pleasures of hearty food, alcohol, sex, and luxurious accommodations. He was to wear clothes of rough hemp, live in a simple lean-to in almost total social isolation, and eat a bland porridge. Lavish burial referred to the practice of burying members of the ruling elite with a great deal of material wealth. Consider the grave of Lord Yi (d. 433 B.C.E.) in Suixian, Hubei, a lord of what was not an enormous or particularly powerful state. Lord Yi went into the next life with a large number of his personal belongings: numerous weapons, eleven *tons* of ritual bronzes, and an enormous set of bronze bells and chime stones (see Figure 2.5). Lord Yi also took with him members of his harem: twenty-one young women, ranging between the ages of thirteen and twenty-six.[13] As this case demonstrates, the practice of accompanying-in-death, although less prominent than it had been in the Western Zhou or in the Shang, still continued.

Not surprisingly, Mozi hated the mourning and burial practices of the elite. Three years of mourning, he complained, wasted the time of the ruling elite—time they should have spent governing the state. What was worse, he noted, was the fact that such practices endangered the health and well-being of the mourner. Lavish burials wasted valuable resources that otherwise could be used to enrich the state and bring benefits to the masses. Because of these factors, Mozi urged rulers to adopt simpler mourning procedures and more frugal burial practices. Instead of observing an extended period of mourning, mourners, he said, "may weep going to and from the burial, but after that they should devote themselves to making a living." And in lieu of lavish burials, such as that of Lord Yi, the ruling elite should just perform functional burials: coffins three inches thick "sufficient to bury rotting bones," shrouds thick enough only to "cover rotting flesh," and graves only deep enough so that the stench of the decaying corpse does not annoy the living.[14]

**FIGURE 2.5** This wine vessel was found in the tomb of Lord Yi of Zeng and dates to around 433 B.C.E. Constructing it must have required many resources, as it weighs 374.79 lbs. Archeologists think that it was used to cool wine, and it has a space at the top to place ice. (© National Museum of China.)

Mozi's position on mourning and burial was characteristic of his antitraditionalism. One must not, he urged rulers, assume that what is customary or traditional is right—to "confuse what is habitual with what is right, and what is customary with what is right." Beyond that, his polemical stance on mourning and burial reflects his iconoclasm. Unlike the *Analects* authors, Mozi asked why a given practice or custom was appropriate or inappropriate and why a given act was moral or immoral. According to Mozi, the only basis for knowing whether something was appropriate or moral was Heaven. "The will of Heaven is to me," he notes, "like a compass to a wheelwright or a square to a carpenter. The wheelwright and the carpenter use their compass and square to measure what is round or square for the world, saying, 'What fits these measurements is right; what does not fit them is wrong.'"[15] This line of reasoning, of course, raised the question of how one was to determine Heaven's will. According to Mozi, the will of Heaven is unambiguous: If a course of action is correct, Heaven will send its rewards usually in the guise of bountiful harvests and peace. If not, then Heaven will send its punishments in the guise of famines, eclipses, and other natural disasters.

# *Mencius*

Mencius or Meng Ke is perhaps the best known self-proclaimed follower of Confucius. According to Sima Qian (c. 145–c. 90 B.C.E.), he was a native of the state of Zou and lived from about 371 to 289 B.C.E. The main source of knowledge about Mencius's life and philosophy is a text known as the *Mencius*. The date of the *Mencius* is difficult to determine with any certainty. The *Mencius*, like both the *Analects* and the *Mozi*, actually was not the work of its reputed author. Instead, it is a collection of sayings of Mencius and reports of conversations with friends, opponents, and rulers. One crucial difference between it and the *Analects* is that the *Mencius* has far more sustained argumentation than the earlier text.

Like Confucius, Mencius was deeply frustrated with his inability to win high office. He traveled in vain from court to court, believing himself to be the only man of his day who could reform the world. Again like Confucius, Mencius eventually abandoned his efforts to find official employment and took on students. Although ignored in his own time, he was to have a lasting impact on Chinese thought and political culture into the twentieth century. During the Song dynasty (960–1279), Mencius's theories about human nature and governance came to be accepted as authoritative.

Mencius is best known for his assertion that human nature is good, an assertion that has drawn characterizations of his thought as being "tender-minded," optimistic, and even naïve. Yet there is more to this statement than meets the eye. For one, Mencius is not claiming that human beings are all good or that they are born good. He is claiming that everyone has the potential to become a sage, which represents the culmination of human achievement. Mencius observed: "the sage, too, is the same in kind as other men." The major difference between sages and ordinary people was that sages were the rare individuals who developed their moral potential through long and hard study and reflection.[16] And, in fact, the sage that Mencius most often held up as a model, Shun, was a man of very humble and even foreign origins. Second, he argues that human beings have in them an innate moral sensibility, which he refers to as the "four sprouts" (*si duan*). All men, he tells one interlocutor, would experience alarm if they were to see a child fall into a well. This spontaneous feeling of commiseration and alarm, according to Mencius, is the beginning or sprout of the virtue of *ren* (humaneness or benevolence) that figures prominently in the *Analects*. Similarly, the other three sprouts (feelings of shame, of courtesy, and of the sense of right and wrong) constitute the basis of duty (*yi*), propriety (*li*), and wisdom (*zhi*). It is not enough, however, to have these spontaneous feelings. One must cultivate these feelings through study and reflection to develop one's full moral potential.

Mencius is also famous for his rebuttal to Mozi's advocacy of universal concern as the solution to societal and political woes. Mencius's rejection of this doctrine is, of course, unsurprising, given the fact that he saw himself as a follower of Confucius. Confucius, who reportedly believed that sons should conceal their father's crimes, would have frowned on the doctrine of universal concern. Mencius argued that it is impossible for a person to show as much concern for the families of others as he shows to his own. Human beings, he claims, are naturally inclined to love their own fathers and kin more than those of others. Failure to do so, he adds, would make a person no different from animals. Second, Mencius rejects the view that partiality to one's own kin is at the root of social/political problems. On the contrary, encouraging people to be good sons, brothers, and members of local communities makes for good social order. "If only everyone loved his parents and treated his elders with deference," Mencius mused, "the Empire would be at peace." This is, he states, because a humane man, a man who loves his parents, can "extend his love from those he loves to those he does not love."[17]

In addition to rebutting the doctrine of universal concern, the *Mencius* also rejects the Mohist position on mourning and burial. Generous burials and extended mourning, the *Mencius* maintained, should not be discarded. Instead, the practice should be preserved because it is rooted in human nature (*ren xing*). It sprang from the spontaneous urge to mourn that all share when faced with the loss of a loved one. As proof of this claim, the *Mencius* describes the practices of men and women in distant antiquity. When a parent died, he observed, the children would take and consign the parent to a ditch. After casting off their parents' bodies, the children passed the place where the bodies lay. There, the children found them eaten by foxes and bitten by flies. Mencius reportedly described their response accordingly:

> A sweat broke out on their brows, and they could not bear to look. The sweating was not put on for others to see. It was an outward expression of their innermost heart.[18]

Two major political doctrines that Mencius advocated were the Mandate of Heaven (*tian ming*) and the rule of virtue. According to Mencius, Heaven gave ruling houses a mandate to rule, but rulers were obliged to rule benevolently and bring benefits to the masses. If a ruling house failed to fulfill its obligations, Heaven would revoke its mandate to rule. Under these circumstances, regicide could be permissible. This had already occurred several times in the past. The last rulers of the Xia (traditionally considered China's first dynasty) and Shang dynasties had been tyrants, and they had been replaced by worthy men who established new dynasties.

Mencius also believed that with Heaven's blessing, it would be appropriate for a ruler to cede his throne to a sage. This had happened in distant antiquity: King Yao had abdicated his throne and passed over even his son, in favor of Shun, a man whose lowly birth did not prevent him from attaining sagely virtue and wisdom. Here ancient history converged with contemporary controversy related to a political crisis that occurred within Mencius's own living memory. The king of Yan had abdicated his throne to a royal favorite, a man named Zizhi, invoking the example of Yao. This decision outraged rulers from neighboring states, who accused the king and his favorite of inverting the political order and blurring the status distinctions that existed between lords and subjects. The rulers of these neighboring states thereupon invaded Yan, executed the pair, and divided among themselves its territory. Mencius certainly was aware of the controversy. But for him, finding a sage who could benevolently govern the masses was more important than preserving the existing political hierarchy. "The people are of supreme importance," he observed, "the altars to the gods of earth and grain come next; last comes the ruler."[19]

Compared to the Confucius of the *Analects,* Mencius seems to place less of a premium on preserving the existing political hierarchy. This is evident not only in his doctrine of the rule of virtue, but also in views on *li.* One episode from the *Mencius* tells of him reportedly disregarding sumptuary rules regulating burial. When his mother died, he lavished on her a thick coffin, an extravagance reserved for higher-ranking individuals. When a friend reproached him, Mencius was prompted to reply that in the golden age of distant antiquity, no one made such distinctions. Men simply buried their parents in a fashion that reflected their feelings of love for their parents. Thus, for Mencius, the natural feelings that all sons share take precedence over considerations of rank and political status.

In several regards, Mencius exemplified the spirit of the Warring States Period and its shift away from a rigidly stratified society to one with greater social mobility. This is seen in his habit of speaking of human as beings with a shared nature, in his assertion that all men shared the same potential for sagehood regardless of birth or origins, and most of all, in his belief that virtue, not birth, ultimately should determine who should govern.

## Xunzi

Born in the state of Zhao around 312 B.C.E., Xun Kuang, known to posterity as Xunzi ("Master Xun"), lived in a turbulent age. Although it is not known exactly when he died, some accounts suggest that Xunzi lived to be a very old man. He witnessed not only the destruction of his native state and the states he lived in but also may have lived long enough to see the unification of China under the First Emperor of Qin in 221 B.C.E.[20]

In some regards, Xunzi was far more successful in his attempt to gain influence than Mencius. He went to the powerful state of Qi to teach at the famous state-sponsored Jixia academy, which was arguably the center of intellectual life at that time. There, he received titles and stipends for a time, but finally was forced to leave because of political difficulties. Before long, however, Xunzi was appointed as an official in the powerful state of Chu. By some accounts, he lived there until the end of his life. He was the teacher of two famous thinkers, Han Feizi (d. 233 B.C.E.) and Li Si (d. 208 B.C.E.). The latter would go on to become the notorious minister and advisor to the First Emperor of Qin (259–210 B.C.E.).[21]

Xunzi is mostly known through a work named for him, the *Xunzi.* Although it is not clear that Xunzi actually wrote the *Xunzi* in part or in its entirety, the *Xunzi* is noteworthy for its format. Unlike the *Analects* or the *Mencius,* the text of the *Xunzi* is organized into essays, each of which possess a great degree of thematic unity. It is also voluminous and systematic, a reflection undoubtedly of Xunzi's longevity.

Xunzi made himself notorious by declaring human nature to be evil. In part, this blanket statement, issued at the beginning of his chapter on human nature, was intended to catch the attention of his audience, and also it was intended to highlight his fierce disagreement with Mencius, although both men considered themselves followers of Confucius. By declaring human nature to be evil, Xunzi means to say that humans lack any inborn inclination to act in an ethical manner. Left to their own devices, human beings would descend into chaos and conflict. "For a son to yield to his father or a younger brother to yield to his eldest brother, for a son to relieve his father of work or a younger brother to relieve his elder brother," Xunzi mused, "acts such as these are all contrary to man's nature and run counter to his emotions."[22]

Despite the fact that he took a rather harsh view about human nature, Xunzi was nevertheless optimistic about the potential of humans to improve themselves. And, perhaps more so than Mencius, Xunzi was committed to the idea that anyone, even the "man on the street," could achieve sagehood by transforming themselves through moral training, study, and hard work. But here again the similarities stop. Whereas Mencius saw the process of sagehood as the development of innate moral sensibilities, Xunzi saw the road to sagehood as radically transformative, comparable to carpentry: "A warped piece of wood must wait until it has been laid against the straightening board, steamed, and forced into shape before it can be straight."[23]

Like other early thinkers, Xunzi was concerned about *li*. But quite unlike any other early thinker, he created a very sophisticated theory about the origins of *li*:

> What is the origin of *li*? I reply: man is born with desires. If his desires are not satisfied for him, he cannot but seek some means to satisfy them himself. If there are no limits and degrees to his seeking, then he will inevitably fall to wrangling with other men. From wrangling comes disorder and from disorder comes exhaustion. The ancient kings hated such disorder, and therefore they established the *li* and duty in order to curb it, to train men's desires and to provide for their means of satisfaction.[24]

This passage reveals much about Xunzi's ideas about the relationship between human nature and cultural institutions. Raw human desires, he declares in no uncertain terms, give rise to chaos. The chaos caused by raw human desires creates a need for the *li*. In other words, although the *li* are not themselves a part of human nature, they are necessitated by human nature. In subsequent discussions, Xunzi goes on to explain how the *li* transform raw human desires and allow for their expression in aesthetically appealing and socially productive ways. All men, according to him, experience grief when their parents die. If men were left to their own devices, they would most likely be incapacitated by their grief and be unable to go about their business. They might express their feelings for their parents by burying them with incredible amounts of material wealth and even human sacrifices. If everyone adopted these practices, states would be ruined. It follows that the *li* are necessary. They put limits on how long one can mourn; they prohibit human sacrifices, and they curtail how much wealth can be buried in the ground.

Another fascinating aspect of Xunzi's philosophy was his agnosticism. He clearly did not believe in life after death and described the dead as "the ones without consciousness." In this regard, Xunzi was not alone. The *Intrigues of the Warring States* (*Zhanguoce*), a pre-Qin text that relates court politics and warfare, also tells a tale about a dying dowager queen of Qin who gave orders for her lover to be buried with her. A friend, a courtier, of her lover thereupon went to talk the dowager out of this plan. The courtier asked her whether she believed in life after death, and she replied that she absolutely did not. Thereupon the courtier pointed out that if there was no life after death, there would be no use to burying her lover with her. But if there did happen to be life after death, she would have some explaining to do in the next life when she met up with her former husband. Satisfied with the courtier's reasoning, the dowager dropped her plans.

In addition to denying life after death, Xunzi, quite unlike Mozi, regarded Heaven as inscient. The natural world proceeds according to its own ways, oblivious to humans. It will rain or not rain regardless of whether people pray or make their sacrifices. The heavenly bodies rotate the same way whether a sage or a villain is on the throne. A well-ordered and prosperous society depends solely on the ruler:

> Respond to nature with good government, and good fortune will result; respond to it with disorder, and misfortune will result. If you encourage agriculture and are frugal with expenditures, then Heaven cannot make you poor. If you provide the people with the goods they need and demand their labor only at the proper time, then Heaven cannot afflict you with illness.[25]

Xunzi's philosophy reflected the concerns of his time in several regards. Living in a period of political change and upheaval, the destructive potential of human beings left a deep impression on Xunzi. And yet, Xunzi was optimistic about people's potential not only to transform their own basic nature, but also to create an efficacious society through human efforts alone. Xunzi's concerns, as well as his basic attitudes about what it meant to be human, would be enormously influential for hundreds of years.

# Laozi and Zhuangzi

Much scholarly attention and energy has been devoted to the task of determining exactly what Daoism (also known as Taoism) was in early China. Religious studies scholars, looking for a Chinese popular religion, like to think of Daoism as a religious movement that emphasized meditation and self-cultivation practices. Students of political thought sometimes conjecture that Daoism was the by-product of a school of statecraft, one that focused on techniques of political control. Philosophers, looking for Chinese analogues to Greek skeptical thinkers, prefer to speak of Daoism as a philosophy that advocated a return of men and women to harmony with nature and its underlying reality, the *Dao* (or *Tao*), an ineffable, eternal, self-activating, omnipresent reality. Regardless of what label we use for Daoism, it is undeniable that two of its texts, the *Daodejing* and *Zhuangzi*, have been enormously influential in Asia, Europe, and North America.

Recent archeological finds strongly suggest that the *Daodejing* is the older of the two. The *Daodejing* ("The Way and Its Power") known by many in the United States as the *Tao te ching*, following an older Romanization. It is also known by the title of *Laozi* (Lao-tzu) or the *Book of Master Lao*, after its putative author, Laozi, who reportedly was an older contemporary of Confucius. Laozi is a shadowy figure, whose identity was very much in doubt even by Han times.

The *Daodejing* is a strange text. Much of it is in verse, leading some scholars, such as Harold Roth, to speculate that it was originally a meditation manual.[26] And much of it is cryptic, paradoxical, and highly suggestive and hence has been the subject of more classical commentary than any other text. It is also, not surprisingly, the most frequently translated book from China. In part, the popularity of the *Daodejing* is due to the inscrutability of its language, which invites a multitude of interpretations. But the popularity of the *Daodejing* also has to do with its mysterious, but powerful, messages.

One such message is the inadequacy of language. The first line of the version of the *Daodejing* accepted as authentic prior to recent archeological dicoveries reads, "The Way that can be named is not the eternal Way." In other words, the totality of the Way—the way things are, as well as the way things should be—eludes codification. Another theme from the *Daodejing* is the limits of conventional notions of value. Is it better to be strong, as opposed to weak? Not necessarily, suggests the *Daodejing*. Weak states, for instance, may outlive strong states, because lacking rich resources and wealth, they may elude attack and conquest. Is it better to be famous for one's knowledge? Again, not necessarily, as "those who know do not speak; those who speak do not know." Or—to touch upon a political theme of the text—would it be preferable, as many Warring States thinkers suggested, to educate and transform the masses to create a tightly governed and prosperous state? Again, the answer, against the conventional grain, is a resounding "no." The best rulers allow the people to return to "ignorance" or to a life of primal simplicity, one in which they are in tune with nature. And to attain this ideal, the ruler must conduct his government with great delicacy and restraint, like a cook boiling a small fish. He must not interfere with the Way and, by taking no action of his own, must allow everything to take its course.

The other well-known Daoist classic is the *Zhuangzi*, which takes its name from its legendary author, Zhuangzi (or Master Zhuang, also known as Zhuang Zhou). As is the case with Laozi, little is known about Zhuangzi. In fact, some scholars doubt very much that he ever existed. The Zhuangzi is certainly not the work of a single hand, but a compilation of different works, ranging in date from the mid-Warring States Period to the first century of the Western Han dynasty. Unlike the *Daodejing,* which comprises short verses or paragraphs, the *Zhuangzi* contains long chapters, filled with colorful anecdotes and fanciful conversations. In some places, Confucius even appears, occasionally as a venerated teacher, and, in other places, as a fool ripe for a verbal thrashing by a famous outlaw.

Many parts of the *Zhuangzi* speak to the importance of withdrawal and reclusion, as opposed to active political engagement. In many respects, this position stands in contrast with the views found in other texts surveyed earlier in this chapter. Unlike the *Analects,* the *Mencius,* or even the *Xunzi,* the *Zhuangzi* does not brim with advice for rulers about how to better administer the realm. The wise man, to put it somewhat differently, is not an active minister, but a hermit who knows that it is better to sit fishing on the banks of a remote mountain stream.

Like many of the texts covered, the *Zhuangzi* also takes a position on the value of traditional mourning rituals. But unlike the *Mozi* or *Mencius,* the *Zhuangzi* does not explicitly condemn or defend the practice. Instead, it recounts an episode from Zhuangzi's own life. Zhuangzi's wife had died. When one of his comrades, Huizi, came to convey his condolences, he found that instead of grieving, Zhuangzi was sitting in his tub singing. This took Huizi aback, and he protested. "You lived with her, she brought up your children and grew old," said Huizi. "It should be enough simply not to weep at her death. But pounding on a tub and singing—this is going too far, isn't it?" Zhuangzi responded:

> You're wrong. When she first died, do you think I didn't grieve like anyone else? But I looked back to her beginning and the time before she was born. Not only the time before she was born, but the time before she had a body. Not only the time before she had a body, but the time before she had a spirit. In the midst of the jumble of wonder and mystery a change took place and she had a spirit. Another change and she had a body. Another change and she was born. Now there's been another change and she's dead. It's just like the progression of the four seasons, spring, summer, fall, winter. Now she's going to lie down peacefully in a vast room. If I were to follow after her bawling and sobbing, it would show that I don't understand anything about fate. So I stopped.[27]

The episode about Zhuangzi's mourning for his wife not only reveals what the authors of the text thought about traditional rites of mourning, but it also illustrates two larger points found in the *Zhuangzi.* The first has to do with the limits of conventional morality, a morality that depends upon distinctions, such as between good and bad or between true and false. For the *Zhuangzi,* drawing distinctions, especially through language, is inherently problematic, because it prevents men and women from grasping the totality of the Way. "What does the Way rely upon," Zhuangzi reportedly asks. "That we have true and false? What do words rely upon, that we have right and wrong? How can the Way go away and not exist? How can words exist and not be acceptable? When the Way relies on little accomplishments and words rely on vain show, then we have the rights and wrongs of the Ru and the Mohists. What one calls right the other calls wrong; what one calls wrong the other calls right. But if we want to right their wrongs and wrong their rights, then the best thing to use is clarity."[28]

Given the limits of language and, indeed, the limits of conventional morality, the *Zhuangzi* urges men and women to stop drawing distinctions. "Discard and confuse the six tones, smash and unstring the pipes and lutes, stop up the ears of the blind musician Kuang, and for the first time the people of the world will be able to hold on to their hearing. Wipe out patterns and designs, scatter the five colors, glue up the eyes of Li Zhu, and for the first time the people of the world will be able to hold on to their eyesight.[29]

The second theme that the episode about Zhuangzi's mourning touches upon has to do with the importance of acquiring the proper perspective on matters, a theme that runs through many anecdotes found in the text. Is death better than life or freedom better than captivity? With respect to these questions, the *Zhuangzi* recounts a memorable anecdote, one drawn from history:

> Lady Li was the daughter of the border guard of Ai. When she was first taken captive and brought to the state of Qin, she wept until her tears drenched the collar of her robe. But later, when she went to live in the palace of the ruler, shared his couch with him, and ate the delicious meats of his table, she wondered why she had ever wept.

The anecdote concludes by posing a more challenging question. That is, given that freedom may not necessarily be better than captivity, how can one know that death might not be better than life—"How do I know that the dead do not wonder why they ever longed for life?"[30]

Anecdotes, such as the one about Lady Li, not only illustrate the importance of perspective but also the uncertainty of human knowledge. The *Zhuangzi* brings home this point in the allegory of the dream, where the text implicitly compares humans' awareness of the world with a dreamer's perception of dreams.

> Once Zhuang Zhou [that is, Zhuangzi] dreamt he was a butterfly, a butterfly flitting and fluttering around, happy with himself and doing as he pleased. He didn't know he was Zhuang Zhou. Suddenly he woke up and there he was, solid and unmistakable Zhuang Zhou. But he didn't know if he was Zhuang Zhou who had dreamt he was a butterfly, or a butterfly dreaming he was Zhuang Zhou.[31]

To realize that human awareness is in itself indeterminate was for the *Zhuangzi* authors a great insight.[32] And indeed, the text refers to this kind of awareness as nothing but "the great awakening," one in which "we know that this is all a great dream."[33]

# *Han Feizi*

Few Chinese thinkers are as notorious as Han Feizi (c. 280–233 B.C.E.), who was one of Xunzi's two famous pupils. His ideas survive in the *Han Feizi,* a text of fifty-five chapters reviled for millennia for its *realpolitik* outlook but appreciated for its clever arguments and colorful writing. In modern times, it has even been compared to Machiavelli's *The Prince.* Like *The Prince,* the *Han Feizi* is replete with historical anecdotes illustrating the author's point, as well as many statements that shocked readers by their cynicism and apparent lack of regard for morality.[34]

A member of the royal house of the small state of Han, Han Fei or Han Feizi ("Master Han Fei") was destined for a career in government. But according to Sima Qian, Han Fei suffered from a stammer. And in an age when statesmen distinguished themselves through brilliant oratory rather than writing, his career suffered. Worried about the fortunes of his small home state, he admonished his royal relatives in written memorials, but all in vain. Ironically, the one ruler who did take Han Feizi's writings to heart was the young Qin ruler, who would become the first emperor of China. The Qin minister, Li Si, brought to his lord's attention the writings of his former classmate, for whom he expressed great admiration. Yet despite his admiration for Han Feizi, the young Qin ruler launched a campaign against Han in 234 B.C.E. Just before the invasion, the ruler of Han dispatched Han Feizi to Qin to plead on behalf of Han, but, following Li Si's advice, the Qin ruler had Han Fei executed. Why Li Si turned on his classmate is not clear. Some suggest he was jealous of Han Fei, whom he acknowledged to be the greater talent. Others suggest that Li Si was concerned that Han Feizi was not trustworthy. Before drinking the poison sent to him by Li Si, Han Fei composed "The Difficulties of Persuasion," a famous work in which he explored the dangers facing statesmen.[35]

Traditional scholars categorize Han Feizi as a Legalist (*fa jia*). Two other famous Legalist thinkers were Shang Yang and Shen Buhai (d. 337 B.C.E.), although little is known about their philosophies. By most accounts, Legalist ideas first emerged around the fourth century B.C.E. along with state consolidation and rationalization. Legalists emphasized practical problems of statecraft and political control over ethical concerns. Unlike Mencius, who frowned upon discussions of profit and political power, Legalist thinkers openly discussed ways in which rulers could maximize their tax revenues, enlarge their corvée labor force, and effectively wage wars. They believed that strict enforcement of law (*fa*) and a system of rewards, rather than ritual norms, would ensure good social order.

In addition to subscribing to these views, Han Feizi's advice to rulers in large part reflects his specific understanding of the political upheaval in his own time. For Han Feizi, as for Xunzi, the roots of the trouble lay in human nature. Human beings, he noted, virtually always act out of self-interest—even at the expense of good political order. Expressions of self-interest were inescapable and manifested in all human relations. This is clearly shown, Han Feizi argued, by the fact that many families kill newborn infants if they are girls because, unlike boys, girls cannot support their parents in old age. If calculations of self-interest influence the re-lationship of parents and child, which are based on natural bonds of affection, how much more is this the case for relationships not bound by ties of natural affection, relations such as those between lord and minister? To illustrate his point about the unreliable nature of political relations, Han Feizi frequently turned to the histori-cal record, which was replete with examples not only of ministers betraying their lords but also of conflicts of interest arising between royal husbands and wives and between brothers.

For Han Feizi, the ills of his time required some drastic measures. Rulers, he warned, should not attempt to return to an idealized past of human government, as some thinkers proposed. To do so would be to emulate a farmer who, while working in a field one day, noticed that a rabbit dashed itself unconscious against a tree stump. That evening the farmer took the rabbit home and feasted on it with his family. The next day and every day thereafter the farmer waited by the tree stump for another rabbit. Just as foolish, according to Han Feizi, were those who believed that the accidental successes of the past would be repeated.

The enlightened ruler is free of illusions about restoring humane government, which had only worked in distant antiquity before population pressures trans-formed society into a world of strife. Instead, the enlightened ruler needs to be aware that human beings act out of self-interest. Therefore, he must always be on guard against his ministers, wives, male favorites, and even children. He realizes that everyone—even those who profess to love him dearly—potentially benefits from his death. The enlightened ruler furthermore, Han Feizi argues, realizes that people deceive, especially when they are aware of the desires and fancies of the ruler. As a result, the enlightened ruler conceals his own thoughts and feelings to discover those of his subjects and to keep his subjects guessing. Finally, the en-lightened ruler avoids activities or favorites who cloud his judgment. "The ruler is easily beguiled by lovely women and charming boys, by all those who can fawn and play at love," complained Han Feizi, "They wait for the time when he is sated with food and wine, and ask for anything they desire, for they know that by this trick their requests are sure to be heeded."[36] For this reason, the enlightened ruler disciplines himself with his favorites and acts only to promote the worthy and ca-pable, knowing in the long run that his chances of survival are greater if he gov-erns in a dispassionate and impartial manner.

Later assessments of Han Feizi have been far from kind. In part, Han Feizi's rhetoric—in particular, his penchant for pithy but extreme statements—inspired harsh assessments of his philosophy. But in large part, these assessments owe much to Han Feizi's association with the policies of the Qin empire and the Legalists. Some scholars even go so far as to see Han Feizi as an advocate of royal tyranny and a theorist of authoritarianism. Yet one could argue that in many re-gards, Han Feizi's ideas, like those of Machiavelli, should be considered in their historical context. True, Han Feizi emphasized the importance of political control and harsh penalties, but his advocacy reflected his desire to bring unity and order to an increasingly chaotic world. Had he lived a little longer perhaps Han Feizi would have seen his dreams realized.

# *Notes*

1. Lothar von Falkenhausen, "Sources of Taoism: Reflections on Archaeological Indicators of Religious Change in Eastern Zhou China," *Taoist Resources* 5.2 (1994): 7–8.

2. Lothar von Falkenhausen, "The Waning of the Bronze Age, Material Culture and Social Developments, 770–481 B.C.E.," in Edward Shaughnessy and Michael Loewe, eds., *The Cambridge History of Ancient China: From the Origins of Civilization to 221 BC* (Cambridge: Cambridge Univ. Press, 1999), pp. 514–525.

3. David Hawkes, *The Songs of the South: An Ancient Chinese Anthology of Poems by Qu Yuan and Other Poets* (London: Penguin Books, 1985), p. 27.

4. Hawkes, *Songs of the South*, p. 69.

5. Hawkes, *Songs of the South*, p. 75.

6. Frank Kierman, Jr., "Phases and Modes of Combat in Early China," in Frank A. Kierman and John K. Fairbank, eds., *Chinese Ways in Warfare* (Cambridge: Harvard Univ. Press, 1974), pp. 26–66.

7. Mark Edward Lewis, "Warring States Political History," in *Cambridge History of Ancient China*, pp. 620–29.

8. Burton Watson, "Introduction," *Basic Writings of Mo-Tzu, Hsün Tzu, and Han Fei Tzu* (New York: Columbia Univ. Press, 1964), p. 5.

9. A. C. Graham, *Disputers of the Tao: Philosophical Argumentation in Ancient China* (La Salle, Ill.: Open Court, 1989), p. 34.

10. Robert Eno, Personal communication, 18 May, 2004. The text that makes this claim is the Han philosophical compendium, the *Huainanzi* (c. 139 B.C.E.).

11. Watson, *Basic Writings of Mo-Tzu*, p. 18.

12. Watson, *Basic Writings of Mo-Tzu*, p. 40.

13. Wu Hung, "Art and Architecture of the Warring States Period," in *Cambridge History of Ancient China*, pp. 721–723.

14. Watson, *Basic Writings of Mo-Tzu*, p. 76.

15. Watson, *Basic Writings of Mo-Tzu*, p. 83.

16. *Mencius* 2A2, trans. D.C. Lau, *Mencius* (Harmondsworth, Penguin, 1970), p. 80.

17. *Mencius* 4A11, pp. 122–23.

18. *Mengzi* 3A5, trans. D.C. Lau, p. 105.

19. *Mencius* 7B14, p. 196.

20. Watson, "Introduction," *Basic Works of Mo-Tzu* (*Hsün* section), pp. 1–2.

21. Ibid.

22. Watson, *Basic Works of Mo-Tzu*, p. 164.

23. Watson, *Basic Works of Mo-Tzu*, p. 157–159.

24. Watson, *Basic Works of Mo-Tzu*, p. 89. Translation slightly modified.

25. Watson, *Basic Works of Mo-Tzu* (*Hsün* section), p. 79.

26. Harold D. Roth, *Original Tao: Inward Training (Nei-Yeh) and the Foundations of Taoist Mysticism* (New York: Columbia Univ. Press, 1999).

27. Burton Watson, *The Complete Works of Chuang Tzu* (New York: Columbia Univ. Press, 1968), pp. 191–92.

28. Watson, *Complete Works of Chuang Tzu*, p. 39. Translation slightly modified.

29. Watson, *Complete Works of Chuang Tzu,* p. 111.

30. Watson, *Complete Works of Chuang Tzu,* p. 47.

31. Watson, *Complete Works of Chuang Tzu,* p. 49.

32. David N. Keightley, "Disguise and Deception in Early China and Early Greece," in Steven Shankman and Stephen Durrant, eds., *Early China/Ancient Greece: Thinking Through Comparisons* (Albany: State Univ. of New York Press, 2002), p. 137.

33. Watson, *Complete Works of Chuang Tzu,* p. 49.

34. Keightley, "Disguise and Deception in Early China and Early Greece," p. 137.

35. Watson, *Complete Works of Chuang Tzu,* p. 47.

36. Watson, "Introduction," *Basic Works of Mo-Tzu* (*Han Fei Tzu* section), p. 4.

37. Watson, "Introduction," *Basic Works of Mo-Tzu* (*Han Fei Tzu* section), pp. 1–15.

38. Watson, *Basic Works of Mo-Tzu* (*Han Fei Tzu* section), p. 43.

# The Early Imperial Period

The Qin unification of China in 221 B.C.E. was the beginning of some 400 years of imperial rule, although the Qin rule was short lived. The Han built on Qin foundations and erected a more lasting political structure. Under the Han, civilization in what is now China was reshaped, and the Han state became a great imperial power comparable in achievements and historical significance to the Roman Empire (see Figure 3.2). Most historians divide the Han into two periods. The first period is the Former or Western Han (206 B.C.E.–9 C.E.), the latter name reflecting the location of the imperial capital in Chang'an in the West. This period came to an end in 9 C.E., when the regent, Wang Mang, usurped the throne and established a short-lived Xin dynasty (9–23 C.E.). By 25 C.E., members of the Liu clan wrestled control of the empire from the Xin and established the imperial capital in Luoyang in the East. This period is referred to as the Later or Eastern Han dynasty (25–220 C.E.).

# I. The Qin

To most people living outside China, the Qin dynasty (221–206 B.C.E.) is famous for two monuments: the army of terra-cotta soldiers found in Xi'an and the Great Wall (of which the much later additions are still visible). It is also arguably the most notorious of all early East Asian regimes. Today, both in China and elsewhere, the Qin has come to epitomize authoritarian rule and imperial tyranny. The truth, however, is more complicated.

## Sources and Historiographical Problems

The negative image of the dynasty is based on traditional assessments that emphasize three themes: the repressiveness of Qin rule, the harshness or severity of its institutions, and the follies of its rulers. The best exposition of the repressiveness of Qin rule is found in "The Faults of the Qin," a famous essay by the Han scholar-official, Jia Yi (201–168? B.C.E.), who observes of the First Emperor or Qin Shihuang:

> He reached the pinnacle of power and ordered all in the Six Directions, whipping the rest of the world into submission and thus spreading his might through the Four Seas. . . . He then abolished the ways of ancient sage kings and put to the torch the writings of the Hundred Schools in an attempt to keep the people in ignorance. He demolished the walls of the major cities and put to death men of fame and talent, collected all the arms of the realm of Xianyang, and had the spears and arrowheads melted down to form twelve huge statues in human form—all with the aim of weakening his people.[1]

One infamous incident of Qin rule that Jia Yi alluded to in the preceding extract was the First Emperor's decision to burn books by a wide array of thinkers in 213 B.C.E. Jia Yi believed that this policy was intended to "keep the people in ignorance."

Most exposition of the second theme revolves around the burdens levied upon commoners through conscript labor. Conscript labor was levied upon all able-bodied adult males in the realm, usually in the form of labor or military service. Periodically the state required local officials to register the name, place of origins, status, and age of every person under his jurisdiction. With this information, the government was able to estimate the size of its conscript labor force and build large-scale public works. The best known of all public works is the Great Wall, built by linking earlier walls raised by states against each other and intended to protect the empire from hostile, nomadic groups. Restored by the Ming dynasty, it still can be seen just north of Beijing. According to Han accounts, the Great Wall was built with conscript labor.

Other important public works projects that used conscript labor include networks of roads that ran from one end of the empire to the other, as well as irrigation and transportation canals. With conscript labor, the Qin state also built a lavish mausoleum for the First Emperor. Although his tomb has yet to be excavated by archeologists, if we believe Han accounts, it was a wonder (see Figure 3.1). According to the famous historian Sima Qian (c. 140–c. 90 B.C.E.), the 700,000 conscripts charged with building it "dug through subterranean streams and poured molten copper for the outer coffin, and the tomb was filled with models of palaces, pavilions, and offices, as well as fine vessels, precious stones and rarities." The First Emperor wanted his tomb to replicate more than his palace; he wanted to recreate the entire world within the tomb. "All the country's streams and the Yellow and the Yangzi Rivers were reproduced in quicksilver and by some mechanical means made to flow into a miniature ocean; the heavenly constellations were shown above and the regions of the earth below."[2]

The third theme in traditional accounts of the Qin focuses on the purported follies of the emperors. For example, the reason, according to Sima Qian, that the First Emperor invested great energy in his mausoleum was because he had a pathological fear of death. And by the end of his reign, like many elites, he became so obsessed with avoiding death that he sponsored futile expeditions to find immortality elixirs, including one that involved sending a score of young men and women to mythical islands. With age, his obsession grew so strong that none of his ministers dared to use the word in his presence. Not only did the First Emperor have a pathological fear of death, but by Sima's account, he was no less than a megalomaniac. Once, at the end of his rule, the emperor made a tour of the realm. Arriving in the East, he visited the most sacred mountain, Mount Tai, and decided to scale its heights and leave three inscriptions, which would bear everlasting witness to his achievements. Rather immodestly, one of the inscriptions, translated by Martin Kern, proclaims:

> The August Emperor
>     embodies sagehood,
> And after having pacified all
>     under Heaven
> He has not been remiss in
>     rulership.
> He rises early, retires late at
>     night;
> He establishes and sets up
>     enduring benefits,
> Radiates and glorifies His
>     teachings and instructions.
> His precepts and principles reach all around,
> The distant and the near are completely well-ordered
> And all receive His sage will.
> The noble and the mean are distinguished and made clear,
> Men and women embody compliance,
> Cautious and respectful to their professions and duties.
> Distinctly demarcated are the inner and outer spheres,
> Nothing that is not clear and pure,
> Extending down to the later descendants.
> His transforming influence reaches without limit:
> May [later ages] respect and follow the decrees He bequeaths
> And forever accept His solemn warnings![3]

**FIGURE 3.1** Terra-cotta warrior guarding the tomb of the First Emperor. Although yet to be excavated, archaeologists have discovered a complete terra-cotta army in the immediate vicinity of the tomb. (© Bridgeman Art Library.)

There are reasons to doubt at least some of the stories that have come down to us about the First Emperor. True, the First Emperor may well have left three inscriptions on Mount Tai, but we must bear in mind that accounts such as Sima's were written by court historians employed by the Han victors. Jens Ostergard Petersen, for one, has questioned the conventional accounts of the repressive measures undertaken by the Qin. With respect to the burning of the books, Petersen, after careful examination of the extant textual record, concluded that the measure was far more limited than previously thought. It did not apply to all philosophical inquisitions but just to compilations of didactic historical anecdotes that the Qin state regarded as having "fragmented form and petty concerns."[4] For another thing, many of these stories are undeniably anti-Qin aiming to discredit, and even slander, the Qin ruling house. Consider the following passage, also by Sima Qian, which describes the mother of the First Emperor as a nymphomaniac:

> While the First Emperor was growing up, the licentiousness of the Queen-dowager did not cease. Lü Buwei feared it might be discovered and that disaster would befall him, so he secretly sought a man named Lao Ai, who had a tremendous penis, and made him his retainer. At times he would indulge in some wild music, and have [Lao] Ai move about [in time with it], with his penis filling up the [hole of] a wheel made of tong wood. He caused the Queen-dowager to hear of this, in order to entice her. The Queen-dowager heard of it, and actually wished secretly to have him. Lü Buwei thereupon introduced Lao Ai, and had someone falsely accuse him of a crime deserving castration. At the same time [Lü] Buwei secretly told the Queen-dowager that if she could have [Lao Ai] falsely castrated, then he could be obtained to serve within [the women's quarters]. At this, the Queen-dowager secretly gave heavy bribes to the official in charge of castration, to have him [that is, Lao Ai] falsely condemned, pluck off his beard and eyebrows, and make him a eunuch. In this way he came to enter the service of the Queen-dowager.[5]

# Reappraisals

Recent scholarship has presented a more balanced picture of Qin rule, acknowledging its achievements. To be sure, although Qin rule was harsh, the Qin were also responsible for significant centralizing measures. The empire was divided into commanderies (*jun*), in turn subdivided into counties (*xian*) with administration entrusted to officials whose assignments, promotions, demotions depended on performance. The physical integration of the realm was fostered by a large-scale road-building program. Written communication was facilitated by the creation of a standard script to replace many local scripts. In addition to standardizing the script, the First Emperor and his advisors also unified weights and measures. Acts such as these no doubt proved invaluable to subsequent generations of Han dynasty emperors, who also struggled to unify an empire prone to dissolution.

Another great, although somewhat more controversial, legacy of the Qin was its legal code. Most standard accounts emphasize that the Qin code was extensive and excessively harsh. One aspect of the code that is often criticized is the practice of collective punishment according to which the spouses, children, and often the extended family of a criminal would be punished, even put to death, if they did not each denounce the offender. The purpose of this practice was threefold. First, it was to ensure that families took responsibility for policing their members; second, it prevented family members from seeking revenge or rebelling against the state; and third, it encouraged family members to denounce, rather than to shield, each other.

Another noteworthy aspect of the Qin legal code was its control of the private conduct of its subjects. A man could not only be punished for failing to show up to do his conscript labor or for murdering his neighbor, he could also be punished for engaging in sexual relations with someone else's wife. In a similar vein, a woman could be severely punished for being rude to her in-laws, as well as for having sexual relations with a slave. The most serious offense with regard to private conduct, however, was a lack of filial piety to one's parents, an offense that was punished by execution in the marketplace.[6]

Although from our perspective, these codes seem harsh and even tyrannical, it is also important to bear in mind that they were far from arbitrary. Consider two excerpts from the Qin code:

> In trying a case, if one can use the documents to track down [the evidence in] their statements, and get the facts on the parties without an investigation by beating, that is considered superior; investigation by beating is considered inferior; in addition, intimidation is considered the worse [course of action].
>
> In general, when questioning parties to a case, you must first listen to everything they say and record it, with each party developing his statement. Although you may know that he is lying, there is no need to interrogate him immediately. When his statements have been recorded in their entirety and there are no explanations, then interrogate him with interrogators. When interrogating him, once again listen and record his explanatory statements in their entirety; once again, inspect the other [points] which lack explanation and reinterrogate him about them. When you have interrogated him to the greatest extent possible and he has lied repeatedly, has changed what he has said but not submitted, should the law match interrogation by beating, then investigate by beating. When you have investigated by beating, you must compose a document which reads:
>
> Transcript:
>
> Because X repeatedly changed what he has said and there were no explanatory statements, we question X by beating.[7]

As seen from these excerpts, although torture was allowed by the Qin code, it was regarded as an undesirable, last resort—to be avoided if possible and only to be used when the proper procedures were followed.

# II. The Han

## *The Formative Years*

Not long after the death of the First Emperor, rebellions broke out against the Qin. Of the rebel leaders, the most formidable were Xiang Yu (233–202 B.C.E.), a Chu aristocrat of great courage and charisma, and Liu Bang (247–195 B.C.E.), a man reputed to be of obscure origin, with little cultural refinement but personal shrewdness. According to later accounts, Liu Bang's shrewdness prevailed over Xiang Yu's courage, and by 202 B.C.E., Liu Bang, known to posterity as Gaozu, became one of the first men of obscure and nonaristocratic origin to found a major dynasty. That dynasty is called the Han, or more narrowly the Former or Western Han (206 B.C.E.–9 C.E.) (see Figure 3.2.).

Administratively the Han built on Qin foundations, but a substantive difference between the early Western Han and the Qin lay in the degree of political centralization. Whereas the Qin attempted to rule the entire realm from the state capital, this was not feasible for the first five Han emperors. For one thing, Liu Bang had to reward the old generals and comrades-in-arms who had helped him to defeat Xiang Yu. Because of this, Liu Bang had to parcel out large territories as vassal states to his former generals or comrades-in-arms. Once firmly established, however, he regretted having given away so much territory and wished to forestall any ambitions his former generals and comrades-in-arms may have entertained. Under one pretext or another, he regained control over the lands assigned and reincorporated the territory into the empire. For another thing, the empire was too vast and difficult to simply rule from the capital in Chang'an, so Liu Bang also established kingdoms in the East for members of his own clan, his many sons, and their grandsons (see Figure 3.3). In many ways, one could say that the early Han had returned to the decentralized system of rule that characterized the Western Zhou.

The decentralized system of rule proved, however, to be a source of trouble. Perhaps more so than Liu Bang's old generals and comrades-in-arms, members of the imperial Liu family entrusted with kingdoms entertained ambitions of their own. And despite rich gifts and titles from the court, by the time of the Emperors Wen (r. 180–157 B.C.E.) and Wu (r. 140–86 B.C.E.), Liu kings openly rebelled against the emperors. Emperor Wen had special difficulty with his wayward younger brother, Liu Chang (c. 199–174 B.C.E.), also known to posterity as King Li. Liu Chang had violated sumptuary rules, using the emperor's own carriage, and he had murdered and participated in a rebellion against his brother. Nevertheless, Emperor Wen had been unwilling to punish Liu Chang because he was the emperor's last surviving brother, and the emperor loved him. Not surprisingly, it was only a matter of time before Liu Chang participated in a rebellion against the emperor. In strongly worded memorials, various statesmen, including Jia Yi, urged the emperor to punish his brother severely. Emperor Wen, Sima Qian tells, acceded, although only reluctantly, and Liu Chang was sent unceremoniously into banishment in the south in a cage. Indignant at his treatment, Liu Chang reportedly refused

**FIGURE 3.2** Map of the Han empire.

**FIGURE 3.3** Jade burial suit of the Princess Dou Wan, wife of Liu Sheng (d. 113 B.C.E.). Mancheng, Hebei, 67.72 in long. The Han court bestowed jade suits only to members of the Liu clan and the highest ministers of the realm. (© Giraudon/Bridgeman Art Library.)

food and water and died before reaching his destination. Hearing the news of his brother's death saddened Emperor Wen, and, again according to Sima Qian, he then made the mistake of enfeoffing Liu Chang's son, Liu An, king of Huainan, with a large territory that had once belonged to Chu.

In his turn, Liu An grew up to entertain dynastic ambitions of his own. Somewhat more refined and subtle than his father, Liu An was also well known during the reign of his nephew, Emperor Wu, as a great patron of learning. He commissioned an encyclopedic work, the *Huainanzi,* which contains essays on topics ranging from myth to philosophy of government, geography, and astronomy. However, in 154 B.C.E., Liu An reportedly rebelled against the emperor, with hopes of superseding him. Although the truth of the charges against him is unclear, Liu An, along with his wife, committed suicide. His children were executed, and his territory was absorbed by the court.

# The Quality of Han Rule

Traditional scholarship tends to emphasize the differences between Qin and Han rule, portraying the latter as less tyrannical and authoritarian and correlating this with differences in theories of governance. The Han ruling house, beginning with Emperor Wu (r. 140–86 B.C.E.), adopted Ru doctrines as its state orthodoxy.[8] Most scholars refer to this policy as "the victory of Confucianism." As such, one would expect that the Han dynastic house would promote traditional values associated with Confucian thinkers, such as filial piety and benevolent rule. To be sure, Han emperors supported traditions of learning scholars now retrospectively regard as Ru or Confucian, and Emperor Wu was responsible for establishing an imperial academy. Finally, the early Han rulers did at least pay lip service to values found in the *Analects,* in particular, filial piety. From the reign of Emperor Wu on, calls to recruit "filial sons" into the imperial bureaucracy became frequent.[9]

Nevertheless, it would seem that some historians exaggerated the differences between the Qin and Han, for the early Han regime was almost indistinguishable from the Qin in a number of ways. For one, Han legal institutions show great continuity with their Qin predecessors, even though Liu Bang reportedly abolished the harsh and intrusive Qin codes. Han administrative documents discovered by archeologists in the last several decades reveal that, like its Qin predecessor, the Han state was indeed harsh.[10] Family members were punished for one individual's crimes. For example, if a man raped or engaged in illicit sexual relations with a woman, not only would he be castrated, but also his wife and the children who lived with him would be imprisoned. A woman, furthermore, who did not denounce her husband for committing a crime would also be punished, although usually somewhat less severely.

Perhaps the best example of how harsh the Han code could be is a legal case narrated in a document buried in a tomb dating to 187 B.C.E. It begins:

> The statute observes: As for those who are responsible for affairs in the county magistrate's office but whose father or mother or whose wife dies, they are allowed a grace leave of 30 days. If their paternal grandfather or grandmother dies or their natural siblings die, they are

allowed 15 days. If they are brazenly remiss in this, then they are to be shaved and made into a wall-builder or grain-pounder of the state. They are to be shackled at the feet and transported to the bureau of the salt mines in Ba prefecture [in the South West]. . . .

Next the document introduces the case of Woman A, whose husband, an army private, had died of illness. As appropriate, A and her mother-in-law named Su wailed all night next to the coffin placed in the front hall of the house before burial. This was as it should be, but:

> A and a man, B, fornicated in the chamber behind the coffin. The next morning, Su denounced A to an officer, who bound A for arrest. There was uncertainty as to what A's offense had been. . . . The [rights of inheritance] of a wife are secondary with respect to the parents of her husband. In the instance that a father or mother had died, and before they had been buried, the child had fornicated by the side of the deceased's [coffin], then the child would have been deemed unfilial. Being unfilial, he or she would have been cast off in the market place. If his or her crime had been secondary in [severity] to being unfilial, then he or she would have merited being tattooed and made into a wall-builder or grain-pounder. Had he or she been brazenly lax, then he or she would be imprisoned. Applying this principle to this case, the wife reveres the husband and [only reveres him] second to her father and mother. Yet A's husband died, and she was not sorrowful or grieved. She fornicated with a man by the side of the deceased's [coffin], and thus [her offense] warrants [the punishments as stipulated by] the two regulations concerning the "unfilial" and the "brazenly lax."[11]

Prurience aside, this case reveals that the Han state, like its Qin predecessor, attempted to regulate relationships between parents and children as well as between spouses and was as interested as its predecessor in penetrating into the daily lives of ordinary people and punishing what most of us now largely consider to be "personal" or "private" matters. But, on the one hand, it was, and remains, hardly unique in this respect. And, on the other, the state's actual ability to influence, let alone control, local daily life was limited in an age before the invention of paper and brush, not to speak of telephones and fax machines.

The early Han state showed great interest, like its Qin predecessor, in maintaining control over and extracting labor from the population. Many of the administrative documents discovered from Han tombs show that the state required every man, woman, and child to register their name, age, place of origin, and sex with local authorities. Each year, every able-bodied adult man and woman was required to perform service or pay for a substitute. Failure to register or perform service was seriously punished. All Han subjects were further categorized into classes, according to their status. As was the case in Qin times, high-status individuals were punished on the whole less severely than commoners or slaves. Criminal offenses, especially minor ones that did not merit death or serious mutilation, also provided the Han state with an additional source of revenue: offenders were often put to work in the state-owned salt and iron mines, as well as on building public works, such as city walls.

# The Xiongnu and Other Neighboring Peoples

From early times the Han traded, negotiated, and fought with neighboring peoples. During the Warring States Period such contacts became quite extensive, including relations with tribal confederations in Manchuria and Korea in the Northeast, with the inhabitants of the steppes to the Northwest, and with the peoples of the South. Before the reign of Emperor Wu, Han foreign policy was generally conciliatory, but that emperor adopted expansionist policies and by force of arms asserted Han control over the Southeast, including what is now Northern Vietnam, and established Han colonies in Korea where they greatly accelerated the diffusion of Han culture into that peninsula and beyond to Japan.

It turned out that both Korea and Vietnam were suitable for the Han-style agricultural way of life and gradually adapted a Han-style government and higher culture while resisting Han political dominance. In contrast, a Han way of life was irrelevant to the people of the grasslands to the Han empire's north and northwest. The frequently antagonistic relations between the nomads of the steppe and the settled people of the plains remained a persistent problem for two millennia.

The greatest nomadic challenge that faced the Western Han emperors came from the Xiongnu, one of the nomadic groups that lived in the North and Northwest. The First Emperor reportedly had the Great Wall built as a cautionary move and had even sent out an expedition against them. The Xiongnu threat became truly formidable under the effective leadership of Maodun, who became the ruler of the Xiongnu confederacy in 209 B.C.E. Under his leadership, the Xiongnu forced the Han court to make frequent conciliatory gestures, such as providing luxury gifts and sending Han princesses in marriage to Xiongnu princes. Eventually the Xiongnu leader had sufficient confidence to suggest marriage to Liu Bang's widow, the Empress Dowager, so that they could spend old age together and unite their realms. Although she was reportedly greatly insulted by such a proposal, the Empress Dowager allowed herself to be talked out of attacking the Xiongnu. Instead, she sent back a conciliatory note to the Xiongnu leader, declining his proposal on the ground that she was too old and ugly to be married!

The Xiongnu, like other nomads, were often formidable opponents because of their skill in warfare. For them war represented merely a special application of the skills of horsemanship and archery that they practiced every day in guiding and defending their flocks. It was thus not difficult for Xiongnu men to conduct frequent raids of Han territory. In contrast, military service for a Han peasant required that he interrupt the normal pattern of his life, leave his work, and undergo special training. The mobility of the nomads was an asset not only in attack but also in defense, for traveling lightly with their flocks and tents, they could elude

Han military expeditions and avoid complete destruction or permanent control, even when the Han were able to mobilize their superior resources in manpower and wealth.

Two strategies for coping with the Xiongnu emerged in the Han court. The first, preferred by the first Western Han emperors and their advisors, was appeasement by sending Han princesses as Xiongnu brides as well as expensive gifts as payoffs. The second strategy, which was adopted by Emperor Wu, involved an aggressive stance: sending large armies into the present-day Ordos Region, Inner Mongolia, Gansu, and Han Turkistan. To maintain surveillance over these areas, he established military colonies in strategic places and pressured local rulers and chiefs to enter into tributary relations with the Han. In addition to accepting Han suzerainty, they were required to send princes to the capital, ostensibly to receive a Han education, but actually to serve as hostages. Proponents of the second strategy argued that appeasement failed on two counts. It did nothing to prevent Xiongnu raids on the frontiers, and it was expensive. All the same, to raise revenue to pay for his wars with the Xiongnu, Emperor Wu instituted state monopolies on salt, iron, liquor, and coinage. The salt and iron industries proved to be an especially rich source of revenues for imperial coffers.

In reality, the proponents of more aggressive measures were correct at least in terms of expense. The costs of payoffs to the Xiongnu were high, perhaps as high as 7 percent of the total imperial budget for one year.[12] Fortunately for Emperor Wu, his aggressive strategy ultimately succeeded. By 53 B.C.E., the Xiongnu were no longer the imposing military threat they had been. By that time, the tribes had split into northern and southern federations, and it was the latter that gave its allegiance to the Han. Splitting the Xiongnu could be construed as a victory for a combination of carrot and stick. Struggles broke out between Xiongnu factions, much to the delight and satisfaction of a relieved Han court.

## Intellectual Movements

Most twentieth-century assessments of Han thought have been far from kind. More charitable commentators stress the relatively conservative nature of Han thinkers, who, unlike their Warring States predecessors, rarely departed from traditional ideas in a radical way. Han thinkers developed, elaborated, and synthesized the insights of Warring States masters.[13] Less charitable commentators lament the derivative nature of Han thought, its sterility, and even its lack of intellectual rigor.[14] The most critical commentators go so far as to condemn Han thought for being fanciful, intellectual, weak, and even inherently antiscientific. The perceived lack of intellectual rigor in Han thought was so serious a problem that the Buddhist "conquest" of China was inevitable, as literati were looking for a new infusion of intellectual creativity that was found lacking in the indigenous tradition.[15] Han thought was depicted as being consumed with textual study and controversies and constrained by imperial orthodoxy.

Underlying these stereotypes are a number of scholarly misconceptions. One is that there was anything approximating a formal state ideology, "Confucian" or otherwise. True, Emperor Wu did ban self-professed *fa* masters (usually translated "Legalist"), and he did indeed promote the learning of the *Ru* (often translated "Confucians"). But this does not mean that he imposed a crackdown on all non-Confucian schools of thought, an impossibility because there were no organized schools of thought at that time.[16] This interpretation is also implausible, when one considers what the terms, often translated as Legalist or Confucian, actually meant in their time. *Fa jia*, for example, referred merely to experts on statecraft—and not to a school that transmitted the doctrines of certain Warring States masters. *Ru*, similarly, referred to men who were versed in the classics in general, as opposed to men who professed their loyalty to a body of doctrines or beliefs. The classics were simply from too many different sources and periods to present any single coherent worldview.[17]

The notion that Han thought was derivative, conservative, and otherwise uninspiring becomes less plausible when one considers some of its major accomplishments in historical writing and natural philosophy.

One such accomplishment was the creation of East Asia's most admired history as well as the first dynastic history. The most famous Han historian by far was Sima Qian (c. 145–90 B.C.E.), the author of the *Shiji* or the *Historical Records*. Sima Qian devoted his life to the completion of a work begun by his father, a history of his world from the legendary Yellow Emperor to his own day. The *Shiji* comprised five sections: the Basic Annals, Chronological Tables, Treatises, Hereditary Houses, and Memoirs. The treatises include essays on rites, music, pitch pipes, the calendar, astronomy, the solemn *feng* and *shan* sacrifices performed at Mount Tai, the Yellow River and canals, and economics. The memoirs contain accounts of the lives of famous men, important political and military leaders, thinkers, and groups such as imperial favorites, merchants, and so forth. They also include accounts of non-Han people.

Sima Qian's work set a pattern for later histories. Its form, somewhat modified, was followed by later historians including Ban Gu (d. 92 C.E.), author of *The History of the Former Han (Hanshu)*. This history, which is a record of the preceding dynasty written during and sanctioned by the succeeding dynasty, was the first in a series of such dynastic histories.

One characteristic of Sima Qian's writing, which is shared by many early and later historians, is extensive quotation from original documents. Another is a careful separation between the narrative text and his own editorial comments. To be sure, Sima Qian and others could no more transcend their times and origins than could their counterparts elsewhere. The very process of selection reveals personal values and ideals. Sima Qian freely expressed his enthusiasm for political valor and virtue, his delight in clever stratagems, and his fascination with character and personality. His deep feelings give life to his prose. A fine stylist and gifted raconteur, he did not hesitate to invent dialogues or turn to poetry to convey the full force of a historical personage's feelings or personality. His flair for the dramatic is exemplified by the following account of a battle:

Tian Dan then rounded up a thousand or more oxen from within the city and had them fitted with coverings of red silk on which dragon shapes had been painted in five colors. He had knives tied to their horns and bundles of grease-soaked reeds to their tails, and then, setting fire to their tails, had them driven out into the night through some twenty or thirty openings which had been tunneled in the city wall. Five thousand of the best soldiers poured out after them. The oxen, maddened by the fires that burned their tails, rushed into the Yan encampment which, it being night, was filled with terror. The oxtail torches burned with a dazzling glare, and wherever the Yan soldiers looked, they saw nothing but dragon shapes. All who stood within the path of the oxen were wounded or killed. The five thousand soldiers, gags in their mouths so they would make no noise, moved forward to attack, while from within the city came an accompaniment of drumming and clamor, the old men and boys all beating on bronze vessels to make a noise until the sound of it shook heaven and earth. The Yan army, taken completely by surprise, fell back in defeat, and the men of Qi were able to capture and put to death its commander, Qi Jie.[18]

A second major Han intellectual accomplishment was the completion of a philosophical order to account for all reality, one that probably began late in the Warring States Period. Basic to the efforts of Han thinkers was the conviction that the world was an organic whole passing through time in identifiable phases. All phenomena, no matter how diverse, that shared any particular temporal phase were held to be interrelated in a set of extensive correspondences.

One of the texts often used by Han thinkers to draw correspondences was the *Changes (Yijing)*. The *Changes* is of uncertain authorship or date, but most scholars believe that it was an ancient divination manual. Sixty-four hexagrams and the commentaries on them form the heart of the book. Each hexagram was created by combining two trigrams, each of which consists of three lines, either broken or unbroken. Because each trigram has three lines of only two kinds, that is, broken or unbroken, only eight combinations are possible:

Combining the eight trigrams into hexagrams in turn yields sixty-four unique figures. A common method of divination was to select the appropriate hexagram by counting the stalks of the milfoil. The very concept of divination is based on the conviction that nature and man are interrelated. By identifying the *yin* with the broken line and the *yang* with the unbroken, the *Yijing* illustrates the way this pair of concepts applies to everything. For example, the first hexagram represents heaven, all *yang,* and the second hexagram represents earth, all *yin*. The rest consist of combinations of the two.

Besides correspondences that use *yin* and *yang,* there were various versions of such correspondences, which employed Five Agents or Phases terminology and other related systems. Table 3.1 is based on the order by which the Five

**TABLE 3.1** Correspondences for the Five-Agents System

| Correspondence | Wood | Fire | Earth | Metal | Water |
|---|---|---|---|---|---|
| Seasons | Spring | Summer | Autumn | Winter | |
| Divine Rulers | Tai Hao | Yan Di | Yellow Emperor | Shao Hao | Zhuan Xu |
| Attendant spirits | Gou Mang | Zhu Yong | Hou Tu | Ru Shou | Xuan Ming |
| Sacrifices | Inner door | Hearth | Inner court | Outer court | Well |
| Animals | Sheep | Fowl | Ox | Dog | Pig |
| Grains | Wheat | Beans | Panicled millet | Hemp | Millet |
| Organs | Spleen | Lungs | Heart | Liver | Kidneys |
| Numbers | Eight | Seven | Five | Nine | Six |
| Stems | *Jia/yi* | *Bing/dingi* | *Mou/ji* | *Geng/xin* | *Ren/guei* |
| Colors | Green | Red | Yellow | White | Black |
| Notes | Jue | Zhi | Gong | Shang | You |
| Tastes | Sour | Bitter | Sweet | Acrid | Salty |
| Smells | Goatish | Burning | Fragrant | Rank | Rotten |
| Directions | East | South | Center | West | North |
| Creatures | Scaly | Feathered | Naked | Hairy | Shell-covered |
| Beasts of the directions | Green Dragon | Scarlet Bird | Yellow Dragon | White Tiger | Black Tortoise |
| Virtues | Benevolence | Wisdom | Faith | Righteousness | Decorum |
| Planets | Jupiter | Mars | Saturn | Venus | Mercury |
| Officers | Minister of Agriculture | Minister of War | Minister of Works | Minister of Interior | Minister of Justice |

From Wm. Theodore de Bary, Wing-tsit Chan, and Burton Watson, *Sources of Chinese Tradition,* Vol. I (New York: Columbia Univ. Press, 1960), p. 199. Reprinted with permission.

Agents were thought to produce each other. Another Han arrangement was fire-water-earth-wood-metal, the sequence in which the Agents overcome each other.

The acceptance of the idea that all phenomena are interrelated in a set of correspondences gave great satisfaction. Not only did it explain everything, but also it enabled humans to feel at home in the world, part of a temporal as well as a spatial continuum. It provided both an impetus to the development of science and the basis for a sophisticated theoretical framework for explaining the world (see Figure 3.4). Because it made Han investigators sensitive to phenomena that interact without apparent physical contact, it enabled them to discover and explain phenomena such as the sympathetic vibration of musical instruments and the workings of magnetism. Among the most noted scientists was Zhang Heng (78–139): mathematician (he calculated the value of pi), practical and theoretical astronomer, cartographer (he invented the grid system for map making), and inventor of a seismograph that registered the direction of earthquakes far from the capital.

**FIGURE 3.4** Mirror back. Bronze, Eastern Han dynasty, diameter 6.77 in (Metropolitan Museum of Art, New York). Mirrors have been found in many elite Han tombs, although it is not clear what their intended function was. Some of them depict the cosmos and constellations. (© A.M.S. Foundation for the Arts, Sciences and Humanities. Photograph courtesy of the Arthur M. Sackler Gallery, Smithsonian Institution, Washington, D.C.: MLS 1802.)

## *Poetry*

Among the poetic remains of the Han are the verses collected by the Music Bureau established by Emperor Wu. These include hymns and songs for ceremonial occasions and also a group of fresh and simple folk songs. Originally they were sung to the accompaniment of instruments such as the flute, a bamboo mouth organ known as the *sheng,* the drum, the lute, or a stringed instrument that was the ancestor of the Japanese *koto.* The music has been lost, and the words alone remain. The dynasty also produced good and important poems in a form limiting lines to five words each.

The most characteristic and popular form, however, was the rhapsody ( *fu*), a literary genre that often ran to great lengths and combined poetry with prose. There were prose introductions and conclusions, and there might be prose interludes between the streams of verse. They were frequently in the form of a poetic debate and drew on both the rhetorical tradition of the Warring States Period and on the rich metaphors and fantastic allegories of the Chu tradition. Exotic terminology, verse catalogs, and ornamental embellishments enriched the verse, but in the hands of less than a master, the form was apt to degenerate into mere ostentation and artificiality. Its thematic repertoire included royal hunts and ceremonies, landscapes, the capital, fauna and flora, female beauty, and musical instruments.

The most highly regarded Han rhapsodist was Sima Xiangru (179–117 B.C.E.), a colorful man who as a young and poor scholar eloped with the widowed daughter of a wealthy merchant. Eventually his poetic gifts were recognized by Emperor Wu, and the poet received a post at court. One of his greatest *fu* describes the imperial park. It is too long to quote in full, but the following segment, in Burton Watson's translation, is sufficiently substantial to suggest its scope and flavor:

> Within the park spring the Ba and Chan rivers,
> And through it flow the Jing and Wei,
> The Feng, the Hao, the Lao, and the Jue,
> Twisting and turning their way
> Through the reaches of the park;
> Eight rivers, coursing onward,
> Spreading in different directions, each with its own form.
> North, south, east, and west
> They race and tumble,
> Pouring through the chasms of Pepper Hill,
> Skirting the banks of the river islets,
> Winding through the cinnamon forests
> And across the broad meadows.
> In wild confusion they swirl
> Along the bases of the tall hills
> And through the mouths of the narrow gorges;
> Dashed upon boulders, maddened by winding escarpments,
> They writhe in anger,
> Leaping and curling upward,
> Jostling and eddying in great swells
> That surge and batter against each other;
> Darting and twisting,
> Foaming and tossing,
> In a thundering chaos;
> Arching into hills, billowing like clouds,
> They dash to left and right,
> Plunging and breaking in waves
> That chatter over the shallows;
> Crashing against the cliffs, pounding the embankments.
> The waters pile up and reel back again,
> Skipping across the rises, swooping into the hollows,
> Rumbling and murmuring onward;
> Deep and powerful,

Fierce and clamorous,
They froth and churn
Like the boiling waters of a caldron,
Casting spray from their crests, until,
After their wild race through the gorges,
Their distant journey from afar,
They subside into silence,
Rolling on in peace to their long destination,
Boundless and without end,
Gliding in soundless and solemn procession,
Shimmering and shining in the sun,
To flow through the giant lakes of the east,
Or spill into the ponds along their banks.[19]

The poet has turned the park into the cosmos, fulfilling the intent of the landscape architect who designed it. The poem, characteristically concluding with a moral or political message, ends with the emperor virtuously giving up his luxuries to benefit the people.

# Gender

The reevaluation of traditional culture that began late in the nineteenth century and prevailed after the May Fourth Movement of 1919 (see Chapter 19, Part II), gave rise to a dismal view of the lot of women as oppressed by *Confucianism,* a term often used as shorthand for classical elite culture. This Confucianism was denounced as a conservative, patriarchal, and highly gendered ideology that prevailed during and after the Han and dictated that women were to be subordinates to fathers, husbands, and sons; that they were to be confined to domestic affairs; and that they were to be submissive and weak. This dismal picture suited the modern agendas of missionaries and progressives bent on contrasting their vision of a modern and Westernized society with a gloomy picture of traditional society as sexually oppressive, unequal, and backward. To cite a famous example, Mao Zedong asserted that his revolution would free women from the four cords that bound them: political authority, clan authority, religious authority, and the authority of husbands.[20]

Support for this view was drawn from a limited number of passages in the classics, such as the observation attributed to Confucius in the *Analects,* "Woman and people of low birth are very hard to deal with. If you are friendly with them, they get out of hand, and if you keep your distance, they resent it."[21] Nor was Confucius the only one purportedly to have a misogynistic view of women. Along similar lines, another classical text observes: "The complaints of a woman are without end."[22]

This picture of both the ideology and the actuality is not without its problems. For one thing, it is based less on careful readings of extant sources than on passages taken out of their larger contexts. Take the just cited excerpt from the *Analects*. Commentators have been fiercely debating its meaning for millennia. Is it a general statement about women and their lack of worth or a more limited observation about male servants and young women? More to the point, however awful, this remark is mitigated by other statements attributed to Confucius in the *Analects*, passages expressing the view that women could serve as ministers to sage kings and crediting virtuous women for having played a role in creating a moral government. Similarly one should be wary of reading too much into the second passage ("A woman's complaints are without end"), often cited in isolation, ignoring the directly preceding sentence: "The virtue of a woman is without bounds." Like the first passage, this passage, when taken in its larger context, suggests a more complicated attitude toward women than one would initially think.

The textual record suggests that Han elites imagined that virtuous men were physically courageous even as children. For example, one account depicts Boyu, an ancient sage, being beaten with a stick by his mother for misbehaving. After he was beaten, he wept. According to one Han account, this took his mother aback because he had never before wept during a beating. When asked by his mother why he wept, Boyu reportedly observed, "Before, when I offended you and you beat me with the stick, I often felt pain. But today your strength could not make me feel pain. This is why I am weeping."[23] As this famous tale of filial devotion reveals, Boyu's devotion to his mother is such that he rejoices in painful beatings. His empathy for her overrode his fear of physical pain or discomfort.

Not only were virtuous men supposed to be physically courageous, but they were ideally intellectually precocious and learned. The theme of intellectually precocious and learned male children frequently recurs in Han-period texts. For example, at the age of eight, Ban Gu, the historian already encountered, was said to have been well-versed in—or even to have completely memorized—the histories and the *Odes*.[24]

Another characteristic commonly admired in men was the ability to mourn a parent or friend deeply—and in accordance with ritual dictates. For example, Ma Guang, a former army general, was reportedly a "man small of stature, cautious in mind, but when he mourned for his mother, he was devastated." Another source notes how Ma Guang mourned his mother. "His sorrow was so very deeply felt, his feelings so wounded, that his form became altered and his bones stood out."[25]

As Michael Nylan has recently shown, Han elites by and large imagined virtuous women in similar terms. Women, like men, were supposed to be physically courageous and intellectually precocious and learned and able to mourn their parents deeply. Take for example, Empress Dowager Deng Sui (81–121 C.E.), who would later become the virtual ruler of the empire. One historical record describes her as follows:

When the future empress was six years old, [her grandfather] Deng Yu doted on her, so he took it upon himself to trim her hair. Now, as he was aged and his eyesight was blurred, Deng Yu once happened to hurt her with the scissors, but she bore the pain without saying anything [because she didn't want to hurt her grandfather's feelings]. . . .

Like Boyu, Deng Sui, even as a small child, was reportedly physically courageous and so solicitous of her grandfather's feelings that she suppressed the rather instinctive desire to cry out. Like Ban Gu, Deng Sui was also intellectually precocious:

At the age of seven, she could handle history texts; at thirteen, the *Odes* and the *Analects*. Whenever her elder brother read the classics and commentaries, she would immediately express her ideas and pose difficult questions.[26]

Finally, virtuous women like Deng Sui mourned the passing of their parents deeply. According to her biographer, when her father died, the future Empress Dowager reportedly cried all night and refrained from eating salty vegetables for three years. She became so emaciated that her friends did not recognize her.[27]

Government and society were patriarchal, but recent scholarship has also pointed out that the classic elite traditions were not patriarchal in the sense of emphasizing a man's relationship to his father and playing down the central importance of the mother-son bond. Han elites and, in particular, Eastern Han elites certainly recognized the central importance of the mother-son bond. Mothers were a man's closest tie.

The closeness of the mother-son bond was celebrated in Han literature as well as art. There were pictorial celebrations of the mother-son bond, for example, that of the sage Zengzi and his mother (see Figure 3.5), who allegedly even had powers of telepathic communication. According to one second-century account, Zengzi was out of the house gathering wood in the wild when a visitor came to the house. Seeing that Zengzi was gone, the guest wanted to leave, but Zengzi's mother urged him to stay, observing that her son would soon be back. She then pinched her left arm, and at that moment, Zengzi also felt a pain in his left arm. Upon returning, he asked his mother why her arm hurt.

There were also, quite strikingly, figurines of mothers nursing newborn infants. One image expresses the ancient conception of the breast (*ying*) as the seat of "closeness" (see Figure 3.6). The closeness of the mother-son bond was also prominent in mourning ritual. Eulogists wrote the most poignant inscriptions for sons who had lost their mothers. Consider the following inscription commissioned by a son whose mother had died in 185 C.E.:

There is a saying among men
"The humane will be long-lived."

**FIGURE 3.5** Zengzi and his mother. This image is taken from the Wuliang shrine in Northeast China, a shrine that most scholars believed belonged to a locally prominent family that flourished in the mid-second century C.E. This particular site contains many depictions of historical and semihistorical episodes. Among the depictions are many that relate tales of filial sons and virtuous stepmothers. (From Feng Yunpeng and Feng Yunyuan, c. 1821. *Jin shisuo*. Reprinted: Shanghai: Shangwo Press, 1934, 3.18–19.)

They ought to enter eternal life,
Become gray and wizened without end.
Bright Heaven has no pity.
It visits upon us this cruel calamity.
Sick in her chamber, left with an incurable chronic illness,
Bitter and pained, wasted and hurt,
Grieving and saddened the filial son.
He was very fearful, very worried
That her spirit could not be raised.
There was no medicine that he did not administer to provide her.
Alas, great sorrow was this indeed!
At this, the filial son wailed out for such a long time
That her vital energies, having stopped, be restarted.
Crying out and calling, he proclaimed his grief.
He did not know his crime.
May Bright Heaven, Lord on High,
Pity the orphan left behind,
Who seeks, longs for her roaming spirit.
Does anyone know where it now resides?[28]

**FIGURE 3.6** Mother and son. This figurine, excavated from Sichuan, dates to the Eastern Han dynasty. In a visually striking image, it captures the very notion of the closeness between mother and children. (© Cultural Relics Bureau of Sichuan.)

# Changes in Political Economy during the Han Period

During the four centuries that spanned the founding of the Western Han and the fall of the Eastern Han, the socioeconomic configuration of the empire was transformed. Whereas early Han rulers attempted to foster economic equality in rural areas, their first- and second-century successors made few attempts to prevent social and economic stratification. The result was not only a considerable widening of the gap between the wealthy and the poor but also the weakening of central power and authority.

From the vanquished Qin, the early Western Han emperors inherited goals of economic rationalization and state building. Their efforts, however, were often thwarted by large landholders and local magnates, many of whom may have been the descendants of Warring States families who had ruled walled settlements.

**TABLE 3.2** Farmer's Budget at the End of the Former Han Dynasty

Out of 100 acres to support a family of 5: total yield is 150 bushels (4500 cash) per annum

Taxes: 15 bushels (450 cash) or 10%

Food for five: 90 bushels (2700 cash) or 60%

Leftover cash = 1350 cash

Sacrifices: 300 cash

Clothes for five per annum: 1500 cash

Based on Nancy Swann, *Food and Money in Ancient China: The Earliest Economic History of China to A.D. 25* (Princeton: Princeton Univ. Press, 1950), pp. 140–43.

Early Han emperors tried to remove them from their local bases, forcing them to relocate either to the capital or to distant frontier regions. Emperor Wu and his advisors also deployed "harsh officials" to various localities through the empire. Armed with directives, these officials eagerly prosecuted the local elites as well as errant members of the imperial families.

Like their Qin predecessors, the founders of the Western Han realized that the fate of their dynasty was linked to the fortune of small peasant landholders. Here more than humanitarianism or philanthropy was at work: there were also solid fiscal reasons. Because taxes in the Han period were collected per household, not per capita, a greater number of households meant greater tax revenues. Furthermore, it tended to be much easier to collect taxes from small households rather than large landholders who had resources for hiding their wealth from tax collectors, or who, in many cases, were themselves the tax collectors. Thus, it was in the interest of the dynasty to have as many small landholders as possible, rather than fewer and larger households maintained on large tracts of land or manors controlled by wealthy and influential masters.

Small landholders were difficult to protect. For one thing, they were always threatened by the possibility of debt.[29] As Table 3.2 reveals, it took very little to drive a peasant over the edge. In good years, the family of a small peasant landholder would run a deficit of 450 cash or 10 percent of their total income for one year. In addition, the costs of illness, death, burial, and special government levies, such as military taxes, were not covered under this budget. Drought, illness, burial costs, and even additional government taxes could force small landholders to go under. If that happened, the landholder would have to sell his or her land to a landlord and become a tenant farmer and dependent. From the standpoint of the central government, manors meant double trouble: they not only entailed less tax revenues but also the concentration of sufficient resources to support armies capable of challenging the dynasty.

In their efforts to keep small landholders solvent, Early Han emperors tried several measures. At some points, they seized land from aristocrats, merchants, and wealthy officials and redistributed it to the poor. They also made grants of public lands to the poor, a practice that continued until the beginning of the second century C.E. These land grants were usually territories in the West and South, territories that were either underpopulated or not yet under cultivation. The situation was something like that in nineteenth-century America when the government gave away land to anyone who was willing to settle it. Another important way in which emperors and their advisors sought to improve the lot of small land-holders was to develop agricultural improvements such as ordering the repair and creation of new irrigation systems. This was necessary because drought was a persistent problem in the North China Plains, the heartland of the Han Empire. In addition, they provided subsidies to small landholders: seed grain, iron farming implements (which replaced lower-quality wooden ones), and draft animals. Finally, they put a monopoly on iron production to lower the cost of more effective iron implements.[30] All of these improvements were intended to increase the agricultural productiveness of peasant farmers and keep them out of debt.

Despite their best efforts, the Western Han government largely failed in their attempt to keep small landholders solvent. One important reason for this was the fact that Han agriculture favored economies of scale in which profits rise as investments increase. The latter included improved farming equipment as well as drought animals to do the work today performed on most American farms by tractors. In theory, small landholders should have benefited from the development of technically advanced ploughs, seed drills, weeders, and the like, but they did not, largely because the improvements were too expensive. As seen earlier, under favorable conditions, small farmers could barely break even, let alone buy cutting-edge farming equipment. Instead, these agricultural improvements only benefited landlords, who could afford to invest in them. And the landlords did in fact make use of these improvements, which resulted in them, as opposed to the small landholders, enjoying greater productivity and more profit and ultimately acquiring more *land*. Ironically, these agricultural improvements not only failed to keep peasants out of debt, but they also contributed to the increasing gap in wealth.[31]

Perhaps the most important reason why early Western Han emperors failed to keep small landholders solvent had to do with the composition of the bureaucracy. Early Han emperors had wanted to keep their military and economic power close to home. As such, they not only made their relatives, maternal as well as paternal, rulers of vast territories, but they also recruited them into the imperial bureaucracy. Yet, as illustrated by Emperor Wen's trouble with his brother, blood ties were far from reliable, and within a generation of the founding of the dynasty, Western Han emperors faced rebellions from their brothers, cousins, and even sons. As a result, by 154 B.C.E., Emperor Wu, after considerable urging, had decided to eliminate potentially troublesome relatives. But by doing so, he left a vacuum in government. To staff his bureaucracy, he had no choice but to turn to men of local prominence, wealth, and standing—in other words, landlords.

By the end of the Western Han dynasty, the consequences of bringing landlords to power became clear, as many of them attempted to reverse state policies not to their liking. In 81 B.C.E., the court convened to discuss the merits of Emperor Wu's economic policies, in particular, the monopoly on salt and iron. The debate and its record came to be known as the "Debate on Salt and Iron" (*Yantielun*). On one side of the debate were officials who defended the late emperor's policies, headed by the Lord Grand Secretary, a man of mercantile background, Song Hongyang (152–80 B.C.E.). On the other side were a group of officials, referred to only as the Ru, who attacked the late emperor's policies and who represented the interests of the landlords. The Lord Grand Secretary and his allies argued that the monopoly was necessary for the security of the empire and beneficial to the population:

> The Xiongnu have frequently revolted against our sovereignty and pillaged our borders. . . . The former emperor [Wu] took pity upon the people of the border areas who for so long had suffered disaster and hardship and had been carried off as captives. Therefore he set up defense stations, established a system of warning beacons, and garrisoned the outlying areas to ensure their protection. But the resources of these areas were insufficient, and so he established the salt, iron, and liquor monopolies and the system of equitable marketing in order to raise more funds for expenditures at the borders. Now our critics, who desire that these measures be abolished, would empty the treasuries and deplete the funds used for defense. They would have the men who are defending our passes and patrolling our walls suffer hunger and cold.

The opponents of the state monopolies, however, disagreed. The policies, they noted, sprung from the pursuit of profit. "Never," they said, "should material profit appear as a motive of government." According to these men, acting on the wrong motives would have dire results, corrupting the morals of the peasants and leading them to abandon agriculture:

> But now in the provinces the salt, iron, and liquor monopolies, and the system of equitable marketing have been established to compete with the people for profit, dispelling rustic generosity and teaching the people greed. Therefore those who pursue primary occupations [farming] have grown few and those following secondary occupations [trading] numerous. As artifice increases, basic simplicity declines; and as the secondary occupations flourish, those that are primary suffer. When the secondary is practiced the people grow decadent, but when the primary is practiced they are simple and sincere. When the people are sincere then there will be sufficient wealth and goods, but when they become extravagant then famine and cold will follow.[32]

Sang Hongyang and his allies lost the argument. Not long after, he and a number of other officials found themselves implicated in a plot to kill the powerful regent. Along with their clans, Sang and his allies were executed. And with Sang's execution came the beginning of the end of an era of dynastic expansion, court power, and policies aiming to regulate and shape the direction of the economy.

The effects of bringing landlords to power can also be seen in the career of the imperial uncle, regent, and usurper, Wang Mang (r. 9 B.C.E.–23 C.E.). Wang Mang rose to power around 9 B.C.E. and apparently made one last effort to save the peasants and deal with the gap in wealth. In 9 C.E., he attempted to "nationalize" and redistribute land, an attempt that hearkened back to earlier calls to implement the "well-field" system, first described by Mencius. Believed to have been an ancient manner of land tenure, the well-field system provided for land to be divided land into nine squares like a tic-tac-toe board. Eight families were given use of the eight outer squares, and the remaining central square was worked by all families with the grain going to the state.

In addition to attempting to implement the well-field system, Wang Mang also tried to limit large landholdings and prohibited slavery. He reintroduced government monopolies on salt and iron and instituted the so-called "Five Equalizations," policies that fixed the price of stable goods and provided government loans to farmers. Unsurprisingly, Wang Mang's policies were unsuccessful, in large part because he met with fierce resistance from powerful landlords. One of these, Liu Xiu, the future Guangwu emperor, was a descendant of the Liu imperial clan. With the support of landed interests from his local base, Liu Xiu overthrew Wang Mang, "restoring" the Han dynasty in 25 C.E. and moving the capital to Luoyang in the East (hence, the name of the Later or Eastern Han).[33] In fact, Guangwu's "restoration" represented a decisive end to attempts to save the small landholders from the encroachment of powerful landlords.

For small landholders, both developments—the unintended effects of agricultural improvements and the political rise of landlords—were disastrous. And indeed, by the beginning of the Eastern Han dynasty, independent small landholders were largely a thing of the past. Instead, more than half of the entire Han

**FIGURE 3.7** Hulling and husking grain. Tomb tiles such as this one provide much information on the lives of ordinary people during the Han dynasty. What is striking about these tiles is that they offer a stunning contrast to the kind of art found in North China in the same period. In Sichuan a more naturalistic perspective emerged. Many of the figures represented are in scale, and they move in real space. (© National Museum of China.)

**FIGURE 3.8** Rent collection. This mural, also taken from a second-century Sichuanese tomb, provides more direct evidence of the existence of manors. This particular mural shows a rent collection scene. Here, the tenant farmers bring their rent in kind, rather than cast, to a representative of the large landholder, possibly a manager. The representative is much better dressed than the peasants bringing him the rent. (© Cultural Relics Bureau of Sichuan.)

population were now tenant farmers, and large manors had come to dominate China's economic scene. By some accounts, manors made up as much as 65 percent of the total land under cultivation.[34]

The manor system, at the heart of the emerging socioeconomic order during the subsequent Six Dynasties Period as well as during Han rule, can be summarized as follows. The owner of the manor was something of a lord, who had dependents. Dependents typically were of two kinds: tenant farmers and retainers. Tenant farmers were often former small landholders and their descendants, who had been forced by economic pressures to sell their land to a large landholder. Possessing no land of their own, they would then rent land from the large landholder. Most times, about half of their agricultural yield would go to the large landholder as rent. Retainers, on the other hand, provided military service, in return for support and protection. The relationship between these two kinds of dependents and the large landholder was certainly not equal and often not entirely voluntary.

The existence of manors is attested to not only by literary sources but also by Han mortuary art (see Figures 3.7–3.10). Some late Eastern Han tombs depict the sources of their occupant's wealth. For example, the mural shown in Figure 3.7 depicts men hulling grain. This is certainly not a representation of a small family operation, for at least three reasons. First, most peasant households would not have had four adult males because of the relatively small size of the family—on average five to six members—and infant mortality. Second, the men are depicted using sophisticated hulling machines that would have been economically out of

**FIGURE 3.9** Salt mining. Some tenant farmers also mined salt and iron, as this mural depicts. The depiction of tenant farmers working the salt and iron mines of a large landholder is quite striking considering that before the end of the Western Han, salt and iron mining was monopolized by the Han state. (© National Museum of China.)

reach for small landholders on the brink of falling into debt. Third, the fact that they are using hulling machines suggests that the men represented were not producing for their own consumption. Hulling and husking removes the outer portion of the grain, leaving behind a refined, white starch, which was the food of the Han elite, not the peasantry. These reasons suggest that the men represented were the tenant farmers who rented their land from large landholders.

# The Fall of the Han

Two late second-century millenarian rebellions in particular proved devastating to the Han state. The first was the Yellow Turbans (*Huangjin*) rebellion, which swept the Northeast in 184 C.E. The second was the Celestial Masters (*Tianshidao*) movement, which is also known by a variety of names including the Five Pecks of Grains (*Wudoumi*) or Rice Thieves (*Mizei*). The latter, which arose during the reign of Emperor Shun (125–144 C.E.), came to control parts of present-day Sichuan, a territory the size of France that had played an important role in the expansion of Qin power. The Celestial Masters were able to hold the prefectural capital of Hanzhong for almost half a century before the warlord Cao Cao

**FIGURE 3.10** Military stockades, second century C.E., Sichuan. One important aspect of manor life was defense. As mentioned above, retainers (*binke*) provided private military service to a large landholder in return for support and protection. Not surprisingly, some murals, such as this one, also show that manors were sometimes fully stocked with weapons. The reason manors had defense systems was that, by the end of the dynasty, central rule in localities had collapsed. Thus, local populations, both poor and rich, were vulnerable to attacks from bandits, as well as rebellions. (© Cultural Relics Bureau of Sichuan.)

(155–220 C.E.) was able to extract a pledge of fealty from the leaders of the movement in 215 C.E.[35] The movement was seriously damaging to the dynasty, not only because of the loss of a huge territory but also because Sichuan was the economic breadbasket of the empire.

Besides the military weakness of the dynasty, one reason the Celestial Masters were able to seize and hold a huge and economically important Han territory for so long was its geography. Sichuan was and continues to have one of the best natural defense systems in present-day China, because it is bordered by mountains on three sides. As such, it was not difficult for the Celestial Master armies to hold off attempts by a politically and militarily weak dynasty.

Another reason the Celestial Masters were able to hold Sichuan, much to the detriment of the Han, was the fact that the Celestial Masters were well organized. Far from being a chaotic peasant movement, once in control of Sichuan, the Celestial Masters reportedly moved to fill the power vacuum. The leaders created their own bureaucracy, one largely modeled after the Han government. But legend has it that the Celestial Masters bureaucracy had one distinctive characteristic: each post was filled not by a single man, but by a man and wife pair.

The Celestial Masters also created a coherent theology, one that served to cement the authority of its leaders and legitimize its rule. To be sure, most information about the Celestial Masters theology is filtered through hostile sources, and, as such, it is often difficult to separate fact from fiction. Nevertheless, judging from what our sources say, the Celestial Masters appear to have been in charge of a faith healing movement. Its origins, unfortunately, are unclear, aside from the fact that the *Daodejing* appears to have been used by some adherents as a sacred text.

Lore has it that the movement's legendary founder, one Zhang Daoling, was from the Eastern Han capital in Luoyang. After bankrupting his family in quixotic attempts to discover the elixir of immortality, he decided to go to Sichuan because he heard that the inhabitants there were easily duped. This is probably a baseless rumor, as the prefectural capital in Sichuan was the second largest city in the Han empire, and its inhabitants were very cosmopolitan and educated. In any event, elements of Zhang Daoling's theories about health merged with native, even non-Han, religion to form a new theology with several unusual characteristics, including the belief that physical illness was the result of a sin. Conversely, cure from an illness was a sign that a person had repented. Another interesting aspect of the theology was "inherited guilt" (*cheng fu*): the idea that the sins of the parents were inherited or visited upon descendants. There was also a heavily deistic component to the theology. Heaven (*tian*) was not simply an impersonal force, but a god who punished sinners and rewarded good people. In this belief system, early death was a sign of personal or familial wickedness; longevity was a sign of personal or familial virtue.

Rebellions were not the only serious threat to the dynasty. Factional fights between eunuch cliques and members of consort clans allied with powerful bureaucrats broke out sporadically in the second century. The roots of these had to do with the fact that eunuchs, like consorts, enjoyed easy access to the emperor. Eunuchs were deliberately chosen from insignificant families to ensure that they would have no outside loyalties but would be solely dependent on imperial favor. This dependency commended them to strong-willed rulers like the founder of the Later Han; his weaker successors, however, sometimes became the instruments rather than the masters of the eunuchs. Earlier, in the Qin and during the last half century of the Western Han, individual eunuchs had become powerful, but never before had eunuchs as a group attained the prominence they achieved in the second century. They were even granted the right to perpetuate their power by adopting "sons" to create ersatz families. Not surprisingly, the power of eunuchs was resented by members of the consort clans and powerful officials. By 166 C.E., tensions came to a head, when a group of eunuchs assassinated an elderly statesman. Open fighting broke out, and eunuchs seized control of the court, executing powerful opponents and banning hundreds of powerful officials and their followers from holding office. This episode, known as the Proscription, lasted eighteen years and was responsible for eroding bureaucratic morale and local support for the dynasty.

Powerful warlords, who had strong economic bases in the provinces, also threatened imperial rule. Such men included the corpulent Dong Zhuo, who was responsible for the burning of the Han capital in 190 C.E. Besides Dong Zhuo, there was Cao Cao, a man of obscure background who held the North and who, as seen earlier, managed to pacify the area controlled by the Celestial Masters. Crafty, ruthless, and ambitious, Cao Cao had rivals. They included Yuan Shao, the scion of an old, aristocratic family; Liu Bei, a member of the Liu imperial clan; and Sun Quan, a southern warlord. The four vied for supremacy, and eventually the Yuans were eliminated. When Cao Cao died, his son, Cao Pi ended the fiction of Han rule. Cao Pi founded the Wei dynasty and state, but he failed in his attempt to reunify the empire.

# *Notes*

1. Theodore de Bary and Irene Bloom, eds., *Sources of Chinese Tradition: From Earliest Times to 1600,* 2nd ed. trans. Daniel W. Y. Kwok (New York: Columbia Univ. Press, 1999), p. 229.

2. Yang Hsien-yi and Gladys Yang, *Records of the Historian* (Hong Kong: Commercial Press, 1974), p. 186.

3. Martin Kern, *The Stele Inscriptions of Ch'in Shih-huang: Text and Ritual in Early Chinese Imperial Representation* (New Haven: American Oriental Society, 2000), p. 17. Translation slightly modified.

4. Jens Ostergard Petersen, "Which Books Did the First Emperor of Ch'in Burn? On the meaning of 'Pai Chia' in Early Chinese Sources," *Monumenta Serica* 43 (1992): 2.

5. Derk Bodde, *Statesmen, Patriot, and General: The Shi-chi Biographies of the Ch'in Dynasty (255–206 BC)* (New Haven: American Oriental Society, 1940), p. 7.

6. Katrina McLeod and Robin D. S. Yates, "Forms of Ch'in Law: An Annotated Translation of the Feng-chen shih," *Harvard Journal of Asiatic Studies* 41.1 (1981): 111–63.

7. McLeod and Yates, "Forms of Ch'in Law," pp. 130–33.

8. Michael Loewe, "The Former Han Dynasty," in *Cambridge History of China, Vol. I: The Ch'in and Han Empires, 221 B.C.E.–A.D. 220* (Cambridge: Cambridge Univ. Press, 1986), p. 107.

9. Hans Bielenstein, "The Institutions of Later Han," in *Cambridge History of China,* p. 516.

10. A.F.P. Hulsewé, "Ch'in and Han Law," in *Cambridge History of China,* pp. 520–37.

11. Zhangjiashan er si qi hao Han mu zhu jian zheng li xiao zu, *Zhangjiashan Han mu zhu jian* (Beijing: Wenwu, 2001), p. 227.

12. Yü Ying-shih, *Trade and Expansion in Han China: A Study in the Structure of Sino-Barbarian Economic Relations* (Berkeley: Univ. of California Press, 1967), p. 64.

13. John Fairbank, *China: A New History* (Cambridge: Belknap Press, 1998), p. 62.

14. For evidence of such views, see Benjamin Schwartz, *The World of Ancient Thought,* (Cambridge: Belknap Press, 1985), p. 418; Jacques Gernet, *A History of Chinese Civilization, 2nd ed.* (Cambridge: Cambridge Univ. Press, 1999), p. 166.

15. Paul Demiéville, "Philosophy and Religion from Han to Sui," in *Cambridge History of Ancient China,* pp. 813, 828; Angus Graham, *Disputers of*

the Tao: Philosophical Argument in
Ancient China* (La Salle, Ill.: Open
Court, 1989), p. 315.

16. Michael Nylan and Mark
Csikszentmihalyi, "Constructing
Lineages and Inventing Traditions
through Exemplary Figures in Early
China," *T'oung Pao* 89 (2003): 1–41.

17. Michael Nylan, "A Problematic Model:
The Han 'Orthodox Synthesis,' Then
and Now," in Kai-wing Chow, On-cho
Ng, and John B. Henderson, eds.
*Imagining Boundaries: Changing
Confucian Doctrines, Texts, and
Hermeneutics* (Albany: State Univ. of
New York Press, 1999), pp. 17–56.

18. Burton Watson, trans., *Records of the
Historian: Chapters from the Shih-chi of
Ssu-ma Ch'ien* (New York: Columbia
Univ. Press, 1969), pp. 32–33.

19. Burton Watson, *Chinese Rhyme-Prose*
(New York: Columbia Univ. Press,
1971), pp. 38–39.

20. Dorothy Ko, *Teachers of the Inner
Chambers: Women and Culture in
Seventeenth-Century China* (Stanford:
Stanford Univ. Press, 1994), p. 3.

21. Arthur Waley, trans., *Analects of
Confucius* (New York: Vintage Books,
1938, 1989), p. 216.

22. Huang Kan, ed., *Chunqiu Zuozhuan
zhengyi* (Shanghai: Shanghai guji,
1990), p. 1.258.

23. Cited in Wu Hung, *The Wu Liang
Shrine: The Ideology of Early Chinese
Pictorial Art* (Stanford: Stanford Univ.
Press, 1989), p. 184ff.

24. Anne Kinney, "Introduction," *Chinese
Views of Childhood* (Honolulu: Univ. of
Hawaii Press, 1995), p. 39.

25. Fan Ye, *Hou Hanshu* (Beijing: Zhong
hua, 1976), p. 858.

26. Cited in Michael Nylan, "Golden
Spindles and Axes: Elite Women in the
Archaemenid and Han Empires," in
Chenyang Li, ed., *The Sage and the
Second Sex: Confucianism, Ethics, and
Gender* (La Salle, Ill.: Open Court,
2000), p. 207.

27. Nylan, "Golden Spindles," p. 207.

28. Cited and translated in Miranda
Brown, "Sons and Mothers in Warring
States and Han China, 453 BCE–220
CE," *Nan Nü* 5.2 (2003): 156.
Translation slightly modified.

29. Hsu Cho-yun, *Han Agriculture: The
Formation of Early Chinese Agrarian
Economy, 206 B.C.E.–A.D. 220* (Seattle:
Univ. of Washington Press, 1980),
pp. 66, 80.

30. Francesca Bray, *Science and Civilisation
in China, Vol. 6: Biology and Biological
Technology Part II: Agriculture*
(Cambridge: Cambridge Univ. Press,
1984), pp. 588–89.

31. Bray, *Science and Civilisation,* p. 591.

32. de Bary and Bloom, *Sources of Chinese
Tradition,* trans. Burton Watson, pp.
360–61.

33. Utsunomiya Kiyoyoshi, *Kandai shakai
keizai shi kenkyū* (Tokyo: Sōbunsha,
1955), p. 393.

34. Utsunomiya Kiyoyoshi, *Chūgoku kodai
chūseishi kenkyū* (Tokyo: Sōbunsha,
1977), pp. 19, 382. For figures, see
Chen Chi-yun, "Han Dynasty China:
Economy, Society, and State Power,"
*T'oung Pao* 70.1–3 (1984): 136.

35. Patricia Ebrey, "The Economic and
Social History of the Later Han," in
*Cambridge History of China,* pp. 628–29.

# Part Two

# China and Japan in a Buddhist Age

A major theme in China* and throughout East Asia during the often turbulent years discussed in this part was the gradual spread and flourishing of Buddhism in China and beyond. Concurrently, major developments in just about every sphere of human activity clearly differentiated this period from what preceded it and, in turn, laid the groundwork for the future.

Gautama Siddhartha† (c. 563–483 B.C.E.), the founder of Buddhism, was roughly contemporary with Confucius, but his teachings did not take hold in China until the collapse of the Han dynasty opened people's hearts and minds to a new and originally foreign faith. Then Buddhism simultaneously transformed and was transformed by its encounter with Chinese civilization until it came to pervade the cosmopolitan culture of Tang China and to serve as a carrier for an intensified spread of Chinese civilization to Korea and Japan.

Buddhist piety found eloquent and sensitive expression in stone sculptures such as this. Note especially the care the artist has taken in rendered the faces. As here Buddhist sculpture was generally colored.

*"China" is here and in the following chapters used in a purely geographic sense, stripped of the ethnographic and nationalistic connotations entailed by the term today.
†Gautama refers to his clan, and Siddhartha was the name he received at birth. He is also known as Sakyamuni (sage of the tribe). After he attained enlightenment he was called the Buddha or the Tathagata.

# 4

# China during the Period of Disunity

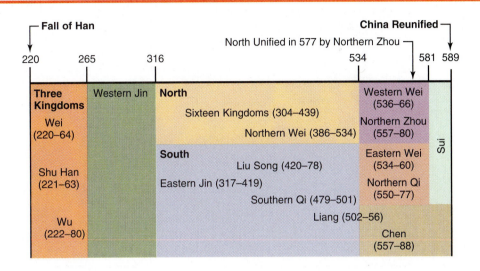

Buddhism has pride of place in our account, but this period also saw the rise of organized Daoism and is noted for the vitality of its literary and visual arts, for institutional innovations as well as political failures, for warfare and coups, but also for economic growth, especially in the South where, by the sixth century, the city now known as Nanjing (old Jiankang) had become the world's largest (see Figure 4.1). When the political center collapsed, China's intrinsic diversity came into full play.

## The Fundamentals of Buddhism

Accounts of the Buddha's life were not committed to writing until centuries after his death. These narratives were the work not of dispassionate scholars but of faithful believers whose aim was to extol the great founder. Tradition has it that Gautama Siddhartha was born a prince and brought up in luxury. He was shocked into a search for religious understanding, however, when on three successive outings from the palace he encountered an old man, a sick man, and a dead man—and learned that such is the fate of humankind. On a fourth trip, depending on the source, he saw either a man laboring or a monk. He abandoned worldly pleasures to seek religious truth, studying with various masters. He then became an ascetic and practiced austerities so severe that they almost cost him his life. Ultimately he found a middle way between self-deprivation and gratification. His subsequent enlightenment under the *bodhi* (wisdom) tree, at which time he be-

**FIGURE 4.1** China c. 500 C.E.

came the Buddha, or "Enlightened One," was achieved despite the efforts of Mara, the evil one, who first sent demons to assail him and then had his daughters (Discontent, Delight, and Desire) tempt him, all equally in vain. The Buddha's success elicited a suitable cosmic response. The whole earth swayed, and blossoms rained from the heavens. After attaining enlightenment, he spent the remainder of his life teaching his disciples, a following whose growth led to the formation of communities of monks and nuns.

At the core of the Buddha's teachings are the Four Noble Truths. The first of these is that life is suffering. Like many religions throughout the world, Buddhism teaches that pain and unhappiness are unavoidable in life. The traditional response of Indian religions is to seek ways to transcend life. Death is not the answer, for in the Indian view, living beings are subject to reincarnation in one painful life after another. According to the law of karma, for every action there is a moral reaction. A life of good deeds leads to reincarnation at a higher and more desirable level in the next cycle; evil deeds lead in the opposite direction. But the ultimate goal is not rebirth as an emperor or millionaire: it is to achieve Nirvana and never be born again. Legend has it that the Buddha himself gained merit in many reincarnations before his final rebirth, and stories of his previous lives have provided rich subject matter for the artist.

The second Truth explains the first, stating that suffering has a cause that we can do something about: attachment produced by our cravings, or desires. This, in turn, leads to the third Truth: that to stop suffering, desire must be stopped. The cause of suffering must be completely understood and halted. This is accomplished by living the ethical life and practicing religious contemplation and the spiritual exercises set out in the last of the Four Truths, which proclaims the Eightfold Path: right views, right intention, right speech, right action, right livelihood, right effort, right mindfulness, and right concentration. The religious life involves vegetarianism, celibacy, and abstinence from alcoholic beverages, as well as positive religious practices. Carried to perfection it leads to release from reincarnation and to Nirvana: that is, to the absolute, the infinite, the ineffable.

There is much that is subtle in the elaboration of these ideas and in their explication by the Buddha and his followers. The doctrine that there is no ego provides an example. That which we think of as the self is merely a temporary assemblage of the five aggregates (material body, sensation, perception, predisposition, and consciousness). At any point in time an individual is a momentary cluster of qualities without any underlying unity. It is a dangerous delusion to think that these qualities pertain to some kind of permanent entity or soul: only by understanding that all is change can Buddhahood be achieved. Transmigration is likened to the passing of a flame from one lamp to another until it is finally extinguished. "Extinguished" is the literal meaning of Nirvana.

Many problems of doctrinal interpretation were left unanswered by the Buddha, for he was a religious teacher concerned with showing the way to salvation, not a philosopher interested in metaphysics for its own sake. The Buddha's concern for spreading the faith was carried on by later missionaries who undertook hazardous journeys to bring the message to distant lands. As with other religions, such as Christianity, later commentators worked out the philosophical implications of the founder's teachings, producing a mass of writings. These holy scriptures were compiled in the Tripitaka, or "three baskets," which consists of monastic rules (*vinayas*), sermons attributed to the Buddha himself (*sutras*), and later commentaries (*abhidharma*, including *shastras*, that is, treatises). The enormity of this body of scripture indicates the vast breadth of Buddhism. It had no centralized organization or ecclesiastical hierarchy and developed in a generally tolerant atmosphere conducive to producing a rich variety of practices and beliefs.

The distinction between the Theravada sects, still predominant in Sri Lanka and Southeast Asia, and the Mahayana schools, most predominant in East Asia, developed before Buddhism entered China. *Mahayana* literally means "greater vehicle," reflecting its claim to more inclusive and powerful teachings than those of the earlier *Hinayana* or "lesser vehicle"—a term generally resented by Theravada Buddhists.

A branch of Mahayana Buddhism important for its development of doctrine was the Madhyamika (middle way) school, which taught that reality is empty or void (*sunya*). Emptiness became an absolute, underlying all phenomena. In innermost essence, everything, including the world of appearances, is Nirvana and empty. If everything is emptiness, then what is it that perceives the emptiness? One school held that the ultimate reality is consciousness; that everything is produced by the mind.

Mahayana Buddhism developed a metaphysical literature whose richness and subtlety are barely hinted at here; it also broadened the appeal of Buddhism to draw in people without the time, training, or inclination for the religious life or abstract speculation. A significant development was Buddha worship, deifying him and placing him at the head of an expanding pantheon. Other Buddhas also appeared and had their following, including Maitreya, the Buddha of the future, who exerted a messianic appeal and was often adopted as a symbol by Chinese rebel movements. Beginning in India in the first century C.E. when the first Buddhas were sculpted, statues, themselves partaking of the holy, inspired the faithful. As a Tang Period inscription puts it:

> The highest truth is without image. Yet if there were no image there would be no possibility for the truth to manifest itself. The highest principle is without words. Yet, if there were no words how could the principle be known?[1]

In addition to the Buddhas, there were numerous lesser gods, but more important than these were Bodhisattvas, who postponed their own entry into Nirvana to help other beings. Somewhat like the Virgin Mary and the saints of Christianity, the Bodhisattvas themselves became objects of veneration and worship, none more than Avalokitesvara (Guanyin in Chinese and Kannon in Japanese), famed for the shining quality of his mercy. Sometimes depicted with multiple hands and arms, Avalokitesvara is a favorite subject of Buddhist sculpture. In China this embodiment of the gentle virtues was gradually transformed into a feminine figure.

Buddhism appealed to many people in East Asia, because it addressed human suffering with a directness unmatched in their native traditions. People were variously attracted by its doctrines, magic and medicine, art, music, and ritual. For those bewildered by abstract Nirvana, there were heavens and hells. Many were comforted by the belief that one could earn merit, "the idea that there is an invisible moral order governing the universe, and that under this system one is rewarded in this life or the next for good deeds."[2] These good deeds could include sponsoring statues and contributing to temples, but also performing acts of kindness such as releasing fish (frequently by ransoming those specially caught for this purpose) or building bridges.

Spread by missionary monks who followed the caravan routes linking the northern part of India with western China, the new religion faced formidable cultural and linguistic barriers in China and might have remained simply an exotic foreign faith had not the fall of the Han set people to questioning traditional verities. During the years of dislocation and confusion that followed, China was ready for new teachings. The history of Buddhism in China cannot be understood apart from other aspects of Chinese history.

# A World in Disarray

The three states (Wei, Wu, and Shu Han) into which China was divided after the fall of the Han inspired China's most beloved historical novel (see p. 271) but lasted less than half a century (see timeline at the beginning of this chapter). Wei was succeeded by the Western Jin (265–317), which unified China from 280, when it conquered Wu, until it was decimated by civil wars beginning in 304. The capture and devastation of Luoyang, the Western Jin capital, in 311 by Xiongnu rebels claiming to be the successors of the Han was followed by the fall of Chang'an in 316. Subsequently, China remained divided until reunited by the Sui in 589.

When the old world disintegrated intellectually as well as politically, thoughtful people were prompted to reexamine old assumptions and find new ways to give meaning to their lives. Whereas the collapse of the old Zhou order gave rise to classical Chinese thought, the new civilizational crisis made men receptive to a new religiosity and ultimately stimulated a cultural flowering in which the aesthetic dimension of human experience and creativity was accorded full recognition and given free play.

Intellectually there was a turning to "abstruse" or "mysterious learning" (*xuanxue*). Its most brilliant thinkers, such as Wang Bi (226–249) and Guo Xiang (d. 312), continued to accept the validity of Confucian social values, whereas their views on the ultimate problems of existence drew on Daoist texts and traditions. Wang, writing on the *Daodejing* and the *Changes* (*Yijing*), gave new depth to the concept of *wu* (non-being emphasized in classical Daoism). For him, original non-being (*benwu*) was the ultimate reality, the origin of all being, of metaphysical unity in a fragmented physical world. He was also the first to introduce two complementary concepts that were to have a long history in Chinese thought: *ti* and *yong*, usually translated "substance" and "function," and understood by Wang Bi also in the sense of latent and manifest.

In contrast to Wang Bi, Guo Xiang, author of a major commentary on the *Zhuangzi*, denied the centrality of *wu*. He understood people to be composed of three elements that they must accept: "spontaneity (a universal, natural, and impersonal force that lies within each of us); limitations in time and society (our span of life, natural endowment, and place in society); and daily renewal (an incessant state of change characteristic of all beings)." Doing so, people will "enter into a 'marvelous coincidence' with themselves and with the oneness of the world, into the mystic fusion with the immanent force that produces everything and has no beginning or end."[3]

Many refined and sensitive men turned to mystical nihilism for an explanation of ultimate reality and sought to attain it through spiritual contemplation, a "sitting in forgetfulness" so complete that forgetting is itself forgotten. To be sure, other, less sublime, ways of forgetting were not forgotten. A favorite pastime of the cultured gentleman was "pure talk." In contrast to the "pure criticism" (*qingyi*) directed against the government by Later Han scholars, *pure talk* (or pure conversation, *qingtan*) was "conversation that is highly witty, refined, and concerned with philosophical matters transcending the concerns and conventions of the mundane world."[4] There were also games of clever repartee for its own sake in which the highest honors went to the man who thought up the most adept and pithy characterization of his acquaintances.

Then there were the free spirits who venerated nature and sought naturalness in conduct, rejecting the social conventions and ideas of propriety that defined the gentleman. There ensued a burst of self-expression in the arts and in the lives of the sophisticated, who let themselves go in music, poetry, and personal attitudes. Most famous are the Seven Sages of the Bamboo Grove (third century), a group of gifted friends noted for their artistic accomplishments and their eccentricity. Wine flowed freely at their gatherings.

One man was always followed by a servant carrying a bottle in one hand and a spade in the other—equipped for all eventualities in life or death. Sometimes he drank stark naked at home. One startled visitor who found him in that state was promptly informed that his house was his pair of trousers; "What are you doing in my trousers?" the "sage" berated him. So much for Confucian propriety!

The men of this age did not invent eccentricity and unorthodox behavior, and they were certainly not the first to enjoy their cups. What was new was that they gave such conduct respectability in a world lacking a credible political as well as intellectual center.

## China Divided

During the long centuries between the fall of the Western Jin in 317 and the reunification of China by the Sui in 589, five dynasties succeeded each other in the South: The Eastern Jin, Liu Song, Southern Qi, Liang, and Chen. Together with the preceding southern state of Wu, they are known as the Six Dynasties.

Meanwhile, in the turbulent and even chaotic North, between 304 and 439 sixteen regional, overlapping short-lived kingdoms barely managed to survive their founders. Military power was paramount, and it was most effectively exercised by mounted warriors in heavy armor, firing volleys of arrows as they rushed by, steadied in their saddles by stirrups now in general use. Many fighting men came from nomadic tribes for whom, in contrast to Chinese peasants, warfare was simply a special application of the everyday skills practiced to protect their flocks.

Thirteen of the kingdoms were founded by men of "non-Chinese" background, including incompletely assimilated people living within as well as beyond "China." As Charles Holcombe has written, "This was a period of general chaos. It is not clear, however, that foreigners really invaded Chinese territories from outside during the fourth century, nor was 'Chinese' as obvious an ethnic identity then as we tend to assume that it is now."[5] Rather than continuing to think in terms of "barbarians" versus "Chinese," it is more accurate to see this as a period of "multi-ethnicity" and bear in mind the "malleability of ethnic identity."[6]

Many people sought refuge from the chaos by fleeing to the South, whereas those who remained found security in fortified citadels commanded by local strongmen. In both the North and the South, the military were the kingmakers and kings (or "emperors"), but Chinese political and literary culture was preserved and developed by the leaders of government and society.

# The Northern Wei (386–534)

The most successful northern state during the fifth and sixth centuries was the Northern Wei, also known as *Tuoba* (in Chinese) or *Tabqac* (in the language of the ruling group) Wei after the nomadic tribal coalition that established the state by military force. Like similar regimes, the Tuoba realized that if they were to enjoy China's wealth on a long-term basis, they needed a political system more sophisticated than the tribal organization they brought from the steppes. In practice, this meant relying on men familiar with Chinese ways of collecting taxes, keeping records, and running a government. But the ensuing sinification had to be kept in check if the conquerors were to retain their power and something of their cultural heritage.

From early on the Northern Wei was attracted to Chinese institutions and culture. When, in 398, they built a Chinese-style capital near modern Datong (Shanxi), they are said to have brought 100,000 craftsmen to work on the project and forcefully relocated 360,000 people to populate the area. At court in the new capital, officials bearing Chinese titles performed Chinese ceremonies accompanied by Chinese music. A Chinese legal code was adopted.

The political system drew on tradition, but the dynasty also innovated. The "equal field system," established in 485, not only outlasted the Northern Wei by more than 350 years but also influenced reformers in Japan. Based on the ancient principle that all land belongs to the emperor, it provided for the allotment of agricultural holdings to each adult farmer for the duration of his or her working life. When a landholder reached old age or died, the land reverted to the state for reassignment. Exceptions were made where the nature of cultivation required greater continuity of tenure. Silk culture, for example, involved permanent planting and continuous care of mulberry trees. Although this was not the original intent, such land came to be held in perpetuity by its proprietors. In return for land, cultivators were obliged to make certain tax payments and render labor services such as road building and military service. Sinification continued apace. A watershed was reached in 493–494 when the capital was moved from the Datong area, close to the old Tuoba tribal home, south to Luoyang in the Chinese heartland, a move partly aimed as a step toward reunifying all to China. The Wei proceeded to gain control of all North China down to the Huai River but no further. In Luoyang itself major changes and improvements were made, and it was divided into regular isolated wards, an innovation adopted in the great Tang capital of Chang'an (see Figure 5.5) and continued in Tang Luoyang.

The implementation of the equal field system in devastated areas did not prevent the regime from cooperating with great landed families entrenched elsewhere. From the outset, the Tuoba rulers employed Chinese advisers and early on gained support among the Chinese elite by adopting the nine-rank system that had originated in 220 as a means for recruiting officials through local recommendation and had by the fourth century become a system for appointing men to office according to their inherited family rank. This emphasis on birth reflected the enduring power and prestige of great Chinese families of distinguished ancestry whose embodiment of Confucian traditions and lifestyle created an aura of distinction that complemented their wealth in land and connections. Their position was further strengthened by the fact that Northern Wei local officials enjoyed considerable autonomy, including the right to appoint their subordinate officials. What they lacked, however, was institutionalized military power.

The growth and triumph of Chinese influence in the end undermined the Northern Wei. During its last half century, men from distinguished families were increasingly attracted into the sinicized central government, in which Chinese was the official language. In Luoyang everyone wore Chinese dress, and even Tuoba nobles had to adopt Chinese names. Many married Chinese wives. This sinification finally alienated those Tuoba tribesmen who had not adopted Chinese ways, including the troops stationed in frontier garrisons. They expressed their displeasure in the usual way—by taking up arms. Although it hung on for close to another ten years, the dynasty never recovered from the Rebellion of the Six Garrisons (524). The Northern Wei state was split. Its legacy included the equal field system, an aristocracy of mixed ancestry from which emerged the leaders who were to unify China, and some superb Buddhist art.

# Buddhism in the North

The more than 1000 Buddhist temples and monasteries that graced Northern Wei Luoyang are no more, but the sculptures of the Yungang caves near Datong and those at Longmen, eight miles from Luoyang (see Figure 4.2), although badly damaged, continue to testify to the success of Buddhism in China and illustrate the process by which the foreign religion found a new home. The creation of temples in caves, as well as the Buddhas and Bodhisattvas, were Indian in origin, but the Bodhisattva in Figure 4.3 shows Chinese artists in the process of assimilating and transforming Buddhist art. In contrast to the lovingly sensuous modeling of the naked body in three dimensions that is the glory of the Indian sculptor, the essentially linear style of the figure, with its geometric composition and frontal orientation, is characteristically Chinese. At its best, this art reproduced in metal and stone the simple piety and sweet spirituality of a religious age.

When Buddhism first reached China during the first century C.E., it was a religion of foreign merchants. Through the period of division the trade routes remained very active, because trade was as advantageous to the nomadic peoples who controlled oases and taxed caravans as it was to the buyers and sellers in the more settled regions. As life became more difficult in China, Buddhism acclimatized itself to Chinese circumstances and became more appealing to people disillusioned with the old ways. In the North devoted missionaries initially won the patronage of rough tribal leaders by using feats of magic to convince them that Buddhism was a more powerful religion than the competition. It was powerful also in other ways, for it enabled tribal chiefs to see themselves in new and grander

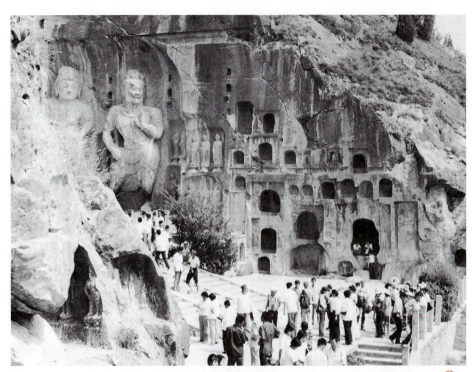

**FIGURE 4.2** Entrance to the Buddhist cave temples at Longmen. (© Lore Schirokauer.)

roles, and it appealed to alien rulers who, through their patronage of this universalistic religion, like themselves foreign to China, could create a broad and venerable base for their claims to legitimacy. And, of course, it was powerful in religious and intellectual terms, inspiring learning and art.

Political patronage was important, but to survive and prosper Buddhism also had to win a wide following among the Chinese people. In this endeavor its foreign origins were not an asset but a liability. Words and ideas, as well as artistic forms, had to be translated into Chinese terms.

Translating Buddhist texts into Chinese proved a formidable undertaking, because they were the products of a radically different culture and were written in a language totally unlike Chinese. The problems faced by the early Buddhist translators were similar to those that much later plagued Christian missionaries trying to render the Bible into Chinese. Particularly vexing was the need to introduce unfamiliar concepts at the very heart of Buddhism. Just as Christians were later to agonize over how to translate *God* into Chinese, Buddhists racked their brains over words such as *Nirvana*. One early solution was to employ Daoist terminology. This terminology had the advantage of sounding familiar. But it could also lead to a great deal of confusion, such as when the Daoist term for "non-action" (*wu-wei*) was used to express the quite different concept of Nirvana. One solution was not to translate at all but to transliterate, that is, to employ Chinese characters to

FIGURE 4.3 Seated Bodhisattva. Stone, Longmen, late Northern Wei. (Photograph © 2005 Museum of Fine Arts, Boston.)

approximate the sound rather than the meaning of the original word. Transliteration was most suitable for reproducing foreign proper names in Chinese. Furthermore, it retained or even increased the magic potency of incantations, but even in relatively modern times, Chinese readers found it difficult to divorce the characters from their meanings.

Despite these handicaps scholar-monks made good progress in their work. The greatest of the translators was Kumarajiva (350–c. 409), like many of his predecessors, a Central Asian. After arriving in Chang'an in 401, he directed a translation project staffed by some thousand monks. In a vivid comment on the translator's art, he once compared his work to that of a man who chews rice in his mouth and then gives it to another to swallow, but he and his staff produced good translations of basic Buddhist texts. They were responsible for the introduction of Madhyamika teachings, foremost among them the doctrine of emptiness (*sunyata*) that became very influential. The translations were an impressive achievement, but the transmission of ideas is always a very complex process. As Robert H. Sharf has emphasized, Chinese Buddhists understood the texts in Chinese terms, largely failing to recognize "the alterity of Indian Buddhism. . . . Like ships passing in the night, seminal features of Indian Buddhist thought simply failed to capture the attention, or at least the imagination, of the Chinese."[7]

Kumarajiva was only one of the many Central Asian monks whose missionary zeal spurred the growth of Buddhism in China. But the traffic was not all one way: Chinese also undertook the long pilgrimage to India following the merchant trade routes, by land or by sea. The monk Faxian, who made the ocean trip during 399–414, left a detailed account of his travels that serves as a prime source for the history of India during this period.

To overcome cultural barriers, early Buddhist apologists argued that their religion was basically compatible with the Chinese heritage and played down areas of potential conflict. That they enjoyed considerable success is shown by inscriptions that reveal that the pious considered the donation of an image not only an expression of their religious faith but also a demonstration of their filial piety and of their reverence for the ancestors whose souls were included in their prayers. (The idea of non-self, or non-soul, never had much currency in popular Buddhism nor was it generally taught even by well-educated Chinese monks.) Yet, not everyone was convinced by this attempt to fuse Buddhism and filiality. After all, the latter demanded the continuation of the family and thus conflicted with the celibate life of the monk and nun.

Withdrawal from the secular world left Buddhists open to charges of antisocial behavior, whereas the growth of monastic wealth and influence made the Buddhist church vulnerable to political attack. A strong competitor both for state patronage and popular support was the Daoist church. Confucians as well as Daoists instigated the persecution of Buddhism during 446–452 by the Northern Wei Emperor Taiwu (r. 424–452) and again by another Northern state during 574–578. Both aimed to destroy Buddhist monasteries and to eliminate the Buddhist religious establishment, which had grown wealthy and powerful, but no attempt was made, then or later, to suppress private Buddhist beliefs. Both persecutions ended as soon as there was a change of ruler, and the new emperor made generous amends. Buddhism had grown too strong to be crushed by government fiat; the persecutions appear to have done little permanent damage.

Religious persecution indicated tension between church and state, but this never developed into the separation of church and state so crucial in Western history. In China the state was always concerned about keeping religions in line. What became the usual pattern was exemplified by the Northern Wei when the state placed controls on the Buddhist establishment so as to prevent the monasteries from becoming havens for tax dodgers or men escaping their labor obligations, to bar fraudulent transfers of land titles to tax-exempt religious institutions, and to enforce standards for ordination and clerical conduct. This was the responsibility of a clerical bureaucracy not unlike its secular counterpart. Northern Wei emperors appointed a monk to be Chief of Monks as head of a network of Regional Chiefs of Monks. He, in turn, supervised the Buddhist orders while also looking after the interests of the religion. The great cave temples were created through a combination of official support by the court and efforts of the Buddhist clergy and laity to gain merit and glory.

# Daoism—The Religion

Although it had deep historical roots, Daoism as an organized religion can be traced to the Celestial Masters of the later Han discussed in the last chapter. As indicated there, the Celestial Masters became the dominant religion of Wei, the state that was the immediate successor of the Han in the North, where the sect remained important. Well organized, it operated "inns of equity," offering travelers free meals. Each inn was supervised by a priest who could be of either sex and was also charged with explaining the *Daodejing* largely in moral terms.

As previously noted, the Celestial Masters owed much of their appeal to their activity as healers. In their case, cure of the sick was achieved through the good offices of an initiate who forwarded the afflicted person's confession, recorded in triplicate—one copy for each of the Officials in charge of Heaven, Hearth, and the Waters to share with his staff. Also of major importance were 1200 officials who were invited to enter the body of the confessing ill person.

Emphasis on healing remained a prominent feature of Daoism, whose practitioners became experts in identifying the cause of illness in the misdeeds of the patient or his progenitors and in identifying which of the countless spirits and demons was responsible for the illness, forcing it to confess and release its victim. Daoist masters also used seals and spells (some carried on the person) to battle disease and prolong life. To assist the progress of the dedicated adept there were meditation and sexual exercises. Breathing exercises to grow embryo of immortality internally and alchemy to produce elixirs externally, although not uniquely Daoist, also found a place in the Daoist repertoire.

The Celestial Masters' vision of an extraterrestrial administration occupied by paperwork much like governments operating here on earth was widely shared, as was the sect's own hierarchical organization, both probably a heritage from the time it actually governed Sichuan. This hierarchy could include the Emperor. The first Emperor to receive cosmic legitimacy through Daoist investiture was Taiwu, the Northern Wei persecutor of Buddhism. The 574–578 persecution was followed by Daoism being proclaimed the official state religion, and we will encounter further cases of the importance of political patronage when we come to the Tang and Song. Political patronage was very helpful, but the relationship between state Daoism and local practitioners is a matter of conjecture. Ultimately, Daoism depended on the credibility and potency of its message to laity and devotee alike.

For the truly dedicated practitioner, willing to spend years in study and practice, Daoism promised more than just good health:

> When he achieves salvation, the adept will wear a feathered garment, will ride on light and straddle the stars, or will float in empty space. He will have wind and light as a chariot and dragons as steeds, His bones will shine like jade, his face will be resplendent, his head will be circled with a halo, and his whole body will radiate a supernatural light as incandescent as the sun and moon. He will be able to realize all his desires and will enjoy an endless youth and a longevity equal to that of heaven and earth. Moreover, he will be able to travel a thousand *li* in a single day, and will be able to immerse himself in water without getting wet or walk through fire without getting burned. Neither beasts nor weapons will have any power over him. He will command the forces of nature and the spirits.[8]

This description pertains to Great Purity (*Shangqing*), also called Maoshan (Mt. Mao) Daoism, but such aspirations were characteristic of Daoist sects generally.

Throughout the period of division and beyond, Daoist abbeys and Buddhist temples competed against each other for political patronage and vied for the support of the populace who they found were addicted to their own local cults, for "no matter whether the mountain is great or small, gods and numinous spirits are found without fail therein."[9] The Celestial Masters' denunciation of false demons became standard fare down through the ages.

Daoists, like the Buddhists, erected statues and had pictures painted to decorate their abbeys and performed mysterious, powerful, and profound rituals. Learned practitioners developed a repertoire of texts so rich and numerous by the fourth century as to require organization and classification. The resulting "three caves" paralleled the three baskets of the Buddhists and included Lingbao (numinous treasure) texts, which had begun appearing in the southeast in the 390s and were to be very influential. Key Buddhist concepts, such as karma, feature prominently in these and other scriptures. Daoists also adopted some Buddhist rituals. A popular Daoist explanation for such shared notions was that Lao Zi had traveled to India where he became the Buddha in order to convert the barbarians, and it took only a small step to make explicit that because the Dao encompassed all, it included Buddhism. Not to be outdone, Buddhist accounts depicted Lao Zi and Confucius as disciples of the Buddha and even portrayed the semidivine founders of Chinese civilization as Bodhisattvas.

After the Period of Division, the Celestial Masters faded from the scene but reappeared under the name Zhengyi (True One) around the mid-eighth century on Mount Longhu (Mt. Dragon-Tiger) in Jiangxi and continue to the present. The immediate future, however, belonged to the sect, founded in the third century, which was headquartered on Mt. Mao and sanctified by and named after three immortal Mao bothers, who are said to have come riding on white swans or cranes and landed on each of the mountain's three peaks. Mt. Mao is located in modern-day Jiangsu, west of Nanjing, capital and hub of the South.

# The South

Spared the nomad incursions and warfare that plagued North China, the South enjoyed relative tranquility, despite a series of political intrigues, palace coups, and the like, which disturbed life at court. Partly through migration from the disturbed North, partly through development of the land, and building on past economic growth, the fertile area of the lower Yangzi River experienced a very substantial increase in population and productivity. Further south, Fujian now became truly Chinese for the first time as a result of increased Chinese settlement. As Chinese settlers moved in, the local aborigines were gradually either pushed back into the hills or absorbed into the Chinese population.

Rice culture was the cornerstone of the agricultural economy of the South. Sophisticated wet-field cultivation of rice took time and effort to perfect. Not only did it involve experimentation with various strains of rice, but it also entailed the construction of paddy fields and careful irrigation to keep the field wet and to maintain the water at an even temperature. When the fields were laid out on sloping ground or when terraces were constructed on hills, a complicated system of dams and reservoirs was necessary.

In the Han the Chinese developed a technique for raising seedlings in a nursery and transplanting them later into paddies when the season was right. Such early planting in nurseries greatly increased the yield, but it also increased the demands for labor. Refugees from the North helped to augment the labor supply and open up new land, making a direct contribution to the growing prosperity of the South. The enlarged labor force was, in turn, sustained by the increased rice yields obtained from wet-field cultivation, which produced more calories per acre than did Northern dry-field agriculture. In good part because of the ability of rice to support high population density, the development of the South was to be of great consequence for the future history of China.

Concurrent with thriving agriculture, the South bustled with trade and commerce—especially Nanjing, where markets could spring up anywhere, for unlike Luoyang, the southern capital was not internally divided into walled-off wards. Money and goods circulated freely in what Shufen Liu has called "a freewheeling market economy."[10] Pottery, textiles, lacquer, bronze mirrors, and paper were produced as well as traded in the South. Especially noteworthy were the luxury goods such as pearls, ivory, coral, and incense as well as gold, silver, and slaves imported through Guangzhou (Canton) from Southeast Asia, South Asia, and even more distant lands. Buddhist texts, statues, and relics also came by sea, complementing those which reached China via the Inner Asian trade routes.

A varied commerce bespeaks a lively society—Nanjing had its merchants, artisans, beggars, and thieves, and as in the North, great families stood at the top of the social hierarchy. They controlled large estates and, combining political and economic power, dominated the governments of a succession of southern dynasties. Not only did they enjoy exemption from taxation and labor service, but they also had ready access to office and set the tone of court life. In the fifth century, they even managed to obtain legislation prohibiting intermarriage between aristocrats and commoners. Their entrenched privileges seriously hampered government efficiency. Yet they were far from invincible. For one thing, their power was constantly being undermined by intense and recurrent conflicts among themselves. Friction between émigré families and those with deeper local roots was endemic. The influence of the great families was also weakened by their lack of military power and their inability to control military strongmen of nonaristocratic background.

When Luoyang was captured by the "barbarians," its fall served to confirm the disillusionment and general pessimism felt by residents of the South. The continuing arrival of émigrés from the North reinforced this spirit. The more sophisticated turned to witty conversation, meditation, alchemy, and wine as a diversion from the depressing social and political problems of the day. It was this discontent and yearning for greater stability that made the society of southern China receptive to Buddhism. But it also served to liberate individual impulses to artistic expression, channeling energies that formerly had been devoted to philosophy and government into the secular arts. The result was an outburst of achievements in those arts that are the most highly prized and most closely identified with the Chinese gentleman: poetry, calligraphy, and painting.

# Poetry

The difficult times produced some lasting poems, many of them from the brush of Tao Qian (365–427), also known as Tao Yuanming, recognized as one of China's greatest poets. After a short career in government, he retired to live the life of a country gentleman, but not without ambivalent feelings toward official life and its obligations. There is in his verse much about wine, the simple country life, books, and nature. Poems such as this have enduring appeal:

> I built my cottage among the habitations of men,
> And yet there is no clamor of carriages and horses.
> You ask: "Sir, how can this be done?"
> "A heart that is distant creates its own solitude."
> I pluck chrysanthemums under the eastern hedge,
> Then gaze afar toward the southern hills.
> The mountain air is fresh at the dusk of day;
> The flying birds in flocks return.
> In these things there lies a deep meaning;
> I want to tell it, but have forgotten the words.[11]

Tao especially loved chrysanthemums and wrote about them often; ever since, this "hermit among the flowers" has been associated with his name. The poem conveys a serene harmony with nature that is a lasting Chinese ideal and a common theme in much later Chinese poetry.

Other fine poets also wrote during this period. But there was at the same time a tendency for poets to indulge in increasingly artificial styles (for example, extreme parallelism in construction, with two lines matching each other word for word) and to exhibit their virtuosity in using an exotic vocabulary, as Han poets had in their rhapsodies. As a result, spontaneity, creative freshness, was gradually lost, and versification was already approaching a dead end when political unification from the North put an end to both the southern courts and their poetry.

More significant than poetic output per se was the development of a new attitude toward literature that grew out of a deep concern with the process of poetic creation. Formerly the poetic art had been primarily, although not exclusively, viewed as a vehicle for moral instruction, but this view was now challenged by those who emphasized free self-expression and pleasure:

> Trying the empty Nothing, and demanding Something
> Banging the silent Zero, in search of Sound.[12]

DRAGON        BOOK        GOOD

These two lines by Lu Ji (261–303) give something of the flavor of the verse of this period, when poetry was appreciated in its own right, They are from Lu Ji's rhapsody (*fu*) on literature, itself a work of high art. More generally, increased emphasis was placed on stylistic devices, exotic language, and the like. When he compiled his famous literary anthology, *Wenxuan,* Xiao Tong (501–531) based his selection on literary merit and adopted a "moderate" view on the nature and function of literature.[13]

**FIGURE 4.4** Basic forms of calligraphy. The top two characters in the "dragon" column and the top characters in the "book" and "good" columns exemplify the Li form (clerical, or official); the third and fourth characters in the "dragon" column and the second characters in the "book" and "good" columns exemplify the Zheng (also called Kai) form (regular, or standard); the fifth character in the "dragon" column and the third characters in the "book" and "good" columns exemplify the Xing form (longhand, or running); and the bottom characters in each column exemplify the Cao form (cursive, or shorthand). (Calligraphy by Dr. Léon L. Y. Chang.)

## Calligraphy

Of all the visual arts, Chinese scholars traditionally have given first place to calligraphy (see Figure 4.4). Behind this high esteem lies the aesthetic appeal and the mystique of the Chinese characters themselves, along with the emphasis on literature in Chinese culture. Moreover, the development of cursive script during the Later Han turned writing into an intensely personal art, a vehicle for self-expression and a creative outlet, well suited for educated people who had been wielding the brush and working with ink since childhood. Calligraphy came to be especially valued as a means for conveying the writer's deepest self, leading a Tang connoisseur to comment that one character was sufficient to reveal the writer. The flow of the lines and the rhythm of the brush creating the abstract beauty of the whole were now far more important than legibility. Thus, Chinese appreciation of calligraphy as high art combined the pleasure and excitement associated with abstract art as well as with graphology.

"In every terrible period of human history there is always a gentleman in a corner cultivating his calligraphy and stringing together a few pearls of expression."[14] Thus wrote Paul Valery in 1915. If so, it is no wonder that calligraphy flourished during the years following the collapse of the Han, nor that the new emphasis on self-expression was particularly conducive to this art.

The greatest calligrapher of the age was Wang Xizhi (321–379), a master whose art served as a model for countless generations. He and two of his sons, also famous calligraphers, drew inspiration from Daoism, with its emphasis on the natural. They sought to express naturalism, itself an abstract quality, through pen and ink. It was a magnificent challenge and typifies the artistic strivings of the age. The effort required years of practice. Wang Xizhi is said to have destroyed everything he had written before age fifty because he was dissatisfied with it. Unfortunately, none of his original work survives. Copies exist, but none is earlier than the Song. Reproduced

**FIGURE 4.5** Portion of a letter from the brush of Mi Fei. (From *Gu Gung Fa Shu*, No. 11 [Taipei, Taiwan: National Palace Museum, 1968], p. 11b). Selected by Dr. Léon L. Y. Chang.

in Figure 4.5 is a letter by a famous Song calligrapher and painter who drew inspiration from Wang Xizhi and one of his sons. The fourth line (reading right to left) is an example of the musical "continuous stroke" style for which they were famous.

# Painting

The human figure remained the main subject matter of painting, although the beginnings of China's great landscape tradition can also be traced back to this period. Preeminent among the painters was Gu Kaizhi (344–407), famed for capturing with his brush the essential character of his subjects, as when, by adding three hairs to a chin, he succeeded in depicting a man's wisdom. Among the most famous of his paintings still extant, although only in the form of a later copy, is a hand-scroll illustrating a poem composed in the third century entitled "Admonitions of the

**FIGURE 4.6** Gu Kaizhi, Scene 5 from *Admonitions of the Instructress to the Court Ladies.* Ink and color on silk. (© The Trustees of the British Museum.)

Instructress to the Court Ladies" in which the painted panels alternate with lines of the text. The scene reproduced in Figure 4.6 illustrates the lines, "if the words you speak are good, men for a thousand *li* will respond; but if you depart from this principle, even your bedfellow will distrust you." Presumably it is the emperor who is mistrusting the lady, although this scene has sometimes been read the other way around. The other panels also illustrate moral edicts and wifely duties. They are basically Confucian in content, although the artist himself was known for his Daoist eccentricity.

The enhanced interest taken in painting led to the development of art criticism and stimulated the formulation of the six classic principles of painting by Xie He, an early sixth-century portrait painter. Most important, but also allowing for the widest latitude of interpretation, is his first principle, which calls on the artist to imbue his painting with a cosmic vitality and sense of life. These terms have been translated by Alexander Soper as "animation through spirit consonance," where "spirit" is a translation of *qi*, the vital force and stuff of man and the universe.[15] *Qi* is also a central concept in Chinese medicine. We will encounter it again when we come to Song metaphysics and cosmology. It also figured in burial customs. The most eminent dead were fitted with jade suits to prevent the *qi* from leaking out of their bodies. Those who could not afford or were not entitled to a complete outfit were equipped with jade stoppers for ears, nose, mouth, and other orifices (see Figure 3.3). In the context of aesthetics, it is the quality that causes a painting to reverberate with life.

Xie He's second principle demands structural strength in the brushwork, demonstrating the vital link between painting and calligraphy, which used the same basic tools and techniques. It was largely in the quality of the artists' brushwork that the Chinese looked for an expression of their vital inspiration.

The next three principles require less explanation because they correspond to criteria familiar in the West. They are fidelity to the object in portraying forms, conformity to kind in applying colors, and proper planning in placing of elements—what we would call composition. The sixth and final principle is very Chinese, for it enjoins the copying of old masters. This is one aspect of the old Chinese veneration for the past. It was a way of preserving old masterpieces such as Gu Kaizhi's *Admonitions* and at the same time provided training and discipline for later artists, who by following the brushwork of a great predecessor would gain technical competence and an understanding of the medium, just as apprentice calligraphers today still begin by copying the great masters of their art, internalizing and making it their own. In neither case is there any intent to deceive.

# Buddhism in the South

In the South as in the North, Buddhism made great headway, winning substantial support among the great families and the personal patronage of rulers. In contrast to the North where Buddhist missionaries had to deal with "barbarian" rulers, in the South erudite and clever monks won favor by adopting the stance and displaying the skills of the sophisticated gentlemen who dominated society. Quick-witted Buddhists became experts in pure talk and engaged also in highly abstract metaphysical discussions in which they displayed their command of the Chinese intellectual heritage.

Accorded new prominence as a model for the sophisticated Buddhist was the figure of Vimalakirti, a wealthy layman who enjoyed life to the fullest and displayed great powers of intellect and a pure and lofty personality (see Figure 4.7). Monasteries and nunneries erected in beautiful surroundings offered a peaceful, scholarly, contemplative setting to those seeking a temporary or permanent respite from the tensions and struggles of life in the world.

Even so, Buddhism did not enjoy universal approval in the South any more than it did in the North. For one thing, Daoism, well established in the South, was always available as an attractive alternative, and there was opposition from other quarters as well. Its enemies attacked Buddhism's alleged subversive effects on state and society and sought to refute its teachings. For example, Fan Zhen, a Confucian official and brilliant debater, argued against the concept of the indestructibility of the soul, now a common tenet of Chinese Buddhism, the original

**FIGURE 4.7** Vimalakirti. Clay, 17.79 in high. Pagoda of the Hōryūji. (© Askaen.)

teaching of the Buddha notwithstanding. Fan Zhen argued that the soul is a passing function of the body, just as keenness is a temporary attribute of a knife. In response, Emperor Wu solicited counterarguments. He received fifty-eight refutations and only two replies supporting Fan Zhen's anti-Buddhist views. The time was not yet ripe for a major anti-Buddhist reaction. On the contrary, the full flowering of Buddhism in China was yet to come.

# China on the Eve of Reunification

After the fall of the Northern Wei, the North remained unstable for another half century, but its leaders demonstrated greater political vigor than those in the South. For models on which to build their state, they relied on classical texts, especially the *The Rites of Zhou* (*Zhouli*), which describes in detail what it claims was the bureaucratic government as it existed under the revered Duke of Zhou. They did this because in the political and moral realms Buddhism and Daoism could not match the native tradition. The memory of the glories of the Han (suitably embellished) and the authority of the remote but exemplary past conveyed in classical texts held firm.

The changes that occurred between the fall of the Han and the Sui reunification were far-reaching and profound. The division of China brought with it foreign rulers and a new religion. It had stimulated a new consciousness, which found expression in literature and art. And it had accelerated the development of the South, thus altering China's economic geography.

These events are comparable to what took place in the West after the fall of Rome, but in China, unlike in Europe, the factors bringing about political integration ultimately prevailed. Buddhism was one such factor and Daoism another. Confucianism as a family ethic, as a state rationale, and as a language of government persisted even when Confucian philosophy was in eclipse. There was a shared sense of what it meant to be civilized and educated.

The ideal of political unity was never questioned. As in the creation of the first empire, reunification came from the northwest, which was again the strongest area militarily. Unification proved to be a great and difficult undertaking—and one that in the end succeeded brilliantly.

# *Notes*

1. Helmut Brinker, "Early Buddhist Art in China," in *Return of the Buddha: The Qingzhou Discovery* (London: Royal Academy of Arts, 2002), p. 20.

2. John Kieschnick, *The Impact of Buddhism on Chinese Material Culture* (Princeton: Princeton Univ. Press, 2003), p. 157.

3. Isabelle Robinet, "Kuo Hsiang," in *The Encyclopedia of Religion* (New York: MacMillan, 1987), with some elisions and rearrangement.

4. *Sources of Chinese Tradition*, 2nd ed., Vol. 1, compiled by Wm Theodore de Bary and Irene Bloom (New York: Columbia Univ. Press, 1999), p. 390.

5. Charles Holcombe, *The Genesis of East Asia, 221 B.C.–A.D. 907* (Honolulu: Univ. of Hawaii Press, 2001), p. 124.

6. David A. Graff, *Medieval Chinese Warfare, 300–900* (London: Routledge, 2002), p. 12.

7. Robert H. Sharf, *Coming to Terms with Chinese Buddhism: A Reading of the Treasure Store Treatise* (Honolulu: Univ. of Hawaii Press, 2002), p. 19.

8. Isabelle Robinet, *Taoist Meditation: The Mao-shan Tradition of Great Purity*, trans. Julian F. Pas and Norman J. Giradot (Albany: State Univ. of New York Press, 1993), p. 45.

9. Go Hong as quoted in Susan Naquin and Chün-fang Yi, eds., *Pilgrims and Sacred Sites in China* (Berkeley: Univ. of California Press, 1992), p. 14.

10. Shufen Liu, "Jiankang and the Commercial Empire of the Southern Dynasties: Change and Continuity in Medieval Chinese Economic History," in Scott Pearce, Audrey Spiro, and Patricia Ebrey, eds., *Culture and Power in the Reconstitution of the Chinese Realm, 200–600* (Cambridge: Harvard Univ. Press, 2001), p. 46. Jiankang is the old name of Nanjing.

11. Liu Wu-chi, *An Introduction to Chinese Literature* (Bloomington: Indiana Univ. Press, 1966), p. 64.

12. Eric Sackheim, *The Silent Zero, in Search of Sound: An Anthology of Chinese Poetry from the Beginning through the Sixth Century* (New York: Grossman Publishers, 1968) p. ii.

13. David R. Knechtes, "Culling the Weeds and Selecting Prime Blossoms," in Pearce, Spiro, and Ebrey, *Reconstitution of the Chinese Realm*, p. 207.

14. Quoted in Etienne Balazs, *Chinese Civilization and Bureaucracy* (New Haven: Yale Univ. Press, 1968), p. 226.

15. Alexander Soper, "The First Two Laws of Hsieh Ho," *The Far East Quarterly* 8(1949): 412–23.

# 5

# The Cosmopolitan Civilization of the Sui and Tang: 581–907

| 581 | 617 | | 755 | 763 | | 907 |
|---|---|---|---|---|---|---|

Sui (China Reunified in 589) — Tang — An Lushan Rebellion — Late Tang

After its reunification in 589, China remained united for approximately 300 years. During this period China became the political model and cultural center for all East Asia. Buddhism and Daoism flourished. Significant changes occurred in government and society. It was the period of classical poetry and law.

Like the Han, the Tang dynasty succeeded a powerful but short-lived regime that had accomplished the original reunification: the Sui. And like the Han, the Tang dynasty may be thought of as having very distinct earlier and later phases, although there was no comparable formal interruption of Tang rule. There are other ways, too, in which the two dynasties are similar, but the differences between them are even more instructive than their points of resemblance.

# The Sui (581–617)

In 577, forty-three years after the demise of the Northern Wei, the Northern Zhou (557–581) reunified the North. Four years later the Northern Zhou general Yang Jian (541–604) usurped the throne and founded his own dynasty, the Sui, which in 589 defeated the last of the southern states. The task of then incorporating North and South into a single political system has been compared to the attempt by Charlemagne (742–814) to create a new Roman Empire in Europe. Although different in outcome, the two situations were quite comparable in terms of land area, diversity of terrain, and variety of local cultures.

Unlike the Qin, the Sui did not seek to impose a new pattern on China but adopted a policy of fusing various local traditions and amalgamating different elements. Although both Yang Jian and his strong minded, influential wife were dedicated Buddhists, the Sui also used Confucian and Daoist traditions to gain support and legitimacy. In formulating a legal code the new dynasty incorporated elements from different legal traditions, North and South, so effectively that it provided the basis for the Tang and all subsequent codes. In other respects too there was much continuity between the Sui and the early Tang, which, unlike the Han, did not repudiate the principles and policies of its immediate predecessor.

Yang Jian or Wendi (r. 581–604), the posthumous name by which the emperor is known in the histories, his wife, and their son, Yangdi (r. 604–618), came from a prominent northwestern family of mixed Chinese and steppe ancestry. Through cultural policies and marriage alliances they undertook reconciliation of the great families of the Northeast and of the South. Yangdi married a southern princess and linked North and South by completing his father's ambitious project of building a canal joining China's two great rivers, the Yellow and the Yangzi, providing the political capital in the North access to the riches of the lower Yangzi. The completed Grand Canal joined Hangzhou and Kaifeng and was linked by extensions both to the area of modern Beijing and to the Sui-Tang capital, the new Chang'an, built near the site of the old Former Han capital. Construction of official granaries helped to establish a government economic network.

The Sui devoted equal care to political consolidation and centralization. The bureaucracy was reorganized, and a tier of local administration was eliminated to make local government more amenable to central direction. Local officials could no longer appoint their subordinates as they had during the period of division, and the "rule of avoidance" prohibited an official from serving in his native place. Nor could he serve more than one tour of duty in the same locality. After this tour, usually lasting three years, he would be reassigned according to merit.

Even more important, the Sui instituted a system of recruiting officials by examination. This deprived the hereditary high aristocracy of the monopoly of power they had enjoyed during the period of division, when appointments had been made by recommendation. Although government service was opened to a somewhat wider class of people, it still remained the prerogative of the wellborn. These measures effectively reduced the ability of officials to establish a personal power base in the areas where they served, reduced the power of the great families to which they belonged, and made officials more responsive to the interests and direction of the central government.

As may be expected of a unifying dynasty, the Sui was vigorous militarily. Expeditions were sent as far south as Central Vietnam, and in the west, nomadic peoples were driven out of Gansu and eastern Turkestan. Colonies were established along the trade routes. Further afield, in Central Asia, states such as Turfan became tributaries. Envoys were exchanged with Japan. The Sui continued the militia system it had inherited from the northern dynasties and settled many troops in garrisons along the frontiers.

The dynasty's aggressive foreign policy demanded the organization and deployment of large military forces. Most costly in terms of casualties and materiel were three unsuccessful campaigns against Koguryo, the state that controlled northern Korea and much of southern Manchuria. Successive defeats placed an unbearable strain on the dynasty's resources. Insurrection and rebellion became widespread. The dynasty was doomed. It had overreached, trying to accomplish too much too rapidly. In the traditional Chinese view, however, the onus for its demise was assigned to Yangdi, who was cast as an archetypical bad last emperor, a self-indulgent tyrant—an image embellished in popular literature, which depicts him as living in luxury while his people were starving, frolicking with the numer-

**FIGURE 5.1** The Tang Empire.

ous women of his harem in a room lined with polished bronze screens to serve as mirrors, when he should have been minding the ship of state.

# The Tang: Establishment and Consolidation

The Tang dynasty emerged from the struggles accompanying the disintegration of the Sui dynasty and built a great empire (see Figure 5.1). Its founder was that dynasty's top general, related through his mother to the Sui ruling house. Many of his officials had also served the former dynasty. There was no sharp break in the composition or the policy of the ruling group, but the fighting was hard and prolonged, taking up most of the reign of the founding emperor, Gaozu (r. 618–626). In 626 Gaozu's second son, a successful military commander, killed the crown prince and another brother apparently to forestall a plot against himself. He then forced his father to abdicate. Known as Taizong (r. 626–649), he directed the consolidation of the new dynasty.

Taizong's physical vigor and military prowess are suggested by the stone panels, which are more than five feet high, showing his favorite mount (see Figure 5.2). Equally vigorous mentally and wise in his knowledge of men, he became one of China's most admired rulers. His most famous Confucian minister was Wei Zheng (580–645). After Wei's death, Taizong compared his minister to a mirror used for

**FIGURE 5.2** General Qui Xinggong of Emperor Tang Taizong's army removes an arrow from the Emperor's horse, Autumn Dew. Stone relief from tomb of Tang Taizong. Design attributed to Yan Liben (d. 673), 59.84 in × 58.15 in. Love of horses and excellence in horsemanship were part of the steppe legacy of the Tang royal family and northwestern elite. (University of Pennsylvania Museum, Philadelphia.)

correcting his judgment analogous to a bronze mirror for straightening out one's clothes and the mirror of the past for understanding the rise and fall of states. But, although he sought Wei Zheng's counsel on moral issues, such as the punishment of officials or the giving and receiving of gifts, the emperor did not allow him to influence major policy decisions such as those concerning peace or war.

Taizong's policies generally built on those of the Sui. He broadened the geographical composition of the bureaucracy by including men from areas other than his native Northwest, but government remained in the hands of the well-born. The most pretentious of these were the high aristocrats of the Northeast, who looked down on the "semibarbarian" northwestern families, not excluding the imperial family, even though it claimed descent from Laozi. Taizong had a genealogy compiled to define the status of families throughout China and rejected the first draft to demote one of the great Hebei lineages and promote the imperial clan to first place.

Following the Sui example, more granaries and schools were built, and a new code of criminal and administrative law was promulgated. This consisted of primary laws, meant to hold for all time, and secondary laws, open to frequent adjustment to allow for changing conditions and local variations. The central government was restructured so that its essential tasks were performed by Six Ministries (personnel, revenue, rites, war, justice, and public works), a system continued by later dynasties.

The early Tang emperors, like those of the Sui, drew on Buddhism and Daoism as well as Confucianism. Taizong gave precedence to Daoism but took care not to alienate the Buddhists. Like his predecessors he took measures to keep the religious establishments under control. Meanwhile, as Howard Wechsler has shown, the early Tang emperors, in contrast to earlier rulers, deemphasized rites centered on their own ancestors in favor of more public rituals performed by the emperor for the good of all. And they extended their own family to form a "political family" of ministers and high officials who were included in rites and granted "satellite tombs" on the vast grounds of the imperial tombs. Such tombs had also been granted in the Han, but not on a scale anything like that of the Tang.[1] The fact that in China, unlike Japan, such tombs continued to be built even in a Buddhist age is not unconnected with issues of legitimation but beyond that also reveals deep-seated differences in attitudes toward burial and perhaps even death.

Statues of foreign envoys (although now headless) still pay homage at Taizong's tomb, confirming

**FIGURE 5.3** Xuanzang, a Tang monk who traveled to India in search of Buddhist scripture. Rubbing in the Schirokauer collection. Making rubbings from stone steles was a popular form of reproducing texts as well as pictures before the invention of printing and remains an inexpensive way to reproduce pictures and calligraphy. (© Lore Schirokauer)

his successful extension of Chinese power even further west than had the Han. But the Tang, like the Sui, failed in Korea. With Chinese power reaching all the way to the Pamirs and the empire at peace, travel of men and goods along the trade routes was more lively than ever. Many foreigners visited and lived in Chang'an during Taizong's reign, but the most famous traveler of the time was a Chinese monk, Xuanzang, who journeyed to India and returned with Buddhist texts and much information about foreign countries (see Figure 5.3).

The emperor was more interested in the latter than the former and even tried to persuade the venerable monk to return to lay life and become a foreign policy adviser. Xuanzang declined, and Taizong financed the translation projects to which the monk devoted the rest of his life. He also ordered Xuanzang to translate the *Daodejing* into Sanskrit for the benefit of the Indian world.

Taizong's last years were spoiled by disappointments in his sons and heirs. The crown prince became so infatuated with nomad ways, even living in a yurt, that he was finally deposed, and the emperor's favorite son was too deeply involved in intrigues over the succession to be trusted. In the end, the succession went to a weak young prince who became Emperor Gaozong (r. 650–683).

## Gaozong and Empress Wu

Gaozong began as quite a vigorous ruler but suffered a stroke in 660. The remainder of his reign was dominated by Wu Zhao (625?–706?), a former concubine of Taizong's who won Gaozong's affection and engineered the removal and often murder of all rivals. After Gaozong's death in 683, two of Wu's sons reigned in succession, but in 690, no longer willing to rule through puppets, she proclaimed herself emperor of a new dynasty, the Zhou, thereby becoming the only woman in Chinese history to rule in her own name.

Gaozong showed his favor for Daoism by proclaiming Laozi "Sovereign Emperor of Mystery and Primordiality," establishing a government abbey in more than 300 prefectures, and requiring the *Daodejing* on the government examinations. Nevertheless, the content of the examination system, the guidelines for gentlemanly conduct and official policies, remained classical, and Confucian-style scholarship was sponsored by the state. In 651 an authoritative edition of the Five Classics (the *Odes,* the *Documents,* the *Rites,* the *Changes,* and the *Spring and Autumn Annals*) was completed, with each classic being accompanied by a definite commentary and subcommentary, in "a sorting out of traditions of scholarship on texts fundamental to civilized life."[2] Such a life was not considered incompatible with Buddhism or Daoism, but it was not defined in Buddhist or Daoist terms.

In contrast to Gaozong, Empress Wu, however, turned mainly to Buddhism, proclaimed herself an incarnation of Maitreya, and ordered temples set up in every province to expound the *Dayunjing,* a sutra prophesying the appearance of a female world ruler 700 years after the passing of the Buddha. Her patronage of Buddhism also extended to other temples and sects; much work was done in the Longmen caves during her reign.

Empress Wu's legitimacy was also bolstered by a genealogy compiled in 659 that listed families according to the official rank attained by their members, rather than according to their traditional inherited social standing, with the Wu family placed first. Under her rule the bureaucracy was expanded, with many new positions filled through the examination system. This opened government careers to a wider group, but in the final stage of the process, candidates continued to be judged on appearance and speech, criteria that inevitably favored the well-born. It was also normal practice for candidates to try to impress an examiner before the tests. Those who could used their family connections for this purpose; others sent samples of their verse.

Under Empress Wu, examination graduates could for the first time rise as high as Chief Minister, although the Empress preferred to bypass this office and work through the "Scholars of the Northern Gate," who formed a kind of personal secretariat. Gradually, however, during the first half of the Tang, examination graduates acquired great prestige and were promoted to the highest offices, even

**FIGURE 5.4** Lady on horseback. Painted clay, Tang, 12.24 in × 15 in. Tang ladies regularly rode horses and played polo, a favorite game among the elite. (Courtesy of Karen Schlansky, www.rosecourtasianantiques.com)

though the majority of officials still entered government service through other means, making use of family connections. Concurrently, government service became the most prestigious career in the empire.

Office-holding remained a male preserve, but Tang women enjoyed more freedom than their predecessors. No doubt conditions varied according to place and social status—documents found in Turfan show women engaged in legal, financial, and religious activities—but, as Patricia Karetzky has suggested, "with dated archeological evidence, a pattern of development can be traced, and it seems to follow the trajectory of female influence at court."[3] That influence reached its zenith under Empress Wu, and, sure enough, the women depicted in paintings now become less stiff and demure. They interact more with others, are more individualized in character and expression, and, perhaps under Indian influence, are more robust. This is confirmed by figurines as well (see Figure 5.4). Art does not mirror life, but it does reflect tastes and values.

Tang power now reached its furthest geographic extent (see Figure 5.1) but at the price of constant fighting, particularly against the Tibetans. In Korea, Empress Wu

先師孔子行教像

**FIGURE 5.5** Portrait of Confucius propagating the teaching. Attributed to Wu Daozi (Qing?). Rubbing, 20.28 in × 43.31 in. (Schirokauer collection.)

supported the successful efforts of the state of Silla to unify the peninsula. Although China was unable to dominate the newly unified state, relations remained cordial throughout her reign. Until around 700 she remained a vigorous, although ruthless, ruler, but during her last years the empress, now in her seventies, came under the influence of sycophantic courtiers. She was deposed in 705, and the Tang was reestablished.

## High Tang

The Tang reached its high point—economically, politically, and culturally—during the reign of Xuanzong (r. 713–756), also known as the "Brilliant Emperor" (Minghuang). His court must have been truly splendid. The emperor, a horse lover, is said to have kept 40,000 horses in the royal stables, including a troupe of dancing horses. Poetry and painting flourished, and horses were a favorite theme for poets, painters, and potters. The most admired of all Tang painters, Wu Daozi, lived during this period. It was later said of him that one day, after painting a scene on a wall, he walked into it, leaving only the empty wall behind. He must have been a remarkable master to have inspired this story. Unfortunately, none of his work is known to have survived, although the most famous depiction of Confucius is attributed to him (see Figure 5.5).

This is one of two portraits of Confucius attributed to Wu Daozi, inscribed on stone and distributed as rubbings. Wearing a simple cloth cap, the venerable "foremost master" is shown as a traveling teacher. Images such as this, although too far removed to testify as to the appearance of the original man or painting, had—and still have—a presence not dependent on their resemblance to the historical persons. And they are invaluable in showing how people imagined the sage and envisioned the painter's style. In 1974 a conference convened by the Taiwan Ministry of the Interior chose this rubbing to distribute to cultural sites around the world. There are even statues of the sage, modeled after this rubbing, in Tokyo and Cleveland as well as Taipei.

Political achievements under Xuanzong included reformation of the coinage, repair and extension of the Grand Canal, and the implementation of a land registration program. To carry out these measures, he employed special commissions headed by distinguished aristocrats. Men of equally imposing background also staffed the Censorate, the organ of the government charged with the surveillance of the bureaucracy. There was a tendency at this time for officials to polarize into two groups: members of the high aristocracy and those of less exalted rank. Nevertheless, factors influencing political alignments were too complex to be reduced to simple family or regional patterns.

Under Xuanzong the power of the Chief Ministers increased and a cabinet of Chief Ministers was established. Near the middle of his reign, the emperor gradually withdrew from active participation in government. From 736 to 752 government was in the hands of Li Linfu, an aristocrat who was an able minister but did not have an examination degree and was often ridiculed by those who did for his lack of scholarship. An expedition to conquer the kingdom of Nanzhao established in 738 in modern Yunnan failed, as did a second attempt in 754, leaving Nanzhao independent and free to expand.

When Li Linfu died in 752, he was succeeded by Yang Guozhong, a much less capable man, who owed his rise to the influence of his cousin, the royal concubine Yang Gueifei, China's premier femme fatale, who so captivated the emperor that he neglected all else and left the burdens of government to her relatives and protégés, unfortunately including An Lushan. In 751 An received the extraordinary honor of adoption into the imperial family in a solemn ceremony for which the rugged middle-aged "barbarian" general was dressed in diapers like an infant. This, however, this did not prevent him from rebelling four years later. The court was forced to flee to Sichuan. Along the way, loyal soldiers blamed Yang Gueifei for the country's difficulties and forced the emperor to have her strangled. Xuanzong then abdicated. The reign that had begun in such brilliance ended in disaster.

# City Life in the Capital: Chang'an

Even the most casual glance at the layout of Tang Chang'an reveals that it was a planned city (see Figure 5.6). Occupying about 30 square miles, excluding the palace area, it was the largest planned city ever built and the largest enclosed by walls. Its roughly 1 million inhabitants also made it the most populous city in the world at the time. Roughly another 1 million people lived in the greater metropolitan area outside the walls.

Many cities grow in response to the social and economic needs of their inhabitants, but planned cities express the values and priorities of their builders. The essential feature of Chang'an is that it was built to be the capital of a great empire.

**FIGURE 5.6** Tang Chang'an.

In accord with tradition, it was oriented so that both the city and the imperial palace faced south. The entire city was, in a sense, the home of the emperor. Its layout resembled that of a typical Tang house, with a service area in front and a garden in the rear. The imposing presence of the emperor and his government was further emphasized by the grand avenue that led from the main city gate to the palace and the government complex. Five hundred feet wide, enough for 45 modern traffic lanes, it was well designed to impress envoys from lesser lands with the might and grandeur of the Tang.

The people of the city lived in rectangular wards, each a self-contained unit enclosed by walls, with entry provided through a gate that was closed each night. Two friends in adjacent wards might be able to see each other's houses but would find it difficult to visit. Because it was the center of government, Chang'an was hardly the place to escape government surveillance and interference. Freedom was to be found in remote mountains and hills. Not everyone wished to rusticate in a remote village, however; many bitterly bemoaned an enforced absence from the great capital—unless, perhaps, they were posted to Luoyang, the secondary capital, or to Yangzhou, the southern metropolis.

Tang culture was cosmopolitan both in its openness to cultural influences from India and the distant west and in serving as model for the other settled societies of East Asia. Both aspects were reflected in the considerable number of foreigners who lived in Chang'an. Some were students. Among these, the most numerous were the Koreans, of whom some 8000 were said to have been in Chang'an in 640. Other foreigners were engaged in commerce, coming from as far away as India, Iran, Syria, and Arabia. The Armenoid wineseller shown in Figure 5.7 probably sold his exotic beverage in the West Market, the center for foreign trade,

**FIGURE 5.7** *Armenoid Merchant Holding Wine Skin.* Pottery with three-color glaze, eighth century, 10 in × 14.65 in. Li Bai (Li Bo) was just one poet much given to this merchant's beverage. (© Seattle Art Museum, Eugene Fuller Memorial Collection, 38.6. Photo by Paul Macapia.)

where his customers could also enjoy other exotic foods and beverages and attend performances of foreign acrobats or magicians or see a foreign play.

Stylish Tang ladies sported foreign coiffures, and painters and potters had a good time rendering the outlandish features of "barbarians" from distant lands. Images of foreigners from all over Central Asia and beyond to Iran were prominent among the clay figurines manufactured in specialty shops to be used for burial with the dead. Among the tomb figures are camel drivers and grooms for the horses, examples of which can be found in almost all museum collections of Chinese art. Information concerning foreign foods, music, and customs can also be found in Tang writings, particularly poetry.

Among the amenities of the capital were the Serpentine Lake and the Hibiscus Garden in the southeast corner of the city, where newly granted degree holders celebrated their good fortune by floating wine cups on the water, and the emperor himself sometimes entered the Purple Cloud Pavilion to observe the festivities. Notably absent, however, were public buildings such as forums, baths, or stadiums found in cities inhabited by citizens rather than subjects. Nor did Chang'an boast great, monumental structures of stone or brick. The men of Tang were under no illusion concerning the permanence of stone. In their view, what endured was the written word.

As the map of Chang'an clearly shows, the city was also a religious center. To its Manichean, Nestorian, and Zoroastrian temples we can now add the abandoned Da Qin Pagoda and Monastery where a mud and plaster nativity and other Christian remains dating from around 780 were discovered in 2001. The places of worship of foreign religions testify to Tang tolerance and cosmopolitanism, but their congregations, like those of Buddhist temples during the Han, remained largely foreign. Not so were the Daoist and even more numerous Buddhist structures. Buddhist pagodas gave Chang'an its skyline, and the influence of Buddhism was everywhere.

# The Flourishing of Buddhism

As a recent study puts it, the Tang saw "the emergence of China as a central Buddhist realm,"[4] home of sacred relics, of Maitreya, and of Manjusri, bodhisattva of meditation and perfect wisdom up on Mt. Wutai (Shanxi). Completely at home, Buddhism flourished institutionally, intellectually, and artistically and penetrated deeply into Chinese life. Many studies have and continue to be written about all these aspects, which we can only outline here.

## Institutionally

Although the state employed Confucian ceremonies and learning whereas individual emperors might favor Daoism, what had become the most prevalent religious organization in the empire could not be disregarded. During the period of division, the southern monk Huiyuan (334–417) had asserted that monks do not bow to emperors, but in the North Buddhism had been expected to serve the state. The Tang, following the Northern Wei, restricted the number of monks and regulated the monasteries, but most emperors also patronized Buddhism as an asset for the empire even if they varied in degree of personal commitment, and Buddhist monasteries flourished economically. In the countryside they operated mills and oil presses, maintained vaults for safe deposit, issued loans for interest, changed money, and performed other banking services including pawnbroking. The temples also held much land that they cultivated with semiservile labor, rented land, and profited from their connections with wealthy patrons who sought to evade taxation by registering land under a temple name.

Urban as well as rural temples provided medical care and put up travelers. They were associated with bridge building and the domestication of sugar. As conduits for Inner and South Asian culture, they influenced Chinese material culture in many ways—including the popularization of chairs. Their grounds served as playgrounds for children and at festival time also for adults. Looking at their buildings and art and listening to the chanting of the monks satisfied people's aesthetic needs.

## Aesthetically

The Guanyin shown in Figure 5.8 is a sculpture in the style seen in eighth-century Chang'an. At their very best, Tang sculptures blend Indian delight in the corporality of mass with a Chinese sense of essentially linear rhythm. It is a combination most suitable for portraying Guanyin, combining the spiritual qualities of a supernatural being with merciful concern for earthly creatures. The balance between movement and restraint, like that between the worldly and the sacred, was difficult to maintain: in later Buddhist art, corporality degenerates into obesity and the robes take on a wild, rococo life of their own.

For those seeking a temporary retreat from the world, Buddhist temples offered a serene place of contemplation:

**FIGURE 5.8** Eleven-headed century, 12.48 in × 39.69 in. The sensuous quality of the body, clothed (not hidden) in diaphanous drapery, owes something to Indian influence, particularly that of the Gupta Period (320–647). (Freer Gallery of Art, Smithsonian Institution, Gift of Charles Lang Freer, F1909.8.)

> I didn't know where the temple was,
> pushing mile on mile among cloudy peaks;
> old trees, peopleless paths,
> deep mountains, somewhere a bell.
> Brook voices choke over craggy boulders,
> sun rays turn cold in the green pines.
> At dusk by the bend of a deserted pond,
> a monk in meditation, taming poison dragons.[5]

The poem is by Wang Wei (699–759), noted also for his landscape painting, music, and calligraphy, all now lost. The dragons are the passions; the scene is visual yet empty.

## Intellectually

Because the analysis of Tang Buddhism in terms of schools has now been questioned, it is safer to think in terms of tendencies, some of which eventually crystallized into major sects. Others, such as the proponents of the Three Stages (Sanjie), did not develop into a powerful sect but did contribute a vision of time as divided into (1) the era of true teaching, (2) the era of counterfeit teaching, and (3) the era of the decay of teaching. Although there was disagreement over exact periodization, the Tang was generally assigned to the period of decay, a view that Tang emperors naturally did not appreciate.

A tendency that became a major sect was Tiantai (Japanese Tendai), named after a mountain range in Zhejiang. Traced back to Zhiyi (538–597), it was patronized by the Sui. Mirroring that dynasty's policy of political and economic integration, Tiantai combined elements of the various doctrines and practices, seeking to combine the scholarly tradition of the South with northern pietism and meditation. The complete Truth for Tiantai was contained in the Lotus Sutra, believed to have been preached by the Buddha to 12,000 arhats (saints), 6000 nuns, 8000 Bodhisattvas, and 60,000 gods. The great god Brahma attended, accompanied by 12,000 dragons, and there were hundreds of thousands of other supernatural beings. As he talked, a ray of light emanated from the Buddha's forehead, revealing 18,000 worlds, in each of which a Buddha is preaching. This text was enormously influential in East Asia and inspired many artistic representations. Through powerful allegories such as that of a man rescued by following a mirage, it recommends the use of "skillful means" (*upaya, fangbian*) to lead people to salvation.

Tiantai doctrine centered on a tripartite truth: (1) the truth that all phenomena are empty, products of causation without a nature of their own; (2) the truth that they do, however, exist temporarily; and (3) the truth that encompasses but transcends emptiness and temporariness. These three truths all involve and require each other— throughout Tiantai the whole and the parts are one. A rich but unified cosmology is built on this basis: temporariness consists of ten realms. Because each of these includes the other, a total of 1000 results. Each of these in turn has three aspects—that of living beings, of aggregates, and of space. The result is 3000 worlds interwoven so that all are present in each. Therefore, truth is immanent in everything: all beings contain the Buddha nature and can be saved. One eighth-century Tiantai patriarch taught that this includes inanimate things, down to the tiniest grain of dust.

Like Tiantai, Huayan taught the doctrine of emptiness and the interpenetration of all phenomena, but added that all phenomena arise simultaneously in reciprocal causation. Deeply interested in doctrinal subtleties, Huayan Buddhists distinguished between *li*, which can be translated as "principle" and is formless, and *shi*, or "phenomena." One of its greatest masters was Fazang (Fa-tsang, 643–712), who was patronized by Empress Wu. In a famous sermon Fazang once explained Huayan doctrine by setting up a Buddha figure surrounded by eight mirrors at the points of the compass. A ninth mirror was placed above the statue and a tenth below. When the Buddha figure was lit by a torch, each mirror reflected not only the Buddha but also all the other mirrors.

Less intellectual but very potent was the esoteric Buddhism patronized by Gaozong, consistent with his abiding interest in Daoist magic. The practitioners of this form of Buddhism, which, like Huayan, stressed the magnificence and mystery of the Cosmic Buddha (Vairocana), used mantras (mystic syllables), mudras (signs made by the position of the fingers and hands), and mandalas (pictorial representations of the cosmos—"cosmograms"). Although influential in China, it did not become a major sect there as it did in Japan, in the form of Shingon. Two other tendencies emphasized practice more than thought.

## Pure Land and Chan

Jingtu (Japanese *Jōdo*), or Pure Land, derived its name from the paradise in the West presided over by Amitabha (*Amituofo* in Chinese; *Amida* in Japanese), Buddha of Infinite Light. Another great favorite of Pure Land Buddhists was Guanyin. Drawing on a long Mahayana tradition, this school emphasized faith as the means for gaining rebirth in the land of bliss. The teaching of salvation by faith was often coupled with the idea that this was the appropriate means for a decadent age. A special practice of Pure Land Buddhism was the invocation of Amitabha's name. This, if done with wholehearted sincerity, would gain anyone rebirth in the Pure Land. The popular appeal of this sect was immense, and its spiritual dimensions probably received their furthest development in the teachings of the Japanese master Shinran (1173–1262).

Chan was also very influential in Japan, so much so that in the West it is generally known by its Japanese name, Zen, but it originated in China and has affinities with Daoism. Chan masters taught meditation as the way for one to pierce through the world of illusion, recognize the Buddha nature within oneself, and obtain enlightenment. Whereas for other schools meditation was only one of many techniques, Chan rejected all other practices, such as the performance of meritorious deeds or the study of scriptures.

Chan came to be divided into "Northern" and a more radical "Southern" school founded by Huineng (638–713) who, according to The Platform Sutra of the Sixth Patriarch, became the sixth patriarch after besting his rival's poem.

> The body is the *bodhi* tree
> The mind is like a clear mirror.
> At all times we must strive to polish it.
> And must not allow the dust to collect

It was under the *bodhi* tree that the Buddha was said to have achieved enlightenment. Illiterate himself, Huineng got a monk to post his response:

> The *bodhi* tree is originally not a tree
> The mirror also has no stand.
> Buddha-nature is always clean and pure
> Where is there room for dust?

Another verse said:

> The mind is the *bodhi* tree,
> The body is the mirror stand.
> The mirror is originally clean and pure;
> Where can it be stained by dust?[6]

In contrast to the so-called Northern branch, which emphasized sitting in silent meditation and attaining enlightenment gradually, Southern Chan taught that illumination comes in a sudden flash, although only after long searching. A

Western analogy might be Newton's experience under the apple tree: he discovered the law of gravitation in a sudden flash, but he would never have done so had he not been constantly thinking about the problem, searching for a solution.

Southern Chan teachers often employed unorthodox methods to prod their disciples on the road to illumination. Their methods included irreverent or irrelevant answers to questions, contradictory remarks, and nonsense syllables—anything to jar the mind out of its ordinary rut. Some masters would strike their disciples in the belief (as with Newton) that enlightenment might come as the result of a sudden physical shock. One widely practiced technique was for the master to assign his pupils a *gong'an* (*koan* in Japanese), an enigmatic statement to be pondered until the pupil attained an understanding that transcended everyday reasoning. One famous *gong'an* asks: "What is the sound of one hand clapping?"

Chan, like some other varieties of Buddhism, was esoteric in that its teachings were fully accessible only to select lifelong practitioners, but, like the Greater Vehicle, Buddhist festivals were for everyone.

## The Hungry Ghost Festival

Hungry ghosts were condemned to suffer in the lowest hells, unable ever to relieve their starvation because their needle-thin throats made it impossible for them to swallow even when food failed to burst into flames on their lips. The festival, still celebrated in East Asia today (and as Obon in Japan), is based on the story of Mulian (Maudgalyāyana in Sanskrit), a deeply filial monk who, with Buddha's help, after searching long and hard in the underworld where he encountered numerous demons, finds and rescues his mother, a hungry ghost condemned to unceasing agony by the bad karma she had accrued through her avarice and stinginess in withholding food and alms from monks.

Recounted in sacred texts but also by popular storytellers using "transformation texts" (*bianwen*) to explain and embellish what was happening in the pictures that were their stock in trade, Mulian's story underwent many variations incorporating material of diverse origin. Scholarly analysis reveals that the demons who staff the underworld include immigrants as well as native born spirits, all equally part of a single system.

Similarly the scholar can detect diverse elements and levels of meaning in the festival, performed on the fifteenth day of the seventh lunar month, long an important date in China. A major theme is the interaction of ancestors and the living, but what is perhaps most impressive is the fusion of meanings and traditions. In that fusion Buddhism, once charged with lack of family values, occupies a central place. As Stephen F. Teiser points out, the spread of the festival in China "signals the movement of Buddhist monkhood into the very heart of family religion."[7]

A document presented to Xuanzong in 739 provides for the Central Office of the Imperial Workshop to supply special bowls for the festival, and the state remained a sponsor and participant, but the festival long outlived the dynasty. This was true of Daoism as well, although it continued to benefit from direct imperial patronage. Xuanzong even strengthened the dynasty's association with Daoism by ordering statues of Laozi and himself to stand side by side in state-sponsored abbeys throughout the empire.

# Daoism

Daoism under the Tang as summarized by Russell Kirkland was "a fairly homogenous blend of nomenclature from the Celestial Masters tradition, meditative practices from the Shangqing tradition, liturgies and social values from the Lingbao tradition, and philosophical texts like the *Daodejing*."[8] This quotation is from an essay on Sima Chengzhen (646–735), a man of distinguished family background who occupied a preeminent place in the Shangqing lineage and was an expert in ritual and meditation. Sima moved easily in polite society, associated with famous literary figures, and enjoyed a fine reputation as a writer, painter, and calligrapher. As a Daoist he emphasized gradually transforming oneself and predicted his own final release from his corporal form.

Shangqing adepts continued to journey through inner and outer space in their quest for wisdom and longevity, whereas ordinary folk too were attracted by longevity techniques, miracles, and the power of local gods: "Ordinary people are saved by the deities, statues in provincial temples take flight when threatened or act in retaliation, nasty demons are slain and good forces are harnessed to the greater prosperity not only of aristocrats but also of the common people and the wider populace."[9] The political landscape might change, but Daoism was deeply rooted in China's sacred landscape dominated by the five sacred mountains that Daoists considered the fingers of the cosmic Laozi.

# The Rebellion of An Lushan (755–763)

The rebellion that drove the emperor into flight to Sichuan and created havoc in the country revealed the underlying weakness in the Tang system. Afterwards, China was never the same again. Today the thesis, first set forth by Naitō Kōnan (1866–1934), that the rebellion marked a major break in Chinese history is generally accepted, and it is only to keep the book reasonably brief that we treat both sides of this divide in a single chapter.

As usual, internal and external troubles reinforced each other. Only strong central leadership could prevent the friction between the aristocratic commissions and the regular bureaucracy from getting out of hand. Old institutions were revealed to be inadequate under new conditions. The dynasty had adopted the "equal field system" of land allotment developed by the Northern Wei as a way of bringing deserted land back under cultivation or opening up new lands, but this system proved unworkable when there was a shortage rather than a surplus of land. The breakdown of the land system brought in its train the failure of the taxation system, which was based on equal land allotments. Because most taxes were collected in kind, that is, goods rather than money, this system required a cumbersome network of transport and storage.

Similarly, the old militia system proved inadequate. The dynasty's military requirements could only be met by large standing armies composed of professional soldiers. In 747 a Tang army crossed the Pamirs, led by a Korean general who had opted for a career under the Tang. This expedition succeeded in preventing Arabs and Tibetans from joining forces, but four years later this same general suffered defeat on the banks of the Talas River near Samarkand. This momentous event not only put an end to Tang ambitions in the area but also opened to Islam what had up to then been a Buddhist-oriented Central Asia.

In 736 the Northwest had been stabilized when the pro-Tang Uighurs became the dominant power. In midcentury, however, the dynasty was challenged by an alliance between Tibet and Nan Zhao, a southwestern state in the area of modern Yunnan Province. The government's response was to create military provinces along the frontiers. These were placed under the direction of military governors (*jiedushi*) who were given logistic as well as military authority and gradually assumed other government functions. With the central army in decline, a serious imbalance of power resulted between the home army and the powerful frontier forces. An Lushan, a general of Turkish extraction, began his rebellion in control of 160,000 troops in the Northeast.

An Lushan seized both Luoyang and Chang'an and proclaimed himself emperor of a new Yan dynasty. But in 757 he was murdered by his son. The rebellion continued, led first by Shi Siming, a general of similar background, and then by his son. In the meantime, the court had fled to Sichuan, the very large (75,000 square miles) and fertile province which, ringed by mountains, is highly defensible. (During the Second World War it served as a bastion for the Nationalist Chinese.)

In 763 the court was able to regain the capital, and the Tang was saved. However, the dynasty was able to recoup only with the assistance of foreign, mostly Uighur, troops. Furthermore, it had to be content with purely nominal submission of the virtually independent "governors" in the Northeast, in the region west of the capital, in parts of Henan, and in Sichuan. Regional differences that before the rebellion had been worked out within the system now threatened to pull it apart.

## Li Bai and Du Fu

The ability to write at least passable poetry was one of the accomplishments expected of a Tang gentleman and was usually required in the civil service examinations. Consequently, a great many poems—more than 48,000, by some 2200 writers—have been preserved. Naturally their quality is uneven, as would be the case if our politicians and business executives were all expected to write poetry.

Li Bai (Li Bo, 701–763) and Du Fu (712–770), China's two most beloved and admired poets, experienced both the brilliance of Xuanzong's reign and the dark times of An Lushan's Rebellion. Neither man was a political success, although Du felt this more keenly than did Li. Both enjoyed friendship and wine and composed beautiful poetry with multidimensional meanings. They were personal friends, and Du Fu greatly admired Li Bai. However, they differed greatly in personality and in their work.

**FIGURE 5.9** Anonymous, *Ming Huang's* (that is, Xuanzong's) *Journey to Shu*. Hanging scroll, ink and color on silk, Tang in style but dates from Song or later, 31.89 in × 22.01 in. (© National Palace Museum, Taiwan, Republic of China.)

Like Wang Wei, Li Bai's subjects included nature, but the nature depicted in poems such as "The Road to Shu Is Steep," describing Xuanzong's flight to Sichuan (see Figure 5.9), is much more exuberant than that of Wang Wei.

Li's fondness for nature and mountains blended well with his freedom of spirit. Although he wrote poems in many forms, he preferred old-style verse, *gushi*, which, unlike the new style, *jintishi*, let poets devise their own rhythmic and verbal structure.

Li Bai was famous as the poet of wine:

> A pot of wine among the flowers:
> I drink alone, no kith or kin near.
> I raise my cup to invite the moon to join me;
> It and my shadow make a party of three.
> Alas, the moon is unconcerned about drinking,
> And my shadow merely follows me around.
> Briefly I cavort with the moon and my shadow:
> Pleasure must be sought while it is spring.
> I sing and the moon goes back and forth,
> I dance and my shadow falls at random.
> While sober we seek pleasure in fellowship;
> When drunk we go each our own way.

**DETAIL FIGURE 5.9** Anonymous, *Ming Huang's Journey to Shu.*
(© National Palace Museum, Taiwan, Republic of China.)

Then let us pledge a friendship without human ties
And meet again at the far end of the Milky Way.[10]

The legend that, when on a nocturnal drinking expedition on a lake, Li fell into the water while trying to fish out the moon and drowned may well be spurious, but it became part of his traditional image. The Song painter Liang Kai captured this image of the slightly inebriated poet floating in space (see Figure 6.4) with an economy of means that would have pleased Li, whose verse is deceptively simple. He knew that true art does not reveal its skill.

Both poets wrote highly compressed verse, but much of Du Fu's poetry, unlike that of Li Bai, is enriched by a patina of allusions that add weight and majesty to the lines. Du was particularly effective in new-style poetry, especially regulated verse *lushi*, in eight lines with five or seven characters per line and elaborate rules governing tone and rhyme as well as verbal parallelism. Along with occasional poems and poems of friendship and wine, Du Fu is most admired for his social conscience and compassion. His sociopolitical commentary can be biting, as in two frequently quoted lines from a longer poem written shortly before the An Lushan Rebellion:

Inside the red gates wine and meat go bad
On the roads are bones of men who died of cold.[11]

Some of his most moving poems describe the suffering and hardships of ordinary people. One concerns the visit at night of a recruiting officer to a village where an aged grandmother informs the officer that only two males are left at home: the old man who has fled and an infant son. She tells him to take her since she can at least cook—and in the morning she is gone.

Du Fu, like his contemporaries, frequently sent poems to those close to him. The following, written while he was living near the upper reaches of the Yangzi River, is addressed to a brother living far away near the mouth of the river. The "wind in the dust" in the third line refers to the warfare that separates the two brothers:

*To My Younger Brother*
Rumors that you lodge in a mountain temple
In Hangzhou, or in Yuezhou for sure.
Wind in the dust prolongs our day of parting,
Yangzi and Han have wasted my clear autumn.
My shadow sticks to the trees where gibbons scream,
But my spirit whirls by the towers sea-serpents breathe.
Let me go down next year with the spring waters
And search for you to the end of the white clouds in the East.[12]

In other poems Du Fu tells of life in the thatched hut he inhabited during exile in Sichuan. Often he voices his dismay at the failure of his political ambitions. His aspirations and disappointments corresponded to the experiences of many of his readers, who admired his artistry and his humanism. Perhaps for all of these reasons, he was venerated as China's foremost poet.

## Late Tang

Major economic support for the dynasty came from the South. The main source of revenue was the salt monopoly, for the government controlled all but one of China's major salt-producing areas and sold monopoly salt to merchants for distribution throughout China. Dezong (r. 780–805) strengthened the dynasty's finances and also built up a large palace army. His successor, Xianzong (r. 806–820), was especially vigorous in fostering institutional renewal and in reasserting central control over some of the lost provinces. But both of these vigorous emperors relied on men directly dependent on them, the "inner court," rather than using the regular bureaucracy. The result was the emergence of eunuch power. Eunuchs commanded the palace armies and, as in the Han, formed self-perpetuating "families" through adoption. Xianzong was murdered by eunuchs, whose power grew greatly in the 820s and 830s—an attempted coup against them in 835 failed. To make matters worse, officialdom at the time was divided into bitterly hostile factions. A dispute that lasted half a century arose out of a disagreement over the results of a special civil service examination held in 808.

Dezong and Xianzong personally favored Taoism, as did Wuzong (r. 840–846), who built a Terrace for Immortals within the palace grounds so that he might "ascend into the mists and wander freely through the nine divisions of Heaven." Personally hostile to Buddhism, he could not resist the temptation to meet the state's pressing financial needs by seizing Buddhist riches. He is, consequently, best known for his persecution of the church: monastic lands and wealth were confiscated, monks and nuns were returned to lay life, and slaves and dependents were released. The emperor himself claimed to have defrocked 260,500 monks and nuns and when it was all over, the regulations allowed for only 49 monasteries with approximately 800 monks in all the empire.

Irreparable damage was done to collections of sacred texts, to the bronze statues that had been the glory of Buddhist sculpture, and to religious buildings, so that today we have only a very few Tang pagodas and halls, the largest of which is located on Mt. Wutai, Shanxi. This is similar in design to the Tōshōdaiji founded by a Chinese monk in Japan. Similarly, large-scale Tang sculpture in wood and bronze has not survived, but the more than life-size bronzes at the Yakushiji in Nara, Japan, are fine representations of the Tang international style. In China a good many stone statues survived, including a very large Vairocana Buddha just outside the caves at Longmen.

The policy of persecution was promptly reversed by Wuzong's successor, but the Buddhist establishments were to suffer another devastating blow during the enormously destructive rebellion of Huang Chao. Particularly hard hit were traditions such as Tiantai and Huayan, which focused on textual studies. Only two sects continued to flourish: Pure Land, grounded in the hearts of the people, and Chan, which took pride in its freedom from texts and patronage.

# Late Tang Poetry and Culture

Poetry continued to thrive. In the 790s Han Yu (768–824) and Bo Juyi (772–846) began to write in their own distinctive and widely imitated styles. The latter was a very prolific poet, author of some 2800 pieces, and beloved wherever Chinese influence reached. His "Everlasting Remorse" is the classic poetic rendition of the tragedy of Xuangzong and Yang Guifei. Unlike Du Fu, he wrote in simple and easy language. Like Du he had a strong social conscience:

*An Old Charcoal Seller*
An old charcoal seller
Cuts firewood, burns coal by the southern mountain.
His face, all covered with dust and ash, the color of smoke,
The hair at his temples is gray, his ten fingers black.
The money he makes selling coal, what is it for?
To put clothes on his back and food in his mouth.
The rags on his poor body are thin and threadbare;

Distressed at the low price of coal, he hopes for colder weather.
Night comes, an inch of snow has fallen on the city,
In the morning, he rides his cart along the icy ruts,
His ox weary, he hungry, and the sun already high.
In the mud by the south gate, outside the market, he stops to rest.
All of a sudden, two dashing riders appear;
An imperial envoy, garbed in yellow (his attendant in white),
Holding an official dispatch, he reads a proclamation.
Then turns the cart around, curses the ox, and leads it north.
One cartload of coal—a thousand or more catties!
*No* use appealing to the official spiriting the cart away:
Half a length of red lace, a slip of damask
Dropped on the ox—is payment in full![13]

In other poems, he tells of his daily life, his family, and routines. He once described himself as addicted to poetry, bursting forth whenever he sees a fine landscape or meets a beloved friend: "madly singing in the mountains."[14]

Han Yu is best known for an essay reaffirming the Confucian Way, a precursor of Song Neo-Confucianism. He championed the Old Literature (or Old Culture, *guwen*) movement in opposition to the elaborate parallelism and rhetorical flourishes of more recent prose. Guwen thinkers were not the only ones dissatisfied with the literary culture of the day, but, unlike some of their contemporaries, assumed an "intellectual position that emphasized personal responsibility over the guidance of 'tradition.'"[15]

In his poetry as in his prose, Han Yu preferred the old styles, writing long poems rich in original and daring similes. A common theme in his work is the classic complaint of the Tang gentleman poet: lack of official recognition. A scholar is like a fine horse, in need of proper care if he is to flourish. The trouble with the world lies not in the lack of horses, but in the absence of a ruler who understands horses. Han Yu also showed a lighter side. He wrote an essay admonishing a crocodile and a poem about losing one's teeth.

Other major secular writers and scholars include Liu Zhiji (666–722), the first to write a critical study of history, the philosopher Li Ao (d. c. 844), and the encyclopedist Du Yu (735–812), all deserving more attention than is possible to accord them here. The same holds for the poets Li He (791–817) and Li Shangyin (812?–858). Li He had a penchant for quaint and even frankly odd language; as one Chinese critic put it: his verse has a demonic quality.

Li Shangyin, the most ambiguous of poets, wrote frequently of love, including his own love for a Daoist nun. The following untitled poem can, but need not, be interpreted allegorically. It is every bit as moving understood literally.

At eight she took a look at herself in the mirror,
Already able to paint her eyebrows long,
At ten she went out to tread on the green,
Her skirt made of lotus flowers.

At twelve she learnt to play the small zither:
The silver plectrums she never took off.
At fourteen, she was his among her relatives,
And, one imagined, not married yet.
At fifteen, she weeps in the spring wind,
Turning her face away from the swing.[16]

During the Tang, calligraphy and painting continued to be prized as the arts of gentlemen. Du Fu, one of the first poets to write on or about paintings, was keenly aware of the perishability of silk and ink. And he was right, for the poems have survived long after the paintings disappeared. Long after the Tang, Wang Wei was credited with establishing a gentleman's style of calligraphic painting in monotone, said to have contrasted with the precision of line and decorative coloring of the court style, illustrated in Figure 5.9. The coloring, blue and green, is a hallmark of Tang art, but the pleasure the artist takes in the fantastic mountains is typical of Chinese landscapists. Here, however, in contrast to later mountainscapes, nature does not overwhelm man. Instead, it provides a setting for his activities. The scene is Emperor Xuanzong's flight to Sichuan during the An Lushan Rebellion, although as Michael Sullivan has suggested, it really looks more like a pleasure excursion than a precipitous retreat after tragedy and defeat.[17] Be that as it may, this painting is probably as close as we can now get to the style of the Tang, an important reference point for later Chinese painting as well as a delightful work in its own right.

In religion and in culture, Chinese gentlemen, confident in their heritage, retained a cosmopolitan attitude. When an Arab's receipt of a prestigious decree in 850 provoked some complaints, Chen An wrote that being Chinese was not a matter of physical appearance or place of birth, but "a civilized state of mind."[18]

# Collapse of the Dynasty

During its last 50 years, the Tang dynasty was weakened by conflict and divided loyalties; by mistrust between officials in the capital and military commanders in the field; and by suspicions, manipulations, and falsifications of all kinds. Even reports concerning natural disasters were falsified, as when an official assured the emperor that a plague of locusts had proven harmless because they had "all impaled themselves on thorns and brambles and died."[19] The story makes a sad litany of mismanagement, corruption, and incompetence. Meanwhile, bandit gangs, a refuge for the desperately poor and dislocated, increased in number, size, and ambition. Forming themselves into confederations, they progressed from raiding to rebellion; what had once been a nuisance now became a threat. Power, whether bandit or "legitimate," went to the strong and ruthless. Ordinary people survived as best they could the depredations of bandits and soldiers alike. Even though the dynasty made occasional gains, each rally amounted to no more than one step forward followed by two steps backward.

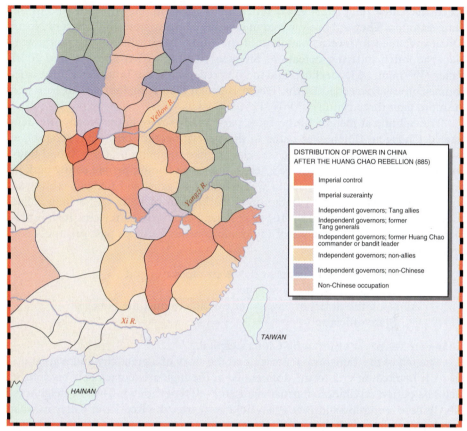

**FIGURE 5.10** Distribution of Power in China after the Huang Chao Rebellion. (Adapted from Robert M. Somers, "The Collapse of the T'ang order," Ph.D. dissertation, Yale University, 1975, pp. 204–205.)

The most serious rebellion was led by Wang Xianzhi and his successor Huang Chao, who destroyed Canton (879), killing many of its foreign as well as Chinese population. He is most notorious for his brutality after he captured Chang'an in 880. Huang failed in his ambition to create a new dynasty; after his rebellion, China was thoroughly fragmented (see Figure 5.10).

The survival of the court now depended on the tolerance of and especially the competition among its neighboring rivals, including the foreign peoples who inhabited the northern borderlands. Among these, the Shatuo Turks were now the most important. Their intervention on behalf of the dynasty rescued it from destruction several times and enabled it to survive the Huang Chao Rebellion. In 905 the Shatuo Turks concluded an alliance with a people from Mongolia called the Khitan, an alliance that continued through the Five Dynasties Period (907–960). The Shatuo Turks themselves formed the second of these dynasties, called the Later Tang (923–934), which as its name implies tried to rule in the Tang tradition. They did not succeed in creating a lasting state, but a part of North China remained in foreign hands until the Ming. Meanwhile in the southwest, Nanzhao, after suffering defeats in Sichuan (829 and 874) and the Red River Valley (Vietnam, 863), declined and in 902 predeceased the Tang. After three brief regimes, it was succeeded by the Tibeto-Burman Dali Kingdom, which persisted for more than three centuries (937–1253).

The fighting at the end of the Tang, particularly severe in the Northwest, devastated Chang'an. There was panic in the streets: people screaming, scrambling over walls, and stampeding while "rebels rage like stamping beasts"; "blood flowing like boiling fountains"; severed heads; houses in flames; people eating bark or human flesh; and deserted palaces where brambles grow and fox and rabbit run wild. These are some of the images in "The Lament of Lady Qi," a long ballad composed by Wei Zhong (836–910) after Huang Chao ruined the city. Its most famous lines capture the essence of the tragic contrast between past greatness and present disaster:

> The Inner Treasury is burnt down, its tapestries and
>     embroideries a heap of ashes;
> All along the Street of Heaven one treads to dust the bones of
>     State officials.[20]

Chang'an was never again to be China's capital.

The fall of the Tang brought to an end the story of a great city and a great dynasty. It marked an end to the dominance of the high aristocracy and brought to a close a period of Chinese martial vigor and self-assertion vis-à-vis its neighbors. No Chinese empire would ever again hold sway over the Red River Valley in what is today Vietnam.

The fall of the Tang was an ending, but it was also a beginning. In considering the Late Tang and its place in history, we should keep in mind that periods when the center was weak have not fared well in the traditional Chinese histories written from the center. Focused on the deadly politics of disintegration, such accounts are apt to obscure developments beneath history's surface, pointing to a happier future. From the vantage point of the High Tang, the Late Tang appears to be a decline, but looking back from the Song and later dynasties, we can see not only major continuities but also new developments, leading to future growth and prosperity. Modern scholars therefore speak of the Tang/Song transition, aware that many later developments, in society and economy, thought, and agriculture, had their roots in the earlier period. We need to keep in mind that we are dealing with a vast and highly diverse land; that changes in the various dimensions of human activity, although interrelated, proceed at their own pace; and that periodization is a necessary analytical (and pedagogical) tool—but no more than that.

Let us end then with two inventions pointing to the future. First is the paddlewheel boat, a Late Tang invention, but not widely used until the great burgeoning of shipbuilding stimulated by Song commercial growth. Next is the truly momentous innovation, woodblock printing, which originated, under Buddhist auspices, no later than the eighth century and was part of the Late Tang scene in the Lower Yangzi and Sichuan, but its full impact had to await the emergence of new conditions under the Song. The Tang is also the last major dynasty for which we have to rely completely on writings and records originally transmitted by hand.

# *Notes*

1. Howard Wechsler, *Offerings of Jade and Silk: Ritual and Symbol in the Legitimation of the T'ang Dynasty* (New Haven: Yale Univ. Press, 1985).

2. Peter K. Bol, *"This Culture of Ours" Intellectual Transitions in T'ang and Sung China* (Stanford: Stanford Univ. Press, 1992), p. 79.

3. Patricia Karetzky, "The Representation of Women in Medieval China: Recent Archeological Evidence," *T'ang Studies* 17 (1999): p. 219.

4. Title and subject of Chapter 2 of Tansen Sen, *Buddhism, Diplomacy, and Trade: The Realignment of Sino-Indian Relations, 600–1400* (Honolulu: Univ. of Hawaii Press, 2003).

5. Burton Watson, *Chinese Lyricism: Shih Poetry from the Second to the Twelfth Century* (New York: Columbia Univ. Press, 1971), p. 175. Reprinted with permission.

6. *Sources of Chinese Tradition*, 2nd ed., Vol. 1, compiled by Wm. Theodore de Bary and Irene Bloom (New York: Columbia Univ. Press, 1999), pp. 496, 498.

7. Stephen F. Teiser, *The Ghost Festival in Medieval China* (Princeton: Princeton Univ. Press, 1988), p. 197.

8. Russell Kirkland, "Ssu-ma Ch'eng-Chen and the Role of Taoism in the Medieval Chinese Polity," in Livia Kohn, ed., *Handbook of Daoism* (Leiden: E.J. Brill, 2000), p. 110.

9. Livia Kohn and Russell Kirkland, "Daoism in the Tang (618–907) in Livia Kohn, *Handbook*, p. 350.

10. Liu Wu-chi and Irving Yucheng Lo, eds., *Sunflower Splendor* (Garden City: Anchor Press/Doubleday, 1975), p. 109.

11. A.R. Davis, *Tu Fu* (New York: Twayne, 1971), p. 46.

12. *Poems of the Late Tang*, translated and with an introduction by A.C. Graham (Penguin Classics). Copyright A.C. Graham, 1965. Reprinted with permission.

13. Liu Wu Chi and Irving Yucheng Lo, eds., *Sunflower Splendor* (Garden City, NY: Anchor Press/Doubleday, 1975), p. 206–207.

14. Arthur Waley, trans., *One Hundred and Seventy Chinese Poems* (London: Constable & Co., Ltd., 1918; reprinted 1947), p. 144.

15. Anthony DeBlasi, *Reform in the Balance: The Defense of Literary Culture in Mid-Tang China* (Albany: State Univ. of New York Press, 2002), p. 50.

16. James J. Y. Liu. *The Poetry of Li Shang-yin—Ninth Century Baroque Chinese Poet* (Chicago: Univ. of Chicago Press, 1969), p. 78.

17. Michael Sullivan, *The Arts of China* (Berkeley: Univ. of California Press, 1973), p. 293.

18. Charles Holcombe's summary in *The Genesis of East Asia 221 B.C.–A.D. 907* (Honolulu: Univ. of Hawaii Press, 2001), p. 51.

19. Robert M. Somers, *The Collapse of the T'ang Order* (Ph.D. dissertation, Yale Univ., 1975), p. 102.

20. Somers, *Collapse*, p. 145.

# 6

# Early Japan to 794

## I. Prehistory

*Geography*

*Paleolithic Culture*

*Jōmon Culture*

*Yayoi Culture*

*Political and Social Developments*

*The Tomb Period (Mid-Third– Late Sixth Century C.E.)*

*The Yamato Kings*

## II. The Emergence of the Japanese State and Elite Culture

*Korean Backgrounds*

*The Late Tomb Period*

*The Seventh-Century Transition (the Asuka Period)*

*Nara as a Center and Symbol*

*Nara as a Religious Center*

*Documents and Structures*

*Literature*

*The Visual Arts*

*The End of the Nara Period*

| | | B.C.E. ⟵ ⟶ C.E. | | | | |
|---|---|---|---|---|---|---|
| ca. 11,000? | | ca. 400? | ca. 250 | 592 | 710 | 794 |

| Jōmon Culture | Yayoi Culture | Tomb Period (Kofun) | Asuka Period | Nara Period |
|---|---|---|---|---|

A major theme in the history of Japan is the interplay between local and imported elements. Although it was deeply influenced by Chinese prototypes and hospitable to Tang civilization, Japan never became simply a smaller replica of China. From the earliest times, the people living on the Japanese archipelago experienced their own challenges, opportunities, and traditions. This chapter begins by introducing the early cultures on the archipelago then goes on to consider the complex internal and external factors that spurred the development of a Japanese state and culture.

The vast centuries dealt with in this part belong to prehistory in that we must rely on archeological evidence supplemented by occasional accounts by outsiders. This is also prehistory in the sense that "Japan," the word and the concept, did not yet exist. In this sense we are dealing with Japan before there was a Japan.

# Geography

Modern Japan occupies the four main islands of Hokkaido, Honshu, Shikoku, and Kyushu (and dozens of smaller ones), stretching some 1500 miles from a latitude of forty-five degrees north (roughly that of Montreal) at the northern tip of Hokkaido to nearly twenty-four degrees north (parallel with the Bahamas) at the southernmost of the Ryukyu, or Okinawa, Islands (see Figure 6.1). With an area of about 146,000 square miles, Japan is much larger than Great Britain, slightly larger than Italy, and a bit smaller than California. Although it is dwarfed by the Chinese giant, it is hardly a small state.

Whereas China occupies a massive subcontinent, Japan is part of a vast chain of islands separated from the eastern edge of the Asian continent by three bodies of water: the Sea of Okhotsk, the Sea of Japan, and the East China Sea. This island chain is part of a larger group of archipelagoes along the northwestern edges of the Pacific Ocean, including the Aleutian Islands to the north and the Philippines to the south. These archipelagos are homes to cultures that heavily de-

**135**

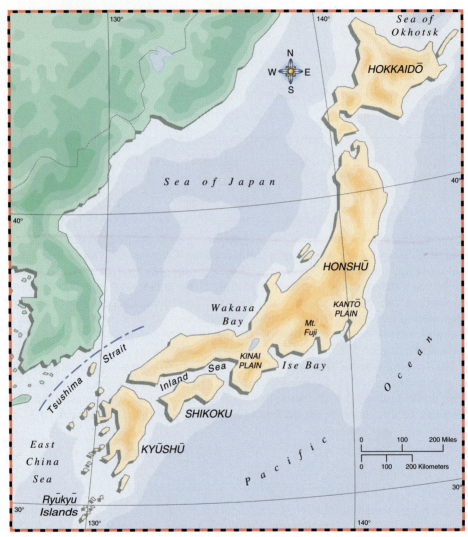

**FIGURE 6.1** The Japanese archipelago.

pend on the ocean for food and transportation and are linked by straits and navigable seas to each other and to the Asian continent.

The Japanese archipelago, like its neighbors, has been shaped by a confluence of powerful tectonic, climatic, and oceanic forces. It sits at the intersection of no fewer than four tectonic plates—the Pacific, North American, Eurasian, and Philippine Sea—and has therefore undergone a great deal of violent geologic upheaval. Even today, there are said to be as many as 1000 earthquakes and tremors per year and more than 40 active volcanoes. Because of this seismic activity, more than two-thirds of the archipelago consists of mountains, which are geologically young (about 5 million years old) and therefore steep and rugged. Such steep mountain ranges produce fast-moving streams, rapid erosion, and attendant landslides and mudslides, preventing cultivation and extensive settlement. Hard to climb, they are also barriers to internal transportation and communication. This has helped preserve regional autonomy and diversity and has resulted in widespread reliance on waterborne travel, especially along coastal routes.

The sediment washed from these steep slopes, as well as the rich volcanic soil produced by numerous eruptions, collected in a few coastal plains, which make up only 13 percent of the archipelago's area but are tremendously fertile. A major factor in Japanese history has been this contrast between the steep mountain ranges and the fertile plains they surround and isolate. There are four important plains. Furthest west is the Tsukushi Plain in northern Kyushu. Close to advanced cultural centers on the Korean Peninsula and the Chinese subcontinent, it was an early center of social and technological development. The other three are on Honshu. At the head of Osaka Bay on the Inland Sea, the Kinai Plain is the site of the famous former capitals at Nara and Kyoto. Further east are the Nobi Plain, at the head of the Ise Bay, and the largest of them all, the great Kanto Plain that surrounds modern Tokyo. This axis of fertile plains lies at the center of Japan's recorded history and even today is the most heavily industrialized and urbanized part of the country.

The archipelago's steep mountains and coastal plains and its location between the Asian mainland and the Pacific Ocean make for distinctive weather patterns. During the winter, prevailing winds blow across Asia, picking up moisture as they cross the Sea of Japan, then depositing it as snow on the northwestern sides of the mountains. However, on the Pacific coast, winters are marked by dry winds and little precipitation. During the summer, warm, moist air comes up from the south, making the climate in southern and central Japan warmer than its latitude would suggest. From the Ryukyu Islands to northeastern Honshu, early summer begins with a rainy season. In general, Japan receives the most rain of the temperate zone. These differences in weather have affected the patterns of human settlement; the areas along the Sea of Japan are much less conducive to intensive agriculture than those on the Pacific side.

Ocean currents are another important environmental factor. Helping warm the Pacific side, the Kuroshio, or Japan Current, flows up from the Philippines, through the Ryukyu Islands, and along the Pacific coast. In contrast, the Oyashio Current, rich in plankton and other nutrients, brings cold water along the Kuril Islands, around Hokkaido, and down both sides of northeastern Honshu. The mixing of these warm and cold currents contributes to the wealth of food sources in the waters surrounding the archipelago, supporting many kinds of edible fish, shellfish, and seaweed.

Except for the semitropical Ryukyu Islands in the south, the archipelago lies entirely in the temperate zone. However, its long north–south expanse, varied terrain, and differing weather patterns make for a variety of flora and fauna. Because of long periods of linkage by land bridges to the Asian continent, most of these are also found elsewhere in East Asia. Ample water and long, warm growing seasons created a paradise for plants, yielding dense forests of trees that are sources of edible nuts and useful wood and fibers. Big animals, such as mammoths, were wiped out by climate change and human predation, but monkeys, boar, bears, deer, and many other small animals survived, as did numerous water and land birds feasting on frogs, other amphibians, and all kinds of insects. This varied repertoire of plants and animals "offered humans a great variety of resources and . . . could make many responses to human encroachment. Unquestionably, that biological diversity has been critical to the archipelago's capacity to support a remarkably dense population for centuries on end."[1]

# Paleolithic Culture

Until the end of the last Ice Age, about 12,000 years ago, land bridges periodically linked the archipelago to the Asian continent along the Sakhalin Peninsula in the north and the Korean Peninsula in the southwest. We may reasonably conjecture that early humans as well as plants and animals took this route. However, although we have evidence that humans lived on the continent from at least 700,000 years ago, there is to date no solid evidence of human presence in the Japanese archipelago before about 35,000 years ago.

It is likely that humans had arrived much earlier than that, but at any rate it is clear that by 30,000 years ago, groups of humans were living throughout the archipelago in the Late Paleolithic (Old Stone Age). These Paleolithic people were foragers who gathered plants, hunted, and fished; they used stone blades and other tools similar in style to those found in sites elsewhere in Asia. Toward the end of the last Ice Age, there are indications of cultural change of such magnitude that archeologists agree on the need to designate a new period.

# Jōmon Culture

The Jōmon is the longest and the first period of what became Japanese culture: it lasted about 10,000 years. Its onset was gradual as distinctive new features appeared. Bows, arrows, and traps facilitated hunting, although there was also greater reliance on seafood and even an incipient awareness of agriculture. Settlements grew in size. As in other Neolithic communities, pottery served many purposes, and it is its distinctive pottery that gives the period its name. Jōmon, literally "rope pattern," refers to the characteristic markings imprinted on many pots by rolling knotted cords over the damp clay.

Subsuming 10,000-odd years of life in such diverse settings under a single designation must not distract us from recognizing a tremendous amount of regional and temporal variety. Neolithic does not imply monolithic! It is best to see Jōmon as what Richard Pearson calls a "large loosely integrated cultural complex."[2] The development of this complex seems to have been spurred by the arrival of new technologies, groups of people (especially from northeast Asia), and responses to changes in climate and environment.

The warming that followed the end of the last Ice Age (12,000 years ago) separated the archipelago from the Asian mainland, leaving the closest point in Kyushu about 120 miles from the mainland, near enough to be influenced by continental developments but removed enough to develop its own ways. Within the archipelago the vegetation transformed. In southwestern Honshu, Shikoku, and Kyushu, broadleaf evergreen trees dominated the forests, whereas broadleaf deciduous trees were common in northeastern Honshu and southern Hokkaido. The latter included many tree species, such as beeches and oaks, that produced edible nuts and acorns, ready sources of food for Jōmon people to gather, store, transport, and consume and to sustain the animals they hunted.

In the northeast, the plentiful marine life carried south by the Oyashio current, especially salmon, was an additional major source of food. Settlements along both the Sea of Japan and the Pacific Ocean subsisted on immense amounts of shellfish, leaving distinctive middens (mounds of discarded shells and other refuse) for archeologists to study. The diet also included venison, yam-like tubers, other wild plants, and freshwater fish. Sustained by such foods, the population was concentrated in central and northern Honshu, but Jōmon sites range from Hokkaido to the Ryukyu Islands.

In addition to dietary evidence, these sites indicate the use of new technologies. There were spears and arrows with stone heads for hunting, pit traps for catching animals, and evidence of domesticated dogs (probably also used in hunting). Fishing equipment included nets, stone and bone hooks, harpoons, and weirs. Canoes could be used for fishing and transportation.

The Jōmon toolkit held other implements of wood and stone. There were shovels for unearthing roots and digging pits and axes for felling trees to clear land for food-bearing plants and for cutting trees into lumber. More direct forms of cultivation appeared around 5000 B.C.E., but agriculture was never the primary means of sustenance. Foraging and hunting generally extracted enough food from the rich environment. There were mortars and pestles for grinding nuts and seeds, drying mats for preserving food, and pits and aboveground structures for storage. Most notably, there was the famous pottery.

Jōmon pots are among the world's earliest. Recently discovered pottery has been dated as far back as 14,500 B.C.E., which would push back the beginning of the period considerably! Ceramics have been found in sites on the Asian mainland dated to the 15th millennium B.C.E., but it is possible that the world's first containers of baked clay were made in the Japanese archipelago. Many Jōmon vessels seem to have been used for storage and cooking, but the more elaborate pieces probably had ritual functions (see Figure 6.2).

Some clay artifacts seem to have had religious or magical significance, including striking doll-like figures with bulging eyes (see Figure 6.3), often found with one of the limbs broken off in what archeologists surmise may have been a fertility rite. If the figure in our illustration concerns female fertility, the numerous stone rods identified as of the Jōmon Period are thought to have been phallic symbols.

**FIGURE 6.2** Pots found in Jōmon sites are often strikingly creative in design, with surface decorations in regular patterns, and sometimes with a riot of abstract flame-like projections along the rims. (© The Cleveland Museum of Art, John L. Severance Fund, 1984.68)

**FIGURE 6.3** Jōmon figurine, perhaps used in fertility rites. (© Scala/Art Resource, NY)

Jōmon culture was marked by much regional variety, and temporal developments linked to changes in pottery styles lead archeologists to divide the period into several subperiods. Around the 7th millennium B.C.E., aboveground and semi-subterranean dwellings appear, and around 5000 B.C.E. characteristic living patterns developed. People now settled in stable communities, living mainly in pit dwellings with roofs of wood and thatch or earth. Villages often had larger, apparently communal wooden structures, which may have been storehouses. Subsequently, there were periods of thriving cultural activity in central Honshu between about 3000 and 2000 B.C.E., and then in the northeast from around 2000 B.C.E. through the first several centuries C.E. There is a tendency to think of hunter-gatherers as living lives of lack and scarcity, but Jōmon culture was surprisingly rich and complex, with sophisticated ceramic arts and extensive settled communities.

## Yayoi Culture

From some point in the middle of the first millennium B.C.E., living patterns and technologies began to appear that are so different from Jōmon that archeologists see it as the beginning of a new culture with its own distinctive pottery (see Figure 6.4). It called Yayoi, after the part of Tokyo in which this pottery was first discovered.

Until recently, the Yayoi Period was thought to have begun around 400 B.C.E., but now carbon-dating results suggest that it may have to be pushed back as much as five centuries! At any rate, it is clear that during the last millennium B.C.E., a cluster of new technologies appeared in northern Kyushu and began to spread through much of the archipelago. Prominent among these were ironworking, bronze casting, glassmaking, weaving, new techniques of woodworking, and, by far the most important, the powerful cluster of food-producing technologies necessary for intensive agriculture.

People now relied extensively on several forms of plant cultivation, most notably wet rice agriculture. Rice was initially grown in low-lying wetlands along rivers, but as earth-working techniques improved and people became better organized, paddy fields were constructed and maintained on higher ground. Yayoi sites also show evidence of a range of dry cultivation, often in swidden (slash-and-burn) fields, of millet, barley, wheat, buckwheat, and beans, to mention the most important crops. Several kinds of fruit trees also contributed to a more varied diet, and people continued to hunt and forage. As in Jōmon times and today, the ocean yielded fish, shellfish, and seaweed, important foods alongside the newer farmed staples. Such continuities between Yayoi and Jōmon are crucial to our understanding of the relationship between the two cultures.

Clearly, the Jōmon–Yayoi transition did not occur all at once. The new pottery and other artifacts, as well as signs of widespread agriculture, first appeared in northern Kyushu, then spread north and east, mainly along the Inland Sea and other waterways, over many centuries. The culture spread in this way was neither unified nor homogenous: individual regions are markedly different in their rates of

**FIGURE 6.4** Pottery jar excavated from Enda Site located in Zao-cho, Miyagi Prefecture: middle Yayoi Period. Small at the base and thin at the neck, the vessel is both functional and pleasing to the eye. It is similar to the form later developed to contain sake, but we do not know what it held originally. (© Tohoku University Archeology Laboratory)

change, patterns of community organization, decorative and burial customs, and so on. Actually, there was no transition to Yayoi in northernmost Honshu and Hokkaido, where Jōmon culture persisted for many more centuries, or in the Ryukyu Islands, where there are few signs of prehistoric agriculture and Jōmon is followed by a Shell Mound culture based on fishing and trading.

Vigorous debate about the nature of the transition between Jōmon and Yayoi continues. Given the locations of the earliest sites and the similarities between their contents and those of contemporary sites on the Korean Peninsula, the mainland provenance of the Yayoi technologies is clear, but scholars disagree about whether their spread was the result of the introduction and diffusion of new ideas or of the migration of large numbers of people. The latter explanation is supported by anthropological and genetic studies of modern inhabitants of the areas in question and by the work of linguists examining the origins of the Japanese language. It seems safe to conclude that both migration and local adaptation were involved.

There is no direct evidence of what languages were spoken by inhabitants of the archipelago during the Jōmon Period or by the Yayoi migrants, but it is likely that the latter arrived speaking a language related to those spoken in the northeast of the Asian continent and the upper part of the Korean Peninsula. The Japanese language, in its modern and earlier forms, is often classified as an Altaic language, related to Korean, Mongolian, and Turkish. In contrast to the Sinitic languages, these languages are agglutinative, which means that much of their expression of meaning involves adding (or "gluing" together) words and word elements. Verbs and adjectives are highly inflected, with differences in tense, mood, level of formality, and so forth expressed by adding to the stem one element after another. The Yayoi language (or languages), which probably absorbed elements of Jōmon tongues, is likely to have been the immediate ancestor of Japanese.[3]

# Political and Social Developments

The emergence of full-blown agriculture and richer material culture supported a rise in population but also brought on more widespread and intense competition for land, water, and other resources. This competition, along with need for greater organization to practice the new forms of agriculture, contributed to the rise of clear division of labor and greater class stratification within communities. There is no reason to think that relations among earlier groups of people were always peaceful, but now hostilities among communities tended to accelerate into full-fledged warfare. This newly hierarchical and violent Yayoi order became the crucible in which more complex and powerful forms of social organization developed.

What happened is clear archeologically. Life during the Jōmon Period was no picnic to begin with, and conditions apparently deteriorated over time. Late Jōmon skeletal remains show signs of disease and malnutrition. A collapse of the food supply, perhaps brought on by climate change, is thought to have reduced the population dramatically in the centuries preceding the arrival of the Yayoi migrants. However, there are few signs of violent conflict in Jōmon sites, and although differences in dwelling structures and grave goods suggest a nascent social hierarchy, there does not seem to have been strong class differentiation. In contrast, Yayoi communities are frequently surrounded by moats and stockades, located on easily defended hilltops, and supplied with tall structures thought to have been watchtowers. Numerous weapons have been excavated from such sites, as have skeletal remains with missing heads or embedded arrow points. At the same time, large structures suggesting storehouses for surplus grain and other foods appear, as do burials accompanied by expensive grave goods. These were placed in special elite areas set apart from less lavish graves. Such evidence confirms the prevalence of an increasingly hierarchical society.

Underlying these developments was the emergence of small but growing political units, headed by chiefs who seem to have been in constant conflict with their neighbors. Some of these chiefs were in contact with Chinese authorities on the Korean Peninsula and beyond. They appear in Chinese records from the first century C.E. onward as "kings" in keeping with the Chinese court's diplomatic model of investiture, according to which "barbarian" rulers on the periphery submitted to the central civilizing power of the emperor and in return received official titles, ceremonial regalia, and valuable trade goods. As they fought among themselves and increased their domains and wealth, these "kings" of the *Wa* (the Chinese term for the inhabitants of the archipelago) relied on the advanced technology, raw materials (especially iron and bronze), and political legitimacy that could only be obtained through such interaction with the societies of the Korean Peninsula and, beyond it, the Chinese imperium.

The most striking and extensive account of such circumstances is from the third-century Chinese history of the Wei dynasty, which includes in its section on peripheral cultures a long description of life in the archipelago during the late Yayoi Period. It describes a society of constant warfare among small kingdoms, temporarily united under a "queen" named Himiko (sometimes pronounced Pimiko), who used magical powers to rule a coalition of chiefdoms from seclusion, assisted by her brother. Because the geographic directions provided by this account are garbled, a perennial topic of debate among archeologists and historians is the location of Himiko's kingdom of Yamatai; the two leading candidates are northern Kyushu and the Kinai region.

The argument about the location of Yamatai concerns the extent of transregional authority during the Yayoi Period and the origins of the central kings who came to power in the subsequent Tomb Period; it is not susceptible to easy solution, but the weight of recent scholarly opinion seems to favor Kinai.

# The Tomb Period (Mid-Third–Late Sixth Century C.E.)

The Tomb Period is named for the great tombs (*kofun,* or "old burial mounds") that became the most ubiquitous and recognizable archeological feature of Japan, dominating the landscape and reminding everyone of the power of the ruling elite. The earliest of these mounded tombs were in the Kinai area, but there are more than 150,000 spread throughout the three main islands (excluding Hokkaido). They continued to be built until supplanted by Buddhist burial methods.

Into the sixth century, the mounds were impressive in their size and in their location away from the settlements of the living. The largest were surrounded by moats and held one or more coffins in chambers that contained grave goods, notably protective or magical objects such as mirrors and swords, and large numbers of valuable tools, utensils, pieces of armor, saddles, ornaments, and so on. Most likely, these great tumuli developed out of the Yayoi mounded tombs. These were probably based on burial methods used on the Korean Peninsula and certainly depended on imported technologies of surveying, earthmoving, and construction. The mounds came in many shapes and sizes, but the classic format was the keyhole shape, which joined a square and a circular mound (see Figure 6.5).

These tombs were clearly sites of ceremonies performed on behalf of, or directed to, the dead. Offerings left outside the tomb included pottery dishes, which probably contained food, but the most characteristic items found on the surface of the tombs are low-fired clay statues called *haniwa.* Many of these are figurative, representing a variety of artifacts, animals, and people, including houses, weapons, musical instruments, boats, and agricultural tools; fish, pigs, birds, deer, monkeys, and especially horses; warriors, shamans, dancers, farmers, and servants (see Figure 6.6). In some cases, these figures seem to have been arranged to represent a ritual procession, perhaps one honoring the occupant of the tomb.

In the early Tomb Period, the mounds were often placed on slopes, or atop preexisting hills, to make them look larger, but during the fifth century they began

**FIGURE 6.5** Daisen Mound, Mozu, Sakai City, Osaka, from the Middle Tomb Period (Fifth Century). Its total length is approximately 892 yards. One theory about the square portion of the keyhole shape is that it originated in a platform for the performance of rituals for the deceased. (© Tomb of Emperor Nintoku, Mozu, Sakai City Osaka)

to be constructed in flat, open areas. The use of such arable land may have suggested a kind of conspicuous consumption, a willingness to take good food-producing land out of service to glorify one's ancestors—or oneself, because the amount of time necessary to build the larger mounds suggests that rulers had theirs constructed while they were alive. This period features astonishingly massive tombs concentrated in the Kinai (see Figure 6.5). In the sixth century, these large mounds were abandoned, and tombs tended to be constructed on mountain slopes.

These changes in the size and location of tombs were accompanied by changes in the style of coffins. With the development of immense mounds, early long wooden containers were replaced by huge chest-like stone sarcophagi, often quarried and shaped with great skill and made from stone transported long distances. Similar stone-working and -moving skills were required for another new

**FIGURE 6.6** Dancing peasant couple. Ht. Left 22.3 in; right 25.2 in. Late Tomb Period. Kōnan site, Osato, Saitama Prefecture, Tokyo National Museum. (TNM Image Archives, http://TNMArchives.jp)

feature of later tombs: massive stone chambers requiring advanced techniques of stone-cutting and -setting originating in China and brought to Japan by stonemasons from the Korean Peninsula, yet another way in which "influence from the peninsula . . . played a crucial role in population growth, economic and cultural development, and the rise of a centralized Yamato state."[4]

# The Yamato Kings

What was the source of the power of those buried in the immense tombs, and what kind of society supported them? As always, there was a relationship between wealth and power, with evidence suggesting that they grew in tandem. Especially from the fifth century, agricultural production grew spectacularly as new agricultural tools and techniques were brought from the Korean Peninsula. These included plows and new iron tools that facilitated clearing land and moving earth. Arable land was also expanded by building canals and improving irrigation, employing many of the skills necessary for constructing the giant mounds. There are also indications that fields were formally divided and allotted to farmers.

Trade grew. In the Kinai region, Osaka Bay developed as a major port, leaving archeological evidence of large complexes of storehouses. Along with more local exchanges, there was trade through the Inland Sea to Kyushu and beyond it to the Korean Peninsula. Surplus production of food and other resources, monopolies over trade, and benefits derived from relationships with peninsular immigrant groups controlling advanced technologies made it possible for elites to muster the massive amounts of labor power necessary to build the huge tombs.

The huge tombs indicate political differentiation, and many scholars argue that they reflect relationships of allegiance and fealty among the elites. The characteristic keyhole-shaped mounds first appeared in the Kinai region. Their subsequent appearance elsewhere throughout Kyushu, Honshu, and Shikoku suggests that a group of central kings, based in the Yamato region (an early name for the Kinai area), controlled the technology of mound construction and distributed it to regional leaders who allied or subordinated themselves to them.

In any case, the distribution, sizes, and shapes of the tombs in various regions suggest a highly developed elite hierarchy within a complex web of allegiances among far-flung regions of the archipelago. A similar network can be traced in the mirrors usually included in the graves: archeologists have been able to work out complex connections among grave occupants based on series of mirrors cast from identical molds. Here, too, what we end up with a picture of a central king distributing mirrors to allies and subordinates.

Tombs and mirrors indicate a major religious component of power or, more probably, a fusion of what we think of as the religious and the secular. They provide for and honor the dead even as they reflect relations among the living.

Later written sources, likely based on oral traditions, suggest that the fifth century also saw the development of a court system, with specialized service groups called *be*. These occupational groups, many composed of immigrants from the Korean Peninsula, supplied the Yamato court with food, tools, weapons, clothing, and ornaments or performed services, such as caring for horses or serving as scribes. The sources also report the development at the court of a system of hereditary kinship groups called *uji*, sometimes translated as "clan," designating corporations of households considered to constitute a kinship unit, inheriting a common name and common religious observances. Actually, they were more political than familial units. Certain lineages within individual *uji* had additional hereditary titles that signified their rank within the putative kinship group and at court.

In the late fifth and especially in the sixth century, the regional great chiefs seem to have become less autonomous as they began to be incorporated into this system of kinship groups, but they retained a great deal of independence. Meanwhile, at court, high-ranking kinship groups, many of them of Korean origin, served the central kings, married into the royal family, and played a significant role in determining succession.

At first the Yamato kings do not seem to have belonged to a single family line, but in the sixth century a dominant lineage emerged. Polygamy and loose principles of succession ensured there was always a large number of candidates to contest the succession on the death of a king. This gave rise to intense factional struggles in which powerful kinship groups associated through service or marriage with the royal family would back different candidates.

Between the third and the sixth centuries, elites gained immense power, but their access to the newly imported technologies and to the technicians who operated them was tightly controlled. This was the primary tool that enabled the central Yamato kings to bind their loose coalition of allies and subordinates into a transregional league that, by the sixth century, stretched across much of the three main islands. As Joan Piggott puts it, the Yamato kings reigned over a "segmented realm" with "fluid" connections to its periphery.[5]

This realm displayed many signs of nascent state formation, including high population concentrations in settled areas, an elite class supported by agricultural surpluses, payment of tribute, trade in luxury goods, construction of imposing structures, military power, craft and technical specialist groups, central kings with a court, and powerful noble families. However, several key developments had yet to come. There was no formal administrative structure, no laws or bureaucracy, and few signs of official ceremonies, taxation, or surveillance and control of outlying regions. The Yamato kings had no capital city and did not rule over an autonomous territory with clear borders.

# II. The Emergence of the Japanese State and Elite Culture

*Korean Backgrounds*

*The Late Tomb Period*

*The Seventh-Century Transition (the Asuka Period)*

*Nara as a Center and Symbol*

*Nara as a Religious Center*

*Documents and Structures*

*Literature*

*The Visual Arts*

*The End of the Nara Period*

Beginning in the late Tomb Period, the interaction between events on the Korean Peninsula and those on the Chinese mainland intensified, and the flows of ideas, technologies, and techniques, as well as people, into the Japanese archipelago, became ever more pronounced, paving the way for the development of the first Japanese state and its elite culture. The changing entity called Japan had its roots in the Yayoi and Tomb Periods, but it was in the seventh century that it first came clearly into view.

# Korean Backgrounds

The Yamato kings had long participated in what some scholars refer to as "the Lelang interaction sphere,"[6] from which emerged the state in Japan and the three kingdoms that dominated the Korean Peninsula from about 300 C.E. until 668 C.E., after Silla eliminated first Paekche (600 C.E.) then Koguryŏ (668 C.E.). The political and cultural history of early Korea, although fascinating and important, is beyond the scope of our "brief" history. Later in this chapter we will need to describe some specific interactions between the Korean states and Japan, but first we consider some broad themes.

Writing, Buddhism, and the state—a technique, a religion, and a form of political organization—were all crucial. Frequently, they also interacted, as indicated by the prominence of writing in Buddhism and statecraft. Both Buddhism and the state relied heavily on written texts, which were produced and consumed by people associated with religious and political institutions.

To begin with writing, the Korean languages were much closer to that spoken by the people on the archipelago than to Chinese. Like Japanese, they did not belong to the Chinese family of languages. When reading and writing, people speaking non-Sinitic languages could pronounce the characters in the then-current Chinese, but they also had every inducement to use them to represent words in their own languages. In the Korean states, such uses of characters involved associating native utterances with entire sentences written in accordance with Chinese grammar, merging reading and translation into one seamless process. This method of reading, which was adopted in Japan as well, yielded a range of possible relations between texts and language: characters could represent Chinese words or non-Chinese words with similar meanings, or they could be used solely for their sounds to spell out non-Chinese words. Like the notations of modern mathematics or science, writing was not limited to any particular place, time, or ethnicity. A similar universality has been and is claimed by the great transcultural religions, and in the case of East Asia that religion was Buddhism.

Buddhism and the state were as intimately related in early Korea as they came to be in Japan. Early Buddhists relied on state tolerance and patronage. According to later histories, even the introduction of Buddhism was accomplished by messages from Chinese states. In the Korean states, as had been the case when they first appeared in North China, Buddhist monks gained support by demonstrating the efficacy of the new religion and the power of their magic in protecting the state and its people. Buddhas and Bodhisattvas readily found their counterparts on the Korean Peninsula, and Maitreya discovered Silla as his native land. Charismatic monks offered ideological legitimacy and advice to kings and elites. For example, in Silla, the famous monk Wongwang gave the following five rules to the Silla military, intellectual, and artistic youth corps known as the Hwarang:

Serve the king with loyalty

Tend parents with filial piety

Treat friends with sincerity

Never retreat from the battlefield

Be discriminate about the taking of life[7]

The first three rules exemplify Buddhism as a carrier of Confucian teachings, and all five demonstrate Buddhist support for king and society and show flexibility in the means used to propagate the faith. As in China, and indeed Christianity in the West, Buddhism was a cultural carrier in such vital areas as medicine, physiognomy, geomancy (divination of placement for graves and buildings), yin-and-yang theory, the calendar (essential for determining when to plant, weed, and harvest), and history (accounts of the past essential for success in the present). State building went hand in hand with church building, in what we might be tempted to call civilization building.

## The Late Tomb Period

By the mid-sixth century, a recently emerged lineage of Yamato kings profited from their connections with agricultural estates and specialist labor guilds within and beyond the Kinai region and presided over a court composed of powerful kinship groups linked with the royal line and each other by networks of intermarriage. At court, polygamy provided many opportunities for building marriage alliances, and imprecise rules for inheriting power insured that succession disputes frequently broke out after the death of a king. The conflicting interests of powerful kinship groups aligned with one or another candidate for the throne often led to violent struggles with serious political consequences. Beyond the court, local chiefs still maintained a great deal of autonomy, especially in more remote areas, but complex webs of allegiance and fealty bound them into a loosely centralized political order.

The emerging states of the Korean Peninsula also figured in the complex politics of the time. They did so not only directly through political and economic connections but also by producing immigrants seeking a new, permanent home. Such people—long-standing residents and recent arrivals—were crucial transmitters of ideas and material culture. They were a source of powerful concepts of political legitimacy, trade goods, and all kinds of advanced technologies, ranging from earth working and construction to writing, and including weaving and metalworking. Those coming across from the Korean Peninsula were not all Albert Einsteins, but most brought with them more powerful technologies and more sophisticated cultural practices than what was current in the archipelago.

Relations with the proto-Korean political entities were not always peaceful. From the late fourth century, in the middle of the Tomb Period, there is evidence of military involvement of Wa troops in fighting on the Korean Peninsula. The first official historians (described later in this chapter) went to great lengths to portray this in terms of conquest and subjugation (claims resurrected during the twentieth-century Japanese colonization of Korea), but these anachronistic and far-fetched depictions cannot be taken seriously. It makes far more sense to see the participation of Wa forces in peninsular conflicts as a form of payment for the raw materials (especially iron), prestige goods, and advanced technologies that flowed from the states of the peninsula into the archipelago and that bound the developing Yamato court to Paekche and the small but well-situated Kaya principalities in the southwestern part of the peninsula.

Conflict among Paekche, Kaya, the southeastern state of Silla, and the northern state of Koguryŏ continued through the fifth and sixth centuries and most likely stimulated the flow of immigrant groups into the Japanese archipelago. Fighting intensified in the mid-sixth century (see Figure 6.7). When Silla con-

**FIGURE 6.7** Map of Korea and Japan.

quered Kaya, it deprived the Yamato court of an important peninsular connection and left Paekche and Koguryŏ as the other two of the famous Three Kingdoms of early Korea. It is no coincidence that early Japanese historical sources record that, around this time, the king of Paekche attempted to formally transmit Buddhism to the Yamato court. Such proselytizing was not unrelated to Buddhist ideals of compassion, but the adoption of the new religion, not unlike the transfer of technology today, was also valued for its this-worldly efficacy. The transmission of such powerful practices when Paekche was threatened by Silla and in need of military assistance from the Yamato court fits neatly with the overall pattern of relations between peninsula and archipelago in this period.

The convergence during the late Tomb Period of internal tendencies as the Yamato court gained in power and prestige and its increasing involvement in the volatile situation on the Korean Peninsula set the stage for a dramatic transformation, which began at the end of the sixth century and became irreversible in the seventh.

# The Seventh-Century Transition (the Asuka Period)

The unification of China under the Sui sent shock waves throughout East Asia. The way this happened demands special attention because it had a profound effect on the nature of the Japanese state. The first major change came at the end of the sixth century with a shift in the power structure at court. Next was the 645 C.E. coup d'etat. Then state formation was accelerated by the catastrophic defeat of a Yamato expeditionary force by Chinese and Korean forces in 663 C.E. Finally came a brief civil war in 672 C.E. Each of these events calls for separate analysis, and each is associated with particular political figures whose names are known through late seventh- and eighth-century written sources.*

In the late sixth century, as conflict intensified on the Korean Peninsula and China headed toward reunification, a kinship group known as the Soga seized power in the Yamato court. Their origins are unclear, but the Soga were almost certainly immigrants or descendants thereof. They were closely associated with groups of artisans recently arrived from the Korean Peninsula, especially from Paekche (see Figure 6.8), and were among the earliest patrons of Buddhism. Setting a powerful precedent, they secured their authority by marrying daughters into the royal family rather than attempting to replace it.

---

* It is noteworthy that for the first time it is possible to talk extensively about discrete, dated occurrences and about named individuals and their exploits. The third-century Queen Himiko of Yamatai and a king of the fifth century whose name appears on two sword inscriptions are exceptions, but in general it is not until the seventh century that the history of the Japanese archipelago takes on such personal dimensions.

The head of the Soga kinship group in the late sixth century was Soga no Umako (?–626 C.E.),[†] whose father had married two of Umako's sisters to a preceding king. Taking advantage of these connections, Umako managed to place a nephew onto the throne in 587 C.E. From then until the middle of the seventh century, he and his descendants maintained power at court by continuing to marry daughters to kings and engineering the succession of grandchildren. (In some cases, a queen with royal blood acceded to the throne after the death of her husband.) The degree to which the royal family had a say in court decisions varied according to the specific ruler and head Soga, but the Soga were the primary driving force of change, even to the point of engineering the assassination of an insufficiently pliable king.

Mostly, however, the political dynamics were less a matter of Soga power versus royal power and more a process of advancing the Soga by solidifying the power and authority of court and ruler. Thus, as they continued to sponsor Buddhism and patronize immigrant artisans and scribes, the Soga were associated with the creation of the new and stronger Asuka court characterized by an increase in the symbolic—and to some extent real—power of the Yamato kings.

Eighth-century state histories portray this as an age of enlightened rule by Umako's niece Queen Suiko (554–628 C.E.) and her famous nephew Prince Shōtoku (574–622 C.E.), Umako's great-nephew. The extent to which this pair was involved in actual decision making at court remains unclear, but an episode in the Chinese dynastic history of the Sui shows that the nature of the Yamato royal institution was transformed in this period. The history describes how the Wa sent an envoy to the Sui emperor's court in 607 C.E., bringing a letter stating that the "son of heaven [that is, the emperor] in the land where the sun rises addresses a letter to the son of heaven in the land where the sun sets." This was a striking depar-

**FIGURE 6.8** Painted-wood Kudara Kannon. Asuka Period, 80.6 in high. Hōryūji, Nara Period. Kudara is Japanese for Paekche, and Kannon is Japanese for Kwanyin (Avalokitesvara). (© Askaen)

---

† The convention for Japanese names is that the family name precedes the given name. Moreover, the names of premodern elites often included the genitive particle "no," so "Soga no Umako" literally translates as "Umako of the Soga." Prominent individuals were often referred to by their given rather than their family names.

ture from the traditional Chinese model of diplomacy (in which kings of peripheral states took a supplicant, tribute-bearing posture in interactions with the
Chinese throne), which had been followed by Wa rulers in the Yayoi and Tomb
Periods. The Sui emperor "was displeased and told the chief official of foreign affairs that this letter from the barbarians was discourteous and that such a letter
should not again be brought to his attention."[8]

Some historians have argued that this breach of protocol was inadvertent, but
it likely reflects a Soga-sponsored attempt to claim a newly prominent and independent position for the royal line of the Asuka court. Furthermore, this diplomatic move seems to have been accompanied by the creation of a more elaborate
palace compound to house the Yamato royals and by attempts to exert more control over long-distance trade.

After Umako's death, his son and grandson played prominent roles at court,
but their increasing power eventually encountered a backlash. In the mid-seventh
century, a young prince, known as Tenji (626–671 C.E.) after he assumed the
throne, and who was unrelated to the Soga, conspired against them with Nakatomi
no Kamatari (614–669 C.E.), the leader of another powerful kinship group.
Kamatari was later given the surname Fujiwara, which was to become one of the
most prominent noble kinship groups of premodern Japan (see Chapter 7).

In 645 C.E. Kamatari and Tenji staged a dramatic coup d'etat. The leading
Soga was summoned to court on a pretext and then assassinated in front of the hor-
rified Queen Kōgyoku (594–661 C.E.), Tenji's mother. After wiping out Soga supporters, Kamatari and Tenji began a program of strengthening the throne, creating
formal structures of taxation and administration and constructing a more extensive
palace surrounded by the beginnings of a capital city. Although the measures taken
were more limited than what later historians celebrated as the Taika (Great
Change) reforms, Kamatari and Tenji do seem to have begun to move toward a
more powerful centralized government. In doing so, they relied on the expertise of
highly educated immigrants and on returned students and priests who had traveled
to China to study Buddhism, statecraft, astronomy, and other practical pursuits.

In response to border disputes dating from the late sixth century, the Sui invaded Koguryŏ three times, in 611, 613, and 614 C.E. The human, economic, and
political cost of the failure of those expeditions contributed to the downfall of the
Sui, but more fighting was to come after the Tang replaced the Sui in 618 C.E.
After a period of jockeying among the competing states and the Tang superpower,
the final stage of conflict began in 642 C.E., when Paekche captured territory from
Silla and a minister at the Koguryŏ court carried out a bloody coup. Two years
later, in 644 C.E., Tang began its own military campaign against Koguryŏ. As
Kamatari and Tenji were overthrowing the Soga and embarking on a program of
strengthening and centralizing the Yamato polity, the threat posed by this burgeoning crisis must have been foremost in their minds.

During the rest of the 640s and through the 650s, the complex four-way interaction among Tang and the Korean states came to a head in a final configuration
of alliances. Silla allied itself with Tang, and in 660 C.E. a unified Chinese–Sillan

force gained the upper hand over Paekche. As remnants of its Paekche ally struggled to resurrect their state, the Yamato court was drawn into the conflict and sent a large expeditionary force of ships and troops to fight on the peninsula. The catastrophic defeat of that force by Tang and Silla at the Battle of Paekchon River in 663 C.E. was a key event in ending the three kingdoms of Korea. Five years later Koguryŏ fell, leaving Unified Silla in control of the entire peninsula.

Tenji and his advisers (Kamatari died in 669 C.E.) were faced with a grave crisis. All too conscious of the continuing threat posed by ascendant Silla and its Tang ally, they fortified the potential invasion route, stationing guards and erecting beacons on islands in the straits separating Kyushu from the southern coast of the Korean Peninsula and constructed fortifications on the northern coast of Kyushu and along the Inland Sea. Most significantly, the Yamato court embarked on a crash program of institution building that included a bureaucracy based on written communication and formal taxation to pay for defense and to finance the construction of imposing capitals to project the central authority of the throne. More direct control over outlying areas organized into administrative districts, attempts to create written laws, a census, and a draft system were other major components of a program of state formation.

These changes seem to have happened quickly, an example as described by Bruce Batten of "foreign threat" inspiring "domestic reform."⁹ The large number of refugees fleeing the conflicts of the 660s played a key role, because it seems that much of the literate, administrative manpower for the new administrative infrastructure was provided by immigrants, first from Paekche and then from Koguryŏ.

The final step in the process of state formation occurred after Tenji died in 671 C.E. Again there was a power struggle. One contender was Tenji's son, a pliable young man apparently favored by Tenji and backed by the majority of high-ranking kinship groups associated with the court. However, Tenji's brother, a powerful, determined man in his forties, later known as Tenmu (c. 631–686 C.E.), had strong support from middle-ranking nobles and military backing by some of the regional authorities. The tension over the succession erupted into violence in 672 C.E., a year after Tenji's death. In a brief civil war of less than two months, Tenmu's forces routed those of his opponent, who was driven to suicide. By then the diplomatic and military crisis had somewhat abated but not dissipated, and the victors were faced with a need to unify the court and the country.

Tenmu and his consort Jitō (645–703 C.E.), who went on to rule in her own right after his death, immediately began to consolidate and extend their rule, continuing the process of state building. They worked to extend and strengthen the bureaucracy, to survey the population as a means of extracting taxes and military service, and to reduce the power of the preexisting regional authorities, partly by enfolding them into an expanded provincial administrative structure in outlying areas. They also added new components, including the compilation of complete legal codes and official histories, the construction of large, new palace compounds (and eventually of immense capital cities), and the official sponsorship and control of religious institutions. The latter included both Buddhist establishments, which had heretofore been largely sponsored by prominent kinship groups, and a variety of non-Buddhist cults of indigenous and imported deities later grouped under the rubric Shinto. Many of these developments are obviously ideological and institutional, but among the most far-reaching and significant innovations of this period was the creation of the political title of emperor (*tennō*) and the country name of Japan (*Nihon* or *Nippon*). The exact dates are not clear, but it is relatively certain that both were created during the reigns of Tenmu and Jitō in a deliberate attempt to legitimize and strengthen the powers of the throne.

*Tennō,* literally "heavenly sovereign," refers to the pole star and is a Chinese term used for the emperor who sits at the center of the realm while everything revolves around him. For a brief period in the mid-seventh century, under Daoist influence, this term (*tianhuang* in Chinese) had been used as the official title for the Tang emperor, but the dominant Chinese term for emperor remained *huangdi*. Both the Chinese and the Japanese terms are usually translated "emperor," but they apply to the heads of different political and ideological systems, even though they share some similar and related institutions. *Nihon* literally means base or origin of the sun, a concept that appeared earlier, as in the 607 C.E. letter to the Sui court, but that now came into its own as a full-fledged term for the country.

Both this association of Japan with the sun and the notion of a heavenly sovereign were by now linked with religious beliefs, especially the notion of a sun deity claimed as the ultimate ancestor of the royal line. It is clear that the intent was for this to be immediately obvious: an absolute ruler, the emperor, and a discrete realm for that emperor to rule. Most significantly, their adoption signified the assertion of an independent, sovereign empire, even though in the late seventh century the new realm was limited to the three main islands of Kyushu, Shikoku, and Honshu, while portions of southern Kyushu and northeastern Honshu were not under its control. Even within those bounds, a great deal of local autonomy and variety remained. The emergence of the new state was not a sudden transition to a fully centralized order but an ongoing transformation with many ups and downs for centuries to come.

Not everyone was immersed in worldly pursuits. The Asuka Period was also crucial in the internal history of Buddhism, represented here by a sculpture ranked as a foremost national treasure of modern Japan (see Figures 6.9 and 6.10). This rendering of a pensive Buddha, which has obvious Korean and Chinese antecedents, can stand as a clear visual reminder of the spiritual and philosophical influence of Buddhism in linking cultures throughout East Asia regions and in enriching and elevating the lives of the people.

# Nara as a Center and Symbol

Another project of Tenmu and Jitō was the establishment of a permanent capital city at the center of the new state. Previously a new palace had been constructed for each new ruler, but during Jitō's reign a new Chinese-style capital was estab-

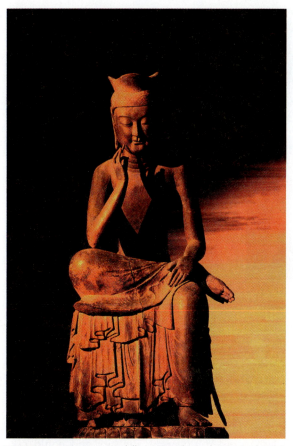

**FIGURE 6.9** Pensive Buddha. Wood, Asuka Period, 48.6 in high. Kōryuji, Kyoto. Earlier identified as Maitreya, at present we do not know which Buddha is represented in this remarkable fusion of piety and sensuousness. (© Chris Lisle/Corbis)

lished. This was followed in the early eighth century by the construction of the great city of Nara, the capital that is the namesake of the Nara Period. Mid-eighth-century Nara was home to about 100,000 people, when the population of the archipelago was around 6 million. Compared with Chang'an's approximately 1 million inhabitants this is not impressive, but for early Japan it was unprecedented. The same applies to the city's dimensions. The great Suzaku Avenue, eighty-one-yards wide, ran from the imposing city gatehouse to the entrance of the palace compound at the north end of the city. It bisected a grid of streets and avenues that was three miles from north to south and three and half from east to west.

Plots within the grid were allotted in accordance with the rank of their occupants. There were two official markets, where various foods and manufactured goods could be exchanged through barter or purchased with some of the official copper coins newly minted by the ambitious state. In addition to vegetables and other crops grown within the city, many staples and supplies were available in these markets, which were connected by canals to rivers leading west to the port city of Naniwa and providing access to coastal routes linking Nara to economic centers throughout western Japan.

The markets provided the economic life of the city, but its priorities were clearly political. As in China, the palace was in the north so that the emperor faced south to receive the homage of his people. The closer one got to the palace compound, the higher the rank of the residents and the grander their dwellings.

**DETAIL FIGURE 6.10** Detail of Pensive Buddha. Wood, Asuka Period. (© Chris Lisle/Corbis)

The great Main Gate of the palace had a tiled roof and was painted in brilliant red, green, and white with gleaming metal ornaments. On both sides stretched a thirty-foot high wall. There were other gates to the imperial compound, all manned by guards who required written passes from entrants other than bureaucrats or regular palace workers. The palace area itself was almost 1100 yards from north to south and more than 1300 yards from east to west. As the ceremonial and administrative center of the state, it contained several grand edifices. The largest was the Great Supreme Hall, or Throne Hall, from which the emperor oversaw such state ceremonies as the enthronement ritual, New Year's celebrations, and visits by foreign dignitaries. Here also the emperor held royal audiences attended by some of the thousands of bureaucrats who worked in buildings that surrounded a huge courtyard just south of the Great Supreme Hall. The royal residence was also located in the palace compound, as were several pleasure gardens; all manner of offices, archives, and workshops; and kitchens, breweries, and storehouses to supply the needs of both state banquets and laborers' lunches.

From this palace compound the emperor oversaw the city and could take pleasure in the laudatory words of an early Nara poet:

> The royal city,
> Nara of the blue-green earth,
> Like blossoming trees
> That shimmer into fragrant bloom,
> Is at the height of splendor now.[10]

The laborers who had built it, or the peasants whose hard-earned foodstuffs supported it, might have had different perspectives on the capital city, but it certainly made possible a glittering, refined lifestyle for the royal family and the nobles and officials who surrounded them at court.

The aesthetic richness of their lives is apparent in the precious articles preserved in the Shōsōin, a remarkable log-cabin-like storehouse still standing on pillars in the compound of the Tōdaiji temple. Inside this great repository of eighth-century art are hundreds of objects and thousands of paper documents; the treasures therein include books; weapons; mirrors; screens; silks; musical instruments; medicines; fragrant woods; and objects of gold, lacquer, mother-of-pearl, and glass. Among them are items used in the dedication ceremonies for the immense central Buddha image of the temple and imported goods from China, Korea, India, Persia, Greece, and Rome. The music, art, and literature of the Nara court formed a similarly sophisticated mixture of elements from Japan, Korea, China, and points beyond.

## Nara as a Religious Center

Tenmu, Jitō, and their successors did not stop at creating the position of emperor and the domain of Japan; they worked to construct elaborate ideological justifications of the legitimacy—even the divine necessity—of these political institutions and the norms they entailed. New religious developments supplied essential support.

This came from two main sources: massive state sponsorship of, and control over, a variety of Buddhist institutions on the one hand and, on the other, partial systematization of a variety of cults of local gods, or *kami,* into a complex hierarchy of shrines associated with divine narratives centered on the royal house.

These religious institutions—with their solemn rites, revered texts, imposing buildings, lavish art, sacred music and dance, and charismatic practitioners—joined secular government institutions in asserting the legitimacy of the new state.

Just as the capital city with its palace complex lay at the center of the polity, a central temple in that capital sat atop a state-sponsored countrywide network of state temples and nunneries. This huge temple was constructed on the eastern edge of the Nara capital in the middle of the eighth century. Its name, Tōdaiji (Great Eastern Temple), reflects its location in the capital but perhaps also Japan's status as the Buddhist country on the edge of the civilized world, out in the ocean to the east of China and India.

The Tōdaiji temple complex encompassed numerous halls, cloisters, service buildings, and belfries, and it boasted two towering pagodas—more than 330 feet, placing them among the highest structures in East Asia at the time. (For its gate guardian, see Figure 11.4.) At the center was the Great Buddha Hall, more than 280 feet wide and 150 feet tall. Even now, in a rebuilt version smaller than the original, it is said to be the largest wooden structure in the world. The Great Buddha itself was a gargantuan gilt bronze image of Vairocana, the cosmic Sun Buddha who was thought to sit at the center of all universes, projecting himself outward in the form of myriad Buddhas manifested in sundry times, places, and worlds. More than fifty feet tall and weighing more than 1 million pounds, this huge image was at the time the largest cast bronze statue in the world. (Unfortunately, earthquakes, fires, and repeated warfare have taken their toll. The Buddha has been so much restored and rebuilt that the present version probably bears little resemblance to the original.)

**FIGURE 6.11** Izumo. Shrine building at the ancient sacred site of Izumo, in western Honshu. (© Lore Schirokauer)

The construction of the statue and the great hall that housed it was an immense undertaking, requiring massive state support and contributions and labor from hundreds of thousands. The dedication ceremony, on the ninth day of the fourth month of 752 C.E., involved 10,000 monks, 4000 musicians and dancers, and 7000 state officials. It centered on the painting in of the eyes of the cosmic Buddha by Bodhisena (704–760 C.E.), an Indian priest. This was surely one of the most magnificent spectacles of Japanese history, staged in a "vast cathedral of state religion," sitting at the center of the network of provincial temples, just as the emperor in his capital city sat at the center of the realm.[11]

Alongside this network was another of cults devoted to apparently indigenous gods (*kami*), worshipped in shrines that paralleled, in their own distinctive manner, the temples devoted to Buddhism (see Figure 6.11). In the early histories, as in the system of official shrines laid out in the legal codes and presided over by the Council of Shrine Affairs, these "native" cults are linked to the power, legitimacy, and putative divinity of the royal line. It is likely that the worship of certain deities, often associated with sacred features of the landscape such as mountains or rivers, had roots deep in the practices and beliefs of early inhabitants of the archipelago, but these cults also drew on an eclectic mixture of elements from overseas, including the Chinese religious practices often grouped under Daoism, the gods and rituals of Korean immigrants, and the ideas and practices developed under Buddhist influence. This conglomerate of ritual spaces and practices eventually came to be grouped under the term Shinto ("way of the gods"), but it is anachronistic to see it as a unified, native faith that preexisted the importation of Buddhism.

# Documents and Structures

If the capital, with its palaces and temples, reveals the body and something of the spirit of the late seventh- and eighth-century state, writing was its lifeblood. Objects with writing on them have been uncovered from the middle of the Yayoi Period, and we know that the Yamato kings of the Tomb Period employed scribes from the Korean Peninsula to produce diplomatic correspondence and ceremonial inscriptions, but there was little reliance on writing as a means of communication and storage of information until the seventh century. The political transformation that occurred during the decades following the anti-Soga coup of 645 C.E. entailed a sudden increase in the quantity and variety of writing. More texts appeared as did people capable of reading and writing them.

The new state engineered by Tenmu and Jitō and expanded by their successors relied on a range of texts and institutions created by and dedicated to their production and storage. In this it resembled the Chinese and Korean states, which served as institutional models. Moreover, especially in the late seventh century, many positions were filled by literate refugees from Paekche and Koguryŏ.

The textual embodiment of the new political system prompted historians to designate the new order the *ritsuryō* state, referring to penal (*ritsu*) and administrative (*ryō*) codes. Based largely on the Tang legal code but modified to reflect Japanese circumstances, these written codes were the official basis of the early state. The administrative code specified the structure of the entire government, from the royal household and its prerogatives down to the procedures to be followed in operating provincial stables. The penal code laid out classes of offenses and stipulated punishments. These two classes of legal texts were supplemented by two classes of government orders: those that gave detailed instructions in how to carry out the stipulations of the administrative code, and others that amended the code through official directives.

The compilation of such codes may already have been under way during Tenji's rule, but the first reliably dated promulgation of at least a partial administrative code took place in 689 C.E. The first full promulgation of penal and administrative codes occurred at the beginning of the eighth century (the Taihō codes). Revisions were promulgated several decades later. Although these revisions were eventually supplanted first by official directives and later by other forms of legal pronouncements, they remained the nominal law of the land (however empty such a designation might have been) until the nineteenth century.

The mere promulgation of the codes does not mean that the nature of Japanese society changed overnight, but it is clear from a variety of historical and archeological sources that the textual vision of an ideal state contained in the codes did correspond to some extent to actual institutions put in place in the late seventh and eighth centuries.

Among those institutions was a range of official government offices housed in the great palace compound that dominated the capital city. The administrative codes provided for a vast bureaucracy arrayed beneath the emperor, staffed by career officials and appointed, at least ostensibly, at the emperor's pleasure. The highest government offices were the largely ceremonial Council of Shrine Affairs and the Council of State Affairs, which was made up of ministers, councilors, and advisers who oversaw the workings of the government. Under the auspices of the council were a variety of ministries with responsibility for different aspects of the state, such as the Ministry of Military Affairs, the Ministry of the Treasury, or the Ministry of Justice. Each ministry was home to multiple levels of bureaucrats and was housed in a dedicated building in the palace compound.

In addition to the many official positions, with specified titles, responsibilities and salaries, the members of the government and of capital society at large were regulated by an elaborate system of ranks. Particular offices were restricted to individuals of specified ranks. On the surface the system appeared meritocratic, with regular promotion a reward for exemplary service, but in practice the sons of high-ranking officials enjoyed a significant head-start in their initial appointments. The rank system was virtually restricted to elite capital residents and especially favored its upper echelons (a separate and unequal system was employed for provincial elites). Although the world of the capital was a small one, it was riven by political factionalism and rivalries between powerful figures and kinship groups. In this context rank was extremely important. In addition to determining eligibility for government offices, rank carried a great deal of social cachet and provided an official stipend that was often a significant source of income.

This central administrative structure was financed by a system of taxation based on the equal-field system founded in Chinese theories and practice. This system was never established in full and began transforming into something else almost as soon as it was instituted. But, at least on paper, it provided for public ownership of all land, which was then parceled out to the people in return for various categories of tax liability.

Several layers of government mediated between the central administration in the capital and the households farming the land, catching fish and game, making salt from seawater, and otherwise producing food and other necessities. The country was divided into around sixty provinces (*kuni*) (the precise number ranged from fifty-eight to sixty-six depending on the period), ruled by governors dispatched from the center. The governors and the senior staff that accompanied them resided in provincial capitals, overseeing a bureaucracy whose middle and lower ranks were staffed by local elites, often members of powerful kinship groups with local roots antedating the advent of the centralized state. Each province was divided into districts with their own chiefs and staffs drawing on similar local elites. Beneath the districts were "townships" (often paper-based administrative units rather than actual physical communities) and, at the bottom of the system, residential units of one to three dozen people living near each other. These residential units were exhaustively surveyed in comprehensive censuses because they were the basis of the system of land distribution and taxation.

Through this system, farmers, fishers, foresters, and others at the bottom of the social hierarchy supported the state and the elites, paying taxes in the form of rice, other grains, other foodstuffs, textiles, and handicrafts and providing forced labor and military service. Shipments of tax goods were funneled from the district offices to the provincial level and up to the central government in the capital, and groups of able-bodied adult men were recruited for a labor tax, or corvée, which obliged them to work on roads, irrigation, and construction of official government structures in the province and beyond. Groups of districts were also responsible for supplying and equipping fixed numbers of conscript soldiers, some of whom were dispatched to the capital or to border regions to serve long, lonely terms of guard duty.

These exactions amounted to a tremendous burden on the population, especially because rural populations were particularly vulnerable to epidemic disease, natural disasters, and failed harvests. Records of the period abound in references to peasants absconding from the districts to which they were legally bound and to men starving by the side of the road as they attempted to return from military service or forced labor.

The official historians on whom we must rely, like the central and provincial bureaucrats, had professional reasons for creating documents conveying the image of a fully centralized, top-down state, but the reality was far more complicated. It is clear that their idealized vision of a multilayered, entirely code-based bureaucratic system ranging from the emperor down to the peasants was never fully realized. The reach of the state was limited in depth and geographic extent. It took the military campaigns of the early eighth century to bring southern Kyushu into the fold, and the frontier in northeastern Honshu remained contested into the ninth century.

Even within the borders of the state, different regions were under varying degrees of centralized control. Archeological finds of wooden labels on shipments of tax goods show that most formal tax payments came from western Honshu, Shikoku, and northern Kyushu: the area surrounding the Inland Sea that had been the traditional realm of the economic power centered in the Kinai region. At least in terms of its tax base, we could argue, with Wayne Farris, that "the eighth-century state was truly a 'western Japanese' phenomenon."[12]

There was a great deal of local and regional variation in the character of interaction among the peripheral populations, their own elites, the officials dispatched from the capital, and the more or less distant offices of the central government. Even so, it is apparent from the vast public works projects of the eighth century that the early state succeeded, on an unprecedented scale, in mobilizing the labor of much of the archipelago's population.

## Literature

Writing was also the lifeblood of the church. Japanese priests made repeated trips to China in search of sacred texts, bringing back works that were copied, studied, and commented upon in the great monasteries of Nara. Several state-sponsored sutra-copying projects were undertaken to gain merit for the sponsoring royals and nobles and to protect the land from external and internal dangers and misfortunes. The result was the production of more than 100,000 volumes of Buddhist works during the eighth century. Many still survive, as do documents in the Shōsōin that present a vivid picture of the lives of the hard-working scribes who labored to produce them.

Important and numerous as they were, Buddhists texts were not the only texts produced in the Nara Period, which also produced the earliest extant historical and literary collections composed in Japan. These included officially sanctioned works, such as gazetteers (*Fudoki*) detailing the history and geography of each province, but the best known examples are the two earliest histories of Japan, the 712 C.E. *Kojiki* (*Record of Ancient Matters*), Japan's oldest extant literary work, and the 720 C.E. *Nihon shoki* (*Chronicles of Japan*).

By using a systematic mixture of characters, employing some phonetically and others to render the meaning of a word, the compilers of the *Kojiki* created a text that can be read in Japanese. In addition to prose narratives, it contains 112 "songs" attributed to the gods and legendary figures. Although they may well have roots in early oral forms, the songs are an organic part of the written work. The *Kojiki* narrates the divine origins and the succession, always legitimate, of early "emperors." The prose passages include fascinating stories, replete with magic, battles, and romance, and there is some compelling poetry in the songs. No doubt one goal was to entertain, but this did not preclude it from providing a grounding for the legitimacy of the royal house and its dominion over the realm. Crucial in this respect were explanations of the genealogies of gods, emperors, their children, and their descendants, which served as a basis for the hierarchical ordering of noble kinship groups.

Like the *Kojiki*, the *Nihon shoki* starts with the origin of heaven and earth and narrates the divine ancestry of the royal house, but in contrast to the earlier work, it does so in an explicitly Sinitic manner, borrowing extensively from Chinese cosmological and historical texts and generally modeling itself on the early Chinese dynastic histories. Unlike the *Kojiki*, it follows the norms of literary Chinese syntax and vocabulary. In the *Nihon shoki*, the legitimacy of the royal house is linked to its putative divine origins, but it is also a matter of adhering to the moral and cultural models of the Chinese classics—and, eventually, of Buddhism. Although its earlier sections contain a great deal of mythic and legendary material (much of which overlaps with the *Kojiki*), as it progresses it becomes more like a historical chronicle.

Because it goes right up to the abdication of Jitō in 697 C.E., the *Nihon shoki* is the major source for seventh-century history and includes valuable material for studying earlier periods. However, it recounts a myth of the founding of "Japan" by the putative first emperor in 660 B.C.E., an impossibly early date; includes dubious exploits of early "emperors" who cannot be directly linked to actual Yamato kings; and depicts the Korean states as inferior to and in some cases as subjugated by early Japan (when nothing called Japan existed). Even in the sections devoted to the seventh century, there is much that should be viewed skeptically, including the image of Prince Shōtoku as a cultural hero and founding sponsor of Buddhism and the portrayal of the period immediately after the anti-Soga coup as a time of dramatic "reform" along Chinese lines. This is not to say that there is no truth to its stories of early and mid-seventh-century institution building. In the final analysis, it is a monumental work, containing an immense trove of detail and narrative incident, and should be appreciated as such even though we cannot accept everything it tells us.

In addition to the two histories, major anthologies of poetry were composed during the Nara Period. One such, the *Kaifūsō* (*Patterned Sea-grasses of Cherished Style*), is a 751 C.E. collection of Chinese-style verse that provides insight into the elegant literary banquets of late seventh and eighth centuries. Another, the *Man'yōshū* (*Collection of Ten Thousand Ages*), is a huge anthology of Japanese-style poetry compiled in several stages over the course of the eighth century. Although it is very much a product of the court, its more than 4500 poems include an astonishing variety of literary forms, attributed to poets ranging from emperors to anonymous border guards from the eastern provinces.

It is also the source of the poem about Nara quoted previously.

Among its authors, the best known is the late seventh-century court poet named Kakinomoto no Hitomaro, whose rich body of work survives only in the *Man'yōshū*. Among his poems are elegies to princes and propagandistic tributes to deified royal figures, but there are also affecting laments such as the following, whose speaker has parted from his wife in the provinces to travel to the capital:

> . . . like the jeweled weed
> That slips and floats in the waves,
> Riding in their embrace,
> Was she in soft and yielding sleep
> Whom I have left behind,
> Helpless as a trace of dew or frost,
> And come upon this road.
> At the fourscore bendings of the way
> Ten thousand times
> I turn and look again,
> But every time
> Our village is yet further sunk away.
> And every mountain
> Taller than the one I crossed before.
> Like summer grasses
> She must droop, sorrowing in her heart,
> Yearning for her love,
> The dear girl whose gates I long to see:
> O mountains, I command you to bow down![13]

We can merely hint at the richness and variety of the poems collected in this splendid anthology. There is space for just one more excerpt to suggest something more of the range of themes and tones found in its pages. This was written by the great poet Yamanoue no Okura (660–730 C.E.), a cosmopolitan and deeply learned man who may have been born in Paekche. As we conclude our consideration of glories of Nara culture, it reminds us of the lives of those whose labor made them possible, although that, all too frequently, did not save them from poverty and hunger. It appears that the village chief of the final lines is out to collect a tax payment from the unfortunate narrator:

> By my pillowside
> My father and my mother crouch,
> And at my feet
> My wife and children; thus am I
> Surrounded by grief
> And hungry, piteous cries.
> But on the hearth
> No kettle sends up clouds of steam,
> And in our pot
> A spider spins its web.
> We have forgotten
> The very way of cooking rice;
> Then where we huddle . . .
> There comes the voice
> Of the village chief with his whip,
> Standing, shouting for me,
> There outside the place we sleep.[14]

# The Visual Arts

Much of the visual art that survives from this period is Buddhist, ranging from sculptures and ritual implements to banners and tapestries and including carefully copied sutra texts that are masterpieces of calligraphy. This is partly because Buddhist temples, much like monasteries in the West, played an important role in preserving and maintaining works of art. But it also reflects the immense cultural and intellectual importance of Buddhism and the central place given to sculpture, architecture, and other visual arts in East Asian Buddhism. Still-extant temples, many of them in and around the modern city of Nara, are treasure troves of seventh- and eighth-century art.

Among the oldest of these surviving temples, said to contain the oldest wooden buildings in the world, is Hōryūji, near Nara (see Figure 6.12). This temple is associated with Prince Shōtoku and is likely to have originated in a private establishment sponsored by him and by members of his kinship group. A fire de-

**FIGURE 6.12** The Hōryūji, Nara Perfecture. (© Askaen) 🏵

stroyed the early structures in 670 C.E. When the temple was reconstructed, links between Buddhist institutions and the nascent state were firmly woven into legends of Shōtoku's achievements. Figure 6.10 shows the nucleus of Hōryūji, a quadrangle enclosed by a cloistered walk. Equal emphasis is accorded the pagoda and the Golden Hall, balanced against each other along a rough east–west axis. This is one of a variety of temple compound layouts, based on Chinese and especially Korean prototypes found in early Japanese temples.

Other buildings commonly found in temples included a lecture hall, usually located to the north or back, a sutra repository to store the scriptures, a belfry, a refectory, and buildings to house monks in their cells. The major buildings stood on stone bases and were roofed in clay tiles. Their heavy roofs were supported by an elaborate system of bracketing that, as on the continent, contributed greatly to the aesthetics of the building. Large exterior wooden units were painted red; yellow paint covered the crosscut faces of the brackets, rafters, and so on; and other, intervening spaces were painted white. In their orientation, structure, and ornamentation, these buildings generally followed Chinese and Korean precedents.

The art housed in these temples was also frequently the work of Chinese and Korean artists and craftsmen. Indeed, Nara Period temples in Japan are among

**FIGURE 6.13** Tamamushi Shrine. Lacquer on wood, seventh century, 92 in high. Hōryūji, Nara Prefecture. (© Archivo Iconografico, S.A./Corbis)

our best sources for studying Chinese Buddhist art through the Tang in its temporal and regional variations. Hōryūji, like several other early temples, is a great treasure house of Buddhist art. One of the loveliest sculptures there is the Kudara Kannon (see Figure 6.8). The overall effect of this elongated figure is one of great elegance and grace. Nara sculptors were also capable of striking realism, as in the miniature figure of Vimalakirti (see Figure 4.7). Among the earliest paintings extant in Japan are those on the cabinet-sized Tamamushi (Jewel-Beetle) shrine, also in the Hōryūji collection. The shrine is so named because it was decorated with iridescent beetle wings set into metal edging, a technique also practiced in Korea. The depicted scene derives from a famous story concerning an earlier incarnation of Sakyamuni. It shows the future Buddha sacrificing himself to feed a starving mother tiger unable to feed her young. The painting begins at the top, where the future Buddha is shown hanging his clothes on a tree, and it ends at the bottom, where the tigress is devouring him (see Figure 6.13).

In seventh- and eighth-century East Asia, the art and architecture of Tang China was a transcultural idiom that projected elegance and power. The spirit of that architecture is well illustrated by the Golden Hall of Tōshōdaiji (see Figure 6.14), an eighth-century temple in Nara.

Tōshōdaiji was founded by the Chinese monk Ganjin (Jianzhen), who finally reached Japan on his sixth attempt, having earlier been frustrated by storms, pia

b

**FIGURE 6.14** The golden hall of Tōshōdaiji, Nara. Although the original roof was more sloping and less steep than the present version, the illustration gives a good idea of the self-assured strength of Tang-style building at its best. (a: © Lore Schirokauer; b: From Robert Treat Paine & Alexander Soper, *The Art and Architecture of Japan* [Pelican History of Art, 2nd Edition. 1974], pg. 186)

**FIGURE 6.15** Portrait sculpture of the Chinese monk Ganjin (Jianzhen).
Dry lacquer, mid-eighth century, 31.77 in high. Tōshōdaiji, Nara.
(© Schirokauer Collection)

rates, shipwrecks, and once by the Chinese authorities. By the time he reached
Japan, he had lost his sight. His portrait sculpture (see Figure 6.15) vividly invokes
his blindness. Like Bodhisena, the Indian priest who painted in the eyes of the
Great Buddha, the story of Ganjin is a reminder of the cosmopolitan Buddhist
culture of the eighth century.

# The End of the Nara Period

During the Nara Period there were no further foreign crises as serious as the Korean conflict of the seventh century and no full-blown civil wars like that of 672 C.E. However, in addition to natural disasters (including famines and a horrible smallpox epidemic from 735 to 737 C.E.), the court was repeatedly shaken by succession problems and power struggles that ended in the losers' exile or death. Frequently, these involved the Fujiwara, whose descent from Kamatari, who had helped plan the anti-Soga coup of 645 C.E., did not prevent them from adopting the Soga strategy of gaining power through intermarriage with the royal line. Thus Emperor Shōmu (701–756, r. 724–756 C.E.), who oversaw the expansion of the eighth-century state and the construction of the Great Buddha, had a Fujiwara mother and wife. Fuhito, the Fujiwara head at the time, was his grandfather and father-in-law.

In addition to such marriage politics, the Fujiwara dominated by monopolizing, or attempting to monopolize, high-ranking positions on the Council of State Affairs and by creating offices not provided for in the official code. But after Shōmu died the marriage politics backfired. His Fujiwara consort had no sons who survived infancy, so the royal couples' *daughter* was named crown prince and eventually placed on the throne. This daughter, Empress Kōken/Shōtoku (718–770 C.E.), actually reigned twice, because she was forced to abdicate but overthrew her successor and returned to the throne. She had no offspring. Histories report that an unsuccessful attempt to abdicate in favor of an influential Buddhist priest was not welcomed by the court. It appears that during her reign royal power faced the dual threat posed by powerful independent Buddhist institutions on the one hand and by the unbridled ambitions of the Fujiwara on the other. Both would persist for centuries to come.

At any rate, in 781 C.E. a great-grandson of Tenji, Kanmu (737–806 C.E.), acceded to the throne. Already middle-aged, he was a strong figure who set about attempting to gain greater control of the state by reducing the influence of powerful temples and noble kinship groups. These goals seem to have contributed to his momentous decision to move the capital from Nara in 784 C.E.

There were precedents for moving the capital, but Kanmu clearly intended to create a new center of power in an area removed from great temples and powerful court families. Other factors in the move to Nagaoka (southwest of modern Kyoto) likely included the exhaustion of natural resources and taxable land in the area around Nara and the improved waterborne transportation available at the new site, which was linked by water to the port at Naniwa and over Lake Biwa to the coast along the Sea of Japan. Problems encountered in building the capital at Nagaoka led to its abandonment after a mere decade, but the next capital site, that of modern Kyoto, would remain the royal seat for eleven centuries.

# Notes

1. Conrad Totman, *A History of Japan* (Oxford: Blackwell, 2000), p. 19.

2. Richard Pearson, *Ancient Japan* (New York: Arthur Sackler Gallery/George Braziller, 1992), p. 62.

3. On the origins of the Japanese language, and more broadly on the issue of the Jōmon–Yayoi transition, see Mark Hudson, *Ruins of Identity: Ethnogenesis in the Japanese Islands* (Honolulu: Univ. of Hawaii Press, 1999).

4. William Wayne Farris, *Sacred Texts and Buried Treasures: Issues in the Historical Archaeology of Ancient Japan* (Honolulu: Univ. of Hawaii Press, 1998), pp. 120–21.

5. Joan Piggott, *The Emergence of Japanese Kingship* (Stanford: Stanford Univ. Press, 1997), p. 65.

6. Hyung Il. Pai, *Constructing Korean Origins: A Critical Review of Archeology, Historiography, and Racial Myth in Korean State-Formation Theories* (Cambridge: Harvard Univ. Asia Center, 2000), pp. 174–236 and passim.

7. Peter H. Lee and Wm. Theodore de Bary, eds., *Sources of Korean Tradition* (New York: Columbia Univ. Press, 1997), p. 54.

8. Ryusaku Tsunoda and L. Carrington Goodrich, *Japan in the Chinese Dynastic Histories* (Kyoto: Perkins Oriental Books, 1968), pp. 40–41.

9. Bruce Batten, "Foreign Threat and Domestic Reform: The Emergence of the *Ritsuryō* State," *Monumenta Nipponica* 41:2 (Summer 1986): 199–219.

10. Edwin Cranston, *A Waka Anthology, Vol. 1: The Gem-Glistening Cup* (Stanford: Stanford Univ. Press, 1993), p. 377.

11. William H. Coaldrake, *Architecture and Authority in Japan* (London: Routledge, 1996), p. 70.

12. Farris, *Sacred Texts and Buried Treasures,* p. 221.

13. Cranston, *A Waka Anthology, Vol. 1: The Gem-Glistening Cup,* p. 205.

14. Cranston, *A Waka Anthology, Vol. 1: The Gem-Glistening Cup,* pp. 362–63.

# Heian Japan

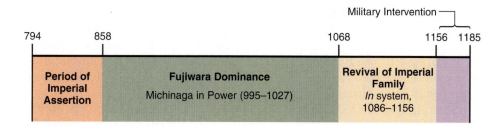

The Heian Period (794–1185) began with a vigorous assertion of imperial power under Emperor Kanmu, but that was not to last. The long-term trend favored an aristocracy that ruled at times with the emperor but more frequently in his stead and presided over a refined culture that left a permanent mark on Japanese life and perceptions of the world. Thereby linked to the future, the Heian Period was also connected to the past, as it was within frameworks in place by the Nara Period that new forms of political power, extraction of resources, religious symbolism, and aesthetic expression arose.

By keeping the temples on the outskirts of the new capital of Kyoto and by patronizing new schools, which had their headquarters in the mountains, Emperor Kanmu was able to evade the political influence of the old, city-based Buddhist orders. Equally energetic and innovative in secular matters, he established new agencies to advise the throne and enforce its decisions, appointed inspectors to examine the books of retiring provincial governors, and replaced the ineffective conscript army with a militia system. In this way, he and his immediate successors were able, for almost half a century, to rule within the framework of the early state system.

This period of relative imperial assertion was followed by two centuries during which a lineage of the Fujiwara house enjoyed political and economic ascendance, ruling by dominating the court without displacing the imperial house. This set a pattern for subsequent Japanese history. Emperors continued to function as titular heads of government, symbols of legitimacy, and objects of veneration based on the myth of their divine descent, their religious authority, and the court's preeminence in matters of high culture. Their extraordinary aura retained its radiance even when they had little actual political power.

# The Fujiwara

The Fujiwara house, as already noted, was founded by Nakatomi no Kamatari (614–669), who was rewarded for his leading role in the coup of 645 by receiving the name Fujiwara, literally "wisteria plain." Subsequently, the Fujiwara had their ups and downs, but they remained an important factor in Nara politics. Toward the end of the period, the opposition to the powerful priest sponsored by Kōken/Shōtoku was led by a Fujiwara. The Fujiwara house grew to the point that it divided into four main branches. One of these (the "Northern," or Hokke) gained great power in the Heian Period.

Intermarriage with the imperial family was a key to Fujiwara power. In 858 Fujiwara Yoshifusa (804–872), head of the Council of State since 857, placed his eight-year-old grandson on the throne and assumed the title of regent for a minor (*sesshō*). This was the first time anyone outside the imperial family had filled this position. Yoshifusa was succeeded by his nephew Mototsune (836–891), who was the first to continue as regent even after the emperor was no longer a minor, assuming for that purpose the new title of *kanpaku*, designating a regent for an adult emperor. This meant a claim to rule on behalf of the emperor as a general prerogative, not just as a temporary measure awaiting his majority. It was as regents that the Fujiwara institutionalized their power.

The ambitions of this house did not go uncontested. After Mototsune died in 891, there was an interlude without a Fujiwara regent until Tadahira (*sesshō*, 939–941; *kanpaku*, 941–949) resumed the tradition. The most famous of the opponents of the Fujiwara was Sugawara no Michizane (845–903). A noted scholar of Chinese studies and a poet, he enjoyed great influence for a time but eventually could not withstand the Fujiwara political machinations or avoid being posted to Kyushu, a form of exile. There he died, but his ghost reputedly returned to punish his enemies, leading to a brilliant posthumous career. To put an end to a series of storms, floods, droughts, fires, and other calamities attributed to his angry spirit, he was promoted several times and finally became the patron god of letters and calligraphy, worshipped at shrines erected in his honor in the capital and elsewhere. His poetry, too, lived on, including the following composed in exile in 902:

> *The Lamp Goes Out*
> It was not the wind—the oil is gone;
> I hate the lamp that will not see me through the night.
> How hard—to make ashes of the mind, to still the body!
> I rise and move into the moonlight by the cold window.[1]

Michizane died the next year, but the light of his poetry continued to shine.

Other rivals of the Fujiwara were considerably less successful, and from 967 on the tradition of Fujiwara regents continued without interruption. A high point in Fujiwara power was reached under Michinaga (966–1027), who demonstrated great skill in the intrigue and political infighting necessary to succeed at court. He was especially skilled at marriage politics; he managed to marry four daughters to emperors, two of whom were also his grandsons. Emperors who were the sons of Fujiwara mothers and married to Fujiwara consorts were unlikely to resent the influence of the great family, let alone to resist it. Michinaga felt so secure that, although he briefly became a *sesshō*, he never assumed the title of *kanpaku*, preferring the reality to the trappings of power. His successors, however, resumed the title and continued to derive legitimacy and prestige from their close association with the imperial family. In the meantime, as the emperor's political power waned, his sacerdotal role grew even more important. Indeed, the ritual and ceremonial demands on the throne were so great that when the imperial family reasserted its power in the eleventh century, the lead was taken by abdicated emperors who, by resigning, had freed themselves from the burdensome routine of official observances.

The importance of marriage politics and control of the emperor should not be underestimated, but lasting political power usually is linked to some kind of economic power, and Heian Japan is no exception. In their heyday the Fujiwara were the wealthiest family in the land; their mansions outshone the imperial palace. To understand the source and nature of their wealth, it is necessary to examine changes in Japan's basic economic institutions, changes that had their origins in the Nara Period but reached their fruition in Heian times. At the heart of these changes was the development of estates (*shōen*).

## The Estates

The estates or *shōen*\* were private landholdings essentially outside government control. Even after Japan officially adopted the Chinese "equal field" system, certain lands were exempt: (1) those held by the imperial family and certain aristocratic families, (2) those granted to great temples and shrines, and (3) newly developed fields, which after 743 could be retained in perpetuity. Furthermore, there was a natural tendency for all land assignments to become hereditary. This was true of lands assigned to accompany certain ranks and offices and of lands assigned to cultivators. It is unclear to what extent the system of public ownership and distribution of land was carried out, but the period from the mid-eighth century onward was marked by an increase in the amount of land officially declared private. Historians disagree about the reasons this happened. Some see the complicated system of land redistribution as unsuited to Japanese conditions; others attribute it to failure to adjust to economic growth; and still others, on the contrary, view it as a response to decline brought on by recurrent epidemics.

Whatever its causes, the growth of estates did not mean the sudden disappearance of public lands: despite the reduction in the areas so designated, state-

---

\* To reduce the proliferation of technical terms, we will call them estates but ask the reader to keep in mind that there was nothing quite like them in Western history.

administered land remained economically and politically important until well after the end of the Heian Period. However, the development of private landholdings was accompanied by a growth of tax exemptions granted to influential aristocrats and temples. In time, these tax exemptions were broadened to include other privileges, such as immunity from inspection or interference by local provincial government officials, who were thus deprived of administrative authority over the estates. In many cases, they could not even enter them.

Landholdings of this type first appeared in the eighth century and grew thereafter largely by a process of commendation. Small landholders placed their fields under the protection of those powerful enough to enjoy tax exemption and immunities. Thus, a small, relatively powerless local landholder might assign his land to a richer and more influential family or religious institution, retaining the right to cultivate the land in exchange for a small rent, less than he would have had to pay to the tax collector. In this way, he secured an economic advantage and received protection from the exactions and pressures of the local officials. The new proprietor might in turn commend the land to one of the truly powerful houses, such as the Fujiwara, with high status at the capital. To obtain their protection, he would in turn cede certain rights.

Furthermore, because the proprietor was usually an absent landlord living in the capital area, he required the services of administrators, and these men received certain rights to income from the land. These rights, called *shiki*, entitled the bearer to a certain portion or percentage of the income from the land and could be divided, passed on to heirs, or even sold without affecting the integrity of the estate. As a result, the system became complicated: one man might hold different kinds of rights in one estate, hold rights in several estates, or both. Women, too, could hold these rights, and the most fortunate were able to enjoy an independent source of income not unlike the modern owners of stocks and bonds.

It was a complicated system, but essentially four levels of people were associated with an individual estate in what Elizabeth Sato characterizes as a "hierarchy of tenures." At the bottom of the scale were the cultivators (*shōmin*). Above them were the resident managers known variously as local lords or proprietors (*ryōshu*), members of influential families resident in the estate (*shōke*), or estate officials (*shōkan*). Still another step up were the central proprietors (*ryōke*), and at the top of the ladder were the patrons (*honke*), who frequently lived in the capital, as did many *ryōke*.[2]

## Government and Administration

The steady growth of large holdings outside government jurisdiction continued despite sporadic government efforts to halt the process by decree, because those profiting from the estates controlled the government. As a result, by the twelfth century more than half of Japan's rice land was incorporated into estates, and the government was faced with a decrease in revenue and a decline in power.

The rise of the estate system can be seen as a kind of privatization. Similarly, provincial governors gained a great deal of autonomy in collecting taxes on the remaining publicly administered land (*kokugaryō*) under their jurisdiction. Originally dispatched as government administrators, they became virtual tax farmers, responsible for supplying a fixed amount annually for the entire province and allowed to keep whatever they could collect above that amount. Consequently, many governors became wealthy, and a class of current, former, and potential provincial governors formed a new noble elite. Ironically, many female authors whose accounts of life in the capital are masterpieces of Heian literature were from this class, and thus depended economically on the very hinterlands they despised as remote and bumpkin-ridden.

The capital remained the arena in which the great families competed for status and its benefits, and there were still officials who took their duties seriously. However, public offices gradually became the hereditary prerogatives of particular noble kinship groups, which treated them as their own possessions. The deterioration of the machinery of governance by the mid-Heian Period undermined even basic institutions for maintaining order. Pedigree, not ability, determined who was appointed chief of the Imperial Police. Established in the early ninth-century reassertion of imperial authority, in its heyday the Imperial Police exercised wide powers in the capital and even in the provinces. It was the only official source of armed support for the throne. But by the time of Michinaga, it lacked the strength even to secure the capital against internal disruptions and disorders. Already in 981, unruly priests from the great monastery on nearby Mt. Hiei encountered no effective resistance as they marched through the streets of the capital to press their demands. In 1040 robbers found their way into the imperial palace and made off with some of the emperor's clothes!

Clearly, government was no longer functioning as it had in Nara or during the period of vigorous imperial rule in Early Heian. The period of Fujiwara ascendancy has been considered a time of deterioration in government, a view consistent with economic growth produced by opening new lands, because not only in Japan have old political institutions often been undermined by economic development (nor is there any necessary correlation between political centralization and economic growth). However, to focus on the decline of certain institutions of the imperial government may blur the part played by nonofficial but legal institutions in the de facto government, now largely privatized.

What affected the lives of people on the estates were, mostly, not the decisions reached at court but rather those made by the aristocratic families or temples that served as the estate's patrons and by the administrators and overseers who supervised things on a daily basis and reported to the patrons. To administer their estate holdings and, for aristocratic families, their household affairs, these patrons had a *mandokoro* or, as translated by G. Cameron Hurst, an "administrative council." Hurst describes the Fujiwara administrative council as consisting of the following:

A documents bureau (*fudono*) "for handling complaints and other types of correspondence"

A secretariat (*kurōdo-dokoro*)

A retainer's office (*samurai-dokoro*) "to coordinate the activities of the warriors in the service of the household"

A stable (*mimaya*)

An attendant's bureau (*zushin-dokoro*) "to control the attendants allotted by the court to high-ranking nobles"

An office of court dress (*gofuku-dokoro*)

A provisions bureau (*shinmotsu-dokoro*), which "handled the receipt and storage of rice and other grains, vegetables, fish, and other foods for the household's meals"

A cook's bureau (*zen-bu*) "in charge of the actual preparation of food"

There was also a judicial office (*monchūjo*) for administering justice in those estates where this right belonged to the patron.[3]

# The Warriors

Heian aristocrats were civilians who preferred intrigue to war and often displayed a marked disdain for the military. However, no society seems able to dispense with military force entirely. Before the introduction of conscription and peasant armies, most fighting had been done by trained warriors affiliated with particular kinship groups. This class of fighters never disappeared. As less and less land was administered under the "equal field" system, raising conscript armies became less and less practical. In 792, two years before the move to Kyoto, the conscription system was abolished. The central government no longer had the means to raise armies—except as the emperor or his ministers raised fighting men in their own domains—and military power and responsibilities passed to provincial government officials and great families.

Because fighting involved costly equipment, such as horse and armor, and training in special techniques, such as archery and swordsmanship, it remained the profession of a rural elite established in both the political and the estate system. Some warrior leaders were originally provincial officials to whom the government had delegated military responsibilities. Others, rising within the estate system, were entrusted with defense responsibilities on the estates. The pace of the development of local warrior organizations and their size varied according to local conditions. They were especially prominent in the eastern part of the Kanto region, still a rough frontier area, where formidable warrior leagues grew and clashed.

It was fighting men of this type who kept order in the provinces, performing police and military functions and fighting for various patrons as they jockeyed for power. For example, such warrior organizations fought on both sides during a rebellion led in 935 by Taira no Masakado, a fifth-generation descendant of Emperor Kanmu. The practice was to keep the size of the imperial family within reasonable limits by cutting off collateral branches after a given number of generations. At that time, they were given a family name and endowed with rich official posts in the capital or the provinces where their prestige, wealth, and political connections were great assets in attracting local warrior followers. Two of the greatest warrior associations were grouped around leaders who claimed such imperial antecedents: the Minamoto (also called Genji) and the Taira (or Heike). The Masakado Rebellion was put down only with great difficulty. Concurrently, there was trouble in the west: Fujiwara no Sumitomo (d. 941) had been sent to suppress piracy on the Inland Sea but instead turned outlaw himself. In the restoration of order, Minamoto no Tsunemoto (d. 961) played a leading role. Tsunemoto's son established an alliance between the Seiwa branch of the Minamoto (or Seiwa Genji) and the Fujiwara house.

During the eleventh century there was more fighting in the Kanto area, with wars from 1028 to 1031, smaller-scale fighting between 1051 and 1062, and another war from 1083 to 1087. These wars provided opportunities for building the strength of local warrior houses and of the Minamoto and Taira leagues. Although both leagues had adherents throughout the country, the Minamoto strength was centered in eastern and northern Honshu and the Taira developed a power base in the Inland Sea and capital areas.

Also in the second half of the eleventh century, the Fujiwara hold on the reins of power at court was challenged when a shortage of daughters hampered their marriage politics. Emperor Go-Sanjō (r. 1068–1072) came to the throne because his brother's Fujiwara empress was childless. Although he was opposed by the Fujiwara regent, he enjoyed the crucial support of another powerful Fujiwara noble. His success was to have far-reaching consequences for court politics.

## Rule by Retired Emperors

This revival of the imperial family begun by Go-Sanjō was continued by his son Shirakawa, who became emperor in 1072. He abdicated in 1086 but continued to exercise great power as retired emperor (*in*) until his death in 1129. Two more vigorous heads of the imperial line followed, Toba (r. 1107–1123; retired emperor, 1129–1156) and Go-Shirakawa (r. 1155–1158; retired emperor until 1192). The position of the retired emperor resembled that of the Fujiwara regent, with the emperor's paternal family replacing his maternal line. Like the Fujiwara and despite the ambivalence of Shirakawa, the general policy of the abdicated emperors was to acquire for the imperial family the same type of assets enjoyed by the Fujiwara. As a result, the imperial house built a vast network of estates and was transformed into the country's largest landholder.

The political situation at this time could and did become complicated when there was more than one retired emperor on the scene. The ambitions and machinations of the courts, the Fujiwara, and the great temples (which had their own armed forces) contributed to political instability complicating the politics and the life of the capital. These complexities and instability provided an opening for the ambitions of the provincial warrior organizations serving the imperial and the Fujiwara families.

The retired emperor system came to an end under Go-Shirakawa. In 1156 military power was, for the first time, directly involved in capital political disputes; once the warriors had been called in, they could not readily be dismissed. Despite the rise of the warriors, however, for another 700 years (until 1869), the imperial family and the Fujiwara remained in Kyoto, and the Fujiwara provided the regents. Indeed, the Fujiwara house grew so large that men came to be called by the names of their branch families, and even in the twentieth century a member of one of these Fujiwara branches (Konoe) became a prime minister.

# Heian Buddhism: Tendai

When Emperor Kanmu turned his back on Nara and moved his capital at the end of the eighth century, he curtailed the political power of the old schools, but Buddhism continued to grow and flourish. It also continued to enjoy imperial patronage. Kanmu himself supported the priest Saichō (767–822) who, dissatisfied with the worldliness of the Nara priesthood, had founded a small temple in 788 on Mt. Hiei northeast of Kyoto. In 804 Saichō traveled to China to advance his understanding of the faith, surely not unaware that Chinese sanction was a must for his temple to gain the high prestige enjoyed by the Nara temples. The trip also enhanced his standing at the court, with which he maintained a close relationship throughout his life.

Saichō originally moved to Mt. Hiei to escape the corrupt atmosphere of Nara, not because he disagreed with the teachings of Nara Buddhism. However, in China he studied Tendai (Tiantai) doctrines (see Chapter 5). On his return from China, Saichō established Tendai in Japan, thereby removing himself both doctrinally and geographically from the Nara temples. The latter resented him bitterly, and when Emperor Kanmu died they fought back with some temporary success, such as when they disputed the new school's right to ordain priests, a right not granted to the Tendai temple on Mt. Hiei until 827, by which time Saichō was dead. The doctrinal content of Saichō's Tendai, like that of its Chinese parent, was grounded in the Lotus Sutra. In contrast to the proponents of some of the older schools, Saichō preached the universal possibility of enlightenment. Everyone could realize his Buddha nature through a life of true religious devotion. On Mt. Hiei, Saichō insisted on strict monastic regimen.

Saichō was more skilled as an organizer than as a theoretician. He laid solid foundations for the subsequent expansion of what he had built, and eventually his little temple grew to a vast complex of some 3000 buildings. It flourished on Mt. Hiei until it was destroyed in the sixteenth century for political reasons. In keeping with the syncretic nature of Tendai, the Buddhism propagated on Mt. Hiei was broad and accommodating, so much so that it remained the source of new developments in Japanese Buddhism even after the temple community had departed from the earnest religiosity of its founder.

After Saichō's death, a line of abbots succeeded him, among them Ennin, the famous traveler to China, whose diary is a major source of information about the Tang. Then late in the ninth century there developed a split between the followers of Ennin and those of his successor. This bitter rivalry, fueled as much by jealousy as by doctrinal differences, led to the introduction of force into religious politics and the appearance of temple militias ("evil monks," or *akusō*) who engaged in brawls and combat. The use of violence increased, and by the eleventh century leading shrines and temples maintained large standing armies. Particularly troublesome was the monastery of Mt. Hiei, which kept several thousand troops. They repeatedly descended on the capital, terrorizing its inhabitants, to demand ecclesiastical positions, titles, and land rights. Ironically, the temple on Mt. Hiei, which was located on a mountain to the northeast partly to protect the capital from supernatural forces thought to approach from that direction, became in the Late Heian Period a major source of disturbances.

## Esoteric Buddhism: Shingon

Contemporary with Saichō was Kūkai (774–835), founder of the other major school of Heian Buddhism, Shingon. He, too, studied in China and benefited from imperial patronage, although in his case it came not from Emperor Kanmu but from that emperor's successors. Like Saichō, he established his main monastery on a mountain, choosing Mt. Kōya on the Kii Peninsula, far removed from the capital. When Kukai returned from China, Saichō befriended him and showed interest in the doctrines Kūkai brought back, but this cordial relationship did not last. A year after Saichō's death, Kukai moved closer to the center when he was appointed abbot of Tōji, the great temple at the main (southern) gateway to the capital.

In contrast to Tendai, which flourished in China as it did in Japan, the type of Buddhism introduced by Kūkai was never prominent in China and failed to survive the mid-Tang persecution of Buddhism. Shingon (*mantra*, in the original Sanskrit; *zhenyan*, in Chinese) literally means "true word," thus conveying the importance of mystic verbal formulae in this school and its insistence on a tradition of oral transmission of secret teachings from master to disciple. Because only the initiated were privy to the full truth, it is known as esoteric Buddhism. Transmitted in addition to the sacred teachings and verbal utterances were complicated ritual observances involving the mudra (hand positions of the Buddha but also used by Shingon priests) and the use of ritual instruments.

Central to Shingon teachings and observances is Dainichi (Vairocana), the cosmic Buddha whose absolute truth is all encompassing and true everywhere and forever. In his *Ten Stages of Religious Consciousness*, Kūkai ranked the various levels of spiritual life. At the lowest level he placed animal life, lacking spiritual dimension. Confucianism he ranked as only the second step upward, with Daoism third. Then came various schools of Theravada and Mahayana Buddhism, including Tendai (eighth). At the top he placed Shingon. In this way, Shingon incorporated and found a place for other schools of Buddhism, although the Tendai monks were hardly pleased with their place in the Shingon hierarchy. No explicit provision was made in this schema for local gods, but the name Dainichi (Great Sun) invited identification with the Sun Goddess claimed as ancestress by the imperial family, and Shingon proved hospitable to local deities through its concept of duality. This concept held that a single truth manifests itself under two aspects, the noumenal and the phenomenal, so Dainichi and the Sun Goddess could be considered as two forms of one identical truth.

The teachings of esoteric Buddhism were complex and difficult to understand, yet it was enormously popular during the Heian Period, even overshadowing Tendai until Ennin introduced esoteric practices into Tendai. One reason for the appeal of Shingon was the mystery of its rites. From the beginning, people in Japan had been drawn to Buddhism at least partly by the magical elements connected with Buddhist observances such as incantations, divination, exorcism, and medicinal use of herbs. Now they were impressed by the mysterious elements in the secret rituals performed in the interior of Shingon temples, hidden from all but the most deeply initiated of the priests. The elites of Heian Japan, with their taste for pageantry, were also attracted by the richness of the colorful Shingon rites.

Much of the prosperity of Shingon can be attributed to the genius of Kūkai (also known by his posthumous name Kōbō Daishi, or Great Teacher Kōbō). He was an exceptional man, famed for his brilliance and learning, his artistic talents, and his calligraphy. He is so associated with writing that later hagiographers even credited him with the invention of the *kana* syllabary that developed during the Early Heian Period. Kūkai is also credited with the introduction of tea to Japan and the building of bridges, and a cluster of miraculous stories grew up around his name. To this day, he lies in his grave on Mt. Kōya awaiting the coming of Maitreya (see Figure 7.1). One of Kūkai's most lasting contributions to Shingon, and a major source of its appeal, was his emphasis on the arts. A gifted artist himself, he saw art as the ideal vehicle for transmitting religious truth. Unlike Tendai, Shingon did not give birth to many new schools of Buddhist thought, but it did leave a rich artistic heritage.

# Pietism

Later in the Heian Period, revulsion at the worldly (and military) success of the established temples, and hope of rescuing a world falling into increasing disorder, stimulated a pietistic movement. This movement was initiated by the priests Kūya (903–972) and Genshin (942–1017) and centered around Amida (Amitabha, the Buddha of the Infinite Light, who presides over the Western

**FIGURE 7.1** Mt. Kōya, Wakayama. The path, almost two kilometers long, leading through a deep forest to Kūkai's resting place is lined with the tombstones, some grand and some humble, of those who will attain salvation when Kūkai rises up to meet Maitreya. (© Lore Schirokauer)

Paradise). So disrupted was Japanese society that many people were convinced they were about to enter the last of the three Buddhist ages (*mappō*), the degenerate age of the decline of the Buddha's law. The pietists taught that only faith in Amida could provide salvation in such dire times, and a famous statue of Kūya shows him with little Amidas issuing from his mouth, symbolizing the power of chanted incantations calling on that Buddha (see Figure 11.2). In a spirit of evangelical zeal, he traveled throughout the countryside, bringing people his message of Buddhist salvation and leading them in dancing and chanting the name of Amida.

It is characteristic of the Heian Period that Genshin's teachings were propagated not only in writing but also in art. His work contains terrifying depictions of hell that inspired lurid scrolls illustrating all manner of posthumous torment, and he is associated with a genre of painting depicting *raigō*, that is, a descent by Amida mercifully coming down to a man's deathbed to gather his soul to paradise. One custom among the devout was for a dying person to hold a string attached to the figure of Amida in such a painting. For example, when Michinaga, the strong-minded Fujiwara who was de facto ruler of Japan, lay dying, he repeated the *nenbutsu,* an invocation to Amida, holding such a cord, while a chorus of monks chanted the Lotus Sutra. This practice became as widespread as the *raigō* depictions themselves.

Another deity worthy of mention is Jizō, who began as the bodhisattva who saves souls in hell but became popular as the embodiment of Amida's compassion. Eventually he merged with other gods, until in time he came to be regarded as the protector of children who had died young. He still graces many a roadside shrine in Japan today.

Amidism continued to attract an increasing following and devoted apostles such as Ryōnin (1072–1132), a Tendai monk who placed additional emphasis on the *nembutsu.* As the Heian Period neared its end, the veneration of Amida and the use of the *nembutsu* spread far and wide through existing temples, but eventually the new religious force established new schools in their own right. The break came when Hōnen (1133–1212) established Pure Land Buddhism as an independent school in the Kamakura era.

# A World Permeated by Religion

No society is composed entirely of the devout—certainly not that of Heian Japan! The degree of piety felt by those who attended religious observances ranged widely. The diarist and essayist Sei Shōnagon famously recorded her belief that a priest should be handsome so that the audience will have no inducement to divert their eyes and thoughts. Frequently, then as now, a visit to a temple was primarily a pleasure trip. On the other hand, in the daily lives of all classes, religion and magic were inextricably interwoven with elements of Buddhism, yin-and-yang theory, geomancy, worship of local deities or *kami,* and popular beliefs of all kinds. (Geomancy, *feng shui* in Chinese, is the Chinese practice of selecting sites for graves, buildings, or cities according to the topographic configuration of yin and yang.) The inhabitants of the capital were forever purifying themselves; they studiously avoided traveling in certain directions on days for which this was inauspicious or even dangerous, and when ill they sought the services of a priest skilled in exorcism. The monastery on Mt. Hiei provides a good example of this fusion of beliefs. Before building his temple northeast of the capital to guard the city against the evils that, according to Chinese beliefs, emanate from that direction, Saicho was careful to pay his respect to the local *kami.*

Alongside and sometimes within the grounds of Buddhist temples were shrines for the worship of *kami.* The deities, the accounts of their origins and activities, and the observances performed in their honor constituted a complex mixture of indigenous and imported elements and provided the sources for the myths showcased in the *Kojiki* and *Nihon shoki,* as well as the foundation for the state-supported shrine system. From the eighth century onward, and increasingly during the Heian Period, aspects of *kami* worship were combined with new and old Buddhist doctrines and deities into new configurations of ritual practice, sacred space, and systems of thought, all strongly influenced by esoteric Buddhism. The development of various mixtures of local deities and Buddhist concepts and practices as worked out by Heian Period thinkers eventually led to the emergence of a Shinto tradition that, ironically, claimed purely local roots. To quote Mark Teeuwen, "it was this *kami* thought and practice, pioneered by monks of the esoteric Buddhist sects, that opened the way for the *kami* cults to develop into something that may be meaningfully referred to as Shinto: a religious tradition that consciously and explicitly defined itself as non-Buddhist and self-contained."[4]

# Literature

The Heian Period is celebrated for a literary efflorescence that produced works at the core of the canon of classical Japanese literature. Many of the authors were women writing in the vernacular, but Chinese-style poetry and prose, although under-represented in translations and scholarship, remained of central importance, revealing dimensions of aesthetic, social, and political life not available elsewhere. This is partly because male courtiers wrote detailed diaries in Chinese-style prose but also because it provided a medium for essays and poetry dealing with topics and settings largely ignored in vernacular works.

Michizane's complaint about his lamp was one of his hundreds of Chinese-style compositions, ranging from descriptions of elegant banquets to vivid portrayals of the suffering poor and including long autobiographical accounts. For a taste of Heian prose and urban life, we turn to "Record of the Pond Pavilion," by Yoshishige no Yasutane (d. 1002), which extols the virtues of the house and garden the author constructed late in life. But he begins by describing city life in general:

> In the eastern sector of the capital . . . there are huge crowds of people living, eminent and lowly alike. Towering mansions are lined up gate by gate, hall in sight of hall; little huts have only a wall between them, eaves all but touching. If a neighbor to the east suffers a fire, neighbors to the west seldom escape being burned out; if robbers attack the house to the south, the house to the north can't avoid the shower of stray arrows . . . And how much the worse when some great mansion is first built and then begins bit by bit to broaden its gates and doors, swallowing up the little huts all around. Then how many of the poor people have occasion to complain, like sons forced to leave the land of their father and mother, like officials of paradise banished to the dusty world of men.[5]

Chinese style poetry and prose remained central, but literature in the vernacular was also much appreciated. Thousands of poems in the vernacular (*waka*) had already been included in the *Man'yōshū,* but such poems now received official recognition in the *Kokinshū* (short for *Kokin wakashū, Collection of Ancient and Modern Poetry).* This was an imperially sponsored anthology that showcased work by Early Heian court poets and was the first of twenty-one imperial anthologies of *waka* compiled over the next five centuries.

As the inaugurator of this tradition, the *Kokinshū* had a shaping influence, dictating standards of taste, imagery, rhetoric, and even vocabulary. Its compilers not only considered the quality of the works that they included but also took pains in the arrangement and juxtaposition of poems in the anthology to create an overall aesthetic experience for the reader that framed and simultaneously transcended the individual short poems. Similarly, the prefaces of the *Kokinshū* set forth a vision of poetry that resounded through the ages:

> Japanese poetry has the human heart as seed and myriads of words as leaves. It comes into being when men use the seen and the heard to give voice to feelings aroused by the innumerable events in their lives. The song of the warbler among the blossoms, the voice of the frog dwelling in the water—these teach us that every living creature sings. It is song that moves heaven and earth without effort, stirs emotions in the invisible spirits and gods, brings harmony to the relations between men and women, and calms the hearts of fierce warriors.[6]

The beauty of the passing seasons and the vicissitudes of love as it moves from infatuation to all-too-brief fruition and ends in embittered separation are the themes that dominate *waka.* Typical of the former is the following poem by Ki no Tsurayuki (d. c. 945), one of the compilers of the *Kokinshū* and a founder of its characteristic style:

> Ah, the autumn moon—
> shining forth with such brilliance
> that I can make out
> the shapes of the crimson leaves
> as they fall to earth.[7]

For verse that "softens the relations between men and women" we turn to Ono no Komachi, a mid-ninth-century woman who was renowned as a passionate poet of love and who later became the subject of a range of legends and anecdotes—some celebratory, others disapprovingly moralizing. In the following she takes up the common theme of lonely lovers reunited, fleetingly, in a dream:

> Did you come to me
> because I dropped off to sleep,
> tormented by love?
> If I had known I dreamed,
> I would not have awakened.[8]

Literary diaries blending prose and verse, life and art, offer rich insights into the lives and thoughts of the elite women and men who wrote and are depicted in them. Many prose passages in these diaries provide settings for the poetry exchanges that give them sparkle. Other personal prose narratives are more concerned with describing the everyday life and opinions of the writer. The most famous of these is the *Pillow Book* of Sei Shōnagon (fl. late tenth–early eleventh century), which is filled with lush depictions of court life and delightfully snide commentaries on contemporary manners and taste.

A classic of the first half of the Heian Period valued for its prose and poetry was the *Tales of Ise,* which tell of the ninth-century poet, Ariwara no Narihira, famous for romantic and literary exploits. The following passage finds Narihira and some friends boarding a rustic ferry to cross a river in remote eastern Japan, far from the capital, the undisputed center of the world for Heian elites:

> They embarked in wretched spirits, for not a soul among them but had left someone dear to him in the capital.
>
> A white bird about as big as a snipe, with a red bill and red legs, was idling on the water, eating a fish. Its like was not to be seen in the capital, and nobody could say what it was. When they consulted the ferryman, he answered, "Why, that's a capital-bird, of course." Someone composed this poem:
>
> If you are in truth
> What your name would tell us,
> let me ask you,
> capital-bird, about the health
> of the one for whom I yearn.
>
> Everyone in the boat shed tears.[9]

In addition to suggesting the Heian elite's sense of geography, this passage exemplifies the sentimentality and the humor of this scintillating collection.

As new forms of vernacular literature developed, the scripts used to write them also changed dramatically. Earlier, it had been possible to write in Japanese by using Chinese characters to write words, syllables, or a combination of the two. As the syllabic use of characters increased, they were gradually abbreviated and simplified, eventually resulting in new syllabaries distinctive from Chinese graphs (see Figure 7.2). Many texts continued to be written entirely or partially with characters, but the development of the new scripts allowed innovative forms of calligraphy and eventually helped promote the spread of new forms of literacy.

Women are strongly associated with texts written in the cursive syllabary (the modern *hiragana* script), but men also wrote in it, and elite women had more access to and understanding of writing in Chinese characters than they are often given credit for. The visual and stylistic variety of Heian Period writing does not map neatly onto divides between languages or genders, but it provided a rich repertoire of expressive strategies and techniques for Heian and later writers. And many of the most gifted of those writers were female.

FIGURE 7.2 Development of *kana* syllabary. The top row contains Chinese characters, and the bottom row shows the *kana* into which they eventually developed. Reading from right to left, the *kana* are pronounced *chi, ri, ri, ni, ho,* and *ho.* In the bottom row, all except the third (from the right) and the last are *hiragana,* the most commonly used form; the third and last illustrate *katakana,* the form now primarily used for foreign terms and emphasis. (Calligraphy by Dr. Léon L. Y. Chang)

The crown jewel of Heian literature is the *Tale of Genji,* a long fictional narrative by Murasaki Shikibu (fl. late tenth–early eleventh century), a court lady who served an empress who was one of Michinaga's daughters. The influence of this masterpiece on Japanese culture was enormous and varied. References to *Genji* echo throughout Japanese literary history down to the present. Motoori Norinaga (1730–1801), who became its most influential interpreter, admired it most of all for its expression of *mono-no-aware,* a word that defies translation but has been characterized as "that power inherent in things to make us respond not intellectually but with a gasp of emotion."[10] To make this classic accessible to a modern audience, it has been translated into modern Japanese by such outstanding novelists as Tanizaki Junichiro (1886–1965) and Enchi Fumiko (1905–1986). It has also provided subject matter for the arts (see Figure 7.7 later in the chapter) and left its mark on the writing of history.

In *Genji,* Lady Murasaki tells the story of the peerless Genji, the son of an emperor and a low-ranking—and short-lived—consort. He is made a commoner by virtue of a lack of powerful maternal relatives and is thus unable to inherit the throne, but with his intelligence, sensitivity, poetic and musical talent, and charisma he is the undisputed center of court society. The *Tale of Genji* traces his many affairs, his involvement in political intrigues, and the tragic consequences of his moral failings; after his death about three-quarters of the way through, the narrative continues with the darker story of his children and grandchildren's generations. In addition to providing a panorama of the world of the Heian elites, replete with poetry, dance, musical performance, and all manner of pageantry, Murasaki's masterpiece demonstrates a delicate but uncompromising understanding of human behavior and emotions. To quote Royall Tyler, her most recent English-language translator:

The narrative is not extensively descriptive, but the telling touches it provides are just those that nourish a living image in the mind. Many people over the centuries have taken it for a record of life itself in its own time. The experience of reading it resembles that of looking through a small but very clear window into a complete and spacious world.[11]

Late Heian vernacular tales also provide a window into another world, or at least into other realms of the world of the *Genji*. Some collections emerge from Buddhist contexts, motivated partly by preachers gathering material for sermons, but they soon came to include material simply because it was striking, funny, or scurrilous. The greatest of these collections, the early twelfth-century *Tales of Times Now Past*, contains over a thousand Buddhist and secular stories of India, China, and Japan. In its unrelentingly entertaining pages, the reader can encounter such memorable characters as a priest with a huge red nose who goes to absurd lengths to shrink it, a high-ranking court official with an irrational fear of cats, and a group of fishermen who aid a giant snake in a battle with an evil centipede.

## Life of the Heian Aristocracy

Heian literature, with its detailed and varied accounts by elite men and women, is a rich source for the daily life of the upper classes, their values, and their tastes. The literary eminence of Heian ladies itself suggests something of their social status. They had ample leisure for reading and writing; the *Tale of Genji* is twice as long as Leo Tolstoy's *War and Peace*. Often, it seemed, they even suffered from an excess of leisure, becoming bored with long days of inactivity spent in the dimly lit interiors of their homes and welcoming the chance to exchange pleasantries and gossip with an occasional caller. If the caller was a man, he had to conduct the visit seated in front of a screen behind which the lady remained demurely hidden. Fortunately, there were numerous festivals to break the monotony of the daily routine, and pilgrimages to temples provided further diversion.

The world described in Heian literature is a small one, because it concerns only the tiny fraction of people at the pinnacle of society in the capital. Although there are descriptions of travel outside the capital area, the focus is on the capital itself. A provincial appointment, lucrative though it might be, was regarded as tantamount to exile. The provinces were viewed as an uncultured hinterland where even the governing classes were hopelessly vulgar. To these aristocratic ladies, the common people whose labor made society possible were so far removed in manners and appearance as to resemble the inhabitants of another world. At best, they seemed uncouth. At worst, they were regarded as not fully human, such as when Sei Shōnagon encountered a group of commoners on a pilgrimage and noted, "They looked like so many basket-worms as they crowded together in their hideous clothes, leaving hardly an inch of space between themselves and me. I really felt like pushing them all over sideways."[12]

Geographically limited and constricted in social scope, the Heian aristocracy was also less concerned than their predecessors with the rest of East Asia. The last official Heian government mission to China was sent in 838. When near the end of the ninth century it was proposed to send another and Sugawara no Michizane was chosen as ambassador, he successfully declined on the grounds that conditions in China were unsettled. Even after order had been restored in China with the establishment of the Song (960–1279), official relations were not resumed. Even so, travel by priests and merchants continued, and the elites of the Heian capital were fascinated by valuable imported luxury goods from abroad.

In Heian court society, elite men and women developed keen sensitivity to beauty and subtle refinement in conduct. The perfect gentleman embodied by Murasaki's Genji is a fictional ideal rather than a real-life portrait, but it suggests the extent to which life and art could be fused through the cultivation of human sensibilities. In this world, where aesthetics reigned supreme, great attention was paid to pleasing the eye. Ladies dressed in numerous robes, one over the other (twelve was standard), which they displayed at the wrist in overlapping layers, and the blending of their colors was of the utmost importance in revealing a lady's taste. Often all a man saw of a lady were her sleeves, left hanging outside her carriage or spread beyond a screen behind which she remained invisible. The men were by no means to be outdone in the care they took over their own attire. The following description is from Sei Shōnagon's *Pillow Book:*

> His resplendent, cherry-colored court cloak was lined with material of the most delightful hue and lustre; he wore dark, grape-colored trousers, boldly splashed with designs of wisteria branches; his crimson under-robe was so glossy that it seemed to sparkle, while underneath one could make out layer upon layer of white and light violet robes.[13]

This concern for appearance extended to the features of the gentlemen and ladies. Both sexes used cosmetics, applying a white face powder, which in the case of the women was combined with a rosy tint. The ladies took great pride in their long, flowing, glossy hair but plucked their eyebrows and painted in a new set. Such customs are not unfamiliar to the modern world, but far more difficult for us to appreciate are the blackened teeth of the refined Heian beauty. Confined to the aristocracy during the Heian Period, this practice, like so many features of Heian taste and sensibility, later spread to the lower classes of society. It became the sign of a married woman and in the Edo Period was adopted by courtesans.

The emphasis on visual beauty did not mean the neglect of the other senses. Musical performances ranging from impromptu solos to marathon sessions involving many musicians played an important part in the lives of the Heian aristocracy, and aural and visual pleasure was often combined in courtly dances. Nor was the sense of smell neglected. The Heian ladies and gentlemen went to great lengths to blend perfumes, and a sensitive nose was a social asset second only to a good eye and ear.

The ideal Heian aristocrat was as sensitive in personal relations as in matters of aesthetics: feelings should be as beautiful as dress. Nowhere was this more important than in the love affairs that gave Heian vernacular literature its dominant theme. Marriages were arranged by and for the family in a game of marriage politics at which the Fujiwara excelled. But for a noble courtier to confine himself to one wife was the rare exception. He was much more likely to have one or more secondary wives and to conduct still other, more or less clandestine, love affairs. Nor were the ladies expected to remain true to one love for their whole lives, although few were as amorous as Ono no Komachi or Izumi Shikibu, another famously gifted poet with a reputation as a great lover. Nevertheless, jealousy posed a recurring problem for a lady of the Heian age, who might have to bear long waits between visits from her lover. For the less fortunate and less hardy, waiting could become a torture.

The qualities most valued in a lover were similar regardless of sex: beauty and grace, talent and sensibility, and personal thoughtfulness. Murasaki's Genji was ever gallant to one lady he had seduced even though he discovered she was unattractive. He found himself in this predicament because Heian men often had no clear idea of the appearance of the women they were wooing, hidden as they were behind screens with only their sleeves showing. Men fell in love with a woman's sense of beauty, her poetic talents, and her calligraphy. As in China, the latter was all-important because it was thought to reveal a person's character. The Heian version of love at first sight was of a gentleman falling hopelessly in love after catching a glimpse of a few beautifully drawn lines.

At every stage of a love affair, and for that matter in other social relationships, the aesthetics of writing were stressed. At least as important as the literary merits of the poems exchanged on all occasions were such matters as the color and texture of the paper, the way it was folded, and the selection of a spray of blossoms on which to tie the note. Most critical and most eagerly awaited of these poetic missives were the "morning-after letters" sent by a lover immediately upon returning home from a night of love, from which he had torn himself away just before dawn with a proper show of reluctance. In this world of sensitive people, men and women were expected to respond as readily to sadness as to joy. As we saw with Narihira and his boat mates, both sexes cried freely and frequently and neither hesitated to express self-pity. Tears were a sign of depth of feeling and of a genuine awareness of the ephemeral nature of beauty, the transient nature of all that is good and beautiful.

## The Visual Arts

For the purposes of art history, the Heian Period is readily divided into two parts. "Early Heian," sometimes called the Kōnin or Jōgan Period, designates roughly the first century in Kyoto (794–897). In architecture, a transformation of taste is

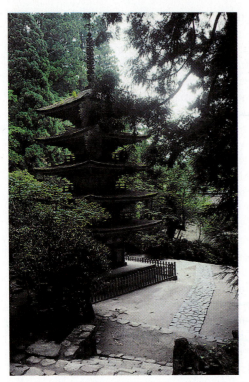

**FIGURE 7.3** Pagoda of Murōji, Nara Prefecture. (© Lore Schirokauer)

apparent in a variety of forms. It is particularly notable in the layout of the new temples, because when Saicho and Kūkai turned from the Nara Plain to build their monasteries in the mountains, they abandoned the symmetric temple plans used around Nara. Down on the plain, architecture could afford to ignore the terrain, but in the mountains, temple styles and layouts had to accommodate themselves to the physical features of the site. On Mt. Hiei and elsewhere, the natural setting, rock outcroppings, and trees became integral parts of the temple, as had long been the case with shrines devoted to *kami*. Even on Mt. Kōya, where there was enough space to build a Nara-style temple complex, the traditional plans were abandoned. Changes were also made in building materials and decoration.

During the Nara Period, the main buildings, following continental practice, had been placed on stone platforms; the wood was painted; and the roofs were made of tile. In the Nara temples, only minor buildings had their wood left unpainted and had been fitted with roofs of thatch or bark shingles. Now, these techniques were also used for the main halls. An excellent site at which to observe the resulting aesthetic is Murōji, a temple set in the mountains some forty miles from Nara among magnificent straight, cedar-like trees (cryptomeria) found on Mt. Kōya and at other locations. Not only in the material but also in the size of its buildings, Murōji is more modest than the Nara temples. Its pagoda (see Figure 7.3) is only half the size of that at Hōryūji but makes up in charm and grace what it lacks in grandeur.

In the Early Heian Period, wood replaced clay, bronze, dry lacquer, and stone as the material of choice for sculpture. Statues, and sometimes their pedestals, were carved from a single block of wood; frequently, the finished sculpture was painted or lacquered. Although some statues of *kami* survive from this period, most Early Heian statuary was Buddhist. Many reflect the demands of the new forms of that religion, particularly esoteric Buddhism. Usually, the statues are formal and symmetric. The flesh is full and firm. The faces are carved in a serious mien, creating an aura of mystery without the hint of a smile or the indication of friendliness. A famous example of Early Heian art is the figure of Sakyamuni (the

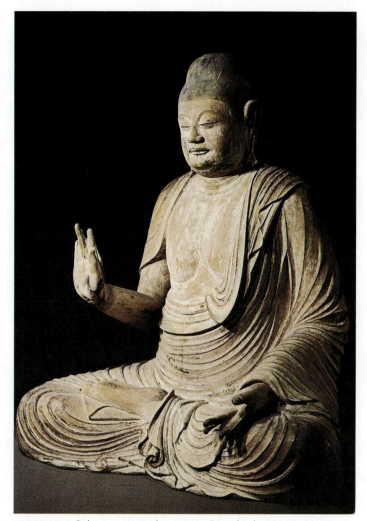

**FIGURE 7.4** Sakyamuni, ninth century, 51 in high. Murōji, Nara Prefecture. It has been suggested that the curious swirls at the bottom may be the result of copying in wood an original calligraphic drawing. (© Murōji Publishers)

historic Buddha) at Murōji (see Figure 7.4). It is, among other things, a fine example of "wave" drapery, so called because its lines flow like the sea. The Shingon school demanded unusual iconographic exactitude in its art, just as it did in its rites. The result was a marked tendency toward formalism, both in reciting the mantras and in creating the religious art. This was especially true of Shingon mandalas, which became complex as artists tried to represent the cosmos graphically,

**FIGURE 7.5** Womb Mandala. Painting on silk, ninth century. Toji, Kyoto.
(© Sakamoto Photo Research Laboratory/Corbis)

including all the various deities that were emanations of Dainichi. Some altars, for example, at Tōji in Kyoto, were arranged in mandala fashion, but more usual were painted mandalas, such as that shown in Figure 7.5.

This is a depiction of the Womb Mandala, representing the world of phenomena. The red lotus at the center symbolizes the heart of the universe. Dainichi is seated on the seedpod of the lotus. Other Buddhas occupy the petals. Altogether there are 407 deities in the Womb Mandala. Its counterpart, the Diamond Mandala, centers on a white lotus and represents the world containing 1314 gods.

A frequent subject of painting and sculpture is Fudō, the Immovable, a ferocious deity bent on annihilating evil. In the *Red Fudo* at Mt. Kōya (see Figure 7.6), the red of the figure and the flames behind him dominate the color scheme and help create a terrifying atmosphere. In his hand he holds a sword, the handle of which is a thunderbolt (*vajra*), a symbol originating in India as the weapon of the god Indra and in esoteric Buddhism thought to cut through ignorance just as lightning pierces the clouds. A dragon coiled around the blade of the sword adds to the threat. The proportions of the figures and the manner in which the picture fills the space produce a feeling of massiveness characteristic of the art of this age.

Early Heian art at its best achieved a certain majesty, but it has a forbidding quality about it that stands in striking contrast to the sweetness of Late Heian art. Shingon continued to influence the production of art after the ninth century, but much of the distinctive work of the period belonged to Amida—and to the Fujiwara. Michinaga had a great temple built in the capital reproducing Amida's paradise, containing "columns with bases of ivory, roof ridges of red gold, gilded doors, platforms of crystal."[14] This temple and a similar one built by Emperor Shirakawa

**FIGURE 7.6** *Red Fudo.* Color on silk, Early Heian, 51.5 in. Myōin, Mt. Koya, Wakayama. (© Red Fudo, Myooin, Koyasan, Wakayama)

are no longer extant. They have to be reconstructed from texts to give us some idea of what Heian Kyoto looked like.

The historical and artistic origins of such temples go back to Chinese images of the Western Paradise and to its closest terrestrial approximation, the Tang palace garden systematically laid out with its lake and bridges. Similarly, a major feature of the Heian mansion (*shinden*) was a garden with one or two artificial hills, carefully placed trees and bamboo, and a pond in which a tiny island was reached by a bridge. A small stream fed the pond and was used to float wine cups at banquets in the Chinese manner. To the north of the garden were the living quarters: rectangular buildings joined by roofed corridors. Like all Japanese-style buildings, these structures were raised a few feet off the ground, and usually a little stream

**FIGURE 7.7** *Genji Monogatari,* section of hand-scroll. Color on paper, twelfth century, 8.5 in high. Tokugawa Museum, Nagoya. (© The Tokugawa Art Museum)

ran under a part of the mansion. Inside, the floors were of polished wood. Flexibility was provided by sliding paper screens, and shutters could be moved to combine small rooms into a larger one. Several kinds of screens (see Figure 7.7) provided some privacy.

## Painting

Sliding doors in the Heian *shinden* mansion were frequently decorated with land-scapes, such as the picture within a picture in Figure 7.7. In painting, as in the other arts, Heian artists added new styles and genres to those inherited from their Nara Period predecessors. This was not a rejection of continental influences but rather an expansion of possible methods of adapting and responding to them, in some cases in strikingly original ways. Japanese-style paintings (*Yamato-e*) de-picted native, not Chinese, subjects, including views of the Japanese landscape. The greatest of such paintings still extant illustrate the *Tale of Genji*. In the Genji Scroll, unlike some later narrative scrolls, the individual scenes are separated by passages of text.

The scene reproduced in Figure 7.7 shows a lady (upper left) looking at pic-tures while one of her attendants reads aloud the story they illustrate. At the lower left, another lady is having her hair combed. In the foreground is a screen such as was used by a lady when receiving a gentleman caller. In this and similar paint-

**FIGURE 7.8** *Animal Caricatures (Chōjū Giga)*, section of hand-scroll. Attributed to Kakūyu (Toba Sōjō). Late twelfth century, 12 in high. Kozanji, Kyoto. (© Kōzanji, Kyoto)

ings, the roofs are removed to afford a view from above into the rooms. The treatment of human features is conventionalized with what art historians refer to as "straight lines for eyes and hooks for noses." The colors were applied quite thickly to produce a richly decorative effect in keeping with aristocratic taste.

Late in the Heian Period there also appeared scrolls (*emaki*) in which no text interrupted the flow of pictorial narrative. Some represent Buddhist hells, but others display a gift for comic caricature.

**FIGURE 7.9** Cosmetic box. Lacquered wood, Late Heian, 8.86 in× 12 in × 5.12 in. Hōryūji, Nara Prefecture. (© Sakamoto Photo Research Laboratory/Corbis)

Particularly well known are the cartoon-like animal scrolls attributed to Kakūyu (Sōjō, 1053–1140) but probably completed near the end of the twelfth century. Here frog-priests and rabbit-nobles gambol and disport themselves. In Figure 7.8, a monkey chants before an altar supporting not a Buddha but a frog.

The decorative arts also illustrate the taste of the Heian aristocrats. See, for example, the cosmetic box shown in Figure 7.9. It is adorned with cart wheels, made of mother-of-pearl and gold, and half immersed in water. The asymmetry of the design and the unifying flow and rhythm, here supplied by the water, are characteristic of Heian achievements in decoration.

**FIGURE 7.10** Byōdōin (Phoenix Pavilion). Uji, Kyoto prefecture. (© Lore Schirokauer)

# The Phoenix Pavilion

Sometimes a single site offers a summary of a whole era; for Late Heian art this is true of the Phoenix Pavilion (Byōdōin) (see Figure 7.10). It is located in Uji, a locale some ten miles from Kyoto that figures prominently in the *Tale of Genji*. The building is associated with the Fujiwaras: it was built by one of Michinaga's sons. It is dedicated to Amida, who occupied the center of a *raigō* in sculpture. Other versions of the *raigō*, painted on the doors and inner walls, show Amida and his entourage descending onto a Japanese landscape. Mother-of-pearl insets in the main dais and in some of the columns contribute to the overall richness of effect.

Amida himself is the work of the sculptor Jōchō. He is fashioned in the joined-wood technique, which affords greater freedom of expression than the Early Heian process of carving from a single piece of wood. It also allows greater and more varied exploitation of the grain. The halo, alive with angels, clouds, and flames, contrasts with the calm of Amida. As Robert Treat Paine so eloquently expressed it, "the tranquility of the Absolute is made to harmonize with the Buddha's sympathy for the finite."[15]

The design of the buildings suggests a bird coming in for a landing or ready for flight. Two bronze phoenixes grace its highest roof. It may be considered a mansion for the Buddha himself. To assure that Amida, too, will enjoy the beauty of the setting and the lovely sight of his hall reflected in the pond, the architect has thoughtfully provided an opening so that he can look out. Here is another example of the unity of building and site that was such a key feature of Heian architecture.

# *Notes*

1. Burton Watson, trans., *Japanese Literature in Chinese, Vol. 1* (New York: Columbia Univ. Press, 1975), p. 122.

2. Elizabeth Sato, "The Early Development of the Shoen," in John W. Hall and Jeffrey P. Mass, *Medieval Japan: Essays in Institutional History* (New Haven: Yale Univ. Press, 1974), p. 105.

3. G. Cameron Hurst, Jr., "The Structure of the Heian Court," in John W. Hall and Jeffrey P. Mass, *Medieval Japan: Essays in Institutional History* (New Haven: Yale Univ. Press, 1974), p. 52.

4. Mark Teeuwen, "The *Kami* in Esoteric Buddhist Thought and Practice," Chapter 6, in John Breen and Mark Teeuwen, eds., *Shinto in History: Ways of the Kami* (Richmond, Surrey: Curzon, 2000), pp. 96–97.

5. Watson, *Japanese Literature in Chinese,* pp. 58–59.

6. Helen Craig McCullough, trans., *Kokin Wakashū: The First Imperial Anthology of Japanese Poetry* (Stanford: Stanford Univ. Press, 1985), p. 3.

7. Steven Carter, trans., *Traditional Japanese Poetry: An Anthology* (Stanford: Stanford Univ. Press, 1991), pp. 106–07.

8. Carter, *Traditional Japanese Poetry: An Anthology,* p. 84.

9. Helen McCullough, trans., *Classical Japanese Prose: An Anthology* (Stanford: Stanford Univ. Press, 1990), p. 43.

10. David Pollack, *The Fracture of Meaning: Japan's Synthesis of China from the Eighth through Eighteenth Centuries* (Princeton: Princeton Univ. Press, 1985), p. 37.

11. Royall Tyler, "Introduction," *The Tale of Genji* (New York: Penguin, 2001), p. xii.

12. Ivan Morris, *The Pillow Book of Sei Shonagon* (New York: Columbia Univ. Press, 1967), p. 258.

13. Morris, *The Pillow Book of Sei Shonagon,* p. 76.

14. Robert Treat Paine and Alexander Soper, *The Art and Architecture of Japan* (Baltimore: Penguin Books, 1955), p. 212.

15. Paine and Soper, *The Art and Architecture of Japan,* p. 45.

# Part Three

# A New and Crucial Phase

*Scholars are generally agreed that Song China and Kamakura Japan mark a major new phase in their respective histories, although they only partially overlap in time and contrast drastically in content. This contrast precludes using a single designation for both histories. In this respect there is a contrast also in that most Western scholars are content to follow their Japanese colleagues and write of "Medieval Japan," as we occasionally do here, while there is no terminological consensus on the China side. Even in the case of Japan, we warn the reader against assuming too easy parallels with the history of "Medieval" Europe.*

*Although some historians of China find "medieval" applicable to the period they study, there is little consistency in their usage. In terms of the classic periodization of European history where "Medieval" gives way to "Early Modern" in the Renaissance, we can well consider the Song "Early Modern" even though from another perspective we could call it the beginning of the "Late Traditional" or "Late Imperial." A term increasingly adopted by specialists is "Middle Period," but we have not followed suit both to avoid suggesting parallels with the European "Middle Ages" and also because, in a sense, every period—hopefully including our own—is a "middle period" between past and future.*

The Song vase in its restrained elegance and subtle coloring, contrasting with the vigorous tri-colored ware of the Tang, as well as with the deliberate roughness and asymmetry of the Japanese bowl. In this part of the book we will observe China and Japan following different trajectories in other respects.

# 8

# China during the Song: 960–1279

960 1127 1234 1279

| Liao (Khitan) (907–1119) | Jin (Jurchen) (1115–1234) | Mongols |
| Northern Song | Southern Song | |

The Song (960–1279) represents a new phase of Chinese history. Although it did not equal the Tang in military power or geographic extent, this dynasty saw, in just about every sphere of human activity, the emergence of features, some of which continued into the twentieth century. Changes in state and society, in the economy, and in technology had a profound effect on China's future while new departures in philosophy and art created a heritage of classic dimensions that for centuries to come inspired and challenged thoughtful people throughout East Asia. As always, these developments were interrelated but proceeded at different tempos.

The Song, like the Tang, is bisected by a major cataclysm into an earlier and a later period.

**Northern Song** designates the period from 960 until 1126 when the dynasty ruled over both North and South from its capital at Kaifeng near the junction of the Yellow River and the canal system leading to the prosperous southeast and thus a location economically superior to returning to repeatedly devastated Chang'an. This "eastward shift of the political center"[1] was to remain permanent.

**Southern Song** applies to the dynasty after 1127 when it was confined to the South, having lost the North to the Jin, a state formed by the Juchen people from what is now Manchuria. With its "temporary" capital at Hangzhou in the lower Yangzi region, the dynasty occupied what by then was clearly the economic heartland.

## The Founding

The dynastic founder was a general of what turned out to be the last of the Five Dynasties of the Tang-Song interregnum. Determined not to have his be simply the sixth minidynasty, he persuaded his fellow generals, who had helped him to power, that it was in their best interest to retire to the comfort of their estates. Although this did not prevent considerable military influence for some time, subsequent emperors and statesmen, determined to avoid the reemergence of warlords who had destroyed the Tang, saw to it that that power was placed in civilian hands. By devices such as the rotation of troops and frequent changes of command, the court prevented generals from developing personal power and succeeded in keeping commanders in line. The military profession suffered a permanent loss of status. It became a truism among the Chinese that good men are not turned into soldiers any more than good iron is wasted to make nails.

# The New Elite

The old aristocratic families that had been so prominent under the Tang dynasty did not survive the violence that characterized the decline and fall of the Tang. Their demise cleared the way for the rise of new families who, ideally, based their prestige on literary learning and an elite lifestyle, their power and formal status on office holding, and their wealth on land ownership. Depending on context, they appear in the secondary literature as gentlemen or literati, scholar-officials, and landlords. Although these attributes frequently did not overlap, when all three were present they reinforced each other. Even though the spread of printing made books cheaper and encouraged the diffusion of literacy, a certain economic level still had to be reached before a family could afford to dispense with the labor of a son and pay for his education. Education, in turn, was a prerequisite for an official career, whereas office holding provided opportunities for the acquisition and protection of wealth.

Song social structure was far more complex than this, however. Then, as now, there were also the overeducated poor and the undereducated rich: the deeply learned scholar who lived a life of frugal obscurity, and the man of wealth who was not fully educated by elite standards and thus ineligible for political appointment and unwelcome in high society. The fact that learning, office, and wealth did not necessarily coincide made for considerable social variety, a variety further enhanced by contrasts between urban and rural life and by major regional differences. Furthermore, status was a function of the social group. Even a criminal (say, a salt smuggler) might enjoy high standing within his community although being despised by the official elite. It is important to remember that in premodern times the web of government rested only lightly on society and that the world of officialdom was remote from most people's lives. This reminder is necessary, because most of the historical sources stem from the world of the scholar-official, which also supplied China's historians. This scholar-official elite played a crucial role in maintaining Chinese unity, but unity should never be mistaken for uniformity.

During the Southern Song there was a shift of focus as elite families tended to concentrate less on obtaining office and more on strengthening their local roots by prudent management of their affairs and property, taking advantage of market forces in a growing economy. To quote Robert Hymes, "What was new in and after the Tang-Song transition was that the means for an elite lifestyle—wealth and the education that depended on it—became available, relatively broadly, apart from the state's extractive and redistributive mechanisms." The local elite assumed leadership roles in the construction of public works such as bridges and waterworks, in social welfare measures, in temple building, and in defense. Marriage ties with similar families helped to confirm and perpetuate their influence. They acted as powerful intermediaries between their local communities and the central state.[2]

In contrast to societies in which status is defined by ancestry, the Chinese system neither guaranteed continuity of status for these elite families nor were there laws barring the way for those trying to rise from below. Economically, movement up and down was facilitated by the ready transferability of land and other forms of wealth and by the custom of dividing estates among heirs rather than leaving them intact to a single son. Yet, once established, some local elite families could persist for generations.

To distinguish the new elite from the old, scholars, particularly those specializing in later periods, sometimes call them the "gentry," divided into the relatively large local gentry and the more restricted upper gentry of office holders or examination system degree holders eligible for office. Both were educated. Although the examinations were open to almost all men, excluding only a small minority such as the sons of criminals and the like, most candidates came from the local gentry. However, obtaining an official degree was always difficult. In the late Northern Song, roughly 100,000 men competed for about 500 degrees; that is, 1 of 200 passed. Later it got much worse, leaving candidates with little hope of earning the highest degree. Nevertheless, an examination degree remained *the* mark of elite status.

# The Examination System

Founded in the Sui and increasingly prestigious during the Tang, the civil service examination system came into its own in the Song and (except under the Mongol Yuan) remained the most prestigious means of government recruitment until it was abolished in 1906. Although during the Song many men continued to enter government through other means, such as sponsorship by an official, in later dynasties the examination route represented the normal route into government service, and possession of a degree replaced pedigree as status signifier. During its long life, the system was refined and greatly elaborated, but its basic features were already clearly in evidence in the Song.

Structurally the system provided for an orderly progression through a series of tests (three during the Song, more later). These began at the local level, included a metropolitan examination given in the capital to candidates from the entire country, and culminated in a palace examination held under the personal auspices of the emperor. The Tang practices inviting candidates to bring personal influence to bear were eliminated. On the contrary, the government now went to great lengths in its attempt to secure impartiality. The papers of candidates, identified only by number, were copied by clerks before being submitted for grading so that the reader would be unable to identify the author of any paper by its calligraphy. The battle of wits between would-be cheaters and the authorities seeking to enforce honesty lasted as long as the examinations themselves and was pursued with great ingenuity by both sides. Nevertheless, despite occasional scandals, the examination system enjoyed a well-deserved reputation for honesty.

Success in the examinations required first of all a thorough command of the classics, which the candidates had to memorize. They had to be able to identify not only well-known lines but also the most obscure passages and even sequences of characters that made no sense to anyone who failed to recognize the context in which they appeared in a classic text. Tests of memory and exercises demonstrating command over formal literary styles were favored by examiners, because they made grading easier and more objective. Formal criteria were stressed in judging candidates' poems and essays. There was a persistent tendency for the examinations to turn into mere technical exercises, testing skills that revealed little about either a man's character or his administrative competence. This remained true even though the candidates were also required to discuss the meaning of designated passages from the classics and to answer questions concerning statecraft that theoretically had some bearing on the policy problems of the day.

Competition was rough. Preparing for and taking the examinations became a way of life. It has been estimated that the average age of Song candidates who completed the entire process and received the coveted *jinshi* ("presented" or "advanced scholar") degree was in the mid-30s. Because some areas, notably the southeast, were more advanced culturally and educationally than others, regional quotas were proposed, but, unlike during later dynasties, they were largely not enacted. As a result, men from the southeast predominated. Even with quotas, competition was bound to be more intense in some areas than others, but the most serious inequity was caused by the increasing importance of alternative examinations given to the relatives of officials. This, along with the special treatment accorded the numerous imperial clansmen, signified the effective abandonment of fairness during the Southern Song.

Despite its shortcomings the examination system did facilitate the careers of China's greatest statesmen during the Song and later. And it graduated administrators who shared a common intellectual heritage and recognized a common set of values, gentlemen who were scholars as well as officials. It provided a measure of social mobility and at least the appearance of meritocracy, largely determined the educational curriculum, and shaped the structure of the lives of those who aspired to a degree. It is no wonder, therefore, that the examinations themselves became a subject of profound concern and intense debate. The tradition of protest against its inadequacies is almost as old as the system itself. There were those who wished to see it abolished altogether, others who argued for reforms of various kinds, and men who felt it their filial duty to participate even though they despised preparation for the examination as unrelated to genuine study. The examination system remained a topic of political debate and scholarly controversy.

# The Northern Song

From the beginning of the dynasty under Taizu (r. 960–976) and his brother, Taizong (r. 976–997), who completed the establishment of the dynasty, the Song had to tolerate a non-Chinese presence in North China. The Liao dynasty (907–1119), which antedated the Song and had been created by the Khitan, a tribal people, held sixteen prefectures on the Chinese side of the Great Wall. To preserve their distinctiveness, the Liao created dual institutions, dividing the government into Northern and Southern Chancelleries, and produced an Inner Asian/Chinese multicultural civilization deserving fuller treatment than we can give it here. Relations between the Song and the Liao were frequently hostile, but neither state was able to subdue the other. The Song and Liao came to terms in 1005 after the Song emperor, Zhenzong (r. 997–1022), had personally taken the field against the Khitan. Negotiations led to a treaty that provided for the cession of some territory to the Song, for diplomatic exchanges, trade, and a Song agreement to send the Liao contributions in silk and silver. For the Song the cost was considerably less than would have been required to finance a military solution.

The Liao were not the Song's only troublesome neighbors. In 1038 there was a challenge from the West as the leader of the Ordos-based Tangut peoples organized the Xi Xia state, which was less successful than the Liao in containing the tensions between sinification and preservation of steppe traditions that had earlier undermined the Northern Wei and other hybrid northern states. In 1038 the Xi Xia invaded Shaanxi, and in 1044, the Song Emperor, Renzong (r. 1022–1063), signed a peace treaty with the Xi Xia along the lines of the earlier agreement with the Liao. The Xi Xia, however, remained a military problem for the Song until all of North China fell to the Jin (1115–1234).

Initially the Song had welcomed the emergence of the Jin as an ally, but the dynasty's attempt to "use barbarians against barbarians" ended in disaster.* The last two emperors of the Northern Song, Huizong (r. 1100–1126) and his son, Emperor Qinzong (r. 1126–1127), were taken to Manchuria as prisoners of the Jurchen and there lived out their lives. The dynasty was able to reestablish itself in the South, but the North, homeland of Chinese civilization, remained lost. Not until the founding of the Ming dynasty in the fourteenth century was the North to come again under Chinese rule (see Figure 8.1).

Mindful of its dangerous neighbors, the dynasty concentrated its military and political attention on the North. In the South, after military conflict and political missions during the eleventh century, relations with Vietnam settled into a more or less stable pattern, with the Chinese dynasty treating Vietnam as a tributary state as it did the Dali kingdom in Yunnan. In contrast to the sixteen prefectures lost in the North and despite some wishful thinking, the prefectures once claimed in Vietnam never again became part of China. However, the Mongol Yuan dynasty was to incorporate Yunnan into the empire.

## Government and Politics

The organization of the Song government basically followed that of the Tang except that the civil and military functions were strictly divided with preference to the former. Even so, the Song maintained a huge army equipped with sophisti-

---

*The dynasty lost the north.

**FIGURE 8.1** Song China—Political and Commercial. 🌐

cated weapons and managed to persevere for more than 300 years against a for-midable succession of enemies. The maintenance and support of the military establishment was expensive, as was the financing of an expanding civilian bureaucracy. Naturally, Song scholars and officials disagreed over economic and fiscal policies much as they did over the examinations and over the linked issues of foreign and military policy.

Song politics were complicated by factionalism and infighting, usually conducted not by stable and legitimized political parties united by a common program but by factions whose members might share some common policy commitments but were more likely to be held together by personal relationships and temporary alliances. Characteristically, factions accused each other of narrow self-interest, and

**FIGURE 8.2** *Five-Colored Parakeet.* Attributed to Emperor Huizong but probably painted for rather than by him, this carefully studied, realistic yet idealized, five-colored parakeet exemplifies the emperor's and the period's taste for elegance and precision. Hanging scroll, colors on silk, 20.87 in high. (© 2005 Museum of Fine Arts, Boston.)

each charged its opponents responsible for the development of factionalism itself, a phenomenon condemned by nearly everyone as inimical to the state.

Each faction sought to obtain the emperor's support. This was as crucial in practice as it was in theory, for, initially at least, the disappearance of an aristocratic counterweight served to increase the power of the throne. Still, even strong-minded Northern Song emperors tended to manipulate rather than to intimidate their officials. Those who fell out of imperial favor usually suffered nothing worse than exile. The dynasty's most imperious ruler, Huizong, harbored elevated ambitions but ended a political failure and owed his lasting fame to his aesthetics, his elegant calligraphy, and the paintings bearing his name (see Figure 8.2). The dynasty did produce a number of dominant ministers, including China's greatest and most controversial reformer.

# Wang Anshi

Wang Anshi (1021–1086) was not the first Song reformer. That honor went to Fan Zhongyan (989–1052), famed for defining a true Confucian as "one who is first in worrying about the world's troubles and last in enjoying its pleasures." Fan and Wang's reforms were part of a major Confucian revival that drew inspiration from shared classical ideals and was fostered by the "Old Culture" Movement (*guwen*) that had begun in the Tang (see Chapter 5, p. 129) and sought the transformation of state and society along with culture and literature. Both men sought to bring government closer to the classical ideal, and Wang, like Fan, initially commanded widespread reformist support. But Wang went far beyond his predecessor in initiating new programs. Able to promote his new policies as long as he enjoyed the support of Emperor Shenzong (r. 1067–1085), he ended up antagonizing his most illustrious contemporaries, chief among them the dynasty's greatest historian, Sima Guang (1019–1086), author of *A Comprehensive Mirror in Aid of Government* (*Zizhi Tongjian*). Other opponents included the poet and theorist of culture, Su Shi (Su Dongpo, 1037–1101), and the Cheng brothers, whose ideas became central to "Neo-Confucianism" (see later). Opposition to Wang spurred these men to some of their greatest achievements and stimulated much of "the subtle art of dissent" in poetry and painting revealed by Alfreda Murck in her admirable book.[3]

One of Wang's first acts, signaling his economic activism, was to establish a finance planning commission (1069). This, like the establishment of a state trade system (1072), was designed to save government money by breaking the monopoly on government procurement held by large merchants. It provided that the government should deal directly with small suppliers who now became eligible for government loans. Wang's willingness to innovate and readiness to delegate authority is exemplified by the "bureaucratic entrepreneurship"[4] he fostered in allowing the officials of the Tea and Horse Agency maximum discretion in operating the Sichuan tea monopoly.

Wang consistently preferred monetary transactions over dealing in commodities. Tax payments in cash were substituted for the customary deliveries of supplies to the palace (1073). Similarly, Wang instituted a tax to finance the hiring of men to perform local government service (1071), a function previously assigned to well-off local families on a rotating basis. He also increased the amount of currency in circulation. Nevertheless, there was a currency shortage brought on by increased demand.

Wang Anshi did not neglect agriculture. To save small farmers from the ruinous short-term interest rates of 60 to 70 percent charged for carry-over loans during the hard months between spring sowing and autumn harvest, he instituted farming loans ("young shoots money") with a maximum interest rate of 20 percent for the season (1069), but pressures to make money soon eclipsed the social welfare aspect of the program. To deal with the perpetual problem of faulty tax rolls and fraudulent records, Wang initiated a land survey in 1072, but that too ended in failure.

Another program organized people into groups of 10, 30, and 300 families to ensure collective responsibility for local policing, tax collections, and loan repayments and to supply men for a local security force that could also function as a military reserve. Another measure designed to cut the dynasty's enormous military expenses placed horses with farmers. In return for maintaining them, the farmers could use the horses in peacetime but were obligated to turn them over to the army in case of military need. This program failed to take into account the fact that farm horses do not make good military steeds.

A number of programs were rendered ineffective because they were sabotaged by officials and/or even used to oppress the very people they were intended to help. Reform of personnel recruitment and of management was crucial. Wang tried to obtain the men he needed by changing the examination system. He included law as a subject to be tested, assigned his own commentaries on the classics as official interpretations to be followed by the candidates in their papers, and stressed the classic known as *The Rites of Zhou (Zhouli)*, because it provided justification for in-stitutional reform and a government that penetrated deep into society. He also tried to circumvent the entire examination system by expanding the state univer-sity and ensuring its graduates direct entry into government. Wang realized that most of the actual work of government, particularly on the local level, was per-formed not by civil service officials serving a tour of duty in a county or prefec-ture but by a sub-bureaucracy of clerks, petty agents, and underlings who re-mained permanently in place. There was little to restrain these men, who shared neither the status nor the learning of the officials, from squeezing maximum profit out of their jobs. Despised as notoriously corrupt, they tended to become still more corrupt to compensate for being despised. Wang's policy was to reduce their number, improve their pay, place them under stricter supervision, and give the most capable among them an opportunity to rise into the regular bureaucracy.

Wang's personality as well as the intrusiveness of his measures made him many enemies. By 1076 he was out of office. In the middle and late 1070s, his program lost momentum, but a full reaction did not set in until the death of his imperial pa-tron, Emperor Shenzong. Subsequently, there was an ambitious revival of reform under Huizong. Still later, individual measures similar to those of Wang Anshi were reinstituted from time to time, but no minister again tried to do so much so rapidly. His program remained an illustration of what government could do and also what it could not and should not attempt to do. Few after the fall of Northern Song shared Wang's vision of an activist government integrating state and society.

As always, political and economic developments were closely intertwined. The economic history of the period is varied and complex, but clearly the Song was a period of dramatic economic change.

# The Economy

Qualitatively and quantitatively Song economic changes were so extensive that they have been called revolutionary. They occurred in all three areas of primary economic activity: industry, agriculture, and commerce (see Figure 8.1). Of this triad, industrial growth peaked during the Northern Song, whereas agricultural and commercial growth continued even after the loss of the North.

Important progress was made in the production of many commodities. Paper making and all the processes involved in book production advanced; there was progress in salt processing and notable developments in ceramics and in hydraulic engineering. Tea processing and shipbuilding gained new eminence. China developed a coal and iron industry that was the most advanced in the world. In North China deforestation provided the major incentive for coal production. Much of this coal found its way into furnaces used to smelt iron mined in an area stretching in an arc from southern Hebei to northern Jiangsu.

Much of the iron and steel went to equip an army of well over 1 million men, providing them with swords, other weapons such as arrows tipped with steel, and armor of various kinds. Iron tools, especially the *tieda*, "a pronged drag hoe that looks like an iron-toothed rake"[5] helped raise agricultural productivity. Other ferrous metal products included tools for carpenters and other workmen, consumer items such as stoves and smaller objects such as nails and needles, bits for drilling wells, and the chains used in suspension bridges. Most bridges, however, were made of stone or wood. Our illustration shows an arched bridge high enough to permit large boats to pass underneath and strong enough to support lively traffic in people and goods as well as numerous stalls. The city depicted in loving detail in Figure 8.3 is almost certainly not Kaifeng as traditionally thought, but it exemplified the growth of cities bustling with life and commerce.

Kaifeng itself originated as a commercial center and continued to function as such after it became the political capital. It housed not only government offices, garrisons, warehouses, and arsenals but also private textile concerns, drug and chemical shops, shipyards, building material suppliers, and so forth. There was also a thriving restaurant and hotel industry. In contrast to the symmetrical, planned layout of the Tang capital, Kaifeng grew organically. Lively streets replaced the old system of enclosed wards, and the population spilled beyond the city walls as its inhabitants sought relief from urban congestion.

Song city dwellers did not escape the grimmer aspects of urban life. Deadly fire was a constant threat. In Kaifeng guard stations were placed at 50-yard intervals; watchtowers were erected, each manned by 100 firefighting soldiers; and huge iron containers were kept filled with water. Despite these precautions, there were frequent and destructive conflagrations. Crime, too, was a fact of urban life. People had to be prepared for confidence men who passed lead off as gold, holdup specialists against whom merchants required special police protection, and all kinds of other petty criminals who eked out a living as best they could. For those who could not make a decent living, honestly or dishonestly, the city still offered advantages not available in the village. On special occasions, public alms were distributed. There were state hospitals and dispensaries and houses for the aged, the decrepit, and the orphaned. If worst came to worst, those dying in poverty at least had the consolation of knowing that they would receive proper burial even if they had no relatives to pay for it.

Some of the mining and manufacturing enterprises were large-scale operations employing hundreds of workers, whereas other concerns were confined to

**FIGURE 8.3** The *Rainbow Bridge,* detail of Qingming Scroll by Zhang Zeduan. Hand-scroll, ink and light color on silk, mid-eleventh century, 10.04 in high. Viewers could travel at leisure through town and country as scrolls such as this were gradually unrolled, an effect recaptured only with difficulty by the modern museum visitor who sees such a painting completely spread out in a glass case. Frequently, as here, a river provides continuity. *Rainbow Bridge* resembles rainbows in both shape and color. For a cogent discussion of this famous scroll, see Heping Liu, *Painting and Commerce in Northern Song Dynasty China, 960–1126* (Dissertation, Yale University, 1997), Chapter 5. (© Collection of the Palace Museum, Beijing.)

small workshops. Various kinds of brokers facilitated commercial transactions, and numerous lines of business were organized into guilds or associations that supervised the terms of trade and also served as intermediaries between their members and the government. As in medieval Europe, members of the same profession or guild frequently (but not always) set up shop in the same city street or district.

The growth of manufacturing and the growth of cities were sustained by an increase in agricultural yields. At the same time, the opening of new markets for rural products stimulated the development of agriculture, now called upon to feed a population of more than 100 million. The size of harvests was increased by the use of improved farm tools, advances in water control, wider application of fertilizers, and the development of new strains of rice. In the southeast it later became common for a rice paddy to produce two crops a year, either two harvests of rice or one of rice followed by a crop of wheat or beans grown on the paddy after it was drained.

Life in the country was hard but could be good: This is how a Late Northern Song poet describes life in his native village:

> At cock crow the whole village rouses.
> Gets ready to set off for the middle fields:
> Remind the wife to be sure to fix some millet,
> Shout to the children to shut the gate behind us.
> Spade and hoe catch the morning light;
> Laughter and hubbub mingle on the road.
> Puddles from the night before wet our straw sandals;
> Here's a wild flower to stick in the bun of your hair!
> Clear light breaks through the distant haze;
> Spring skies now are fresh and gay.
> Magnolia covers the wandering hills;
> In the empty field, a brocaded pheasant preens.
> The young people have come like racing clouds;
> Owl-like, an old man squats on his heels alone.
> The yellow earth glistens from the rain that passed;
> Clouds of dust race before the wind.
> Little by little, the whole village gathers,
> Calling greetings from field to field.
> The omens say it will be a good month;
> Let's keep on working, dawn to sundown![6]

Whether in the country or in town, economic growth rarely benefits all people equally. It does not prevent corruption ultimately at the expense of those too poor to afford bribes and presents. Nor does it preclude the wealthy from increasing the size of their holdings by taking advantage of the numerous peasants who held insufficient land to maintain their families or themselves and had to work as tenant sharecroppers or as field servants in conditions of legal inferiority. Wang Anshi's reforms notwithstanding, farmers remained burdened by inequitable taxation and exorbitant interest rates. Rural uprisings during the dynasty were rare, but there was unrest and rebellion in the 1120s. Much of the good that Huizong accomplished by building schools and sponsoring charities was undone by the heavy burden of taxation and government exactions. Especially notorious were the emperor's demands for rare plants, stones, and novelties. His reign also saw the most ambitious imperial sponsorship of Daoism.

## The Religious Scene

From the outset Song emperors patronized Daoism. Then, roughly a century before Huizong, Zhezong, the emperor who personally led the army against the Liao, promoted it in a major way, sponsoring the compilation of Daoist texts, the performance of Daoist ceremonies, and the construction of Daoist edifices while claiming imperial descent from the Yellow Thearch, a mythical sage-ruler in a tradition going back to pre-Han times, and revering "heavenly texts" of supposedly supernatural provenance. The emperor patronized old sects such as the Celestial Masters and Shanqing while also bringing in new deities. Discussing Zhezong's Daoist projects, Edward L. Davis has traced the transformation of the Black Killer, a fierce god with angry eyes and unkempt hair who rides a dragon and carries a huge sword, from his origins as "the dark, militaristic god of a tenth century cult into the Perfected Lord of an eleventh century text—into a supporting minister of the Jade Emperor and defender of the Song dynasty" and noted it paralleled "the transformation of the military elite of tenth century kingdoms into the bureaucratic servants of eleventh century emperors."[7] Davis goes on to connect what was happening at court with the practices of Daoist Ritual Masters who interacted with spirit mediums and Buddhist Tantric exorcists, borrowing and competing with each other for elite patronage.

Huizong went a good deal further than Zhezong. He began by giving Daoists priority over Buddhists and ended by attempting to turn Buddhists into Daoists, even ordering that the Buddha's name be changed to "The Golden Immortal of Enlightenment." The emperor drew on practitioners from all over the empire to compile texts, and he sponsored the first printing of the Daoist cannon. In the course of time Huizong became convinced of his own elevated place in the universe, declaring himself an incarnation of the "Great Thearch of Long Life" or "Imperial Lord of the Supreme Empyrean," charged with the salvation of the realm. He was so convinced of his own sacredness that he ordered the basic five musical notes of the Chinese scale recalibrated using the length of his fingers as the standard.

Although imperial patronage of Daoism helped, its strengths were manifold. A number of new sects were established during the Song, but the most influential development occurred under Jin when Wang Zhe (1112–1370) taught that Daoism, Confucianism, and Buddhism were all three of equal value and stressed nourishing both one's nature and one's life force. The Celestial Realization sect, founded by Wang, continues today with its headquarters at Beijng's White Cloud Abbey.

Perhaps Daoism's greatest strength lay in its ability to admit local gods into its pantheon and in the vigor of its local Ritual Masters. Prominent among the latter during the Southern Song were practitioners of Thunder Rites, perhaps making effective use of gunpowder (the earliest record of the formula for gunpowder is dated 1044). With local cults proliferating in a veritable "deity explosion,"[8] gods and practitioners alike had to show that they could deliver.

Deities with sufficiently strong, enthusiastic, and influential support could hope for official recognition and an official title. A major asset of the Daoists that set them off from their competitors was their access to all the resources of a celestial bureaucracy as revealed in their sacred texts. But they did not have the field to themselves. Deeply rooted local gods promising their followers a more personal, nonbureaucratic relationship represented a countervailing trend studied by Robert Hymes, who has characterized Song religion as "the meeting point of a relatively few common assumptions, an extremely wide variety of usages, gods, rituals, and practitioners, and several organized or semi-organized bodies contending to impose order on the variety."[9]

FIGURE 8.4 Liang Kai, *Li Bai*. Ink on paper, mid-thirteenth century, 31.10 in high. Chan-inspired paintings by artists such as Muqi and Liang Kai are mostly preserved in Japan where they continue to be influential and much appreciated. (© TNM Image Archives, http://TnmArchives.jp/.)

Some of these organizations were Buddhist, established not only by monks but also by lay leaders as Buddhism grew and flourished to such a degree that the Song has been called its "golden age." This certainly was true of Chan, which built on Tang doctrinal developments to create its own sectarian identity and developed strict and detailed monastic rules covering the entire day from how to wash your face and brush your teeth in the morning; to rules for bath, toilet, and meals; down to the directive to sleep on your right side. Chan temples became the most numerous in the land. Up north, Chan flourished, the Shaolin monastery was just one of a number of major Chan centers, and Xingxiu (1161–1246), "The Old Man of a Thousand Pines," who was also well versed in Confucianism, played a key role in the development of what remained the influential "Northern" school of Chan. Beyond China, Chan became a major presence in Korea and Japan.

The influence of Chan beyond the temple was manifold. Expressiveness and spontaneity were prized by Chan painters, some of whom worked in an untrammeled, spontaneous style developed in late-ninth-century Sichuan and best represented by Wang Mo ("ink-Wang"), who made pictures by splashing ink on silk, usually while drunk. Chan masters of this ink-splash technique dashed off their work, destroying what did not come out right, but never laboring over their art, confident that artistic inspiration, like religious enlightenment, comes in a flash. A favorite subject of Chan painters was a pair of Tang recluses wearing expressions of divine lunacy: Han Shan ("Cold Mountain"), who is famous for his poetry, and Shide, who worked in a monastery kitchen and is usually holding a broom. The finest Southern Song Chan painters were as unrestricted in subject matter as in style. For Muqi six persimmons could mirror the truth as faithfully as any portrait of the Buddha (see Figure 12.1). Liang Kai's famous portrait of Li Bai (see Figure 8.4) suggests that he and the Tang poet were kindred spirits.

Along with Chan, a resurgent Tiantai flourished intellectually and institutionally. The prominence of Guanyin is reflected in gilded wooden figures of the Bodhisattva seated in a position of "royal ease," with one leg raised, supporting an arm. Housed in temples more delicate and refined than their Tang predecessors and now more generally capped by gracefully curved roofs, such figures were among the best products of the last phase of Buddhist art. Although not the center of focus, Guanyin is present too among the figures in the cliffs at Dazu in Siquan, just one of the places where indigenous and Tantric elements were combined into a unique local tradition. More broadly, belief in karma and the accumulation of merit came to be widely held throughout the culture.

# The Confucian Revival

Confucian ceremonies, political ideals, and moral teachings had never been abandoned, but new circumstances gave the tradition new life. A major source of energy early on were advocates of literary and political reform affiliated with the *guwen* movement. Among those who turned to government, hoping to realize their ideals, were both Wang Anshi and his bitter opponent Sima Guang. Sima, rather than confining himself to a single dynasty, had the confidence and vision to do something not attempted since the Han: a study of virtually the whole of Chinese history (beginning where the *Zuo Zhuan,* a classic account of the period covered by the *Spring and Autumn Annals,* had left off). Sima's title, *A Comprehensive Mirror in Aid of Government,* reflects his focus on the state along with his conviction that an accurate account of the past is an indispensable guide for the present. Departing from precedent, he included in the finished work discussions of the discrepancies he had found in the sources and his reasons for choosing one version of an event over another. This approach was in keeping with a new widely shared spirit of rereading and rethinking old texts.

The examination system, along with the emphasis on correct understanding of tradition as a guide to politics and life, implied a commitment to education. Confucius himself had become a teacher when he failed in his search for a ruler to implement his ideas. Thus, it is no accident that the Confucian revival under the Song was accompanied by the burgeoning of schools: government schools during the Northern Song and private academies during the Southern Song. Many of these academies embraced ideas first advanced in the eleventh century but not prominent until the twelfth (see "Neo-Confucianism"). The growth of schools both stimulated and was stimulated by the spread of printing.

# Poetry and Painting

Thanks to printing, a huge number of poems by more than 9000 Song authors survive. The poem quoted earlier is an example of five-character old-style verse. Many fine poems were written in the old forms including poems by Su Shi, a ver-

satile, open-spirited exponent of the centrality of cultural creativity. Su is also famous for expanding the song lyric (*ci*) form of poetry. Written to tunes, of which
only the titles now remain, it required great skill to fit the words to the music but
allowed unusual freedom in diction and used colloquial expressions. Actually Su
Shi's genius was not bound by any set form. Perhaps his most famous works are
two rhapsodies (*fu*) on the Red Cliff, site of a crucial battle fought during the
Three Kingdoms Period. Su also wrote many poems on friendship, drinking, and
nature. Like other Song poets he knew and loved the literature of the past. But he
also brought to it a critical spirit. For example, his view of the highly respected and
beloved Tang poet Meng Jiao was hardly shared by his contemporaries but will
surely strike a responsive chord in anyone who has ever labored over a poem only
to discover that the reward was not worth the effort:

> *Reading the Poetry of Meng Jiao—First of Two Poems*
> Night: reading Meng Jiao's poems,
> Characters fine as cow's hair.
> By the cold lamp, my eyes blur and swim.
> Good passages I rarely find—
> Lone flowers poking up through the mud—
> But more hard words than the *Odes* and *Li sao*—
> Jumbled rocks clogging the clear stream,
> Making rapids too swift for poling.
> My first impression is of eating little fishes—
> What you get's not worth the trouble;
> Or of boiling tiny mud crabs
> And ending up with empty claws.
> For refinement he might compete with monks
> But he'll never match his master Han Yu.
> Man's life is like morning dew,
> A flame eating up the oil night by night.
> Why should I strain my ears
> Listening to the squeaks of this autumn insect?
> Better lay aside the book
> And drink my cup of jade-white wine.[9]

Su Shi was at the center of a circle of talented friends devoted to poetry, calligraphy, and painting, the three arts of gentleman-scholars who frequently wrote
their poems on a painting, thus combining the three arts in a single work. Su himself saw a close relationship between poetry, "pictures without form," and paintings, "unspoken poems."[10] The bamboo branch attributed to Wen Tong and reproduced in Figure 8.5 illustrates what the painter can accomplish by employing
the ink and brush of the calligrapher. Bamboo was a favorite subject of painters
and poets. Sima Guang planted some in his famous "Garden of Solitary
Enjoyment" in Luoyang. Unfortunately this garden is long gone, but we have
Robert E. Harrist, Jr., to lead us through another eleventh-century garden.[11]

**FIGURE 8.5** *A Broken Branch of Bamboo,* attributed to Wen Tong. Album leaf, ink on paper, 19.02 in × 12.20 in. (© National Palace Museum, Taiwan, Republic of China.) The analysis by Roger Goepper (*The Essence of Chinese Painting* [Boston: Boston Book and Art Shop, 1963], p. 134), is worth quoting in full:

> All the elements have been drawn with a single confident brush stroke: the sections of the stem and the branches with a firm and elastic writing brush (*ganbi*), the counter-pressure of whose springy tip can be felt in the hand; the leaves with a softer and limper brush (*shuibi*), which submits obediently to the slightest pressure of the hand. The interaction of the graphic forms resulting from these two techniques largely determines the general impression created by the painting, the individual elements becoming fused in a composition filled with tension and vitality. The diagonal upward movement of the stem is answered contrapuntally by the smaller twigs, while the sudden break diverts the thrust from the top left-hand corner and causes it to fade out into the largest blank space in the composition. At the same time this break introduces an element of the unexpected and exciting into the picture; it disturbs the harmonious bamboo and determines its fate, as they do with man. The fixed points of composition lie on the one hand in the knots of the stem, accentuated by small brush dashes, and on the other in the areas of radiation formed by the rhythmic play of the overlapping leaf spears.

**FIGURE 8.6** Fan Kuan, *Traveling among Streams and Mountains.* Hanging scroll, ink and light color on silk, 29.49 in × 51.02 in. Impressive scope, strength, and dark tones have replaced the rich colors, the clarity of line, and the decorative charm of earlier landscape paintings (compare Figure 5.9). (© National Palace Museum, Taiwan, Republic of China.)

A new age evoked a new vision. The towering achievement of Song art was in landscape painting. Developing styles that first appeared during the Five Dynasties between Tang and Song, Song artists produced classic works. Fan Kuan (c. 960–c. 1030) sought to encompass the whole of nature in his work (see Figure 8.6). Here we can observe the classic Chinese perspective dividing the picture surface into three planes, one near and one distant, with the middle plane occupied by water or mist. Whereas nature in earlier paintings provided a setting for man, here man is reduced to his proper dimensions. A road invites the viewer to enter the painting and contemplate the grandeur of nature.

Fan was a northerner. In the South, masters like Dong Yuan (d. 962) and his disciple Juran (fl. c. 975) depicted the softer, more atmospheric mountainscapes of their region and founded another influential tradition. The difference between the southern and northern painters was not only a matter of tone and technique, but as Richard M. Barnhart has suggested of Dong Yuan, "The southern master appears to have wished to meditate upon the land, as a poet; the northern masters to dramatize it."[12]

# The Southern Song (1127–1279)

Despite the deployment of catapults, flamethrowers, and incendiary devices made with gunpowder, the Song lost the North. The dynasty carried on under a son of Huizong known as Gaozong (r. 1127–1162), who was forced to flee from the Jurchen troops and take refuge on some islands off the southeast coast before the tide of war turned. In 1138 Gaozong designated Hangzhou as the "temporary capital," and a peace agreement with the Jin followed in 1142. The previous year had brought the death in prison of Yue Fei (1103–1141), one of China's most celebrated generals still today extolled as a hero who had paid for his patriotism with his life. Conversely, Qin Guei (1090–1155), the minister who engineered Yue's death and effected the peace, came to be despised as the prototype of the traitor. Later, iron statues representing Qin Guei and his wife in chains were placed on the grounds of Yue Fei's tomb beside Hangzhou's West Lake. In the past visitors expressed their contempt by spitting on the statues, but that is now prohibited.

In the treaty of 1142 the Song accepted the Huai River as its northern boundary, agreed to make annual payments to the Jin, and recognized the Jin as its superior. Nevertheless, relations between the two states remained uneasy. Fighting broke out again between 1161 and 1165 and again the dynasty was saved by its superior fleet, both at sea and in the Yangzi River where its maneuverable paddle-wheel boats, ramming enemy vessels or using gunpowder missiles to incinerate them, carried the day. After a period of unfriendly coexistence, cold war again turned into active warfare from 1206 to 1208. This time the war came to an end only after the Song handed over to the Jin the severed head of the minister responsible for starting the war. The Jurchen state was gradually sinified during the twelfth century, adopting the examination system and other Chinese institutions, but this did not induce the Song to look any more kindly on its northern neighbor.

The Southern Song government was therefore by no means unhappy when the new Mongol power rose in the North to challenge the Jin. When the Mongols destroyed the Jin and occupied North China in 1234, the Song's situation became precarious. The dynasty held on for another 40 years, however, largely because of its maritime strength and the effectiveness of its mountain fortresses. When the end did come, it was hastened by naval treachery.

## Southern Song Cities and Commerce

Politically and psychologically the loss of the North was a grave blow to the dynasty, but economically the loss was much less severe, because by this time a good two-thirds of China's population and wealth were in the South.

Trade accounted for much of this wealth. Commerce was facilitated by the use of paper money, a Chinese innovation that originated in Sichuan with the circulation of private certificates of deposit secured by funds placed in private shops. In the eleventh century, paper money was issued for the first time by the government. As long as these notes were adequately secured by goods or specie (hard cash) they worked well. However, the government could not resist the temptation to issue more paper money than it could back with solid reserves. When this became generally known, the value of the notes depreciated.

A large part of China's internal as well as foreign trade was waterborne, for it cost less to transport goods on rivers and canals than to cart them overland. China's oceangoing ships were large, capable of carrying several hundred men. They were navigated with the aid of the compass, a product of China's traditional expertise in magnetism. In other ways, too, the ships were technologically advanced. Their features included "watertight bulkheads, buoyancy chambers, bamboo fenders at the waterline, floating anchors to hold them steady during storms, axial rudders in place of steering oars, outrigger and leeboard devices, oars for use in calm weather, scoops for taking samples off the sea floor, sounding lines for determining the depth . . . , and small rockets propelled by gunpowder for self-defense."[13] Merchant ships could be converted to military use. The superiority of its navy was crucial to the Southern Song's military security.

The trading cities of the South were known for their prosperity, the fast pace of life, and the reputed frivolity and shamelessness of their inhabitants. The greatest city was Hangzhou. Situated between the Yangzi River (to which it was linked by canal) and the international ports of the southeast coast, it was a government and trade center, home of merchants and officials. Flanked by the Zhe River and the West Lake, Hangzhou was a city of bridges and canals. All kinds of merchandise, ranging from staples to luxury goods, were sold in the city. Olive, crab, ginger, water-chestnut, and orange dealers had their own guilds, as did cap makers, goldsmiths, and twine makers, among others. There were many medicine shops, among them The Ever Honest Pharmacy. The Lin Family Toothbrush Shop, Tong

Family Candle Store, Niu Family Belt Store, and Xu Family Funerary Paper Shop were among the numerous family enterprises offering their wares. There were florists, fan shops, and bookstores and retailers selling pearls, jade, fine silk, and even rhinoceros hide. Among the amenities offered by the city were exquisite restaurants, tea houses, cabarets, and baths. Entertainment was also provided by a host of popular performers, chess masters, fortunetellers, acrobats, storytellers, and puppeteers as well as numerous practitioners of the world's oldest profession, ladies "highly proficient and accomplished in the use of endearments and caresses,"[14] according to Marco Polo, whose testimony on life in the city after the Mongol conquest when it was no longer the capital, is usually reliable if not necessarily based on personal observation. Outside the city, the surrounding hills with their Buddhist temples provided opportunities for pleasure excursions. A favorite pastime then as now was boating and partying on West Lake.

Quanzhou in Fujian now displaced Guangzhou (Canton) as the main port and became "the emporium of the world"[15] with a beautiful mosque to serve the Arab population and a skyline dominated by two pagodas decorated with scenes from the Ramayana, the Indian epic beloved throughout Indianized Southeast Asia. Until 1160 when monetary considerations prompted a change in policy, the government, which derived considerable revenue from foreign trade (through customs duties, licensing fees, sales and transit taxes, and so forth), encouraged overseas commerce by maintaining harbors and canals, building breakwaters, erecting beacons, operating warehouses, setting up hotels, and rewarding merchants who attracted foreign shipping to Chinese ports. Among the major imports were aromatics and drugs, textiles, minerals, and miscellaneous luxury items, and the primary exports included silks, metals (especially copper coins exported to Japan and found as far away as Somalia and Zanzibar), and ceramics. The export of the latter was actively encouraged by the government, and the discovery of Song shards not only throughout South and Southeast Asia but also in the Middle East and along the east coast of Africa attests to the wide popularity of Song products. This was the precursor of the later export trade that was to make the word *china* synonymous with *porcelain*.

# Literary and Visual Arts

Song men and women were great collectors. One result was the scholarly compilation of several impressive compendia of historical and natural data. Another was Huizong's great palace art collection as well as the rare plants, birds, and animals in his magnificent and costly garden. But there were also much more modest private collections. Li Qingzhao (1094–c. 1152) has described how she and her husband used to enjoy their throve of old books and art, pawning some clothes to buy rubbings and fruit to enjoy together at home before war put an end to all that. Li's account is in prose, but she is best known for her poetry. Here she described the fall festival held on the ninth day of the ninth month in a poem with allusions to her favorite poet, Tao Qian, allusions that her contemporaries, like the careful readers of our Chapter 4, would immediately recognize:

**FIGURE 8.7** Ma Yuan was known as "One Corner Ma" because of his tendency to concentrate his compositions in one corner. The scene of the scholar quietly contemplating and enjoying nature is charming but lacks the grandeur of Fan Kuan (see Figure 8.6). (© National Palace Museum, Taiwan, Republic of China.)

> The mists—thick clouds—sad all day long,
> The gold animal spurts incense from its head.
> Once more it's the Festival of Double Nine;
> On the jade pillow—through mesh bed curtain—
> The chill of midnight starts creeping through.
> At the eastern hedge I drink a cup after dusk;
> Furtive fragrances fill my sleeve.
> Don't say one can't be overwhelmed:
> When the west wind furls up the curtain,
> I'm more fragile than the yellow chrysanthemum.[16]

Other Southern Song poets wrote widely on themes too numerous to list but include eloquent complaints on the government's peace policy: "Stabled horses die of obesity; strings unstrung break on the bow."[17]

Painters who lived after the period of monumental masters such as Fan Kuan knew that the classical achievement could not be repeated. One solution was to paint a part of nature rather than the whole, for example, a branch to represent the tree. One who did this was Ma Yuan (c. 1160–c. 1225). Figure 8.7 shows a gentleman-scholar communing with nature. Ma was greatly appreciated in Japan, as was Xia Gui (c. 1190–1230). *A Pure and Remote View of Rivers and Mountains* (see Figure 8.8) is a masterpiece in which the artist made the most of the musicality of the hand-scroll as a temporal as well as visual medium.

**FIGURE 8.8** Xia Gui, *A Pure and Remote View of Rivers and Mountains*. Section of hand-scroll, ink on paper, 18.27 in high. Many have imitated Xia's style, but very few were able to achieve the subtlety and strength of his brushwork animating the austerity of his composition. (© National Palace Museum, Taiwan, Republic of China.)

Song ceramics also represent a classic achievement, combining the vigor of earlier pottery with the grace of later ware. As in painting, there were major differences between northern and southern styles, reflecting in this case not only different tastes and a varied clientele but also differences in the chemical composition of the clays used by potters. Song wares include stoneware and porcelain, vessels covered with a slip (clay coating) that has been carved away to produce a design, and vessels covered with enamel or decorated with a painting. Colors run from white and grays to black, as well as various hues from lavender to olive. Perhaps most prized is the celadon, blue-green ware often decorated with a crackle (network of fine cracks) formed by the glaze cooling more rapidly than the vessel (see p. 203). Some of this exquisite ware was made especially for the imperial household, and such pieces are fitting representatives of Song refinement and elegance.

# "Neo-Confucianism"

It was the great strength of the new Confucianism that it was at once a creed that gave meaning to the life of the individual, an ideology supporting state and society, and a philosophy that provided a convincing framework for understanding the world. It conceived of the world as an organic whole and itself constituted an rganic system in which each aspect reinforced the other in theory as well as in practice.

Education remained at the forefront. One of the most famous academies was the White Deer Grotto Academy, and it was primarily through private academies that the new way of thought was perpetuated. At the famous White Deer Grotto Academy, headed for a time by Zhu Xi (1130–1200), students were exposed to a heavy mixture of moral exhortation and scholarship so that they might emerge both virtuous and erudite. Like dedicated teachers everywhere, committed Confucians were forever pleading with their students to forget careerist considerations such as passing examinations and to concentrate on the serious business of learning and self-improvement.

The guidance of a mentor was believed to be extremely important, but for the sake of those who lived in remote places without teachers, Zhu Xi and Lu Zuqian (1137–1181) compiled *Reflections on Things at Hand* (*Jinsi 1u*), an anthology that drew on the writings of the four Northern Song thinkers who came to be considered the founders of a new Confucian philosophy, Zhou Dunyi (1017–1073), the brothers Cheng Hao (1032–1085) and Cheng Yi (1033–1107), and Zhang Zai (1020–1077). *Reflections,* which became enormously influential in Korea and Japan as well as in China, deals with many matters of practical concern ranging from guidance on how to manage a family to advice on when to accept political office and when to decline. It includes discussions of political institutions and behavior. Its main emphasis, however, is on self-perfection, which alone makes all the rest possible.

The authors of *Reflections* carefully distinguished their teachings from those of Buddhism and Daoism and attacked the Buddha and Laozi. Yet, even the staunchest Confucian was not immune to the attractions of Chan, and interest in Daoism remained high. It is therefore not surprising that Song Confucians were influenced by these two traditions even as they sought to undermine them by creating the sophisticated philosophy often known in the West as "Neo-Confucianism" but not referred to by any one designation in China or East Asia generally.

The intellectual atmosphere was further enlivened by Confucians who rejected theoretical speculation and insisted that the true vocation of a scholar lay in concentrating on matters of practical statecraft. But by narrowing their intellectual focus, these thinkers also narrowed their appeal at a time when fewer men looked to the state for a solution of society's ills and their own careers. In contrast, many found Zhu Xi's classic formulation of Neo-Confucianism persuasive, and some accepted it as an identity that, to quote Peter K. Bol, "could provide social and moral guidance in their role as the elite of a local society relative to which they could be powerful, and it provided moral and political justification for their autonomy from a government relative to which they felt powerless."[18]

Zhu Xi's deep and broad impact did not come until after his death. Neither he nor his four Northern Song predecessors were accepted as orthodox in their own day. It was not until the second quarter of the thirteenth century that Zhu's teachings received official recognition and his commentaries on the *Four Books* were officially accepted. Of these four core texts, revered repositories of fundamental truth, only the *Analects* had been part of the Confucian cannon through the ages. The other three, *The Mencius, The Great Learning,* and *The Doctrine of the Mean* (the last two are chapters from the *Rites–Liji*), remained subjects of controversy for most of the Song Period.

It was characteristic of East Asian thinkers that they did not present their ideas in systematic treatises but as commentaries on the classics, in miscellaneous writings (including letters), and in conversations recorded by disciples. This made the study of their ideas very demanding but also encouraged successive generations of scholars to reinterpret texts in their own way. Neither in the Song nor later was Neo-Confucianism a monolithic philosophy.

Song thinkers, like earlier Chinese philosophers, found it congenial and fruitful to think in terms of complementary opposites, interacting polarities such as inner and outer, substance (*ti*) and function (*yong*), knowledge, and action. Perhaps they were particularly attracted to this mode of thought because it enabled them to make distinctions without doing violence to what they perceived to be an ultimate organic unity. In their metaphysics they naturally employed the ancient *yin* and *yang,* but more central to their thought was the conceptual pair *li* and *qi*.

This *li*, not to be confused with the term for rites written with a different character, is frequently translated as "principle" or "pattern." Because the Chinese word does not distinguish between singular and plural, *li* can also be understood as a network of principles. Indeed, the accepted Song etymology of the word was that it originally signified veins running through jade. Each individual *li* is part of the entire system, and in the philosophy of Cheng Yi and Zhu Xi, this system constitutes the underlying pattern of reality. In this view nothing can exist if there is no *li* for it. It is characteristic of the Confucian cast of mind that this applies as much to the realm of human conduct as it does to the physical world. The *li* of fatherhood has the same ontological status (order of being or order of reality) as the *li* for mountains. No distinction is made between the former, which is defined in moral terms, and the latter, for the world of moral action and that of physical objects is held to be one and the same. Both are comprehensible and equally "natural."

*Qi*, which we already encountered in our discussion of painting in Chapter 4, is an even more difficult word to render into English. It is the vital force and substance of which man and the universe are made. It is energy, but energy that occupies space. In its most refined form it occurs as a kind of rarefied ether, but condensed it becomes the most solid metal or rock. Zhu Xi envisioned the world as a sphere in constant rotation, with the heaviest *qi* held in the center by the centripetal force of the motion. *Qi* then becomes progressively lighter and thinner as one moves away from the center. This explains why the air at high altitude is thinner than that at sea level.

It was theoretically possible to construct a philosophy based on either concept. Zhang Zai based his theories entirely on *qi,* whereas Zhu Xi's contemporary Lu Jiuyuan (1139–1193) asserted that *li* alone exists. Cheng Yi and Zhu Xi, however, accepted both as irreducible entities, although *li* had logical and ontological (but not temporal) priority over *qi*. In Zhu Xi's system *li* was further identified with the Supreme Ultimate (*taiji*), which had formed the basis of Zhou Dunyi's metaphysics. In this way *li* was elevated to a level superior to *qi*. Nevertheless, in the actual world *li* never occurs without *qi*. This very important doctrine enabled the Song philosophers to accept Mencius's theory of the essential goodness of humankind and to explain man's frequent departures from that goodness: people were composed of good *li* and more or less impure *qi*. The ancient sages were born with perfectly pure *qi:* they were born perfect. But ordinary folk have to cope with more or less turgid *qi:* we must work to attain perfection.

The way for ordinary people to attain perfection is by truly grasping the *li*, but because these are found within everyone as well as out in the world, there was disagreement over the proper method of self-cultivation. Zhu Xi generally stressed the "investigation of things," by which he meant primarily the study of moral conduct and especially the timeless lessons contained in the classics. Consequently his school was associated with an emphasis on scholarly learning, even though it by no means ruled out more inner-directed endeavors such as silent meditation and reflection. Lu Jiuyuan, in contrast, foreshadowing the teachings of the major Ming dynasty philosopher Wang Yangming, stressed inner illumination. For him, without the reader's innate understanding, even the classics remain without meaning. The truth is within: he once went as far as to say, "The classics are all footnotes to me."

The Song philosophers gave the old concept of *ren* (humaneness) a new metaphysical dimension. Zhang Zai proclaimed, "All people are my brothers and sisters, and all things are my companions."[19] In keeping with this ideal was a new growth in secular charities. Meanwhile, high-minded moral seriousness, demands for vigilance against selfish desires, and ideal selflessness were repeatedly challenged by real life politics, by market forces that obeyed no moral laws, and by social change as people went about their daily affairs guided more by notions of decency than by moral perfection. This is borne out by the family-oriented *Precepts for Social Life* by Yuan Cai, who earned the highest examination degree in 1163.

## Values and Gender

In Confucian theory widows should not remarry, but Song widows did so regularly, and if necessary went to court to protect their property rights. Similarly, theoretically women were not permitted to divorce their husbands, but in the Song, although the system still favored husbands, wives could initiate divorce and easily remarry. Li Qingzhao, for one, remarried after being widowed, but when the marriage did not work out, she petitioned for divorce. Whether married, divorced, or widowed, women controlled the dowries they brought into the marriage and could use them as capital. This could amount to a considerable estate, because Song dowries were larger than those in the Tang, thereby compensating, as Robert Hymes suggests, for the decline of value of a bride's pedigree.[20] The stone portraits of two Song ladies in Figure 8.9 suggest the self-assured grace of women wealthy enough to patronize the Buddhist establishment.

**FIGURE 8.9** Two Song ladies. Cave 165, Maijishan, Gansu. These portraits in stone convey something of the character of their subjects. The Buddhist caves at Maijishan have escaped much of the destruction seen at Longmen, Yungan, and other sites. Sculpture remained associated with religion, whereas painting could be religious or secular. (Courtesy of Michael Sullivan and Dominique Darbois.)

Although girls did not study for the examinations, they were not excluded from literacy. On the contrary, many families took joy and pride in a well-educated daughter or daughter-in-law. With men now admired for their learning, taste, and refinement rather than their martial qualities, there was a trend for elite women and men increasingly to resemble each other. At the same time, there was a countertrend to accentuate or even invent differences. This is apparent in the slender women that inhabit poetry and painting as well as in the development of women's medicine as a distinct field of specialization (there was no corresponding category of male medicine), emphasizing female vulnerability.

The most visible change in women's appearance was in their feet. The practice of footbinding probably originated among court dancers during the Five Dynasties Period and spread first to dancing courtesans and then among the Song upper classes. Under later dynasties it became prevalent among the elite and was also widely practiced in other social strata. It continued well into the twentieth century. Its purpose was to restrict the growth of the feet. The procedure may not have been fully developed in the Song, when the toes of young girls may have been bent upwards. But in its mature form, the feet of young female children were wrapped tightly in bandages about two inches wide and ten feet long. Over a period of time, the four toes of each foot were bent into the sole, and the sole and heel were brought as close together as possible. The great toe was left unbound. The result was thought to enhance a woman's grace and attractiveness. Footbinding was not part of a Confucian social program, but it was tolerated by a society supposedly governed by Confucian values.

The spread of footbinding suggests that the influence of courtesans on standards of feminine beauty reached deeply into elite society. The same was true of their song lyric poetry (*ci*), which circulated widely and was emulated by the wives and daughters of the elite to the consternation of moralists who would keep women focused on family and home. Cheng Yi reports of his mother that "she loved literature but did not engage in flowery composition. She considered it wrong for present-day women to pass around literary compositions, notes, and letters."[21] Instead, she set an example in running her family, kind but firm with servants and children. Female literacy was an asset to be used to educate the children.

Similarly the Neo-Confucians sought to channel, not suppress, women's managerial skills. The ideal was for wives to run the household, including the family's finances, leaving the husband free to pursue his studies and to deal with the outside world. This could be, and later was, interpreted literally to entail the seclusion of upper class women at home. That interpretation came later, but it roots are in the Song. The Neo-Confucian ideal also demanded the wife's total identification with her married family. First, women were praised for using their dowry for the sake of their new family; then efforts were made to change marriage and property laws, efforts that were to come to fruition during the Yuan.

# The End

Among the reasons for the Southern Song's ability to sustain itself for a century and a half were the geographic defensibility and the prosperity of the South as well as the government's ability to command acceptance as the legitimate regime and to perform the traditional functions of government. However, it also suffered from internal ills: unstable imperial leadership (the first three emperors ended their reigns by abdicating), factional divisiveness in officialdom, a general decline in government effectiveness, and a lack of confidence in the government's ability to solve society's problems.

The government's monetary policies eventually produced rampant inflation, and a shrinking tax base resulted from the decline of small landholders and tax evasion by those who held much land. To deal with the latter situation, an ambitious land reform program was launched by Chief Councilor Jia Sidao (1213–1275) during the 1260s. Large landowners were required to sell to the government a portion of their holdings, which the government then managed itself. The economic gains thus realized, however, were counterbalanced by the disaffection of the wealthy and powerful at a time when the state required maximum unity against the Mongol threat.

The government had its troubles, but the dynasty continued to inspire loyal devotion to the end—and even beyond. Not only did men sacrifice their lives in its defense even after the cause was hopeless, but there were also others who remained loyal even after its demise. This was a new phenomenon in Chinese history, and, as with so many Song innovations, set a precedent for later ages.

# Notes

1. F. W. Mote, *Imperial China, 900–1800* (Cambridge: Harvard Univ. Press, 1999), pp. 17–20.

2. Robert Hymes, in Denis Twitchett and John W. Chaffee, eds., *The Cambridge History of China, Vol. 4: Sung China* (forthcoming) (draft p. 126).

3. Alfreda Murck, *The Subtle Art of Dissent: Poetry and Painting in Song China* (Cambridge: Harvard Univ. Press, 2000).

4. Term coined by Paul J. Smith. Cf. his *Taxing Heaven's Storehouse: Horses Bureaucrats, and The Destruction of the Sichuan Tea Industry, 1074–1224* (Cambridge: Harvard Univ. Press, 1991).

5. Li Bozhong, "Was There a Fourteenth Century Turning Point? Population, Land, Technology, and Farm Management," in Paul J. Smith and Richard von Glahn, eds., *The Song-Yuan-Ming Transition in Chinese History* (Cambridge: Harvard Univ. Press, 2003), p. 156.

6. Qin Guan, in Kojiro Yoshikawa, *An Introduction to Sung Poetry*, trans. Burton Watson (Cambridge: Harvard Univ. Press, 1967), pp. 16–17.

7. Edward L. Davis, *Society and the Supernatural in Song China* (Honolulu: Univ. of Hawaii Press, 2001), p. 80.

8. Robert Hymes, op. cit. (draft p. 103).

9. Robert Hymes, *Way and Byway: Taoism, Local Religion, and Models of Divinity in Sung and Modern China* (Berkeley: Univ. of California Press, 2002), p. 21. Reprinted with permission.

10. Susan Bush, *The Chinese Literati on Painting: Su Shih (1037–1101) to Tung Ch'i-ch'ang (1156–1636)* (Cambridge: Harvard Univ. Press, 1971), p. 25.

11. Robert E. Harrist, Jr., *Paintings and Private Life in Eleventh-Century China: Mountain Villa by Li Gonglin* (Princeton: Princeton Univ. Press, 1998).

12. Richard M. Barnhart, "Tung Yiian," in Herbert Franke, ed., *Sung Biographies— Painters,* Münchener Ostasiatische Studien, Vol. 17 (Wiesbaden: Franz Steiner Verlag, 1976), p. 141.

13. Mark Elvin, *The Pattern of the Chinese Past* (Stanford: Stanford Univ. Press, 1973), p. 137.

14. R. E. Latham, trans., *The Travels of Marco Polo* (Baltimore: Penguin Books, 1958), p. 187.

15. Angela Schottenhammer, *The Emporium of the World: Maritime Quanzhou, 1000–1400* (Leiden: Brill, 2001).

16. Eugene Boyang, trans., in Kang-I Sun Chang and Haun Saussy, *Women Writers in Traditional China: An Anthology of Poetry and Criticism* (Stanford: Stanford Univ. Press, 1999), p. 94.

17. Liu Wu-chi, *An Introduction to Chinese Literature* (Bloomington: Indiana Univ. Press, 1966), p. 119.

18. Peter K. Bol, "Neo-Confucianism and Local Society, Twelfth to Sixteenth Century: A Case Study," in Smith and Glahn, *Song-Yuan-Ming Transition,* p. 245.

19. Wing-tsit Chan, *A Source Book in Chinese Philosophy* (Princeton: Princeton Univ. Press, 1963), p. 497.

20. Robert Hymes, in *Cambridge History of China,* Vol. 5 (forthcoming).

21. Wing-tit Chan, trans., *Reflections on Things at Hand: The Neo-Confucian Anthology compiled by Chu His and Lü Tsu-ch'ien* (New York: Columbia Univ. Press, 1967), pp. 180–81.

# The Mongol Empire and the Yuan Dynasty

**Fall of North China**

1206     1234                          1279                                    1368

**MONGOL CONQUESTS**
Chinggis Khan (1206–27)

**YUAN DYNASTY**

Khubilai Khan (1260–94)

The Mongols are famed as the world's foremost conquerors, creators of the largest empire in the history of the planet (see Figure 9.1). They established their supremacy over most of Eurasia, including Russia and Persia, all of Central Asia, China, and Korea. Mongol armies reached as far West as the Adriatic; in the East they took to ships to attack Japan, where they hastened the demise of the Kamakura Shogunate, and in the southeast they sent a naval expedition against Java. Even those lands that, like Japan, preserved their independence were affected by the Mongol challenge. For a time, communication between East and West was facilitated by Mongol domination and encouragement of trade. But the Mongol territory was too vast, local cultures were too various and deeply rooted, and the centrifugal forces were too strong for the Mongol Empire to last very long. Ultimately the empire disintegrated, leaving a much disputed legacy.

# Chinggis Khan: Founding of the Mongol Empire

Temujin, the future Chinggis Khan (c. 1167–1227), was the son of a Mongolian tribal chieftain. When his father was killed, the boy was forced to flee and spent a number of years wandering. Eventually he returned to his tribe and began his career as a world conqueror by avenging the murder of his father. Gradually he gained ascendancy in the hierarchy of tribal chiefs, forming a new nomadic federation in a process that gave rise to a new sense of Mongol ethnic identity that came to include not only those who had considered themselves Mongols earlier but also anyone who had been with Chinggis at this founding time.

Chinggis was almost forty by the time he established his leadership over all the Mongol tribes, which, at a great meeting held in 1206, recognized him as the supreme ruler, the Chinggis Khan. As supreme ruler he unified the tribes, organized them into a superb fighting force, and started them on the road to world conquest. Unifying the tribes was a difficult task because they were widely dispersed and also

**FIGURE 9.1** The Mongol Empire, 1294.

because the tribesmen were excellent fighters, jealous of their independence. It required great determination, political skill, knowledge of men, and manifest ability to lead and weld these tribal groups into a people. It also required ruthlessness, drive, military skill, and courage. Apparently Chinggis Khan had these qualities. He was able to obtain the support of the hardy tribesmen. Equally significant as a testament to his personal power was his ability to attract a following of *nökhör,* "companions," who, renouncing all other ties to clan or tribe, gave their patron their sole and complete loyalty. Many of Chinggis Khan's best generals were *nökhör.*

It does not detract from Chinggis Khan's personal achievement to note that more impersonal forces were also at work, inducing the Mongols to unify and attack the settled peoples who sometimes broke off trade vital to the steppe nomads. Particularly serious was a drop in climactic temperature that reduced the amount of grass available to feed the animals vital for Mongol subsistence.

Clans and tribes remained the basic units of Mongol organization, but at a higher level the people were also bound together by loyalty to the Great Khan and by a law code (*jasagh*) first promulgated in 1206 and later expanded. Also transcending tribal divisions was the army, organized on a decimal system in units of tens, hundreds, and thousands. An elite corps, which grew to 10,000 men, formed its core. At the height of the campaigns, the total army may have numbered nearly 130,000 men. It was joined in those campaigns by almost an equal number of non-Mongol warriors, the forces of other peoples who joined the Mongols after 1205 rather than attempt to resist the whirlwind.

The Mongol army was a superb force in its overall direction, organization, and the toughness and ability of its individual fighting men. These fighters lived in the saddle: they could even sleep on horseback while their horses marched. When necessary they withstood great privation and endured all kinds of hardship. They were able to cover enormous distances at great speed, changing mounts several times in the process. The Mongol horses too were very hardy, able to endure extremes of climate, and in winter to find food by digging it out from under the snow or stripping twigs and bark from trees. Moreover, on the command level, the Mongols achieved masterly feats of planning and carrying out their operations. Their enemies were defeated as much by the Mongols' rapid movements and the precise coordination of their far-flung armies as by their ferocity and superb tactical discipline.

Whatever the Mongols could not use they destroyed. That was the fate of cities that resisted: their women and children were enslaved, and the men were either killed or used as living shields in the next battle or assault on a city. Mongol brutality left terror in its wake. Even for Europeans, who lived in a far more military culture than that of China, the encounter with Mongol arms was an overwhelming experience that could only be explained in supernatural terms. According to *The Chronicle of Novgorod,* "God alone knows who they are and whence they came."[1] In Russia, Poland, and Hungary the merciless Mongols appeared as manifestations of God's wrath and their cruelties as acts of divine punishment meted out to sinners.

By the time of his death in 1227, Chinggis Khan had established Mongol supremacy in Central Asia, begun the offensive against Russia, destroyed the Xi Xia, fought the Jin, and captured Beijing. His headquarters remained in Mongolia with Karakorum as the capital, although it did not become a major city with a city wall and permanent buildings until 1235. This was the work of Ögödei (r. 1229–1241), who as Great Khan inherited the richest part of his father's empire. According to Mongol custom, however, other portions had been assigned to Ögödei's brothers, who ruled over three major khanates in Turkestan, Russia, and Persia.

The death of Chinggis Khan and the division of his patrimony did not diminish the momentum of Mongol conquests: in 1231 Mongol troops crossed the Yalu River into Korea and continued their advance in North China, taking Kaifeng in 1233 and Luoyang in 1234. Also in 1234 they completed the destruction of the Jin. In 1236–1238 they took Sichuan. The Dali kingdom fell in 1252–1253. Mongol armies were equally successful in the West, where they seized Kiev in 1240 and Baghdad in 1258. In 1241 a Mongol army was on the Adriatic. And then they turned back. Western Europe was spared, not because the Mongols were beaten in battle or awed by the Western defense—they had already thoroughly defeated the largest army in Europe by far, that of King Bela of Hungary— but by a command decision of the Mongol general. The exact reason for the turnabout is not known, but geography most likely played a role: the vast number of horses required by the Mongol army needed great open plains on which to graze.

The Mongols developed a courier system to link their empire; couriers could cover up to 200 miles a day. They also had a written language based on that of the

Uighurs. They were bound by the *jasagh* laws. Where complex political institutions existed, as in China and Persia, the Mongol laws were grafted on to the local culture, but the Mongols lacked a formalized system of succession as well as an organized political system capable of molding their vast and diverse conquests into a lasting unity.

Under Chinggis Khan's grandson Khubilai (1215–1294), who became Great Khan in 1260, the conquest of the Southern Song was completed in 1278. In 1264, early in his reign, Khubilai transferred the capital from Mongolia to Beijing, and in doing so tacitly relinquished the Mongol claim to rule the entire world. Once again the political balance of East Asia was dominated by China, although this time not by Chinese.

# China under the Mongols: The Early Years (1211–1260)

Almost half a century passed between Chinggis Khan's first attack on territory traditionally Chinese (1211) and the beginning of Khubilai's reign. By the twelfth century the Jin had, through its examination system and other policies, developed strong claims that it, rather than the Southern Song, was the legitimate successor to the Northern Song, whose culture it did much to continue. As already noted, people living under the Jin also developed their own form of Daoism and contributed importantly to Buddhism. Unfortunately for the dynasty, the Mongol advance put an end to "High Jin,"[2] the forty years of peace from 1165 to 1206 that saw the dynasty's greatest achievements. The Mongol invasion of North China was a catastrophe for many ordinary farmers as well as for members of the elite such as Yuan Haowen, whose poems of "death and disorder" from 1233 to 1235 attest both to Jin literary sophistication and to the devastation of those years.

In their military operations against the Jin as well as the subsequent civil administration of North China, the Mongols made use of non-Mongols, particularly Khitan leaders who were traditionally hostile toward the Jin and also Chinese who felt no great loyalty toward the Jurchen. The services of such men were essential to the Mongols, operating as they were in unfamiliar terrain and outnumbered by their enemy. Indeed, the service of men of non-Mongol background was indispensable, as the Mongols themselves numbered only around 1 million people. Thus, non-Mongol military leaders were accepted as *nökhör* and granted the privileges that went with that status, including the receipt of lands to rule.

Among the non-Mongols in the service of the Khan, Yelü Chucai (1189–1243) was the most outstanding. As a sinicized Khitan of royal Liao lineage and a first-place examination graduate under the Jin, Yelü was well equipped to mediate between the Mongols and their Chinese subjects. Summoned to Mongolia by Chinggis Khan in 1218, he became influential as a court astrologer and is said to have played a role in the Mongol decision to stay out of India. But his real prominence came under Ögödei when he was able to persuade the Khan to reject the proposal by a group of Mongols that all the territory conquered in North China be turned into pasturage. This was a serious proposal consistent with the Mongol way of life and with the crucial need for great quantities of horses if the Mongols were to retain their power. Other nomadic peoples, most recently the Jurchen, although much less involved than the Mongols in maintaining power outside China, had pondered the same alternatives. In the end, Yelü's position prevailed. He persuaded the Khan, not by appealing to Chinese theories of government, but by demonstrating the profits to be gained through an orderly exploitation of a settled and productive population. Yelü was thereupon, in 1229, placed in charge of taxation and created a tax system staffed by civilian officials.

Rising eventually to highest office, he worked hard to fashion a centralized administration along Chinese lines but achieved only partial success. For example, he failed in his attempt to subject privileged non-Chinese in North China to the same taxes imposed on the Chinese population. He did obtain enactment of a census, but he could not dissuade Ögödei from granting lands to supporters, who were beyond the government's fiscal control. In this case his proposal would have affected Chinese as well as non-Chinese leaders whose self-interest was at stake. The division of China into large-scale and loosely controlled military commands continued throughout the Mongol period; these commands later evolved into the large provinces into which China was divided during the Ming and Qing.

Yelü rescued Chinese scholars from captivity and found positions for them, including posts as tutors to Mongol nobles, but always faced stiff opposition. Toward the end of his life he suffered increasing setbacks. Throughout his career he appealed to Mongol greed. In the end he was outbid by Central Asian merchants who argued that Yelü's centralized tax system was less lucrative than opening China to tax farming with the right to collect taxes going to the highest bidder. Any amount the contractor collected in excess of what he owed the government was his to keep. This arrangement appealed to the rapaciousness of both the government and the tax farmer and resulted in the most ruthless measures to exact ruinously high taxes. Despite Yelü's protests that this was a short-sighted policy harmful to the people who produced the wealth, in 1239 a Muslim businessman was granted the right to collect taxes in North China. At the time of Yelü Chucai's death in 1243, it looked as though his work was coming undone. He did not live to see how Khubilai Khan went about creating a Sino-Mongolian state.

# Khubilai Khan and the Early Yuan

In 1271 Khubilai Khan (r. 1260–1294), following the transfer of the capital to Beijing, adopted Yuan ("The Origin") as a Chinese-style dynastic name, explaining in an edict that it is derived from the principle of "Great Origin" (*qianyuan*), the first hexagram of the *Changes*. Thereby the Yuan became the first dynasty named not after a place or the founder's original fiefdom but for a potent and auspicious idea. Chinese court ceremonials were adopted. Chinggis Khan now received a posthumous Chinese title (Taizu), and Khubilai himself appears in the Chinese histories under the name of Shizu. Previous khans had preferred to live among their herds and tents instead of taking up permanent residence in the capital and spent as much time hunting as they did looking after government operations. Khubilai, in contrast, spent most of his time in Beijing or in the summer capital at Shangdu in Inner Mongolia. He was careful to give at least an appearance of ruling in a Chinese manner while engaged in "a delicate balancing act between ruling the sedentary civilization of China and preserving the cultural identity and values of the Mongols."[3] Among measures designed to accomplish the latter were a prohibition against Mongols marrying Chinese, his own practice of taking only Mongol women into the palace, and a policy of discouraging Mongols from associating with Chinese. That he also saw himself as a universal ruler is indicated by an unsuccessful attempt to propagate a new alphabet that he hoped could become a universal script. On the other hand, he did not try to devise a uniform code of law applicable to all the different peoples under his rule, and the Yuan remained the only Chinese dynasty lacking such a code.

Khubilai's first priority was to make himself truly master of all China, completing the military conquest initiated by his grandfather and continued by Chinggis Khan's successors. The subjugation of the Southern Song was difficult, for resistance was stiff, and the Mongols had to learn new techniques to operate successfully in the South. They were finally victorious, assisted by the defection of much of the Song navy. When the Southern Song fell in 1279, the Mongols became the first nomadic conquerors to rule all of China (see Figure 9.1). By this time gunpowder warfare was well established. Mongol soldiers carried side arms resembling miniature cannons, whereas Yuan and Song ships fired bombards at each other.

The fall of Southern Song did not bring an end to warfare. Although Khubilai's empire was China based, his ambitions were not confined to China. He sent an expedition against Japan in 1274, and, after he was master of all of China, organized a second, more massive attack in 1281. Both attacks failed. Plans for a third attempt were never carried out. This was largely because in the 1280s Mongol forces were occupied with operations in Southeast Asia, where repeated attacks were made on Vietnam and Burma. In 1281 and again in 1292 the Khan's fleet attacked Java. These expeditions forced local rulers into ritual submission but did not expand the territory under actual Yuan control. At the same time Khubilai could not afford to neglect the inner Asian frontier, where he was repeatedly challenged by Ögödei's grandson, Khaidu. Khubilai and his successors concentrated on securing Mongolia. This they accomplished but at the cost of giving up their ambition to dominate Central Asia.

Within China a significant number of men remained loyal to the old dynasty, continued to employ Song terminology, and dreamed of a Song restoration while refusing to serve the new power. For their part, Mongols relegated southerners to the lowest category in their fourfold division of society along ethnic lines. Highest status was accorded to the Mongols. Next came persons with special status (*semuren*). These were Mongol allies, largely from Central Asia and the Near East, such as Turks, Persians, and Syrians. They played an important role in government financial administration, often served as managers for Mongol aristocrats, and enjoyed special privileges as financiers. Organized into special guilds, they financed the caravan trade and loaned out money at usurious rates. The third status group, although termed *hanren*, which usually means "Chinese," included all inhabitants of North China at the time of the Mongol conquest of the Jin: those of Khitan, Jurchen, or Korean family background as well as ethnic Chinese. Finally, at the bottom, were the 80 percent of the Chinese population who lived in the South, the *nanren* or "southerners," also referred to by the less-neutral term *manzi*, that is, "southern barbarians" even though the most cultured scholars lived in the South. The fourfold division of society was expressed in the recruitment and appointment of government officials, in the conduct of legal cases, and in taxation.

Most Chinese literati resigned themselves to the new order and accepted the Yuan as the recipient of the Heavenly Mandate, but others remained unreconciled even though Khubilai had placed Chinese Confucians in high advisory or educational posts and had shown himself so receptive to their advice that he even had his son and heir educated in the Confucian manner. The emperor was also a generous patron of Chinese arts and letters, but he refused to reinstitute the civil service examinations and continued to give top priority to expensive military campaigns. To avoid dependence on Chinese officials, Khubilai employed foreigners, including Muslims, Tibetans, Uighurs, and other Central Asians, and even men from the Far West such as the Persian astronomer Jamal al-Din and, quite probably, the Venetian Marco Polo.

Khubilai made a start in the reconstruction of the shattered economy of the North, but the South remained the main economic region. One policy that the Yuan adopted from their Jin and Song predecessors was the use of paper money. Concerned with not disrupting economic life, Khubilai even provided for conversion of Southern Song paper money into that of the Yuan and made paper money the sole legal currency. As long as the paper currency was well backed, this policy was a success despite the slow inflation that set in after 1280. In other areas too, including the rehabilitation and extension of the Grand Canal, Khubilai's regime accomplished much. He displayed an ability to learn and to adjust to new circumstances in administrative as well as in military matters. What he could not do was to construct a system that would run smoothly of itself, and, unfortunately for the dynasty, there was not to be another Khubilai Khan.

# The Yuan Continued, 1294–1355

Although the Yuan accomplished more than traditionally hostile Chinese historians would later admit, it never achieved the strength and longevity of a major Chinese dynasty. Lacking a tradition of orderly succession, the dynasty was troubled by numerous succession disputes. During the 40 years after Khubilai's death, seven emperors came to the throne, often with accompanying bloodshed and murder. After 1328 men from the Mongolian steppe no longer played a major role in these struggles. Earlier, in 1307, the Mongolian homeland had been reduced to a province under civil administration. But the elimination of the steppe as a power base did not alleviate internal tensions. Nor was the dynasty able to devise a lasting formula for balancing the diverse elements in government and society.

Court politics were dominated by factionalism, which found expression in fluctuating government policies. Personnel policies were a particularly sensitive area. Not until 1313 was an imperial edict issued, reviving the civil service examinations based on the Confucian classics and the commentaries of Zhu Xi, as was to remain the case for the duration of the system. The first tests were given in 1315. Although the curriculum was a major concession to the Confucian literati, the system favored the Mongols and their non-Chinese allies, who were given simplified examinations. Even so, degree holders occupied less than 2 percent of government posts. Under these circumstances some Chinese, hungry for office, could not resist the temptation to assume non-Chinese names.

In 1335 Bayan (Chancellor from 1333 to 1340), as part of a program to restore the political system as it had operated under Khubilai Khan, obtained an imperial decree canceling the examinations. This was consistent with his policy of reinforcing ethnic separation and appointing officials on the basis of lineage and practical experience. He managed to cut costs, but gained the enmity of all who viewed the reinstitution of the examinations as a step toward the normalization of government and as an opportunity for personal advancement.

Bayan was overthrown by Toghtō (d. 1356), who served as Chancellor from 1340 to 1344 and again from 1349 to 1355. Toghtō revived the examination in 1342. Although degree holders enjoyed great prestige, the examinations did not regain the prominence they had enjoyed during the Song. Still worse from the Chinese scholar's point of view was the persistent Yuan policy of according military officials supremacy over civilian officials.

A major problem during the 1340s was the Yellow River, which broke its dikes, flooded, and, most disastrously, began to change its course away from its previous outlet south of the Shandong Peninsula. One part of the river now flowed north of the Shandong Peninsula; another emptied into the Grand Canal, putting it out of commission. Not only did this cause great dislocation and suffering to the inhabitants of the affected areas, but it also threatened the economic survival of the dynasty by interrupting shipments of grain from the South. The only alternative to the Grand Canal route was by sea, but the maritime route was in constant danger from an increasingly bold and assertive pirate, Fan Guozhen. Clearly a massive effort was required for the government to reestablish control over the river or over the sea route, and it lacked the resources to do both. Given the choice, Toghtō decided to concentrate on the more immediately threatening and more manageable inland problem. Furthermore, rather than settle for a superficial and temporary solution, he proposed the digging of a new channel for the Yellow River south of the Shandong Peninsula. Although his plan ran into political opposition, this great feat of hydraulic engineering was successfully carried out during Toghtō's second administration. Under the direction of a Chinese engineer it was completed with the labor of 150,000 civilians and 20,000 troops.

The Yellow River problem was solved, but the cost was high, for it strained to the utmost the economic resources of the government and the people. An excessive issue of inadequately backed paper money produced growing inflation, which added its toll to the hardships of the population already suffering from government exactions. In mid-century the government was beset by dire problems, but these were much more severe in the north than in the south.

## The Economy

Recent demographic studies conclude that the population of China dropped by around 30 percent from 108 million in 1220 to 75 million in 1229, rose back to 87 million by 1252, but amounted to only 67 million in 1381. Although warfare accounts for much of the initial drop, factors that were out of government control also took their toll during "the calamitous fourteenth century," to use the title of Barbara Tuchman's famous book. As John Dardess reminds us, "from Iceland and England at one end of Eurasia to Japan at the other, societies were suffering plagues, famines, agricultural decline, depopulation, and civil upheaval. Few societies were spared at least some of these symptoms. China was spared none of them."[4] Global cooling produced harsh winters. Repeated floods and droughts in North China were also related to the severe weather. The epidemics of mid-century China, disasters China shared with the rest of Eurasia, probably were a consequence of the new ease of travel for disease as well as for people.

Like the Yellow River problem, these natural disasters affected everyone in the land but some more than others. Regional and local developments, such as the silting up or widening of a river, often governed the rise and fall of market/temple towns in the Southern Yangzi basin, which was much less hard hit than the North by the destruction wrought by warfare and nature. The Mongol conquerors did not disturb the class structure of South China, nor did they inflict permanent damage on the southern economy. There the ceramics and silk industries continued to flourish, and a new cotton industry also developed. (Cotton culture may have been borrowed from the aboriginal inhabitants of China's southern provinces; a species of cotton was cultivated in Western Yunnan by the third century C.E. However, cotton did not become important economically until the Yuan.)

In the Yangzi basin the spread of advanced farming techniques from the lowlands to the highlands as well as better techniques for drying fields, turning marshes into fertile farmland, were among the agricultural advances that linked the Yuan to the Song on the one hand and prepared the ground for what was to follow in the Ming on the other. Current research suggests that while the Southern Yangzi basin did not escape all harm, the fourteenth century was hardly calamitous for this vital region, which was confirmed as the most productive in the empire.

# Society

Some Mongol social policies, such as creating hereditary families of artisans, appear to have had little lasting effect on Chinese social structure. But for the history of women and thus the family, this was a crucial period marked by numerous twists and turns as policies changed to take into account Mongol and Chinese views, which in certain cases and times strongly diverged, pulling in different directions, but in other cases pulled in the same directions.

A striking example of divergence is the levirate, practiced by the Mongols and other nomadic people, providing for men to inherit their brother's widows. It seems that this practice was well suited to life on the steppe, but it was regarded with abhorrence by the Chinese. Conversely, an example of convergence is the Mongol concern for having males as heads of household so that they would be available for military service, which was consistent with Neo-Confucian views on the priority of sons over daughters in inheritance. This entailed placing the wife's property under the jurisdiction of the family she married into. An official measure dated 1313 states:

> Regarding dowry lands and other goods that a woman brings into her marriage: henceforth if a woman who has once been married wishes to remarry, regardless of whether she is divorced while her first husband is alive or living as a widow after her husband has died, all the dowry property and other assets she originally brought into her marriage should be taken over by the family of her former husband. She is absolutely not permitted to take them away with herself, as was formerly done.[5]

This passage comes from a recent work by Bettine Birge, who goes on to point out that actual practice no doubt lagged behind changes in law. However, the direction of change was to be confirmed under the dynasties that succeeded the Yuan, and the actual situation of the majority of women did change.

# Religion

The Mongol tolerance of foreigners also extended to foreign religions. The early khans liked to sponsor religious debates at their courts, and under the Mongols all religions were granted tax exemption. Nestorians and Muslims and Christians and Jews were welcome. Integral Perfection Daoism got a temporary boost after Qiu Chuji (d. 1227) visited Chinggis Khan in Central Asia, but in the end the intense competition for official patronage was won by the proponents of Tibetan Buddhism. After gaining the submission of Tibet, the Mongols used a prominent Tibetan abbot to rule on their behalf over this mountainous land, where the dominant religion was an amalgam of Indian Buddhism and the native Bon religion. Known as Lamaism, after the Tibetan word designating a monk, this religion was more sophisticated and universal than the native shamanism of the Mongols. The Mongol rulers were impressed by the Lamaist formulae and charms infused with magic power to cure or harm, and they were attracted to the Tibetan religion as a form of Buddhism practiced by a hardy, nonagricultural people like themselves. In 1260 a Mongol lama was established as State Preceptor, and in 1261 he was given responsibility for the entire Buddhist clergy. Khubilai's successor continued to favor Lamaism, and as a result of imperial munificence, there was a proliferation of Buddhist art. Much of this art showed Tibetan or Nepalese influence, but it never won the esteem of students of Chinese art. A very different expression of official favor took the form of an edict, issued in 1309, stipulating that anyone striking a lama would have his hand cut off and that an offender would lose his tongue for insulting a lama. However, the conversion to Lamaism of the Mongols who remained on the steppe did not take place until the sixteenth century.

Lamaism had little impact on the Chinese population whose religious life and institutions showed a great deal of continuity with the past. Shanqi Daoism continued to be strong on Mt. Mao, whereas another sect claimed succession from the Celestial Masters. Pure Land Buddhism had a vast following, and Chan remained influential, beginning with Yelü Chucai, who turned to Chan after the fall of the Jin. During a period of monastic training under Xingxiu, "The Old Man of a Thousand Pines," Yelü acquired a profound knowledge of Chan.

Many people belonged to the lay Buddhist societies that had developed under the Southern Song. As summarized by Daniel Overmyer:

> By the Yuan period these sects were characterized by predominantly lay membership and leadership, hierarchical organization, active proselytism, congregational rituals, possession of their own scriptures in the vernacular, and mutual economic support.[6]

The southern Yangzi basin was an area of vigorous religious and economic activity. There Buddhist temples displayed their power to attract people and wealth and thus stimulated as well as participated in the growth of towns, centers of religion and commerce.

## Cultural and Intellectual Life

Although some earnest scholars saw it as their mission to promote the Way by serving (and civilizing) the Mongols, others found withdrawal from active politics morally preferable and the demands of study and/or self-cultivation more compelling and fulfilling. Private academies with their Neo-Confucian curriculum offered an attractive alternative to government service, as did local activism. Followers of Zhu Xi drew confidence from their claim to be continuing a tradition that Zhu Xi had firmly rooted in the work of the ancient sages and that provided ample food for thought about issues such as the proper balance between internal moral cultivation and scholarly study.

A local tradition that was to have great influence on the Ming founder was that of Jinhua (Wuzhou), 125 miles south of Hangzhou, where Neo-Confucians found room for the appreciation of literature, on the one hand, and practical considerations of governance and reform on the other—two strands that had at times appeared as alternatives to rather than as elements within Neo-Confucianism. Most significantly, the leaders of this movement "used the Neo-Confucian style of self-cultivation to define a style of leadership that valued moral independence, individual responsibility and scholarly authority."[7]

The South remained the center of intellectual life, but the North also contributed in many ways. For example, the great mathematician Zhu Shijie drew on both northern and southern mathematical traditions. His *Introduction to Mathematics*, although long lost in China, became very influential in Japan, but his stature as not only the Yuan's but also China's leading algebraist is based on *Mirror of the Four Elements* (preface 1303), a book nonetheless remarkable for being long neglected. Little is known of Zhu's life other than that he came from the North and taught in Yangzhou around 1300, but the preface to his book suggests that he had quite a following and why:

> People come like clouds from the four quarters to meet at his gate in order to learn from him. . . . By the aid of geometrical figures he explains the relations of heaven, earth, men and things (technical terms for the algebraic notation). . . . By moving the expressions upward and downward, and from side to side, by advancing and retiring, alternating and connecting, by changing, dividing, and multiplying, by assuming the unreal for the real and using the imaginary for the true, by employing different signs for positive and negative, by keeping some and eliminating others and then changing the positions of the counting rods, by attacking from the front or from one side, as show in the four examples—he finally succeeds in working out the equations and the roots in a profound yet natural manner. . . .[8]

Zhu would probably have been a mathematician under any circumstances, but other talented men, who in more normal times would have taken up a political career, now found an outlet in poetry and painting. Yuan paintings often contain an element of self-portraiture, although rarely was this as explicit as in *Emaciated Horse* (see Figure 9.2) by the Song loyalist Gong Kai (1222–1307), who belonged to the generation that experienced the change of dynasties. His painting expresses the self-image of the Chinese scholars who found themselves condemned to live in a world that did not respect their talents or prize their values; a world in which, as indicated in the poem Gong added to his painting, the stables of the former dynasty remained empty. The horse, long a symbol of the scholar-official, was an especially fitting symbol for the neglected Confucian living under a conqueror who prided himself on his horsemanship. The very gauntness of Gong's haggard horse brings out the essential strength of its splendid physique. To those who understood its meaning, the painting was an eloquent, proud, and poignant statement of a bitter shared fate.

**FIGURE 9.2** Gong Kai, *Emaciated Horse*. Hand-scroll, ink on paper, 22.44 in × 11.81 in. The very gauntness of Gong's haggard horse brings out the essential strength of its splendid physique. (© Abe Collection, Osaka Municipal Museum of Fine Arts.)

The uncertain times prompted a good number of educated men to make a living by pursuing occupations that brought them into close daily contact with ordinary, common people. Some became doctors, others took up fortune-telling, and still others turned to the theater for their livelihood. Great dramas were produced as well as powerful paintings.

## "Northern" Drama

The performance arts had a long history in China. Early shamanistic religious dances, performances of music and acting staged for the amusement of the imperial court; "ballets" such as the Tang poet Bo Juyi's favorite, *Rainbow Skirts and Feather Jackets;* and possibly Indian influences form part of the background of Chinese drama that first emerged during the Song and reached its classic form during the Yuan. Equally important to the emergence of mature Yuan music drama was the heritage of popular entertainment, including the various theatricals staged for the benefit of the inhabitants of Song Kaifeng and Hangzhou (both of which had thriving theater districts), featuring not only performances by live actors but also puppet shows, acrobats, and shadow plays, genres with their own histories. In the puppet theater some puppets were on strings, others were on sticks, still others were controlled by explosive charges, and some productions featured "live puppets," that is, children manipulated by a "puppeteer." In the shadow plays, the audience observed silhouettes of figures manipulated behind a screen and in front of lights.

Among the precursors of the Yuan drama, none are more important than the storytellers who had enlivened the Song urban scene. In Song Hangzhou they were numerous enough to form "guilds." Set up in their stalls, they recited their stories, sometimes to the accompaniment of musical instruments. Each man had his specialty: realistic stories, stories of ghosts and the miraculous, religious tales, or stories based on historical episodes. Their art consisted not of simply relating an old story but making it come vividly alive by dramatic modulations of the voice and other dramatic devices. Cyril Birch tells of a fairly recent practitioner of the art who "in one breath could produce seven distinct sounds to represent in realistic fashion the screams of a pig in the successive stages of its slaughter."[9] Thus, the development of the theater did not inhibit the continuing flourishing of the art of the storyteller, but this art did leave its mark on the formal conventions not only of the theater but also of the novel, and it influenced the content as well as the form of both of these popular genres.

Chinese drama always involved music and never lost its character as a performance art, although in the Yuan northern performance and southern literary traditions converged to produce the written opus that came to define the genre after undergoing considerable editing, in the course of which much was lost:

> The taming of a ragged physical format, the regularization of shape and style, was paralleled by the suppression of the equally chaotic and unbounded world the text represented. In a harnessing of both behavior and presentation, regicide, forced abdication, bloody retribution, and unleashed sexual desire and predation were winnowed out, just as miswritten characters or misunderstood passages were rewritten.[10]

The plots of many of the plays still extant are based on earlier materials. Historical episodes such as the marriage of the Han palace beauty Wang Zhaojun to a Xiongnu chieftain; the political and military ploys devised by Zhuge Liang and his contemporaries of the Three Kingdom Period; the tragedy brought on by East Asia's most famed femme fatale, Yang Gueifei; the story of Xuanzang's pilgrimage to India; and other historical and semihistorical events provided the Yuan dramatists with some of their most effective and popular themes. And the plays for their part did much to fix in the popular mind colorful, larger-than-life images of these personages, creations of the poetic imagination embellishing the more prosaic historical accounts.

Theatergoers also enjoyed dramatic renditions of old love stories, such as that of the beautiful Yingying and a student named Zhang recounted in the celebrated thirteenth-century play *The Romance of the Western Chamber* by Wang Shifu. In adapting the old tale to the stage, Wang did not hesitate to rework his materials for greater theatrical and literary effect. Thus, the play makes skillful use of Yingying's mother's refusal to honor her promise to marry her daughter to whomever would rescue them when they are surrounded by rebels. Yingying, already greatly attracted to the young rescuer, now gives him her heart. And the injustice of the mother's act also transforms Nurse Huaining from an obstacle into a highly resourceful ally. To please his audience, the playwright departs from the Tang version of the story and has the drama end with the couple overcoming all obstacles to their happiness, including Yingying's mother. After Zhang passes his examinations, they are united in marriage. Love triumphs in the end. This happy resolution is characteristic of the genre, for these plays were designed to appeal to an audience not only of connoisseurs but also of ordinary people with little or no formal education, who desired happy endings.

The repertoire of the Yuan theater included many plays expressing a longing for justice. Some featured that model of official rectitude and wisdom Judge Bao (based on a real official, Bao Zheng [999–1062]), a champion of justice who repeatedly uncovers even the most ingenious deceptions of the wicked. Prominent among the villains of such plays are greedy and unscrupulous officials who subvert the moral order they are theoretically committed to uphold. Among the heroes are Robin Hood-like figures, outlaws who have right on their side even as they defy the state and its laws. (Many of these heroes also appear in the Ming novel *The Water Margin;* see Chapter 10). No doubt many members of the audience derived vicarious pleasure from witnessing the punishment of venal and corrupt officials resembling those who in real life went uncorrected. The plays do not deal with contemporary events in any obvious way nor do they directly cast aspersions on the regime. Yet one wonders what a Mongol spectator would have made of the scene in *Autumn in the Palace of Han,* in which the playwright described the hardships facing Wang Zhaojun among the "barbarians" when she will have only "tasteless salted flesh" to eat and for drink "clabbered milk and gruel."[11]

The plays were written for standard actors' roles: leading man, leading lady, villain, and so on. The characters too can be classified into easily recognizable types such as the faithful lovers of *The Romance of the Western Chamber,* the corrupt officials and wise judges of the courtroom dramas, the uncouth but virtuous outlaws, and the beautiful, talented, and strong-minded courtesans. Most plays consisted of four acts between which short interludes, or "wedges," could be inserted. Because stage props were few, characters regularly made speeches of self-identification. The playwrights also used occasional recapitulations, carryovers from the tradition of the storyteller.

Music played an important part in the theater. The songs or song sequences in each act were in a single mode or key. The lute and zither were the standard instruments of the Yuan northern drama. In contrast to the mellow, refined music of the southern drama that reached its height under the Ming, the Yuan sound was vigorous and spirited. The Yuan drama's roots in the tradition of oral narrative are also revealed in the assignment of all arias to a single performer. Thus, in *Autumn in the Palace of Han,* only the emperor sings.

The products of the Yuan playwright frequently achieved high literary excellence. Dialogue written in the spoken language of the time lent an earthy freshness to texts, which at times included bawdy vulgarisms that no respectable Confucian scholar of later times would have allowed to flow from his brush. Such language contributed to the bad repute in which the Yuan drama was held in polite circles under later dynasties, until it was appreciatively rediscovered in the twentieth century. What was valued by the critics were the plays' poetic passages, particularly the lyric songs (*sanju*), which rank with other major forms of Chinese poetry in their technical intricacy, musical subtlety, and employment of various poetic devices, including the effective use of imagery. Just as connoisseurs judged paintings by the quality of their brushwork, critics focused on the merits of the poetry in the plays. Thus, a fifteenth-century critic praised the poetry of Ma Zhiyuan, author of *Autumn in the Palace of Han,* as resembling "a phoenix gliding and singing in the highest clouds."[12]

*The Romance of the Western Chamber* is beloved for its poetry. In it Yingying herself is deeply moved when Zhang sings to her of love, and "word follows word like the endless dripping of a water-clock."[13] Here Zhang's song was accompanied by his zither, but the *sanju* were sung without accompaniment. In the great plays the poetry is an integral part of the work, contributing to dramatic development. Thus, the recurrent image of the moon, which appears more than fifty times in the poetry of *The Romance of the Western Chamber,* helps to give the drama unity and depth. It is present, of course, when after a long courtship, the lovers are united. Then, "the bright moon, like water, floods the pavilion and terrace."[14]

The lovers have to suffer through a long period of separation and uncertainty before their union is made permanent at last, but they are fitting representatives of an essentially optimistic and life-affirming theater that combined high art with wide appeal to all classes.

# Painting

In contrast to the theater, in which individuals from all kinds of backgrounds participated and which had something for everyone, elite painting was a much more esoteric pursuit. But whereas literary men later disdained the drama as plebeian, the achievements of the great Yuan painters were admired by all later connoisseurs.

The distinction between the professional who sells his wares to the aesthetically naive and the amateur who paints for himself and his friends did not originate in the Yuan but was confirmed by those critical of the taste of the Mongol court. Professional artists continued to take pride in the perfection of their techniques and the excellence of their craftsmanship. Gentlemen-amateurs, no less serious about their art, found in brush and ink a vehicle for self-expression and for the cultivation of self as in Gong Kai's horse.

The most famous Yuan horse painter was also the outstanding exception to the rule that the gentleman-artist avoided the imperial stable. Zhao Mengfu (1254–1322) held high office under the Mongols and paid the price in lost friendships and inner conflict. Later Chinese scholars, although not approving of his career, were compelled to recognize the force of his genius as a major painter and one of China's truly great calligraphers. Indeed, his paintings of horses were so prized that forgeries abound. Zhao's work is illustrated here not by a horse but by a landscape painting (see Figure 9.3), which exemplifies a deliberate archaism that appealed to the Yuan literati.

As is apparent in *Autumn Colors on the Qiao and Hua Mountains,* Zhao's archaism demanded the complete rejection of the aesthetics of his immediate pre-

**FIGURE 9.3** Zhao Mengfu. *Autumn Colors on the Qiao and Hua Mountains.* Hand-scroll, ink and colors on paper, dated 1296, 36.6 in × 11.18 in. Here Zhao has discarded developments in perspective and ignored size relationships in his attempt to recapture an earlier noble simplicity. (© National Palace Museum, Taiwan, Republic of China.)

decessors. No trace can be found here of the styles of Ma Yuan and Xia Guei, and there is a deliberate, consistent avoidance of prettiness. Zhao and his contemporaries, somewhat like the Pre-Raphaelites of nineteenth-century England, tried to return to the rugged honesty of an earlier age and to unlearn the lessons of the classic period of their art. The Chinese painters, however, were more ready than the Pre-Raphaelites to sacrifice surface beauty for the sake of attaining what Zhao called "a sense of antiquity" (*guyi*). They also differed in that they conceived of their art in terms of calligraphy: both painting and calligraphy served the purpose of writing down on paper or silk the ideas the gentlemen had in their minds. In the two paintings reproduced in Figures 9.2 and 9.3, the unused space does not serve as a horizon, nor does it contribute to the overall composition. Therefore, the use of this space for calligraphy does not disturb the painting. In a sense the painting, too, is calligraphy just as, in another sense, the calligraphy is painting.

Now, as earlier, calligraphy was prized as a revelation of the lofty character of its cultivated practitioner, an emphasis that made for variety in style in painting as in writing. The master painters of the Yuan did not share a uniform style nor did individual artists necessarily limit themselves to a single style. There is, for example, a famous anecdote, recorded in the late Ming, concerning the painter Ni Zan (1301–1374), who one night, while inebriated, painted bamboos that a friend the next day criticized for not looking like bamboos. Exemplifying the Yuan literati

**FIGURE 9.4** Ni Zan, *The Rongxi Studio.*
Hanging scroll, ink on paper, dated 1372, 13.98
in × 29.41 in. This painting exemplifies Ni Zan's
calligraphic talents and the cool restraint of his
unpeopled landscapes. (© National Palace
Museum, Taiwan, Republic of China.)

painter's disdain for representation, Ni laughed and replied, "Ah, but a *total* lack of resemblance is hard to achieve!"[15] Yet, Ni often painted ordinary bamboos. Bamboos, which, like the gentleman-scholar, bend before the wind but do not break, were a favorite subject of the literati painters, who could also find Daoist significance in the fact that the center of this plant is hollow, that is, empty. In the painting shown in Figure 9.4, Ni, like Zhao Mengfu, has avoided all painterly tricks. He achieved a calm, bland poetry. This aesthetic of the cool and clean is also found in the white and in the blue-and-white ceramics of the age.

At the opposite stylistic pole from Ni Zan are the paintings of Wang Meng (c. 1309–1385), especially his later work (see Figure 9.5). Whereas Ni Zan works in monochrome, Wang delights in bright colors. In the painting of Ni, nature is stable and empty, but Wang fills his space with natural forces surging around the abodes of his recluses and threatening to burst forth beyond the borders of the painting. Perhaps this was an appropriate statement for a period when social and political forces in China were about to burst through the Yuan dynastic framework.

In considering the cultural achievements of the Yuan, it is worth noting that foreign influence did not enter the world of the literati painters. Conversely, no appreciation or even an awareness of their art is to be found in the literature of the European visitors, such as Marco Polo and his successors of the fourteenth century. Although there was a Catholic archbishop in Beijing and relations across the great Eurasian land mass were often cordial, these relations had a low priority on both sides of the world, for the distances were enormous, and Europe as well as China was faced with far more immediate challenges and opportunities in politics, economics, art, and thought closer to home. In many respects China was ahead of Europe at the time. Literati painting of the type prized in the Yuan was not even considered worthy of note by Europeans before the nineteenth century, and it was not until the twentieth century that people in the West learned how to see and value these paintings.

## Rebellions and Disintegration

By the middle of the fourteenth century the dynasty was threatened by popular rebellions as well as by the growing independence of its own regional commanders. People caught in a seemingly hopeless situation increasingly put their hopes in charismatic leaders and

**FIGURE 9.5** Wang Meng, *The Forest Grotto and Juqu.* Hanging scroll, ink and colors on paper, 16.73 in × 27.05 in. This painting employs "unraveled hemp fiber" and S-shaped strokes. (© National Palace Museum, Taiwan, Republic of China.)

messianic teachings. Under a leader who claimed descent from the Song imperial line, the White Lotus Society attracted the miserable: dismissed clerks, deserters from the Yellow River project, peddlers, outlaws, the idle, and the displaced. Known as the Red Turbans after their headdresses, these people turned to open rebellion in 1352, and for the next three years much of Central and South China was lost to the Yuan. Under Toghtō's leadership, the dynasty was able for the time being to put down this challenge, ultimately employing forces composed mainly of Chinese soldiers.

Because of court politics, Toghtō was dismissed in 1355, ousted just as he was conducting what promised to be a siege of a town on the Grand Canal seized by a former salt smuggler who, in leading a major rebellion, had seized a town on the Grand Canal and proclaimed a new dynasty. Under Toghtō, the government maintained control over its military forces by taking great care in the making of appointments, by separating command and supply functions, and by generally exercising central leadership, but after his fall no other political strongman appeared to prevent the formation of regional power centers.

Between renewed rebellions and concessions made by the government to various commanders supposedly defending it, the central government itself deteriorated to the point where it was just one more local power. During the last twelve years of the Yuan, the issue was not so much the survival of the dynasty as the determination of its successor. The dynasty had the misfortune to rule during a time when the floods, plagues, and famines that tormented the people and fueled rebellion were beyond the powers of government control. John Dardess concluded,

> The various late Yuan regimes all tried seriously to alleviate these disasters. None ignored them. Yuan medical and food relief efforts, by all appearances, were both conscientious and sophisticated. . . . It might well be that the long term cumulative effects of such repeated natural calamities were too great for any government to handle and that if normal conditions had prevailed in China, the Yuan dynasty might have lasted much longer than it did.[16]

As it turned out, the future belonged neither to the regional commanders nor to the rebel Song regime in the North, but to an organization led by Zhu Yuanzhang (1328–1398) in the South. Zhu had been born into a poor family and as a youth served as a novice in a Buddhist monastery. Later he became a beggar and eventually was drawn into the Red Turbans, where he rose to become a military commander. After the defeat of the Red Turbans, he became a leader of his own rebel organization. In contrast to the Red Turbans, who had directed their animosity as much against local landlords as against the dynasty, Zhu undertook reconciliation of the local elite. By abandoning the messianic radicalism of the earlier rebels and by demonstrating his intention to reconstruct the traditional kind of imperial government, he was able to gain valuable support among the gentry. Although some of the Chinese elite remained faithful to the Yuan and one of the most valiant and loyal defenders of the dynasty was a Chinese general, Zhu Yuanzhang could not be stopped. By 1368 it was all over: the Mongol court fled to Mongolia, and a new dynasty, the Ming, was established with its capital at Nanjing. Early in his reign Zhu Yuanzhang, known posthumously as Taizu, issued an order proscribing unorthodox religious sects, foremost among them the same White Lotus sect that had inspired his own campaign to power.

Although traditionally they had a bad reputation, the Mongols accomplished the reintegration of the North and the integration of Yunnan into the Chinese body politic and allowed the South Yangzi basin to continue its economic development. The effect of the Mongol period on Chinese political culture is more complex: scholars have looked to this period to explain the contrast between the rather benign government of the Song and the more authoritarian rule of the Ming. The Mongols had set an example of strong imperial rule and, in their declining years, had provided a lesson of what could happen in the absence of strong central direction. The lesson was not lost on the Ming founder.

# Notes

1. R. Mitchell and N. Forbes, trans., *The Chronicle of Novgorod 1016–1471*, 3rd Series, Vol. 25 (London: Camden Society, 1914), p. 64.

2. Hoyt C. Tillman and Stephen H. West, *China under Jurchen Rule: Essays on Chin Intellectual and Cultural History* (Albany: State Univ. of New York Press, 1995), p. 4.

3. Morris Rossabi, *Khubilai Khan: His Life and Times* (Berkeley: Univ. of California Press, 1987), p. 115.

4. John W. Dardess, in Herbert Franke and Denis Twitchett, *The Cambridge History of China*, Vol. 6 (Cambridge: Cambridge Univ. Press, 1994), p. 385.

5. Bettine Birge, "Women and Confucianism from Song to Ming: The Institution of Patrilineality," in Paul J. Smith and Richard von Glahn, eds., *The Song-Yuan-Ming Transition in Chinese History* (Cambridge: Harvard Univ. Press, 2003), p. 235.

6. Daniel Overmyer, "Chinese Religion—An Overview" in Mircea Eliade, ed., *The Encyclopedia of Religion*, Vol. 3 (New York: Macmillan, 1987), p. 282.

7. Peter Bol, "Neo-Confucianism and Local Society, Twelfth to Sixteenth Century: A Case Study," in Smith and von Glahn, pp. 166–67.

8. Joseph Needham, *Science and Civilization in China, Vol. 10: Mathematics and the Sciences of the Heavens and the Earth* (Cambridge: Cambridge Univ. Press, 1959), p. 47.

9. Cyril Birch, trans., *Stories from a Ming Collection: The Art of the Chinese Story-Teller* (New York: Grove Press, 1958), pp. 10–11.

10. Stephen W. West, "Texts and Ideology: Ming Editors of Northern Drama," in Smith and von Glahn, pp. 329–30.

11. Cyril Birch, ed., *Anthology of Chinese Literature*, Vol. 1 (New York: Grove Press, 1965), p. 483.

12. Chung-wen Shih, *The Golden Age of Chinese Drama: Yuan Tsa-chü* (Princeton: Princeton Univ. Press, 1976), p. 160.

13. Shih, *The Golden Age of Chinese Drama*, p. 192.

14. Shih, *The Golden Age of Chinese Drama*, p. 159.

15. James Cahill, *Hills Beyond a River: Chinese Painting of the Yüan Dynasty, 1279–1368* (New York: Weatherhill, 1976), p. 175.

16. Dardess, *The Cambridge History of China*, pp. 386–87.

# 10

# The Ming Dynasty, 1368–1644

| 1368 | 1424 | 1505 | 1590 | 1644 |
|---|---|---|---|---|
| EARLY MING | EARLY MIDDLE PERIOD | LATE MIDDLE PERIOD | LATE MING | |

The Ming, the last native Chinese dynasty, reincorporated northern territories separated from the rest of China for almost two and a half centuries and for a short time even reestablished rule over what is now northern Vietnam. The stability of the regime and the general prosperity of the people, as well as notable achievements in literature, philosophy, and the arts, demonstrated the continued vitality of the Chinese tradition and its capacity for growth and transformation. When, toward the end of the Ming period, the first modern Europeans arrived in China, they found much to admire.

# The Early Ming (1368–1424)

The Early Ming was a period of vigorous Chinese military resurgence abroad and assertion of imperial autocracy at home. The dynastic founder, Zhu Yuanzhang or Taizu (see Table 10.1), ruled for 30 years (1368–1398) and left a deep imprint on the reigns that followed. For his era name he chose Hongwu, "grand military achievement," and his military accomplishments were certainly impressive.

By the end of his reign, the Ming controlled all China, dominated the frontier region from Hami, in Xinjiang, north through Inner Mongolia and into northern Manchuria, and, beyond that, had won the adherence of Korea as well as various Central and Southeast Asian states that sent tribute (see Figure 10.1.)

Chengzu (r. 1402–1424), the third Ming emperor, often referred to by his reign name, Yongle ("perpetual happiness"), personally led five expeditions against the Mongols, intervened in Annam (now northern Vietnam), which he incorporated into the empire, and, most spectacularly, sent out great maritime expeditions marking China as the world's premier naval power.

Taizu was a harsh, suspicious, and autocratic ruler. In a move to weaken the bureaucracy and ensure that it not speak with a single voice, he abolished the position of Chancellor. Ministers now had to kneel before the emperor, whereas in the Song they had stood and in the Tang they had sat in the imperial presence. As F. W. Mote has pointed out, it was typical of Taizu that "while the emperor was

**FIGURE 10.1** Ming China, middle sixteenth century. 🌐

determined to produce a universal code that could be minutely followed, he undermined that intent by constantly issuing laws which met immediate needs and which often contradicted the Great Ming Code."[1] Taizu insisted on deciding personally even matters of secondary importance. A very hard worker, he went through stacks of memorials: in one period of ten days he is reported to have perused 1660 memorials dealing with 3391 separate matters. In 1382 he appointed four grand secretaries to help him with this workload, but it was not until later in the dynasty that the Grand Secretariat developed into an institution.

Taizu energetically furthered the work of reconstruction and of relief for the poor, some of whom were resettled, and he established a tax system. But he overreached in aiming at "nothing less than the ethical and behavioral transformation of the entire population of China in accordance with ancient mores laid out in the Confucian canon."[2] To reform the people he ordered placards set up in all villages admonishing people to behave virtuously. Government regulations were posted on village kiosks along with the names of evildoers deemed deserving of public humiliation. Localities were ordered to set up schools for commoners, people and deities were registered, and unacceptable gods were banned.

To control the countryside and provide a check on officials, Taizu established the *li-jia* as a basis for labor-service and local security. Under this system, every ten families in an area constituted a *jia,* and ten *jia* formed a *li.* Each household was required to post a notice on its door indicating the names, ages, and occupations of its members, and all members of a *li* were responsible for each other's conduct. However, overlapping systems of authority made for inefficiencies as "the urgent concern with corruption overrode careful hierarchy."[3] Sarah K. Schneewind further points out, "The new dynasty could not create local social institutions by fiat, but competed for resources with local subjects and clergy, and with its own representatives."[4] Even under the Taizu the local forces more than held their own, and that was still more the case later.

Taizu reestablished the imperial university, founded many schools, and reinstituted the civil service examinations. Confucianism again became the official state doctrine. But the emperor rejected the antiauthoritarian aspects of the thought of Mencius and had 85 sections (about one-third of the text) expurgated before accepting *The Mencius* as a legitimate book. Merciless in exterminating those who stood in his way or were suspected of doing so, Taizu obtained information through a secret service provided with its own prison and torturing apparatus. Officials who displeased the emperor were subjected to beating in open court. Always painful and terribly humiliating, the beating was sometimes so severe that the victim died. *The Cambridge History* singles out 1382 to 1392 as "years of intensifying surveillance and terror."[5]

Chengzu (or Yongle) was as vigorous and severe as his father but did not hesitate to pursue a far more aggressive foreign policy and to move the capital from Nanjing to Beijing. This he did after defeating his nephew, the second emperor, in a massive civil war. He went on to rebuild Beijing into a magnificent city. To assure Beijing's supplies, Chengzu reconstructed the Grand Canal, "the world's longest manmade waterway" compared by Shih-Shan Henry Tsai to a route linking Florida and New York.[6] Just as harsh as his father when it came to purging real or suspected opponents, he was better educated than Taizu and more generous in his patronage of Confucianism. Not only did he hold more frequent civil service examinations, but he also sponsored major scholarly projects. The most grandiose of these was the compilation of a huge literary treasury, which employed more than 2000 scholars and when completed in 1408 resulted in a compendium of 22,877 rolls, or chapters. Under Chengzu the complete, unexpurgated *Mencius* was also once more made available. He also sponsored the compilation of a new Daoist cannon and venerated a number of Daoist deities.

It is sometimes said that the Ming reaction against the hated Mongols led to an overreaction against all things foreign, but this is not entirely true. Not only did the Ming continue Mongol institutions such as the system of hereditary military households and employing their own Mongol soldiers, but they also followed a broad cultural policy.

Thus, Chengzu not only sponsored a great compendium of Song Neo-Confucianism but also patronized the publication of Buddhist works, including a new edition of the Tripitaka. After the death of his wife, he had a Buddhist monastery near Nanjing repaired and built there an octagonal porcelain pagoda nine stories tall, more than 276 feet high. It remained standing until it was destroyed in 1854 during the Taiping Rebellion.

# Maritime Expeditions (1405–1433)

Chengzu, reversing Taizu's policy of avoiding maritime expansion, sent a number of trusted eunuchs as envoys to Southeast Asia before launching seven great maritime expeditions under the command of Zheng He, a Muslim eunuch. The first of these included 27,800 men, 62 or 63 large ships, and 255 smaller vessels, and the third was of similar dimensions, far larger than the seventeen vessels and 1500 men who participated in the second and largest of Columbus's expeditions (1493–1495). They visited not only various areas of Southeast Asia but also the Indian Ocean, Arabia, and the east coast of Africa. These voyages were unique in their scope and official sponsorship, but the technology that made them possible had previously been employed in private ventures not considered worth recording by official historians. Thus, it is interesting to observe that on their first voyage the expedition had dealings with Chinese settlers in Sumatra. Reportedly they also defeated a Chinese "pirate" in those waters, killing 5000 men and bringing the leader back for execution in Beijing.

The Chinese sources, composed by scholars hostile to the undertaking and ever ready to attribute self-interest to a usurper emperor, emphasize Chengzu's desire to find the nephew from whom he had seized the throne but who had eluded capture. More broadly they may be viewed as an aspect of early Ming military and political assertiveness, for they effectively demonstrated Chinese power and brought tributary envoys to the Ming court such as the King of Borneo, who died in China in 1408 and was buried outside Nanjing, where his grave can still be seen. It is recorded that as a result of the fourth voyage, nineteen countries sent tribute.

Foreign envoys coming to render submission enhanced the court's glory and prestige. Also forthcoming from foreign lands were exotic objects and animals. The emperor was particularly delighted by giraffes, represented in Beijing as auspicious *qilin* or "unicorns." Most probably trade was also a motive for the voyages; we know that ships of the first voyage carried silk and embroideries on board. And trade was a major factor in inducing foreign lands to send envoys to China. On the Chinese side, however, the Ming court never looked upon trade as something intrinsically worthwhile.

From the official Chinese point of view, these expeditions did not have an economic rationale. Furthermore, their eunuch leadership did not win them friends among Confucian officials. When Chengzu died, they lost an enthusiastic supporter, although his successor Xuanzong (r. 1426–1435) did send out one last expedition.

Just as the expeditions can be seen as part of a general Early Ming assertiveness toward the rest of the world, their abandonment forms part of a broader pattern as the dynasty trimmed its ambitions and abandoned the attempt to annex Annam (1426). An incentive for maintaining an ocean navy was removed with the completion, in 1417, of a system of locks that maintained a water level sufficiently high to allow the grain vessels supplying the capital to use the Grand Canal throughout the year. No longer was the capital dependent on sea transport about six months a year. Furthermore, the crucial land frontier once again demanded military attention: fighting Mongols was a vital enterprise, whereas ocean expeditions were a luxury.

In the absence of a strong naval effort, Chinese waters became the domain of pirates and smugglers, a situation not ameliorated by the dynasty's regulations to control and curb maritime trade. For example, already during the Yongle period, the Japanese had been officially limited to one tribute mission every ten years, composed of only two ships with a maximum of 200 men (later raised to 300) to call at Ningbo (Zhejiang Province). These regulations were not always enforced, for private Chinese interests as well as the Japanese stood to profit by the trade conducted on these occasions. But the regulations illustrate the dynasty's negative attitude toward relations with maritime countries.

# The Early Middle Period (1425–1505)

The seventy-five years of the Early Middle Ming were, on the whole, a time of peace, stability, and prosperity, under emperors less ambitious for military glory and personal power than Taizu and Chengzu. Xuanzong (1426–1436) abandoned the Ming effort to control Annam but did lead one expedition against Mongol raiders in the North. The Mongols were particularly troublesome under his successor, Yingzong, whom they actually captured and held prisoner for a year. On his return he endured six and one-half years of confinement in a palace in the capital while his brother, Taizong, remained on the throne, but then was able to conduct a second reign (see Table 10.1). In the 1460s and 1470s there was a revival of Chinese military strength. The Great Wall was strengthened and extended for 600 miles to protect the northern border of Shaanxi. The wall as it stands today owes much of its imposing mass and extent to the Ming.

To save himself from drowning in paperwork, Xuanzong relied on the Grand Secretaries to screen memorials, draft edicts, and the like. This informal group of two to six officials became increasingly influential during the last quarter of the fifteenth century. At the same time eunuch influence increased. Eunuchs enjoyed unique opportunities for informal, relaxed conversation with emperors who often turned to them for advice and entrusted them with important missions. Because elites did not castrate their sons, eunuchs invariably came from humble families without political influence and were thus entirely dependent on imperial favor. Going a step further than his predecessors, Xuanzong established a school for eunuchs, but this did not prevent the continuing hostility of Confucian officials, who tended to criticize even honest and able eunuchs as a matter of principle.

Ming emperors believed in doing things on a grand scale. For example, in 1425 the court reportedly had 6300 cooks in its employ, preparing meals not only for the considerable palace population but also for government officials on set occasions. Xuanzong was very fond of Korean food and sent eunuchs to Korea to bring back, among other things, virgins, eunuchs, and female cooks. He also took an active interest in the arts and was probably the only emperor after Huizong of

**TABLE 10.1** Ming Emperors

| Temple Name | Era Name | Era Dates |
| --- | --- | --- |
| Taizu | Hongwu | 1368–1399 |
| Huizong | Jianwen | 1399–1402 |
| Chengzu | Yongle | 1403–1425 |
| Renzong | Hongxi | 1425–1426 |
| Xuanzong | Xuande | 1426–1436 |
| Yingzong | Zhengtong | 1436–1450 |
| Taizong | Jingtai | 1450–1457 |
| Yingzong (restored) | Tianshun | 1457–1465 |
| Xianzong | Changhua | 1465–1488 |
| Xianzong | Hongzhi | 1488–1506 |
| Wuzong | Zhengde | 1506–1522 |
| Shizong | Jiajing | 1522–1567 |
| Muzong | Longqing | 1567–1573 |
| Shenzong | Wanli | 1573–1620 |
| Guangzong | Taichang | 1620–1621 |
| Xizong | Tianqi | 1621–1628 |
| Sizong | Chongzhen | 1628–1645 |

The Ming founder initiated the practice followed by all subsequent emperors of retaining a single era name (*nianhao,* literally "year designation") throughout his reign. Normally the era name remained in use until the end of the Chinese lunar year in which the emperor died. Transposing the Chinese dates into the Western calendar, it turns out that all except three Ming emperors (Chengzu, Muzong, and Shenzong) died during the year preceding the change in reign name. (For example, Taizu died on June 24, 1398, but Hongwu was used through January 5, 1399. Huizong was enthroned on June 30, 1398, but the era name remained Taizu for the remainder of that lunar year.

Ming emperors are often known by their era names rather than by their posthumous temple names. To comply with the style of most English language materials, we will refer to Ming emperors by their temple names but use era names for the emperors of the Qing (1644–1911).

the Song to be a gifted painter and poet. Among the noted painters who served for a time at his court was the flower and bird specialist Bian Wenzhi (c. 1356–1428). Another famous painter was Dai Jin (1388–1462), who worked in the Ma-Xia tradition of the Southern Song. His artistic talents did not, however, save him from dismissal when he painted the coat of a fisherman red, a color reserved for the garments of officials. Returning to his native Zhejiang, he became a leader in what was known as the Zhe school of painting.

Xuanzong's reign is also known for its bronzes and especially for its porcelain. Under the Ming, private kilns continued to produce ceramics in traditional styles, but it was the imperial kilns, turning out vast quantities of vessels in many different shapes, that stood at the forefront of technical and artistic development. Whereas the Yongle period is noted for its white porcelain, by Xuanzong's reign blue-and-white ware had come into vogue and reached its classic peak (see Figure 10.2).

During the following reign the imperial kilns enjoyed a monopoly of blue-and-white porcelain, protected by an order prohibiting its private sale. But this could not be maintained for very long. Ming blue-and-white porcelain had such appeal that it soon stimulated imitation and went on to win admiration not only in East Asia but in distant lands such as Persia and Holland. The porcelain of each reign had its own characteristics. During the fifteenth century, its color

**FIGURE 10.2** Plate with bird decoration. Blue-and-white porcelain, Early Ming, probably Xuande, diameter 19.76 in. This kind of fine ware grew so popular in the West that in English "china" became synonymous with porcelain. (© The Asia Society, Mr. and Mrs. J.D. Rockefeller Collection, photograph by Lynton Gardiner.)

range was broadened when white porcelains were decorated by painting them with various enamel colors. The five-colored enamels made during the reign of Emperor Xianzong (r. 1465–1488) are particularly prized.

The Early Middle Period came to an end with the death of Xiaozong (r. 1488–1505), a model of Confucian propriety and a rare monogamist among the Ming emperors. His was generally a calm reign, but after more than 130 years, the dynasty was beginning to show signs of deterioration. The trends that would trouble government during the sixteenth century were already at work beneath the surface.

# The Later Middle Period (1506–1590)

During this period, which includes most of the sixteenth century, the government suffered from inadequate imperial leadership, but the political system still showed a capacity for reform.

Wuzong, who reigned from 1506 to 1521, devoted his time and energy to sports, entertainments, sex, and drink while neglecting government and allowing

eight eunuch "tigers" to run wild. Unclear and overlapping administrative juris-
dictions, present from the beginning of the dynasty, as well as conflicting interests
reaching up to and down from the highest levels of government worked against
government efficiency. In his study of the endemic and widespread violence in the
capital region David Robinson traces patronage networks that connected court
eunuchs, local officials, and men of force who, depending on shifting circumstances, "often effortlessly changed hats from garrison soldiers to enterprising local bandits, from military retainers on the staff of provincial governors and local
magnates to rebel leaders. In many cases services rendered and reputation acquired in one capacity directly increased one's value in another."[7] In 1510, faced
with drought and government incompetence, bandits turned into rebels, creating
havoc as far south as the Yangzi and reaching from the ocean west to the Taihang
mountains. It took the government two years to suppress the rebellion, but it did
not go beyond restoring the previous situation.

For the remainder of the Later Middle Period the center remained weak.
Under Shizong, the Jiajing emperor (1522–1567), the arts flourished but government did not. This emperor became engrossed in increasingly longer Daoist ceremonies. By the end of his reign, there were ceremonies that continued for twelve
or thirteen days and nights. He was followed by Muzong (r. 1567–1572), who is
said to have devoted his five years on the throne more to his private pleasures than
to public business. Next came Shenzong, the Wanli Emperor (r. 1573–1620), who
was a minor until 1590.

Grand Secretaries and eunuchs now wielded great power while a decline in
government honesty and efficiency was apparent both in the capital and in local
government. The local elite increasingly avoided taxation and frequently moved to
cities and towns. Then, as now, the lure of social, cultural, political, and economic
opportunities was a major attraction of urban life. As absentee landlords, they often succumbed to the temptation to charge high rents, allocate taxes unfairly, and
charge exorbitant interest on mortgage loans.

From early on, the tax system left a great deal to be desired. According to
Martin Heijdra,

> The tax and corvee system as it was conceived in the late fourteenth
> century had many internal contradictions: it hovered uncertainly be-
> tween land-based and population-based criteria for tax collection; it
> was not designed to accommodate changed in the population over
> time. . . .[8]

Inequalities in taxation hurt the government as well as peasants, but there
were also reformers. Most notable was Hai Rui (1513–1587), who had a reputation for uprightness, courage, and concern for the common people. As a magistrate he reassessed the land to make taxes more equitable, wiped out corruption so effectively that government clerks were reduced to poverty, and himself
led a life of exemplary frugality. His refusal to toady to his superiors earned him

powerful enemies, and he came close to losing his life when he submitted a scathing memorial that, among other things, charged the emperor with neglect of government and excessive indulgence in Daoist ceremonies. During the Ming one did not denounce an emperor with impunity: in prison Hai Rui was tortured and condemned to death by strangulation. He was saved only by the death of the emperor. On his release from prison he resumed his career but was forced into retirement when he offended powerful families by forcing them to return lands they had seized illegally. Late in life, in 1585, he was recalled to office, and after he died he was idealized as the perfect official incarnate. About four centuries later, in the 1960s, Hai Rui became the focus of a major controversy (see Chapter 23).

A very different kind of reformer was Zhang Juzheng (1525–1582), who dominated government during the reign of Muzong and for another ten years during Shenzong's minority. He has been described as a Confucian Legalist, for he was convinced that strong and strict government was ultimately for the people's benefit. Efficiency and control were the hallmarks of his policy. Among his achievements were a repair of the Grand Canal, reform of the courier system, new regulations designed to strengthen central control over provincial officials, and a reduction in the total number of officials. He eliminated eunuch influence from the Six Ministries, prevented censors from abusing their authority, and tried to reform the provincial schools.

To improve government finances, Zhang directed an all-China land survey (1581) and extended to the whole country the "single whip method of taxation," previously tried in Zhejiang and Fujian. This replaced once and for all the Two Tax System first instituted during the Tang. Implementation remained incomplete, but, in principle, the new method provided for the consolidation of tax obligations into a single annual bill.

Another important innovation was the use of silver as the value base for tax assessment. Although Zhang thereby recognized the importance of silver, which had become widely used in commercial transactions, he based his monetary policy on high-quality copper coins because silver, unlike copper, had to be imported and was therefore of uncertain supply. But he could not prevent the continued popularity of silver, and ultimately, as we shall see, Zhang's apprehension about depending on a foreign supply of silver turned out to be well founded. The silver *tael* (ounce) remained the standard monetary unit into the twentieth century.

Zhang was also troubled by what was happening in the civil service examinations. Ever since Taizu had lent imperial favor to an essay form composed of eight rigidly stipulated sections and known as the "eight-legged essay," the tendency had increasingly been to judge papers on the basis of form rather than content. This eased the task of the examination readers but threatened to turn the examinations into mechanical exercises. Zhang, who served as an examiner in 1571, wanted the questions to emphasize current problems and the answers to be graded on content. But in his contempt for "empty" theorizing, he went beyond this and ordered the suppression of private academies. These he also considered undesirable, as potential breeding grounds for political associations and as holders of tax-exempt land. However, the decree banning academies (1579) did little permanent damage to these institutions.

Zhang Juzheng made many enemies. They had their revenge after his death, when his family property was confiscated and his sons were tortured. But he left the regime in sound financial condition at a time when it was incurring heavy military expenditures, fighting Mongol invasions between 1550 and 1570 and maintaining military preparedness thereafter. The government's fiscal health at this time reflected the general economic strength of sixteenth century China.

## Economy and Society

Peace and stability made for prosperity. During the first century of the Ming, northern agriculture was rehabilitated. Taizu discriminated against the people in the Yangzi delta who had resisted him when he was founding the dynasty, but by the fifteenth century this area resumed its economic growth. The Southeast remained China's most populous and prosperous region. The gradual spread of superior strains of rice, which had begun during the Song, permitted a steady increase in China's population, which rose from 65 to 80 million in the fourteenth century (well below that of the Song) to about 150 million by the end of the sixteenth. The introduction in the sixteenth century of new crops from the Americas laid a foundation for still further population increases that were to follow in the Qing.

Although it is difficult to find major breakthroughs or radically new technologies or industries, change was so substantial that scholars speak of a "second commercial revolution." There was an increase in interregional trade in staples as well as an increase in the growing of cash crops, most notably cotton in the Yangzi delta, where grain now had to be imported. Although this was not the original intent, the Grand Canal was kept going in large part by the private trade of private merchants and also by the seamen who serviced the official boats. Suzhou, located near the juncture of the Grand Canal and the Yangzi River, emerged as a major economic and cultural center.

An increased use of money and participation in an impersonal market influenced the behavior of rich and poor even as the growth of commerce increased class differentiation. In addition to Suzhou, Nanjing, Yangzhou, and Hangzhou, numerous smaller cities prospered. Among the important industries of the period were the porcelain and ceramic kilns centered in Jiangxi, the cotton manufacture of Nanjing, and the silk weaving in Suzhou.

Enthusiastic customers for silk and porcelain were found not only domestically but overseas in Europe and Japan. As payment for these prized commodities, silver flowed into China from Japan and increasingly from Spanish America through Manila, fueling a truly global trade network. Silver also financed a flourishing domestic market. Hebei remained the center of iron manufacture, and Anhui was known for its dye works. Indigo and sugar cane, along with cotton, were important cash crops grown for the market. A well-known seventeenth-century technical manual, *Creations of Man and Nature,* offers impressive evidence of the inventiveness of Chinese craftsmen.

Much of what happened was beyond the government's purview. At the local level the central government was represented by the magistrate, who in theory was responsible for everything that happened in his district. He was supposed to supervise tax collection, provide public security, administer justice, and see to the economic as well as moral needs of the population. However, because his staff was small and the average Ming district had a registered population of more than 50,000, the magistrate's control and influence were restricted.

Local society operated according to its own rhythms, with its patterns influenced and affected by government to be sure, but not determined by it. Particularly important was the role of the local gentry elite, the magnitude of whose influence has induced a Japanese scholar to write of "gentry rule," that is "indirect regional rule that went beyond the boundary of mere tenant-landlord relations" and included political rule (administering justice, mediating quarrels, maintaining public order, administering relief, etc.), cultural rule (education, culture, guidance of public opinion, etc.), and economic rule (control of the market, etc.).[9] This characterization no doubt needs qualification, but the gentry did preside over provincial life and gave it much of its tone.

There is no reason to believe that regional variations in social structure and economic relationships were of lesser magnitude in the Ming than later because they reflect differences between ecosystems as well as local traditions. A major development in the most economically advanced regions was for "descent groups" (groups larger than a family descended from a common ancestor) to organize into "lineages" with shared ceremonies and assets (usually land). In her exemplary study of a county in Anhui, Hilary J. Beattie found that the local gentry dated back to the Early Ming, that gentry lineages were formally organized in the sixteenth century, and that they were able to survive the rebellions and upheavals of the late years of the dynasty and even the great nineteenth-century Taiping Rebellion.[10] They were able to accomplish this by maintaining solid economic roots in local land ownership and by investing their income in education. Education, in turn, secured their local status, in addition to providing the requisites for competing in the civil service examinations. Members of the gentry who succeeded in becoming officials used their political influence and their economic assets to benefit the lineage, but the gentry were able to sustain themselves even during periods lean in examination success. This suggests that local social and economic status was the primary source of their power and that there was greater continuity in the family background of the local elite than there was among that much smaller subgroup of their members capable and fortunate enough to gain access to a career in the imperial bureaucracy.

Among the means used to secure lineage cohesion were the periodic compilations of genealogies. These not only fostered a sense of historic continuity among lineage members but also identified the individuals belonging to the lineage. Prominent gentry lineages also maintained ancestral halls and graveyards and conducted ceremonial sacrifices to lineage ancestors. Not infrequently, the income from lineage land was used for these purposes. Lineage solidarity was also maintained by general guides for the conduct of the members and by formal lineage rules. One penalty for severe infractions of these rules was expulsion. The contrast in status between the local elite and the government underlings who served in the sub-bureaucracy is revealed by the stipulation found in many lineage rules that any member sinking to the occupation of government clerk or runner be promptly expelled. The gentry lineages also profited from participation in a complicated network of marriage relationships.

The general trend was for the strongest lineages to develop in the Southeast, but the present state of research is not sufficient to attempt a social/historical map or timeline. Similarly, although we know that there were bondservants on landed estates in the sixteenth century as well as tenants and hired workers, the situation was complex (for example, bondservants could also be landlords), sources are unequally distributed, and geographic parameters are as yet unclear.

## Literacy and Literature

Along with prosperity came an increase in literacy, not only among the well-educated and ambitious but also among the more humble and less sophisticated. Bookshops did a brisk business selling collections of model examination papers used by candidates to cram for tests as well as encyclopedias, colored prints, novels, collections of short stories, guides that explained the classics in simple language, and books of moral instruction illustrated with tales of wrongdoing and retribution.

The audience for wood block prints was even wider than that for books. Although it was the Japanese who developed the colored wood block print to its highest aesthetic form, the colored print originated in China. The earliest extant Chinese colored print formed the frontispiece of a Buddhist sutra dated 1346, but the best prints were produced in the seventeenth century and included five-color illustrations of erotica.

Some gifted men turned to literary careers after failing to advance through the examination system. Two such men were Feng Menglong (1574–1646) and Ling Mengqi (1580–1664), authors of widely read anthologies of short stories. Both men were also dramatists and scholars. Feng's interests ranged particularly widely; for instance, he wrote books on gambling as well as on Confucianism. But he is most famous for publishing *Stories, Old and New,* three collections of colloquial short stories based on the promptbooks of the storytellers, who had long formed part of the urban entertainment. Liu Wu-chi's description of the subject matter of Feng's stories reveals their diversity:

> Their range includes: quasi-historical tales of kings and generals, faithful friends and filial sons; romantic yarns of strange lands and peoples; supernatural stories of marvels and prodigies, spirits and ghosts, Buddhist monks and Daoist immortals; realistic stories of scandals in monastic establishments; daring exploits of brigands and thieves; murders, lawsuits, and court trials; domestic tragedies and bloody revenges; social comedies and family reunions.[11]

Ling, son of a noted publisher and scholar, rewrote and retold the stories in the two collections he published, both entitled *Striking the Table in Amazement at the Wonders.*

# The Novel

The novel, like the short story, was only gradually freed from its antecedents in the oral tradition of storytelling, with the eliminating of extraneous material and refining of crudities. It remained essentially episodic in structure and often included poems. Despite the literary excellence and subtlety of works written by and for the educated elite and the interest they stimulated among Late Ming scholars, even the greatest novels did not gain Confucian legitimacy as high literature. In Japan the novel was an honored part of literary culture, but in China reading a novel was a surreptitious pleasure indulged in by students when their teacher was not looking—or vice versa. Many novels of the Ming period retold old stories or embellished historical episodes; others were adventure stories, serious or comic; and still others were pornographic. The four major novels that have come down to us from the Ming are *The Romance of the Three Kingdoms, The Water Margin* (translated also as *All Men Are Brothers*), *Journey to the West,* and *The Plum in the Golden Vase* (also translated as *The Golden Lotus*).

The Romance of the Three Kingdoms (*Sanguozhi yanyi*) was first published in 1522, although it may have been written in the late Yuan. It is a fictionalized account of the conflict between Wei, Wu, and Shu in the third century C.E. In its pages the gifted but badly flawed character of Cao Cao, the martial heroics of Guan Yu, and the strategic genius and devoted loyalty of Zhuge Liang come vividly alive. It is no wonder that ordinary people in China formed many of their perceptions of history from this and other novels. This literature was also popular in Korea and Japan where *The Romance of the Three Kingdoms* was widely read and much loved. The tale remains popular throughout East Asia even in our age of videos and DVDs.

A different kind of history supplied the materials for *The Water Margin* (*Shuihuzhuan*). Based on a Yuan play, it is set in the closing years of the Northern Song and recounts the deeds of 108 bandit heroes driven by the cruel corruption of a decadent government to take justice into their own hands, outlaws who champion the oppressed and avenge the wronged. Numerous episodes, rendered in everyday speech, tell of feats of strength and daring, clever stratagems, and acts of savage but righteous vengeance. The novel's theme did not endear it to the political authorities, and during the Qing dynasty it was officially proscribed. However, it continued to be sold under the counter and enjoyed a broad readership. Among the eminent twentieth-century leaders who read it with profit as well as delight was the young Mao Zedong.

The third major Ming novel, *Journey to the West* (*Xiyuji*, translated also as *Monkey*), first published in 1592, describes the trip to India of the Tang monk Xuanzang (see Figure 5.3). The trip is transformed into a fantastic journey, a heroic pilgrimage, and a tale of delightful satire and high comedy. Monkey is one of three supernatural disciples assigned by Buddha to accompany the priest and protect him from the monsters and demons that threaten him along the way. Many times Monkey saves the day, for he is endowed with penetrating, although mischievous and restless, intelligence and has acquired many magical gifts: he can somersault through the air for leagues with the greatest of ease, has the power to change into all kinds of shapes, and can transform his body hairs into a myriad of monkeys. Over his ear he wears a pin, which becomes an enormous iron cudgel when needed. The novel can be enjoyed as sheer fantasy, or for its satirical accounts of the bureaucratic organization of Heaven and the underworld, or as a religious allegory.

Either the authors of these three novels are obscure, or the attribution of authorship is itself in doubt. The identity of the author of *The Plum in the Golden Vase* (*Jinpingmei*) is even more obscure, and for good reason, because no respectable gentleman would have wanted his name linked to an erotic novel condemned by the Chinese as pornographic. In its 100 chapters, *Jinpingmei* gives a detailed account of the dissipations of a wealthy lecher. It offers a naturalistic tableau of amorous intrigues within the household and beyond, of drinking parties, and of sumptuous feasts and portraits of go-betweens and fortunetellers, doctors and mendicants, singing girls, and venal officials, and so on. After a life of sex without love, the hero, reduced to an empty shell, meets a fitting death, and the novel rolls on for another twenty chapters to recount the unraveling of the household.

## Drama

In the Ming, drama in the southern style reached its peak. It differed from the northern drama (discussed in the preceding chapter) in language, form, and music. Southern plays were much longer, running to forty and more scenes, and the songs, accompanied by the bamboo flute, were assigned to choruses as well as to the leading players. The result has been described as an "undulating cavalcade"[12] composed of scenes varying in length, number of players, and importance. Because of the length of the plays and the familiarity of the audience with their plots, performances of Ming drama, as of Japanese Nō, came to feature selected scenes from a number of plays rather than a single one played all the way through. The authors were often sophisticated literary men, writing as much for their peers as for the wider public, who at times were more concerned about achieving literary excellence than creating effective theater. Ming playwrights were prolific: some 1200 titles are still known.

Acknowledged as the greatest Ming playwright was Tang Xienzu (1550–1616), who earned a *jinshi* degree but had a frustrating official career. In his *The Dream of Han Tan* a young man falls asleep as he is trying to prepare a meal of millet. He then sees his whole life in a dream: he comes in first in the *jinshi* examination, performs great deeds, is slandered and condemned to death, is cleared, and then is promoted. As he is about to die, he wakes up to discover that the millet on the stove is nearly ready to eat. This makes him realize that life itself passes as rapidly as a dream. Tang wrote three other dream plays, and a dream also features importantly in his most admired work, *The Peony Pavilion*. This long play of fifty-five scenes centers on a love so strong that it is able to bring the dead back to life.

Other well-known Ming plays were written on the theme of love. A perennial favorite was the disastrous love of the Tang emperor Xuanzong for Yang Guifei. The repertoire also contained plays on more contemporary matters. One of the last southern masterpieces was *The Peach Blossom Fan,* completed in 1699 and depicting the end of the Ming half a century earlier. In it the conflict between traitorous villains and loyal heroes is intertwined with the story of the love shared by a loyal young scholar and a virtuous courtesan. Southern dramas continued to be performed and written, but toward the end of the eighteenth century there arose a new form of theater, based more broadly on popular taste. This was Peking Drama, famed for its actors and singers more than for its writers. Its repertoire consisted largely of adaptations of older works.

# Painting

The most notable center for painting in the Later Middle Ming was Suzhou, where the Wu school flourished from about 1460 to 1560. Famed for its poetry, painting, calligraphy, drama, and garden retreats, conceived and designed as miniature replicas of vast nature, Suzhou offered a place of refuge for sophisticated people fleeing the uncertainties of political life, a place where the literati could pursue their own interests in peace, the home of the gentleman cultivating his artistic talents apparently without regard for money or career as well as of the professional artist like Tang Yin (1470–1524) who, combining the "education of the upper class and the material needs of the lower,"[13] enjoyed the patronage of the wealthy for whom he painted commemorative paintings such as one celebrating the eightieth birthday of a virtuous widow who, although reportedly poor, brought up two sons by herself. Between commissions, Tang, like his compeers, supplemented his income by painting fans for a wider market, including, but hopefully not limited to, those who aspired to acceptance as cultivated gentlemen. Then, as now, other producers and consumers of a vibrant visual culture satisfied their own tastes with little regard for the latest theories or fashions current among elite (or would-be elite) sophisticates.

Designations such as "Zhe school" and "Wu school" are Chinese classifications based on the artist's residence, style, and/or social status. Unfortunately for

**FIGURE 10.3** Wen Zhengming, *The Seven Junipers of Changshu.* Section of hand-scroll, ink on paper, 142.52 in × 11.34 in. (© Honolulu Academy of Arts, Gift of Mrs. Carter Galt, 1952 [1666.1].) In the rhapsody *(fu),* which Wen added to his painting, he invites the viewer on a flight of the imagination:

the modern student, these criteria did not always coincide: not all amateurs resided in Suzhou, some professionals adopted "amateur" styles, and so forth. However, in stylistic terms, the Zhe school declined in the sixteenth century. Its most characteristic contribution to Chinese art was the continuation of Southern Song academic painting. For fresh departures, one must turn to Suzhou.

The man whose work stands at the beginning of the Wu tradition was Shen Zhou (1427–1509), who was also a talented poet and calligrapher. He lived in comfort on an estate about ten miles out of town and loved to paint the local landscape. Although deeply influenced by Yuan painting, he gradually developed a style of his own that conveyed a genial warmth and a sense of ease and naturalness.

Wen Zhengming (1470–1559) studied painting under Shen Zhou and befriended Tang. He admired and frequently took as his model Zhao Mengfu, the great Yuan painter, but was too talented an artist to follow one model only. Nor did he spend a lifetime perfecting a single style or refining a single vision. Instead he worked in many different manners during his long and productive life. Some of his paintings contain references to painting styles going back to the Tang, styles previously revived during the Southern Song and the Yuan. Such multiple historical references were among the qualities most admired in his work by Ming and later connoisseurs. It is not possible to illustrate the work of an artist like Wen Zhengming with a single "representative" painting, but *The Seven Junipers of Changshu* is one of his most distinctive and powerful (see Figure 10.3).

Wen's inscription states that he was copying Zhao Mengfu, but this is "copying" at its most creative, for what it shares with the Yuan painter is the power of its abstraction and the expressiveness of its brushwork. It also shares a love for the old: the trees were originally planted in 500 C.E., and four were replaced in the

Like creaking ropes the junipers dance to the wail of the wind, conjuring up a thousand images: split horns and blunted claws, the wrestling of the dragon with the tiger, great whales rolling in the deep, and giant birds who swoop down on their prey. And now, like ghosts, they vanish, now reappear, vast entangled forms. (Tseng Yu-ho, in Richard Edwards, *The Art of Wen Cheng-ming* [1470–1559] [Ann Arbor: Univ. of Michigan Museum of Art, 1976], p. 122.)

eleventh century. But here the accent is not on venerable age, but on strength and an explosive vitality that cannot be contained by the edges of the paper.

Poems on paintings, as in the case of *Junipers*, remained common, and some poems were paintings in words:

> A slim bending egret,
> Flies to alight on a riverbank.
> Like a patch of snow that does not melt,
> It dots the emerald of the river sky.[14]

The author of this poem, Zhou Saizhen (fl. 1496), by birth and marriage belonged to the upper stratum of Ming officialdom. Apparently her poem "Encouraging My Son to Study and Abstain from Wine" did not fall on deaf ears, for he was awarded the *jinshi* degree in 1496. Zhou was one of a number of talented and sophisticated Ming women whose poems often express the grief of separation, loneliness, and/or the melancholy of the seasons.

## Ming Thought: Wang Yangming

Like Wen Zhengming's junipers, Ming thought could not be confined within its traditional frame. It was Wen's and Zhou's contemporary, Wang Yangming (Wang Shouren, 1472–1529), who opened up new intellectual vistas within Neo-Confucianism. Unlike the gentlemen-painters of Suzhou, Wang had a very active official career. At its low point he suffered two months in prison and a beating of 40 strokes followed by exile in Guizhou, but he subsequently served with great

courage and distinction both as a civil administrator and as a military commander, rendering outstanding service by suppressing rebels.

Ming thinkers had to cope with the problems of living a Confucian life in a
world that remained stubbornly un-Confucian. Despite the state's official support
for Confucianism, Chinese government and society were as far from resembling
the Confucian ideal as ever. How was one to live a proper life in a society that was
not right and proper, amid the venality of officials, the social changes induced by
economic expansion, and the continuing politicization of government administration? They also had to redefine the role of the educated gentleman as the growth
of commerce created a new prosperity, new sources of power, and, de facto, new
value systems. At the same time, the spread of literacy undercut the monopoly of
classical thought, classical culture, and the status of those with a classical education. Moreover, there was a sense that in a postclassical age perhaps the only way
the scholar could make a personal contribution was through specialization, recognizing that the traditional aim of universal knowledge was no longer attainable. In
an effort to define their personal and social roles, the educated were forced to return to the question of the nature of their own nature:

> Was it static or dynamic, metaphysical or physical, an abstract ideal
> or an active force, a moral norm or a trans-moral perfection? . . . How
> was the individual to understand that nature in relation to his actual
> self and his society?[15]

The issue at stake was not purely intellectual. It involved a quest not only for
knowledge but also for wisdom and sagehood.

For Wang Yangming the essential insight came suddenly at the age of 36 after
a period of intense thought while in exile in Guizhou. His experience has often
been likened to the sudden enlightenment sought by Chan Buddhists. Like Zhu
Xi's contemporary, Lu Jiuyuan, Wang identified human nature with the mind-
heart (*xin*), in turn identified with principle (*li*). For Wang, as for Lu, *li* alone exists. Everyone is endowed with goodness and has an innate capacity to know good
(*liangzhi*). Self-perfection consists of "extending" this capacity to the utmost.
Everyone can attain perfection because we are all endowed with the gold of sagehood. People may differ quantitatively in their abilities, but qualitatively they are
the same, just as the gold in a small coin is in no way inferior to that in a large one.
Thus, Wang took it very calmly when a disciple reported going out for a walk and
finding the street full of sages. That was only to be expected. However, there is
need for strenuous effort to refine the gold by eliminating the dross, that is, "selfish desires." Sagehood does not come easily.

External sources of doctrinal authority, including the classics, repositories of
the words and deeds of the sages, have only a secondary, accessory function.
According to Wang Yangming, "If words are examined in the mind and found to
be wrong, although they have come from the mouth of Confucius, I dare not accept them as correct."[16] Conversely, if the mind finds them correct, it does not
matter if the words have been uttered by ordinary folk. The truth is in and of the
mind. It remains one whole because the mind and *li* are universal.

As is the case for all Confucians, the knowledge that concerns Wang Yangming is at once metaphysical and moral. It is not to be grasped by abstract intellectualization but must be lived. What is true of sensory knowledge holds for all knowledge: a person can no more know filial piety without practicing it than he can know the smell of an odor or understand pain without direct personal experience. Knowing and acting are inseparable, two dimensions of a single process: "Knowledge in its genuine and earnest aspect is action, and action in its intelligent and discriminating aspect is knowledge."[17] A man may discourse with great erudition and subtlety on filiality, but it is his conduct that will reveal his depth of understanding. To employ a modern example, a person who "knows" smoking is bad for him but persists in the habit reveals that he does not really "know" this with his whole being. A perfectly integrated personality is, of course, a mark of the sage.

Wang Yangming had an abiding influence because he spoke to some of the persistent concerns of East Asian thinkers and activists. One may, for example, detect in Mao Zedong's discussions of the relationship between theory and practice overtones of the Ming philosopher's insistence on the unity of knowledge and action. One reason for his influence is that he was the kind of thinker who opens many doors rather than laying down a rigid system.

# Religion

Both Buddhism and Daoism had by now permeated Chinese culture, including popular festivals and medical practices. On the Buddhist side, we can cite the popularity of *Journey to the West* in many genres and for various audiences. Meanwhile among the literati the *Laozi* and *Zhuangzi* continued to delight and inspire. An example of the Daoist religious influence is Wen Zhengming's painting, for his seven junipers represent the seven stars of the Northern Dipper, important in Daoism, and depict an actual group of trees in the grounds of a Daoist temple not far from Suzhou.

Imperial patronage remained important. Shizong (1521–1566) was such a generous patron of Daoism that he has been called "The Daoist Emperor." Like so many of his subjects he turned to Daoists for ways to preserve and prolong life (although ingesting immortality medicine had cost two of his predecessors their lives). Shizong raised Daoists to the highest positions of state and neglected government in favor of Daoism. Hai Rui was jailed when he tried to persuade the emperor to give up further investigations into attaining immortality.

Daoists often formed alliances with eunuchs, but that eunuch ascendancy did not necessarily harm Buddhism is indicated by their power during the reign of Wuzong, a fervent Buddhist who in 1507 personally ordained 40,000 monks. As Chün-fang Yü has indicated, the history of Ming Buddhism falls readily into three periods.[18] As in other respects, the Ming began with a period of state activism with the government undertaking control of the number of monks and supervision of temples and monasteries. This was followed by a middle period of decline in spiritual vigor and rigor, although Buddhist institutions continued strong. Finally, the Late Ming, beginning with the Wanli reign period

(1573–1615), experienced a revival. An example of a new intensity was the four years Hanshan Deqing (1546–1623) devoted to copying a sutra in his own blood mixed with gold, invoking Amitabha after each word.

Deqing, who was ultimately recognized as a Chan patriarch, was typical in his serious study of and writing on a wide range of Buddhist texts. He also wrote commentaries on Daoist and Confucian classics. A number of outstanding Late Ming Buddhist masters were similarly open to and learned in other teaching while remaining Buddhist at heart.

Both the fervor and the willingness to cross boundaries in search of intellectual and spiritual fulfillment were characteristic of many areas of Late Ming thought and behavior. An extreme form of Confucianism is demonstrated notably by the celebration of young women whose filial devotion induced them to slice their own flesh, hoping to cure an ailing parent.

## Ming Thought after Wang Yangming

Some of Wang Yangming's followers and disciples led courageous but quite conventional lives of public service, self-cultivation, and teaching, but others developed the more radical implications of his thought. Wang Yangming taught that the mind in itself is above distinctions of good and evil, an idea with a strong Buddhist flavor and compatible with Daoist ideas. The tendency to combine Confucianism, Buddhism, and Daoism was a very old one now given new vitality. Present in Wang Yangming, it was carried further by Wang Ji (1498–1585), who freely employed Buddhist and Daoist terms, valued Daoist techniques of breath control, but remained a Confucian in his rejection of empty abstract speculation and in his moral values.

Wang Ji and Wang Gen (1483–1541) are considered the founders of the Taizhou branch of Wang Yangming's teaching, named after Wang Gen's native prefecture where he established a school. Wang Gen was born into a family of salt producers and remained a commoner throughout his life. In 1552 his enthusiasm for the teachings of the sage prompted him to build himself a cart such as the one he imagined Confucius to have used. He then rode in it to Beijing to present a memorial. He attracted much attention in the capital until persuaded by fellow disciples of Wang Yangming to return south, where he remained a vigorous and fervent popular teacher, attracting a good many commoners as students.

In their personal conduct as well as in their teachings, the more radical followers of Wang Yangming stretched the parameters of Confucianism to the utmost and went beyond the limits tolerated by the state. He Xinyin (1517–1579) was a courageous defender of free discussion in the academies and so devoted to all humanity that he turned against the family as a restrictive, selfish, exclusive institution. His unorthodox ideas, courageous personal conduct, and reputation as a troublemaker eventually helped land him in prison, where he died after being beaten. Li Zhi (1527–1602), another controversial figure, carried the individualism implicit in Wang Yangming's philosophy to the point of defending selfishness. A thorough nonconformist, he denounced conventional scholars who, he claimed, lacked an authentic commitment to the core values of Confucianism. In 1588 Li

Zhi shaved his head and became (at least in appearance) a Buddhist monk. But he continued to offend the literati; in 1590 local gentry organized a mob that demolished the temple where Li was staying. Imprisoned in 1602, he committed suicide. Until a modern revival of interest in his ideas, he was best known as an editor of *The Water Margin*, and the novel's opposition to the establishment accords very well with Li's own attitudes.

Meanwhile, Jiao Hong (c. 1548–1620) went beyond earlier theorists who had considered Confucianism, Buddhism, and Daoism as independent and complementary. Instead he saw the three teachings as forming a single teaching so that each could help explain the others.

The significance of He, Li, and Jiao may lie not so much in their intellectual influence, which was limited, but rather in demonstrating the limits to which Ming thought could be stretched. Li Zhi shocked not only members of the official establishment but also activist Confucians, who were dismayed by the radical subjectivism of this line of thought and appalled by the Buddhistic notion that human nature was beyond good and evil.

At the same time, others struggled with how to contain social change and restore what they considered a proper relationship between state and society and yearned for a simpler age such as an Early Ming, which they idealized. Timothy Brook has described the "panicked indignation" of Late Ming writers:

> Many became obsessed with the extent to which Chinese society had grown away from what they were trained to believe it had originally been: an agrarian realm where superiors knew their responsibilities and inferiors their places. But, they felt, people no longer stayed put: class distinctions had become disturbingly fluid; the cultivation of wealth had displaced moral effort as the presiding goal of the age.[19]

And he goes on to say:

> However artificial, the classical status hierarchy of gentry, peasantry, artisanate, and merchants may have seemed in the opening years of the dynasty, by the end of the Ming it was nothing but a quaint trope invoked by a few censorious gentry authors to mourn the erosion of what they deemed to be their near-hereditary claim to elevated status.[20]

# Dong Qichang and Late Ming Painting

Dong Qichang (1555–1636) was a major painter and calligrapher, the leading connoisseur of his generation, and China's foremost art historian. Many of the ideas of Dong and his circle were not new, but he gave them their final authoritative expression. The key to his analysis was the division of painters into Northern and Southern schools resembling the Northern and Southern branches of Chan Buddhism. The assignment of a painter into one group or the other was not based on geography but on the man's social standing and on his style. A "Northern" painter was defined as a professional who stressed technical excellence and fine

**FIGURE 10.4** Dong Quichang, *The Qingbian Mountain*. Hanging scroll, ink on paper, dated 1617. 26.38 in × 88.58 in. Natural forms are tilted, compressed, and juxtaposed, not to represent nature but to emphasize the painting's formal organization and the interplay of light and dark. (© Cleveland Museum of Art, 2003. Leonard C. Hanna, Jr. Bequest, 1980.10)

craftsmanship to produce handsome paintings of maximum visual appeal. In contrast, "Southern" painters were literati, men of wide reading and profound learning for whom painting was an experience of self-expression, a chance to allow their genius and sensibility free play, much as in calligraphy. Dong traced these two lines all the way back to the Tang and cast Wang Wei as the founder of the Southern tradition. He also included painters of his own dynasty in his analysis. Furthermore, Dong and his friends affirmed their affiliation with the Southern tradition.

Self-identification with a tradition of amateurism did not preclude the study of earlier masters. Dong himself was influenced in calligraphy by Zhao Mengfu and Wen Zhengming and greatly admired the master painters of the Yuan. But he emphasized the need to "unlearn," and a painting such as his picture of the Qingbian Mountains (see Figure 10.4) has only a faint resemblance to its purported tenth-century model. Nor is there in this painting any desire to represent mountains as they actually appear to the eye or to define the depth relationships between them by clearly placing them one behind the other. The effect of Dong's theories and art on seventeenth-century painting is suggested by Wang Yuanqi (1642–1715), a famous painter who in 1700 became the chief artistic advisor to Emperor Kangxi and who described Dong as having "cleansed the cobwebs from landscape painting in one sweep."[21]

In the final years of the Ming there were artists painting in a number of different styles, many playing on earlier modes. A painter who took as his point of departure the classic Song landscape but turned it into an expression of his own fantastic imagination was Wu Bin (c. 1568–1626): Figure 10.5 shows a landscape that never was nor ever could be. Paintings such as this suggest both some of the potentialities and some of the dangers inherent in Ming individualism. In the seventeenth century, the dynasty, like the painting, found itself balanced on too narrow a base.

## Late Ming Government (1590–1644)

A conspicuous feature of the last fifty years of the dynasty was the inadequacy of its emperors. When Zhang Juzheng died in 1582, Emperor Shenzong, then not quite nineteen, determined that during his reign no minister would again dominate the government, but soon the emperor himself ceased to bother very much with government. From 1589 to 1615, a period of more than 25 years, he did not hold a single general audience, and from 1590 to his death in 1620, he only conducted personal interviews with Grand Secretaries five times. Nor, except on matters of taxation and defense, did he respond to memorials. As a result much government business was simply left undone. He was particularly remiss in personnel matters. By the end of his reign, not only were the offices in the capital seriously understaffed, but it has also been estimated that as many as half of the prefectural and district posts were also unfilled. Whereas at the start he had punished officials who criticized him in their memorials, during the last 20 years he largely ignored even them. Some high officials withdrew from their posts without authorization—they too were ignored.

**FIGURE 10.5** Wu Bin landscape. Hanging scroll, ink and light color on paper, 38.78 in × 120.47 in. (© Asian Art Museum of San Francisco, Gift of the Avery Brundage Collection Symposium Fund and the M.H. de Young Memorial Museum Trust Fund, B69D17. Used with persmission.) James Cahill has said it best: "Solids evaporate into space, ambiguous definitions of surface unsettle the eye as it moves over them, and the towering construction of spires and cliffs, like the creation of some titanic, demented sculptor, balances on an absurdly narrow base." (James Cahill, *Fantastics and Eccentrics in Chinese Painting* [New York: The Asia Society, 1976], p. 36.)

The emperor did take an interest in military matters. From the 1580s on there was fighting in the southwest against various tribal peoples as well as against the Thais and especially against the Burmese. In the 1590s there were campaigns in Inner Mongolia, and large Ming armies fought a Japanese invasion of Korea. These military actions were generally successful but enormously expensive. Also costly but not as successful was the Ming military effort in Manchuria, where the Manchu chief Nurgaci founded a state and fought the Ming to a draw (see Chapter 15).

The political deterioration that marked the decline of the Ming did not escape the attention of earnest Confucians who saw it as their duty to protest forcefully against political abuses and to object against un-Confucian conduct such as the refusal of Zhang Juzheng to retire from office to observe mourning on the death of his father. Early in the seventeenth century, the Donglin Academy, founded in 1604 in Wuxi northwest of Suzhou, became a center for such "pure criticism," which cost many Donglin men their lives. Conflict between pro-Donglin and anti-Donglin factions lasted through the final thirty years of the dynasty.

Emperor Xizong (r. 1620–1627) was peculiar even by Late Ming standards. He "did not have sufficient leisure to learn to write"[22] but spent all his time on carpentry, creating many pieces of fine furniture, which he lacquered himself. Factionalism, which in the absence of strong imperial leadership had flourished under Shenzong, now turned vicious. Wei Zhongxian (1568–1627), a very capable and equally unscrupulous eunuch, gained power due to his influence over the emperor. Wei purged all opponents, foremost among them the members of the Donglin faction, six of whom died in prison after torture. One of these men, Zuo Guangdou, in his notes to his sons left vivid descriptions of agonizing pain and suffering, which he interlaced with exclamations of his fervent devotion to the emperor, such as "my body belongs to my ruler-father."[23] Like He Xinyin and Li Zhi, Zuo demonstrated his Confucian selflessness even to the point of death, but his martyrdom, unlike theirs, testifies to the persuasiveness of a kind of Confucian authoritarianism in which even a carpenter-emperor could command the loyalty others might think due, if at all, only to a sage. To the end, the dynasty retained the loyalty of most of its officials.

Not content with actual power, Wei also thirsted for public recognition. He heaped honors on himself and even had a nephew take the emperor's place in performing sacrifices in the imperial temple. He also encouraged a movement to have temples housing his image built throughout China. But he did not survive Emperor Xizong for long, and the temples perished shortly after the man. The succeeding emperor, Sizong (r. 1627–1644), attempted reform during his reign, but the lack of a consistent policy is suggested by the high turnover of the regime's highest officials: from 1621 to 1644 the presidents of the Six Ministries were changed 116 times.

Bureaucratic infighting and corruption was something the dynasty could no longer afford, for during the reign of Shenzong the earlier fiscal surplus had been turned into a mounting deficit. But the trouble went deeper:

> The Ming fiscal administration was in essence built on the foundation of a grain economy. With its diversified rates and measurements, self-supporting institutions, regional and departmental self-sufficiency,

divided budget, separate channels of cash flow, numerous material and corvee labor impositions, and local tax captains, the fiscal machinery was grossly unfit for a new monetary economy. . . . However, [these unsatisfactory features of the Ming fiscal administration] would not have been so appallingly evident had not the wide circulation of silver thoroughly changed the nation's economic outlook. The archaic fiscal structure became more outdated than ever because it was set against the background of a mobile and expanding economy.[24]

The wide circulation of silver also left China vulnerable to inflation when silver imports, largely from the Spanish Americas through Manila, were interrupted.

The delicate balance between the central government and the local elite was upset when the dynasty made too many concessions to the gentry. Too much was given away; too many fields were removed from the tax rolls. Large landowners were able to find tax shelters through various manipulations, and only peasant freeholders remained to pay taxes. Locally resentment against the gentry grew, and the shortage of funds forced the dynasty to neglect vital public works. Grain stored for emergency use was sold off. Even the postal system was shut down. Finally, the regime failed to pay even its most strategically placed troops: when the end came, the capital garrison had not been paid for five months.

Military deserters and dismissed postal employees were among those who took the lead in forming the outlaw gangs that appeared first in Northern Shaanxi and then spread from there. As they grew in size and strength, they progressed from disorganized raiding to more ambitious objectives. Two groups emerged as the most powerful. One, established in Sichuan, was led by Zhang Xianzhong (c. 1605–1647), a leader notorious for his brutality. The other was led by Li Zicheng (c. 1605–1645), a former postal attendant, whom the official sources depict as a cruel but dedicated leader, and who, in the twentieth century, came to be celebrated in the People's Republic as a hero. In 1644 Li Zicheng seized Beijing, and the Ming emperor committed suicide, but Li proved unable to found a new dynasty, for he had not taken the necessary ideological and administrative steps to win over the members of the scholar-official elite. For them he represented at best an unknown force, and no one could rule China without their cooperation. This was understood by Li's most powerful and capable competitors even though they came from Manchuria. When they built their dynasty, they made extensive use of Ming precedents.

# *Notes*

1. Frederick W. Mote, *Imperial China 900–1800* (Cambridge: Harvard Univ. Press, 1999), p. 570.

2. John W. Dardess, in Paul J. Smith and Richard von Glahn, eds., *The Song-* *Yuan Ming Transition in Chinese History* (Cambridge: Harvard Univ. Press, 2003), p. 123.

3. Sarah K. Schneewind, *Community Schools and Improper Shrines: Local*

*Institutions and the Chinese State in the
Ming Period, 1368–1644* (Ph.D. dissertation, Columbia Univ., 1999), p. 101.

4. Schneewind, *Community Schools and
Improper Shrines,* p. 120.

5. Frederick W. Mote and Denis
Twitchett, eds., *The Cambridge History
of China, Vol. 7: The Ming Dynasty,
1368–1644,* Part I (Cambridge:
Cambridge Univ. Press, 1988), pp.
149–81.

6. Shih-Shan Henry Tsai, *Perpetual
Happiness: The Ming Emperor Yongle*
(Seattle: Univ. of Washington Press,
2001), p.121.

7. David Robinson, *Bandits, Eunuchs, and
the Son of Heaven: Rebellion and the
Economy of Violence in Mid-Ming China*
(Honolulu: Univ. of Hawaii Press,
2001), p. 97.

8. Martin Heijdra, "The Socio-Economic
Development of Rural China during
the Ming," in Denis Twitchett and
Frederick K.W. Mote, eds., *The
Cambridge History of China, Vol. 8: The
Ming Dynasty, 1368–1644,* Part 2
(Cambridge: Cambridge Univ. Press,
1998), p. 477.

9. Shigeta Atsushi, as discussed in Mori
Masao, "The Gentry in the Ming: An
Outline of the Relations between the
Shih-ta fu and Local Society," *Acta
Asiatica* 38 (1980): 31–53.

10. Hilary J. Beattie, *Land and Lineage in
China: A Study of T'ung-ch'eng County,
Anhwei, in the Ming and Ch'ing
Dynasties* (Cambridge: Cambridge
Univ. Press, 1979).

11. Liu Wu-chi, *An Introduction to Chinese
Literature* (Bloomington: Indiana Univ.
Press, 1966), pp. 216–17.

12. K'ung Shang-jen, *The Peach Blossom
Fan,* trans. Chen Shih-hsiang and
Harold Acton (Berkeley: Univ. of
California Press, 1970), p. xiv.

13. Anne De Coursey Clapp, *The Painting
of T'ang Yin* (Chicago: Univ. of Chicago
Press, 1991), p. 46.

14. Norman Kutcher, trans. in Kang-I Sun
Chang and Haun Sausy, eds., *Women
Writers of Traditional China: An
Anthology of Poetry and Criticism*
(Stanford: Stanford Univ. Press, 1999),
p. 170.

15. Wm. Theodore de Bary and the
Conference on Ming Thought, *Self and
Society in Ming Thought* (New York:
Columbia Univ. Press, 1970), p. 12.

16. Wing-tsit Chan, trans., *Instructions for
Practical Living and Other Neo-
Confucian Writings* (New York:
Columbia Univ. Press, 1963), p. 159.

17. Wing-tsit Chan, *A Source Book in
Chinese Philosophy* (Princeton:
Princeton Univ. Press, 1963), p. 681.

18. Chün-fang Yü, "Ming Buddhism"
Chapter 14, in *Cambridge History, Vol. 8.*

19. Timothy Brook, Communication and
Commerce," in *Cambridge History, Vol.
8,* p. 579.

20. Brook, p. 580.

21. Quoted in James Cahill, *Fantastics and
Eccentrics in Chinese Painting* (New
York: The Asia Society, 1967), p. 22.

22. Quoted in Arthur W. Hummel, ed.,
*Eminent Chinese of the Ch'ing Period,*
Vol. 1 (Washington, DC: GPO, 1943),
p. 190.

23. Quoted in Charles O. Hucker,
"Confucianism and the Chinese
Censorial System," in David S. Nivison
and Arthur F. Wright, eds.,
*Confucianism in Action* (Stanford:
Stanford Univ. Press, 1959), p. 208.

24. Ray Huang, "Fiscal Administration
during the Ming Dynasty," in Charles
O. Hucker, ed., *Chinese Government in
Ming Times* (New York: Columbia Univ.
Press, 1969), pp. 124–25.

# The Kamakura Period in Japan

1156        1185      Jōei Code → 1232                         1333

**TAIRA**                  **KAMAKURA**

Gempei War            Mongol Invasions
(1180–1185)           of Japan
                       (1266–1274)

The ascent of the Japanese warrior was a slow process that began well before the Kamakura period and remained incomplete. Although the period, now often identified as early medieval, gets its name from the seat of warrior power at Kamakura in eastern Japan (Kanto), it was a time of shared power. The sanctity of the throne as the ultimate source of authority remained intact. Furthermore, the leaders of both the Minamoto and Taira groups were not just commanders of warriors pure and simple but also, to quote Jeffrey Mass, "bridging figures—military nobles in the truest sense—between the great central aristocrats, who were their patrons, and the great provincial warriors, who were their followers." This helps explain the slow development of warrior power and "the incompleteness of the warrior revolution."[1] Rivalries among the provincial fighting men overshadowed potential ties of common class interests or feelings of solidarity. The same was true of the imperial court. Political intrigues and fighting pitted not only warriors and aristocrats against each other but also warriors against warriors, court nobles against court nobles, and even fathers against sons in a complicated struggle for power.

# Triumph and Fall of the Taira (1156–1185)

In 1156 open conflict broke out between the retired emperor and the reigning emperor, and military men were called in on both sides. On one side, supporting the cloistered emperor, was a force led by Minamoto no Tameyoshi (1096–1156); on the other side, the emperor, Go-Shirakawa, had the backing of a coalition led by Taira no Kiyomori (1118–1181), which also included among its leaders Tameyoshi's own son, Yoshitomo (1123–1160). Military victory in what is known as the Hōgen Conflict went to Kiyomori's coalition, but the real losers were the court and the old civil nobility.

The outcome left Kiyomori in a position of great power, but the victorious coalition was soon dissolved, and further fighting ensued in the Heiji War (1159–1160). Once again Kiyomori won, this time defeating his former ally, Yoshitomo. These Hōgen and Heiji conflicts were brief and localized but extremely bitter. They were followed by manhunts and executions, because warriors did not share the civilian aristocrats' qualms about taking life. Gone were the days when the usual penalty for being on the wrong side politically was exile.

These military victories gave Kiyomori a new power base, but he operated within the old framework, seeking to dominate the court and government machinery in the capital. He married his daughters into the imperial line and to Fujiwara regents, but he also relied and depended on his connection to Emperor Go-Shirakawa, whose wishes he could not ignore. In 1180 he placed his grandson on the throne.

In his personal deportment, too, he conformed to the standards of taste set by the court. But to the grand Kyoto aristocrats, he remained an arrogant provincial parvenu, worthy only of contempt. An attempt to exert greater control over the court by transferring it to a site near modern Kobe failed. More successful was Kiyomori's handling of the troublesome temple armies. He attacked and burned two of the worst offenders, both in Nara: the Tōdaiji and Kōfukuji, the prime temple of the Fujiwara family.

Conditions in the capital were unusually harsh during these years. Storms, earthquakes, and disease afflicted the city, which, as always, was also susceptible to the ravages of fire. A major conflagration destroyed a third of the city in 1177; in one two-month period after the fire, more than 40,000 corpses were found in the streets of the capital.

Kiyomori's most serious problem was that during his ascendancy the old institutions remained as weak as ever. He could no more exercise complete control over the provinces than he could over the cloistered emperor. Led by Yoshitomo's son Yoritomo (1147–1199), the Minamoto took advantage of this situation to rebuild their power. With the support of many eastern Taira and Minamoto families, Yoritomo initiated the Gempei War (1180–1185), which ended in the permanent defeat of the Taira. Contributing to this outcome was the brilliant generalship of Yoshitsune (1159–1189), Yoritomo's younger brother, who defeated the Taira at sea and on land. Later, Yoshitsune incurred the suspicion of his powerful brother, who, in the end, turned his armed might against him and brought about his death.

The wide extent of the fighting, a style of combat that placed a premium on personal valor, contrasts between the Taira (who had adopted many of the ways of Kyoto) and the rougher eastern warriors, and the effect of the war on subsequent developments have assured it a lasting place in the Japanese imagination and in literature. It is recounted in Japan's major literary epic, *The Tale of the Heike* (*Heike monogatari*), a tale widely chanted among all classes, and it generated a host of minor romances, including some that embellished the story of Yoshitsune, transforming it into a heroic legend.

## Establishment of the Bakufu

Yoritomo was not a great general, but he was a good judge of men, a consummate politician, and an effective organizer. Carefully, he consolidated his position in the east. With his headquarters in the small fishing village of Kamakura, he built a se-

Route of Mongol invastion attempts

**FIGURE 11.1** Japan, 1200–1600.

cure base for warrior power (see Figure 11.1). There he established his *bakufu*, literally "tent government," a term that evokes the military origins of his power. Legitimization for the new order came from the emperor, who in 1192 "appointed" Yoritomo shogun or, to use the full term, *seii taishōgun* (barbarian-suppressing general). Under the theoretical sovereignty of the emperor, the shogun's government exercised substantial "delegated" power. This was the beginning of an institution (the shogunate) that lasted until 1868.

At the heart of Yoritomo's power in eastern Japan were ties of vassalage, aptly defined by Peter Duus as "a personal bond of loyalty and obedience by which a warrior promised service to a lord or chieftain in return for military protection, security, and assistance."[2] The ties of vassalage were more inclusive and expandable than the old kinship bonds, which, however, did not disappear. Vassalage was contractual in the sense that there was at least a tacit understanding of mutual obligations, but these were never spelled out or incorporated in legal documents. Nor were there legal mechanisms for altering or dissolving the arrangement. Ideally, it called for deep personal devotion of vassal to lord rather than the more abstract loyalty demanded in an impersonal bureaucratic state; but in practice, especially in turbulent and unsettled times, much depended on the individuals involved.

From his vassals (*gokenin*, "honorable housemen") Yoritomo demanded and expected absolute loyalty. Such loyalty was granted him partly as a result of the confidence he inspired in his men, some of whose families had served the Minamoto for generations. Others, particularly in western Japan, cast their lot with Yoritomo only after they had been impressed with his visible accomplishments. Calculations of military and political advantage on the part of the lesser lords helped augment Yoritomo's strength, which after the defeat of the Taira surpassed that of any possible rival, military or civil. Economic inducements also provided powerful motivation. Those who served him could expect confirmation of the land rights (*shiki*) they already held, and they could hope for further rewards in the form of rights over land confiscated from the enemies of the Minamoto. Economic self-interest reinforced the bonds of personal vassalage in Japan just as in feudal Europe; it was the cement that ensured the cohesiveness of the system.

There are certain striking resemblances between Kamakura Japan and feudal Europe. Both featured rule by a military aristocracy that held predominant local power, a system of vassalage, and land as a source of wealth. However, the Kamakura system functioned in uneasy tandem with the political and economic system centered on Kyoto. Yoritomo had neither the power nor the intent to eliminate the old order but used it to his own advantage in consolidating his power. His vassals received land rights, not land, and at least until the early thirteenth century the old Kyoto nobility and religious establishments retained much of their political influence and wealth.

## Local Governance

The most important power "delegated" to Yoritomo was legal control over the staffing of provincial posts, which enabled him to appoint his own men to administrative positions in the provinces. He was also authorized to appoint his men to the newly created position of land steward or overseer (*jitō*) and as military protectors (*shugō*).

Land stewards were appointed to estates and given official responsibility for the collection of rents and the forwarding of dues to the absentee holders of rights in the estates—that is, the court aristocracy, the imperial family, and the great religious establishments. The stewards also received considerable police and judicial authority over the estates and were rewarded by grants of rights (*shiki*) to a portion of the estate income. The function of the military protectors, appointed to most provinces, was to provide liaison between the *bakufu* and its retainers and to maintain security. They were responsible for suppressing rebels and punishing major crimes. The appointment of stewards and military protectors thus served both the cause of *bakufu* power and that of public order, but it left the imperial system of provincial governance basically intact.

The restoration of order benefited everyone, and the new system recognized the economic prerogatives and the continued legitimacy of the Kyoto establishment.

However, tensions inevitably resulted from the intrusion of a lord–vassal system into the old estate structure, as well as between the continued coexistence of private estates and publicly administered lands (*kokugaryō*). Disputes between stewards and estate proprietors were endemic. In the long run, the advantage clearly lay with the local warriors, but the *bakufu,* determined to uphold the system, frequently ruled against stewards' attempts to extend their powers at the expense of proprietors or peasants. Tensions likewise arose between military protectors and officials of the much older imperial provincial office. The former, with their military prowess, eventually eclipsed the latter in terms of de facto control, but this was a slow process and not necessarily accompanied by open conflict.

Early medieval peasants varied widely in status and wealth. At the top were the *myōshu,* managers and later owners of some land with responsibilities for tax collection who also derived wealth from entrepreneurial village activities such as money lending and sericulture. Cultivators received a share of the harvest. At the bottom were transient laborers and the hereditary household servants of wealthy families. There were no restrictions on geographic and social mobility. Peasants were free to leave, but when they did, they lost any claim to the land.

The coexistence between Kamakura and Kyoto was tested in 1221, when Emperor Go-Toba (1190–1229) used imperial lands and Buddhist monasteries to raise a force of dissatisfied warriors in an attempt to restore imperial power. He was soundly defeated. The end result was to strengthen the shogunate, which used the occasion to confiscate 3000 estates, appoint additional stewards in central and western Japan, and establish its own deputies in Kyoto. Faced with widespread general disorder, the *bakufu* sought to strengthen its own place within the system rather than to devise a new system.

# The Hōjō Regents

Yoritomo established the Kamakura shogunate on a firm foundation but did not succeed in founding a dynasty of shoguns. He killed off rivals within his own family, but his death in 1199 was followed by a struggle for power.

Emerging victorious was the Hōjō, the family of Yoritomo's remarkable, strong-minded widow, Masako (1157–1225), who herself dominated shogunal politics for a time and was dubbed the "nun shogun." Her father became the first in a line of de facto Hōjō rulers, although they never assumed the office of shogun. That was held by a puppet, who after 1219 was not even a Minamoto, because in that year a Fujiwara infant received the appointment. Meanwhile, the Hōjō, by placing family members in key posts, exercised control over the *bakufu*. In this way, real power was doubly divorced from apparent authority: in theory, the country was ruled by an emperor, but this emperor was largely under the control of his abdicated father (the retired emperor); meanwhile, in Kamakura, the other locus of government, the power ostensibly "delegated" to the shogun was exercised by Hōjō ministers.

Although the overall structure seems complex, organization of the Kamakura shogunate remained relatively simple in keeping with its modest scope of government. An Office of Samurai looked after the affairs of the shogunate's vassals (*go-kenin*) and generally supervised military and police matters. A board of inquiry (*monchūjo*) dealt with various judicial matters and under the Hōjō handled cases arising outside of Kamakura. General administration was under the jurisdiction of an Office of Administration similar to the household offices used by the great Heian families. Yoritomo designated it the *mandokoro,* the usual name for such a household bureau. The heads of these three bureaus participated in a council that advised Yoritomo, who made the final decisions himself. The council was led by the chief of the *mandokoro,* and it was in this capacity that the Hōjō exercised their power. In 1225 an innovative Hōjō statesman created a Council of State to allow broader warrior participation in government, but the Hōjō soon dominated this body.

The Hōjō concept of government is reflected in the law code of 1232, the Jōei Code, the first codification of warrior law. One of its purposes was to define the duties of stewards and military protectors. Another major concern was to clarify matters of land tenure and succession. Included among the latter were the property rights of warrior women. For example, women had some inheritance rights, and divorced women could retain the land they had originally brought into the marriage.

The code emphasized the impartial administration of justice in settling disputes among warriors, disputes that usually concerned land rights. The adjudication of such matters was one of the shogunate's prime functions, and much of its power and prestige rested on samurai confidence in the equity of its decisions. The Jōei Code sought to achieve this by setting forth its provisions in a simple and direct manner and by restricting itself to a small number of regulations. For cases not covered by precedent, it advised recourse to common sense. As the need arose, additional articles were added to the code. Its reputation as a symbol of justice was so strong that a revised version of it was adopted by the next shogunate in the fourteenth century.

Another indication of Hōjō effectiveness and the resilience of the institutions of the *bakufu* was the ability of the regime to withstand a most formidable military challenge and to survive the strains it produced in the body politic.

# The Mongol Invasion and Its Aftermath

The Mongol conquest of East Asia was in full swing when the Jōei Code was issued, but it was another third of a century before its momentum was felt in Japan. Before they needed to defend themselves against the Mongols, the Kamakura statesmen had successfully avoided political or military entanglement in continental affairs, although they did nothing to discourage trade with the Song, which flourished both before and after the founding of the shogunate. Although this trade consisted mostly of luxury items, for China it brought a drain of copper coinage, which posed a problem for Song finances. A major effect in Japan of the trade with China was to stimulate a renewed interest in Chinese culture. The shogunate also maintained cordial relations with Korea: when, in 1227, the depredations of Japanese pirates off the Korean coast prompted Korean complaints, the *bakufu* ordered the offenders arrested and executed.

The Mongols changed all that. In 1266, even before the conquest of the Southern Song had been completed, Khubilai Khan dispatched his first messenger to Japan demanding submission. This threat produced great consternation at court in Kyoto, but the shogunate remained calm, determined to resist. It took the Mongols until 1274 to organize a military expedition, but in that year a force of about 30,000 was sent to Japan. They landed near Hakata, in northern Kyushu, and fought briefly with a Japanese force assembled by the *bakufu* but consisting mostly of local warriors. Fortunately for the Japanese, a great storm destroyed this expedition. Heavy casualties did not deter Khubilai Khan from trying again. He renewed his demands only to meet with rebuff; the Japanese showed their determination to resist by executing his envoys. In 1281 Khubilai sent a much larger force, estimated at 140,000 men, to crush the Japanese. But the shogunate, too, had used the intervening years in military preparation: they built a stone wall along Hakata Bay, amassed troops, and trained them in the techniques of group fighting employed by the Mongols, which contrasted with the individual combat customary in Japanese warfare. They fought for seven weeks before nature intervened once more; another great storm, called *kamikaze* ("divine wind") by the Japanese, settled the issue. About half the men sent by Khubilai perished in this fruitless attempt to add Japan to his empire.

Still the Great Khan did not give up. Preparations for a third attempt were in progress when he died in 1294. Only then was the project abandoned. But the *bakufu* did not know that: it continued the policy of military preparedness until 1312. In repulsing these attacks, the shogunate achieved a great success and further increased its power vis-à-vis the civilian court. But it had to share the glory of victory with temples and shrines, which claimed credit for securing divine intervention. Indeed, the notion of Japan as a special land protected by its deities gained currency from this time. This idea was central to the teachings of Nichiren (described later).

For the shogunate, however, the Mongol invasions proved its eventual undoing. Fighting the Mongol invaders, unlike internal warfare, brought in no new lands or booty with which to meet the expectations of warriors demanding their just rewards. When the shogunate proved unable to satisfy warrior claims, the *bushi* lost confidence in the regime. Their loyalty was weakened, and as they increasingly turned for support to local authorities (military protectors and the stronger stewards), centrifugal forces came to the fore. The characteristic Hōjō response was to draw more power into their own hands, a policy not designed to deal with the underlying causes of their deteriorating situation. At the same time, economic pressures and the realities of power worked against aristocratic civilian interests, as military stewards proved increasingly reluctant to forward payments to Kyoto. Vis-à-vis the peasants, too, the stewards were assuming ever-greater powers. If a steward departed too far from custom in his demands, the peasants could appeal to higher authority (including Kamakura), or they could negotiate with the steward himself. However, the stewards' local authority was so extensive that increasingly they treated the estates as though they were their own property. The shogunal policy of balancing military with civilian prerogatives was breaking down. As the shogunate declined, the peculiar dual governance by court and *bakufu,* aristocrat and warrior, was also coming to an end.

## The Warrior and His Ideals

By background and training, the ideal *bushi* was a man different from the Heian aristocrat. As a warrior, he was called upon to exhibit martial skills and to demonstrate valor and manly pride. Many of the features later idealized and incorporated into a "code of the samurai" are evident in medieval epics such as *The Tale of the Heike.* Virile, selfless, and incorruptible, the ideal samurai showed disdain for death and concern for maintaining his honor. He should even be ready to commit ritual suicide by disembowelment (*seppuku*) rather than face capture or dishonor.

In Kamakura Japan as elsewhere, the ideal must not be confused with the reality. Indeed, the more demanding an ideal, the rarer those who attained it. Even in the fictional *Tale of Genji* there is only one shining prince, and surely Heian Kyoto was not totally lacking in boors! Similarly, warriors who fled from combat, turned on allies, or allowed themselves to be captured were numerous. In practice, skills in negotiation and alliance building and careful management of the extended family and its property were as much hallmarks of the successful medieval warrior as martial ability and valor in battle. Moreover, there were cases of women successfully leading *bushi* houses without a male head.

## Religion: The Pure Land Sect

The turbulence and uncertainties accompanying the transition from aristocratic to warrior rule tended to confirm the belief that history had indeed entered its final phase of degeneracy (*mappō*) and made people all the more receptive to the solace of religion. One result was the continuing growth and development of the popularizing and pietistic trends exemplified earlier by the activities and teachings of Kūya and Genshin. A major leader in this tradition was Hōnen, who advanced the Pure Land School of Buddhism (Jōdo; Qingdu in Chinese), named after the paradise in the West over which presides Amida (Amitabha), the Buddha of Infinite Light. To the faithful it offered the hope of rebirth in the land of bliss. In practice, it stressed the *nembutsu*, and Hōnen carried the invocation of Amida further than his predecessors by teaching that the *nembutsu* was not just one method for attaining salvation but rather the best and indeed the only method suitable for the age.

When Hōnen expressed his ideas in writing, his book was burned by the monks on Mt. Hiei, the bastion of Buddhist orthodoxy. He remained a controversial person, suffering in his seventies an exile of four years from which he was allowed to return only a year before he died. Underlying the emphasis on the invocation of Amida was a belief in salvation through faith rather than through works or religious observances. Hōnen himself, on his deathbed, declined to hold the usual cord connected to an Amida to draw him to paradise. His persistent rejection of traditional ritual and scholasticism helps explain the hostility of the older schools.

Pure Land Amidism was further developed by Hōnen's greatest and most renowned disciple, Shinran (1173–1262), founder of the True Pure Land School (Jōdo Shinshu). Although he lived much earlier, Shinran has been compared with the founders of Christian Protestantism because, like them, he insisted that humans were so debased that they could not possibly gain salvation through their own efforts or "self-power" but must depend on the "other power" of Amida. Specifically, salvation comes through faith—frequently experienced by the individual in an act of conversion. The boundless compassion of Amida embraces the bad man or woman and the good. Indeed, bad individuals, conscious of their lack of worth, may be closer to salvation than good people who are incapable of resisting self-congratulation on their merits and who rely on their own efforts to attain rebirth in paradise. Once converted and granted faith, each person will naturally bring the message to others, repeating the *nembutsu* not out of a desire to be saved or for reassurance but out of gratitude and joy.

Shinran was himself filled with a sense of his own sinfulness. "A baldheaded old fool" is the name he adopted for himself. He also carried rejection of the old monastic observances further than any of his predecessors; he ate meat and even married. Exiled for his radical views, he spent his life proclaiming his religious message among the common people as one of themselves.

Shinran did not intend to found a new school, nor did he acknowledge having disciples. But he left many followers who further developed the True Pure Land School, attracting many adherents. In the fifteenth century, Rennyo (1415–1499) organized the community of believers into a disciplined body, ready and able to fight for their beliefs. The True Pure Land School is still one of the largest religious organizations in Japan, now divided into two branches, each headed by descendants of Shinran. This tradition of hereditary leadership was made possible by the abandonment of celibacy. It is also consistent with the value placed on family and with Jōdo faith in the benign "other power" of Amida.

Other popular forms of Pure Land Buddhism also flourished in medieval Japan. One of the best-known Pure Land evangelists was Ippen (1239–1289), who, like Kūya (see Figure 11.2), practiced the dancing *nembutsu* and who became the subject of a famous narrative scripture scroll.

# Nichiren

**FIGURE 11.2** Kōshō, *Kūya*. Wood, Kamakura, approx. 46 in high. Rokuharamitsuji, Kyoto. (© National Commission for Protection of Cultural Properties of Japan)

Many older schools of Buddhism practiced invocation of the Buddha of the Western Paradise without, however, abandoning their older rituals or beliefs. But tolerance was not universal. A vociferous and vehement opponent of Pure Land teachings, as of the doctrines of all the other rival schools new and old, was Nichiren (1222–1282), one of Japan's most flamboyant religious leaders. Like Hōnen and Shinran, he was exiled for his advocacy of unacceptable beliefs, but unlike the others, he was almost put to death; he was saved, according to his followers, only by a miracle, as lightning struck the poised executioner's sword. Nichiren's conviction of the correctness of his teachings was buttressed by his belief that he was a reincarnation of a bodhisattva specially entrusted with the Lotus Sutra, the only text incorporating Buddha's teachings in all their dimensions.

Nichiren, although born into a family of poor fishermen, was a learned man. But like Hōnen and Shinran, his message was simple: faith in the Lotus Sutra, rather than a mastery of its contents, was the requirement for salvation. In place of the invocation of Amida practiced by Pure Land Buddhists, he substituted *namu myōhō renge-kyō* (hail to the Lotus Sutra of the wonderful law), usually chanted to the beat of a drum.

In adversity Nichiren demonstrated a depth of conviction and strength of character readily appreciated by warriors who valued similar virtues. Perhaps his origins in eastern Japan also enhanced his standing among the *bushi* who had established the shogunate. Furthermore, he was greatly attached to the land and was Japan-centered to an unusual degree, envisioning Japan as the headquarters for his faith, which from there would spread throughout the world. The very name he chose for himself, Nichiren (*nichi* = sun, *ren* = lotus), indicated his dual devotion to the Land of the Rising Sun and the Lotus Sutra. In his view, the one required the other. Repeatedly, he warned that the Lotus was essential for Japan and predicted dire consequences if other schools remained in favor. He prophesied the Mongol invasions, thereby increasing his credibility. Convinced that Buddhism had made its long journey across Asia to Japan to attain perfection, he cited the failed Mongol invasions as proof of Japan's special, divinely protected status. Nichiren's concern for state and country, his courage, and his zeal remained an inspiration for his followers in later times. One man is even said to have journeyed to Siberia as a missionary. Nichiren, the man and the faith, have retained their magnetism to the present. Today he is venerated not only by the traditional Lotus sect but also by the Sōka Gakkai (Value Creation Society), a religious body whose membership has burgeoned since World War II.

# Zen

Pure Land Buddhism and the teachings of Nichiren appealed widely to warriors, but Zen, with a more limited following, enjoyed official favor and *bakufu* support. In Japan, as in China, Zen (Chan in Chinese) was taught and practiced before it became institutionalized with its own temples during the Kamakura shogunate. In Japan it was promoted by two monks, Eisai (1141–1215) and Dōgen (1200–1253), both of whom traveled to China.

Eisai made two trips and brought back not only religious ideas but also great enthusiasm for tea, thus initiating the long association between that beverage and Japanese Zen. He was a follower of the Rinzai (Linji in Chinese) school, practicing the use of the *kōan* riddles. Eisai found support in Kamakura, but in Kyoto he accommodated himself to the religious life of the old capital by observing Tendai and Shingon practices and Zen rules. He even recommended the *nembutsu* and allowed chants and prayers.

Dōgen, in contrast, was uncompromising in his attitude toward secular authority. He eventually settled in the mountains remote from Kamakura and Kyoto, consistently declined worldly honors, and built a small temple, which later grew into the great monastery of Eiheiji. Dōgen differed from Eisai also in the type of Zen he preached, because he brought back from China the doctrines of the Sōto (Caodao in Chinese) school, which emphasized sitting in silent meditation (*zazen*) without a specific object or goal in mind, a gradual process of realizing the Buddha nature through the body and the mind. In his attitude toward the transmission of the truth, Dōgen was a moderate, accepting scriptural authority and the authority of the personal transmission from patriarch to patriarch. The influence enjoyed by the Sōto school in Japan was much greater than that accorded Caodao in China.

The proper practice of Zen made great demands on its practitioners, demands no less severe than those encountered in military training. Seekers after illumination did not, like the second patriarch, have to sever an arm to demonstrate their seriousness of purpose, but they did have to endure a period of waiting and abuse before they were admitted to the spartan, rigorously regulated life of the temple (see Figure 11.3).

**FIGURE 11.3** Zazen. Even now, the average day of the Zen Buddhist monk in Japan may run from 3 A.M. to 9 P.M. and is filled with a steady round of religious observances, manual labor, and *zazen*. The latter is itself a rigorous discipline, a period of formal meditation in which no bodily movement is allowed. A senior monk makes the rounds with a long flat stick to strike those who show signs of losing concentration. (© Michael S. Yamashita/Corbis)

The fortunes of Zen were furthered not only by native Japanese monks but also by Chinese masters who traveled to Japan and won considerable influence in Kamakura. For example, the Kenchōji, one of the great Kamakura temples, was built by a Hōjō regent who invited a Chinese monk to become its abbot. Several of the regents became deeply versed in Zen. With Zen, the monks brought from China a variety of artistic and cultural influences of which tea is just one example. The secular influence of Zen became even more marked in the succeeding Muromachi period. The continuity of Zen influence is reflected in the career of Musō Sōseki (1275–1351), also known as Musō Kokushi (Musō the National Master), who successively enjoyed the favor of the Hōjō regent, the emperor Go-Daigo, and the Ashikaga shogunal house (see Chapter 12).

## Kami Worship

No account of the religious scene in the Kamakura period is complete without mentioning the continuing appeal of the native spirits, in the so-called Shinto tradition. In the medieval period, *kami* worship had been subsumed within Buddhism institutionally, doctrinally, and even to a great extent physically, with temple compounds typically containing a shrine. Shinto's influence on Buddhism in turn was profound: Ippen, for example, identified individual Buddhas and bodhisattvas with *kami,* and Tendai and Shingon remained hospitable to the *kami. Kami* worship in turn borrowed freely from Buddhism. The Inner and Outer Shrines at Ise were regarded as Shingon mandalas. It may well be that there was a special affinity between Shingon and Shinto; indeed, the major Shinto writer and champion of the imperial house, Kitabatake Chikafusa (1293–1354), ascribed the success of Shingon in Japan, as opposed to in China, to its compatibility with Shinto.

Another syncretic religion was preached by mountain priests (*yamabushi*), who embodied a combination of shamans, monks, and Daoist mountain ascetics. They identified mountain *kami* with Buddhist incarnations and emphasized the role of religious retreats in the mountains. In their ceremonials and incantations they blended Shinto and Buddhist elements. This mountain religion (Shugendō) had enjoyed aristocratic patronage during the Heian period but now turned increasingly toward the common people for support. In the process, it furthered the spread of Buddhism to northern Japan.

# Religious Art

When the Taira destroyed the Tōdaiji and Kōfukuji temples in Nara, they inadvertently prepared the way for a great revival of Buddhist sculpture, stimulated by a happy conjunction of artistic talent and generous patronage. Old works that were damaged or destroyed had to be restored or replaced. Patronage for this effort came from both the *bakufu* and the court, giving rise to a school of highly talented artists (all of whom chose names ending in "kei"). Artistic inspiration came partly from the sculpture in the old capital area, but the best Kamakura sculptures also convey a new realism and robust vigor. The leading figure of the new school was Unkei (active 1163–1223), whose career exemplified the blending of the old and the new. He participated in the restoration of some traditional Nara sculptures, but he also traveled and worked in eastern Japan, where he was exposed to the values and tastes of the warrior class. Both experiences influenced his work.

A good example of the new style is provided by the guardian figures flanking the main entrance of Tōdaiji, a joint enterprise in which Unkei participated (see Figure 11.4). In such guardian figures, ferocity tends to take precedence over realism, but this is not the case in sculpture portraits of milder Buddhist saints and monks. A new device that appeared at this time was the use of crystal for the eyes to give them a life-like sparkle. The figure of Kūya (see Figure 11.2) goes beyond realism: even the words of the priest were portrayed as a string of small Amidas emerging from his mouth. Amidas came in all sizes. In his compassionate benevolence the massive Kamakura Amida, paid for by funds raised from the common people, leans forward to look down on pilgrim and sightseer (see Figure 11.5).

Along with Amida, Kannon continued to enjoy great popularity. Dating from the middle of the thirteenth century, and thus roughly contemporary with the

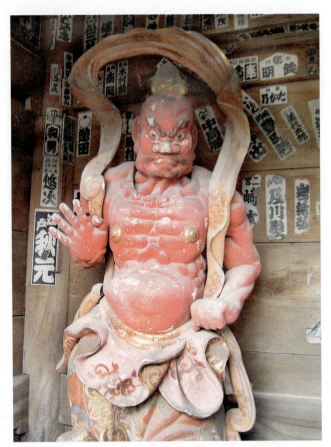

**FIGURE 11.4** *Nio* (Guardian Figure), Great South Gate. Wood, approx. 30 ft high. Tōdaiji, Nara. These figures are constructed of many pieces of wood carefully fitted together. Kamakura sculptors rejected the delicate serenity of Late Heian sculpture but not its new technique. The wood is undercut to emphasize tendons and muscle, imparting an effect of virility and strength. (© Mark Schumacher)

Kamakura Amida, are the breathtaking contents of the Sanjusangendō (Rengeōin) in Kyoto. It features a seated "thousand-armed" Kannon, which is flanked by a thousand standing statues of the same Kannon in ranks, a Kamakura manifestation of the Buddhist proclivity for repetition. Of greater artistic appeal are some of the realistic Kamakura sculptures also found in this hall.

The vitality of early Kamakura sculpture gradually waned, and the decline in the quality of Buddhist sculpture turned out to be permanent. Craftsmen contin-

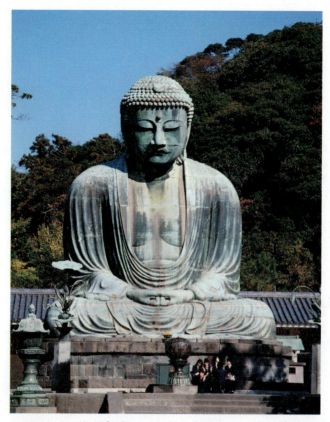

**FIGURE 11.5** *Amida.* Bronze, Kamakura, approx. 49 ft high, completed in 1252. Artistically, this figure compares favorably with the poorly restored giant Buddha at Nara, but its effectiveness is probably more a function of its dimensions than of any inherent artistic excellence. It is partially hollow; inside, steps lead to a little window in Amida's back, through which visitors may look out. (© Royalty-Free/ Corbis)

ued to produce Buddhist figures in imitation of older styles, but there was a dearth of new departures or even creative revivals. The Buddhist religion and the visual arts continued to enrich each other, but after the Kamakura period the relationship between them took a new form.

Chinese influence, visible in some fourteenth-century religious sculpture, can also be seen in architecture, which drew on at least two distinctive Chinese traditions. One style of great power was known in Japan as the "Indian style" (Tenjikuyō), although it was actually imported from Fujian in China. Its best example is the gate of Tōdaiji (see Figure 11.6), which shelters the two guardian figa

b

**FIGURE 11.6 (a AND b)** The Great South Gate. Tōdaiji, Nara, with detail showing the hallmark of the "Indian style" bracketing constructed along a single, transverse axis and inserted through, rather than mounted on, the supporting columns. As Sherman Lee observes, "The gate structure is logical but simple, almost heavy rather than lucid, with a brute strength that overpowers memories of the refined Heian architectural style and which finds no later repetition." Sherman Lee, *A History of Far Eastern Art* (New York: Harry N. Abrams, 1964), p. 324. (a and b: © Lore Schirokauer)

FIGURE 11.7 Engakuji Relic Hall. Thirteenth century, Kamakura. Unfortunately, the Chinese prototypes have not survived, and the building is now covered with an incongruous Japanese-style thatched roof. (a and b: From Robert Treat Paine and Alexander Soper, *The Art and Architecture of Japan* (Pelican History of Art, 2nd rev. ed., 1974). Reprinted with permission of Penguin Books Ltd.)

ures described previously. This style was short lived in Japan but survived in Fujian, from which a later version was reintroduced to Japan in the seventeenth century with the Ōbakusan (Huangboshan) sect of Zen.

Perhaps the Japanese called this style "Indian" because it ran counter to the prevailing fashions of Song architecture and taste. In any case, they reserved the term "Chinese style" (Karayō) for buildings modeled on the prevailing continental style. In Kamakura, the Kenchōji (1253) was supposed to be a copy of a famous Chan temple in Hangzhou, and the Engakuji (see Figure 11.7) is said to have been built by an architect who had traveled to Hangzhou to study the Chinese model.

# Literature

The crosscurrents of Kamakura history and the styles of life prevalent at court, in the military, and in the temple found expression in a rich and varied literature, much of it of the highest quality. Collections such as the late Heian *Tales of Times Now Past* gained popularity. Among the best known is the thirteenth-century *Tales from the Uji Collection*, which in vivid and direct language recounts tales of the morals and miracles of Buddhism and a range of other, nonreligious anecdotes. One story, made famous by a twelfth-century narrative scroll, concerns the holy man of Mt. Shigi who obtained his daily food by sending his begging bowl flying down from his mountain to be filled. When one day the bowl was disdained by a wealthy man, it flew back up the mountain with his entire rice-filled warehouse. The painter had great fun depicting the consternation of the rich man as his store-house flies off. The episode ends happily when the holy man decides to return the rice, and the bowl flies back down the mountain carrying one bag, followed by all the other bags flying through the air in single file.

The *Confessions of Lady Nijō*, completed in the first decade of the fourteenth century and thus quite late in the Kamakura period, takes us back to the familiar world of the court lady. In the early chapters we find her conducting her love affairs and paying attention to the fine points of aesthetics against a general background of melancholy awareness that reminds us of the *Tale of Genji*. The last two sections, however, are an account of her life as a Buddhist nun, fulfilling vows to copy the sutras, and traveling to holy sites (including Ise). She also travels to Kamakura, where her advice on dress and decoration is eagerly sought, because in these matters the prestige of the court remained paramount.

Poetry, too, remained an integral part of court life. Some fine poetry was produced in the late twelfth and early thirteenth centuries under the auspices of two great poets, father and son: Fujiwara Shunzei (1114–1204) and Fujiwara Teika (1162–1241). They were descendants of Michinaga, although poetry, not politics, was their world.

In addition to his fame as a poet, Shunzei was recognized by his contemporaries as an arbiter of poetic taste and was influential in developing a new aesthetic, which sought to deepen the expression of melancholy (*aware*) by adding to it a new dimension of profound mystery (*yūgen*). A mood of sadness also colors the word *sabi*, first used as a term of praise by Shunzei, for whom it basically meant "loneliness." These qualities permeated the aesthetic climate of the subsequent Ashikaga period and will be encountered again in our description of the characteristic achievements of that era.

Teika presided over the committee that compiled the *Shinkokinshū* (*New Kokinshu*, 1205), one of the great collections of Japanese verse and often considered the last of the great imperial anthologies. The following poem by the priest Saigyō (1118–1190) is an example of the poetic qualities found in the best court poetry:

Even one who claims
to no longer have a heart

feels this sad beauty:
snipes flying up from the marsh
on an evening in autumn dusk.[3]

Buddhism demands that a devout man give up the feelings of his own heart even when they are humbly aesthetic.

One of Teika's poems included in the anthology is from a series of 100 poems on the moon. (The composition of such series was one way Japanese poets transcended the limitations of the *tanka*.)

On her straw of straw
she waits as the autumn wind
deepens the night,
spreading moonlight for her robe—
the maiden of the Uji River.[4]

Even in translation the beauty of the original imagery remains apparent. In contrast, the following is just one example of a poem that dispenses with imagery—a practice not unusual in *tanka*. It was written by Lady Jusammi Chikaku, who lived around 1300 (after the great age of Saigyū, Shunzei, and Teika). It is included here to remind us that poetry did not end with them and that ladies and gentlemen continued to excel in this medium. It deals with one of the recurrent motifs in statements of the woman's side of love, the breaking of love's promises.

In recent days
I can no longer say of wretchedness
That it is wretched,
For I feel my grief has made me
No longer truly capable of grief.[5]

The theme is ageless. The private, delicate yet resilient world of the court poet seemed far removed from the hurly-burly of politics and warfare; affected though these poets were by the events of their age, in their poetry they did not deign to notice the intrigue and the fighting.

A literary man who wrote excellent prose and fine poetry was Kamo no Chōmei (1153–1216), who withdrew from the turbulent world to live quietly in a hut on a mountainside near Kyoto. His *An Account of My Hut* is a carefully constructed essay about the world around him: the calamities such as fire, famine, and earthquake suffered by those who remained behind in the world and observations on the simplicity and solitude of his own life. Deeply religious, he fell short of the complete detachment taught by Buddhism but found consolation in repeating the *nembutsu.*

Kamakura literature also devotes much attention to the world of the warrior, as reflected in the military tales and romances. We have already mentioned the tales that grew around Yoshitsune, the younger brother of Yoritomo. Often retold were accounts of his heroic exploits and those of his right-hand man, the stout monk and formidable fighter Benkei, who became his lifelong follower after the young Yoshitsune bested him in a sword fight on a bridge. Stories extolling bravery in battle, engaging accounts of clever stratagems, and celebrations of victory were as appreciated by the Kamakura warrior as by warriors everywhere, but the ultimate tone of the tales is somber. Yoshitsune was, in the end, vanquished (even if one legend has him fleeing to the continent to become Chinggis Khan). Defeat is also the fate of the Taira in *The Tale of the Heike,* an oratorio given its final, classic form after the Kamakura *bakufu* had passed away by the blind musician-priest Akashi no Kakuichi (d. 1371), praised by Barbara Ruch as "one of the greatest composer-performers in history."[6] The main theme of his work is the fall of Taira pride, not the glory of the victorious Minamoto.

Underlying *The Tale of the Heike* is a sense of the transience of victory, the ultimate emptiness of success. Buddhist consciousness of the fleeting nature of all that is best in life saved the age of the Heian courtier from sinking into mere shallow hedonism and likewise rescued the world of the Kamakura warrior from the futile pomposity of the vainglorious. The sweetness of the warrior's triumph is just as ephemeral as the joy of lovers. The opening words of *The Tale of the Heike* sound a note that reverberates throughout the medieval period:

> In the sound of the bell of the Gion Temple echoes the impermanence of all things. The pale hue of the flowers of the teak-tree show the truth that they who prosper must fall. The proud do not last long, but vanish like a spring-night's dream. And the mighty ones too will perish in the end, like dust before the wind.[7]

# Notes

1. Jeffrey Mass, "The Kamakura *Bakufu,*" in Kozo Yamamura, ed., *The Cambridge History of Japan, Vol. 3: Medieval Japan* (Cambridge: Cambridge Univ. Press, 1990), p. 49.

2. Peter Duus, *Feudalism in Japan* (New York: Alfred A. Knopf, 1969), p. 8.

3. Steven Carter, *Traditional Japanese Poetry: An Anthology* (Stanford: Stanford Univ. Press, 1991), p. 161.

4. Carter, *Traditional Japanese Poetry: An Anthology,* p. 197.

5. Earl Miner, *An Introduction to Japanese Court Poetry* (Stanford: Stanford Univ. Press, 1968), p. 133.

6. Barbara Ruch in *The Cambridge History of Japan, Vol. 3: Medieval Japan,* p. 531.

7. Donald Keene, *Japanese Literature* (New York: Grove Press, 1955), p. 78.

# Muromachi Japan

Culturally and politically, the more than two centuries described in this chapter were an unusually rich and complex time in the history of Japan. The political ascendancy of warriors, so long in the making, was completed, but the period's cultural efflorescence owed much to elements of aristocratic and commoner culture as the Ashikaga *bakufu* took up residence in Kyoto. The period is called Muromachi after the section of northeast Kyoto where the Ashikaga shoguns resided, although it is sometimes applied only to the time after 1392. It is also crucial to bear in mind that after 1477 the *bakufu's* area of effective control shrank to the capital area, even if a shogun continued to play some political role until 1573.

# The Kenmu Restoration (1333–1336)

Between the Kamakura and the Ashikaga shogunates, as earlier between the Heian and the Kamakura Periods, there was a brief interlude. The Kenmu (Kemmu) Restoration of Emperor Go-Daigo (1288–1339) was an attempt to reassert the prerogatives of the throne similar to the earlier efforts of Emperor Go-Toba. Because it confronted a much-weakened shogunate, the restoration had considerable initial success. Even after Kyoto was lost, there was sufficient momentum to sustain a government in exile in the mountains of Yoshino, south of Nara, which for more than half a century provided at least a potential rallying point for those opposed to the Ashikaga. Not until 1392 did it come to an end.

The origins of the restoration go back to an imperial succession dispute in the middle of the thirteenth century. After the reluctant intervention of the *bakufu,* a compromise was reached whereby the two disputing branches, northern and southern, would alternately occupy the throne. Go-Daigo was determined to break this agreement and retain the succession in his own line. To that end, he gathered a coalition of warriors to defy the bakufu.

Fighting began in 1331 when the shogunate tried to force Go-Daigo to abdicate. At first Go-Daigo suffered setbacks, including capture and exile to the Oki

Islands in the Sea of Japan. But the *bakufu* was unable to suppress Go-Daigo's coalition, and in 1332 the emperor escaped from the Oki. He returned to Kyoto in triumph after Ashikaga Takauji (1305–1358), commander of a *bakufu* force sent to destroy him, changed sides. Behind Takauji was the wealth and prestige of the Ashikaga family, which, like Yoritomo, the founder of the first shogunate, belonged to the Seiwa Minamoto lineage. Another important Go-Daigo warrior ally, Nitta Yoshisada (1301–1338), seized Kamakura in the name of Go-Daigo and put an end to the power of the Hōjō family and to the Kamakura *bakufu*.

When Go-Daigo adopted a policy to merge military and civil power and put it in the hands of civil governors, however, his warrior supporters were dismayed. When he appointed his own son shogun, Takauji's support for him dwindled, and the throne's policies cost him the military support required for his survival. The Kenmu Restoration came to an end in 1336 when Takauji defeated Nitta Yoshisada and then dethroned Go-Daigo. Go-Daigo escaped south to the mountains of Yoshino, and with his remaining followers occasionally mounted an offense against the Ashikaga forces for more than fifty years. Ironically, a major casualty of the military turbulence was the civil provincial administration that had survived the Kamakura Period, because now the military governors (*shugo*) increasingly assumed control of public land. The emperor's attempt to turn back the clock misfired badly.

Go-Daigo's significance is still debated. Some see him as an anachronism, desiring restoration of imperial power and thus a reduction of warrior power. Others, however, credit him with a vision for the future, including an understanding of the importance of commerce in national life and of reviving relations with China, then under Mongol rule. Still others point to his policies as despotic beyond anything seen previously in an emperor.

# *The Establishment of the Ashikaga Shogunate (1336–1368)*

The power of the Ashikaga, enhanced after the defeat of Nitta Yoshisada, was legitimated in 1338, when Takauji received the coveted title of shogun from the new emperor he had installed in Kyoto. Go-Daigo's rival court continued in exile for another twenty-two years until 1392, when Yoshimitsu, the third and very vigorous Ashikaga shogun, brokered an end to the conflict and to the so-called period of the northern and southern courts (Nambokucho, 1336–1392). The basic foundations of the new shogunate were firmly in place.

The de facto defeat of an emperor by warriors was an event that stirred discussion among contemporary intellectuals. The genealogical and theoretical bases for Go-Daigo's claims to legitimacy were supplied by the aristocrat Kitabatake Chikafusa. In his *The Records of the Legitimate Succession of the Divine Sovereigns*, Chikafusa argued not only for the legitimacy of Go-Daigo but also for the sanctity of correct imperial succession leading back all the way to the Sun Goddess. It was this, he claimed, that made Japan uniquely divine and set it apart from other lands. Meanwhile, the *Taiheiki,* a military epic, supplied stirring accounts of the feats of imperial loyalists, such as Kusunoki Masashige (d. 1336), an early and faithful adherent to Go-Daigo's cause, and Nitta Yoshisada. It turned these men into popular heroes, adding luster to the cause they served. Thus, one legacy of the Kenmu Restoration and the Yoshino court was an embellished and fortified imperial myth.

In contrast, Ashikaga Takauji was somewhat unreasonably cast as the villain of this historical drama. After all, although they denied the throne any real power, he and his successors wanted to preserve the status of the throne, the theoretical source of Takauji's own authority. For his part, even Chikafusa admitted that the warriors had a legitimate role given the ineffectiveness of the imperial course. A contemporary anecdote vividly illustrates its tarnished reputation: a warrior, probably under the influence of alcohol, refusing to dismount when he encountered the procession of the abdicated emperor, is quoted as saying, "Did you say 'cloistered emperor' (*in*) or 'dog' (*inu*)? If it's a dog, perhaps I'd better shoot it."[1] He then struck the retired emperor's carriage with an arrow. The upshot was that the carriage overturned and its occupant tumbled into the street. Takauji promptly had the warrior beheaded.

## Japanese and Continental Culture

The life of Zen Master Musō Soseki is an indication that the vicissitudes of political and military fortune did not disrupt all careers, because he enjoyed in turn the favor and patronage of the Hōjō, Go-Daigo, and Takauji. Of the latter it is said that he often practiced Zen before going to sleep after a heavy dinner party.

Musō straddled spheres of influence as well as reigns, and he left his physical mark on the capital. He was responsible for the fine garden at Tenryūji, the great Zen monastery built by Takauji for Musō and dedicated to the memory of Go-Daigo. Its building and grounds covered almost 100 acres west of the capital. Musō also deserves much of the credit for the Saihōji, popularly known as the "moss garden." He also persuaded Takauji to establish a nationwide system of Zen temples.

Musō's role extended beyond that of spiritual mentor: it was on his advice that Go-Daigo in 1325 had sent an official embassy to China, resuming relations broken off almost 500 years earlier. Similarly, his influence is seen in Takauji's decision to send another mission in 1339. In the latter case, the ship was named after the monastery Tenryūji, which was involved in lucrative voyages to China, and Zen monks provided the major impetus for renewed interest in Chinese culture. In this way religion, commerce, culture, and relation with the continent were deeply intertwined.

In the arts, as elsewhere, the Japanese selected from China what appealed to them. They ignored the monumental Northern Song landscapes, preferring the more intimate Southern Song painting of Ma Yuan and Xia Gui and especially the vigorous brushwork and bold imagery in the paintings by Zen monks such as Muqi. Even though these artists never traveled to Japan, much of their work has

FIGURE 12.1 *Six Persimmons*, Muqi. Ink on paper, 14.2 in wide. Daitokuji, Kyoto. (© Daitokuji Temple)

been preserved only there. For Muqi, six persimmons mirrored the truth as faithfully as any portrait of the Buddha (see Figure 12.1). This painting is still owned by the Daitokuji temple, founded in 1326 with the backing of the retired emperor and Go-Daigo.

Monasteries and nunneries continued to provide a haven for those seeking to retire from the trials and tribulations of an unstable world. Among them was Yoshida Kenkō (1283–1350), poet, court official, and author of *Essays in Idleness* (*Tsurezuregusa*), a collection of brief jottings long admired in Japan as a repository of good taste in social conduct as in art. Despite the randomness of its organization, like Sei Shōnagon's *Pillow Book* and Kamo no Chōmei's *An Account of My Hut*, Kenkō's work is held together by recurrent themes. Particularly significant is his celebration of the aesthetics of the impermanent, because to Kenkō perishability is an essential component and a necessary precondition for beauty. And he voices aesthetic judgments that have since become closely associated with Japanese taste, displaying a preference for objects that bear the signs of wear and have acquired the patina of age (*sabi*). He loves the old literature: "The pleasantest of all diversions is to sit alone under the lamp, a book spread out before you, and to make friends with people of a distant past you have never known."[2] His antiquarianism is pervasive: he admires the old whether it be in poetry, carpentry, or even torture racks for criminals. His style is fresh and succinct, observant yet detached.

## Government and Politics

Unlike their predecessors, the Ashikaga shoguns did not establish a new center of power but conducted their affairs from Kyoto and appointed a deputy to look after their interests in the Kanto region. Other deputies were established in Kyushu, west-central Japan, and in the north. Although the shoguns held the highest civil offices, their power depended on their control over their vassals. But the old bonds had been weakened, and the system of loyalties on which the Ashikaga depended proved highly unstable.

The military protectors of the Kamakura Period developed into provincial military governors, although their title, *shugo*, remained the same. At its height, the Kamakura *bakufu* had limited the power of the *shugo* by assigning men to provinces in which they had no family roots or property; by asserting its right to dismiss and confirm the *shugo*, even though the positions eventually became hereditary; and by maintaining direct control over lesser vassals. In the Ashikaga age, however, warriors in the provinces steadily whittled down the absentee proprietors' control of land. The Ashikaga, eager to obtain warrior support, played into the hands of the military governors in particular by assigning them virtually unlimited rights to taxation and adjudication. Increasingly, the *shugo* were able to turn local warriors into vassals. Frequently, the term *shugo-daimyo* is applied to these provincial power holders who, like the later full-fledged daimyo, held extensive territory and grew increasingly autonomous of the *bakufu* in Kyoto.

*Bakufu* and *shugo* were involved in a complicated balance of power, which all parties tried to manipulate to their own advantage. Until the Onin War, the fulcrum of this balance remained in Kyoto. The situation offered military governors and their deputies opportunities, but it also posed dangers. They might be able to recruit local warriors as vassals to augment their own military power, but they could not count on the loyalty of these men, who put family interests first and were not reluctant to switch sides.

On a lower level, too, the trend favored local warriors. Instead of retaining *shiki* in scattered areas, the land stewards (*jitō*) gradually consolidated their holdings. They became strong enough to make peasant leaders their vassals, and they took on the character of local overlords. The estate (*shōen*) system, badly battered by the conflict of the fourteenth century, was severely damaged, and aristocratic and religious control of land dwindled as a result. The old system did not disappear completely, however, until the period of reunification (see Chapter 14).

To complicate matters still further, the great military families (*shugo* and *jitō*) faced internal family conflicts as single inheritance became common. The old tradition of dividing an estate equally among heirs, feasible in times of peace and security, created fragmentation that was too dangerous in a period of unrest. Therefore, to secure the family's future, the property was left intact and passed to a single heir designated by the family head. This was not necessarily the eldest son, but it was always a son: a daughter would be unable to protect the property militarily. This system frequently led to bitter rivalries and hard-fought family succession disputes. These, like all serious conflicts in this period, were settled by force of arms.

John Whitney Hall succinctly defined the Ashikaga body politic when he wrote, "The imperial system was now in effect dead, but the system of military allegiances and feudal controls had not fully matured."[3] Based on unstable alliances, the system nevertheless worked, at least to a degree, and was indeed the closest thing to a government in an era of political diffuseness. It neither hampered considerable economic growth nor inhibited fine cultural achievements. Indeed, under Ashikaga Yoshimitsu (1358–1408), Japan experienced a cultural and political renewal.

# Yoshimitsu and His Age

In 1368 Yoshimitsu, not yet ten, became the third shogun. Initially, however, the shogunate was controlled by the capable Hosokawa Yoriyuki, a member of one of the Ashikaga collateral families powerful in Kyoto and the provinces. Yoriyuki's official appointment was as chief administrator (*kanrei*), the top position in the *bakufu*, which was always assigned to one of the three most powerful vassal families (Hosokawa, Shiba, or Hatakeyama). His services to the *bakufu* included administrative reform, settlement of conflicting land claims, and a strengthening of the shogunate's finances. Spending was reduced, and new sources of revenue were opened by taxing the wealth of commercial enterprises such as *sake* breweries and moneylenders. (These two establishments frequently belonged to the same proprietor because the original capital of the pawnshops often came from the profits of the *sake* trade.) Indeed, the Ashikaga shogunate, unlike either the Kamakura or the Tokugawa shogunates, drew substantial revenues from commercial sources in the capital.

When Yoshimitsu took power into his own hands, he continued efforts to strengthen the shogunate. He successfully met several military challenges, and in 1392 he secured the reunification of the two imperial courts. A final campaign in 1399 achieved a workable balance of power in the country. Through a series of impressive processionals to religious sites, such as Mount Kōya and Ise, Yoshimitsu further displayed his power and inspected local conditions firsthand. His lavish patronage of religious establishments no doubt helped win him support in those quarters.

Yoshimitsu, unlike the first two Ashikaga shoguns, was born and raised in Kyoto and sought to combine his warrior heritage with the values long cherished there. In gratifying his taste for fine architecture and beautiful gardens, he spared no expense. Unfortunately, his Palace of Flowers (Hana no Gosho) has not survived. Politically, he demonstrated his dual legacy by assuming the title of chancellor and shogun, and he even managed to have his wife made empress dowager! Yoshimitsu truly believed in doing things in royal style: once he entertained the emperor with twenty days of banqueting, music, and theatrical performances, a display of wealth that the emperor could not match. In this period the shogunate controlled the imperial budget through its tax collecting authority and did not hesitate to demonstrate to the emperor its ability to withhold needed funds. Yoshimitsu and his successors expressed formal deference toward the emperor but kept his finances rather underfunded.

Many of Yoshimitsu's entertainments took place on his estate in the northern hills (Kitayama) just beyond Kyoto, graced by the Golden Pavilion (Kinkakuji), a symbol of his good taste and affluence. Although the roofline and parts of the building were covered with gold leaf, the plain surfaces of natural wood, the pavilion's shingled roofs, and the grilled shutters and solid doors of the second floor preserved the Japanese tradition of natural simplicity. On the other hand, the paneled doors and arched windows of the top story derive from the standard repertoire of Chinese Zen architecture. With artful casualness, the building is set on an artificial platform in a pond. It combined Chinese and native elements harmoniously and tastefully.

Chinese elements in the Golden Pavilion are but one facet of Song influence on Ashikaga art. Indeed, without the patronage of such men as Yoshimitsu, many valuable Chinese paintings would have been lost. The shogun's fondness for things Chinese extended to Chinese dress. He even reported that the emperor of China visited him in his sleep. When awake, he made an effort to cultivate good relations with the Ming, and diplomatic communiqués between him and the Chinese court referred to Yoshimitsu as the "king" of Japan. As usual, the Chinese responded to foreign tribute by giving even more impressive gifts in return. A lucrative trade ensued, in which the officially patronized Five Zen Temples of Kyoto (*gozan*) played a leading role and from which they derived much wealth. Along with the Zen temple Tenryūji, Shōkokuji played a prominent part in these undertakings. Here, communications intended for the Ming were drafted by monks in Chinese. At Chinese request, Yoshimitsu took measures against unofficial Japanese traders ("pirates") in East Asia.

It is characteristic of the age that Zen monks were welcomed by the Ashikaga rulers not only for their religious insights but also for their managerial abilities, their command of Chinese learning, their poetic talents, and their expertise in the various arts. For example, the Zen monk Josetsu of the Shōkokuji was famous as an ink painter and was patronized by both Yoshimitsu and his successor. His *Patriarchs of the Three Creeds* (see Figure 12.2) reflects the religious, cultural, and artistic ambiance of the period. In it, the three great teachers Sakyamuni, Confucius, and Laozi are shown in harmonious agreement. The "abbreviated" brushwork is in the manner beloved by Zen artists. Each figure is rendered in its own style, and every stroke, every line, counts. The style of this painting is Chinese, and its subject inspired Song artists, although none of their paintings survive. It is a theme that reflects the Chinese trend toward religious and philosophical syncretism. Such syncretism was readily accepted in Japan, which had never experienced an institutionalized Daoism competing with a Buddhist establishment, and where Buddhism had from the first been mixed with Confucianism. The close relationship between Daoism and Zen has already been noted. Josetsu's own name is a case in point. It was given to him by a great priest of the Shōkokuji and was derived from the *Daodejing* passage, "the greatest skill is like clumsiness ( *josetsu*)."[4] This was his artistic ideal and his achievement.

# The Nō Drama

When Yoshimitsu hosted the emperor for twenty days, among the entertainments offered were performances of Nō, the classic drama of Japan. The roots of Nō are in less-formal singing, dancing, music, and mime, but its developed form was truly the creation of a remarkable father and son, Kan'ami (1333–1384), a Shinto priest, and

**FIGURE 12.2** *Patriarchs of the Three Creeds.* Attributed to Josetsu. Hanging scroll, ink on paper, 8.58 in × 38.7 in. (© "Patriarchs of the Three Creeds," by Josetsu Ryosokuin, Kyoto)

Zeami (or Seami, 1363–1443). Both composed plays and acted in them, and Zeami formulated the critical and aesthetic criteria of the art. When Yoshimitsu first saw them performed, he was especially captivated by Zeami, then a good-looking boy of eleven, because the shogun was eclectic in his sexual as in his artistic preferences.

A performance of Nō is presented on a highly polished square wooden stage open to the audience on three sides. A raised passageway leads from the actors' dressing room through the audience to the stage. Both stage and passageway are roofed. Three small pine trees in front of the passageway and a band of pebbles in front of the stage replicate the drainage area surrounding gutterless buildings, symbolic reminders that Nō performances were originally held outdoors. The stage is bare or almost bare. Occasionally, there are symbolic representations of scenery: an outline of a boat, a cube to suggest a well. Likewise, stage properties are few and generally symbolic.

The Nō is often compared with Greek drama, but the differences are as important as the similarities. For example, both use a chorus, but the chorus in Nō does not participate in the dramatic action. Seated at the side of the stage, the chorus expresses what is in the actor's mind and sings his lines when he dances. The music, produced by a flute and some drums, provides accompaniment and accent.

The actors and the chorus are all male. Some actors wear highly stylized and exquisitely fashioned masks. The carving of these masks is a prized art. The one reproduced in Figure 12.3 represents a young woman. It illustrates the characteristic features of a classic Heian beauty, with her powdered complexion, artificial eyebrows, and blackened teeth. By subtle body movements and just the right tilt of the head, a great actor can suggest remarkable nuances of mood and emotion, and the frozen faces of the unmasked actors attain a mask-like anonymity. The effect allows full concentration on the spiritual message of the play and not on the identity of the actor. Attired in all the elegance of Heian courtier costumes, the actors "dance" their roles, moving with slow and deliberate grace.

Nō plays are classified by the Japanese according to subject matter: plays about a god, a warrior, a woman, a mad person, or a demon. It later became customary to include one of each type, in this order, in a full program that would take about six hours to perform. The texts are short, and although they contain some fine poetry, they were always meant for the stage. The plots draw heavily on the literary tradition, recreating some of the most poignant scenes from earlier literature, including the *Tale of Genji, The Tale of the Heike,* and the *Tales of Ise.* As one might expect, there are plays about Yoshitsune and other notable figures, including the great poetess Komachi, who is portrayed as an old woman suffering because she caused others to suffer when she was young and beautiful. Others deal with legends; the story of the fishermen who stole the angel's cloak (*Hagoromo*) is a favorite.

FIGURE 12.3 Nō mask. (© Tokyo National Museum)

The tone is serious; the presentation symbolic. The typical Nō play is not an enactment of a dramatic episode or a dramatic rendition of a historical or mythological occurrence; it is a retelling after the event. Consider the play based on the death of the young Atsumori, reluctantly slain in battle by the warrior Kumagai, as recounted in *The Tale of the Heike.* The main actors in Zeami's play on this theme are the priest who was once Kumagai and a young reaper who is actually the ghost of Atsumori. Here, the purpose of art is not to mirror life but to transform it; setting the action in the play's own past allows a meditation on the Buddhist themes of permanence and the folly of worldly ties. It is an art that eschews realism and aspires to convey a sense of profound meaning beyond the words and scenes on stage. The ultimate criterion, according to Zeami, is a play's success in creating *yūgen,* the sense of underlying mystery.

A tone of grave sadness is hard to sustain for hours. Even a refined Kyoto aristocrat with his penchant for melancholy must have welcomed the comic relief provided by *kyōgen* (mad or wild words), performed in the interlude between Nō plays. Often in the nature of farce, they show a fondness for broad humor and foolery: servants outwitting their master, a dull country bumpkin sent to purchase a sculpture of the Buddha and taken in by the trickery of an apprentice posing as a statue, and so on. Livelier than Nō, *kyōgen* are less demanding of the audience, but they lack the aura of profundity and poetic mystery that has sustained the Nō tradition in Japan.

## Political Decline and Cultural Brilliance

When Yoshimitsu died in 1408 and was succeeded by his son, there was no radical discontinuity in shogunal politics or even in cultural policies, although his death brought an end to the favor shown to Zeami. Under the fifth shogun there were signs of fiscal and political weakness, but the following shogun, Yoshinori (r. 1428–1441), was able to rally the Ashikaga fortunes. However, Yoshinori's policy of strengthening the *bakufu* necessarily involved checking the power of strong military governors (*shugo*), and this turned out to be a dangerous and difficult game. It cost Yoshinori his life when he was lured to a mansion by a military governor and assassinated.

Yoshinori was the last strong and vigorous Ashikaga shogun. His son was eight when he inherited the office and died two years later. He was followed by another child, Yoshimasa (1436-1490). Yoshimasa remained shogun for thirty years (1443–1473) then retired, having presided over the political collapse of the regime. From Yoshinori's assassination in 1441 through the Onin War (1467–1477), governance, such as it was, disintegrated. But the Ashikaga shogunate benefited from its historical momentum and the absence of a viable alternative, because the power of the provincial families, afflicted by succession disputes, was also declining. It is characteristic of the age that the Ashikaga downfall came not at the hands of a more powerful family or coalition but as the result of disputes within its own ranks. In 1464 Yoshimasa, still without an heir, designated his brother as next in line, but the following year his ambitious and strong-minded wife Masako bore him a son. Anxious to have her son be the next shogun, she found support in a powerful provincial governor's family, and another family backed the older claimant. Thus, the ground was prepared for the succession struggle that set off the disastrous Onin War. The outcome of the war did not lead to the triumph of either family, but it did destroy the authority of the Ashikaga and half of the city of Kyoto, and it wreaked havoc on much of the surrounding country. During these violent years, Yoshimasa continued to emulate Yoshimitsu in patronizing the arts; he had the exquisite aesthetic sensibilities long cultivated in Kyoto. But he lacked the qualities of command and decisiveness required of a shogun, a holder of what was, after all, a military office.

Yoshimasa was as lavish as Yoshimitsu in financing building projects and in giving entertainments. He, too, was a great patron of Nō and an admirer of Heian and Song aesthetics. Like Yoshimitsu, his name is associated with a district in the outskirts of Kyoto to which he retired (Higashiyama). As a counterpart to Yoshimitsu's Golden Pavilion, there is Yoshimasa's Silver Pavilion (Ginkakuji), somewhat smaller, more intimate, and more subdued than its predecessor, having two stories instead of three (see Figure 12.4). It, too, combines, or at least juxtaposes, Chinese and native elements, featuring a continental second story placed on a Japanese first story.

A Chinese theme is echoed in the Ginkakuji's sand garden, identified as a rendition of the West Lake outside Hangzhou, frequented by Song painters and poets such as Su Shi on their pleasure outings. Near one bank, however, stands a volcano, also of sand—a miniature Mount Fuji. Such gardens were the objects of much care and careful planning. Wealthy patrons such as Yoshimasa went to great expense to obtain just the right effect. Transportation costs were disregarded when a stone was discovered precisely right in shape and texture and presenting the exact contrast between its rough and its smooth surfaces required for the composition of the garden.

As in China, stones themselves were objects of connoisseurship. Similar care went into the selection and pruning of plants and into performing the myriad chores necessary for maintaining a garden at its aesthetic best.

In Japan as in China, the aesthetics of garden design and landscape painting were closely related. Like the painter, the garden artist could choose rich, colorful landscapes—using tree and shrub, rivulet and waterfall, pond and bridge—or he could confine himself to stone and carefully raked sand, much like the ink painter who rejected color. Such sand and stone gardens can be viewed as three-dimensional monochrome landscapes with the sand representing water and the rocks functioning as mountains, or they can be enjoyed as abstract sculptures inviting the viewer to exercise imagination. Like Zen, they concentrate on the essentials.

**FIGURE 12.4** Ginkakuji (Silver Pavilion), Kyoto. (© Lore Schirokauer)

The finest are found in the Zen temples of Kyoto (see Figure 12.5). Not all of the Ryōanji's fifteen stones are visible in this photograph because the garden is designed so that there is no single point from which they can all be seen at once.

The compound of the Silver Pavilion also contains a small hall, the interior of which is divided between a Buddhist chapel and a new element: a room for the performance of the tea ceremony. Tea grew in popularity after its enthusiastic advocacy by Eisai, the Zen monk who introduced Rinzai to Japan. Even Kyoto commoners enjoyed creating formal occasions for its consumption. It was not until the time of Yoshimasa, however, that it developed into a ritual art with its own strict rules and regulations.

The accent in the classic tea ceremony is on simplicity and tranquility of spirit. Through a small doorway no bigger than a window, the guests crawl into a room about nine feet square to enjoy in silent calm the movements of their host as he prepares the tea with motions as deliberate as those of an actor on the Nō stage. After they have drunk the deep green tea, they may exchange a few remarks about the bowl or the flower arrangement prepared for the ceremony. Among the unrefined, the ceremony may be exaggerated into ostentation; in incapable hands it easily degenerates into an empty and pedantic formalism. But when performed

**FIGURE 12.5** Sand and Stone Garden. Ryōanji, Kyoto
(© Lore Schirokauer).

with an easy grace by a master, it can convey Japanese good taste at its best. The cult of tea—for such it was—reached perhaps its greatest height during the Momoyama Period (1568–1600).

The tea ceremony influenced secular architecture, which during the Ashikaga Period adopted many of the features of the tea room. Rush matting (*tatami*) now covered the whole floor—previously, individual mats had been placed on wooden floors as needed to provide a place for people to sit. Sliding doors consisting of paper pasted on a wooden frame (*shoji*) came into common use, supplementing the earlier sliding partitions (*fusuma*) with their painted surfaces. Another standard feature is the alcove (*tokonoma*) with its hanging scroll and flower arrangement. Flower arrangement, like tea, became an art, with its own rules and styles passed through the generations by the masters of distinct schools. It became one of the polite accomplishments expected of those with a claim to refinement.

In all the arts, the influence of Zen aesthetics remained strong even after the Onin War disrupted the network centered on the Five Zen Temples of Kyoto, which by then included some 300 monasteries, or several thousand institutions if sub- and branch-temple affiliates are counted separately.

## Poetry and Painting

In Yoshimasa's time, poetry continued to be an important part of Kyoto life. In the Heian Period it was not uncommon for one poet to supply the first three lines of a *tanka* (a thirty-one-syllable poem), leaving it to his companion to complete the poem with a suitable couplet. From such origins grew the linked verse (*renga*), which became a favorite Muromachi pastime. Its instability was an important part of its appeal. Nijō Yoshimoto (1320–1388), a champion of *renga*, put it this way:

> The poet of *renga* does not seek to tie the idea of one moment in with that of the next but, like this fleeting world, shifts through phases of both waxing and waning, of sadness and joy. No sooner does he reflect on yesterday than today has passed; while thinking about spring it becomes autumn, and even as he admires a scene of new blossoms it turns into one of crimson leaves. Is this not proof that everything is impermanent, like scattered flowers and fallen leaves?[5]

Reflecting its social nature, the composition of *renga* came to be governed by complicated rules:

> Of the opening verse (the *hokku*) it was said, "The *hokku* should not be at variance with the topography of the place, whether the mountains or the sea dominate, with the flying flowers or falling leaves of the grasses and trees of the season, with the wind, clouds, mist, fog, rain, dew, frost, snow, heat, cold, or quarter of the moon. Objects which excite a ready response possess the greatest interest for inclusion in a *hokku*, such as spring birds or autumn insects. But the *hokku* is not of merit if it looks as though it had been previously prepared." The requirements for the second verse were somewhat less demanding; it had to be closely related to the first and to end in a noun. The third verse was more independent and ended in a particle; the fourth had to be "smooth"; the moon had to occur in a certain verse; cherry-blossoms could not be mentioned before a certain point; autumn and spring had to be repeated in at least three but not more than five successive verses, while summer and winter could be dropped after one mention, etc.[6]

A master such as the Zen monk Sōgi (1421–1502), the greatest of the *renga* poets, was able to create fine poetry within this framework. Sōgi also composed *tanka* in the old tradition of court poetry, now coming to an end. The last imperial anthology was compiled in the fifteenth century. The *renga* may not have been a great poetic form, but it pointed in new directions.

In painting as in poetry, Zen monks continued to contribute greatly. Josetsu's style of monochrome painting was continued by two Zen monks, Shubun (d. 1450) and Sesshū (1420–1506), both trained at the Shōkokuji. In their work the influence of Song painting remains clearly visible. The fifteenth-century painter-monks in the great Zen temples could draw on Japanese ink paintings in the Chinese manner going back to the Kamakura Period, and the more eminent or fortunate among them might also see the Chinese paintings kept in Japan. The prime source for these was the shogunal collection systematized and catalogued for the first time under Yoshimasa. Most fortunate were those who were able to travel abroad. Thus, Shubun drew inspiration from a journey to Korea, and Sesshū

**FIGURE 12.6** *Ama-no-Hashidate*, Sesshū. Hanging scroll, ink and light color on paper, 70 in long. (© Shimizu Kohgeisha Co., Ltd.)

was able to travel to and in China. There was no need for him to paint Chinese landscapes from imagination alone.

Sesshū's versatile genius expressed itself in a variety of styles. One of his greatest paintings shows the man who was to become the second Zen patriarch offering his severed arm as a token of religious commitment to Bodhidharma, the reputed Indian founder of Zen in China. Another is a long landscape scroll (more than fifty-two feet long) guiding the viewer on a leisurely trip through scenery and seasons. Reproduced in Figure 12.6 is his painting of a renowned beauty spot on the Sea of Japan, Ama-no-Hashidate (the Bridge of Heaven). It was evidently painted on the basis of personal observation shortly before his death. The written identification of the various localities confirms the realism of this solidly constructed painting, and the softness of the painter's brush is appropriate for the gentle Japanese landscape.

Although Zen monks and temples had the greatest influence on the arts, some major contributions were made by believers in the *nembutsu*, who demonstrated their faith in Amida by incorporating his name in theirs. The aesthetics of Nō may be compatible with the teachings of Zen, but the greatest names in this theater were, as we have seen, Kan'ami and Zeami. And among the main painters in the monochrome style imported from the continent were the three Ami: Nōami (ca. 1394–1471), Geiami (1431–1485), and Sōami (d. 1525)—father, son, and grandson. These three men not only were fine painters but also served as the shogun's advisers in aesthetic matters, cataloguing and evaluating his art collection and passing as masters in the gamut of Ashikaga art from flower arranging, tea, and incense to music and the stage.

Also part of the artistic scene were professional painters. Two names that were to remain important as major schools of painting enjoying official favor first appear in the fifteenth century. These schools, like the schools of Nō and other arts, were continued from father to son or, if necessary, to adopted son, perpetuating their traditions much like warrior or merchant families. Their secrets were just as carefully guarded as the formulae of sake brewers or pharmacists. Painting in the old native style (Yamatōe), Tosa Mitsunobu (1434–1525) became official painter to both the imperial court and the *bakufu*. Provided with a generous grant of land, he was able to establish the social and economic position of his family. Meanwhile, his contemporary Kanō Masanobu (1434–1530) painted in the Chinese manner, although without all the religious and literary associations found in the work of the nonprofessional artists. Of the two, the Kanō line was the more creative. Masanobu's son Motonobu (1476–1559) added color to his paintings. In this he was likely influenced by the Tosa school.

Especially in the city of Kyoto, commoners enjoyed various cultural pursuits. Wealthy merchants such as moneylenders collected objects including ceramics, illustrated screens, poetry books, and kimono. Some commoners rubbed elbows with aristocrats at cultural events such as tea ceremonies, poetry rounds, and the more sophisticated linked-verse competitions. Commoners could be found in the audience at Nō performances, at public recitations of literary epics, and sometimes even as actor participants in comic *kyōgen* and in *sarugaku,* a mime-based theatrical art. Some wealthier commoners produced amateur ink paintings. Festivals, usually based at a local shrine, were a very visible and popular cultural activity; Kyoto's Gion Festival is the main example of this genre. A religious ceremonial core was lavishly elaborated by the townspeople, who prepared the ornate floats for the festival parade. The ostentatious display of wealth and a street-level energy were important elements of the culture of commoners.

This rich hybrid culture of Muromachi—the blending of the imported and the native, the high and the low—was new to Japan. The interpersonal contact that was a feature of tea ceremony and linked-verse gatherings imparted a socially mixed character to the culture of the age. Muromachi taste was exquisite, expressed in the aesthetic of the Nō mask, the sand garden, the tea ceremony, and a Sesshū landscape, a taste for the old (*sabi*), the solitary and poor (*wabi*), the astringent (*shibui*), and the profound (*yūgen*). The prestige of Chinese culture was enormous, and Sinophiles versified and painted in Chinese. But, unlike their predecessors of the Nara Period, they were selective in their borrowing and rapidly assimilated the new. In later ages Muromachi aesthetic sensibility was challenged, assailed, and even displaced, but it never disappeared entirely.

# Economic Growth

The economy grew during the Kamakura epoch, and in Ashikaga times there was considerable if unevenly distributed prosperity. Frequently, developments that originated in the earlier period reached fruition in the later. The basis of the economy remained agricultural, and an increasing agricultural yield provided the means for growth. Improvements in farm technology employing better tools and devices such as the waterwheel, new crops, double-cropping, and new strains of rice and greater use of draft animals were some of the major developments that increased the productivity of the land. This, in turn, positively affected commerce and manufacturing. Technical progress in such endeavors as mining, *sake* brewing, and paper production, to mention just a few, further contributed to this process. The resulting wealth produced a prosperous stratum of peasants and townspeople, many of whom engaged in several livelihoods simultaneously, including moneylending, sericulture, estate management, and transportation. However, poor laborers and peasants were forced to live at subsistence level, led precarious lives, and famine was still frequent. At the very bottom of society was the outcast class, especially numerous in the Kyoto area, where they were employed especially by religious institutions as manual laborers and security guards.

An added economic stimulus came from trade with China and Korea. Initiated by Yoshimitsu, it continued, with minor interruptions, to grow and flourish. To control this commerce and keep the number of ships within agreed-upon limits, the Ming issued official tallies valid for trading at a specified port. This system also had the effect of restricting unofficial trade; it lasted until the middle of the sixteenth century. Japanese imports included cotton from Korea, and from China came great quantities of copper coins as well as porcelain, paintings, medicine, and books. A major Japanese export was fine swords. Japan also exported copper, sulfur, folding fans (a Japanese invention), screens, and so forth. The ability to trade products of sophisticated craftsmanship is another index of Japanese accomplishments during this period.

With the growth of commerce, of markets, and of market towns, there appeared guilds (*za*)—product-specific groups of merchants and artisans exercising monopoly rights over the exchange and production of various commodities. In return for protection of their rights and privileges, these guilds paid taxes to their overlords, great religious institutions, and powerful families. The moneylenders of Kyoto, for example, enjoyed the protection of the Tendai monastery on Mount Hiei, which occasionally sent its armed agents into the capital on behalf of its clients. Temples and shrines, aristocratic families, and the *bakufu* itself, as their hold on the provinces loosened, welcomed the guilds as an additional source of revenue and increasingly depended on income from this source. As noted earlier, already under Yoshimitsu the Ashikaga shogun relied heavily on income from these quarters, and this trend continued. The prosperity of the moneylenders is only one of several signs of the increasing use of money, a development both a product of and a stimulus to commercial growth. To facilitate transactions between places distant from each other, bills of exchange also came into use.

Around ports and markets, cities grew. The most impressive was Sakai, near modern Osaka, which in the sixteenth century became an autonomous political unit governed by a group of elders who were mostly merchants. Hakata in Kyushu, the center for trade with Korea, also flourished, as did several other well-placed cities.

The growth of cities and similar economic developments suggest parallels with European history, but such parallels hold only to a limited degree. Japanese merchants and cities did not achieve autonomy; instead, the merchants provided a source of revenue for feudal lords. Social and political institutions were not shattered, but society was enriched by the emergence of a new urban population. One result of political decentralization combined with economic growth was the diffusion of higher culture to the provinces. Conversely, students of Nō and linked verse have pointed out that these arts owe much to popular culture. Sōgi, the great master of linked verse, was himself of obscure parentage. Many more opportunities for men of low birth were created during the warfare that marked the last phase of Ashikaga rule.

# A Century of Warfare

The Onin War (1467–1477) was the beginning of a century of sporadic warfare and political instability and became a major turning point in Japanese history, but it took almost a century before the direction of change became clear. The war drastically curtailed the power of the Ashikaga *bakufu,* ending the system of alliances on which it was precariously based. The military governors, who had been drawn into Kyoto, were mostly superseded by local deputies. Not only was the old balance of power demolished but its very constituents were also eliminated. Rupture and indeterminacy are the themes that resound in Mary Elizabeth Berry's fine study of Kyoto during this difficult time, summarized as follows:

> Kyoto went through seven bloody transitions in government between 1467 and 1568, as well as numerous failed coups and invasions. Marches on the city by debtors occurred almost annually for thirty years; a radical movement of townspeople under the banner of Lotus sect reverberated for a decade. The landscape was stark: residents of a repeatedly assailed and burned city retreated into two separate enclaves that they protected with moats, walls, and watchtowers.[7]

*Gekokujō*—those above overthrown by those below—was a watchword of the day. During this period, the shogun was unable to control even the provinces near Kyoto and occasionally was driven out of the capital temporarily by warlords. Even so, the Ashikaga *bakufu* could not be counted out completely as late as the 1550s; in Kyoto, at least, the *bakufu* remained the only recognized authority to adjudicate disputes.

Not the capital alone but people throughout Japan were affected when, to quote William Butler Yeats, "the center did not hold" and local armies motivated by local causes bitterly fought each other. Disruption and uncertainty affected the people at the bottom of society at least as much as the elites. This was a period of great popular unrest. During the middle of the fifteenth century, numerous peasant uprisings demanded debt cancellation. Skillful in organization and timing, some of these even laid siege to Kyoto, stopping commercial activity there until debt amnesties could be negotiated. In earlier times as well, villages had banded together in leagues to press demands against estate overlords. By the late fifteenth century, large-scale peasant uprisings against local warriors could dominate entire provinces. In the most famous case, in Yamashiro province near Kyoto, peasants were able to hold power for eight years (1485–1493).

The proliferation of popular Buddhist movements, some with a militant character, was another feature of the age. Particularly prominent was the well-organized Ikkō sect, whose members followed Shinran's True Pure Land Buddhism. In the sixteenth century, these sectarians were able to obtain control of the province of Kaga, on the Sea of Japan; extend their power into neighboring Echizen; and maintain a strategic stronghold in the Kyoto–Osaka area. The Lotus sect followers of Nichiren, commoners and elites alike, multiplied rapidly in the fifteenth century and were dominant in Kyoto by the early sixteenth century. In the authority vacuum of the 1530s, they established loose rule of the city through a confederation of congregations only to be brutally suppressed by an alliance of warriors and monks of the Enryakuji on Mount Hiei in 1536.

What had been decentralized governance gave way in the mid-sixteenth century to radical fragmentation as Japan was divided into many separate principalities, directed by feudal lords known as daimyo who became major players in the next phase of Japanese history, as recounted in Chapter 14, where we will begin by considering some of the effects of this century of warfare. This has the advantage of emphasizing the indeterminacy of the war years and of suggesting that, like any period of major conflict, it needs to be considered in relation to both its past and its future. Furthermore, placing it at the end of one chapter and at the start of another that marks the beginning of a new part of our text may partly compensate for our inability to devote a whole chapter to it and still keep our history reasonably brief.

# Notes

1. H. Paul Varley, *Imperial Restoration in Medieval Japan* (New York: Columbia Univ. Press, 1971), p. 131.

2. Donald Keene, trans., *Essays in Idleness: The Tsurezuregusa of Kenko* (New York: Columbia Univ. Press, 1967), p. 12.

3. John W. Hall, *Japan from Prehistory to Modern Times* (New York: Dell Publishing, 1970), p. 110.

4. Jan Fontein and Money L. Hickman, *Zen Painting and Calligraphy* (Boston: Museum of Fine Arts, 1970), p. 93.

5. Quoted by H. Paul Varley, in Kozo Yamamura, ed., *The Cambridge History of Japan, Vol. 3: Medieval Japan* (Cambridge: Cambridge Univ. Press, 1990), p. 475.

6. Donald Keene, *Japanese Literature* (New York: Grove Press, 1955), pp. 34-35.

7. Mary Elizabeth Berry, *The Culture of Civil War in Kyoto* (Berkeley: Univ. of California Press, 1994), p. xviii.

# East Asia and Modern Europe: First Encounters

## Key Dates

| | |
|---|---|
| **1514** | Portuguese Reach China |
| **1543** | Portuguese Reach Japan (Shipwreck) |
| **1549** | St. Francis Xavier Lands in Kyushu |
| **1571** | Spanish Conquest of Philippines |
| **1601** | Matteo Ricci Received by Emperor of China |
| **1614** | Persecution of Christians in Japan |
| **1630** | Japan Closed to Foreigners |
| **1700** | 300,000 Christian Converts in China |
| **1742** | Pope Decides against Jesuits in Rites Controversy |

The story of the early contacts between post-Renaissance Europe and East Asia can be conceived as an overture setting the tone, introducing basic themes, and establishing the harmonics of the history to come. We have already noted the trade nexus, and we now turn to consider more direct encounters. To avoid breaking up the story, as indicated by the subheadings, this chapter straddles some of the following as well as preceding chapters. In the long run, the general failure of the early intermediaries to build viable bridges of mutual understanding made it all the harder to do so later when East Asia had to deal with a Europe transformed by the French and Industrial revolutions.

## The Portuguese in East Asia

The pioneers of European global expansion were the Portuguese, who reached India in 1498, China in 1514, and Japan in 1543. Having wrested control of the seas from their Arab rivals, they established their Asian headquarters in 1510 at Goa, a small island off the coast of West India. In 1511, they captured Malacca, a vital center for the lucrative spice trade, located on the straits separating the Malay Peninsula from Sumatra (see Figure 13.1).

The desire to break the Arab spice monopoly supplied the economic motive for this initial European expansion. Spices were highly valuable relative to their bulk and weight. Easily transported and fetching a high price, they formed an attractive cargo. And there was an assured market for them in Europe, where they added flavor to an otherwise dull diet and made meat palatable in an age when animals were slaughtered in the fall for want of sufficient fodder to sustain them through the winter. They were also used in medicine and in religious ceremonies.

Prospects for trade were hampered, however, by the absence of any European commodities that could be marketed in Asia. Lacking access to silver, the Portuguese initially financed themselves by a mixture of trade and piracy, taking advantage of their superior ships, weapons, and seamanship. They derived income from transporting goods from one Asian country to another: Southeast Asian wares to China, Chinese silk to Japan, and Japanese silver to China. They used their profits from this trade to purchase spices and other products for European markets. But before this trade could prosper, they had to secure entry into China

**FIGURE 13.1** Eastern Europe and Asia in the sixteenth and seventeenth centuries. 

and Japan. This posed problems quite different from those they had encountered in seizing a small island off the coast of politically divided India or in driving the Arabs from Malacca.

In China they got off to a very bad start. Not waiting for official permission to trade, they engaged in illegal commerce and even built a fort on Lintin Island, located at the mouth of the river that connects Canton to the sea. Their unruly behavior did not endear them to the Ming authorities and served to confirm the opinion that these "ocean devils" were a new kind of barbarian. The outrageous behavior of the Portuguese traders was further embellished by the Chinese imagination. When the Portuguese bought kidnapped Chinese children as slaves, the Chinese concluded that their purpose was to eat them. The Chinese long continued in the firm belief that they were dealing with barbarous child-eaters. More than just a popular rumor held by the ignorant, this belief found its way into the official history of the Ming dynasty.

The first Portuguese envoy to China not only failed to obtain commercial concessions, but he also ended his life in a Cantonese prison. It was a most inauspicious beginning. But the Portuguese would not leave, and their superiority on the seas made it impossible for the Chinese to drive them out. In 1557 an arrangement was reached, permitting the Portuguese to establish themselves in Macao in exchange for an annual payment. There the Portuguese administered their own affairs, but the territory remained under Chinese jurisdiction until Macao was ceded to Portugal in 1887.

# The Jesuits in Japan

Trade and booty were not the only objectives of the Europeans who ventured into Asian waters. Missionary work was also important: mid-sixteenth-century Goa boasted some eighty churches and convents. From the beginning, the missionary impulse provided a strong incentive as well as religious sanction for European expansion, and it was the missionary rather than the trader who served as the prime intermediary between the civilizations of East Asia and the West from the sixteenth to the twentieth centuries.

Among the early missionaries, the great pioneers were the Jesuits, members of the Society of Jesus. Founded in 1540, this tightly disciplined religious order formed the vanguard of the Catholic Counter-Reformation. They were the "cavalry of the church," prepared to do battle with Protestant heretics in Europe and/or the heathen in the world beyond. Along with its stress on martial discipline and intensive religious training, the Society was noted for its insistence on intellectual vigor and depth of learning. The latter included secular as well as sacred studies, and the ideal Jesuit was as learned as he was disciplined and devout.

In 1549, less than ten years after the founding of the Jesuit order, St. Francis Xavier (1506–1552), one of the original members of the Society, landed on Kyushu, the most accessible of Japan's four major islands. This was just six years after the Japanese had first encountered Europeans, some shipwrecked Portuguese who had landed on the island of Tanegashima. Xavier was well received and was soon able to establish relations with important men in Kyushu. First impressions on both sides were favorable. The Japanese were impressed by the strong character and dignified bearing of the European priests. The Jesuit combination of martial pride, stern self-discipline, and religious piety fit well with the ethos of sixteenth-century Japan, and the Christian religion did not seem altogether strange. On the contrary, Christianity, when initially brought to Japan from Goa, seemed like just another type of Buddhism. Some of its ceremonies were similar, and it was difficult for the early priests to convey the subtleties of theology, to explain the difference between God and the cosmic Buddha, for example, or to distinguish Paradise from the Buddhist Pure Land. At last the Jesuit fathers concluded that the devil, in all of his malicious cleverness, had deliberately fashioned Buddhism to resemble the true faith so as to confound and confuse the people.

The initial meeting of the Jesuits and the Japanese was facilitated by similarities in their feudal backgrounds. In Japan, the Europeans found a society that resembled their own far more than did any other outside Europe. "The people," wrote Alessandro Valignano (1539–1606), "are all white, courteous and highly civilized, so much so that they surpass all the other known races of the world."[1] Only the Chinese were to receive similar praise—and, indeed, to be regarded as "white." Donald F. Lach has summarized the qualities the Jesuits found to admire in the Japanese: "their courtesy, dignity, endurance, frugality, equanimity, industriousness, sagaciousness, cleanliness, simplicity, discipline, and rationality."[2] On the negative side, besides paganism, the Jesuits were appalled at the prevalence of sodomy among the military aristocracy and the monks. They criticized the Japanese propensity to commit suicide and also found fault with the "disloyalty of vassal to master, their dissimulation, ambiguity, and lack of openness in their dealings, their bellicose nature, their inhuman treatment of enemies and unwanted children, their failure to respect the rule of law, and finally their unwillingness to give up the system of concubinage."[3] Nevertheless, the similarities between Japanese culture and their own gave the Jesuits high hopes for the success of their mission.

In their everyday behavior the Jesuits tried to win acceptance by adapting themselves to local manners and customs, as long as these did not run counter to their own creed. "Thus," Valignano observed, "we who come hither from Europe find ourselves as veritable children who have to learn to eat, sit, converse, dress, act politely, and so on. . . ."[4] They learned how to squat Japanese style, learned to employ the Japanese language with its various levels of politeness, and mastered the art of tea—the Jesuit dwelling was usually equipped with a tea room so that their guests could be properly entertained. C. R. Boxer has pointed out that the Christian monks came from a land with rather different standards of personal cleanliness: "Physical dirt and religious poverty tended to be closely associated in Catholic Europe where lice were regarded as the inseparable companions of monks and soldiers."[5] But in Japan the devoted monks even learned to wash, a major concession to Japanese sensibilities. Still there were limits: Valignano could not bring himself to endorse the Japanese custom of taking a hot bath every day. That would really be going too far!

Careful attention to the niceties of etiquette was required of the Jesuit fathers in their strategy of working from the top down. It was their hope to transform Japan into a Christian land by first converting the rulers and then allowing the faith to seep down to the populace at large. The purpose of their labors was not to Europeanize Japan or China but to save souls. They realized that the enthusiastic support of the ruling authority would be an invaluable asset, whereas without at least the ruler's tacit approval they could do nothing.

This approach met with considerable success in Kyushu, where they converted important local lords, who ordered their people to adopt the foreign faith. Although there were numerous cases of genuine conversion, some lords simply saw the light of commerce, adopting a Christian stance in the hope of attracting the Portuguese trade to their ports. On at least one occasion, when the great Portuguese ship did not appear, they promptly turned their backs on the new faith. The Jesuits themselves became involved in this trade and also in politics. For seven years they even held the overlordship of Nagasaki, granted to them by a Christian lord.

Xavier and the monks who came after him realized that real progress for their mission depended on the will not only of local Kyushu lords but also of the central government. Xavier's initial trip to Kyoto came at an unpropitious time—the city was in disorder. But Nobunaga (1532–1584), the first of Japan's three great unifiers after a century of division, soon became a friend of the Jesuits. Attracted by their character and interested in hearing about foreign lands, perhaps he was also happy to talk with someone not part of the hierarchical order that he himself headed. This personal predilection coincided nicely with reasons of state. It was consistent with his hostility toward the Buddhist orders and with his desire to keep the trading ships coming in. Hideyoshi (1536–1598), Nobunaga's successor, was at first similarly well disposed toward the foreign religion. He liked dressing up in Portuguese clothes, complete with rosary, and once said that the only thing that kept him from converting was the Christian insistence on monogamy.

The political and economic success of the Jesuits helped the spread of Christianity, but power, or the semblance of power, always entails risks. There was the danger that the ruler might perceive the activities of the monks not as assets bolstering his own position but as liabilities, actual or potential threats to his authority. A portent of future disaster came in 1587 when Hideyoshi issued an order expelling the monks. Eager to encourage trade and not really feeling seriously threatened, he did not enforce the decree, but it foreshadowed the persecutions that were to begin in earnest 36 years later.

Meanwhile, there was a surge of popularity for things Western, for instance, "Southern barbarian screens," showing the giant black ships of the foreigners and the foreigners themselves (see Figure 13.2). Other scenes, based on paintings from Europe, depicted various barbarian topics: the battle of Lepanto, an Italian court, European cities, and maps of the world, not to mention religious subjects. Whereas some artists painted European subjects Japanese style, others experimented with Western perspective and techniques of shading to produce three-dimensional effects. Western motifs were not limited to painting. Western symbols were widely used in decoration: a cross on a bowl, a few words of Latin on a saddle, and so forth.

# The Impact of Other Europeans

Despite the order of 1587, Western influences continued to enter Japan. The situation was further complicated when the Portuguese were followed by other Europeans. The first of these to reach Japan were the Spanish, whose conquest of the Philippines (named after Philip II) was completed in 1571. To the Japanese, Manila presented a new source of profitable trade, but the colonization of the Philippines also alerted them to the imperialist ambitions of the Europeans and revealed connections between Christian evangelism and colonialism. With the arrival of the Dutch and English Protestants in the early 1600s, there were also Europeans in Japan who broke the link between trade and missionary activity and did their best to fan Japanese suspicions of their Catholic rivals. Now, as later, the "West" did not represent a single interest, nor did it speak with a single voice.

The Spanish empire differed from that of Portugal in kind as it did in scale. Whereas the Portuguese maintained themselves by the proceeds from the inter-Asia trade, the Spanish commanded the precious metals of the New World, especially the silver that reached China by way of Manila to pay for Chinese silks. The immediate effect on Japan of the coming of the Spaniards was to complicate the situation of the Jesuits. The Spanish were every bit as committed to the mission-

**FIGURE 13.2** "Southern Barbarians" in Japan. Namban screen. (© Freer Gallery of Art, Smithsonian Institution, Washington, DC. [F1965.22].)

ary enterprise as were the Portuguese, but they patronized Franciscan monks rather than Jesuits. The first Franciscan arrived in Japan from Manila in 1587. Much less well informed about conditions in Japan than the Jesuits, the Franciscans were less discreet in their work. They rejected the Jesuit strategy of working from the top down, and, instead of associating with the elite, worked among the poor and forgotten, the sick and miserable—those at the very bottom of society. The Jesuits did not disguise their contempt for the ignorance and poverty of the Franciscans, the "crazy friars" (*fraile idiotas*) as they called them, and these sentiments were heartily reciprocated by the friars, who scoffed at Jesuit pretensions.

## The "Closing" of Japan

It was an omen of things to come when, in 1597, Hideyoshi crucified six Franciscan missionaries and eighteen of their Japanese converts after the pilot of a Spanish ship driven ashore in Japan reportedly boasted about the power and ambitions of his king. Like Nobunaga and Hideyoshi, Tokugawa Ieyasu, the third and last of Japan's three unifiers, was at first friendly to the Christians, but he too turned against them. In 1606 Christianity was declared illegal, and in 1614 he undertook a serious campaign to expel the missionaries.

By 1614 there were more than 300,000 converts in Japan. The destruction of Christianity was long and painful. Tortures, such as hanging a man upside down with his head in a pit filled with excrement, were used to induce people to renounce their faith. Before it was all over, more than 3000 persons were recognized as martyrs by the Vatican, of whom fewer than seventy were Europeans. Others died without achieving martyrdom. From 1637 to 1638 there was a rebellion in Shimabara, near Nagasaki, against a lord who combined merciless taxation with cruel suppression of Christianity. Fought under banners on which Christian slogans were written in Portuguese and led by some masterless samurai, it was a Christian version of the rural uprisings characteristic of the century of warfare before Nobunaga. In its suppression, some 37,000 Christians lost their lives.

Persuasion as well as violence was employed in the campaign against Christianity. Opponents of Christian dogma argued that the idea of a personal creator was absurd and asked why, if God were both omnipotent and good, he should have tempted Adam and Eve and devised eternal punishment in Hell for non-Christians even though they led exemplary lives. According to Christian teaching, even the sage emperors Yao and Shun would end in hell. The First Commandment was attacked as leading to disobedience of parents and lord; a loyal retainer should accompany his lord even into hell.

Such arguments suggest that the Japanese saw Christianity as potentially subversive, not only of the political order, but of the basic social structure, for it challenged accepted values and beliefs and demanded a radical reappraisal of long-revered traditions. Its association with European expansionism posed a threat from abroad, and, as exemplified by the Shimabara Rebellion, it also harbored the seeds of radical disruption at home. Thus, the motivation for the government's suppression of Christianity was secular, not religious. The government was not worried about the state of its subjects' souls, but it was determined to wipe out a dangerous doctrine.

New restrictions followed. The Spaniards were expelled in 1624, one year after the English had left voluntarily. In 1630 Japanese were forbidden to go overseas or to return from there or to build ships capable of long voyages. The Portuguese were expelled after the Shimabara Rebellion on the grounds of complicity with that uprising. When they sent an embassy in 1640, its members were executed. The only Europeans left were the Dutch (see Figure 13.3), who kept other Europeans from trying their luck in Japan until the English and Russians challenged Dutch naval supremacy in the late eighteenth and early nineteenth centuries. In 1641 the Dutch themselves were moved to the tiny artificial island of Deshima in Nagasaki Harbor, where they were virtually confined as in a prison. The annual Dutch vessel to Deshima was all that remained of Japan's contact with Europe, but it sufficed to spark the "Dutch Learning" discussed in Chapter 15.

Japan's closing was far from complete. Trade and diplomatic contacts with Korea and the Ryukyu Islands continued. Japan refused to participate in the Qing tribute system, but this did not prevent an annual average of almost twenty-six Chinese ships from coming to Nagasaki.

**FIGURE 13.3** *A Dutch Dinner Party.* Prints such as this satisfied the public's curiosity about the strange customs of the Westerners—and may or may not have been accurate portrayals. Color print, 12.99 in × 8.66 in. (© Charles E. Tuttle & Company, Tokyo.)

# The Jesuits in China

Xavier had hoped to begin the work in China himself, considering that this was not only a great project in itself but also a major step in the Christianization of Japan, providing an answer to the question he was constantly asked there: "If yours is the true faith why have not the Chinese, from whom comes all wisdom, heard of it?"[6] Xavier died before he could reach his goal, and three further Jesuit attempts to enter China also failed. Then Valignano established a special training center in Macao so that missionaries could study the Chinese language and culture in preparation for work in China. As elsewhere, it was Jesuit policy in China to concentrate on gaining the support and, if possible, the conversion of the upper classes. To this end, they once more went as far as possible to accommodate themselves to native sensibilities and ways of doing things.

Again, the strong character and attractive personalities of the first missionaries were of great importance in gaining them entry. The outstanding pioneer was Matteo Ricci (1551–1610). A student of law, mathematics, and science, he also knew a good deal about cartography and something of practical mechanics. Once in the East, he was able to master the Chinese language and the classics. Slowly Ricci made himself known in Chinese officialdom, impressing scholars and officials with his knowledge of mathematics, astronomy, and cartography; his command of Chinese classical learning; and his prodigious memory. At last in 1601, after eighteen strenuous years, Ricci was received in an imperial audience and won permission for himself and his colleagues to reside in the capital. (By this time they had discarded the Buddhist robes worn by Jesuits in Japan and had adopted the gowns of Confucian scholars that were more acceptable to the Chinese.) In Beijing he was able to win over and convert a number of prominent men. By the time Ricci died in 1610, the mission was well established in the capital and accepted by the government. Ricci's body was laid to rest in a plot donated by the emperor.

During the period when the Japanese were persecuting Christians with increasing ferocity, the Jesuits in China labored fruitfully, building on the foundations laid by Ricci. They were particularly successful in demonstrating the superior accuracy of European astronomical predictions. Thereby they succeeded in displacing their Muslim and Chinese competitors and established themselves in the Bureau of Astronomy, an important and prestigious office. Jesuit gains in this area were solidified by the work of Adam Schall von Bell (1591–1666), a German Jesuit who was a trained astronomer and served as chief government astronomer in Beijing. Schall von Bell also assisted in casting cannon for the Ming, although it did not save the dynasty.

The Jesuits made some notable converts among the literati, particularly during the troubled years of the declining Ming. Most notable was Xu Guangqi (Paul Hsu, 1562–1633), who translated Euclid's *Elements* and other works on mathematics, hydraulics, astronomy, and geography, thereby becoming the first Chinese translator of European books. With the help of such men, Western science and geography were made available to China, but European influence remained limited. Thus, when Li Zhi (1527–1602), one of the most forceful and independent Late Ming thinkers, met Ricci, he was impressed with the Jesuit's personality but saw no merit in his proselytizing mission.

The triumph of the Manchus did not seriously disrupt Jesuit activity. Schall von Bell was retained by the new dynasty as their astronomer. He was followed by the Belgian Jesuit, Ferdinand Verbiest (1633–1688), the last of the trio of great and learned missionary fathers. Verbiest, like Schall von Bell, cast cannon and in other ways won the favor of Kangxi. A good account of Jesuit activities at court comes from the emperor's own brush:

> With Verbiest I had examined each stage of the forging of cannons, and made him build a water fountain that operated in conjunction with an organ, and erect a windmill in the court; with the new group. . . . I worked on clocks and mechanics. Pereira taught me to play the tune "Puyanzhou" on the harpsichord and the structure of the eight-notescale, Pedrini taught my sons musical theory, and Gheradini painted portraits at the Court. I also learned to calculate the weight and volume of spheres, cubes, and cones. . . .[7]

The Emperor accepted the Jesuits' science with alacrity and took their quinine for the sake of his health. He also discussed religion with them, but here they were less successful: "I had asked Verbiest why God had not forgiven his son without making him die, but though he had tried hard to answer I had not understood him."[8] In China, as in Japan, the fathers found it most difficult to explain the central tenets of their faith to people with very different ideas about the nature of the universe and of the divine.

The high point for early Catholicism in China came in the middle years of Kangxi's reign, but by 1700 there were no more than 300,000 Christians in China, roughly the same number as in much smaller Japan a century earlier. In both cases the missionaries were there on sufferance, dependent on the good will of the authorities. And in China, as earlier in Japan, divisions between the Europeans themselves strongly contributed to their undoing.

# The Rites Controversy

The controversy that brought an end to the missionary activity in China centered on the Jesuit policy of accommodation, which was opposed by rival orders, particularly and vigorously by the Dominicans. It revolved around the question of the proper attitude a Christian should adopt toward Confucianism, its doctrines, and its practices. This kind of dispute also undermined the Jesuits in Vietnam but not in Japan, where Catholic fathers of all orders agreed in their condemnation of Buddhism and Shinto and in their absolute refusal to allow their converts to have anything to do with such heathen religions.

In China, however, the basic strategy used by Ricci and followed by his successors was to accept the teachings of Confucius, "the prince of philosophers." They argued that they had come not to destroy Confucius, but to make his teachings complete, capping his doctrines with the truths of revealed religion. Like Chinese thinkers intent on using Confucius in new ways, the Jesuits also discarded and condemned previous interpretations and commentaries on the classics. They attacked Neo-Confucianism and developed new theories of their own. In their enthusiasm for the classics, the Jesuits turned Confucius into a religious teacher.

Some members of the order went as far as to trace the origin of the Chinese people to the eldest son of Noah. The most extreme even claimed to find Christian prophecies in the *Changes.* Meanwhile, the Dominicans held that the ancient Chinese were atheists and argued against the Jesuit portrayal of Confucius as a deist. The resulting literature greatly influenced Western understanding of Chinese philosophy. At its best it was a serious effort by Europeans to understand Chinese thought in what they believed to be universally valid terms.

The status of Confucius and the acceptability of the classics were major issues for missionaries operating in a society dominated by the Confucian examination system. Even more troublesome, however, was the related problem posed by Confucian observances. Were the ceremonies in veneration of Confucius, held in the temples of Confucius throughout the land, acts of religious devotion and therefore anathema to a Christian? Or were they social and political in character, secular expressions of respect for China's greatest teacher? Even more important, what about the rites performed by every family in front of the tablets representing its ancestors? Was this a worship of the departed spirits and thus the most iniquitous idolatry? Or did these acts of commemoration for one's forebears merely convey a deep sense of filial piety? Were the two kinds of ceremonials civic and moral in nature, or were they religious, and therefore sacrilegious? Consistent with their stand on Confucianism, the Jesuits claimed the ceremonies were nonreligious and therefore permissible. The Dominicans disagreed.

The issue was fiercely debated, for much was at stake. Theology aside, it is easy to see the practical reasons for the Jesuit standpoint. To exclude Christians from performing the ceremonies for Confucius would be to exclude them from participation in Chinese political life. Worse still, to prohibit the ritual veneration of ancestors would not only deprive Chinese Christians of their sense of family but would make them appear as unfilial, immoral monsters in the eyes of their non-Christian fellows. If the advocates of Christianity rejected the classics and insisted on this kind of nonconformist behavior, it would be turned into a religion subversive of the Chinese state and society. Suffering persecution and widespread condemnation, Christianity would be unavailable to many souls, who would thus be deprived of their chance for salvation.

But the Dominicans could muster strong counterarguments. Why should a church that condemned Protestant Christianity condone Confucian Christianity? The issue was not the acceptability of Christianity to the Chinese but whether the salvation of souls would be fatally jeopardized by tolerating false Confucian doctrines. In their eyes, nothing could be allowed to interfere with the Christian's sacred duty to maintain the purity of the faith.

# The Decline of Christianity in China

The question, "When does Christianity cease to be Christianity?" was to reappear in the nineteenth century and is not all that different from the question, "When does Marxism cease to be Marxism?" which agitated some thinkers in the twentieth century. Such questions are never easy to resolve, and perhaps only true believers need grapple with them. Be that as it may, in the papacy, the church had a source of authority that could rule on what was acceptable and what was not. The process of reaching a decision was complicated and involved.

What is important here is that the outcome went against the Jesuits. In 1704 the pope condemned Chinese rituals, and in 1742 a decree was issued that settled all points against the Jesuits. This remained the position of the Catholic Church until 1939. Grand and powerful emperors such as Kangxi, however, resented Rome's claims of authority over their subjects and saw no reason to abide by the papal judgment as to what was fitting for their realm. They naturally favored the Jesuit point of view. In the end, the pope would send only those missionaries the emperor of China would not accept.

Some missionaries remained in China after the break, including the Jesuit Giuseppe Castiglione, who served as court painter for half a century, from 1715

**FIGURE 13.4** A lady's portrait in Western-style costume (inspired by Daiyu). Anonymous, mid-eighteenth century. (© Palace Museum, Beijing.)

to 1766. Among other things, he designed a miniature Versailles for the Summer Palace, destroyed in the nineteenth century. Michael Sullivan has described his fusion of artistic traditions as a "synthetic style in which with taste and skill and the utmost discretion, Western perspective and shading, with even an occasional hint of chiaroscuro, were blended to give an added touch of realism to painting otherwise entirely Chinese in manner."[9] Figure 13.4 shows a painting in the European manner done at the Chinese court. Just as Louis XV of France sometimes amused himself by having his courtiers and their ladies assume Chinese dress, the Qing emperor Qianlong enjoyed exotic Western costume on occasion. Meanwhile a Western perspective appeared in color prints intended for a broad popular market.

Regardless of the Rites Controversy, the Christians also had opponents in China itself, motivated by the usual combination of self-interest and conviction. There was no Chinese counterpart to Nagasaki: instead, the view of foreigners in Canton and the surrounding area, the part of China most exposed to the Europeans, at this time was already negative. Christianity was proscribed in 1724. Some churches were seized, and other acts of persecution occurred, but the suppression of Christianity was not as thorough as that which had taken place in Japan. This was probably because there was no Chinese equivalent to the Shimabara Rebellion—at least not yet. Not until the nineteenth century did the potential of Christianity as an ideology of peasant rebellion become evident in China. By the end of the eighteenth century, the number of Chinese converts had been reduced to about half what it had been at the beginning of the century.

Western contact did influence some areas of intellectual life, such as astronomy and cartography, but remained peripheral, far removed from the mainstream of Chinese intellectual life. There was no revolution in thought or art. Those of the Qing elite who came in touch with things Western rarely progressed much beyond the appreciation of European exotica, such as clocks and other mechanical de-

**FIGURE 13.5** The Canton waterfront, c. 1760. Artist unknown. One of four panels creating a panorama of the waterfront. Notice the flags of Western nations in front of their respective warehouses. Gouache on silk, 29.02 in × 18.78 in. (© Peabody Essex Museum, Salem, MA.)

vices. Ricci himself lived on as the patron saint of clockmakers. The influence was much stronger in the other direction, for the Jesuit reports on China were well received in Europe and helped to create the image of an ideal China dear to the philosophers of the European Enlightenment.

A major difference between the course of events in China and Japan was that in China trade considerations did not influence government decisions concerning missionary policies.

## Trade with the West and the Canton System

After 1683, the Qing, recognizing that the flourishing maritime trade with Southeast Asia was of great economic importance to coastal communities and posed no security problems for the empire, basically left its management to local authorities. Although Kangxi instituted some restrictions on foreigners trying out the Chinese market, it was Qianlong who restricted them to Canton, where a special area was set aside for the warehouses (called "factories") of the foreign traders, who were allowed to reside there but not to bring their wives and settle down (see Figure 13.5).

There were other restrictions under this Canton System (1760–1842). In all their transactions foreign traders were required to deal with a group of Chinese merchants who had been granted a monopoly of foreign trade. These merchants belonged to the Cohong, an association of firms (or *hong*) established for that purpose. In theory the Cohong was composed of a maximum of thirteen *hong,* but in practice there were only seven or eight such establishments, supervised by an imperial official who usually squeezed a good deal of personal profit out of his position. Each foreign ship was placed under the responsibility of a particular *hong,* which handled not only commercial matters but also saw to it that duties were paid and that the foreigners conducted themselves properly.

Under this system, the foreigners were not granted direct access to Chinese officials, nor were there any provisions for government-to-government relations. On the British side, the prime agent was the East India Company, which, under government charter, enjoyed a monopoly of trade between England and China and governed much of India, an arrangement not challenged until the nineteenth century, when the idea and forces of free trade triumphed.

The Qing taxed foreign maritime trade more heavily than that of Chinese ships, but both were administered separately from the tributary system of conducting foreign relations. Consequently, when Macartney, in 1793, and Lord Amherst, in 1816, came to China to try to expand trade and open European-style diplomatic relations, they ran head-on into a well-established dynastic practice that the Qing court saw no reason to change. The system continued to operate until China faced a Europe that could no longer be contained.

# Notes

1. C.R. Boxer, *The Christian Century in Japan* (Berkeley: Univ. of California Press, 1951), p. 74.

2. Donald F. Lach, *Asia in the Making of Europe, Vol. I: The Century of Discovery* (Chicago: Univ. of Chicago Press, 1965), p. 728.

3. Ibid.

4. Quoted in Boxer, *The Christian Century in Japan,* p. 214.

5. Ibid.

6. A.H. Rowbotham, *Missionary and Mandarin* (Berkeley: Univ. of California Press, 1942), p. 46.

7. Quoted in Jonathan Spence, *Emperor of China* (New York: Alfred A. Knopf, 1974), pp. 72–73.

8. Spence, *Emperor of China,* p. 84.

9. Michael Sullivan, *The Meeting of Eastern and Western Art* (New York: New York Graphic Society, 1973), pp. 66–67.

# Last Dynasties

*U*nder the last dynasty of Chinese emperors and Japanese shoguns, both lands experienced unprecedented prosperity before they ran into considerable difficulties. In most respects, however, the differences between them remained as striking as ever. This includes the pattern of their histories, because the Manchu conquest of China—lengthy, bloody, and traumatic as it was—in the end only temporarily disrupted the continuity of Chinese culture and society, so scholars often lump Ming and Qing under a single rubric. In Japan, however, a century of warfare eliminated old structures and set the stage for a new system that differed so markedly from its predecessors that scholars generally consider it the beginning of a new historical period.

During these years, European civilization was transformed in ways that were to have profound effect all over the globe. But that came later. For now, China and Japan were for the last time left free to deal with overseas challenges on their own terms and to develop each according to its own internal dynamics. However, in both China and Japan the end of the last dynasties came when this was no longer the case, so this part of our book ends before they do.

The Hall of Annual Prayer is 32 meters in diameter and 38 meters tall. Four inner pillars represent the four seasons; twelve middle and twelve outer pillars stand for the twelve months and the twelve hours of the traditional Chinese day. In its dimensions as well as symbolism, the building radiates the strength of tradition and of the emperor who prayed there to Heaven for good harvests.

# 14

# Tokugawa: Background, Establishment, and Middle Years

| 1336 | 1600 | 1651 | 1787 |
|---|---|---|---|

| Period of Unification<br><br>Momoyama (1568–1600) | EARLY TOKUGAWA | TOKUGAWA SHOGUNATE: THE MIDDLE YEARS<br><br>Genroku (1688–1704) · Kyōhō Reforms (1716–1736) |
|---|---|---|

In this chapter, we will consider the unification of Japan and the first two centuries of the Tokugawa shogunate, when Japan underwent changes so deep that scholars often refer to this period as "early modern" (*kinsei*), comparable to the European Renaissance. This designation is useful because it highlights the continuities with what was to come and the considerable discontinuities with earlier history. Conversely, however, it may distract from what the Tokugawa shared with its past or cause us to overestimate its links to the future. We begin with its recent past, the century of warfare and the period of unification out of which it emerged.

# I. The Legacy of War

In Chapter 12 we left a fragmented Japan with daimyo (lords) warring against one another to preserve their territories and, if possible, to expand them. The sizes of these principalities varied widely; some were no larger than a small castle town, and others might be as large as one of the old provinces. Regardless of the size of his holdings, the daimyo's fate depended on his success in the field of battle. What counted was power. Although some of the mid-sixteenth-century daimyo belonged to the old families, many emerged out of the class of local warriors. In these strenuous, difficult times, capable, ambitious, and unscrupulous men struggled to the top using any means at hand; frequently, betrayal was the price of upward mobility. The introduction of formal oaths, unnecessary in an older and simpler age, did not change the situation. Vassals could be counted on for their loyalty only as long as it was in their best interests to be loyal.

To obtain and hold their vassals, the daimyo originally granted or confirmed landholdings, much like European fiefs, thereby bringing to a final end the old and complicated system of estates and *shiki*. In return for these grants of land, the vassals were obliged to render military service to their lord and provide the services of a set number of their own fighting men. The traditional elites in the capital area, aristocrats and religious institutions, could not compete with local warriors for control of land, so the old *shōen* system disappeared.

Despite uprisings and social turbulence, the future was to belong to warriors, not peasants or religious institutions. In the long run, success in this precarious age went to those daimyo who could most effectively mobilize the resources of their domains, turning them into small states. The ultimate consequence of the breakdown of central unity was the creation of smaller but more highly integrated political entities. Daimyo normally asserted their authority over the succession of their vassals and, because political combinations were involved, they had a say concerning their vassals' marriages. Some daimyo, in their house laws, asserted rights to tax the land in their territory and to regulate economic activities. Frequently, spies were employed to keep the lord informed of the activities and plans of his vassals.

A potent force for integration was the changing nature of warfare. It was found that massed foot soldiers, recruited from the peasantry and armed with spears and the like, were an effective force against the traditional, proud, and expensive mounted warriors. Armies grew larger, and vassals tended to serve as officers commanding troops of commoners.

Sixteenth-century Japan was no exception to the rule that changes in offense stimulate new developments in defense. The Japanese answer to the new armies was the castle. It was often built on a hill, crowned with a tower, protected by walls, and surrounded by a moat or a natural body of water. These castles often served as the centers of daimyo-states, and there appeared a tendency for warriors to be gathered there, removed from the land and supported by hereditary stipends the daimyo financed through taxation.

An added impetus to the use of the new type of armies came after the Portuguese introduced European firearms to Japan in 1543. Within ten years, the daimyo of western Japan were using imported and domestic muskets in their armies. In response, bigger and more elaborate castles became necessary, so that in defense as well as in offense the larger daimyo with ample means had a decisive advantage.

By the middle of the sixteenth century, trends toward political consolidation were apparent on the macro and micro levels, but that did not come quickly or easily.

# II. Unification and Consolidation (1573–1651)

*Oda Nobunaga*

*Toyotomi Hideyoshi*

*The Invasion of Korea*

*Grand Castles and the Arts*

After the demise of the last Ashikaga shogun, there was not another for thirty years, but there was always an emperor. The imperial court, although impoverished and dependent on warrior patronage, was generally well led and succeeded in remaining Japan's most prestigious ceremonial and cultural center, setting standards of refined taste in poetry, flower viewing, kickball, and other arts and conferring honors and ranks on warriors eager for recognition. In a period with numerous complex crosscurrents in values and ideas as in politics and society, the court benefited from what Lee Butler has called "an ideology that upheld the traditional social order and confirmed the centrality of the court in the political and social world of medieval Japan."[1]

When Tokugawa Ieyasu (1542–1616) had himself appointed shogun in 1603, he confirmed the status of the emperor as well as the hegemony he had established at the decisive battle of Sekigahara in 1600, a victory marking the effective beginning of the Tokugawa rule. In establishing a new order, he built on the work of two forceful predecessors: Oda Nobunaga (1534–1582) and especially Toyotomi Hideyoshi (1542–1616).

# Oda Nobunaga

Nobunaga inherited control of Owari, not one of the great territories but one of strategic importance in central Honshu. From this base, he embarked on a ruthless drive for supremacy carried out with great military and political skill. In 1560 he won one of the key battles of his career by defeating an enemy army of some 25,000 with only 2000 men of his own. In 1568 he entered Kyoto. For another five years, the last Ashikaga shogun precariously retained his title, but from 1573 to 1603, there was no shogun.

An important element in his military success was Nobunaga's effective use of firearms. As already noted, after their introduction by the Portuguese in 1543, daimyo were using imported and homemade muskets in their armies. Nobunaga was quick to employ the new weapons and techniques; he had the will and the means to do so with great effectiveness. Thus, in 1575 he won a crucial battle through the superior firepower of his 3000 musketeers. For defense he built a great castle at Azuchi on the shore of Lake Biwa.

Secular opponents were not alone in feeling the full force of Nobunaga's wrath. After he seized Kyoto, he turned his attention to the monks on Mount Hiei and ended the military proclivities of the great Tendai monastery. He did this by destroying its buildings, slaughtering its monks, and eliminating the unfortunate inhabitants of nearby villages. "The roar of the huge burning monastery, magnified by the cries of countless numbers of the old and young, sounded and resounded to the ends of heaven and earth."[2] An estimated 1600 people lost their lives in this terrible bloodletting. Nobunaga was similarly set in his hostility toward the Ikkō sect. In Echizen province, he was responsible for the deaths of 30,000 to 40,000 Ikkō adherents, although he did not eradicate the sect completely. Even Mount Kōya only narrowly escaped Nobunaga's wrath. His hostility toward organized Buddhism was one of the factors influencing the friendly reception he accorded the first Jesuit missionaries to enter Japan.

Nobunaga was politically adroit. He forged valuable alliances through his marriage policies, managed to keep his enemies divided, and retained his followers and allies. A major element in his growing power was his ability to attract new vassals, frequently men who had been the vassals of his rivals. By going over to Nobunaga, they could secure their own positions and hope to participate in future gains. Thus, success fed on success.

By opening markets, breaking up guild monopolies, destroying toll stations, and encouraging road construction and shipbuilding, Nobunaga fostered trade. He also reorganized the administration of his lands, introducing a new system of tax collection and initiating a land survey. And he began to disarm the peasantry. Both were in full swing when Nobunaga died, betrayed by one of his own generals avenging a wrong. At the time of his death, he controlled about a third of Japan but clearly indicated his intent to be master of all.

# Toyotomi Hideyoshi

Hideyoshi was born a peasant but rose to become one of Nobunaga's foremost generals. After Nobunaga's death, he defeated other contenders for the succession and then continued to increase his power much in the manner of Nobunaga, inducing daimyo to acknowledge his supremacy. Hideyoshi continued to increase his power by diplomacy. Unable to subdue the strongest daimyo, Tokugawa Ieyasu, he gave his sister to Ieyasu in marriage and assigned him substantial holdings in the Kanto in exchange for domains of less value in central Japan. In this way, he saw to it that Ieyasu was both content and at a distance.

Hideyoshi also relocated his own vassals to assure maximum security. Those he trusted most were placed in strategic positions, and those thought to harbor territorial ambitions were provided with hostile neighbors to discourage them. To demonstrate their loyalty, vassals were sometimes required to leave wives and children with Hideyoshi as virtual hostages. Feudal bonds were further strengthened through marriage alliances. Thus, through conquest, diplomacy, and manipulation Hideyoshi became, in effect, overlord of all Japan. By 1590 all daimyo swore oaths of loyalty to him. Because he did not belong to the Minamoto lineage, he was ineligible to become shogun. He did have himself adopted into the Fujiwara family, and in 1585 he was appointed regent (*kanpaku*). This association with the imperial throne gave added legitimacy to his place at the apex of a system of feudal loyalties.

Hideyoshi was intent on keeping the daimyo in their places but not eliminating them. On the contrary, his policies strengthened the daimyo locally vis-à-vis their warriors and farmers even as he took steps to assure their subordination. When a daimyo was relocated, he took many of his vassals with him into his new domain, where they had no hereditary links to the land. This accelerated a tendency, already visible earlier, for samurai to be concentrated in castle towns where they received stipends collected from land but were divorced from direct supervision of the land. On the one hand, this severed the samurai from an independent power base and made them dependent on the daimyo. On the other, villages were left to provide their own leadership and to run their own affairs with little outside interference as long as they fulfilled their tax obligations. The village was freed from samurai control even as it was deprived of warrior leadership in case of conflict.

One of Hideyoshi's most important acts was the great "sword hunt" of 1588, when all peasants who had not already done so were ordered to surrender their weapons, the metal to be used in building a great statue of the Buddha. By depriving peasants of their weapons he did more than discourage them from rioting or rebelling—although he did that, too. A major, and intentional, consequence of the measure was to draw a sharp line between peasant and samurai, to create an unbridgeable gulf between the tiller of the soil and the bearer of arms where hitherto there had been low-ranking samurai who had also worked the land.

By this time, Hideyoshi's land survey, begun in 1582 but not completed for all of Japan until 1598, was well under way. In this great survey the value of cultivated land was assessed in terms of average annual productivity, measured in *koku* of rice, a *koku* being equal to 4.96 bushels. The resulting listings were used to assess the taxes due from each village, and the holdings of the daimyo were calculated in terms of the assessed value rather than acreage. From this time on, a daimyo, by definition, held land assessed at a minimum of 10,000 *koku*. Large daimyo held much more than that. Some of the greatest had several hundred thousand *koku*, and there were a few with more than 1 million. Hideyoshi personally held 2 million, not including the lands of his most trustworthy vassals. Tokugawa Ieyasu held 2.56 million. Like the confiscation of weapons, the land survey, which listed the names of the peasant proprietors, effectively separated farmers and fighters.

An edict of 1591 carried the process further. The first of its three articles prohibited fighting men from becoming peasants or townsmen, and the second banned peasants from leaving their fields and becoming merchants or artisans and prohibited the latter from becoming farmers. The third prohibited anyone from employing a samurai who had left his master without permission. If discovered, the offender was to be returned to his master. If this was not done and the culprit was knowingly allowed to go free, then the edict declared that "three persons shall be beheaded in place of the one, and their heads sent to the offender's original master. If this threefold substitution is not effected, then there is no alternative but to punish the new master."[3] In this way, Hideyoshi, who had himself risen from the peasantry to the greatest heights, did his best to make sure that henceforth everyone would remain within his hereditary social status.

# The Invasion of Korea

Hideyoshi's vision of the world and his own place in it extended well beyond Japan. He took an active interest in overseas trade. After he subjugated the Kyushu daimyo, he undertook suppressing the pirates and freebooters who had long plagued the Chinese and Korean coasts. In East Asia as elsewhere, the line between trade and piracy was often obscure, as was the actual nationality of the so-called Japanese pirates (*wako*), many of whom were Chinese. Hideyoshi undertook other measures to encourage international commerce. One of his two great castles was at Osaka, which soon eclipsed Sakai as a trading center and remains today the second largest city in Japan.

But Hideyoshi looked abroad for more than trade: he thought in terms of empire. In the 1590s, he demanded the submission of the Philippines by their Spanish governor, although no steps were ever taken to enforce the demand. He also made plans to conquer China, which he then intended to divide among his vassals, much in the same way he had dealt with his Japanese conquests. After China would come India and, indeed, the rest of the world as he knew it. Hideyoshi's invasion of the continent can partially be seen as an attempt to satisfy the perpetual land hunger of his vassals or, at least, to find employment for restive samurai. It would also convince the Japanese and the rest of the world of Hideyoshi's power and glory. Another factor surely was his personality, but Jurgis Elisonas has suggested that "not so much megalomania as ignorance moved the entire enterprise."[4]

Whatever Hideyoshi's motivation, he dispatched a force of 150,000 men to Korea in 1592, after Korea had refused free passage for his troops to march to China. The Japanese force had great initial success and captured Seoul within a month. But they ran into difficulties further north and were bested at sea by the superior ships and seamanship of the Korean fleet under Admiral Yi Sun-sin, famous for his armed "turtle ships." Chinese military intervention and Korean guerrilla fighting also took their toll, and in 1593 peace negotiations were under way. These talks were fruitless, however, and in 1597 Hideyoshi sent another force of 140,000 men to Korea. This time they met with stronger resistance. The whole attempt was suddenly abandoned when Hideyoshi died in 1598, and the Japanese forces immediately returned home.

The expense of the campaign helped undermine the Ming dynasty in China, but the real losers were the Korean people, who suffered pillage and rape at the hands of their Chinese allies as well as their Japanese enemies. In the second campaign, the Japanese announced that all Korean officials along with their wives and children would be killed, as would any farmer who did not return to his house and land. Following through, the Japanese conducted manhunts, and as proof of their exploits commanders sent back to Hideyoshi casks filled with noses preserved in salt. Careful records were kept, and nose counts figured in determining promotions and rewards. Other Koreans were brought back to Japan in bondage. One result was an infusion of Korean influence on Japanese pottery and printing.

Hideyoshi never joined the Korean campaigns but left command to his vassals, several of whom were seriously weakened as a result. As it turned out, not only his continental ambitions but also his hopes to found a lasting dynasty at home came to naught. Before he died, he made his most powerful vassals solemnly swear allegiance to his five-year-old son, Hideyori, whom he left in their care as regents. But this proved useless, and in the ensuing struggle for power Ieyasu emerged the winner. His victory at Sekigahara in 1600 was followed by his designation as shogun in 1603, after he had acquired a suitable Minamoto ancestry. Final confirmation of Ieyasu's triumph came with the fall of Osaka Castle and the death of Hideyori in 1615. Ieyasu inherited Hideyoshi's power, but unlike Hideyoshi, he concentrated on building a lasting state at home.

# Grand Castles and the Arts

The period of unification is usually called the Azuchi–Momoyama Epoch (or Momoyama for short) after Nobunaga's Azuchi Castle near Lake Biwa and Hideyoshi's Momoyama Castle in Fushimi, close to Kyoto. In many ways, these castles, along with those of the daimyo, are fitting representatives of the age. Dominating the surrounding countryside, they featured massive keeps and strong fortifications designed to withstand the new armies and weapons. Their great size was made possible by the wealth obtained by the unifiers and the daimyo as they achieved greater local control. The castles formed nuclei around which grew new cities, as first samurai and then merchants and artisans were attracted to castle towns. The most grandiose of all the castles was built by Hideyoshi in Osaka and boasted forty-eight towers. Unfortunately, Hideyoshi's and Nobunaga's castles were all destroyed, although the Osaka Castle was later rebuilt.

Most admired among Japan's castles is that at Himeji, which dates from the early seventeenth century. In recognition of its suggestive white silhouette, it is commonly known as the "Heron Castle" (see Figure 14.1). Like European castles, it is a stronghold surrounded by moat and wall and protected by massive foundations. Aesthetics were an important consideration in building a castle, and not only to please its owner, because "its purpose was to impress rivals by its elegant interiors as well as to frighten them by its strength."[5] One way to impress people was through richness of decor. The dark interiors of the castle were "lavish to the point of absurdity."[6] Hideyoshi's castle even had locks and bolts of gold and columns and ceilings covered with the precious metal.

Paintings on walls, sliding doors, and screens decorated and brightened the castle interiors. To meet new needs and tastes, the paintings were frequently large and used striking colors. Gold leaf was employed to create a flat background with the result that "its unreality reinforces the assertive substance of painted objects."[7] The artist Kanō Eitoku (1543–1590) epitomized the new style and spirit. Generously patronized by both Nobunaga and Hideyoshi, Eitoku worked at both the Azuchi and the Momoyama castles. The Eitoku screen shown in Figure 14.2 was originally one of a pair, but its companion is now lost. It is about twenty feet long and eight feet high and was obviously intended for use in a large room.

The Kanō school was continued by Eitoku's adopted son, Sanraku (1559–1653), in a trend that culminated in the great decorative screens of the early Tokugawa Period. In another medium, Momoyama fondness for rich deco-

**FIGURE 14.1** Himeji Castle. Himeji, Hyōgo. (© Lore Schirokauer)

**FIGURE 14.2** *Chinese Lions* (*Kara-shiki*), Kanō Eitoku. Section of sixfold screen, 88.58 in high. (Imperial Household Collection, Tokyo.) (© Sakamoto Photo Research Laboratory/ Corbis)

ration produced elaborate wood carvings such as those on the Kara Gate of the Nishi Honganji in Kyoto, popularly known as the gate that requires a whole day to be properly seen.

Ostentatious and profuse, the Momoyama aesthetic is far removed from Ashikaga restraint. Nothing could be more alien to the aesthetics of the tea ceremony than the monster tea party given by Hideyoshi in 1587 to which literally everyone was invited for ten days of music, theater, and art viewing.

This was not the only occasion on which Hideyoshi displayed a penchant for great gatherings and lavish entertainment; however, he also patronized Sen no Rikyu (1522–1591), greatest of the tea masters, who stressed harmony, respect, purity, and tranquility in his writings on tea. A story told about the great tea master and his son has them visiting another practitioner of the art. When they entered the garden, the son admired the wooden gate, covered with moss, at the end of the path leading to the tea hut, but the father disagreed:

> That gate must have been brought from some distant mountain at obvious expense. A rough wicket made by the local farmer would give the place a really quiet and lonely look, and not offend us by bringing up thoughts of difficulty and expense. I doubt if we shall find here any very sensitive or interesting tea ceremony.[8]

Sen no Rikyu is said to have influenced the potter Chōjiro (1576–1592), originator of Raku ware, illustrated by the tea bowl that accompanied the vase on our part opener. Eschewing the technical virtuosity of Chinese ceramics, the Japanese potter delights in bringing out the earthiness of the clay. The tea master, Furuta Oribe (1544–1615), originated a ceramic tradition characterized by thick glazes and rough brushwork and not only intentionally made misshaped bowls but even broke some so he could mend them.

Yet, as Lee Butler has written of Sen no Rikyu, "His practice of tea was at the same time very simple and deeply complex: it presented an image of poverty while revealing and requiring considerable wealth, and it adopted and revered the simplest of objects, thereby giving them great value."[9] From the beginning, a tendency toward wealth and ostentation coexisted with the aesthetics of poverty and simplicity, although the fantastic prices paid by wealthy daimyo competing for ownership of a famous bowl or jar were not exactly in keeping with the original spirit of tea. It is also worth noting that both tea masters became embroiled in the world of power and politics to the point that they were ordered to commit suicide. Tea survived, worldly yet refined. The second Tokugawa shogun was a connoisseur, and it remained the occasion for the display and appreciation of the best of taste.

As in China, painters in Japan often worked in more than one style. Both Eitoku and his great contemporary, Hasegawa Tōhaku (1539–1610), worked both in monochrome and in color. In scale, Tōhaku's masterly *Pine Grove* (see Figure 14.3) is typically Momoyama, because it occupies two screens more than five feet (sixty-one inches) high, but it is ink on paper and subtle rather than ostentatious.

# III. The Tokugawa Political Consolidation (1600–1651)

The political structure of Tokugawa rule was devised by Ieyasu and completed by his two immediate successors, Hidetada (1616–1623) and Iemitsu (1623–1651). By the middle of the seventeenth century, the system was in full operation.

**FIGURE 14.3** *Pine Grove*, Hasegawa Tōhaku. Section of a sixfold screen. 136.6 in × 61 in. (© Tokyo National Museum.)

Ieyasu rose to supremacy as the leader of a group of daimyo, each of whom was backed by his own vassals and supported by his independent power base. The daimyo were by no means all deeply committed to the Tokugawa. Hideyoshi's recent failure to establish a dynasty had demonstrated, if any demonstration was needed, the folly of relying solely on the loyalty of such men, especially when passing the succession to a minor. Ieyasu assured the smooth transfer of power to his son by resigning from the office of shogun in 1605, after holding it for only two years. But he continued in actual control until his death, working to ensure the continuity of Tokugawa rule.

All the daimyo were the shogun's vassals, bound to him by solemn oath, and when a daimyo's heir succeeded to his domain, the new daimyo had to sign his pledge of vassalage to the shogun in blood. Still, some vassals were more reliable than others, and the Tokugawa classified them into three groups. Least trusted and potentially the most dangerous were the "outside," or allied, daimyo (*tozama*), who were too powerful to be considered Tokugawa subordinates. Virtually all of these, like Ieyasu, had been vassals of Hideyoshi. Some had supported Ieyasu at the battle of Sekigahara, but others came over to the Tokugawa only after the outcome of that battle left them no choice. More trustworthy were the house daimyo (*fudai*), most of whom had been Tokugawa family vassals raised to daimyo status by the Tokugawa; thus, unlike the *tozama*, they were indebted to the *bakufu* for their status and domains. The third group, the collateral daimyo (*shimpan*), was composed of daimyo belonging to Tokugawa branch families. The Tokugawa also held its own lands, which supported its direct retainers. Some of these held fiefs of less than the 10,000 *koku* required for daimyo status, but many of them received stipends directly from the *bakufu*.

When Ieyasu was transferred to the Kanto region by Hideyoshi, he chose as his headquarters the centrally located village of Edo (modern Tokyo), then consisting of about a hundred houses but destined to become one of the world's great cities. The shogunate also maintained castles at Osaka and Shizuoka (then called Sumpu) and the Nijō Castle in Kyoto, residence of a *bakufu* deputy responsible for the government of the capital city and serving concurrently as the shogun's representative at the imperial court.

To secure itself militarily, the Tokugawa placed its *fudai* in strategic areas. It dominated the Kanto, central Japan, and Kyoto–Osaka regions, and the *tozama* had their territories in the outer areas. Several policies were initiated to keep the daimyo from acquiring too much strength. They were restricted to one castle each and had to secure *bakufu* permission before they could repair this castle. They were allowed to maintain only a fixed number of men at arms and, in line with the seclusion policy, were forbidden to build large ships. To keep the daimyo from forming political alliances that might threaten the *bakufu*, they were required to obtain *bakufu* consent for their marriage plans.

During the first half of the seventeenth century, the shogunate enacted a vigorous policy of increasing its own strength at the expense of the daimyo. In this period there were 281 cases in which daimyo were transferred from one fief to another, shuffles that strengthened some and weakened others. Another 213 domains were confiscated outright. This happened sometimes as a disciplinary measure, such as when a lord proved incompetent or the domain was torn by a succession dispute. More often, confiscation resulted from failure to produce an heir. Deathbed adoptions of an heir were not recognized. By such means, the Tokugawa more than tripled the size of its holdings, until its own domain was calculated as worth 6.8 million *koku* of rice. The distribution of their holdings also favored the Tokugawa economically, as it did militarily, because they possessed many of Japan's mines and most of the important cities, such as Osaka, Kyoto, and Nagasaki. In the mid-Tokugawa Period, *shimpan* held land worth 2.6 million *koku; fudai,* 6.7 million; and *tozama,* 9.8 million. It is indicative of the decline of their economic and political power that religious institutions held only around 600,000 *koku,* and the emperor and the court nobility could draw on land worth only 187,000 *koku.*

To see to it that the daimyo obeyed *bakufu* orders, the shogunate sent out its own inspectors. It also devised a highly effective system of strengthening itself politically (while draining the daimyo financially) by requiring them to spend alternate years in residence in Edo, where the *bakufu* could keep them under surveillance. When they did go back home to their domains, they had to leave their wives and children behind as hostages. This system of alternate attendance (*sankin kotai*) forced the daimyo to spend large sums traveling with their retinues. The maintenance of suitably elaborate residences in Edo was a further strain on daimyo resources. The daimyo were also called upon to support public projects such as waterworks or the repair of the shogun's castle at Edo, but such exactions were not as burdensome as the constant expense of alternate attendance. The residence requirement had the additional effect of turning Edo into a capital not only of the *bakufu* but of all Japan.

In theory, the shogun was both the emperor's deputy and the feudal overlord of all the daimyo. Thus, he had political legitimacy and the authority of a supreme commander standing at the apex of the military hierarchy. This dual role made him, in effect, responsible for the conduct of foreign affairs. The early *bakufu* also asserted its financial predominance when it reserved for itself the right to issue paper currency. Its regulations extended even to the dress of the daimyo. The final provision of a code issued in 1635 declared, "all matters are to be carried out in accordance with the laws of Edo."[10] The *bakufu*'s own domain comprised about a fourth of Japan.

# IV. The Middle Years (1653–1787)

Bakufu–Han Relations

Economic and Social Change

Classes and Values

The Aesthetic Culture of the Aristocracy

Genroku Urban Culture

    The Print

    Theater and Literature

Intellectual Currents: Confucianism

    Historiography and Nativisim

    Dutch Learning

Reform and Its Limits

Art and Literature After the Genroku Period

Ieyasu founded a long dynasty of shoguns and found the stability he sought, but that stability in itself generated change. Under the Tokugawa Japan enjoyed peace, experienced economic growth, and developed a flourishing urban culture. At the same time, there were stresses inherent in the system and, over time, new conditions arose to strain the body politic and society.

## Bakufu–Han Relations

Whatever the shogun might wish, the daimyo remained largely free to manage affairs in their own *han*. The tendency of daimyo and their samurai to identify with their own domain, at times even generating *han* chauvinism, was strongest among the *tozama,* but the others also focused on managing their *han.* Thus, they had a stake in maintaining and enlarging the decentralized aspect of the larger political system. Under the fourth shogun, Ietsuna (1651–1680), the daimyo regained much lost ground. *Bakufu* policy was reversed. There was a drastic decline in the number of daimyo transferred and *han* confiscated. Deathbed adoptions were recognized as legitimate. The shogunate even began permitting *han* to issue their own paper money. A proliferation of local currencies ensued. To protect their own money, some *han* in the eighteenth century prohibited the use of outside currencies—including the *bakufu*'s money!

The vigorous but eccentric fifth shogun, Tsunayoshi (1680–1709), presided over a reassertion of *bakufu* power, which earned him the enmity of the daimyo and lasting ignominy and ridicule. He was an easy target because he carried to an extreme his Buddhist devotion to the preservation of animal life and especially his solicitude for dogs, sometimes even at the cost of human life. This earned him the epithet "dog shogun." Nevertheless, his period saw a great flowering of culture and a resurgence of centralizing activity. But this did not lead to a permanent shift in the power balance, nor did it initiate a long-term trend toward greater *bakufu* control. If it had, this shogun's historical image would have been different.

Until the end of the Tokugawa, the pendulum continued to swing between the *bakufu* and the *han.* In his analysis of the history and dynamics of this process, Harold Bolitho has shown that periods of *bakufu* assertiveness tended to occur under vigorous shoguns working with trusted advisers drawn from among the shogunate's low-ranking retainers. Unencumbered by fief or vassals, totally dependent on the shogun, they became his men, free from potential conflicts of interest. Under such regimes, the high-ranking senior councilors, always selected from among the *fudai,* were treated with an outward show of respect while they were actually bypassed and disregarded. Little love was lost between the *fudai* and the new men.

When the shogun was a minor or incompetent, control over the *bakufu* reverted to the senior councilors, descendants of the Tokugawa's most favored and highly trusted vassals. The service of these vassals had formed the core of Ieyasu's strength, and he relied on their descendants for continued loyal service to his house. Although these men were conscious of their heritage of special obligations toward the shogunate, they also had responsibilities and opportunities as daimyo.

The tensions between shogunate and *han* were mirrored in their own persons as they faced the often-conflicting demands of *bakufu* and *han.* The usual pattern was for them to act more as daimyo than as *bakufu* officials. Such senior councilors were not prepared to sacrifice *han* privileges for the sake of the larger body politic. There were even cases of *han* held by incumbent senior councilors refusing to export grain badly needed to combat famine elsewhere. There were periodic shifts in the balance of power between the *bakufu* and the *han,* but the issue was never lastingly resolved in favor of one or the other. It can be argued that this proved beneficial in the long run because it allowed considerable divergence yet still maintained a center.

The more than 250 *han* varied widely in size, natural resources, and local conditions. All the lands held by a daimyo were not necessarily contiguous; some domains were more easily organized than others. But in general, operating on a smaller scale than the *bakufu,* the daimyo were more successful in controlling their retainers. The trend for the samurai to be concentrated in the *han* capitals divorced from the land continued strong. By the last decade of the seventeenth century, more than 80 percent of the daimyo were paying stipends to their samurai. By the end of the eighteenth century, 90 percent of samurai depended entirely on their stipends. Only 10 percent retained local roots in the country.

## Economic and Social Change

During the Tokugawa, peace made economic growth possible. There was a rise in demand to meet the needs of the samurai and the growing expenses of the daimyo. The system of alternate attendance stimulated the commercialization of agriculture, and agricultural productivity increased substantially, especially in the seventeenth century. Cultivated acreage doubled because of vigorous irrigation and land reclamation. Technological improvements, the practice of multiple-cropping, better seed strains, and improved fertilizers helped, as did the dissemination of knowledge through agricultural handbooks and manuals. The spread of market networks was accompanied by regional specialization in cash crops such as cotton, mulberry trees for rearing silk worms, indigo, tobacco, and sugar cane, but grain continued to be grown in all parts of Japan.

Population rose from about 18 million at the beginning of the Tokugawa to around 30 million by the middle of the period. Afterward, there were fluctuations in population, but there was no major long-term increase during the rest of Tokugawa; in 1872 the population stood at only 33.1 million. Although famine and disease took their toll, mortality rates were comparatively low, and the average life span was likely longer than that in premodern Europe because Japan was free from war and was less susceptible to epidemics. Late marriage, the custom of having only one son marry and inherit, and abortion and infanticide kept population growth under control. Family planning was widespread. Even when times were good, life was by no means easy for Japanese peasants who remained at the mercy of the elements. Many were poor, but for most of the period, the standard of living rose.

With samurai now largely removed from the land, the villages were left virtually free to collect the taxes due their overlord. Within the village, neither the benefits of agricultural growth nor the burdens of taxation were shared equally: there were wide gradations in wealth, status, and power backed by the state. Because tax reassessments were infrequent, wealthy peasants who were able to open new lands and otherwise increase their yields found their incomes rising.

Traditionally, the main house of an extended family had claims on the services of the lesser households and some obligations to look after the poorer members. Furthermore, the heads of the main houses formed the traditional village leadership. Now, with more money in circulation, wealthy villagers turned increasingly to hired laborers or tenant farmers to work their land. They also put their money

to work in rural commerce, moneylending, and such rural industries as processing vegetable oils, brewing sake, producing soy sauce, and making paper. Because
the wealthy villagers did not necessarily belong to the old main houses, tensions
ensued.

These tensions were aggravated by economic disparities, because poorer villagers and the landless did not share in the prosperity of the countryside but suffered as contractual relationships replaced those based on family. Most often they
endured in silence, but at times they vented their resentment in uprisings. Peasant
unrest was on the increase in the late Tokugawa. In contrast to early Tokugawa
rural uprisings, often led by village headmen, those of the later period were frequently directed against those wealthy and powerful villagers. However, neither
the uprisings nor the changes in agricultural technology seriously threatened the
basic stability of the village. Violence was a form of protest, not a means toward
revolution.

Changes in agriculture increased yield but did not alter the basic pattern of
rice farming, with its need for intensive labor and community cooperation. At the
same time, the experience of calculating work in terms of money and time was to
prove a legacy useful in the future.

Internal peace and economic vigor were conducive to expansion of the
Japanese presence in the far north, homeland of the non-Japanese Ainu people
who, by the end of the eighteenth century, accounted for only about half the population of Hokkaido. The Japanese presence then accelerated, partly out of concern
over Russian expansion. In the early nineteenth century in eastern Hokkaido, they
pursued a policy of turning the Ainu into Japanese, forcing them to abandon their
bear festival, to cut their hair in the Japanese manner, and to give up tattooing and
ear piercing. The decline in Ainu numbers and identity proved a long-term trend.

Economic expansion also left a dubious ecological legacy. In the seventeenth
century, both the *bakufu* and the domains promoted land clearance. Old-growth
forests were cut. By the end of the century, producers and consumers were faced
with a lumber shortage. In the eighteenth century, there was a countervailing
move to save natural resources and even to reforest cleared areas. However, government policies were inconsistent, because agriculture brought in more much
needed tax revenue than did forestry. Conrad Totman concludes, "How best to
balance the need for both woodland and arable was a dilemma that early modern
Japan never resolved."[11]

Much of the lumber went to the cities, home not only of officials but also of
merchants, who became rich as the economy flourished and the political authorities found their services indispensable. Merchants supplied an economic link between the cities and the rural hinterlands and between the localities and the capital. They handled the transport, warehousing, and sale of rice and other
commodities. Frequently, they were licensed to operate *han* monopolies and organize commodity production. Important merchants acted as financial and forwarding agents for the daimyo, handling shipments to Osaka for exchange or to
Edo for the daimyo's consumption. They supplied banking services, dealing in the
manifold *han* currencies, transferring funds, and issuing loans to political author-

ities and hard-pressed samurai. They were the backbone of widespread and diverse commercial networks. The position of individual commercial establishments could be precarious—in extreme cases, a wealthy merchant with heavy loans out to the powerful might suffer confiscation so that the loans could go unpaid, as happened to a great Osaka merchant in 1705. However, these cases were exceptions. Government measures forcing creditors to settle for less than full repayment, or even cancellation, simply had the effect of raising the cost of new loans, because the authorities never found a way to eliminate the need for such borrowing.

With the *bakufu*, daimyo, and samurai dependent on them, the merchants prospered; in the second half of the eighteenth century, there were more than 200 mercantile establishments valued at more than 200,000 gold *ryō*, a monetary unit worth roughly a *koku* of rice. Such merchants were fully the economic equals of daimyo. Some of the great modern commercial and financial empires go back to the early Tokugawa, including the house of Mitsui, founded in 1620.

By the beginning of the eighteenth century, Edo had a population of about a million, a little more than half of them townspeople (*chōnin*). Osaka, too, developed as a prosperous commercial and shipping center, and Kyoto remained a major city. The capitals of the *han* also became trade centers, with merchants and artisans playing an active role in shaping the character of each city. The most prominent merchants, as city elders, ward representatives, and the like, had a role in administration.

As in the villages, there were also great differences in status and wealth among the town dwellers; for every great merchant, there were many more humble shopkeepers, peddlers, artisans, laborers, and servants. At the bottom of society, constituting less than 2 percent of the population at the end of the Tokugawa Period, were *hinin* (nonpeople), mostly beggars, and *eta*, or outcasts (today called *burakumin* because *eta* is considered pejorative), who, most prominently, engaged in butchering and tanning, tasks considered unclean. The *bakufu* supported one powerful outcast house to lord over all outcasts in its domain in return for supplying leather goods and men to serve as prison guards and executioners. As Eiko Ikegami has pointed out, "The identical action of killing, whether human beings or animals, was, however, interpreted variously as either a source of pollution and exclusion (in the case of the outcasts) or a source of honor and power (in the case of the samurai)."[12]

# Classes and Values

To create an enduring order, Ieyasu followed Hideyoshi in drawing a clear line between samurai and commoners. It did happen that destitute *rōnin*, masterless samurai, dropped out of their class or that through marriage an alliance was formed between a wealthy merchant family and that of an impoverished samurai, but such cases remained uncommon. And yet time and economics drew an increasing wedge between theory and practice.

Assigned to various duties, the samurai staffed the increasingly bureaucratized administrative machinery of the domains and the *bakufu*. Most were now occupied more with civil than with military affairs. The most visible sign of the samurai's privilege was his sole right to wear swords, symbols of his status even after they had ceased to be his major tools. Although he was expected to acquire some proficiency in at least one of the martial arts, these became "a matter of formal gymnastics and disciplined choreography."[13] The samurai's status and stipend depended on heredity rather than merit. Nevertheless, the ethos of the samurai remained that of a loyal military vassal imbued with a strong and prickly sense of personal honor.

One way to tame the samurai was to encourage them to become learned. Although Ieyasu patronized the Confucian scholar Hayashi Razan (1583–1657), whose family continued to supply the heads of the *bakufu*'s Confucian academy, it was not until the end of the century that Confucianism came to prevail. The ideal was for the samurai to combine the virtues of Confucian scholar and warrior. An early proponent of a fusion of Confucian and warrior values was Yamaga Sokō (1622–1695). A student of Hayashi Razan and of the martial arts, he is considered a founding father of the modern way of the warrior (*bushidō*).

One of Yamaga's followers became the leader of the famed forty-seven *rōnin* who persevered in seeking vengeance for the wrong done their dead lord. In 1703 their carefully nurtured plans were rewarded with success as they stormed into the Kyoto mansion of the offending daimyo and killed him. They were immediately considered heroes and have remained popular examples of ideal loyalty. Theirs was an act of warrior courage and devotion, but it was also illegal! For a time the shogunate debated what should be done but then found a solution that would both uphold the substance of civil law and preserve the warriors' honor: they were ordered to commit ritual suicide. Playwrights lost no time in adapting the story for the stage. *Chūshingura (Treasury of Royal Retainers)*, to give the drama its proper title, was popular with commoners and samurai alike and has remained a Japanese favorite; in the twentieth century both the cinema and the television versions enjoyed great success.

In Tokugawa times, there was much on which samurai and commoner could agree. The official morality was promoted in periodic lectures and spread by the many schools founded during the Tokugawa Period so that by 1800, 40 to 50 percent of Japanese males were literate to some degree. Fewer girls went to school, but, as in China, special texts were published for their benefit. It is estimated that 10 percent of girls were in school by the end of Tokugawa in 1868.

Hierarchical principles of organization operated throughout the society, as did a tendency to rank people in grades. Like samurai, even the inhabitants of the demimonde of the urban pleasure quarters were carefully ranked. The great merchant houses resembled feudal fiefs not only in their wealth but also in their expectation of lifelong loyal service from their employees, who in turn were entitled to be treated with paternalistic solicitude. A similar relationship survives in Japanese industry to this day.

Although merchant and samurai held many values in common, it was a mark of samurai pride to regard financial considerations with contempt. Fukuzawa

Yukichi (1853–1901), in his famous autobiography, tells how his father took his children out of school when, to his horror, their teacher began to teach them arithmetic, a subject fit only for merchants and their offspring. But business had its defenders, including the Kaitoku Academy in Osaka, which taught the importance of trade and of those who engaged in it. Also legitimating the merchants' calling was the strain of Buddhism that considered all occupations valid forms of devotion. Heart Learning (Shingaku), a religion founded by the Kyoto merchant and philosopher Ishida Baigan (1685–1744), combined elements of Shinto, Confucianism, and Buddhism to create an ethic for the artisan and merchant stressing honesty, frugality, and devotion to one's trade. Diversity in classes and lifestyles made for similar diversity in the visual, literary, and performing arts and in thought.

# The Aesthetic Culture of the Aristocracy

The aristocracy inherited a rich cultural tradition. The subtle arts of the tea ceremony and flower arranging continued, and the Nō drama that had flourished in Muromachi times had its devotees, including the shogun Tsunayoshi, who performed in Nō plays. In architecture, the classic aesthetic of restraint was exemplified by the imperial villa at Katsura, outside Kyoto, but it coexisted with a love for the ornate, displayed at Nikko, the mausoleum north of Tokyo where Ieyasu's remains are interred. Here, brightly painted and gilded decorations luxuriate in chaotic flamboyance, saved from empty vulgarity by their setting in a magnificent forest and creating, in Alexander Soper's words, "a serene depth of shadow into which their tumult sinks without an echo."[14]

In Kyoto, aristocratic aesthetics enjoyed a surge of vitality in a movement led by Hon'ami Kōetsu (1558–1637), who established a community of artists and craftsmen on a site granted him by Ieyasu in recognition of his prominence as a member of that city's Nichiren Buddhist community. Kōetsu was trained in his family's hereditary art of sword repair and connoisseurship, but his far-reaching talents found masterly expression in tea bowls, lacquer inlay work, and cast metal vessels; in painting; and, above all, in calligraphy. Frequently, he collaborated with other artists, such as in the bold and free calligraphy he contributed to the handscroll *Thousand Cranes*, painted by Tawaraya Sōtatsu, a highly gifted younger contemporary (see Figure 14.4). The result is a decorative elegance that honors an aristocratic tradition going back to the Heian Period (794–1185).

The third great Kyoto artist was Ogata Kōrin (1658–1716), represented here by a pair of iris screens, which Elise Grilli has compared with Mozart's variations on a musical theme, the artist "first stating his motif, then adding variations, shifts, repetitions, pauses, leaps, intervals, changes of tempo, accents, chords, rise and fall, with changes of mood from major to minor."[15] Kōrin's color orchestration and his superb eye for the decorative are apparent even in a reproduction, which by its very nature cannot completely capture the vibrant original (see Figure 14.5).

**FIGURE 14.4** *Thousand Cranes*. Section of a hand-scroll. Painting by Tawaraya Sōtatsu, calligraphy by Hon'ami Kōetsu. Gold and silver underpainting on paper, 11.2 feet × 47.9 feet. (© Kyoto National Museum.)

# Genroku Urban Culture

The achievements of aristocratic culture demand recognition, but it was the commoner culture of the cities that stood out as the period's most vital and fascinating development. Urban culture reached a high point during the Genroku Era, technically the era name for the sixteen years from 1688 to 1704 but more broadly used for the cultural life of the fifty-year period beginning in the last quarter of the seventeenth century, when some of Japan's most creative artists were at work. These include the playwright Chikamatsu (1653–1724); the short story writer Saikaku (1642–1693); Moronobu (1618–1694), generally credited with developing the Japanese print; and Matsuo Bashō (1644–1694), master of the haiku.

Most large cities have "pleasure districts," parts of town devoted to bohemian life, erotic activities, entertainment, and gambling. Tokugawa cities were no exception. But rarely, if ever, have such quarters produced a first-rate aesthetic as they did in seventeenth-century Yoshiwara, the home of Edo's "floating world." Here, and in similar quarters in the other large towns, was a world that savored sophisticated stylishness in dress, coiffure, perfume, gesture, and life itself. The tone was set by the

**FIGURE 14.5** *Irises,* from a scene of the *Tales of Ise,* Ogata Korin. One of a pair of sixfold screens. Color on gold foil over paper, 11.8 feet × 5 feet. (© Sakamoto Photo Research Laboratory/Corbis.)

worldly flair of the man-about-town and the elegance of the spirited courtesans who presided over this world and who looked down with disdain on the country boor.

## The Print

Courtesans and actors were favorite subjects of the *ukiyo-e,* "pictures of the floating world," woodcut prints preceded by *ukiyo-e* paintings and by illustrations for books such as the *Yoshiwara Pillow* (1660), a combination sex manual and "courtesan critique." To produce the prints, portraits of courtesans, theater scenes, nature subjects, or scenes from urban life were carved into wood blocks. These were then inked and printed on paper. The process was highly experimental until Hishikawa Moronobu consolidated the early efforts.

At the beginning the prints were in black and white, but soon color was added, first by hand, then by developing techniques for printing red and green. By the eighteenth century, three- or four-color prints were produced. A versatile master and major contributor to the development of the print was Okumura Masanobu (c. 1686–1764), who, in Figure 14.6, shows an eighteenth-century beauty, dressed in a characteristically sumptuous kimono, gracefully at play.

Masanobu, a master of a variety of styles, influenced other artists, including the creator of the handcolored print shown in Figure 14.7, which conveys a wealth of information about the material culture. Depicting the interior of a house in Yoshiwara, the composition experiments with the receding perspective of European painting.

Masanobu was a publisher and an artist, but usually these functions were carried out by different people. Numerous people had a hand in creating a print. The publisher not only distributed and sold the prints but also commissioned them from the artist with more or less explicit instructions on subject and style. The artist drew the picture and designed the print but then turned it over to the engraver and the printer.

The craftsmanship of these men helped determine the quality of a print, but the artist contributed the essential vision.

## Theater and Literature

An unceasing source of inspiration for the print artist was the kabuki theater, whose celebrated actors enjoyed as much acclaim and attracted as avid a following as did the most elegant of Yoshiwara courtesans. Kabuki originated in the dances and skits performed in Kyoto early in the seventeenth century by a troupe of female performers. But this women's kabuki lasted only until 1629, when it was banned by the *bakufu* to put an end to the outbursts of violence that erupted as rivals competed for the favors of these ladies. For the next two decades young men's kabuki flourished, until it ran into similar difficulties and was prohibited in 1652. After that, all actors were mature men. Even then, kabuki continued to be under restrictions, tolerated but licensed and controlled because, like other indecorous pleasures, it could not be suppressed.

Kabuki's spectacular scenery, gorgeous costumes, and scenes of violent passion enchanted audiences. It was an actor's art, dominated by dynasties of actors who felt free to take liberties with the texts of plays. The audience greeted the virtuoso performances of the stars with shouts of approval. Particularly esteemed was the artistry of the men who played the female roles. These

**FIGURE 14.6** *Courtesan Striking a Shuttlecock with a Battledore*, Okumura Masanobu (1710s). Poetic verses written in calligraphic script decorate the courtesan's kimono. Woodblock print, ink on paper, 12.7 in × 25.7 in. (© Allen Memorial Art Museum, Oberlin College, Ohio. Mary A. Ainsworth bequest [1950.202].)

masters devoted their lives to achieving stylizations of posture, gesture, and voice, conveying the quintessence of femininity, always operating in that "slender margin between the real and unreal"[16] that Chikamatsu, sometimes called Japan's Shakespeare, defined as the true province of art.

**FIGURE 14.7** *A Tea House in the Yoshiwara, with a Game of Backgammon.* Attributed to Torii Kiyotada (fl. c. 1720–1750). The image shows such standard features of Japanese interior architecture as rooms separated by sliding partitions, the *tatami* floor, and the sense of spaciousness created by the virtual absence of furniture. Color woodcut, 25.2 in × 17 in. (© Fine Arts Museums of San Francisco, Achenbach Foundation for Graphic Arts Purchase [A057901 1970.25.14].)

Chikamatsu wrote for the kabuki stage but preferred the puppet theater (*bunraku*), where his lines were not at the mercy of the actors. In *bunraku*, large wooden puppets, each manipulated by a three-man team, enacted a story told by a group of chanters accompanied by three-stringed samisen. This theater became so popular that live actors came to imitate the movements of the puppets. Even after kabuki carried the day in Edo, *bunraku* continued to flourish in Osaka. The puppets, like the masks employed in Nō, assured that the action on stage would not be a mere mirror of ordinary life but would be more stylized and symbolic. It also made possible scenes of violence and fantastic stage business that, impossible for live actors, pose no problems for figures that do not bleed and are not bound by the usual limits of human physiology. Chikamatsu frequently used spectacular elements in his plays on historical subjects, such as *The Battle of Coxinga,* his most famous work in this genre.

Chikamatsu also wrote more subtle domestic plays. These center on conflicts between moral obligation (*giri*) and human emotion (*ninjō*). Feeling usually wins out over duty, but at a heavy price. One play, for example, tells of the tragic love of a shopkeeper and a lovely courtesan whom he cannot ransom from her house for lack of funds. Frequently, the poetic high point of the play is the lovers' flight to death. Often, the women exhibit greater strength of character than the men, but both are turned into romantic heroes through the purity and intensity of their emotions. Art imitates life, but life also imitates art: the plays produced such a rash of love suicides that the *bakufu* finally banned all plays with the words "love suicide" in the title.

Ihara Saikaku loved to write about love in his stories and books. Sometimes he wrote about samurai, but his best works deal with recognizable city types: the miser and money-grubber, the playboy who squanders his patrimony, the young beauty mismatched to an elderly husband, men and women in love with love. Exuberant and witty, he mixed humor and sex and wrote with a robust directness. He was also a prolific composer of *haikai*, light verse that grew out of *renga*, linked verse in which one poet started off, leaving it up to friends to continue.

Enlivened by infusions of everyday speech and humor, *haikai* turned its back on aristocratic refinement, as seen in this famous pair of links in a sixteenth-century anthology:

> Bitter, bitter it was
> And yet somehow funny.
> Even when
> My father lay dying
> I went on farting.[17]

Vulgar as it is, the second verse contrasts sharply with the first, as required in this poetic form. The popularity of *haikai* is attested by several seventeenth-century anthologies, one containing verses by more than 650 contributors.

Classical poems (*tanka*) and *renga* often began with seventeen syllables arranged in three lines (five/seven/five), which, when standing alone, form a *haiku*. The greatest haiku master was Matsuo Bashō, who was born a samurai but gave up his rank to live the life of a commoner, earning his living as a master poet with pupils from all strata of society.

Not every seventeen-syllable poem is a true haiku, because the real measure of a haiku lies not in its formal structure or surface meaning but in its resonance, not in what it says but in what is left unsaid. It presents the reader with a series of images, which, when connected in the imagination, yield a wealth of associations, visions, and emotions. Consider, for example, Bashō's best-known haiku:

> An old pond
> Frog jumps in
> Sound of water.

The inner spring of the poem is the juxtaposition of two contrasting natural elements, a juxtaposition that (like the frog in the water) sets off waves in the reader's mind. The old pond supplies the setting, but implies a condition of ancient stillness that contrasts with the sudden action and results in a delightful image. It raises the question, "How does one explain the relationship between the pond, which has been there for centuries, and a tiny splash that disappears in a moment?" This question was raised by Professor Makoto Ueda, who commented, "Different

**FIGURE 14.8** *Portrait of the poet Bashō,* Yokoi Kinkoku (1761–1832). Matsuo Bashō, the greatest haiku master, composed some of his finest poems on his travels and appears here ready for his next trip with his traveling hat. Ink and color on paper, hanging scroll, 7.2 in × 8.5 in. (© University of Michigan Museum of Art. Museum purchase, gift of the Margaret Watson Parker Art Collection [1968/2.22].)

people will give different answers, though they will all experience the same sort of 'loneliness' when they try to give an explanation. It seems that Bashō was more concerned with the loneliness than with the answer."[18] Some of his finest poems were composed on his travels and are contained in his *The Narrow Road of Oku.* One reads as follows:

At Yoshino
I'll show you
cherry blossoms
Cypress umbrella.[19]

He wrote the poem on his umbrella, and there is a gentle whimsy in Bashō's idea of sharing the beauty of the cherry blossoms with his umbrella. The word translated "umbrella" can also mean "hat." Figure 14.8 is a portrait of Bashō dressed for travel with this haiku inscribed on it.

This painting is an example of the genre known as *haiga* in which a *haiku* and a painting (*ga*) are integrated. It is by Yokoi Kinkoku (1761–1832), in the general manner of Yosa Buson (1716–1783), the most eminent artist in the literati mode. Like Chinese gentleman painters, the creators of Japanese "literati painting" (*bunjinga*, Chinese *wenrenhua*) cultivated calligraphy and poetry as means of self-expression. They looked to China for inspiration but did not limit themselves to Chinese subjects in their art.

# Intellectual Currents: Confucianism

Tokugawa Confucians were deeply influenced by developments in China, but their writings also reflect the vast differences between the two countries. In Japan there was no civil service examination system to reward mastery of Confucian texts.

Most Confucian scholars came from lower samurai or commoner ranks and made their living as teachers or doctors. One attraction of Confucianism to such men was its advocacy of government by the meritorious rather than the well-born. At the same time, even the Sinophiles among them took pride in Japan. Some argued that Japan came closer to Confucian ideals than Qing China, and others played an ingenious "game of one-upmanship."[20]

The beginnings of Tokugawa Confucianism are usually traced back to Fujiwara Seika (1561–1619), an aristocrat who did not find it beneath his dignity to write a letter for a Kyoto merchant sending a trade mission to Vietnam. He drew up a ship's oath, which began: "Commerce is the business of selling and buying in order to bring profit to both parties." He defined profit as "the outcome of righteousness" and admonished merchants not to be greedy.[21]

In Japan, as in China and Korea, Confucian teachings found a home in academies. Edo's premier Confucian academy was founded by Hayashi Razan (1583–1657) under *bakufu* patronage, but Edo did not dominate Tokugawa thought. The fragmentation of political authority made for intellectual diversity.

An outstanding early exponent of Song Confucianism was Yamazaki Ansai (1618–1682), a stern and forceful teacher who stressed "devotion within, righteousness without" and was so dedicated to Zhu Xi that he said he would follow the master even into error. When asked the hypothetical question, What should be done if Confucius and Mencius were to lead a Chinese invasion of Japan? he answered that he would capture the two sages and put them at the service of his own land. Deeply versed in Shinto, Ansai attempted to fuse Confucian ethics with Shinto religion. Most Confucians justified the shogunate by incorporating it into the hierarchy of loyalty, but Ansai's contemporary Muro Kyūso (1658–1734) argued that the Tokugawa ruled because of a heavenly mandate.

Muro Kyūso found it necessary to defend the thoughts of Zhu Xi against increasingly vigorous challenges from other schools. The man considered to be the founder of the rival Wang Yangming school in Japan was Nakae Tōjū (1608–1648). Like the Chinese philosopher, he stressed the inner light and insisted on the importance of action. His lofty and unselfish character attracted the admiration of his contemporaries and of later activist intellectuals. His best-known disciple, Kumazawa Banzan (1619–1691), ran into political trouble, not because of his philosophical ideas but because of such policy recommendations as relaxing the daimyo's attendance requirements to save expenses. His deep concern for the wellbeing of the peasantry went hand in hand with lack of sympathy for the merchant class, as reflected in his advocacy of a return to a barter economy using rice in place of money.

Like Yamazaki Ansai and Kumazawa Banzan, Kaibara Ekken (1630–1714) found much of value in Shinto, but his philosophy of nature was based on *qi*. The writings of this remarkable man range from botany to ethics, from farming to philology, and include precepts for daily life and a primer for women. They express his breadth of mind, commitment to the welfare of society, and faith in the unity and value of knowledge.

In Japan, as in China, there were men who denied the authority of Song thinkers and insisted on going back to the foundation texts. This was the stance of Yamaga Sokō, the formulator of *bushidō,* and of Itō Jinsai (1627–1705), who drew inspiration from the *Analects:* "The *Analects* is like the boundless universe which men live in without comprehending its full magnitude. Enduring and immutable throughout the ages, in every part of the world it serves as an infallible guide. Is it not, indeed, great!"[22] Jinsai rejected the distinction between *li* (principle) and *qi* and stressed self-cultivation with an emphasis on *ren* (humaneness).

Another opponent of Song philosophy was Ogyū Sorai (1666–1728), who insisted on going back even earlier than the *Analects* to the classics and has been described by Kate Nakai as effecting an intellectual "sea-change." Rejecting the unity of the inner human realm and the outer world of heaven and earth, "Sorai challenged the notion that through the practice of *li* [rites and propriety] the individual realized an innate capacity for alignment with a natural order."[23] A complex, many-sided thinker and prolific writer, he emphasized rites and institutions all the more and wrote on many topics: philosophy and politics; literature, linguistics, and music; military science; and economics.

A younger contemporary of Sorai, Goi Ranshū (1697–1762), head of the Kaitokudo Academy, did not believe that the ancients had exhausted all knowledge and even envisioned intellectual progress. A member of the next generation who studied at the academy was Tominaga Nakamoto (1715–1746), a skeptic who argued that all historical texts were unreliable. In the work of these and others were the roots for ideas that exceeded the confines of the Tokugawa order and, indeed, the normal bounds of Confucian thought. But Confucian thought, too, could take men's minds in unanticipated directions.

## Historiography and Nativism

A perennial field of Confucian scholarship was the study of history. Hayashi Razan began work on a history of Japan that was completed by his son and accepted as the official history of the shogunate. Another major contributor to scholarship was the statesman and scholar Arai Hakuseki (1657–1725), noted for his careful attention to evidence and willingness to reexamine traditional beliefs.

A different emphasis appeared in *The Great History of Japan (Dainihonshi),* begun in the seventeenth century and sponsored by Mito, a Tokugawa collateral house. Begun under the lord of Mito, Tokugawa Mitsukuni (1628–1700), it was not completed until the twentieth century. Mitsukuni, a grandson of Ieyasu, enlisted the services of a Chinese émigré and Ming loyalist, Zhu Shunshui (1600–1682). The resulting history was highly moralistic and exalted the Japanese imperial house. Because the shogun derived his legitimacy from the emperor, there was nothing inherently anti-*bakufu* in this, but its focus on the emperor rather than on the shogun was potentially subversive. Indeed, it later became an emperor-centered source for nationalistic sentiments and eventually supplied intellectual ammunition for the anti-*bakufu* movement to "restore the emperor," which culminated in the Meiji Restoration of 1868.

Interest in Japan's past often went hand in hand with a new appreciation of native traditions. Ansai had advocated both Confucianism and Shinto, but Kada Azumamaro (1669–1736) urged a return to a Shinto purified of Confucian elements. Rejection of Confucianism and celebration of the native tradition became a defining theme in the nativist thought of the National Learning (*kokugtaku*) scholars.

Frequently, this was linked to a championship of Japanese literature and aesthetics. Thus Tokugawa Mitsukuni commissioned the Shingon priest Keichū (1640–1701), a great philologist, to write a commentary on the Man'yōshū, the oldest anthology of Japanese poetry. Motoori Norinaga (1730–1801), a gifted philologist, enjoyed wide influence as a teacher, political adviser, and champion of a supposedly pure Shinto found in antiquity and as yet uncorrupted by Buddhist and Confucian influences. Admitting that there was much that was immoral in the *Tale of Genji,* he wrote the following:

> Genji's conduct is like the lotus flower that grows in muddy water yet blooms with a beauty and fragrance unlike any other in the world. Nothing is said about the water's filth; the monogatari [that is, the *Tale*] concentrates instead on Genji's deep compassion and his awareness of what it means to be moved by things and holds him up as the model of a good man.[24]

Motoori's views on *Genji* remain influential, but his life's work was the study of the *Kojiki,* (see Chapter 6). He thought it wrong to try to understand its accounts of the *kami* rationally and arrogant not to recognize the limitations of the human intellect. Indeed, the irrationality of the old legends was a sign of their truth, because "who would fabricate such shallow sounding, incredible things?"[25] Supreme among the *kami* was the Sun Goddess, and although she spread her favor everywhere, foremost among the countries of the world was the land of her birth. Motoori left a dual heritage: academic philology and ideological nativism. Of those who drew on the latter aspect of his thought, the most influential was Hirata Atsutane (1776–1843), whose narrow Japanism proved attractive to many nineteenth- and twentieth-century ultranationalists.

## Dutch Learning

Because the Dutch were the only Westerners allowed even limited access to Japan (see Chapter 13), it is from them that the Japanese got their information about the West. Their annual audience with the shogun allowed the Japanese to satisfy their curiosity about the exotic:

> He [the shogun, mistaken for the emperor by the Dutch chronicle] order'd us to take off our Cappa, or Cloak, being our Garment of Ceremony, then to stand upright, that he might have a full view of us; again to walk, to stand still, to compliment each other, to dance, to jump, to play the drunkard, to speak broken Japanese, to read Dutch,

to paint, to sing, to put our cloaks on and off. . . . I join'd to my dance a lovesong in High German. In this manner, and with innumerable such other apish tricks, we must suffer ourselves to contribute to the Emperor's and Court's diversion.[26]

This is from a report of the embassy of 1691 or 1692. "The red-haired barbarians," as the Dutch were commonly known, continued to be the objects of wild rumor. But they also drew the attention of serious scholars after 1720, when the *bakufu* permitted the import of books on all subjects except Christianity. These scholars wrestled with the difficulties of the Dutch language, laboriously made translations, compiled the first dictionaries, and wrote treatises on geography, astronomy, medicine, and other Western subjects. Shiba Kōkan (1738–1818), the first in Japan to produce copper engravings, was fascinated by the ability of Western art to portray objects as they appear to the eye. Arai Hakuseki had earlier recognized the practical value of Western studies, and this, too, is what Shiba valued. For spiritual nourishment, such men continued to turn to their own heritage, thus foreshadowing the nineteenth-century formula "Eastern ethics–Western science." Because of *bakufu* policy, they knew little about Western political, philosophical, or religious thought.

By the end of the eighteenth century, there were also scholars of Dutch Learning who, alarmed by Western expansionism, discussed political, military, and economic matters at considerable personal risk. Hayashi Shihei (1738–1793) was arrested for defying a *bakufu* prohibition by publishing a book dealing with political issues: he advocated defense preparations against the threat he saw impending from abroad. Honda Toshiaki (1744–1821), who wanted to turn Japan into the England of the East, complete with mercantile empire, escaped persecution by not publishing his ideas.

Implicit in the views of the scholars of Dutch Learning was dissatisfaction with the Tokugawa seclusion policy, which stood in the way of their learning more about Western civilization and prevented them from traveling overseas. Meanwhile, by stressing the royal line, Mito Confucians and National Learning scholars helped weaken the *bakufu* ideologically. And even orthodox Confucianism did not really require a shogun or a *bakufu*. Thus, by 1800 there were fissures in the Tokugawa's intellectual, as well as in its political and economic, foundations.

## Reform and Its Limits

The underlying discrepancy between official theory and socioeconomic reality was brought home to the *bakufu* in a series of financial crises, some aggravated by poor harvests resulting from natural causes. Major famines during 1732 to 1733 and again after 1783 brought death and starvation, as well as rural uprisings and urban riots, highlighting the government's ineptness.

Repeatedly, revenue failed to keep up with government needs. Retrenchment was one standard response. Often, as in the Kyōhō Reforms (1716–1736), a spending cut was seen as morally desirable and as fiscally necessary. Calls for reduction in government spending were accompanied by admonitions for samurai to revive warrior morality and detailed laws to limit merchant expenditure. More effective was the granting of merchant monopolies in exchange for an annual fee. To make it easier to fill high offices with capable men of low inherited rank, the practice of granting such men permanent high hereditary rank was abandoned in favor of raising their rank and stipends only during their tenure of office.

Among the sources of needed revenue were special payments imposed on the *daimyo*, programs of land reclamation, and campaigns to squeeze more taxes out of the peasantry, but in the long run these yielded diminishing returns. The same can be said of the *bakufu*'s attempts to set prices of essential commodities. Some initially successful measures backfired, such as when monetary deflation quelled a destructive inflation only to bring on a deflation so severe that it provoked urban riots in 1733.

Later in the century, the *bakufu* made some additions to its reform repertoire— such as when, under the leadership of Tanuma Okitsugu (1719–1788), it encouraged foreign trade, tried to develop mines, created new monopolies, imposed new merchant licenses, and showed interest in developing Hokkaido. Tanuma, however, was resented for favoring the *bakufu* vis-à-vis the *han*, and his enemies emphasized his corruption. In 1787, food shortages caused by crop failures the previous year led to uprisings throughout Japan and violent rioting in Edo. Tanuma died in disgrace. Whether the *bakufu* was capable of leading the country in new directions remained a question for the future.

# Art and Literature after the Genroku Period

Genroku was the classic age of popular theater, prints, fiction, and haiku, but artists and writers continued to work in these genres and create works that are often considered to mark another highpoint in cultural history. Notable among the later *ukiyo-e* artists was Tōshūsai Sharaku, famous for the psychologically penetrating and bitterly satiric prints of actors he turned out during a ten-month outburst of creativity in 1794. More in keeping with the spirit of the time was Suzuki Harunobu (1724–1770), who excelled in the subtle use of color and the freshness of his young beauties. Controversial and uneven was the prolific Kitagawa Utamaro (1754–1806), who achieved great popularity with his prints of the ladies of the "floating world" (see Figure 14.9).

Toward the end of the eighteenth century, there was a falling off in the quality of the figure print, but, as if in compensation, the landscape print flourished. A master of this art was the "old man mad with painting," Katsushika Hokusai (1760–1849), an eclectic genius. He is represented here by one of his depictions of

**FIGURE 14.9** *A Flirt,* from the series *Ten Studies in Female Physiognomy,* Kitagawa Utamaro. Woodblock print, ink, color, and mica on paper, 9.9 in × 14.9 in. (© Mr. and Mrs. John D. Rockefeller, third collection of Asian Art 1979.219. Asia Society, New York: Photograph by Lynton Gardiner.)

Mount Fuji (see Figure 14.10). Less versatile, but at his best producing works imbued with a delicate lyricism, was Andō Hiroshige (1797–1858), who lived to see Commodore Matthew C. Perry of the United States Navy arrive in Japan in 1853.

Various genres of literature, energized by "a complex fusion of Japanese and Chinese cultures, and by a mixture of popular and elite culture"[27] continued to flourish and delight, as did the haiku, that most Japanese of poetic forms. Perhaps the best loved of the later haiku poets, Kobayashi Yatarō (1763–1827), better

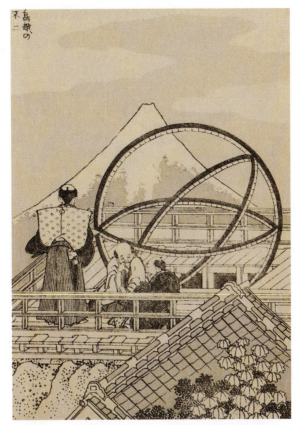

**FIGURE 14.10** "Fuji at Torigoe" from *Fugaku Hyokkei,* Katsushika Hokusai. The instrument shown here is an orrery, a mechanical model of the solar system. (© Spencer Collection [SOR579: Hokusai], New York Public Library, Astor, Lenox, and Tilden Foundations.)

known by his pen name Issa (cup of tea). He achieved wide identification with nature and showed sympathy for even the humblest animals and insects.

> Lean frog,
> don't give up the fight!
> Issa is here![28]

# *Notes*

1. Lee Butler, *Emperor and Aristocracy in Japan 1467–1680: Resilience and Renewal* (Cambridge: Harvard Univ. Asia Center, 2002), p. 287.

2. Ryusaku Tsunoda, Wm. Theodore de Bary, and Donald Keene, comps., *Sources of Japanese Tradition* (New York: Columbia Univ. Press, 1958), p. 316.

3. David John Lu, *Sources of Japanese History, Vol. 1* (New York: McGraw-Hill, 1974), p. 189. Translated from Okubo Toshiaki et al., eds., *Shiryo ni yoru Nihon no Ayumi: Kinseihen (Japanese History Through Documents: Early Modern Period)* (Tokyo: Toshikawa Kobunkan, 1955), pp. 40–41.

4. Jurgis Elisonas, "The Inseparable Trinity: Japan's Relation with China and Korea," in John W. Hall, ed., *The Cambridge History of Japan, Vol. 4: Early Modern Japan* (New York: Cambridge Univ. Press, 1991), p. 271.

5. George Sansom, *A History of Japan, 1334–1615* (Stanford: Stanford Univ. Press, 1961), p. 380.

6. George Sansom, *Japan: A Short Cultural History* (New York: Appleton-Century-Crofts, 1931), p. 437.

7. Carolyn Wheelwright, "A Visualization of Eitoku's Lost Paintings at Azuchi Castle," in George Elison and Bardwell L. Smith, eds., *Warlords, Artists, and Commoners: Japan in the Sixteenth Century* (Honolulu: Univ. of Hawaii Press, 1981), p. 99.

8. Langdon Warner, *The Enduring Art of Japan* (Cambridge: Harvard Univ. Press, 1958), p. 95.

9. Butler, *Emperor and Aristocracy in Japan 1467–1680,* p. 264.

10. Harold Bolitho, *Treasures among Men: The Fudai Daimyo in Tokugawa Japan* (New Haven: Yale Univ. Press, 1974), p. 17.

11. Conrad Totman, *Early Modern Japan* (Berkeley: Univ. of California Press, 1993), p. 229.

12. Eiko Ikegami, *The Taming of the Samurai: Honorific Individualism and the Making of Modern Japan* (Cambridge: Harvard Univ. Press, 1995), p. 116.

13. Ronald P. Dore, *Education in Tokugawa Japan* (Berkeley: Univ. of California Press, 1965), p. 151.

14. Robert Treat Paine and Alexander Soper, *The Art and Architecture of Japan* (Baltimore: Penguin Books, 1955), p. 274.

15. Elise Grilli, *The Art of the Japanese Screen* (Tokyo and New York: John Weatherhill, 1970), pp. 111–12.

16. Attributed to Chikamatsu by his friend Hozumi Ikan. Hozumi's account of Chikamatsu's views has been translated by Donald Keene as "Chikamatsu on the Art of The Puppet Stage," in Donald Keene, ed., *Anthology of Japanese Literature* (New York: Grove Press, 1955), p. 389.

17. Tsunoda, de Bary, and Keene, *Sources of Japanese Tradition*, p. 454.

18. Makoto Ueda, *Matsuo Basho* (New York: Twayne, 1970), p. 53.

19. Calvin French, *The Poet-Painters: Buson and His Followers*, exhibition catalog (Ann Arbor: Univ. of Michigan Museum of Art, 1974), p. 132.

20. Kate Wildman Nakai, "The Naturalization of Confucianism in Tokugawa Japan: The Problem of Sinocentrism," *Harvard Journal of Asiatic Studies* 40 (1980): 157–99.

21. Tsunoda, de Bary, and Keene, *Sources of Japanese Tradition*, p. 349.

22. Tsunoda, de Bary, and Keene, *Sources of Japanese Tradition*, p. 419.

23. Kate Wildman Nakai, "Chinese Ritual and Japanese Identity in Tokugawa Confucianism," in Benjamin A. Elman, John B. Duncan, and Herman Ooms, eds., *Rethinking Confucianism: Past and Present in China, Japan, Korea, and Vietnam* (Los Angeles: UCLA Asian Pacific Monograph Series, Univ. of California, 2002), p. 272.

24. Haruo Shirane, ed., *Early Modern Japanese Literature: An Anthology, 1600–1900,* trans. Thomas Harper (New York: Columbia Univ. Press, 2002), pp. 624–25.

25. Shirane, *Early Modern Japanese Literature*, p. 524.

26. Engelbert Kaempfer, quoted in Donald Keene, *The Japanese Discovery of Europe* (Stanford: Stanford Univ. Press, 1969), p. 4.

27. Ryusaku Tsunoda, Wm. Theodore de Bary, and Donald Keene, comps., *Sources of Japanese Tradition* (New York: Columbia Univ. Press, 1958), p. 524.

28. Harold G. Henderson, *An Introduction to Haiku* (New York: Doubleday, 1958), p. 133.

# 15

# The Qing Dynasty

| c. 1600 | 1644 | | | |
|---|---|---|---|---|
| **Rise of Manchu Power** | | QING DY | | |
| Later Jin (1616–1636) | Kangxi (1662–1722) | Qianlong (1736–1795) | | Opium War (1839–1842) |

In this chapter we will consider the Qing Dynasty (1644–1911) to around 1800. This was a century and a half of major achievements: the state reached its greatest geographical extent (Figure 15.1); the economy grew, as did the population; scholars and artists were productive; and popular culture flourished. In terms of cultural and political sophistication and the dynamics of economic development, China was comparable to the most advanced societies on earth, including Europe, whose "great divergence"[1] into sustained industrial growth was still to come. But by 1800 the Qing had seen its best days, even if no one could yet imagine that it was to be China's last dynasty.

The establishment of the new dynasty was a momentous event, but by no means did it represent a radical break with the past. Social and cultural transformations tend to be more gradual than political change, and, given the limitations of seventeenth-century communication and transportation technology, the new rulers could not have refashioned China had they wanted to. In recognition of the considerable continuity between the Qing and its Ming predecessor (1368–1644), scholars interested in the long view frequently include both under the rubric "late imperial" China.

## The Founding of the Qing

As we have seen, a major theme in Chinese history is the interaction between the Chinese and their nomadic and seminomadic neighbors whose way of life made them formidable horsemen and fierce warriors. One military alternative was the kind of static defense that induced the Ming dynasty to rebuild The Great Wall into the impressive structure it is today. In the northeast, the Ming relied on the Willow Palisades, a barrier formed by lines of willows and a deep trench fortified by military checkpoints.

**FIGURE 15.1** The Qing Empire, 1775. 🌐

Beyond the Willow Palisades lay Manchuria, home of the Jurchen, who spoke a language related to Korean but not to Chinese. Although the Jurchen traced themselves back to the Jin Dynasty (1115–1234) that had once dominated north China, they had long been divided into tribes. In the north they subsisted by hunting and fishing, but in the south, where they were in contact with Chinese speakers, they farmed, raised livestock, and took pleasure and pride in their horsemanship and hunting skills. The ethnic origins of the inhabitants of the agricultural lands of Liaodong and southern Manchuria were diverse. They were not necessarily descended from Chinese settlers, but they spoke Chinese and by and large were Chinese culturally. There was also a major Mongolian presence in Manchuria, and the Mongol influence on the Jurchen was strong.

To bring the various peoples of Manchuria into a state and create a regional power took Nurgaci (1559–1626), clan and tribal chief, more than twenty-five years as he fought, negotiated, and married his way to leadership and power. To facilitate building of the state, he ordered the creation of a script, based on Mongolian, to write the Jurchen language. Originally favored by the Ming, Nurgaci continued to send tribute to Beijing until 1609, but in 1616, he declared himself Emperor of the Later Jin. In 1625, Nurgaci established his capital at Shengyuan but died the following year. It was his son, Hong Taiji (r. 1626–1643), who created a new ethnic identity called "Manchu" and envisioned a broader empire. Defeated by Ming cannon in a battle in 1626, the Manchus made good use of Chinese artillery experts they captured in a 1629 invasion of North China that came close to Beijing. As a result, two years later Manchu forces were able to employ the new weapons effectively. At the same time Hong followed a policy of centralization of power and the use of Chinese officials to build a state capable of conquering and ruling Ming China.

In 1636, while remaining "divine khan" to his tribal subjects, Hong Taiji signaled his ambition to rule China by founding the new "Qing" (pure) dynasty. Nothing in the Chinese tradition stipulated that the imperial house had to be ethnically Chinese. From the beginning, the new dynasty drew support from an alliance with Mongols and Chinese speakers, mostly from Manchuria. This was reflected in the organization of its armies into "banners," each with its own colors. By the time of the conquest, there were eight Manchu banners (278 companies), eight Mongol banners (120 companies), and eight "Chinese" banners (165 companies). Membership in the banners was hereditary. After the conquest, they were stationed in garrisons strategically located throughout the empire. There the bannermen lived apart from the local population under a general who reported directly to Beijing.

After Li Zicheng overthrew the Ming, the key to the military situation was in the hands of the Ming general Wu Sangui (1612–1678), whose army guarded Shanhaiguan, the strategic pass between the mountains and the sea that formed the eastern terminus of the Great Wall. When Wu threw his lot in with the Manchus, Li Zicheng's fate was sealed.

After the Manchus entered the capital, Beijing, in June 1644, the Qing ruler announced he had come to punish the rebels, buried the deceased Ming emperor and empress with full honors, and claimed to be the legitimate successor of the old dynasty. To consolidate and expand their control, the new rulers needed the support and participation of Chinese officials and the tacit assent of the Chinese populace. Even before they gained the capital, the dynasty sought to draw on the talents of Chinese scholars and reassure the Chinese elite by holding its first examinations.

Also before the conquest they formed a political system that balanced an Assembly of Princes and High Officials composed almost exclusively of Manchus with traditional Chinese institutions such as The Six Ministries (personnel, revenue, rites, war, justice, and public works), and the Censorate, charged with reporting on the conduct of the civil service with the right and duty also to criticize the emperor.

Despite such reassuring measures, the subjugation of the rest of China, especially the South, involved long and bloody warfare, including a terrible ten-day massacre in Yangzhou that left the city's gutters filled with corpses. After the capture of Nanjing, which Ming loyalists had made their capital, the Qing emperor forced all men to shave the forward portion of their heads and braid their hair in back into a long queue (pigtail). The Manchus were not the first to force their hair style on their subjects; the Ming had done the same in Vietnam.

After the fall of Nanjing, the Qing still faced prolonged resistance. For some forty years warfare, banditry, and peasant uprisings, along with periods of starvation and epidemics, took a heavy toll. From 1646 to 1658 much of the southeast coast was controlled by Zheng Chenggong (1624–1662), the son of a Chinese pirate-adventurer and a Japanese mother, widely known as Coxinga. From 1661 to 1669, to deprive Zheng of support and supplies, a seventeen-mile strip along the coast, extending from Zhejiang to the Vietnamese border, was completely cleared of people. Barriers, guard posts, and watch towers were erected to prevent anyone from entering. Originally based in Xiamen (Amoy), Zheng moved to Taiwan (Formosa) from which he expelled the Dutch in 1662. His son held out against the Manchus, who finally subdued the island in 1683 and placed it under the administration of Fujian Province. By then the Southwest, too, was pacified, but only after the War of the Three Feudatories (1673–1681), one of whom was Wu Sangui, who had created a practically autonomous state for himself in Yunnan and Guizhou.

In their new empire, the Manchus, who comprised only about 2 percent of the population, and their Mongol associates formed a conquest elite who were conscious of their non-Chinese heritage, forbidden to intermarry with the Chinese, and distinguished from them in dress, family rituals, diet, and lifestyle. For example, Manchu women were not allowed to have bound feet. An inner circle of this elite dominated the inner court and exercised profound influence on government throughout the life of the dynasty.

Along with claiming to be heirs of the Ming and recipients of Heaven's Mandate, Qing emperors, as Manchus, concurrently asserted the claim to rule as khans. In addition, they demonstrated an ability to draw on Buddhist traditions to make their rule acceptable to people beyond the Great Wall. Ritual observances, the rulers solemnly acting like rulers, demonstrated that they were meant to be rulers. Potent symbolism was a major component of Qing authority and power.

China proper was divided into eighteen provinces, which were further subdivided into circuits, prefectures, and counties, but Inner Asian affairs were handled by the Court of Colonial Affairs using the peoples' own languages and appealing to their own political traditions. The emperors themselves regularly studied Mongolian, Manchu, and Chinese. Although the trend was toward increasing bureaucratization, Inner Asians saw themselves as subjects of a universal empire. But China was the Center.

## Early Qing Thinkers and Painters

Although many literati accepted service under the new dynasty, the most original work came from the brushes of men who refused to serve the Qing. Among those who in these turbulent times found tranquility in a Buddhist monastery was Hongren (1610–1663; see Figure 15.2), who "represented the world in a dematerialized cleansed vision . . . revealing his personal peace through the liberating form of geometric abstraction."[2]

Although Hongren had his followers, other painters who lived through the change of dynasties were too individualistic to attract followers or perpetuate styles. One such was Zhu Da, also called Bada Shanren (c. 1626–1705), whose personal behavior was distinctly odd: he sang and laughed frequently but refused to speak. His painting was equally unusual: surging landscapes, huge lotuses, and birds and fishes with the eyes of a Zen patriarch. His hand-scroll *Fish and Rocks* (see Figure 15.3) begins with a section (not shown here) done with a dry brush, and the brushwork becomes wetter as the painting proceeds. Although there are references to the Ming dynasty and himself in the poems on and in the painting, the work remains enigmatic. Zhu Da had to wait several centuries for his fame, but he exemplifies the self-expression favored by the aesthetic theory of his time, which regarded representation as crude and unworthy of gentlemen amateurs even if the distinction between amateur and professional was one more of theory than of practice.

Like Zhu Da in the world of painting, Wang Fuzhi (1619–1704) had no followers in his own time, but late in the dynasty came to be admired as a philosopher who gave primacy to *qi* and as a student of history who emphasized the fact that institutions and policies of one age or culture were not necessarily applicable to another. Another Ming loyalist with trenchant political views that had to wait for centuries for a hearing was Huang Zongxi (1610–1695), who complained that in antiquity the people had been the master, the prince the tenant, but that now the situation was reversed. "Thus he who does the greatest harm in the world is none other than the prince."[3] Among the policies advocated by Huang was restoring pre-Ming strong chief ministership, institut-

**FIGURE 15.2** Hongren's masterpiece, *The Coming of Autumn*, displays a marvelous sense of structural depth. Hanging scroll, ink on paper, 48.19 in high. (© Honolulu Academy of Arts, Gift of Wilhelmina Tenney Memorial Collection, 1995 [No. 2045.1].)

ing tax and land reforms, increasing the authority of local officials, and strengthening education, including the creation of independent schools.

Huang's most influential work was a great compendium of Ming thought still widely used. The writings and teachings of Huang's contemporary, Gu Yanwu (1613–1682), made a deep impression on mainstream Qing scholarship. Objecting to the abstract speculations of Song and Ming philosophers, Gu insisted on what he considered real and practical learning, solidly based on scholarship in the original sources rather than on later commentaries. He himself wrote important studies on historical geography and inscriptions but is most famous for work in historical phonetics. His essays, collected under the title *Records of Daily*

**FIGURE 15.3** *Fish and Rocks*, Zhu Da (Bada Shanren, 1624–c. 1705), Qing Dynasty. Note the water plants and lotuses on the left and the strange rock that invites speculation. Section of hand-scroll, ink on paper, 62.01 in × 11.49 in. (© Cleveland Museum of Art, John L. Severence Fund [1953.247].)

*Knowledge* (*Rizhilu*), discuss government, the examination system, and economics as well as the classics and history and show a range and critical spirit representative of the best of seventeenth-century thought. As summarized by Kai-wing Chow, "His statecraft essays addressed a wide range of issues from political structure, excessive number of degree holders and problems of overcentralization, to taxation and monetary policy."[4] Gu was influential in founding Qing philological scholarship and what came to be known as "evidential learning." Subsequent Qing scholars contributed greatly to textual scholarship.

Not all painters of the early Qing were eccentric or even persistently loyal to the Ming. Outstanding among the more orthodox painters were four artists all named Wang, among whom Wang Hui (1632–1717) was the most gifted. One of his paintings is a rendition of Fan Kuan's *Traveling among Streams and Mountains* (see Figure 8.6). His *Summer Mountains, Misty Rain* (see Figure 15.4) is representative in that Wang here follows the style and composition of the masters of the Song and Yuan in "an almost magical composite" to create a painting very much his own. Wang himself formulated his agenda and expressed his aspiration: "I must use the brush and ink of the Yuan to move the peaks and valleys of the Song and infuse them with the breath-resonance of the Tang. I will then have a great synthesis."[5]

In 1691 Wang Hui received an imperial command to supervise the painting of a series of scrolls commemorating Kangxi's southern tour. He was only one of a number of painters and other men of talent to enjoy the patronage of Kangxi and in turn enhance the aura of the throne and the glory of its occupant.

# The Reign of Kangxi

Kangxi was on the throne from 1662 to 1722 and actually ruled from 1668 on. As already noted, he was able to complete the Manchu conquest of China and did so in campaigns fought largely by Chinese troops under Chinese generals. After the

**FIGURE 15.4** *Fishermen Returning Home,* third and last panel of *Summer Mountains, Misty Rain* (1668), Wang Hui (1632–1717). Hand-scroll, ink on paper, 19 in × 17 in. (© Asian Art Museum of San Francisco, Gift of the Tang Foundation. Presented by Nadine, Martin, and Leslie Tang in celebration of Jack C. C. Tang's sixtieth birthday [B87D8]. Used by permission.)

## TABLE 15.1 The Qing Emperors

Beginning with the Ming period emperors used a single era name (*nianhao,* literally "year designation") throughout their reigns. Consequently, the emperors are often referred to by their era names rather than by their formal posthumous temple names, although these are also employed in the scholarly literature.

| Era Name | Temple Name | Personal Name | Era Dates |
|----------|-------------|---------------|-----------|
| Shunzhi | Shizu | Fulin | 1644–1661 |
| Kangxi | Shengzu | Xuanye | 1662–1722 |
| Yongzheng | Shizong | Yinzhen | 1723–1735 |
| Qianlong | Gaozong | Hongli | 1736–1795 |
| Jiaqing | Renzong | Yongyan | 1796–1820 |
| Daoguang | Xuanzong | Minning | 1821–1850 |
| Xianfeng | Wenzong | Yizhu | 1851–1861 |
| Tongzhi | Muzong | Zaichun | 1862–1874 |
| Guangxu | Dezong | Zaitian | 1875–1908 |
| Xuanzong | None | Puyi | 1909–1911 |

incorporation of Taiwan, he allowed people to return to the southeastern coast and turned his military attention to China's borders in the North and West. In the Amur River region his army destroyed a Russian Cossack base. This success was followed by the Treaty of Nerchinsk, signed with Russia in 1689, which settled frontier problems between the two great expansive empires and regularized relations between them. It also removed the threat of a possible alliance between the Russians and a confederation of Western Mongols. Against the latter, Kangxi personally led his troops in 1696–1697 and won a great victory.

Around the middle of the seventeenth century, Western Mongols had intervened in the political-religious struggles taking place in Tibet and had remained as conquerors. In 1720 Kangxi's armies entered Tibet and installed a pro-Chinese Dalai Lama (the spiritual and secular ruler of Tibet). This was the first but not the last Qing intervention in Tibet.

Kangxi's martial exploits reflected his identification with his forebears and his desire to preserve a Manchu way of life, which he saw as essential for maintaining Manchu supremacy. Another expression of this feeling was his zest for great hunts. To help preserve Manchu distinctiveness, one of the first acts of Kangxi's reign was the closing of Manchuria to Chinese immigration. Kangxi was very much the Manchu, but he was by no means anti-Chinese. Kangxi maintained a strict balance between Manchus and Chinese in the top central administrative posts, and in the provinces, generally, a Chinese governor was counterbalanced by a governor-general, usually placed over two provinces, who was a Manchu, a Mongol, or a Chinese bannerman. Banner garrisons continued to be the main source of security. The emperor also used his Chinese bondservants, who managed the imperial household and the emperor's personal treasury. They also performed confidential tasks such as sending in secret reports on conditions in the provinces.

Kangxi was a vigorous man. He rose well before dawn each day to go through a great stack of memorials before receiving officials, beginning at 5 A.M. (later changed to 7 A.M. to accommodate officials not living near the palace). His personal tours of inspection in the south are famous. To show his benevolence, he reduced taxes and forced Manchu aristocrats to desist from seizing Chinese lands. He was also a man of wide intellectual interests, including, as we saw in Chapter 9, Western learning. He won the affection of many Chinese literati by holding a special examination in 1679 and not only patronized artists but also sponsored the compilation of the official Ming history, a great phrase dictionary, a giant encyclopedia, and an exhaustive dictionary of Chinese characters. He gave special support to the philosophy of Zhu Xi.

# Yongzheng

Kangxi was one of the most successful emperors in all of Chinese history, but he was unable to provide for a smooth succession. Although he had fifty-six children, only one son was by an empress. He was designated heir apparent but disappointed his father, who complained that he was "dissolute, tyrannical, brutal, debauched."[6] He also showed signs of mental instability, and in the end Kangxi placed him in confinement but failed to appoint a successor. The claim that fourteen years later he named his fourth son on his deathbed looks very much like a later fabrication. During these years, various sons, suspicious of each other and each backed by his own political faction, conspired and maneuvered for the succession. The result was that after Kangxi's death, the throne was seized in a military coup by the fourth son, who became Emperor Yongzheng (r. 1723–1735).

Yongzheng censored the record of his accession and also suppressed other writings deemed inimical to his regime or hostile to the Manchus. Like his father, he used military force to preserve the dynasty's position in Mongolia. When Tibet was torn by civil war from 1717 to 1728, he intervened militarily, leaving a Qing resident backed by a military garrison to pursue the dynasty's interests. After the dynasty came to an end in the twentieth century, this provided a basis for Chinese claims of sovereignty over Tibet.

Yongzheng was a tough, hard-working ruler bent on effective government. During the early Qing the emperor had been assisted by the Grand Secretariat, a six-man board composed of three Manchus and three Chinese, but under Kangxi the Grand Secretariat lost its influence. In a move toward greater efficiency and control, Yongzheng created a five-man Grand Council whose members linked the inner court with the outer bureaucracy, headed by the chiefs of the six ministries. By expanding the number of officials entitled to submit secret memorials and sending them confidential replies, he operated his own channel of communication apart from the general bureaucracy and managed local government activities in unprecedented detail.

The emperor saw the need for administrative and fiscal reform and restructured the financing of local government to free magistrates from dependence on private and informal funding. Active in tax reform, he simplified the system of tax registers by combining the land and personal service taxes. This and other measures, along with strong imperial oversight, led to increased government efficiency, although in the long run effective reform below the county level proved unattainable.

Yongzheng's reign was despotic, efficient, and vigorous. By the simple device of sealing the name of the heir-apparent in a box kept in the throne room, he was able to assure that on his death there would be no struggle over the succession. Thus, he prepared the way for what was to be the dynasty's most splendid reign, that of Qianlong.

# Qianlong

During Qianlong's reign (1736–1795), the Qing achieved its greatest prosperity. Expansion into Central Asia reached its greatest extent (see map, Figure 15.1). This was partly the result of Qing diplomatic skill in practicing "divide and rule" policies, their ability to work with local leaders and manipulate inner Asian symbols of authority, and the sheer power of their armies. The Qing also took advantage of the disunity and declining strength of the Inner Asian peoples. The weakening of these peoples has been subject to various interpretations. According to Morris Rossabi, the most plausible explanations include the diminishing importance of the international caravan trade in an age of developing maritime commerce, a trend toward the development of sedentary societies marked by urbanization, and Russian expansion that reduced the area to which tribes could flee in retreat, thereby reducing their mobility.[7]

Under Qianlong, Chinese Turkestan was incorporated and renamed Xinjiang. To the West, Ili was conquered and garrisoned. This brought into the empire Muslim leaders, including followers of the activist Naqshbandiyya order, difficult to convince as to the legitimacy of Qing rule. The Qing also dominated Outer Mongolia after finally defeating the Western Mongols. Its policy there was to preserve Mongol institutions, but it allowed Chinese merchants to enter and exploit the people, thus reinforcing the anti-Chinese animosities of the animal-herding Mongols. It is no accident that after the Qing fell in the twentieth century, the Mongols promptly declared their independence.

Throughout this period there were continued Mongol interventions in Tibet and a reciprocal spread of Tibetan Lamaism in Mongolia. Qianlong fought two wars of bloody repression against the Tibetan minority in western Sichuan. He again sent armies into Tibet and firmly established the Dalai Lama as ruler, with a Qing resident and garrison to preserve Qing suzerainty. Other than that, no further attempt was made to integrate Tibet into the empire after the manner of Xinjiang. To foster the loyalty of Mongols and Tibetans, Qianlong drew on the Buddhist tradition. Six tangkas (Tibetan religious paintings) survive, portraying the emperor as Manjusri, bodhisattva of compassion and wisdom. Tibetan records often refer to him by that name.

Further afield, military campaigns against Vietnam and Burma and over the Himalayas into Nepal forced local rulers to accept Qing hegemony and render tribute. Qianlong's expansion involved millions of square miles and brought into the empire non-Chinese peoples, such as Uighurs, Kazakhs, Kirghiz, and Mongols, who were at least potentially hostile. It was also a very expensive enterprise. The dynasty enjoyed unprecedented prosperity and managed in the mid-1780s to accumulate a healthy financial reserve, but its resources were not inexhaustible. Yet Qianlong delighted in the glory and wealth. He built a sumptuous summer residence, partly of Western design, and undertook grand tours of the empire. In his policy toward the literati, he combined Kangxi's generous patronage of scholarship with Yongzheng's suspicion of anti-Manchu writings. The greatest project he sponsored was the *Complete Library of Four Treasuries* (*Siku quanshu*), employing 15,000 copyists working twelve years to produce 3462 complete works in 36,000 volumes. This "final affirmation of the unity of knowledge and power in Chinese history"[8] preserved many books but also merged with a campaign to ferret out and suppress writings offensive to Manchu sensibilities.

Some 80 percent of Qianlong's officials were Chinese, but the emperor was much concerned that Manchus not become Chinese. To this effect he ordered compilation of Manchu genealogies and histories, promoted study and use of the Manchu language by Manchus, and insisted on adherence to all customs that set Manchus apart from Chinese down to the details of feminine adornment. Three earrings in each ear were mandatory for Manchu ladies, and woe to her who made do with just one in the Chinese manner. Qianlong's measures standardized Manchu lore and practices; they reaffirmed Manchu identity but rendered the tradition inflexible.

## Eighteenth-Century Governance

The eighteenth century was generally a time of prosperity, when institutions functioned as smoothly as they ever had. A system of state and local granaries ensured adequate and affordable food supplies. In the rich Lower Yangzi region, local elite-run lineages constructed and operated lineage and community granaries, but elsewhere government assumed a more active role in providing these sources of emergency food. In the eighteenth century it also performed formidable feats of information gathering and coordination over the breadth of the land.

The state's concern for upholding popular morality was expressed in the promotion of village lectures based on edifying imperial pronouncements and its compilation of an officially sanctioned pantheon of local gods and spirits, although it tolerated others as long as they were not considered downright subversive. It also fostered schools. As in the case of community granaries, in the more advanced areas education was left to local initiative, but in outlying provinces officials played a more active role. Thus, a dedicated eighteenth-century governor of Yunnan provided the leadership for establishing 650 schools for the instruction of the numerous minority peoples of the province.

When the system operated effectively, as in the eighteenth century, state and society formed a continuum without a fixed boundary. Although local gentry might resist tax collection and examination candidates resent the bitter competition that left them little hope for success, essentially officials and elite shared a broad spectrum of values and ideas, pushing them to cooperate rather than compete and to work in harmony rather than conflict. As a recent study puts it:

> Because the state understood the art of ruling to include shaping people's moral behavior, it was inclined to be meddlesome, authoritarian, and censorious. But at the same time, because only people who freely choose to do the right thing can be said to have high moral standards, the state accepted and even promoted initiatives among its subjects that it saw as likely to make people take their moral and social agency seriously.[9]

# Eighteenth-Century Literati Culture

Following the lead of Gu Yanwu, but without his breadth, Qing scholars engaged in "evidential learning," rejected philosophical speculation, and relied on careful textual study to reveal the meaning of the classics:

> If only they [those who seek the Way] correct primary and derived characters, discern their pronunciation, read the explanations and glosses, and master the commentaries and notes, the meaning and principles will appear on their own, and the Way within them.[10]

Scholars of evidential learning made important, even iconoclastic, discoveries concerning the questionable historicity of parts of such canonical texts as the *Changes,* the *Documents,* and the *Rites (Liji).* One effect was to undermine the examination system orthodoxy, but the concentration on philology (historical linguistics) easily led to the view that textual studies alone were truly "solid" (in the sense that they avoided abstract speculation) and "practical."

Yan Yuan (1635–1704) was one prominent scholar who focused on practice and condemned both quiet meditation and book learning as standing in the way of true self-cultivation, which should lead to the practice of classical virtues and rites, thereby engendering the capability of changing the world. He studied military science and medicine and emphasized rigorous adherence to classic rites, specific guidelines on how to reform society and conduct one's life. During the eighteenth century scholarly and social interests converged as performance of classic and expensive rites became "an emblem of sociocultural superiority."[11]

Yan's chief disciple Li Gong (1659–1733), like many of his peers, expounded his teachings in the form of commentaries on the classics. A major eighteenth-century thinker was Dai Zhen (1723–1777), who made important contributions to linguistics, astronomy, mathematics, and geography as well as philosophy. Like most of the creative seventeenth-century thinkers, he rejected the metaphysical existence of *li,* which he considered simply the pattern of things. He also disputed Zhu Xi's dualistic theory of human nature, insisting that it contradicts the teachings of Mencius that human nature is one whole and all good and that moral perfection consists in fulfilling one's natural inclinations.

Dai Zhen shared his age's faith in philology, but this was not true of his contemporary Zhang Xuecheng (1738–1801), who strongly disliked philological studies and sought meaning in the study and writing of history. Zhang is perhaps most famous for his thesis that "the six classics are all history," by which he meant that they are not "empty" theoretical discussions but that they document antiquity and illustrate the *Dao.* A scholar must not stop at the facts but get at the meaning. Zhang once compared a work of history to a living organism: its facts are like bones, the writing is like the skin, and its meaning corresponds to the organism's vital spirit.

Along with history and philosophy, another subject of perennial concern to Chinese scholars was the function and value of literature—and the criteria by which it should be judged. The poet Yuan Mei (1716–1797) held that the purpose

of poetry is to express emotion and that it must give pleasure; he rejected the didactic view, held by Zhang Xuecheng, among others, that it must convey moral
instruction.

Yuan's poetry and prose reflect the life of a talented, refined eighteenth-
century hedonist, unconventional within the bounds of good taste, and marginally
aware of the exotic West. One of his prize possessions was a large Western mirror
much admired by his female pupils. Among Yuan's less conventional works are a
cookbook and a collection of ghost stories. His interest in ghosts was shared by his
friend, the painter Le Ping (1735–1799), the youngest of the "Eight Eccentrics of
Yangzhou," a man who claimed to have seen the apparitions he painted.

Yuan, a champion of women's poetry, encouraged women, including two of
his sisters, to write poetry and publish their verse. Qing literary people disdained
the verse of courtesans highly popular in the Late Ming and increased poetry's
thematic scope. Although "the lovelorn poems of lonely ladies" remained popular,
Susan Mann emphasizes the "growing number of poems exploring other domains
of feminine sensibility: education and the acquisition of learning, spiritual development and the rewards of old age, female friendship and its intimacies, parental
heartache and its intermittent release in joy and pride."[12] Furthermore, to have a
published female in the family was now a source of pride.

In the eighteenth century, painters of various schools developed their manners
and styles: professionals working in the meticulous and mannered "Northern"
style, eclectics drawing on diverse traditions and models, and individualists striv-
ing, sometimes excessively, for originality. An unusually interesting and prolific
artist was the painter Gao Qipei (1660–1734). Even in the Song dynasty and earlier, artists had experimented with unconventional materials instead of using a
brush, but none had gone as far as Gao (see Figure 15.5).

Qing painters and scholars generally perceived themselves as latecomers in a
long and revered tradition. As such they faced a dilemma similar to that of
painters, poets, and composers of our own time who no longer feel they can contribute to the traditional lines of development in their arts, that is, be another
Rembrandt or Beethoven. What had been valid for one age could not serve another. Thus, some literati artists cultivated the notion that the epitome of art was
non-art, that is, the deliberate cultivation of innocent awkwardness. Unusual behavior was tolerated, and it became quite acceptable to sell one's paintings.

Both Gao and Le did so without jeopardizing their "amateur" status. Meanwhile,
openly professional artists, who did not claim literati status, sold their work to ordinary, unsophisticated folk who appreciated bright colors and verisimilitude. Colored
woodblock prints also appealed to a wide audience, as did popular drama and vernacular literature. The latter, in particular, reached new heights.

# Fiction

Many of the dynasty's best writers and thinkers were men who had failed in the examination route to success, an experience that probably helped them to view society with a measure of critical and even satiric detachment. The examinations them-

**FIGURE 15.5** *Tiger Seen from Above* (c. 1700), Gao Qipei (1660–1734). Ink and colors on paper, 20.24 in. × 41.46 in. At the upper right, Gao Qipei wrote the following text: "Life with the fingers from the man from outside the Shanghai gate." Beneath it are several red stamps. (© Rijksmuseum, Amsterdam [AK-RK-1991-10].)

selves were a favorite target. Pu Songling (1640–1715) wrote this account of the seven transformations of a candidate in the provincial examination:

> When he first enters the examination compound and walks along, panting under his heavy load of luggage, he is just like a beggar. Next, while undergoing the personal body search and being scolded by the clerks and shouted at by the soldiers, he is just like a prisoner. When he finally enters his cell and, along with the other candidates, stretches his neck to peer out, he is just like the larva of a bee. When the examination is finished at last and he leaves, his mind in a haze and his legs tottering, he is just like a sick bird that has been released from a cage. While he is wondering when the results will be announced and waiting to learn whether he passed or failed, so nervous that he is startled even by the rustling of the trees and the grass and is unable to sit or stand still, his restlessness is like that of a monkey on a leash. When at last the results are announced and he has definitely failed, he loses his vitality like one dead, rolls over on his side, and lies without moving, like a poisoned fly. Then, when he pulls himself together and stands up, he is provoked by every sight and sound, gradually flings away everything within his reach, and complains of the illiteracy of the examiners. When he calms down at last, he finds everything in the room broken. At this time he is like a pigeon smashing its own precious eggs. These are the seven transformations of a candidate.[13]

This examination was held in a labyrinthine compound, with the candidates housed in individual cells where they had to spend the night. It was an eerie place sealed off from the rest of the world, for during an examination session the great gates remained firmly shut: if a man died during the examination, his body was wrapped in straw matting and thrown over the wall. Thus, it was a perfect setting for numerous tales of ghosts, usually the spirits of jilted maidens come to wreak vengeance on the men who had done them wrong.

As David L. Rolston points out, "neither landscape painting nor traditional Chinese fiction is structured around the use of the convention of fixed perspective or viewpoint so important in western painting or fiction."[14] *The Scholars* (*Rulinwaishi*), a novel by Wu Jingzi (1701–1754), is a good case in point. Characterized by Shang Wei as "a literati novel driven by conflicting impulses toward irony and the Confucian moral imagination,"[15] it satirizes the examination system, catches in its net an assortment of human follies, and unveils the intricacies of social life in vignettes of the pompous and the ignorant, the unworldly scholar and those who cheat him, and the hypocrite and other unsavory types even as it struggles with "the question of how a literatus can live a meaningful life in a time of disenchantment."[16] Although it is episodic in organization and somewhat uneven in quality, it incorporates certain technical advances in the art of storytelling, notably in the way it allows its characters to reveal their personalities gradually rather than labeling them at the very start.

China's most beloved and exhaustively studied novel is *The Dream of the Red Chamber* (*Honglou Meng*), also translated as *The Story of the Stone*. Like *The Scholars*, it offers priceless insights into Qing society, this time from the vantage point of a large, eminent family in decline. With rich detail and a cast of hundreds, it reveals how such a family was organized and how it functioned, the relationships between the generations and the sexes, the lives of women, and the status of servants, and it does all this with fine psychological characterizations based on the personal experience of the author, Cao Zhan (d. 1763). But it is far more than a novel of manners. Conscious of its own fictionality, it prompts the reader to contemplate the distinction between the real and the unreal and to ponder the nature of love and desire. C. T. Hsia has written that "it embodies the supreme tragic expression in Chinese literature"[17] and that "the ultimate tragic conflict lies in a tug of war between the opposing claims of compassion and detachment."[14] In the twentieth century this novel stimulated a mountain of serious scholarship and was finally admitted to the world of high literature.

# A Buoyant Economy

During the initial forty cataclysmic years after the founding of the Qing, warfare, destruction, dislocation, and cold weather combined to bring widespread hardship, famine, disease, and population decline. But then both the economy and the population revived and went on to reach new heights. By the end of the eighteenth century, the Chinese population was around 300 million, about double what it had been around 1600. More people lived in China than in Europe. The century saw an increase in life expectancy and an all-around improvement in standard of living.

In agriculture, increased production and commercialization went hand in hand. Yields improved with the geographical spread of crops, such as specialized strains of rice suitable to local conditions, and with improved irrigation techniques and better fertilizers, such as soybean cakes. Production was also significantly increased by the introduction of new plants from the Americas: sweet potatoes, peanuts, tobacco, and corn. These could be grown on land previously left uncultivated as unsuitable for traditional Chinese crops.

An increase in the food supply induced people to refrain from female infanticide, thereby spurring population growth. A rising population spurred demand. The economy became more complex with the expansion of markets for commercial crops such as tea, sugar, cotton, hemp, and tobacco, and for other products of agricultural activity, most importantly mulberry trees for feeding silkworms. Rice was grown commercially not only to supply cities and towns but also for sale to farmers who had converted rice paddies to more profitable cash crops.

The developments in agriculture had their counterparts in manufacturing. The products of China's kilns were world famous; Chinese ceramics were copied in Europe and Japan. Brewing, papermaking, mining, and metal working industries thrived. China led the world in silk and cotton textile production. The demand for raw cotton exceeded what could be grown in China, so it was imported from India by way of Thailand. Until the 1770s, Chinese shipping predominated not only in coastal trade but also in foreign shipping, as Chinese junk owners took advantage of the monsoons and engaged in business dealings with a thriving overseas Chinese community. By the end of the eighteenth century Chinese shipping no longer dominated, but China's maritime trade with the West continued to contribute to Chinese well-being.

Throughout the century the balance of overseas trade was in China's favor, as it had been ever since the sixteenth century, when China became the world's "sink" for silver, which flowed in from Japan and the Spanish colonies of Mexico and Peru to pay for Chinese textiles and ceramics. To quote William Atwell, writing of the 1570s:

> Within a short time Chinese silks were being worn in the streets of Kyoto and Lima. Chinese cottons were being sold in Filipino and Mexican markets, and Chinese porcelain was being used in fashioning homes from Sakai to London.[18]

Although this trade was disrupted by the troubles of the seventeenth century, silver imports resumed after trade restrictions were lifted in 1683. The silver flow declined in the 1720s and again at mid-century, but it rose again after 1760. The demand for silver in China and China's ability to absorb the silver without triggering inflation attest to the productivity of the Chinese economy and to the absence of a market for European products in China.

Eighteenth-century China, like all large countries at this time, was primarily agricultural, but Beijing remained the world's largest city until London surpassed it in around 1800. Nanjing and Suzhou prospered as centers of the silk industry and handicrafts—more than seventy different handicraft trades enlivened Suzhou. Increased trade fostered growth of market towns linked by empire-wide merchant groups and serviced by a sophisticated banking system. As William T. Rowe has concluded, "the uniquely efficient water-transport system and marketing mechanism of preindustrial China allowed it to overcome the barriers of long distance and low technology, and to develop a national market by mid-Qing, even though in Europe and elsewhere such a development may have been conditional upon the advent of steam-powered transportation."[19]

Despite the spread of a "national market," generalization about China's local social and economic foundations remains difficult and potentially misleading, because conditions varied greatly from area to area then as they do today. Economic growth and transformation were most evident along the coast and along the major river arteries, with the Yangzi and Pearl River delta areas profiting most from the new prosperity.

## Social Change

One consequence of economic growth was that, at least in the economically advanced parts of China, the market often prevailed over traditional status considerations. It was a time of both great riches and striking poverty, of increased opportunities for some but distress for others. Among the winners were the prosperous merchants of the major cities. The salt merchants of Yangzhou grew so wealthy from their government monopoly that some thirty of them even maintained their own theatrical troupes to entertain at banquets. A rich material culture provided for luxurious living for the wealthy. Meanwhile, the losers included impoverished Manchu bannermen as well as Chinese, giving rise to a vigorous discussion on the causes of poverty. Memorialists asked whether it was a result of insufficient productivity or of faulty distribution and inquired into the causes for the rise in rice prices, the roles of granaries, and so forth.

The uncertainties of the market were matched by those of the examination hall, where the vast majority of candidates had little hope for success. The civil service was not expanded to keep pace with the growth of the population or the economy or to accommodate the growing number of thwarted candidates, many of them superbly qualified. The average candidate had little hope for success, and those who did succeed were worried by the very real danger of downward mobility, because no amount of tutoring could make examination success hereditary.

Already in the Song there had been men who spent a lifetime taking examinations—when the emperor asked his age, one such man replied, "fifty years ago twenty-three." Now the aged candidate became a stock figure in literature. The government even relaxed standards for men older than 70 so that, past retirement age, they could at least enjoy the psychological satisfaction of receiving a degree. In an effort to weed out candidates, new examinations were introduced. Thus, in 1788 the reexamination of provincial and metropolitan graduates was introduced. That brought the total minimum number of examinations required for the final degree to eight, not counting a final placement examination. By this time the criteria for judging papers had become exceedingly formalistic. Candidates spent years practicing highly complex, artificial "eight-legged essays" required in the examinations, and bookshops did a thriving business selling model answers. In the meantime, the old battle of wits between examiners and cheaters remained a draw (see Figure 15.6).

Fear of decline in status and wealth, the dynamics of local society and economy including competition for resources, and the emphasis on family values in classic texts all contributed to the increasing prevalence, especially in the Southeast, of lineages, many of the largest of which dated to the Ming (see pp. 269–270). Those who could made it a practice to place promising boys with kinsmen located in places where examination competition was less stiff than at home. In fields such as education and maintenance of granaries, lineage activism was welcomed by some officials and thinkers as supplementing government activity, but the local power of lineages set limits on what a government official could do, and lineage conflicts generated much violence.

Below the lineage and throughout the realm in practice, as in theory, the basic social unit was the family, but the ideal joint family with "five generations under one roof," including the nuclear families of brothers, required a degree of wealth seldom enjoyed by commoners. The family was normally headed by the senior male, although a widowed matriarch could be the major force. Age prevailed over youth, but men generally outranked women.

**FIGURE 15.6** *A Cheating Shirt.* Before entering the examination compound where they were to spend three days and two nights, candidates underwent a thorough body search. Absolutely forbidden to bring anything with writing on it, the wearer of this undershirt clearly hoped to beat the system. (© Fujii Museum, Kyoto, Japan. Photograph by Lore Schirokauer.)

The "interior" world of the household was regarded as the women's sphere, whereas men dealt with the external world. Marriages were arranged by and for families, with the bride becoming a member of her husband's family and subject to supervision and discipline by her mother-in-law. Giving birth to a child, preferably a boy, raised her standing in the family, and, in the end, "the lonely disaffected young bride became the pillar of the joint family as a mother-in-law" and "the girl who shrieked her childhood away in agony as her foot bones were crushed grew up to insist on binding her daughter's feet."[20] Women as well as men accepted prevailing norms. Dorothy Ko has pointed to the common saying "a plain face is given by heaven, but poorly bound feet are a sign of laziness" as evidence "that a pair of nicely shaped small feet represented the triumph of individual willpower and effort."[21]

We should note here the variety of lifestyles in a land as vast as China. There were regional differences: small feet were more common in the south than in the north and were a mark of status and prosperity in both regions. Poor and low-class women had hard lives but normal feet. There were differences between urban and rural and between rich and poor. Within China proper, in the south and southwest there were many ethnic minorities with their own ways, and beyond the Great Wall non-Chinese traditions prevailed.

# Ecology

The population continued to increase even though Chinese families took various measures to limit the number of children. People married young but practiced sexual abstinence in the early years of marriage when living with their parents. Infanticide, especially female infanticide, as well as neglect, also reduced the number of offspring. Still the population grew. With more people there was mounting pressure related to land. As an official put it in a memorial to Yongzheng, "while the population increases daily, the land does not."[22] Under Yongzheng the government actively pursued a policy of land reclamation, whereas under Qianlong market forces encouraged the maximum spread of agriculture up into the hills, with terraces all the way to the summits, and out into the hinterlands. In 1793 Hong Liangji (1748–1809), whose main focus was on problems of consumption, became the first official to warn against excessive population growth.

These developments changed the balance between the human and the natural environment. Deforestation, which began long before this period, became more acute. "The earth was loose; when the big rains came, water rushed down from the highlands and mud and silt spread out below. Fertile areas near the mountains were repeatedly covered with sand and were abandoned."[23] Another result of a long-term trend toward deforestation was the shortage of wood that already in the sixteenth century prompted salt extractors to shift from boiling to less effective solar evaporation. In the sixteenth and seventeenth centuries, highland and lowland communities frequently fought over woodlands to the point that the state had to intervene. As more accessible forests were cut down, the primary sources of timber were increasingly distant from the center; Guizhou in the southwest and the Yalu region in the northeast became the major suppliers.

The environmental history of much of China and East Asia is complex, because there were major differences within as well as between regions, and much remains to be learned. But a start has been made, revealing the frequently complex interrelations among technology, commerce, climate, government policies, and social practices. Indications are that major parts of China were heading into environmental crisis by the late eighteenth century as forests disappeared, soil eroded, and rivers silted and flooded, rendering human life more dire and condemning to extinction animals deprived of habitat. However, the worst was still to come. As Kenneth Pomeranz has shown, China, environmentally as well as economically, did not yet compare unfavorably to Europe, which was able to avoid intensified land use by exploiting the ecological "windfall" provided by the New World.[24]

# Dynastic Decline

Merchants played a major role in financing Qianlong's wars, but as the expense of military campaigns far beyond the bounds of China proper mounted, the resources of even the prosperous Qianlong regime were strained, while laxity and corruption were rendering government less effective and more expensive. The execution of fifty-six provincial officials between 1774 and 1784 failed to alleviate, let alone solve, the problem. The most notorious offender was Heshen (1750–1799), a handsome and clever young Manchu guards officer, who, for reasons unknown, won and retained the aging emperor's complete trust for twenty-three years, during which he built a network of corruption and amassed an enormous fortune. Although bitterly detested, he could not be removed, for he never lost Qianlong's confidence and affection. An attack on Heshen implied an attack on His Majesty's own judgment and suggested the presence of factionalism. Perhaps Qianlong was especially sensitive to any signs of factionalism because his father, Emperor Yongzheng, had written a strong critique on this subject. Like his political authority, the moral and intellectual authority of the emperor were beyond question.

Qianlong abdicated as emperor after his sixtieth year so that he would not rule longer than his illustrious grandfather, but he continued to dominate the government until his death in 1799. Only then was Heshen removed.

As always, the common people bore the burden of extravagance and corruption. As a result, many of them joined in the White Lotus Rebellion (1796–1804). At its height it affected Sichuan, Hubei, Henan, Gansu, and Shaanxi. The rebellion drew its following by promising the coming of Maitreya (the Buddha of the future), a restoration of the Ming, and the rescue of the people from all suffering. It gained momentum as it attracted the destitute and displaced and proved the power of its cause. The ineffectiveness of the dynasty's response assisted the movement: government generals used the occasion to line their own pockets and bannermen proved their total incompetence. Not until after Heshen's fall did the government make real headway. A new, very capable commander was appointed, disaffected areas were slowly taken back from the rebels, and militia bands organized by the local elite proved effective in putting down insurgency.

The tendency of the government to tinker and elaborate rather than reform and innovate suggests a dangerous hardening of the institutional arteries just as China's place in the world was about to change.

# Notes

1. The term is taken from Kenneth Pomeranz, *The Great Divergence: China, Europe, and the Making of the Modern World Economy* (Princeton: Princeton Univ. Press, 2000).

2. James Cahill, *The Compelling Image: Nature and Style in Seventeenth-Century Chinese Painting* (Cambridge: Harvard Univ. Press, 1982), p. 183.

3. W. Theodore de Bary, trans., *Waiting for the Dawn: A Plan for the Prince (Huang Tsung-hsi's Ming-i Tai-fang lu)* (New York: Columbia Univ. Press, 1993), p. 92.

4. *RoutledgeCurzon Encyclopedia of Confucianism*, Xinzhong Yao, ed. (London: RoutledgeCurzon, 2003), p. 233.

5. Chin-sung Chang, *Mountains and Rivers, Pure and Splendid: Wang Hui (1632–1717) and the Making of Landscape Panoramas in Early Qing China* (Ph.D. dissertation, Yale University, 2004), pp. 118, 126, with the quotation as translated by Wen Fong in Wen Fong, et al., *Images of the Mind: Selections from the Edward L. Elliott Family and John B. Elliot Collections of Chinese Calligraphy and Painting at the Art Museum, Princeton University* (Princeton Art Museum, 1984), p. 184.

6. Jonathan D. Spence, *Emperor of China: Self-Portrait of Kang-hsi* (New York: Alfred E. Knopf, 1974), p. 128.

7. Morris Rossabi, *China and Inner Asia— From 1638 to the Present Day* (New York: Pica Press, 1975), pp. 139–40. Rossabi does not think Buddhism was a major factor, although it may have contributed to the decline (pp. 140–41).

8. R. Kent Guy, *The Emperor's Four Treasures: Scholars and the Rise of the State in the Late Ch'ien-lung Era* (Cambridge: Harvard Univ. Press, 1987), p. 37.

9. R. Bin Wong, Theodore Huters, and Pauline Yu, "Introduction: Shifting Paradigms of Political and Social Order," in Huters, Wong, and Yu, *Culture and State in Chinese History: Conventions, Accommodations, and Critiques* (Stanford: Stanford Univ. Press, 1997), pp. 4–5.

10. Wang Mingsheng (1725–1798) as translated in Benjamin A. Elman, "Social Roles of Literati in Early to Mid-Ch'ing," Chapter 7 of Willard J. Peterson, ed, *The Cambridge History of China, Vol. 9, Part 1: The Ch'ing Empire to 1800* (Cambridge: Cambridge Univ. Press, 2002) p. 395.

11. William T. Rowe, "Social Stability and Social Change," in *Cambridge History*, Vol. 9, Part 1, p. 531.

12. Susan Mann, "Women, Families, and Gender Relations" Chapter 8 in *Cambridge History,* Vol. 9, Part 1, p. 447.

13. Quoted in Ichisada Miyazaki, *China's Examination Hell,* trans. Conrad Schirokauer (New Haven: Yale Univ. Press, 1981), pp. 57–58.

14. David L. Rolston, *How to Read the Chinese Novel* (Princeton: Princeton Univ. Press, 1990), p. 14.

15. Shang Wei, *Rulin Waishi and Cultural Transformation in Late Imperial China* (Cambridge: Harvard Univ. Press, 2003), p. 279.

16. Wei, *Rulin Waishi and Cultural Transformation,* p. 285.

17. C.T. Hsia, *The Classical Chinese Novel* (New York: Columbia Univ. Press, 1968), pp. 246, 264.

18. William Atwell, in Frederick W. Mote and Denis Twitchett, eds., *The Cambridge History of China,* Vol. 7 (Cambridge: Cambridge Univ. Press, 1988), p. 587.

19. William T. Rowe, *Hankow: Commerce and Society in a Chinese City, 1796–1889* (Stanford: Stanford Univ. Press, 1984), p. 62.

20. Susan Mann, "The Education of Daughters in the Mid-Ch'ing Period," in Benjamin A. Elman and Alexander Woodside, eds., *Education and Society in Late Imperial China, 1600–1900* (Berkeley: Univ. of California Press, 1994), p. 21.

21. Dorothy Ko, *Teachers of the Inner Chambers: Women and Culture in Seventeenth-Century China* (Stanford: Stanford Univ. Press, 1994), p. 171.

22. Han Liangfu, as quoted in Robert B. Marks, *Tigers, Rice, Silk, and Silt: Environment and Economy in Late Imperial South China* (Cambridge: Cambridge Univ. Press, 1998), p. 291.

23. Quoted from the Gazetteer for Chengde (Hunan) in Peter C. Perdue, *Exhausting the Earth: State and Peasant in Hunan, 1500–1850* (Cambridge: Harvard Univ. Press, 1987), p. 88.

24. See Note 1. Another major factor in Europe's "great divergence" was the proximity of coal to the center of textile production, whereas in China they were far apart.

# Part Five

# China and Japan in the Modern World

*I*n the nineteenth century the whole world came to feel the might of Europe, where intellectual, political, and economic forces at work since the Renaissance were producing unprecedented wealth and power. This process was accelerated in the late eighteenth century by the Industrial and French Revolutions, gaining momentum with the emergence of new technologies, new appetites, new ideas, new values, and new problems setting off tremors that were to reverberate throughout the globe. It was a tumultuous period of intense economic competition, stringent national rivalries, bitter class conflicts, and sharp clashes between old and new values and ideas. Yet few Europeans questioned the superiority—moral, intellectual, economic, and political—of their civilization or, indeed, of their century.

A major development still with us was that the nation-state won unprecedented and enthusiastic acceptance as the "natural" and uniquely legitimate political entity worthy to be the primary object of political loyalty. Although just what constitutes a "nation" remained ill-defined; nevertheless, the nation-states were able to mobilize human and natural resources to an unprecedented degree, as demonstrated in World War I, which, triggered and fueled by nationalism, brought an end to Europe's global predominance while destroying Czarist Russia and Austro-Hungary, Europe's last old-style multinational empires.

Nineteenth-century nationalism prompted European patriots to revolt against foreign rule, and it also glorified commercial, military, and cultural expansion abroad. Consequently, Qing China faced external challenges to the dynasty and to the society and civilization on which it was built. At the same time, it had to deal with an uprising unprecedented in scope, intensity, and bloodshed. The two chapters in this part deal with how China met these challenges and take us through the collapse of the dynasty and its aftermath. We begin in the middle of the eventful and pivotal nineteenth century. Although in terms of European and even global history, the century came to a close with the First World War, the pivotal event in East Asia occurred twenty years earlier, for the Sino-Japanese War radically affected Korea, China, and Japan.

The West was never uniform, nor its course of events smooth. It helps to place East Asian turbulence in perspective if we keep in mind that the forces of nationalism and republicanism erupted in revolutions on the European continent in 1830 and 1848, that in 1839 English Chartists took to the streets demanding political reforms, that warfare played a crucial role in the creation of Italian and German national states (completed by 1870), that Americans slaughtered each other in civil war, and that bitter fighting and strife marked the transition from Napoleon III, through the Paris Commune, to the establishment of the conflicted Third Republic in France (1870). The violence of the nineteenth century is matched only by that of its successor.

The streetcar played a worthy part and can stand as a symbol for the transition of traditional cities into the new and trans-national modernity. It became an essential part of the urban landscape and of a world on the move.

# China: The Troubled Nineteenth Century

| 1793 | 1800 | 1816 | 1839 | 1842 | 1850 | 1856 | 1860 | 1864 | 1874 |

| Macartney Mission | Amherst Mission | Opium War (1839–1841) | Anglo-French War on China (1856–1860) Taiping Rebellion (1850–1864) Other Rebellions: (1853–1868) (1855–1873) (1862–1875) |

Canton System (since 1760)

Nineteenth-century China was beset by internal and external difficulties, each contributing to the severity of the other. The disintegration of the dynasty continued, as noted in the preceding chapter, and the dynasty was beset by unrest and uprisings, as well as by new threats generated by internal and external forces. Opium, for example, came from abroad, but the fact that its spread in China was made possible by official corruption and by the appeal of the drug to bannermen did not bode well.

The Qing now faced long-term problems that would have taxed the ingenuity and energy of even an honest and effective government. Foremost were the problems created by population pressures, for the population continued to increase in the nineteenth century as it had in the eighteenth. By 1850 the number of inhabitants in China had risen to about 430 million, without any comparable increase in productivity or resources. As the pressures of the struggle for survival strained old humanistic values to the breaking point, it left little room for honesty, let alone charity. Life became brutish and hard. As ever, the poor suffered most, and they were legion, for the uneven distribution of land left many people landless, destitute, and despairing. The situation was made worse by government neglect of public works.

Emperor Jiaqing (1796–1820) tried to remedy the government's financial problems by cutting costs and selling official posts and titles but was unable to solve the underlying fiscal and economic problems, reform the bureaucracy, or help the people, who ultimately supplied the funds. Emperor Daoguang (1820–1850) continued his father's policy of frugality but could not stem the decay. Internal pressures were building, but external crisis preceded internal eruption.

# The Opium War (1839–1841) and Its Causes

Before turning to the opium crisis that triggered the war, we need to consider the long-range factors that made it a turning point in China's foreign relations. Underlying the tensions between China and the West was the incompatibility of the Chinese and Western views of themselves and the world. Both were supremely self-confident and proud of their own civilizations. Both were narrowly culture-bound. Thus, when the Macartney mission arrived in Beijing in 1793 with the hope of broadening the terms of trade and initiating treaty relations, the presents sent to Emperor Qianlong by England's George III were labeled as "tribute" by the Chinese. Qianlong responded to the English monarch by praising his "respectful spirit of submission" and, in the gracious but condescending language appropriate for addressing a barbarian king residing in the outer reaches of the world, turned down all his requests, political and economic. He saw no merit in the British request for representation in Beijing, nor did he favor increased trade: "As your Ambassador can see for himself, we possess all things. I set no value on objects strange or ingenious, and have no use for your country's manufactures."[1]

Sources are inconsistent about whether or not Lord Macartney performed the ceremonial kowtow expected of inferiors and performed by emperors themselves toward Heaven, but he was confident that the Chinese would perceive "that superiority which Englishmen, wherever they go, cannot conceal."[2] The English sent another mission to China in 1816, headed by Lord Amherst, but he was not granted an audience at court.

The British motive for coming to China remained primarily economic. In contrast to China's self-sufficiency and Emperor Qianlong's disdain for foreign products, there was a Chinese product in great demand in Britain. This was tea. First imported in tiny quantities in the late seventeenth century, tea was initially taken up as an exotic beverage with medicinal properties, then popularized as a benign alternative to gin, and finally was considered a necessity of English life. The East India Company, which enjoyed a monopoly of trade with China until 1834, was required by Act of Parliament to keep a year's supply in stock at all times. Tea imports reached 15 million pounds in 1785 and double that amount in the decade preceding the Opium War. Not only did the East India Company depend on the income from the tea trade, but the British government also had a direct stake in tea, because about one-tenth of its entire revenue came from a tax on Chinese tea. Not until the 1820s did the Company begin experimenting with tea growing in India, and it was many years before Indian tea would provide an alternative to the tea of China. The importance of Chinese tea extended even to American history: it was Chinese tea that was dumped from East India Company ships in the famous Boston Tea Party (1773).

The British problem was how to pay for this tea. There was no market for British woolens in China, and the "singsong" trade in clocks, music boxes, and curios was insufficient to strike a balance of trade. Until the last third of the eighteenth century, the sale of British imports covered 10 percent or less of the cost of exports, with the rest paid for in cash and precious metals. Unable to find anything European that the Chinese wanted in sufficient quantity, the English turned to-

**FIGURE 16.1** *Opium Smokers.* Those who could afford to do so indulged in high-quality opium prepared for them by servants at home. The less affluent had to prepare their own. But the least fortunate were left to smoke opium ash or refuse on rudimentary benches in shoddy surroundings in dismal opium dens. (© Mansell/Timepix Collection [838558].)

ward India and the "country trade" between India and China, conducted under East India Company license by the private firms of British subjects. Money obtained in Canton by the "country traders" was put on deposit there for the Company against bills of exchange on London. In this way, England, India, and China were connected by a trade-and-payments triangle.

Until 1823 the largest commodity imported to China from India was cotton, but this volume never reached the amount necessary to balance the trade. That feat was accomplished with opium. Opium had long been used for medicinal purposes, but the smoking, or more accurately, the inhaling of opium fumes through a pipe, began in the seventeenth century. The spread of the practice was sufficient to provoke an imperial edict of prohibition in 1729, but this and subsequent efforts to suppress use of the drug were unsuccessful, and opium consumption continued to increase. Distributed partly through older salt-smuggling networks and protected by the connivance of corrupt officials, use of opium spread steadily and proved particularly attractive to soldiers and government underlings. The drug was habit forming and its effects were debilitating (see Figure 16.1).

Withdrawal was excruciatingly painful. Over time the addict developed a tolerance for opium and needed more and more of the drug to achieve a "high." Thus, to pay for tea, the Chinese were sold a poison. Because private country traders brought the opium to China, the East India Company disclaimed responsibility for the illegal traffic in China. At the same time, however, it profited from the sale of opium in India. However, within India, where the British, as the paramount power, felt a certain sense of responsibility, consumption of opium for non-medicinal purposes was strictly prohibited.

The Chinese market for opium developed at such a pace that the balance of trade was reversed. During the 1820s and 1830s large quantities of silver seem to have left China to pay for opium imports. This caused an increase in the number of copper coins needed to buy a specific amount of silver, thereby destabilizing the Qing monetary system. What began as a public health problem now became a fiscal problem as well. In 1834, the East India Company's monopoly of the China trade was abolished by the British government. This opened the gates of trade still wider on the British side, resulting in an increased flow of opium to China and an increased flow of silver out of China.

Abolition of the Company's trade monopoly was a victory for English advocates of free trade, who were as antagonistic to restraints on trade abroad as at home. The immediate effect in China was to put an end to the system of Cohong-Company relations in Canton. Now in place of the Select Committee of the East India Company, an official of the crown represented the British side. To initiate the new relations, Britain sent out Lord Napier as First Superintendent of Trade with instructions to establish direct contact with the Qing viceroy, to protect British rights, and to assert jurisdiction over Englishmen in Canton. To accomplish these aims, he was ordered to use a moderate and conciliatory approach. Napier, however, more ambitious than diplomatic, immediately took an adamant stand on the issue of direct communication with the viceroy. He violated Chinese regulations by not waiting in Macao for permission to proceed to Canton and by sending a letter rather than petitioning through the *hong* merchants. With neither side willing to back down, the impasse developed into a showdown. All Chinese employees were withdrawn from the British community, food was cut off, and trade was stopped. Napier finally withdrew to Macao, where he died. This all took place in 1834. Unfortunately, in the ensuing lull, no progress was made toward finding a new modus vivendi between the two sides.

For a brief moment the Chinese considered legalizing opium, but in 1836 the emperor decided on suppression. In doing so, he sided with the Spring Purification Circle of reform-minded literati officials, who were seeking influence in government decision making. Thus, an "Inner Opium War," to use James M. Polachek's formulation, developed parallel to and intertwined with the external conflict.[3]

Opium dealers and addicts were prosecuted with great vigor, and imprisonments and executions were widespread, with the result that the price of opium dropped precipitously. This program was well under way when the vigorous and determined reformer Lin Zexu (1785–1850) arrived in Canton in March 1839. As imperial commissioner, he was charged with stamping out the drug trade once and for all.

Lin conducted a highly successful campaign against Chinese dealers and consumers. He also severely punished corrupt officials who had connived in the trade. To deal with the foreign source of the opium, he appealed to Queen Victoria:

"Suppose there were people from another country who carried opium for sale to England and seduced your people into buying and smoking it; certainly your honorable ruler would deeply hate it and be bitterly aroused."[4] He also admonished the foreign merchants, and he backed moral suasion with force. He demanded that the foreigners surrender all their opium and sign a pledge to refrain from importing the drug in the future at the risk of confiscation and death. To effect compliance, he used the same weapons of isolating the foreign traders employed successfully in 1834 against Napier. Elliot, the British Superintendent of Trade, took a fateful step in response when he ordered the British merchants to turn their opium over to him for delivery to the Chinese authorities. By this act he relieved the merchants of large amounts of opium they had been unable to sell because of the efficacy of the Chinese prohibitions, and he made the British government responsible for eventual compensation. No wonder that the merchants enthusiastically dumped their opium: 21,306 chests were delivered to Lin Zexu. It took twenty-three days to destroy it all.

In England, firms interested in the China trade exerted great pressure on the government for prompt and vigorous military action. Lin, meanwhile, pleased with his victory, continued to press Elliot on the issue of the pledges, but here he did not succeed. The Superintendent of Trade argued that it was against British law to compel the merchants to sign the pledges and that the imposition of the death penalty without the benefits of English judicial procedure was also contrary to British law. What was at stake here was the issue of British jurisdiction over British subjects, a source of Anglo-Chinese friction since 1784, when the British had refused to submit to Chinese justice. The issue came to the fore again in the summer of 1839, when a group of English sailors killed a Chinese villager in the Canton hinterland. Refusing to turn the men over to Lin Zexu, Elliot tried them himself, but when they were returned to England the men were freed, because the home court ruled that Elliot had exceeded his authority.

The first clash of the war took place in November 1839, when the Chinese tried to protect one of the only two ships whose captains had signed the bond despite Elliot's stand and who now wanted to trade. When a British ship fired a shot across the bow of the offending vessel, the Chinese intervened with twenty-one war junks, which, however, were no match for the foreign ships. In December, trade with the British was stopped, and on January 31, 1840, a formal declaration of war was announced by the governor-general of India, acting in the name of the home government.

In June 1840, the British force, consisting of sixteen warships, four armed steamers, twenty-seven transports, a troop ship, and 4000 Irish, Scottish, and Indian soldiers, arrived in China. First the British blockaded Canton, and then they moved north. Lin and his associates remained confident of victory, holding that the British, like their maritime pirate predecessors, depended on the spoils of war to finance their military operations and thus had grossly overextended themselves.

The British were fired on at Xiamen (Amoy) while trying to deliver a letter from Prime Minister Palmerston under a white flag of truce, a symbol the Chinese did not understand—just one example of mutual cultural misunderstanding. They then seized Chusan Island, south of the Yangzi estuary, and Dinghai, the chief city there. The main body of the fleet sailed another 800 miles north to Beihe, near Tianjin, where Palmerston's letter was accepted. By this time the emperor had lost confidence in Lin Zexu, whose tough policy had led to the military retaliation.

Lin was dismissed, disgraced, and exiled to Ili in Central Asia. His place was taken by the Manchu prince Qishan (d. 1854), who, in September 1840, by flattery and accommodation, got the British to return to Canton for further negotiations. When these came to naught, the British resumed military operations, with the result that in January 1841 Qishan was forced to sign a convention that provided for the cession of Hong Kong, payment of an indemnity to Britain, equality of diplomatic relations, and the reopening of Canton. Both Qishan for the Qing and Elliot for the British thought they had done very well, but neither government accepted their work. The Chinese emperor was indignant at how much had been conceded, whereas Palmerston fumed that Elliot had demanded too little. The reactions of the Chinese and British governments showed all too clearly how far apart they still were. Caught in the middle were the negotiators. Like Lin Zexu earlier, now Qishan came to feel the imperial displeasure: his property was confiscated and he was sent to exile on the Amur. Elliot too was dismissed; his next position was as consul-general in Texas.

In the renewed fighting, the British besieged Canton in February 1841, but the siege was lifted on payment of a ransom of 6 million Spanish silver dollars. However, before their departure, the British experienced the growing hostility of the local population. They were attacked by a body of troops organized by the local gentry. Although militarily ineffective, the attack was an indication of popular sentiment, and its results were embellished by hard-liners to support their advocacy of continued intransigence toward the British. In August, Elliot was relieved by Pottinger, and the last phase of the war began when the British moved north, occupying Xiamen in August and Dinghai in October. Reinforcements were sent from India, increasing the naval force and bringing troop strength up to 10,000. With this force, Pottinger continued the campaign, advancing up the Yangzi until his guns threatened Nanjing. There on August 29, 1842, the treaty that ended the war was signed. It was a dictated peace imposed by the Western victor on the vanquished Chinese.

# The Treaty of Nanjing and the Treaty System

The Treaty of Nanjing (together with the supplementary Treaty of the Bogue, October 1843) set the pattern for treaties China later signed with the United States and France in 1844, established the basic pattern for China's relations with the West for the next century, and supplied the model for similar treaties imposed on Japan. The Canton System and the Cohong monopoly were abolished. Five ports—Canton, Xiamen, Fuzhou, Ningbo, and Shanghai—were opened to British trade and residence. Britain received the right to appoint consuls to these cities. The treaty also stipulated that henceforth official communications were to be on a basis of equality.

The Qing was forced to pay an indemnity of 21 million Spanish silver dollars. Of this, 12 million was for war expenses, in keeping with the European practice of forcing the loser to pay the costs of a war. Another 6 million was paid as reparations for opium handed over to Commissioner Lin, and the remaining 3 million went to settle the debts owed by the *hong* merchants to British merchants.

An important provision of the treaty established a moderate Chinese tariff of from 4 to 13 percent on imports, with an average rate of 5 percent. The Chinese, whose statutory customs had been even lower, did not realize that by agreeing to this provision they were relinquishing the freedom to set their own tariffs. On the British side there was the conviction that, as Adam Smith had taught, the removal of constraints on trade would benefit all by allowing everyone to concentrate on what he did best.

The British, having acquired an empire in India, with all the burdens of government that it entailed, did not seek to create another in China. Trade, not territory, was their aim. But they did demand and obtain a Chinese base. Hong Kong Island, at that time the site of a tiny fishing village, was ceded to them in perpetuity. Well located and with an excellent harbor, it developed into a major international port.

The issue of legal jurisdiction over British subjects was settled by the Treaty of the Bogue, which provided for extraterritoriality—that is, the right of British subjects to be tried according to British law in British consular courts. Having only recently reformed their own legal system, the British were convinced of its superiority. There were precedents in Chinese history for allowing "barbarians" to manage their own affairs, but in the context of modern international relations, extraterritoriality amounted to a limitation on Chinese sovereignty.

The Treaty of the Bogue also provided for most-favored-nation treatment. This obliged China to grant to Britain any rights China conceded in the future to any other power. Its effect was to prevent China from playing the powers off against each other. It meant that once a nation had obtained a concession, it was automatically enjoyed by all the other states granted most-favored status. In the 1844 treaties, the United States and France gained this status. In the American treaty, China agreed to allow for the maintenance of churches in the treaty ports and to treaty revision in twelve years, whereas the French won the right to propagate Catholicism.

The status of the opium trade was left unsettled in the original treaties. An agreement to outlaw smuggling did not slow down the growth of the traffic, which was legalized under the next round of treaty settlements, 1858–1860, and opium even functioned as a kind of money. From the annual 30,000 chests before the Opium War, the trade expanded to reach a high of 87,000 chests in 1879. It then declined as Chinese production of opium increased. British opium imports were down to about 50,000 chests when, in 1906, the Qing took strong measures against the drug. British imports finally came to a stop in 1917, but opium smoking remained a serious social problem until the early 1950s.

For China, the treaties solved and settled nothing. A particularly ominous development was the permission granted for foreign gunboats to anchor at the treaty ports, for when additional ports were opened, foreign powers had the right to navigate China's inland waterways. Today, with the benefit of hindsight, it is apparent that the cumulative effect of the treaties was to reduce China to a status of inequality unacceptable to any modern nation.

Although it is now universally regarded as a milestone, the treaty settlement did not seem so to the Qing authorities who, as John Fletcher has shown, had made many of the same concessions as recently as 1835 in reaching a settlement with the tiny Central Asian state of Kokand. This treaty involved an indemnity, a tariff settlement, the abolition of a merchant monopoly, and a special position exceeding that of most-favored-nation status and seen by the Qing as simply a case of "impartial benevolence."[5] From the vantage point of Beijing, Hong Kong seemed as remote as Kokand.

Foreign policy remained deeply imbedded in political conflicts, revealing deep lines of division in the body politic. When the Manchu-led centralizers, who advocated peace, came into power, they purged their opposition so thoroughly that Chinese scholar-officials of various intellectual persuasions found common ground in pressing for open discussion in official channels, administrative decentralization, and a policy of determined resistance against the foreigners. Few men had any inkling of the dimensions of the challenge facing the empire. For example, Wei Yuan (1794–1857), author of the influential *Illustrated Treatise on the Sea Kingdoms* (first version, 1844), limited himself to incorporating new information into old categories, and felt no need to break with tradition. Despite his geopolitical orientation, he persisted in underestimating the British threat.

Under the circumstances, the best that experts could suggest was for China to acquire "barbarian" arms and to employ the old diplomacy of playing off one barbarian against another. Less well-informed officials suggested that future military operations take advantage of the supposed physical peculiarities of the barbarians, for example, their stiff waists and straight legs, which made them dependent on horses and ships, or their poor night vision.

## Internal Crisis

The encroachments of the foreign powers were ominous, but the internal crisis was even more dangerous. Government leadership remained totally inadequate. Earlier, Emperor Daoguang's partial success in reforming the official salt monopoly system had not compensated for his failure to reinvigorate the Grand Canal or Yellow River managements. The Grain Transport Administration was "in effect a free-wheeling taxation agency that preyed upon officialdom and populace alike."[6] By 1849 the Grand Canal was impassible. From then on, tax grain had to be shipped by sea. The abandonment of the canal cost thousands their jobs. Emperor Daoguang did not live to see the Yellow River disaster of 1852. Since 1194, the greater river had flowed into the sea south of the Shandong Peninsula, but now it shifted to the north, spreading flood and devastation over a wide area.

The next emperor, Xianfeng (1851–1861), was nineteen when he inherited the throne and proved equally incapable of dealing with an increasingly menacing situation. Even while rebellion threatened the dynasty, a major scandal involving bribery and cheating shook the examination system.

Famine, poverty, and corruption gave rise to banditry and armed uprisings, as had so often happened in the past. The most formidable threat to the dynasty came from the Taiping revolutionaries. To aggravate the crisis, the dynasty also had to contend with rebellions elsewhere. In the border regions of Anhui, Jiangsu, Henan, and Shandong, there was the Nian Rebellion (1853–1868) led by secret societies, probably related to the White Lotus Society. There was also a Muslim rebellion in Yunnan (1855–1873) and the Dongan Rebellion in the Northwest (1862–1875). Yet it was the Taiping who came closest to destroying the Qing in a civil war that, in terms of bloodshed and devastation, was the costliest in human history. It is estimated that more than 20 million people lost their lives.

## The Taiping Rebellion (1850–1864)

The founder of the Taiping movement was a village schoolteacher named Hong Xiuquan (1814–1864), who belonged to the Hakka, ethnically a Han subgroup, which many centuries earlier had migrated from the north to the southeast, where they remained a distinct ethnic group. Originally, Hong hoped for a conventional civil service career, and four times went to Canton to participate in the civil service examination, only to fail each time. In 1837, shocked by his third failure, he became seriously ill, and for forty days was subject to fits of delirium during which he experienced visions. These visions he later interpreted with the aid of a Christian tract he picked up in Canton, where Protestant missionaries had made a beginning in their effort to bring their faith to China. He also received some instruction from an American Southern Baptist missionary. On the basis of his limited knowledge of the Bible and Christianity, he proceeded to work out his own form of sinicized Christianity.

Central to Hong's faith was his conviction that in his visions he had seen God, who had bestowed on him the divine mission to save humankind and exterminate demons. He also met Jesus and was given to understand that Christ was his own elder brother. This recasting of Christianity into a familistic mode had appeal for Hong's Chinese audience but dismayed Western Christian missionaries, who were further appalled by Hong's claims that he himself was a source of new revelation.

The emphasis in Taiping Christianity was on the Old Testament—on the Ten Commandments, not the Sermon on the Mount. Hong's militant zeal in obeying the first commandment by destroying "idols" and even Confucian ancestral tablets soon cost him his position as a village teacher. He became an itinerant preacher among the Hakka communities in Guangxi, gaining converts and disciples among the downtrodden and dispossessed, whom he recruited into the Association of God Worshippers. To the poor and miserable, he held out a vision of the Heavenly Kingdom of Great Peace (*Taiping tianguo*), an egalitarian, God-ordained utopia.

In keeping with both Christianity and native traditions, Taiping Christianity stressed a strict, even puritanical, morality. Opium, tobacco, gambling, alcohol, prostitution, sexual misconduct, and foot binding were all strictly prohibited. Women were made equal to men in theory and, to a remarkable extent, also in practice. Consonant with both Christian egalitarianism and native Chinese utopian ideas was a strong strain of economic egalitarianism, a kind of simple communism. Property was to be shared in common, and in 1850 the members of the Association were asked to turn over their funds to a communal treasury that would provide for everyone's needs.

The Taiping land program was based on a system of land classification according to nine grades found in *The Rites of Zhou,* long a source of Chinese radical thought. The idea was that everyone would receive an equal amount of land, measured in terms of productivity of the soil. Any production in excess of what was needed by the assignees was to be contributed to common granaries and treasuries. The system did not recognize private property.

The basic political structure was a unit of twenty-five families consisting of five groups of five families each. The leaders of these and larger units were to combine civil and military duties and look after the spiritual welfare of their people by conducting Sunday religious services. The Taiping developed their own hymns, primers, and literature, which served as the subject matter for a new examination system open to women as well as men. Similarly, there were female as well as male military units. Marriages took place in church and were monogamous.

What stood in the way of realizing this utopia were the "demons," mostly Manchus. By July 1850 the Association had attracted 10,000 adherents, primarily in the remote and neglected province of Guangxi. In defiance of the Qing, they now cut off their queues, the long braids of hair hanging down from the back of the head, which had been forced upon the Chinese by the Manchus as a sign of subjugation. Because they also refused to shave the forepart of their heads, the government called them the "long-haired rebels." Millenarian religious beliefs, utopian egalitarianism, moral righteousness, and hatred of the Manchus proved a potent combination when fused into a program of organized armed resistance. In November 1850 there were clashes with government troops, and on January 11, 1851, Hong's thirty-seventh birthday, his followers proclaimed him "Heavenly King," thus formally defying the Qing.

At this stage, the Taiping enjoyed good leadership. One of the outstanding secondary leaders was Yang Xiuqing, originally a charcoal burner, who was a talented organizer and strategist. Starting from their base in Guangxi, the Taiping forces made rapid military progress. One of their favorite tactics in attacking cities was to use their contingent of coal miners to dig tunnels to undermine the defending walls. The incompetence of the government forces also helped. As the Taiping armies advanced, they picked up strength. It has been estimated that their number reached more than 1 million by the time they took Nanjing in 1853.

After such a quick advance, with their ranks swollen by new adherents only partially versed in Taiping tenets, it was time to call a halt and consolidate. The movement had formally been proclaimed the Heavenly Kingdom of Great Peace in 1851. Now, with its capital at Nanjing, the leaders attempted to turn it into a solid regime. To continue military operations, two expeditions were sent out. A small force was dispatched north and came within twenty miles of Tianjin before suffering reverses and defeat. Large forces went west and enjoyed considerable success until 1856, but they too were eventually defeated.

Taiping treatment of Westerners was cordial but clumsy. The regime lost much good will by employing condescending language and expressions of superiority not unlike those used by Beijing. After the British failed to obtain Taiping recognition of their treaty rights, they decided on a policy of neutrality, and the other powers soon followed suit. This remained the policy of the foreign powers through the 1850s.

A turning point for the Taiping regime came in 1856 in the form of a leadership crisis they could ill afford. Yang Xiuqing had increased his power to the point of reducing Hong to a mere figurehead. Yang, too, went into trances, and claimed to be acting on God's orders, but he was unable to convince the other leaders. When he overreached, they turned on him. Yang, along with his family and thousands of followers, was killed, but no strong successor appeared to take his place. By the time Hong's cousin Hong Rengan (1822–1864) came into prominence in 1859, it was too late to restructure the regime. Hong Rengan was the most Westernized of the Taiping leaders but had neither the time nor the power to build the centralized and modern state he had in mind. His leadership lasted only until 1861. Hong Xiuquan himself was immersed in his religious mission, occupied in writing elaborate comments on the Bible, and was totally lost to the world.

Failure of its leadership was one source of Taiping weakness. Inadequate implementation of stated policies was another. Practice did not conform to theory. For example, Hong Xiuquan himself, as well as other Taiping leaders, kept numerous concubines despite the Taiping call for monogamy. Moreover, there were many missed opportunities: the failure to strike before the dynasty could regroup; the failure to cooperate with secret societies and other opponents of the regime who did not share the Taiping faith; and the failure to cultivate good relations with the foreign powers.

To make matters worse, Taiping revolutionary ideas repelled all those Chinese who identified with the basic Confucian way of life and understood that the Taiping program was not merely anti-Manchu but anti-Confucian and thus subversive to the traditional social order. Consequently, the Taiping leaders not only failed to recruit gentry support, but they also antagonized this key element in Chinese society. To the literati, rule by "civilized" Manchus was preferable to rule by "barbarized" Chinese.

## Zeng Guofan and the Defeat of the Taiping

What ultimately prolonged the Qing dynasty's life was a new kind of military force organized by Zeng Guofan (1811–1872), a dedicated Confucian and a product of the examination system. Unlike the old armies organized under the Qing banner system (see p. 381), Zeng's army was a strictly regional force from Hunan, staffed by officers of similar regional and ideological background personally selected by him. They, in turn, recruited soldiers from their own home areas or from members of their own clans. A paternalistic attitude of officers toward their men, a generous pay scale honestly administered, careful moral indoctrination, and common regional ties all helped to produce a well-disciplined force high in morale.

Qing statesmen were aware that strong regional armies such as Zeng's threatened the balance of power between the central government and the regions and were ultimately dangerous to the authority of the dynasty. But the traditional armies of the regime had proved hopelessly inadequate, and the Manchu rulers had no choice but to trust their defense to Zeng. Although organized in Hunan, where it began its operations, the army also fought the Taiping in other provinces. It was not always victorious: twice Zeng suffered such serious reverses that he attempted suicide. But in the long run a well-led and highly motivated army, honestly administered and true to its purpose, proved superior to the Taiping forces.

The dynasty also benefited from the services of two other remarkable leaders: Zuo Zongtang (1812–1885) and especially Li Hongzhang (1823–1901), whose Anhui Army became the strongest anti-Taiping force. After the treaties of 1860, the Western powers sided with the regime that had made such extensive concessions to them, and Western arms were of great assistance, particularly to the Anhui Army. An American adventurer was succeeded by a British officer as leader of 4000 or 5000 Chinese in the "Ever Victorious Army." Meanwhile, French officers commanded the "Ever Triumphant Army," composed of Chinese and Filipino mercenaries. Customs revenues helped loyalists purchase foreign arms and steamers and establish arsenals.

After a series of victories, the loyalist armies laid siege to Nanjing. When the situation became desperate, Hong Xiuquan relied on divine intervention, ordering the starving people to eat manna. According to a Taiping general, "The Sovereign himself, in the open spaces of his palace, collected all sorts of weeds, which he made into a lump and sent out of the palace, demanding that everyone do likewise."[7] The same source attributes Hong's subsequent fatal illness to his eating of these weed concoctions. Shortly after Hong's death, on July 19, 1864, the city fell to an army commanded by Zeng Guofan's brother. As had happened often in this bitter war, the fall of Nanjing was followed by a bloodbath. Hong's son managed to flee, but was discovered in Guangxi and executed. The Taiping, once so close to victory, were completely eradicated. Similarly, the loyalist forces succeeded in quelling the Nian, Muslim, and other rebels.

The Taiping's example was to inspire future revolutionaries, whereas conservatives continued to admire Zeng Guofan. That others were restless and defiant is suggested by the famous life-size self-portrait of Ren Xiong (1820–1857), who served in a military headquarters but did not rest easily with his choice (see Figure 16.2). Painted in Shanghai, which was beginning to assume its role as a major meeting place between China and the West, this original, unsettling work of art mirrors the stress of its time and foreshadows future conflict and distress.

# China and the World from the Treaty of Nanjing to the End of the Taiping

As we have seen, the Treaty of Nanjing established a pattern but satisfied neither side. Frustrated in attempts to negotiate locally, the British demanded direct representation in Beijing. They also pressed for treaty revision, because the opening of the new ports had not led to the anticipated increase in trade. Behind the demands for freer trade was the persistent belief that only artificial restrictions prevented the development of a giant market in China for British textiles and other products.

One cause of friction between the English and the Chinese was the repeated postponement of the opening of Canton because of the strong antiforeign feeling of its people. The continuation of the opium trade did not help matters, nor did the development of a new commerce in Chinese laborers. These men were often procured against their will, crowded into dismal "coolie" vessels, and transported as contract laborers to work the plantations of Cuba and Peru. The boom set off by the discovery of gold in California in 1848 also brought Chinese immigrants to the United States, but they came as free laborers, their passage organized by Chinese merchants. By 1852 there were 25,000 Chinese in the American West, and by 1887 there were twice that number in California.

**FIGURE 16.2** Ren Xiong. In a self-portrait unlike any ever painted before, Ren depicts himself with a military haircut and expresses both belligerence and anxiety. Hanging scroll, ink and color on paper. 31 in × 69.9 in.

There were some efforts for cooperation during these years, as the foreign powers sided with the dynasty rather than with the Taiping. With Chinese consent, the British set about suppressing piracy. More important was the establishment of the Foreign Inspectorate of Customs in Shanghai in 1854 after the Qing officials had been ejected by rebels. The Inspectorate became responsible for the collection of tariffs and the prevention of smuggling. By the new treaties of 1858, its authority was extended to all treaty ports. It remained an important source of support for the dynasty during and after the Taiping Rebellion.

Nevertheless, there was more discord than harmony, and in 1856 war broke out once more. The immediate cause of war was the Arrow Affair. The Arrow was a Chinese-owned but Hong Kong registered vessel which, although flying the British flag, was boarded by Chinese officials, who seized twelve Chinese men whom they charged with piracy. When the viceroy returned the men but refused to apologize and guarantee that it would not happen again, the British responded by seizing Canton. There was a lull in the fighting while the British were occupied fighting a war in India set off by the Mutiny of 1857. When the war in China was resumed in December 1857, the English were joined by the French.

As in the first war, the Europeans again moved north, and in Tianjin the British and French negotiated the Treaties of Tianjin, providing for permanent residency of diplomats in Beijing, the opening of ten new ports, foreign travel throughout China, reduction of inland transit dues, an indemnity, and freedom of movement for all Christian missionaries. However, hostilities resumed after the British envoy discovered that the Qing planned to exchange ratifications in Shanghai rather than Beijing. Although the Chinese defeated the British at Taku, where the river leading to Tianjin enters the sea, victory went to the allies who entered Beijing, where Elgin, the British commander, vented his anger by burning down the imperial summer palace of around 200 buildings northwest of Beijing. In October the Conventions of Beijing were signed to supplement the Treaties of Tianjin, which now also took effect. In addition to the usual indemnity, China was forced to open eleven new ports, to grant rights to travel in the interior, and to allow foreign envoys to reside in Beijing. In 1860 the French also surreptitiously inserted into the Chinese text a provision granting missionaries the right to buy land and erect buildings in all parts of China.

The peace agreements were secured through the mediation of the Russian ambassador to Beijing, who used the opportunity to consolidate the gains Russia had made to date and to obtain new concessions for his country. Under Peter the Great and Catherine the Great, Russia's land empire had expanded into the area west of the Pamirs then known as Russian Turkestan, and in 1851 Russia obtained trading privileges and the right to station consuls at Kuldja and Chuguchak (Dacheng) in the Ili region of Chinese Turkestan (now Xinjiang) east of the Pamirs. Now areas southwest of Kuldja and Urga (Ulan Bator) in Outer Mongolia were also opened to them, but, having suppressed Muslim rebellions, the Qing were able to retain their position in Central Asia.

Meanwhile, Russia made massive gains in the northeast. In the Amur region Nikolai Muraviev, governor-general of Siberia, began putting pressure on the Qing in 1847. In 1860, the entire area north of the Amur was ceded to the Russians, who also received the lands east of the Ussuri River, which were incorporated into the Russian Empire as the Amur and Maritime Provinces. In the latter, Muraviev founded Vladivostok ("Ruler of the East" in Russian). Russia also now received most-favored-nation status. The gains Russia made at this time remain a source of conflict between the Russians and Chinese.

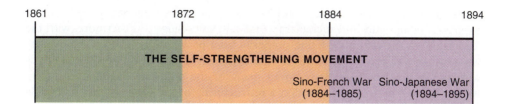

| 1861 | 1872 | 1884 | 1894 |
|------|------|------|------|

**THE SELF-STRENGTHENING MOVEMENT**

Sino-French War     Sino-Japanese War
(1884–1885)          (1894–1895)

# II. 1870–1894

*The Post-Taiping Revival*

*Self-Strengthening—The First Phase*

*Self-Strengthening—The Theory*

*The Empress Dowager and the Government*

*Education*

*Economic Self-Strengthening*

*The Traditional Economic Sector*

*Missionary Efforts and Christian Influences*

*Old and New Wine in Old Bottles*

## The Post-Taiping Revival

During the Tongzhi Period (1862–1874), Zeng Guofan, Li Hongzhang, and other leaders in the victory over the Taipings sought to cope with the dislocations wrought by warfare and to revive the dynasty by launching a program of Confucian reformism: expenses and taxes were cut in the ravaged south, relief projects were instituted, public works projects were initiated, land was reclaimed and water was controlled, and granaries were set up. As always, agriculture had priority.

An aspect of the revival dear to its Confucian sponsors was a strengthening of scholarship by reprinting of old texts, founding of new academies, opening of libraries, and the like. Examination system reform was similarly a high priority, as was the elimination of bureaucratic corruption. Questions dealing with practical issues of statecraft were introduced, and attempts were made to limit the sale of degrees and offices. By such measures the reformers sought to raise the level of honesty.

However, the reforms did not penetrate to the crucial lower level of the bureaucracy—many county magistrates continued to gain office through purchase—

and nothing effective was done to curb the rapacity of the solidly entrenched and notoriously corrupt sub-bureaucracy of clerks and underlings. Furthermore, with the leadership for the reforms coming primarily from provincial governors, the dynasty was powerless to reverse the trend toward regionalism. The disruption of old bonds with the central government removed many of the political constraints on local wealth and power and set in motion a restructuring of local society that ultimately proved dangerous for both the state and the social order.

# Self-Strengthening—The First Phase

The aim of the Self-Strengthening Movement was to fortify the Qing through selective borrowing from the West. It began in the Tongzhi Period with a focus on military modernization and international relations and was expanded in its middle phase (1872–1885) to encompass transportation (shipping and railways), communications (telegraph), and mining. Finally, after China's defeat by France in 1885, it was further broadened to include light industry.

During the first phase, Li Hongzhang created gun factories in Shanghai (1862) and Suzhou (1864), established an arsenal in Shanghai with Zeng Guofan (1865), and founded another in Nanking (1867). In 1870, Li also expanded machinery works first built in Tianjin in 1867. Another leader in Fuzhou founded a shipyard with machinery from France that had a shipbuilding and a navigation school attached, one teaching French and the other English.

With the emperor being a minor, foreign policy was largely under the direction of Prince Gong, who expressed the regime's order of priorities thus:

> The situation today may be compared (to the diseases of a human body). Both the Taiping and the Nian bandits are gaining victories and constitute an organic disease. Russia, with her territory adjoining ours, aiming to nibble away our territory like a silk worm, may be considered a threat at our bosom. As to England, her purpose is to trade, but she acts violently, without any regard for human decency. If she is not kept within limits, we shall not be able to stand on our feet. Hence she may be compared to an affliction of our limbs. Therefore we should suppress the Taiping and the Nian bandits first, get the Russians under control next, and attend to the British last.[8]

It was apparent to Prince Gong that new approaches to foreign policy were required to meet these objectives. In 1861, to deal with the foreign powers and related matters, he sponsored the establishment of the Zongli Yamen (Office of General Management) as a subcommittee of the Grand Council to supervise a number of offices (see Figure 16.3). Because its influence depended on that of its presiding officer and his associates, it was most influential during the 1860s, when Prince Gong was at the height of his authority. An important innovation introduced by the Zongli Yamen was appeal to international law, using Henry Wheaton's *Elements of International Law*, a standard text translated by the American missionary W. A. P. Martin.

**FIGURE 16.3** Three members of the Zongli Yamen and statesmen of the Tongzhi Period. Left to right: Shen Guifen, President of the Ministry of War; Dong Xun, President of the Ministry of Finance; Mao Changxi, President of the Ministry of Works. (© Hulton-Deutsch Collection/CORBIS [HU038080].)

Prince Gong, recognizing that Chinese officials would be at a disadvantage in dealing with foreigners unless they had a better understanding of foreign languages and learning, was instrumental in having the Zongli Yamen establish a school for foreign languages and other nontraditional subjects in 1862. The language staff was foreign and included Martin, who became the school's president in 1869. By that time astronomy and mathematics had also been introduced, despite the objections of the distinguished Mongol scholar General Secretary Woren (d. 1871), who memorialized: "From ancient down to modern times your slave has never heard of anyone who could use mathematics to raise the nation from a state of decline or to strengthen it in time of weakness."[9] Woren was not alone in his objections to this extension of "barbarian" influence.

Nevertheless, similar schools were established at Shanghai, Canton, and Fuzhou. Foreigners were relied on to run both the military and educational establishments. In this way the foundations of self-strengthening and modernization were laid, but the emphasis remained heavily military. This was true even of Feng Guifen (1809–1874), an advocate of learning from the barbarians, who had the audacity to propose that examination degrees be presented to men demonstrating accomplishment in Western mechanical skills.

During the 1860s an important area of Chinese cooperation with the foreign powers was the Maritime Customs Service. Its first director, Horatio Nelson Lay, had acquired a fleet of eight gunboats for the Chinese in England. Although these were paid for by the Chinese, he arranged that the captain of the fleet should receive all his orders through and at Lay's own discretion. This was unacceptable to the Qing, and there were protests. China's first effort to acquire a modern navy ended with disbandment of the little fleet, and Lay was pensioned off. Matters improved, however, when Robert Hart succeeded Lay in 1863. Hart's attitude was the opposite of Lay's. He insisted that the customs was a Chinese service and that Chinese officials were to be treated as "brother officers," and he gave the Qing government well-intentioned and frequently helpful advice on modernization, while building the service into an important source of support for the dynasty.

Cooperation between the Qing and the powers produced the first Chinese diplomatic mission to the West, which was headed by the retiring American minister to Beijing, Anson Burlingame, on Robert Hart's recommendation. For a multiethnic Confucian state like the Qing to employ a trusted foreigner on such an important mission did not appear as extraordinary as it would have later, after nationalism took hold. Accompanied by a Manchu and a Chinese official, Burlingame left China in 1867 for a trip to Washington, several European capitals, and St. Petersburg, where he died. Carried away by his own eloquence, he told Americans that China was ready to extend "her arms toward the shining banners of Western civilization."[10] In Washington, he concluded a treaty rather favorable to China.

The most important negotiations for treaty revision were conducted in Beijing by the British. These culminated in the Alcock Convention of 1869, which included some concessions to the Chinese on duties and taxes, and stipulated that, under the most-favored-nation clause, British subjects would enjoy privileges extended to other nations only if they accepted the conditions under which those privileges had been granted. It also allowed China to open a consulate in Hong Kong. These concessions may appear minor, but the English merchant community felt threatened by them, and their opposition proved strong enough to prevent ratification of the convention.

A fatal blow to the policy of cooperation came in 1870 in Tianjin. A Catholic nunnery there had made the mistake of offering small payments for orphans brought to the mission. Rumors spread that the children had been kidnapped and that the sisters removed the children's hearts and eyes to make medicine. The tense situation erupted into violence. A mob took the life of the French consul and twenty other foreigners, including ten nuns, in what came to be known as the Tianjin Massacre. The powers mobilized their gunboats. Diplomacy finally settled the issue, largely because

France's defeat in the Franco-Prussian War in the same year deprived France of military power and forced the French to concentrate on domestic problems.

# Self-Strengthening—The Theory

Confucian pragmatism was nothing new. Willingness to adopt new means to strengthen and reform the state had animated a long line of Confucian scholars from the Song on, and, as it became clear during the early years of the nineteenth century that the Qing was in serious trouble, some scholars turned against philology to focus on what today would be called policy studies. The *Anthology of Qing Statecraft Writing* (*Huangchao jingshi wenbian*), published in 1827, is a case in point. It is a collection of essays on social, political, and economic matters written by Qing officials and published by He Changlin (1785–1841), with the actual work done by Wei Yuan. Concern for reform and willingness to take a hard, critical look at financial and political institutions characterized the writings of leading intellectuals, and Wei Yuan began to merge these concerns with an interest in the West. The first person to see the West as a source for solving the problems it had created was Feng Guifen, who urged China to use "barbarian techniques" against the "barbarians," the hallmark of the Self-Strengthening Movement.

Although self-strengthening was well established by the 1870s, its classic formulation came in 1898 from the brush of Zhang Zhidong (1837–1909), a governor-general and practitioner of self-strengthening. Like Sakuma Shōzan earlier in Japan, Zhang wanted to preserve traditional values while adopting Western science and technology. The idea was that Chinese learning would remain the heart of Chinese civilization, whereas Western learning would have a subordinate, supporting role. This was expressed in terms of the traditional Neo-Confucian dichotomy of *ti* (substance) and *yong* (function): Western means for Chinese ends. The basic pattern of Chinese civilization was to remain sacrosanct, but it was to be protected by Western techniques.

Conservative opponents of self-strengthening feared that Chinese civilization would be contaminated by borrowing from the West, because ends cannot be separated from means. In the Confucian formulation, *ti* and *yong* are aspects of a single whole. The Confucian tradition had always been concerned with means as well as ends, and generations of scholars had insisted that the Way did not consist merely of "empty" abstractions, but concerned practical realities. There was no essence apart from application. And there was a great deal more to the West than mere techniques. It was fallacious to believe that China could merely borrow techniques from the West without becoming entangled in manifestations of Western culture. If China went ahead with efforts to adopt Western techniques while preserving traditional culture, the best that could be hoped for would be an uneasy compartmentalization. To preserve tradition in a period of modernization, the country would have to be protected from the kind of radical social reappraisal hailed in Japan by champions of "reason" such as Fukuzawa Yukichi.

The contrast with Japan is instructive, for there social change was sanctioned by an appeal to nationalism as symbolized by the throne, whereas in China Confucianism was much too closely associated with the social structure to allow for a similar development. Meiji Japan demonstrated that elements of Confucianism were compatible with modernization, but also that modernization involved changes reaching into the very heart of a civilization.

# The Empress Dowager and the Government

The dominant figure at court from the mid-1870s until her death, just three years before the demise of the dynasty, was the Dowager Empress Cixi (1835–1908) (see Figure 16.4). The intelligent, educated daughter of a minor Manchu official, she entered the palace as a low-ranking concubine and had the good fortune to bear the Xianfeng emperor his only son. After that emperor's death, she became coregent for her son, the Tongzhi emperor, whom she dominated. It was also rumored that she encouraged him in the debaucheries that weakened his constitution and brought him to the grave in 1875 at age nineteen. She then manipulated the succession to place on the throne

**FIGURE 16.4** The Empress Dowager Cixi (1835–1908) seated on the Imperial Throne. Scholars, too, grew long fingernails to show the world that they worked with their minds, not their hands. (Courtesy Arthur M. Sackler and the Freer Gallery of Art, Smithsonian Institution [SC-GR2.56].)

her four-year-old nephew, the Guangxu emperor (r. 1875–1908) and continued to make the decisions even when he ostensibly assumed the imperial duties in 1889. At first Prince Gong had provided a counterforce, but his power declined in the 1870s, and in 1884 he was removed from the government altogether.

The Empress Dowager was a strong-willed woman, an expert in political infighting and manipulation. One of her most reliable supporters was the Manchu bannerman Ronglu (1836–1903), to whom she gave important military commands. Yet, it was an anomaly to have a woman in control of the court, and her prestige was not enhanced by rumors that she was responsible for the murder of her rivals. Corruption in high places also took its toll. The powerful eunuch Li Lianying (d. 1911) was totally loyal to his mistress but also totally corrupt, using his influence to amass a fortune. Cixi herself accepted payments from officials and misspent funds. The most notorious case of financial abuse was her use of money

**FIGURE 16.5** On the shore of Kunming Lake, the Marble Pavilion has become a popular recreational site attracting ordinary Chinese visitors as well as foreign tourists—the kind of folk it was intended to exclude. Summer Palace, Beijing. (© Lore Schirokauer.)

intended for the navy. The Navy Department, established in 1885, became a branch of the imperial household, and China's most famous and magnificent "ship" was made of marble (see Figure 16.5).

Cixi's prime political aim was to continue in power. She had no aversion, but neither did she have any commitment, to the policy of selective modernization advocated by the champions of self-strengthening, and her understanding of the West was very limited. It was to her immediate political advantage to avoid dependence on any single group of officials and to manipulate a number of strong governors-general who had gained in power while suppressing the Taiping Rebellion. These indispensable provincial administrators could no longer be controlled by the court at will, but, fortunately for Beijing, they remained absolutely loyal to the dynasty. The governors-general operated their own political and financial machines and commanded substantial military forces, but they were still dependent on Beijing's power of appointment. Major policy decisions continued to be made in Beijing. The central government was also strengthened financially by receipts from the Maritime Customs. Thus, the West helped to preserve the dynasty even as it was undermining its foundations.

Most powerful of the governors-general was Li Hongzhang, from 1870 firmly established in Tianjin, where he commanded an army, sponsored self-strengthening efforts, and successfully avoided transfer. A protégé of Zeng Guofan, he shared his master's devotion to the dynasty, but not his Confucian probity. From his headquarters, not far from Beijing, Li dominated China's policy toward Korea, but he could not control its foreign policy elsewhere. Arguing for the priority of maritime defense, he objected to overemphasis on inner Asia and unsuccessfully opposed two military campaigns conducted there during the 1870s.

In the next decade he failed to prevent the war of 1884–1885 with France over Vietnam. In this war, fought not only in Vietnam but also on Taiwan and the Pescadores, the Qing suffered the destruction of the Fuzhou dockyards as well as the loss of the fleet built there. Because the defeated dynasty was forced to relinquish all claims to Vietnam, Li was vindicated, but his opposition to going to war against France earned him the denunciations of his enemies, who castigated him as an arch traitor.

Li, however, survived these attacks and remained the most important patron of self-strengthening, now broadened to include light industry in the hope for better results.

# Education

Crucial to every phase was the need for officers, managers, and technical personnel such as scientists and engineers. The fastest way to fill this need was to send students abroad. However, the success of this approach was mixed. The most extensive effort of this sort was made between 1872 and 1881, when 120 students were sent to the United States under the supervision of Yung Wing (Rong Hong, 1828–1912), Yale class of 1854, and the first Chinese to graduate from an American university. The boys were between fifteen and seventeen years old, young enough to master new subjects, but also immature and easily swayed by their foreign environment. To assure continued Confucian training, they were accompanied by a traditional Confucian mentor. Nevertheless, they soon adopted American ways, participating in American sports, dating and in some cases eventually marrying American girls, and in a few instances even converting to Christianity. Yung Wing himself married an American and ended up living in Hartford, Connecticut. The mission had been launched with the backing of Zeng Guofan and Li Hongzhang, but Li withdrew his support when the students were denied admission to West Point and were fiercely attacked by Beijing officials for neglecting their Confucian studies. The mission, poorly managed from the start, was abandoned. Among its participants were some of the first, but by no means the last, Chinese students who, during their overseas stay, became alienated from their culture.

The obvious alternative to study abroad was to supply instruction in modern subjects at home. This was the purpose of the language school established by Prince Gong and other schools at several arsenals and the Fuzhou dockyard. By 1894 a telegraph school, a naval and military medical school, and a mining school were also in operation. The curricula of these schools typically encompassed both the classical studies required for success in the examination system and the new subjects. Because command of traditional learning remained the key to entry into government service, the students naturally tended to concentrate on that, for otherwise their career opportunities were very limited. The most famous graduate of the Fuzhou dockyard school was Yan Fu (1853–1921), who was sent to England to continue his studies at the naval college in Greenwich, but after returning home to China was unable to pass the provincial examination and gained fame not as an admiral, but as a writer and translator.

It did occur to some reformers to broaden the content of the examinations and allow candidates credit for mastering modern subjects, but suggestions along such lines encountered formidable opposition, because they affected the Confucian core of the civilization. A minor concession was finally made in 1887. Three of some 1500 provincial examination candidates might now be granted that degree after being examined in Western along with (not in place of) traditional subjects. They would then be eligible for the highest examination (the *jinshi*) on the same terms as the other candidates!

## Economic Self-Strengthening

The accomplishments of the second phase of self-strengthening included a shipping company, textile mills, the beginnings of a telegraph service, and the Kaiping Coal Mines. Li Hongzhang took the lead in sponsoring and protecting the new ventures. During the first phase, the new factories, arsenals, and other enterprises, run by officials with the help of foreigners, had suffered from bureaucratic corruption and poor management. To avoid this, Li enacted a policy of "government supervision and merchant operation." Capital came from both the public and private sectors. Private financing was very much desired, but capital was scarce, and other forms of investment were more lucrative and prestigious. Private investment came primarily from Chinese businessmen residing in the treaty ports and familiar with modern-style business ventures and techniques.

The records of these companies were mixed. The China Merchants Steam Navigation Company is a good example. When private capital proved insufficient to finance the company, Li Hongzhang put up the rest from public funds. To help the company make a go of it, Li secured for the shipping line a monopoly on the transport of tax grain and official freight bound for Tianjin. He obtained tariff concessions for the company and protected it from its domestic critics and enemies. In exchange, Li exercised a large measure of control, appointing and dismissing its managers, employing its ships to transport his troops, and using its payroll to provide sinecures for political followers. He also used its earnings to buy warships. To advance his policy in Korea, Li had the company lend money to the Korean government.

In the end, the investors made money and their political sponsor benefited, but, after an initial spurt, the companies stagnated. Moreover, they failed to train Chinese technical personnel and were plagued by incompetent managers, nepotism, and corruption. Even their political sponsors exploited the companies, regarding them as sources of patronage and revenue rather than as key investments for the modernization of the country. By the mid-1890s, there was a modern sector in the Chinese economy, but it was largely limited to the periphery of the empire, where Chinese merchants were able to hold their own successfully against foreign competition.

# The Traditional Economic Sector

Although the new enterprises proved disappointing, developments in the traditional sector were hardly encouraging. Chinese tea merchants, despite sophisticated institutions and techniques adequate to sustain dominance of the domestic market, found it increasingly difficult to compete internationally against tea growers in India and Sri Lanka (Ceylon). The large-scale producers in these countries had an advantage over the small Chinese growers in their ability to sustain a high-quality product by investing in fertilizer, replacement bushes, and labor at the crucial picking time. Furthermore, the elaborate structure of the Chinese collection system, which worked so well internally, was too unwieldy to organize an adequate response to international competition. After 1887, with the decline of exportation of tea, raw silk became China's main export. In the mid-1890s China was the world's largest exporter of silk, although by 1904 Japan had supplanted China in this role.

Beyond the treaty ports and their immediate hinterlands, the penetration of foreign imports appears to have been slow and their impact varied. Statistics are hard to find, and there is no consensus about the ways in which the world economy interacted with forces already at work in the Chinese countryside. Thus, Philip C. C. Huang's study of an area of North China where farmers had been growing cotton for a long time remains controversial as well as suggestive. According to Huang, because cotton brought a better price than grain but, being susceptible to drought, also entailed larger risks, the gap between the successful rich and those pushed into poverty by failure increased. Combined with population pressure and an absence of other opportunities for employment, this set in motion an invidious process of *agricultural involution,* a term first applied by the anthropologist Clifford Geertz to Java, where poor peasants worked the land for marginal and diminishing returns. According to Huang, while the men farmed, their wives and daughters supplemented family income by laboring at spinning wheel and loom, often at less than subsistence wages. Whereas spinning was practically eliminated by machine-made thread, the low prices paid to the weavers kept the price of native cloth below that of the factory-made product, which had to be shipped into the interior. "The world economy thus did not undermine the rural economic system or stimulate new departures but accelerated processes already underway. The incorporation of Chinese agriculture into the world economy telescoped and greatly accelerated change in the small peasant economy."[11]

# Missionary Efforts and Christian Influences

The Western presence in nineteenth-century China was no more confined to trade and politics than it had been during the Late Ming encounter. Once again, missionaries were drawn to China, but now there were Protestants as well as Catholics. An early Protestant arrival was Robert Morrison of the London Missionary Society. He reached Canton in 1807, learned the language, brought out a Chinese-English dictionary and a Chinese version of the Bible (later used by the Taiping), founded the school where Yung Wing received his early education, and set up a printing press. Other missionaries, many of them Americans, brought modern medicine and other aspects of Western secular knowledge to China.

The missionaries made a notable effort in education: by 1877 there were 347 missionary schools in China with almost 6000 pupils. Such schools helped spread knowledge about the West as well as propagate the religion. A notable missionary-educator was W. A. P. Martin, who contributed to the Self-Strengthening Movement and became the first president of Beijing University. The first foreign language newspaper published in China was a missionary publication, and missionaries also contributed to scholarship. Outstanding among the missionaries who became sinologists was James Legge, a master translator who rendered the Chinese classics into sonorous Victorian prose. In this and other ways, missionaries with varying degrees of sophistication and self-awareness served as cultural intermediaries.

As indicated by the growth of their schools, the missionaries met with some success, but their strength was largely in the treaty ports, and the results were hardly commensurate with their efforts. By the end of the century, the number of Catholic missionaries in China had climbed to about 750, and there were approximately half a million Catholics in China, up from around 160,000 at the beginning of the century. The Protestants had less success. In 1890 there appear to have been only slightly more than 37,000 converts served by roughly 1300 missionaries, representing forty-one different religious societies. The Tianjin Massacre of 1870 had demonstrated the potential fervor of antimissionary sentiment, and nothing happened to reduce hostilities during the next quarter century.

The reasons for the poor showing of Christianity are many and various. They include difficulties in translation and communication analogous to those that plagued Buddhist missionaries a millennium and a half earlier. The most important concepts of Christianity, such as sin or the Trinity, were the most difficult to translate, but none was more so than the most sacred idea of all, the idea of God. Agreement on how to translate *God* into Chinese was never reached; three versions, one Catholic and two Protestant, remained current. As before, differences in culture compounded the difficulties in communication.

Nineteenth-century missionaries, however, also encountered problems that they did not share with their predecessors, for the Chinese associated Christianity with both the Taiping Rebellion and the unequal treaties. The former showed Christianity as subversive to the social and political order, whereas the latter

**FIGURE 16.6** *The [Foreign] Devils Worshipping the Incarnation of the Pig [Jesus].*
This print employs a homonym for the transliteration of 'Jesus' to depict Christ
as a pig. (From *China and Christianity* by Paul A. Cohen [Cambridge: Harvard
Univ. Press, 1963]. Courtesy Department of East Asian Studies, Harvard
University.)

brought the missionaries special privileges. Both were resented. Furthermore, the
aura of power also attracted false converts, individuals attracted by the possibilities of a treaty port career, and opportunists seeking to obtain missionary protection for their own ends. Popular resentment of the missions was fired by scurrilous
stories and bitter attacks (see Figure 16.6). This hostility was encouraged by the
elite, who saw in Christianity a superstitious religion that threatened their own status and values.

It was no accident that anti-Christian riots often occurred in the provincial capitals during examination time, when they were filled with candidates committed to
the status quo. Here there is an interesting contrast with the situation in Japan,
where 30 percent of Christian converts during the Meiji Period were from samurai
backgrounds. Christianity served the spiritual needs and provided a vehicle for social protest for samurai who found themselves on the losing side of the Restoration
struggle. As a result, in the 1880s and 1890s a prestigious native clergy was developing in Japan, and Christianity remained more influential than the slow growth of

the churches would indicate. In post-Taiping China too, Christianity continued to appeal to people dissatisfied with the status quo, and it counted among its converts some notable protesters, including Sun Yat-sen. But the elite remained hostile, and the real cutting edge of protest was to be elsewhere: too radical for the nineteenth century, Christianity turned out to be insufficiently radical for the twentieth.

In the meantime, missionaries contributed to the Western perception of China. Working in the treaty ports, dealing not with Confucian gentlemen but with men on the margin of respectable society, the missionaries frequently developed a negative view of China and its inhabitants, an image that was the reverse of the idealistic picture painted earlier by the Jesuits.

# Old and New Wine in Old Bottles

In this difficult age, as in most, there were artists and poets whose aim was "transcending turmoil"[12] by working within the rich tradition to which they were heirs. Their accomplishments can give much pleasure, but others more directly convey a sense of the anxieties and hopes of an age. For example, the poetry of Wang Pengyun (1848–1904), an official who served as a censor, sounds notes of uncertainty, apprehension, and regret in an age of dynastic decay.

*In Reply to a Poem from Cishan, Thanking Me for the Gift of Song and Yuan Lyrics I Had Had Printed (To the Tune "The Fish Poacher")*

Now that the lyric voice wavers in wind-blown dust
Who is to speak the sorrows of his heart?
Two years of carving, seeking from each block
The truest music of the string unswept,
Only to sigh now
Finding my grief in tune
With every beat that leaves the ivory fret!
I sigh for the men of old
Pour wine in honor of the noble dead:
Does any spirit rhymester
Understand my heartbreak?
The craft of letters
Furnishes kindling, covers jars:
True bell of tinkling cymbal, who can tell!
Du Fu,* who lifelong courted the perfect phrase
—Did his verse help him, though it made men marvel?
Take what you find here,
See if an odd page, a forgotten tune

*For discussion of Du Fu, see Chapter 5.

**FIGURE 16.7** China During the Self-Strengthening Period.

Still has the power to engage your mind.
My toiling over
I'll drink myself merry, climb the Golden Terrace,
Thrash out a wild song from my lute
And let the storms rage at will.[13]

Late Qing writers were much given to writing sequels, new versions, and parodies of China's classic novels, often at great length. *The Dream of the Red Chamber* was a favorite (see the discussion in Chapter 15). Publication of *The Dream of the Green Chamber* (about a brothel) in 1878 was preceded by *A Precious Mirror for Judging Flowers* (1849), a homosexual romance. *Quell the Bandits* (1853), characterized by David Der-wei Wang as anticipating China's modern political novel,[14] plays off *The Water Margin,* the classic novel recounting the deeds of 108 bandit heroes driven by the cruel corruption of a decadent government to take justice into their own hands (see Chapter 10). Such works, for all their flaws, looked toward the future.

A literary man and political reformer hopeful of the future was Huang Zunxian (1845–1905), who spent 1877 through 1879 in Tokyo as part of the Chinese legation. A collection of his poems describing Japan was published by the Zongli Yamen in 1879. He also wrote a history of Japan and served as a diplomat in San Francisco, Singapore, and London. Rejecting the conventional poetic genres, he sought to preserve tradition through innovation.

Among those who welcomed the winds from the West were a small group of remarkable men, some with experience abroad in official or unofficial capacities. Guo Songdao (1818–1891) was China's first minister to England and the first Chinese representative to be stationed in any Western country. Wang Tao (1828–1897) spent two years in Scotland assisting James Legge in his translations and also visited Japan. One of the founders of modern journalism in China, he favored the adoption of Western political institutions as well as science and technology. Another remarkable man was Zheng Guangyin (1842–1921), a famous scholar-comprador, modernizer, and writer. Such men were interested in Western "substance" (not just "function"), while remaining committed to the Confucian tradition.

Important for the future were a number of younger men whose formative years fell into this period, although they did not become influential until the late 1890s. There are three names in particular to which we will return: Yan Fu, born in 1853; Kang Yuwei, born in 1858; and Sun Yat-sen, born in 1866. The discussion of their ideas must wait, however, for it was not until China was jolted by her defeat in the Sino-Japanese War that they came to the fore.

# III. Foreign Relations

*Continued Pressures*

*Vietnam and the Sino-French War of 1884–1885*

## Continued Pressures

Western pressures continued to affect China's foreign relations in the twenty years before the Sino-Japanese War, but the nature of these pressures began to alter. The initial conflicts had been over Western efforts to open trade and diplomatic relations with China proper; in the 1870s and 1880s foreign intervention in lands constituting peripheral areas of the empire or traditionally tributary states were the major causes of friction (see map, Figure 16.6). Even as Japan was engaged in the Taiwan expedition, the Qing government was troubled by a dangerous situation in Central Asia. In 1871 the Russians used a Muslim rebellion in Xinjiang as a pretext for occupying the Ili region, where a lucrative trade had developed. In Xinjiang itself, Yakub Beg (1830–1877), a Muslim leader from Kokand in Central Asia, obtained Russian and British recognition for his breakaway state. In response to these alarming developments, the Qing court assigned the task of suppressing the rebellion to Zuo Zongtang, who had just finished crushing Muslim rebellions in Shaanxi and Gansu.

He carried out the task with great success. By 1877, the government's control over Xinjiang was being reestablished and Yakub Beg was driven to his death. After difficult and protracted negotiations, the Russians returned nearly all of Ili (1881).

This strong showing in Central Asia, an area to which the Chinese were traditionally sensitive, bolstered morale, and Chinese successes in the diplomatic negotiations that followed encouraged those who were opposed to accommodation with the West. Indeed, the success of China's Central Asian policy encouraged them to demand an equally strong policy in dealing with the maritime powers. Pressure from this source was too strong to be ignored and constituted a major factor leading to confrontation and then to war with France in 1884–1885. At issue was French expansion into Vietnam.

# Vietnam and the Sino-French War of 1884–1885

North Vietnam had been annexed by the Han in 111 B.C.E., but after C.E. 939 native Vietnamese regimes prevailed, the major exception being the short period of Ming domination (1406–1426). The leader of the resistance against the Ming, Le Loi, established the Later Li dynasty (1428–1789), with its capital at Hanoi and its government organized along Chinese lines. As in Korea, the determination to maintain political independence from China went hand in hand with admiration for Chinese culture and institutions. The Chinese influence on Vietnam is what sets it apart from the other, more Indian-oriented states of Southeast Asia.

China also served as the model for the Nguyen dynasty (1802–1945), which from its capital at Hue in Central Vietnam ruled the country through a bureaucracy modeled as closely as possible on that of China. The Chinese model was powerful, yet differences in size and culture between China and Vietnam required adjustments and compromises. To give just one example, Chinese influence was much stronger on civil government than on the military, for military theory and practice in Vietnam (as in the rest of continental Southeast Asia) centered on the elephant.

Vietnam's location in a cultural frontier area provided a rich and complex culture but was also a source of political weakness. One result was that the social and cultural gap between village and bureaucracy was greater in Vietnam than in China. Another result was the difficulty the Vietnamese state experienced in its efforts to incorporate the South, which had been gradually taken over from the Cambodians (regarded by the Vietnamese as "barbarians") during the century from roughly 1650 to 1750. Under the Nguyen dynasty this continued to be an area of large landlords and impoverished peasants, a region where the central bureaucracy operated inadequately. The area also suffered from educational backwardness, with the result that very few southerners were able to succeed in Vietnam's Chinese-style civil service examination system.

Vietnam's long coastline and elongated shape, as well as the presence of minority peoples within its boundaries, further hampered government efforts to fashion a strong unified state capable of withstanding Western encroachments. French missionaries and military men had early on shown an interest in the area and had assisted in the founding of the Nguyen dynasty itself. Nearly 400 Frenchmen served the dynasty's founder and first emperor, Gia-long (r. 1801–1820). Catholicism also made headway: it has been estimated that there were more Catholics in Vietnam than in all of China. For much the same reasons as had earlier animated anti-Christian policies in China and Japan, the Vietnamese authorities turned against the foreign religion, but their suppression of Catholicism gave the French an excuse for intervention.

French interest in Vietnam increased during the reign of Louis Napoleon. In 1859 France seized Saigon. Under a treaty signed three years later, the French gained control over three southern provinces, and five years later they seized the remaining three provinces in the South. These southern provinces became the French colony called Cochin China. During 1862–1863 the French also established a protectorate over Cambodia. French interests were not limited to the South but included Central and North Vietnam (Annam and Tonkin). Treaties concluded in 1862 and 1874 contained various provisions eroding Vietnamese sovereignty, and when disorders occurred in North Vietnam in 1882, France used the occasion to seize Hanoi.

Throughout this period of increasing French penetration, the Vietnamese court had continued its traditional tributary relations with Beijing. When the French took Hanoi, the Vietnamese court responded by seeking both help from the Qing and support from the Black Flags, an armed remnant of the Taiping, which had been forced out of China and was fighting the French in Vietnam.

The Qing responded by sending troops. Considerable wavering and diplomatic maneuvering followed in both Beijing and Paris, but in the end no means were found to reconcile the Chinese wish to preserve their historic tributary relations with Southeast Asia and the French determination to create an empire in this region. The resulting war was fought in Vietnam, on Taiwan and the Pescadores, and along the nearby coast of China proper, where the Fuzhou dockyards and the fleet built there were among the war's casualties.

In the peace agreement that followed, China was forced to abandon her claim to suzerainty over Vietnam. The French colony of Cochin China and the French protectorates of Annam and Tonkin were joined by protectorates over Cambodia and (in the 1890s) Laos to constitute French Indochina. Chinese influence in Southeast Asia was further diminished in 1886 when Britain completed the conquest of Burma, and China formally recognized this situation as well. Then in 1887, China ceded Macao to Portugal, officially recognizing the de facto situation there. Thus, in the last third of the nineteenth century the foreign powers tried to gain further concessions and proceeded to establish themselves in tributary areas that had been part of the traditional Chinese imperial order, although not of China proper. In the face of this challenge, the Chinese made concessions where necessary and resisted where feasible. When areas of major importance were at stake, their policy was quite forceful. As we shall see in Chapter 18, this included Korea, although in the end the Qing was unable to avert disaster there.

# *Notes*

1. Franz Schurmann and Orville Schell, *The China Reader: Imperial China* (New York: Vintage Books, 1967), pp. 105–13, which reproduces Harley F. MacNair, *Modern Chinese History, Selected Readings* (Shanghai: Commercial Press Ltd., 1923), pp. 2–9.

2. John K. Fairbank, *Trade and Diplomacy on the China Coast: The Opening of the Treaty Ports, 1842–1854* (Cambridge: Harvard Univ. Press, 1953), p. 59, which quotes H. B. Morse, *The Chronicles of the East India Company Trading to China, 1635–1834,* 5 Vols. (Oxford, 1926, 1929), Vol. 2, pp. 247–52.

3. James M. Polachek, *The Inner Opium War* (Cambridge: Harvard Univ. Press, 1992).

4. Ssu-yü Teng and John K. Fairbank, *China's Response to the West: A Documentary Survey, 1839–1923* (Cambridge: Harvard Univ. Press, 1954), p. 26.

5. John Fletcher, *The Cambridge History of China*, Vol. 10, ed. John K. Fairbank (Cambridge: Cambridge Univ. Press, 1978), pp. 375–85.

6. Philip A. Kuhn, *Origins of the Modern Chinese State* (Stanford: Stanford Univ. Press, 2002), p. 56.

7. Quoted in Jonathan D. Spence, *God's Chinese Son: The Taiping Heavenly Kingdom of Hong Xiuquan* (New York: W.W. Norton, 1996), p. 325.

8. Teng and Fairbank, *China's Response to the West*, p. 48. Parentheses inserted by the translation.

9. W. Theodore de Bary and Richard Lufrano, eds., *Sources of Chinese Tradition*, 2nd ed. (New York: Columbia Univ. Press, 2000), Vol. 2, p. 238. Adapted from Ssu-yü Teng and John K. Fairbank, *China's Response to the West*, p. 76.

10. Quoted in Immanuel C.Y. Hsu, *China's Entrance into the Family of Nations: The Diplomatic Phase, 1858–1880* (Cambridge: Harvard Univ. Press, 1960), p. 168.

11. Philip C. C. Huang, *The Peasant Economy and Social Change in North China* (Stanford: Stanford Univ. Press, 1985), p. 137.

12. Claudia Brown and Ju-hsi Chou, *Transcending Turmoil: Painting at the Close of China's Empire, 1796–1911* (Phoenix: Phoenix Art Museum, 1992).

13. Cyril Birch, ed., *Anthology of Chinese Literature* (New York: Grove Press, 1971), Vol. 2, p. 294. Reprinted with permission.

14. David Der-wei Wang, *Fin-de-siecle Splendor: Repressed Modernities of Late Qing Fiction, 1849–1911* (Stanford: Stanford Univ. Press, 1997), p. 125.

# Japan: Endings and Beginnings: From Tokugawa to Meiji, 1787–1873

Internal crisis and Western intrusion are the main themes of this chapter. Although there were some good years before the 1830s, the Tokugawa system was showing many symptoms of stress even before challenges from abroad put the old order to a final test. However, the dynamism of the forces subverting the Tokugawa state and society ultimately helped Japan develop into a modern country.

## I. Late Tokugawa

## II. The Meiji Restoration

| 1787 1793 1800 | | 1837 | | 1853 | | 1868 1873 |
|---|---|---|---|---|---|---|

Osaka Uprising    Perry's Arrival

**LATE TOKUGAWA**

**MEIJI (First Phase)**

Kansei Reforms (1789–1791)

Famine (1833–1836)

Mizuno Tadakuni (1841–1843)

Ii Naosuke (1858–1860)

There was a sense during the late Tokugawa that change was in the offing, but the trajectory from Tokugawa to Meiji was by no means clear and direct.

## *The* Bakufu (*1787–1841*)

Nature rescued the land from the famine of the 1780s, but it took government action to relieve the *bakufu*'s financial distress. The Kansei Reforms (1789–1791) were led by Matsudaira Sadanobu (1787–1793), an earnest Confucian who served a young shogun and owed his position as head of the *bakufu* to the support he received from an inner circle of daimyo. Matsudaira encouraged a return to simpler times. He launched a much-needed campaign against corruption and made an effort to improve public services in Edo, but his fiscal and economic program relied on edicts mandating lower prices for rice, restrictions on merchant guilds, cancellation of some samurai loans, and rent control. Matsudaira also sought to freeze foreign policy, reducing contact with the Dutch and proposing to leave Hokkaido undeveloped as a buffer to foreign intervention.

To improve administration, he not only sought to advance "men of ability" but also tried to control what they thought by furthering education and by making the Neo-Confucianism of Zhu Xi the official doctrine. He proscribed heterodoxy from the official *bakufu* school, but this had little effect elsewhere. There was also a hardening of censorship. All told, these measures "institutionalized and hardened tradition . . . and left a regime less flexible and more concerned with preserving a tradition that had now been defined."[1]

It did not take long for the *bakufu*'s systemic fiscal ills to reappear. By 1800 its annual budget showed a small deficit, the beginning of a trend. Forced loans and nineteen currency devaluations between 1819 and 1837 brought only temporary relief. The political authorities remained dependent on the market and on the merchants, who understood and manipulated the market. The government could not simply borrow, because there was no system of deficit financing. When famine struck again, beginning in 1833 and reaching a crescendo in 1836, the *bakufu*'s response was again inadequate. As before, reform was urgently needed.

# Economy and Society

Reflecting Japan's geographic and political diversity, there were major local differences in the economy and society. Fortunately, several local studies are currently helping correct overemphasis on the center, which was less central then than it is now. Thus, in his study of the herring fisheries in Hokkaido, which supplied fertilizer to the rest of Japan, David L. Howell found "a vibrant proto-industrial complex of commodity production for distant markets, dominated by merchant capitalists who used their ties to the local feudal authorities to good advantage."[2]

Several other domains pursued market-oriented policies, and commercial networks developed that linked communities in ways beyond the control of individual political authorities.

Change varied geographically and was complex socially. Some flourished; others suffered. Among the losers were lower-ranking samurai who had to convert a substantial portion of their rice stipend into cash and who were constantly at the mercy of a fluctuating market that they did not understand and would not study. When daimyo, burdened with periodic attendance in Edo and the need to maintain establishments in both Edo and their own *han* capitals, found themselves in financial difficulty, they frequently reduced samurai stipends. This hurt even the small minority of high-ranking men with large stipends but was devastating for the bulk of samurai, who ranked low in status and stipend.

Some samurai married daughters of wealthy merchants, but many lived in increasingly desperate circumstances. They pawned their swords, worked at humble crafts such as umbrella making and sandal weaving, and tried to hide their misery from the world. A samurai was taught that his mouth should display a toothpick even when he had not eaten. The samurai were not dissatisfied with the premises of a social system in which, after all, they formed the ruling class, but they were enraged by the discrepancy between the theoretical elevation of their status and the reality of their poverty. Not only was their poverty demeaning, but the spectacle of merchant wealth also hurt their pride. It seemed the height of injustice that society should reward the selfish moneymakers and condemn to indigence the warriors whose lives were ones of service. They harbored deep resentment against incompetence and corruption in high places, and they called on governments to employ more capable men from the lower samurai ranks.

City merchants and rural entrepreneurs flourished, but the increasing scope of the market had diverse effects on ordinary folk. In the Kanto there were villages left with untilled fields as people fled rural poverty in the hope of a better life in industry or commerce, but the market often proved a hard taskmaster. Consolation when things turned out badly and hope for a better future were offered by charismatic religious teachers and by cults such as Fujiko, which offered a potent combination of pilgrimage to Mount Fuji and worship of Maitreya, the Buddha of the future who would bring a new and better world.

When, as during a famine, things became unbearable, people resorted to violence. The best estimate has it that during 1830–1844 there were 465 rural disputes, 445 peasant uprisings, and 101 urban riots. A great impression was made by the 1837 uprising led by Ōshio Heihachiro (1793–1837), a low-ranking *bakufu* official and follower of Wang Yangming's philosophy of action. Although poorly planned and quickly suppressed, the uprising expressed a general sense of malaise and of the disintegration of authority. This was the case also in the countryside, where, in earlier conflicts, villagers had united behind their headmen, but now the gap between the rich and the poor had reached the point at which interests diverged too widely for the village to speak with a single voice.

# Reforms

In response to the financial and social crisis, there was one more concerted effort at reform both in the domains and at the center. On both levels, large doses of antiquated remedies such as economic retrenchment, bureaucratic reform, and moral rearmament were administered, but there were also some innovative policies. In the *bakufu*, reforms began in 1841 under Mizuno Tadakuni (1793–1851), a house daimyo who rose to *bakufu* leadership. His measures included recoinage, forced loans, dismissal of officials to reduce costs, and sumptuary laws intended to preserve morals and save money. Censorship became stricter. An effort (by no means the first) was made to force peasants to return to their lands. This was in keeping with the Confucian view of the primacy of agriculture and with the Tokugawa policy of strict class separation—but it hardly solved any problems.

A program to create a solid area of *bakufu* control around Edo and Osaka called for the creation of a *bakufu*-controlled zone of twenty-five square miles around Edo and twelve square miles around Osaka by moving certain daimyo and direct retainers out of these areas. This could have rationalized administration and strengthened the shogunate, but the plan proved too ambitious and could not be carried out. In the hope of fighting inflation, merchant monopolies were broken up and an attempt was made to bar the daimyo from engaging in commercial monopolies. Despite the retrenchment policy, an expensive and ostentatious formal procession to the Tokugawa mausoleum at Nikko was organized in an effort to reassert the *bakufu*'s preeminence. But the daimyo were not easily bridled, and the reform lasted only two years.

Various domains, faced with similar problems, attempted local reform programs of their own. Here and there *han* government machinery was reformed, stipends and other costs were cut, and some domains even rewarded the expert assistance of outstanding members of the merchant community by promoting them to samurai status. Agriculture was encouraged and commercial policies were

**FIGURE 17.1** Map showing Satsuma in Kyushu and Choshu in southwest Honshu, 1850s–1860s.

changed. In general, in the *han* as in the *bakufu*, the reforms ended, "some whimpering their way into oblivion, others culminating in an explosion in which the reformers were dismissed . . . and sometimes thrown into prison as well. . . . Whatever the end, they were ignored until their resurrection as models for fresh reforms in the 1850s and 1860s."[3]

A major domain in which the reforms did take hold was Satsuma in Kyushu (see Figure 17.1). Subsequently, Chōshu in southwest Honshu enjoyed similar success. In important ways these were untypical domains. For one, they were both large, outside *han* that had accepted Tokugawa supremacy only when they had no other alternative. Both had had their domains transferred and reduced in size. One consequence was that they kept alive an anti-Tokugawa tradition. Another was that the reduction in the size of their domains left them with a higher-than-average ratio of samurai to the land. In Satsuma, this led to the formation of a class of samurai who worked the land (*goshi*) and maintained a tight control of the countryside, which experienced not a single peasant uprising throughout the Tokugawa Period. Satsuma backwardness was also an asset to the domain in the sense that it worked against the erosion of samurai values found in economically more advanced and urbane regions. Both Chōshu and Satsuma also had special family ties with the court in Kyoto, the most likely focus for any anti-*bakufu* movement.

In both *han,* finances were put in order and a budget surplus was built up, although by different means. In Chōshu, rigorous cost cutting was initiated, major improvements were made in *han* financial administration, and the land tax was reformed. Most monopolies were abolished because they were unprofitable for the government and unpopular among the people. Only the profitable shipping and warehouse monopolies at Shimonoseki were continued. Otherwise, commodity transactions were turned over to merchants for a fee. Satsuma, in contrast, derived much of its income from its monopolies, especially the monopoly on sugar from the Ryukyu Islands, a Satsuma dependency, which was directed to continue sending tribute to China to foster trade. Thus, the Ryukyu Islands were a source of Chinese goods for Satsuma. The sugar monopoly was strictly enforced: private sale of sugar was a crime punishable by death. The sugar was brought to market in Osaka in the *han*'s own ships, and at every stage, from production to sale, everything was done to maximize profit for the Satsuma treasury.

These programs required vigorous leadership, because they naturally ran up against the opposition of merchants and others who benefited from doing things the old way. Both Chōshu and Satsuma were fortunate in having reform-minded daimyo who raised to power young samurai of middle or low rank, men who tended to be much more innovative and energetic than conservative samurai of high rank. Particularly in Chōshu, such differences in background and outlook among the samurai class led to bitter antagonism and political turbulence.

That reform was more successful in Chōshu and Satsuma than in the *bakufu* suggests that it was easier to implement reform in a well-organized, remote domain than in the central region, where the economic changes were most advanced and political pressures and responsibilities were far greater. Reform attempts in other *han* varied in success, but Chōshu and Satsuma are particularly important because these two large and wealthy domains were to play a crucial role in the eventual overthrow of the Tokugawa.

# Intellectual Currents

Economic, social, and political changes were accompanied by intellectual restiveness. Perceptions and ideas advanced by Shinto Revivalists of the School of National Learning, the Mito school with its emphasis on the centrality of the emperor, followers of Dutch Learning, and advocates of social restructuring ate away at the intellectual foundations of Tokugawa rule.

From the world of Osaka merchants came the bold ideas of Yamagata Bantō (1748–1821), a great Osaka financier with a well-established place in society. Yamagata based his ideas on astronomy and formulated a view of the world that allowed achievements to occur anywhere on the globe. He had great regard for utility and trust. One of his recommendations was to make written Japanese more accessible by using only the phonetic *kana* script and eliminating all Chinese characters.

An even more unorthodox thinker was Kaihō Seiryō (1748–1821), who spent his life traveling Japan free from encumbrances of status or family and saw all relations, including that between lord and samurai, in economic terms: the samurai sells his service to the lord in exchange for a stipend. For Kaihō, this was merely accommodating to *li* (principle). Here, a key Neo-Confucian concept is employed to structure a new theory of social conduct. The old bottles were capable of holding remarkably new wine.

In political thought, the respective roles of emperor and shogun continued to be subjects of discussion. In Mito, noted for its work on history, scholars emphasized that the emperor ruled because of his unique descent and that the shogun's legitimacy came from the mandate he derived from the emperor. Aizawa Seishisai (1782–1863), a leading Mito thinker, combined Confucian values and *bushidō* with Shinto mythology in discussing Japan's unique polity (*kokutai*). In 1825 he wanted the emperor to create in Japan the kind of unity that he saw as the basis for the strength of Western states and attributed to (iniquitous) Christianity. As Bob Tadashi Wakabayashi has indicated, in 1825 Aizawa's "argument for using the emperor's religious authority to bolster *bakufu* political supremacy was sensible and compelling."[4] But thirty years later the emperor and shogun had grown so far apart that this would have been inconceivable. Aizawa's glorification of the emperor, however, was to outlast the very idea of a *bakufu*.

Attitudes toward the West varied widely. Hirata Atsutane (1776–1843), for example, drew on the ideas of Motoori Norinaga and advocated an irrational and frequently naive nativism, but as a physician he admired Western medicine and studied Dutch medical texts. To reconcile his adulation of Japan with his appreciation for the foreign science, Hirata maintained that Japan had originally been pure and free of disease: the need for a powerful medical science arose only after Japan was infected by foreign contacts.

Most students of Dutch Learning took a more positive attitude. Interest in practical Western sciences such as astronomy, medicine, and mathematics continued to grow. The *bakufu* itself, in 1811, set up a bureau to translate Dutch books even though it maintained its closed-door policies toward the West. Takano Chōei (1804–1850) and Watanabe Kazan (1795–1841), persecuted for disagreeing with the *bakufu*'s seclusion policy, ended as suicides.

Outstanding among the students of Western science was the Confucian scholar Sakuma Shōzan (1811–1864), who conducted experiments in chemistry and glassmaking and later became an expert in the casting of guns; he was a serious thinker about the principles and the products of Western technology. There was ample room in his thought for Western learning, which he saw as part of the ultimate unity of *li* as taught by Zhu Xi; supplementing, not supplanting, his own tradition. His formula, "Eastern ethics and Western science," conveying the primacy of Japanese values and the compatibility of Western science, became an influential slogan after the Meiji Restoration. But Sakuma did not live to see the day; he was murdered by an antiforeign extremist from Chōshu in 1864.

Sakuma's intellectual strategy was essentially one of compartmentalization. The basic framework was left intact, with native and foreign traditions assigned different functions. Each had its distinct role. Most students of Dutch painting would have agreed, because they valued Western techniques more for their practical results than for any aesthetic merit. Yet, like all generalizations, this demands qualification. Hokusai, who lived until 1849, once contrasted the use of shading for decorative purposes in Chinese and Japanese art with its employment to create an effect of three-dimensionality in the West. He concluded, "One must understand both methods: there must be life and death in everything one paints."[5]

## The Opening of Japan

The opening of China to the West was a result of the Opium War and subsequent treaties with European powers. In Japan, the opening resulted from an armed mission by Commodore Matthew C. Perry of the United States Navy in 1853 (see Figure 17.2). The treaties that followed that momentous event ended the Tokugawa policy of seclusion. This undermined the authority not only of the *bakufu* but also of the entire Tokugawa system.

Before 1853 there were several Western attempts to induce the Japanese to broaden their foreign policy, but these efforts were sporadic, because they were not supported by substantial economic and political interests of the kind at work

**FIGURE 17.2** Commodore Matthew C. Perry (1794–1858) of the United States Navy. Artist unknown. In 1853–1854, Perry successfully led an armed mission to force isolationist Japan's agreement to open trade and diplomatic relations with the United States. Woodcut, nineteenth century, 9.6 in × 10.2 in. (© Courtesy Peabody Essex Museum, Salem, Massachusetts) in China. Regarded as poor and remote, Japan was considered a low priority by the great powers. The first approaches came from Japan's nearest Eurasian neighbor, the Russian Empire, and took place in the north, in the Kurile Islands, Sakhalin, and Hokkaido. In 1778 and again in 1792 the Russians requested trade relations in Hokkaido, and in 1804 a similar request was made in Nagasaki. All were refused. British ships seeking trade or ship's stores were also turned away. British whaling ships sometimes requested supplies, but in 1825 the *bakufu* ordered that all foreign ships should be driven from Japanese waters. In 1837 a private American–British attempt to open relations with Japan fared no better. But in 1842 the shogunate relaxed the edicts of 1825 and ordered that foreign ships accidentally arriving in Japan were to be provided with water, food, and fuel before being sent on their way.

China's defeat in the Opium War and the opening of new ports increased the number of Western vessels in East Asia and hence the pressure on Japan. This changing situation could not be ignored. To begin with, the lessons of Chinese weakness and Western strength were not lost on Japanese observers. Information concerning Western science, industry, and military capabilities continued to be provided by scholars of Dutch Learning and by the Dutch at Nagasaki. Information also came from China: Wei Yuan's *Illustrated Treatise on the Sea Kingdoms* was widely read after it appeared in a Japanese edition in 1847. Furthermore, the Japanese were making progress in mastering Western technology. By the 1840s, Mito, Hizen, and Satsuma were casting guns using Western methods. In 1850 Hizen possessed the first reverberatory furnace needed to produce iron suitable for making modern cannons. As already noted, a few courageous students of the West had suggested abandoning the policy of seclusion well before the arrival of Perry. The Dutch, too, had warned the *bakufu* of the designs of the stronger Western nations.

In 1846 an American mission to Japan ended in failure, but with the acquisition of California in 1848, the interest of the United States increased because Nagasaki, 500 miles from Shanghai, was a convenient fueling stop for ships bound from San Francisco to that port. Thus, the United States, rather than Britain or Russia, whose interests remained marginal, took the lead, sending Perry with four ships. Perry and his fleet reached Japan in July 1853, forced the Japanese to accept a letter from the American president to the emperor, and announced that he would return for an answer the following spring.

No match militarily for the American fleet, the *bakufu* realized that it would have to accede at least partly to American demands. In preparation for that unpopular move, it took the unprecedented step of soliciting the opinions of even the outside daimyo. This turned out to be a serious miscalculation, because instead of hoped-for support, the *bakufu* received only divided and unhelpful advice and seriously undermined its exclusive right to determine foreign policy.

When Perry returned in February 1854 with eight ships, an initial treaty was signed that provided for the opening of Shimoda and Hakodate to ships seeking

**FIGURE 17.3** *Harris's Procession on the Way to Edo.* Artist unknown. Townsend Harris, first American consul to Japan, traveled to Edo (Tokyo) in 1856 to negotiate a commercial treaty with Japan—a treaty that contained terms unfavorable to Japan. Watercolor, 21 in × 15.3 in. (© Peabody Essex Museum, Salem, Massachusetts)

provisions, assured that the shipwrecked would receive good treatment, and permitted the United States later to send a consul to Japan. Similar treaties with Britain and France followed in 1855, and the Dutch and Russians negotiated broader agreements in 1857. The task of negotiating a commercial treaty was left to the first American consul, Townsend Harris, who arrived in Japan in 1856 and gradually succeeded in persuading the shogunate to make concessions (see Figure 17.3). The resulting treaty was signed in 1858, and another round of treaties with the Dutch, Russians, British, and French followed.

At the end of this process, Japan's international situation was essentially that of China under the unequal treaty system. First there was the matter of opening ports. This began with Shimoda on the Izu Peninsula and Hakodate in Hokkaido; it was extended to Nagasaki and Kanagawa (for which Yokohama was substituted). Dates were set for the opening of Niigata, Hyogo (modern Kobe), and the admission of foreign residents, but not trade, into Osaka and Edo. As in China, the treaties gave foreigners the right to be tried by their own consular courts under their own laws (extraterritoriality). Japan lost its tariff autonomy and was limited to relatively low import duties. Most-favored-nation treatment obliged Japan to extend to all states any concession it granted to any one of the others.

## Domestic Politics

For the *bakufu,* forced to accede to foreign demands without enjoying support at home, these were difficult years. Each concession to the powers provided additional ammunition to its domestic enemies. Compounding its difficulties, the *bakufu* itself was divided by factionalism and policy differences. An attempt was made after Perry's arrival to broaden the shogunate's base by drawing on the advice of nonhouse daimyo. The lord of Mito, Tokugawa Nariaki (1800–1860), a persistent advocate of resistance to the West, was placed in charge of national defense. These measures, however, failed to strengthen the *bakufu*—too many men were pulling in opposite directions.

When the shogun died without an heir in 1858, a bitter dispute took place over the rival claims of two candidates for the succession. One was still a boy but had the strongest claim by descent. He also had the backing of most of the house daimyo (*fudai*), including that of Ii Naosuke, greatest of the *fudai.* The other candidate was Tokugawa Yoshinobu (then known as Hitotsubashi Keiki), the capable son of the lord of Mito.

The immediate issue in the succession dispute concerned control over the *bakufu,* because Keiki's accession was seen as a threat to the continued control over the shogunate by the *fudai.* Foreign policy was also involved because the *bakufu* officials, as men on the spot, were inclined to make concessions to the foreigners. The great lords, however, demanded a vigorous defense policy against the intruders from the West. Furthermore, the lord of Mito and some of his peers envisioned their own *han* as playing important roles in building military strength. Thus, his advocacy of a strong foreign policy was consistent with his desire to strengthen his own domain at the expense of the center. Meanwhile, the split in the *bakufu* increased the political importance of the imperial court. Nariaki even appealed to Kyoto for support for his son's candidacy. And when the shogun tried to obtain imperial approval for the treaty negotiated with Harris, he failed.

The crisis of 1858 was temporarily resolved when Ii Naosuke took charge of the *bakufu* as grand councilor (*tairo*), a high post more often than not left vacant and one that had previously been held by several members of the Ii family. The effective power of this position depended on the authority of the incumbent, and the strong-minded Ii Naosuke used it to dominate the shogunate. He proceeded to sign the treaty with the United States without prior imperial approval; vigorously reassert *bakufu* power; purge his enemies; force into retirement or house arrest the daimyo who had opposed him and were on the losing side in the succession dispute, including the lord of Mito; and punish some of the court nobles and Mito loyalists. For a moment, the *bakufu* was revitalized. But only for a moment: in March 1860, Ii was assassinated by a group of samurai, mostly from Mito. They were advocates of *sonnō*, "revere the emperor," and *jōi*, "expel the barbarians."

## Sonnō Jōi

As we observed earlier, Mito was the home of an emperor-centered school of historiography and political thought, and its lord was one of the most fervent advocates of a strong military policy to "expel the barbarians." It is therefore not surprising that Mito thought influenced the passionate and brilliant young man who became the main spokesman and hero of the Sonnō Jōi movement. This was Yoshida Shōin (1830–1859), the son of a low-ranking Chōshū samurai. Yoshida was influenced by *bushidō* in the tradition of Yamaga Sokō, by books on military science, and by Confucianism. From Sakuma Shōzan he learned about the West. Then he became acquainted with Mito ideas on a study trip to northern Japan, which, because it was unauthorized, cost him his samurai rank. Apprehensive of the West and convinced of the importance of knowing one's enemy, he tried to stow away on one of Perry's ships but was caught and placed under house arrest in Chōshū. After his release he started a school there and attracted disciples, including Kido Kōin (or Takamasa, 1834–1877), one of the three leading statesmen of the Meiji Restoration, and the future leaders Itō Hirobumi and Yamagata Aritomo. Yoshida condemned the *bakufu* for its handling of the foreign problem. He charged that its failure to expel the barbarians reflected incompetence, dereliction of duty, and a lack of proper reverence for the throne. Like many men of lower samurai origins, he resented a system that rewarded birth more than ability or talent, and he blamed the *bakufu*'s inability to reject the foreigners on this system. What was needed to redress the situation were pure and selfless officials who would act out of true loyalty rather than mindless obedience. Thus, Yoshida's teaching combined elements of moral revival at home, opposition to the foreigner, and championship of the throne.

Initially, Yoshida favored the appointment of new men to the *bakufu,* but after the signing of the treaty with the United States in 1858, he concluded that the *bakufu* must be overthrown. Both personal fulfillment and national salvation required an act of unselfish self-sacrifice by a national hero. In 1858, Yoshida, seeking to achieve both aims, plotted the assassination of the emissary sent by the shogun to the imperial court to persuade the emperor to agree to the commercial treaty with the United States. Word leaked out. Yoshida was arrested and sent to Edo, where he was beheaded the following year.

# Mixed Responses to the West

In this turbulent era, Japanese reactions to the West varied widely. Some Japanese, like the Confucian Shinoya Tōin (1810–1867), had an absolute hatred for everything Western. Shinoya even belittled the script in which the foreigners wrote, describing it as follows:

> [It is] confused and irregular, wriggling like snakes or larvae of mosquitoes. The straight ones are like dog's teeth, the round ones are like worms. The crooked ones are like the forelegs of a mantis, the stretched ones are like slime lines left by snails. They resemble dried bones or decaying skulls, rotten bellies of dead snakes or parched vipers.[6]

It is not surprising that a culture that prized calligraphy should find the strictly utilitarian Western script aesthetically unappetizing, but Shinoya's invective goes beyond mere distaste. Every word betrays, and indeed is meant to express, horror and disgust at the beasts that had come among them.

But there were others who were determined to learn from the West, even if only to use that knowledge to defeat the foreigner. Their slogan was *kaikoku joi:* "open the country to drive out the barbarians." The learning process continued. In 1857 the *bakufu* opened the Institute for the Investigation of Barbarian Books near Edo Castle. Not only the *bakufu* but also some of the domains sent men on study trips abroad; in the case of the *han,* this was often done illegally. The process of adopting Western technology, begun even before Perry's arrival, was accelerated.

An indication of the people's receptivity to the new knowledge is provided by the popularity of the writings of Fukuzawa Yukichi (1835–1901), who went abroad twice in the early 1860s and published seven books before the restoration, beginning in 1866 with the first volume of *Conditions in the West* (*Seiyō jijō*), which appeared in 1866 and promptly sold 150,000 copies. Another 100,000 copies were sold in pirated editions. These works, written in a simple style easy enough for Fukuzawa's housemaid to read, were filled with detailed descriptions of Western institutions and life: hospitals and schools, tax systems and museums, climate and clothes, cutlery, beds, and chamber pots. Fukuzawa went on to become a leading Meiji intellectual, but the turbulent years just before the restoration were dangerous for men of his outlook.

Unlike Yoshida Shōin, some people hoped for a reconciliation of the court and *bakufu,* and there were some who still hoped the *bakufu* could transform itself and take the lead in creating a more modern state. These issues, at work during the 1860s, were finally buried in the restoration.

# Last Years of the Shogunate (1860–1867)

After the assassination of Ii Naosuke in 1860, the *bakufu* leadership tried compromise. An effort was made to effect a "union of the court and military" that was confirmed by the shogun's marriage to the emperor's sister. In return for affirming the emperor's primacy, the *bakufu* obtained assent for its foreign policy. It also sought to win daimyo support by relaxing the requirements for attendance at Edo. However, this policy ran into the opposition of Kyoto loyalists, activists of the Sonnō Jōi persuasion, samurai, and voluntary rōnin who had escaped the bonds of feudal discipline by requesting to leave their lords' service. Psychologically, this was not difficult, because their loyalty to their lords had become bureaucratized and they now felt the claims of a higher loyalty to the throne. Men of extremist dedication, ready to sacrifice their lives, to kill and be killed, for the cause, terrorized the streets of Kyoto in the early 1860s and made the capital unsafe for moderates, who risked losing their heads and having them displayed as a warning to others. This also happened to statues: their location in a temple did not save the statues of Ashikaga shoguns from decapitation at the hands of some followers of Hirata Atsutane who, unable to reach prominent living targets, exercised vengeance on the Ashikaga for wronging the emperor in the fourteenth century. Mito, too, was notably unsafe for moderates.

For ordinary people this was a time when their frustrations came to a head, a time of messianic visions and religious fervor, of amulets falling from the sky, and of people finding temporary escape from misery by dancing wildly in the streets, shouting *ee ja nai ka* ("ain't it great," or "what the hell"), barging into the houses of the rich and powerful demanding food and drink, forcing them to join the dance, and wreaking general havoc. Beginning in the cities of central Japan and spreading along the Tokaidō, these riots showed that the Tokugawa order was falling apart. George M. Wilson says of the Meiji Restoration that "a pervasive urge to remedy distress at home was just as compelling to most participants as the patriotic intent to elevate Japan in the international area."[7]

Westerners, too, were blamed for the distress because the opening of the ports was followed by a marked rise in the price of rice, causing great hardship and reinforcing nativistic hatred of foreigners. Several foreigners were assassinated by fervent samurai in 1859, and in 1861 Townsend Harris's Dutch interpreter was cut down and the British legation in Edo was attacked. In 1862 a British merchant lost his life at the hands of Satsuma samurai. When the British were unable to obtain satisfaction from the *bakufu,* they took matters into their own hands. In August 1863, they bombarded Kagoshima, the Satsuma capital, to force punishment of the guilty and payment of an indemnity.

A similar incident involving Chōshū took place in the summer of 1863. By that time, extremists had won control of the imperial court and, with Chōshū backing, had forced the shogun to accept June 25, 1863, as the date for the expulsion of the barbarians. The *bakufu,* caught between the intransigent foreigners and the insistent court, interpreted the agreement to mean that negotiations for the closing of the ports would begin on that day, but Chōshū and the loyalists interpreted it more literally. When Chōshū guns began firing on foreign ships in the Straits of Shimonoseki, the foreign ships fired back. First American warships came to shell the fortifications, then French ships landed parties that destroyed the fort and ammunition. Still Chōshū persisted in firing on foreign vessels, until in September 1864 a combined French, Dutch, and American fleet demolished the forts and forced Chōshū to come to terms. These losses, plus a defeat inflicted on Chōshū adherents by a Satsuma–Aizu force in Kyoto in August 1864, stimulated Chōshū to overhaul its military forces. It had already arranged to purchase arms and ships. Now peasant militia were organized and mixed rifle units were formed, staffed by commoners and samurai, a radical departure from Tokugawa practice and from the basic principles of Tokugawa society. One of these units was commanded by Itō Hirobumi (1841–1909), recently returned from study in England.

Satsuma's response to defeat, although not as radical as Chōshū's, was similar in its appreciation of the superiority of Western weapons. With British help, the domain began acquiring Western ships, forming the nucleus of what was to become the Imperial Japanese Navy. The British supported Satsuma partly because they were disillusioned with the *bakufu* and partly because the French were supporting the shogunate with arms, hoping to lay the foundations for future influence in a reconstituted shogunate. By now many *bakufu* officials appreciated the need for institutional change and for modernization. During the closing years of the Tokugawa, the issue changed from preserving the old system to determining who would take the lead in building the new. In Chōshū and Satsuma, too, there was less talk about "expelling the barbarians" and more about "enriching the country and strengthening the army," at least among the leaders.

The politics of these years were even more than usually full of complications and intrigues, and as long as Chōshū and Satsuma remained on opposite sides, the situation remained fluid. Traditionally unfriendly to each other, competing for power in Kyoto, and differing in their policy recommendations, they were nevertheless unified in their opposition to a restoration of Tokugawa power. There were two wars against Chōshū. In the first, 1864–1865, a large *bakufu* force with men from many domains defeated Chōshū. This set off a civil war in Chōshū from which the revolutionaries, with their mixed rifle regiments, emerged victorious.

This led to a second *bakufu* war against Chōshū, but before this second war began, in 1866, Chōshū and Satsuma made a secret alliance. When war came, Satsuma and some other powerful *han* remained on the sidelines. Although outnumbered, the Chōshū forces, better trained, better armed, and higher in morale, defeated the *bakufu*.

After this defeat by a single *han,* the *bakufu,* under Tokugawa Yoshinobu (who inherited the position of shogun in 1866), tried to save what it could. There were attempts to work out a daimyo coalition and calls for imperial restoration. In November the shogun accepted a proposal that he resign in favor of a council of daimyo under the emperor. According to this arrangement, he was to retain his lands and, as the most powerful lord in Japan, serve as prime minister. However, this was unacceptable to the *sonno* advocates in Satsuma and Chōshū and to the restorationists at court, including the court noble Iwakura Tonomi (1825–1883), a master politician. On January 3, 1868, forces from Satsuma and other *han* seized the palace and proclaimed the restoration. The shogunate was destroyed. Tokugawa lands were confiscated, and the shogun himself was reduced to the status of an ordinary daimyo. A short civil war ensued. There was fighting in Edo and in northern Honshu, but no real contest. Last to surrender was the *bakufu* navy in May 1869.

# II. The Meiji Restoration

*Formation of a New Government*

*The Charter Oath*

*Dismantling the Old Order*

*Disaffection and Opposition*

*The Crisis of 1873*

*The Meaning of the Restoration*

The end of the shogunate brought to the fore new leaders to deal with a world full of dangers and opportunities—perhaps in equal measure.

## Formation of a New Government

The men who overthrew the Tokugawa in January 1868 did not subscribe to any clear and well-defined program. There was general agreement about the abolition of the shogunate and "restoration" of the emperor, but this meant no more than that the emperor should once again be at the center of the political system, functioning as the source of legitimacy and providing a sense of continuity. It most certainly did not mean that actual power should be given to the sixteen-year-old Meiji Emperor (1852–1912; r. 1867–1912),* nor did it necessarily imply the destruction of feudalism, because there were those who envisioned the restoration in terms of a new feudal system headed by the emperor. On the other hand, Japanese scholars had long been aware that the Chinese system provided a bureaucratic alternative to feudalism. This surely eased the shift to bureaucratic centralization.

The new leaders did not always see eye to eye, but they shared certain qualities: they were all of similar age (thirty-five to forty-three years) and rank, and they came from the victorious *han* or the court aristocracy, although the *han* coalition was soon broadened to include men from Tosa and Hizen. The three most eminent leaders in the early years of the restoration were Ōkubo Toshimichi (1830–1878), Kido Kōin (1833–1877), and Saigō Takamori (1827–1877). Both

---

* His name was Mutsuhito, but as in the case of the Qing emperors in China, it is customary to refer to him and his successors by the designation given to their reign periods.

Ōkubo and Kido had risen to leadership in their own domains (Satsuma and Chōshū) through their influence in the domain's bureaucratic establishment and among the loyalist activists. Of the two, Ōkubo was the stronger personality—disciplined, formal, and somewhat intimidating; dedicated to the nation, cautious, and practical. Kido was livelier but more volatile, less self-confident but more concerned than Ōkubo with strengthening the popular base of the government. But he was just as devoted to building a strong state.

Ōkubo's was the single strongest voice in government from 1873 to 1878. One of his initial tasks was to retain the cooperation of Saigō, the military leader of the Satsuma forces who had joined with Chōshū to overthrow the Tokugawa. Saigō was a man of imposing physique and great physical strength. He was known for his outstanding courage and possessed many of the traditional warrior virtues, such as generosity and contempt for money. More conservative than the others, he was devoted to Satsuma and its samurai but worked with the others at least until 1873. They were united in their conviction that the country must be strengthened to resist the West.

For national self-preservation, the leaders were prepared to enact vast changes, but it took time to plan and carry these out and, indeed, to consolidate their own power in a land where, as Kido complained, "we are surrounded on four sides by little *bakufu*."[8] To insure that the emperor would not become a focus of opposition to reform, Ōkubo argued that he should be moved to Edo, renamed Tokyo (Eastern Capital) in September 1868. This took place the following year when the emperor moved into the shogun's former castle, which in 1871, after much debate, was renamed the "imperial palace."

# The Charter Oath

Even before the move, in April 1868, while the emperor was still in Kyoto, a Charter Oath was issued in his name to provide a general, if vague, statement of purpose for the new regime. It consisted of five articles:

1. An assembly widely convoked shall be established and all matters of state shall be decided by public discussion.

2. All classes high and low shall unite in vigorously promoting the economy and welfare of the nation.

3. All civil and military officials and the common people as well shall be allowed to fulfill their aspirations so that there may be no discontent among them.

4. Base customs of former times shall be abandoned and all actions shall conform to the principles of international justice.

5. Knowledge shall be sought throughout the world and thus shall be strengthened the foundation of the imperial polity.[9]

Although the government was reorganized to provide an assembly in keeping with the first article, power remained with the original leadership and the attempt to implement this provision was soon abandoned. In contrast, the end of seclusion, the acceptance of international law, and the openness to foreign ideas conveyed by the last two articles took place. Symbolic of this shift was the audience granted to representatives of the foreign powers by the emperor in Kyoto just a month before the Charter Oath was issued. The document itself was drafted by two men familiar with Western thought; it was then revised by Kido. The ramifications of the Charter Oath were far from clear, but the last article, to seek for knowledge "throughout the world," was taken very seriously. Furthermore, with its call for an assembly and its strong internationalism, the entire document illustrates the gulf between Japanese and Chinese leaders at this time. No Chinese government would have issued such a document in an attempt to gain political strength.

## Dismantling the Old Order

Although the machinery of the central government underwent various reorganizations, the prime need was for the government to extend and consolidate its authority and ability to collect taxes. Because the continued existence of the feudal domains was a major obstacle to this, the government leaders undertook the delicate but essential task of abolishing the *han*. In March 1869, Kido and Ōkubo were able to use their influence to induce the daimyo of Chōshū and Satsuma to return their domains to the emperor. They were joined in this act by the lords of Tosa and Hizen. Many others followed suit, anxious to be in the good graces of the new government and expecting to be appointed governors of their former domains, which they were. The real blow came in 1871 when, in the name of national unity, the domains were abolished and the whole country was reorganized into prefectures. This was made palatable to the daimyo by generous financial arrangements. They were allowed to retain a tenth of the former domain revenue as personal income while the government assumed responsibility for *han* debts and financial obligations. The daimyo were also assured continued high social standing and prestige. Finally, in 1884, they were elevated to the peerage.

By background and experience, the new leadership was keenly sensitive to the importance of military power. Initially, the new government depended entirely on forces from the supporting domains, but this would hardly do for a government truly national in scope. Accordingly, the leaders set about forming a new army freed from local ties. Rejecting the views of Saigō, who envisioned a samurai army that would ensure the warrior class a useful and, he hoped, brilliant role in Japan's future, the leaders decided in 1872 to build their army on the basis of commoner conscription. In January 1873, the new measure, largely the work of Yamagata Aritomo (1838–1922), "father of the Japanese Army," became law.

The restoration had a profound effect on the samurai. The new army, by eliminating distinctions between commoners and samurai, cut to the heart of the status system. Anyone could become a warrior now. Other marks of samurai distinctiveness were eliminated or eroded. In 1870 commoners were allowed to acquire surnames and were released from previous occupational and residential restrictions. In 1871 the wearing of swords by samurai became optional; five years later it was prohibited entirely.

The samurai's position was further undermined by the abolition of the *han,* which left them without political or social function. Furthermore, continued payment of their stipends at the customary rate was more than the central government could afford. Accordingly, they were pensioned off. But in view of their number, the government could not afford to treat them as generously as it did the daimyo. At first, samurai stipends were reduced on a sliding scale from half to a tenth of what they had been, then they were given the right to commute these into twenty-year bonds (1873), and finally they were forced to accept the bonds (1876).

Reduction and commutation of samurai stipends was only one of the measures taken to establish the new government on a sound financial basis. In addition to monetary and banking reform, a tax system was created (1873). The fiscal measures were largely the work of Ōkuma Shigenobu (1838–1922), a man from Hizen who was to remain prominent in Meiji politics, and Itō Hirobumi (1841–1909) of Chōshū. The main source of government revenue was, as before, agriculture, but in place of the old percentage of the crop payable by the village to the daimyo, the tax was now collected by the government in money in accordance with the assessed value of the land. It was payable by the owner, and for this purpose ownership rights had to be clearly established. This was not done in favor of the absentee feudal interest long divorced from the land, nor did ownership pass equitably to all peasants. Instead, certificates were issued to the cultivators and wealthy villagers who had paid the tax during Tokugawa times. In this way tenancy was perpetuated. Because poor peasants, often unable to meet their taxes, were forced to mortgage their land, the rate of tenancy increased, rising from about 25 percent before the new system to about 40 percent twenty years later.

## Disaffection and Opposition

The creation of a modern political, military, and fiscal system benefited the state but hurt some of the people. The peasantry was unhappy not only about the land system but also about forced military service and showed its bitter displeasure by staging uprisings with increasing frequency from 1866 to 1873. Many large merchant houses that had developed symbiotic relationships with the *bakufu* or daimyo also suffered during these years, and some went bankrupt.

More serious for the regime was samurai discontent. The new government was led by former samurai, and for many men the new order meant a release from old restrictions and the opening of new opportunities. Because the samurai were the educated class with administrative experience, they supplied the personnel for local and national government, officers for the army, teachers for the schools, and colonists for Hokkaido. Casting aside tradition, some entered the world of business and finance. Yet there were many who did not make a successful transition, who were unable to take advantage of the new vocations opened to them or to use their payments to establish themselves in new lines of endeavor. And among the leaders and the supporters of the Meiji government were men who firmly believed that its purpose was literally the restoration of the old, not the creation of the new. A split between conservatives and modernizers developed early in the restoration and came to a head in 1873.

# The Crisis of 1873

The crisis of 1873 centered on the issue of going to war with Korea to force it to open its doors to Japan. Those who advocated war, such as Saigō and Itagaki Taisuke (1836–1919) from Tosa, did so not only out of nationalist motives but also because they saw war as a way to provide employment for the samurai, an opportunity to give them a greater role in the new society and a means to preserve their military heritage. Saigō, a military leader with great charisma and devotion to the way of the warrior, asked to be sent to Korea as ambassador so that he could deliberately get himself killed and thus provide a cause for going to war.

A decision for war was made in the summer of 1873 in the absence of Ōkubo, Kido, and other important leaders who were abroad in America and Europe. They were on a diplomatic and study mission headed by Iwakura Tonomi, the noble who had played a leading role at court in bringing about the Meiji Restoration. The purposes of the Iwakura mission were to convey the Meiji Emperor's respects to the heads of state of the treaty powers and build goodwill, to discuss subjects for later treaty revision, and to provide its distinguished members with an opportunity to observe and study the West at first hand. It took 631 days, including seven months in the United States, four in England, and seven in continental Europe. The Japanese leaders did not just have audiences with heads of state and observe parliaments and courts. They were interested in everything:

> They toured cotton mills, iron foundries, shipyards, newspaper plants, breweries, prisons, banks, stock exchanges, cathedrals, telegraph offices, military fortifications, lunatic asylums, libraries and art galleries. . . . [They] visited zoos; attended the theater and opera; and took in endless concerts, ballets, and an occasional masked ball, circus performance, and fox hunt.[10]

They returned home in September 1873 with a new appreciation of the importance and complexity of modernization and new realization of the magnitude of the task facing Japan in its quest for equality. They were convinced of the urgent priority of domestic change.

When the mission returned, Ōkubo led the opposition to the Korean venture on the grounds that Japan could not yet afford such an undertaking. Ōkubo,

Kido, and Iwakura prevailed, with the support of many officials and the court. In October it was decided to abandon the Korean expedition and to concentrate on internal development. The decision split the government. Bitterly disappointed, the war advocates, including Saigō and Itagaki, resigned. They provided leadership for those disaffected by the new government and its policies, an opposition that would prove troublesome to those in power. But their departure left the government in the hands of a group of men unified by a commitment to modernization. Most prominent among them were Ōkubo, Itō, Ōkuma, and Iwakura.

By 1873 the Meiji government had survived the difficult period of initial consolidation. It had established the institutional foundations for the new state, had found a means of defense and national security, and with the resolution of the 1873 crisis had charted the basic course of development at home and peace abroad that was to dominate Japanese policies during the next twenty years.

# The Meaning of the Restoration

Like other major historical events, the Meiji Restoration meant and continued to mean different things to different people. Most visible was increased openness to the West in matters small and large. Already in the early 1870s the gentleman of fashion sported a foreign umbrella and watch and, as recommended by Fukuzawa Yukichi, strengthened his body by eating beef. Faddish Westernism was satirized in one of the best-sellers of the day, *Aguranabe (Sitting around the Stew Pan)* (1871) by Kanagaki Robun (1829–1903). Ōkubo ate bread, drank dark tea for breakfast, and wore Western clothes even at home. In 1872 Western dress was made mandatory at court and other official functions. The Gregorian calendar was adopted the same year. After the Tokyo fire of 1872, the city's main avenue, the Ginza, was rebuilt under the supervision of an English architect. It boasted brick buildings, colonnades, and gas lamps (see Figure 17.4). The inhabitants of Tokyo could take pleasure and pride in the Ginza, but the glitter of the capital was not shared by the countryside. Already in 1874, the widening contrast between the prosperous modern capital and the hinterland prompted Fukuzawa Yukichi to warn of the following:

> The purpose [of the government] seems to be to use the fruits of rural labor to make flowers for Tokyo. Steel bridges glisten in the capital, and horse-drawn carriages run on the streets, but in the country the wooden bridges are so rotten one cannot cross them. The cherry blossoms bloom in Kyōbashi [in Tokyo] but weeds grow in the country fields. Billows of smoke such as rise from city stoves do not rise from the farmer's furnace. . . . We must cease making Tokyo richer and concentrate on rural districts.[11]

Unfortunately for those at the bottom of society, this was not to be.

Ideologically, the main thrust was to use the old to justify the new, a process that produced new visions of the past and of the future. Invoking the name of the em-

**FIGURE 17.4** The Ginza, 1873. The Ginza's facade and lampposts represent the Meiji Restoration's most visible feature—an increased openness to the West in matters small and large. (© Tsisei Corporation, Japan. Used by permission)

peror, a symbol of continuity with the old, the Meiji leaders were able to innovate even as they assured the survival, in new forms, of old values and ideas. Along these lines, there was an effort to turn Japan into a Shinto state. In 1868 Shinto was proclaimed the basis for the government and a Department of Shinto was established, with precedence over the other departments. There was a drive to purify Shinto, to eliminate Buddhist influences that had steadily seeped into Shinto, and to make Shinto the only religion of Japan. This drive, however, ran into opposition from Buddhists and conflicted with Western pressures for the legalization of Christianity. In 1872 the Department of Shinto was abolished, and in 1873 the ban on Christianity was lifted. Settlement of the legal status of Shinto had to wait until 1882.

The restoration was revolutionary in that it destroyed the old system and created a centralized state. It eliminated the old class lines and legally opened all careers to all men. In all areas of human activity it prepared the way for the profound changes that, during the next century, were to transform the very countryside of Japan. But if it was a revolution, it was a revolution from above, an "aristocratic revolution," to borrow a term from Thomas C. Smith.[12] Although popular unrest helped undermine the Tokugawa, the restoration was not the product of a mass movement or of a radical social ideology. It did not radically change the structure of village life or the mode of agricultural production. It eliminated the samurai elite as a legally defined, privileged class but, led by men who were themselves samurai, did so in terms samurai could understand.

The legacy of the restoration was complex and perhaps is not even yet fully played out, because it provided a base for both the successes and the failures that were to come.

# *Notes*

1. Marius Jansen, ed., *The Cambridge History of Japan,* Vol. 5: *The Nineteenth Century* (Cambridge: Cambridge Univ. Press, 1989), p. 60.

2. David L. Howell, *Capitalism from Within: Economy, Society, and the State in a Japanese Fishery* (Berkeley: Univ. of California Press, 1995), p. 91.

3. Harold Bolitho, in Howell, *Capitalism from Within,* p. 159.

4. Bob Tadashi Wakabayashi, *Anti-Foreignism and Western Learning in Early Modern Japan: The New Theses of 1825* (Cambridge: Harvard Univ. Press, 1986), p. 134.

5. Michiaki Kawakita, *Modern Currents in Japanese Art: Heibonsha Survey of Japanese Art,* Vol. 24, Charles S. Terry, trans. (New York and Tokyo: Weatherhill/Heibonsha, 1974), p. 29.

6. Marius Jansen, ed., *Changing Japanese Attitudes toward Modernization* (Princeton: Princeton Univ. Press, 1969), pp. 57–58; quoting van Gulik, "Kakkaron: A Japanese Echo of the Opium War," *Monumenta Serica* 4 (1939): 542–43.

7. George M. Wilson, *Patriots and Redeemers in Japan: Motives in the Meiji Restoration* (Chicago: Univ. of Chicago Press, 1992), p. 2. For *ee ja nai ka,* see p. 98.

8. Albert Craig and Donald H. Shively, eds., *Personality in Japanese History* (Berkeley and Los Angeles: Univ. of California Press, 1970), p. 297.

9. Ishii Ryosuke, *Japanese Legislation in the Meiji Era,* William J. Chai, trans. (Tokyo: Pan-Pacific Press, 1958), p. 145.

10. John Hunter Boyle, *Modern Japan: The American Nexus* (Fort Worth: Harcourt Brace Jovanovich, 1993), p. 92.

11. Quoted in Mikiso Hane, *Peasants, Rebels, and Outcastes: The Underside of Modern Japan* (New York: Pantheon Books, 1982), p. 33.

12. See Thomas C. Smith, "Japan's Aristocratic Revolution," *Yale Review* 50 (Spring 1961), 370–83. Also see Marius Jansen, "The Meiji State: 1868–1912," in James B. Crowley, ed., *Modern East Asia: Essays in Interpretation* (New York: Harcourt Brace Jovanovich, 1970), pp. 95–121, which cites Smith on p. 103.

# The Emergence of Modern Japan:
## 1874–1894

| 1868 | 1877 | 1889 1890 | 1894 1895 | 1912 |
|---|---|---|---|---|
| The Restoration | Satsuma Rebellion | Promulgation of the Constitution | End of Sino-Japanese War | |
| | | | Start of the Sino-Japanese War | |
| | | Rescript on Education | | |
| | MEIJI JAPAN | | | |

After the Meiji leaders consolidated their new regime, their top priority was to transform Japan into a modern nation accepted as an equal by the powers of the world. During the next twenty years, a new political framework was devised, the foundations for a modern economy were laid, and profound change occurred in institutions as in values and ideas. Just as tradition meant different things to different people, throughout the nineteenth and twentieth centuries there were diverse (and changing) versions of modernity. Rather than attempting a substantive definition of modern, we use the term in a purely temporal sense, to mean "up to date." During the nineteenth and twentieth centuries, modernity was largely defined by the West because of its great power.

Change was neither smooth nor simple. In the intricate interweaving of old and new, some old customs went the way of the samurai's sword and topknot, but others were retained or transformed and put to new uses. Early Meiji saw not only the appearance of what was patently new and seen as such, but also the emergence of new versions of the past. John W. Dower, summarizing a body of recent scholarship, has written the following:

> Thus they [recent scholars] called attention to the careful and adroit manner by which elites and molders of popular opinion, in Japan as elsewhere, routinely create modern myths under the rubric of "tradition" or cultural uniqueness—whether these be myths involving the emperor, or an idealized hierarchical "family system," or a code of "obedience and filial piety," or a harmonious "traditional employment system," or a simple and egalitarian rural community, or a pure "national essence" rooted in the past before the corruption of foreign influences from China and the West.[1]

As we have seen, myths centered on a "national essence" could draw on Tokugawa nativist thought, but they became modern myths participating in Japan's process of becoming modern. That process knows no end, but Japan's victory over China in 1895 marked the conclusion of the crucial initial phase, because by then it had achieved many of its initial objectives: a centralized government, a modernizing economy, and sufficient military strength to warrant international respect.

## Political Developments

Acting in the name of the emperor, a small inner circle dominated the government during the 1870s and 1880s, but not without opposition. To mollify those disappointed by the abandonment of the Korean expedition so earnestly sought by Saigō Takamori and his friends, in 1874 Japan sent a military force to Taiwan, ostensibly to punish aborigines who had killed some shipwrecked Okinawans. This expedition was a smaller and less dangerous undertaking than a military confrontation with Korea. It was successful, with the result that China was forced to pay an indemnity and to recognize Japanese sovereignty over the Ryukyu Islands, thus ending the ties that the Ryukyus had maintained with China even while they were Satsuma vassals.

The success of the expedition, however, did not alleviate the situation of disoriented and embittered samurai who felt betrayed by the Meiji leaders. Such men resorted to arms in an uprising in Hizen in 1874, western Kyushu in 1876, and, most seriously, in Satsuma in 1877. The Satsuma Rebellion was led by Saigō, who had withdrawn from the government after the 1873 decision against the Korean expedition. The number of those who threw in their lot with the rebellion rose as high as 42,000. Its suppression strained the military resources of the restoration government, but after half a year the rebellion was crushed.

The Satsuma Rebellion was the last stand of the samurai. When the military situation became hopeless, Saigō committed ritual suicide. His was a martyr's death for a lost cause.

Saigō died under official condemnation as a traitor, but the Meiji government soon rehabilitated him, and government leaders joined in expressions of admiration and acclaim. Not only conservatives but also representatives of the most diverse political persuasions praised the magnanimity of his spirit and transformed Saigō into a legendary hero celebrated in poems and songs (including an army marching song), portrayed on stage and in an extensive literature, depicted in portraits and prints, and even identified with the planet Mars.

Protest against the government continued, on occasion, to take a violent turn. Less than half a year after Saigō's death, some of his sympathizers assassinated Ōkubo Toshimichi, also from Satsuma, who had worked so hard and successfully to create the new Japanese state. There were other assassination attempts, both successful and not. More important in the long run, however, was the formation of nonviolent political opposition, animated not only by objections to one or another aspect of government policy but also by protest against the political domination exercised by a few men from Chōshū and Satsuma who had exclusive control over the centers of power. Basing their position on the first article of the 1868 Charter Oath, early in 1874 opposition leaders demanded the creation of an elected legislature. Prominent among them was Itagaki Taisuke, the Tosa leader who, with Saigō, had left the government over the Korean issue.

In Tosa and elsewhere, antigovernment organizations voiced the discontent of local interests, demanding political rights, local self-government, and formation of a national assembly. The advocates of a constitution and the leaders of what became known as the movement for popular rights drew upon Western political theories. Constitutionalism itself was an idea with wide currency and long pedigree in the West, where it was associated with ideas concerning the supremacy of law, a "social contract," and human rights highlighted in eighteenth-century political thought. In the West, constitutions limited the powers exercised by heads of state by providing representative institutions to share in governing, but a strong argument advanced in Japan was that representative institutions would create greater unity between the people and the emperor. In this view, a constitution was needed not to limit the emperor's powers but to control his advisers. The men in power were not averse to some kind of constitution as a necessary and even desirable component of modernization. Indeed, Kido, as a participant in the Iwakura mission to Europe, became persuaded of the need for a constitution.

By 1878, Kido, Ōkubo, and Saigō were all dead. Of the older men only Iwakura remained important, and three younger men who had already contributed significantly to the Meiji state assumed leadership: Itō Hirobumi and Yamagata Aritomo, both from Chōshū, and Ōkuma Shigenobu from Hizen. Yamagata was the creator of the new army, Itō took the lead in political modernization, and Ōkuma served as finance minister. They agreed that Japan should have a constitution, but they could not agree on the structure of the constitution or on a schedule for drawing up and implementing it. Tensions between Itō and Ōkuma came to a head in 1881 when the latter wrote a memorandum advocating the adoption of an English-style political system. His proposals that the majority party in parliament form the government, that the Cabinet be responsible to parliament, and that the first elections be held in 1883 clashed with the conservative and gradualist views of his colleagues. First, his proposals were rejected; then, when Ōkuma joined in public criticism of the government over its sale of a certain government project in Hokkaido, the emperor consented to having Ōkuma ousted from the government. At the same time, the government announced that the emperor would grant a constitution, to take effect in 1890.

## Formation of Parties

In response, Itagaki and his associates formed the Jiyutō (Liberal party), and Ōkuma followed by organizing the Kaishintō (Progressive party). Both parties advocated constitutional government with meaningful powers exercised by a parliament, but they differed somewhat in ideology and especially in composition. The

Jiyutō, linked to Tosa, drew much of its support from rural areas, where peasants and landlords were unhappy that their taxes were as high as they had been under the Tokugawa and resented bearing a heavier tax burden than that required of commerce and industry. The Jiyutō proclaimed itself "devoted to the expansion of liberty, protection of rights, promotion of happiness, and reform of society."[2] Ōkuma's party (linked to Hizen) was, in contrast, more urban and more moderate, advocating English-style liberalism and setting forth more specific proposals. It had the backing of merchants and industrialists. Although both opposed the government and advocated representative government, the two parties fought each other energetically. At the same time, the parties were troubled by internal factionalism; party splits were based on master–follower and patron–client relations rather than on differences in programs.

The organized opposition was further hampered by the need to operate under restrictive laws, including those promulgated to control political criticism. One source of such criticism was the press. The first newspaper appeared in 1871. Early papers had a small but elite readership and focused on politics, but restrictive press laws enacted in 1875 and revised in 1877 gave the home minister power to suppress publications and fine or imprison offenders. The 1880 Public Meeting Law placed all political meetings under police supervision. Included among those prohibited from attending such meetings were teachers and students. Nor were political associations allowed to recruit members or to combine or correspond with similar bodies. Finally, the 1887 Peace Preservation Law increased the home minister's powers of censorship and gave the police authority to expel people from a given area if they were deemed a threat to public tranquility. Some of the 570 shortly removed from Tokyo were criminals, but many were party members.

The Jiyutō was hurt not only by differences among its leaders but by antagonism within its membership, including conflicts between tenants and landlords. It proved impossible to contain within one party both the radicals who supported and even led peasant riots and the substantial landowners who were the objects of these attacks. In 1884 the party was dissolved. At the end of the same year, Ōkuma and his followers left the Kaishintō, although others stayed to keep it in existence. Criticism of the government continued, but this initial attempt to organize political parties turned out to have been premature.

In addition to suppressing its critics, the government was taking steps to increase its effectiveness. A system of centralized local administration was established that ended the Tokugawa tradition of local self-government. Villages and towns were now headed by officials appointed by the Home Ministry in Tokyo, which also controlled the police. From 1878 to 1880, local assemblies were created as sounding boards of public opinion, but their rights were limited to debate and their membership was restricted to men of means. The details of bureaucratic procedure were worked out and a civil service system was fashioned. A new code of criminal law was enacted, and work began on civil and commercial codes.

For the parties and the government alike, the promulgation of a constitution was seen as an essential component in fashioning a modern state uniting the people and the nation, as exemplified by the advanced countries of the West. However, the West offered a range of ways to accomplish this, with varying degrees of popular participation and power. To prepare for drawing up a constitution, Itō spent a year and a half in Europe during 1882 and 1883, mostly studying German theories and practices, which were most in keeping with the kind of constitution he and the other oligarchs wanted. After his return, several steps were taken in preparation for the constitution: a new peerage was created in 1884 composed of the old court nobility, former daimyo, and some members of the oligarchy; in 1885 a European-style Cabinet was created with Itō as premier; and in 1888 the Privy Council was organized as the highest government advisory board.

## The Emperor and the Constitution

In the last chapter we noted the abandonment of the original effort to turn Japan into a Shinto state and the granting of religious tolerance, but this did not settle how such tolerance was to coexist with the belief in the divine descent of the emperor and in the legends in which it was grounded. The matter was settled in 1882 with the division of Shinto into Shrine Shinto and Sect Shinto. Most Shinto shrines, including the most prominent, such as Ise and Izumo, sacred to the Sun Goddess and her brother, respectively, came under Shrine Shinto. Thus, they were transformed into state institutions operating on a higher plane than the merely "religious" bodies, such as the various forms of Buddhism, Christianity (legalized in 1873), and ordinary Shinto shrines subsumed under Sect Shinto. This formula permitted the government to identify itself with the Shinto tradition from which it derived the mystique of the emperor, source of its own authority, and also meet the demands for religious tolerance voiced by Japanese reformers and Western nations.

In the name of the "restoration" of the emperor, strands of nativist thought and notions of modern monarchy were combined to form an image of the emperor—promoted by careful manipulation of the emperor himself and spread by word and picture. In his person, he represented both old and new: he was a divine being embodying a timeless spirit, but this was a modern divinity, resplendent in his flashy, new, world-class uniform (see Figure 18.1).

In 1889, after work on the constitution was completed, it was promulgated as a "gift" from the emperor to his people. The Meiji constitution remained in force until 1945. The emperor, "sacred and inviolable" father of the family state, was supreme. He was the locus and source of sovereignty: the land and people belonged to him. He had the power to declare war, conclude treaties, and command the army. He also had the right to open, recess, and dissolve the legislature, the power to veto its decisions, and the right to issue his own ordinances. The ministers were responsible not to the legislature but to the emperor. The legislature, called the Diet (derived from *dieta,* Late Latin for public assembly) consisted of two houses, the House of Peers and the House of Representatives. The latter was

**FIGURE 18.1** *Portrait of the Meiji Emperor,* Takahashi Yuichi. Oil, 1880. Emperor Meiji—the reign name of the emperor of Japan from 1867 to 1912 (his given name was Mutsuhito)—ascended the throne when he was fifteen. He is depicted here in a modern medium, dressed in a manner appropriate to an emperor appearing on the world stage during the "long nineteenth century" that ended in 1914. (© Collection Imperial Household, Tokyo, Japan.)

elected by a constituency of tax-paying property owners amounting to about 450,000 men, or 1.1 percent of the total population. The most consequential power of the Diet was the power of the purse, but following the example of the Prussian constitution, the Meiji constitution provided for automatic renewal of the previous year's budget whenever the Diet failed to pass a new budget.

Only the emperor could take the initiative to revise the constitution. The emperor was the final authority, but he was also above politics; the actual exercise of imperial authority was divided between the Privy Council, the Cabinet, the Diet, and the general staff. Because the constitution failed to provide for coordination among these bodies, this was done by the men who had been governing in the emperor's name all along. Gradually, the practice developed of deciding on the selection of prime minister and other major questions by consulting the *genrō*—elder statesmen and leaders of the Meiji Restoration, such as Itō and Yamagata, who talked things out in private. Obviously, this could work only as long as there were *genrō* to consult.

The oligarchs who framed the constitution viewed the government, like the emperor in whose name it functioned, as above the divisive and unedifying world of party politics. But the parties turned out to be stronger than the oligarchs had expected. In the first election of 1890, the reconstituted Jiyutō won 130 seats; the Kaishintō, led again by Ōkuma, won 47; and only 79 members favoring the government were elected. As a result of this growing party strength, there was a stiff parliamentary battle over the budget in the first session of the Diet, which was resolved only after the premier, Yamagata, resorted to bribery and force. When the budget failed to pass the following year, the Diet was dissolved. During the subsequent elections (1892), the government used the police to discourage the opposition but failed to obtain a more tractable Diet. Imperial intervention in 1893 worked only temporarily. Another election was held in 1894, but the majority remained opposed to the government, and the Diet was dissolved after only a month and a half.

The war with China over Korea broke the political deadlock and provided temporary unity in the body politic. During the war, the government enjoyed enthusiastic support at home. By that time, Japan was quite different from what it had been twenty years earlier, when the oligarchs rejected intervention in Korea. The political developments were just one dimension of the transformation of Japan.

# Western Influences on Values and Ideas

Enthusiasm for aspects of Western science and technology went back, as we have seen, to Tokugawa proponents of Dutch Learning, and from the start of Meiji there was a fashion of Western styles, including styles of dress. Representative of Japanese attitudes, the Meiji Emperor himself wore Western clothes and dressed his hair in the Western manner, as in his portrait by Takahashi Yuichi (1828–1894), shown in Figure 18.1. Not only the subject but also the artist was influenced by Western styles. Takahashi was conscious of his precursors: he revered Shiba Kōkan. Like Shiba and his own teacher, the prominent Western-style painter Kawakami Tōgai (1827–1881), Takahashi placed great value on realism. Most of his works, unlike the emperor's portrait, were still-life studies of familiar objects, and his most famous work is a realistic painting of a salmon. A major difference between Kawakami and Takahashi is that whereas the former saw Western art as no more than a necessary component of Western learning to be mastered for technical reasons, Takahashi also valued it as art.

Similarly, men turned to the West in other fields, not only because of practical reasons but also because they were attracted by the intrinsic nature of Western achievements. Prominent among such men were the intellectuals who, in 1873, formed the Meirokusha, a prestigious society devoted to all aspects of Western knowledge. These same men led what was known as the movement for "civilization and enlightenment" (*bummei kaika*). A leading theorist of this movement was Fukuzawa Yukichi, whose books on the West were mentioned earlier.

# "Civilization and Enlightenment"

In eighteenth-century Europe, the intellectual movement known as the Enlightenment sought to put all traditional ideas and institutions to the test of reason. Impressed by the achievements of science as exemplified in the work of Sir

Isaac Newton (1642–1727), such philosophers as Voltaire (1694–1778) and Diderot (1713–1784) believed that reason could produce similar progress in solving human problems and that the main obstacles to truth and happiness were irrationality and superstition. Their greatest monument was the encyclopedia compiled by Diderot and his associates, a summation of the accomplishments of reason in all fields of human knowledge.

Japanese intellectuals such as Fukuzawa were strongly influenced by the European Enlightenment, particularly the emphasis on reason as an instrument for achieving progress. Their faith in progress was also confirmed by influential Western historians such as H. T. Buckle (1821–1862) and Francois Guizot (1787–1874). Firm belief in progress remained widespread during the nineteenth century, even after faith in reason had faded.

A corollary to this new concept of historical progress, in Japan as in the West, was a negative reevaluation of Chinese civilization, now regarded as unchanging and therefore decadent. No longer did the Japanese look up to China as the land of classical civilization; on the contrary, China was now a negative model, and, as China's troubles continued, the Japanese tended to regard it with condescension and concern. Now the source of "enlightenment" was in the West.

One of Fukuzawa's prime goals in advancing the cause of "civilization and enlightenment" was to stimulate in Japan the development of an independent and responsible citizenry. "It would not be far from wrong," he complained, "to say that Japan has a government but no people."[3] Tracing the lack of individual independence back to the traditional family, Fukuzawa advocated fundamental changes in that basic social institution. Ridiculing the ancient paragons of filial piety, he urged limitations on parental demands and authority. Although he viewed the role of women in terms of family and home, Fukuzawa also, on occasion, recommended greater equality between the sexes, championed monogamy, argued that women should be educated and allowed to hold property, and compared the Japanese woman with a dwarfed ornamental tree, artificially stunted.

According to Fukuzawa, history was made by the people, not by a few great leaders, and he thought it wrong to place too much faith in government or to give the political authorities too much power. His view of the role of government resembled the concept of the minimal state held by early European liberals. Consistent with these ideas, he did not enter government himself but disseminated his views in books and through a newspaper he founded. He also established what became Keiō University, a distinguished private university in Tokyo whose graduates played an important part in the world of business and industry.

In Fukuzawa's mind, the independence of the people and the independence of the country were linked; indeed, the former was a prerequisite for the latter. This view was widely held among the proponents of "enlightenment." For instance, the translator of the best-seller *Self-Help* by Samuel Smiles, whose Japanese version was published in Tokyo in 1871, explained that Western nations were strong because they possessed the spirit of liberty. John Stuart Mill's *On Liberty* appeared in Japanese translation the same year; Rousseau's *The Social Contract* was published in installments from 1882 to 1884. Fukuzawa, with his faith in progress, believed that the ultimate universal movement of history is in the direction of democracy and that individual liberty makes for national strength.

Fukuzawa's liberalism of the early 1870s was based on the Western Enlightenment concept of natural law, that is, that human affairs are governed by inherent concepts of right just as the physical world is governed by the laws of nature. This belief resembled the Neo-Confucian concept of *li* (principle) in linking the natural and human orders, but the European doctrine, unlike the Chinese, included the affirmation of innate human rights. It postulated an affirmative body of law stating the inherent rights of people in society, in whose name societies could overthrow unjust governments and establish new ones. It was to natural law that the American colonists appealed when they declared their independence in 1776; this was also the case when the French revolutionaries promulgated their Declaration of the Rights of Man in 1789.

# Social Darwinism

After the "civilization and enlightenment" of the 1870s, discourse became more many-sided, but the concept of natural law was soon displaced by another, more recent, Western import: Social Darwinism. There were various versions of this doctrine, most notably those developed by the enormously influential Herbert Spencer (1820–1903), but all were based on the theory of evolution by natural selection presented in Charles Darwin's famous *On the Origin of Species* (1859). Darwin held that over time the various forms of life adapt to changing natural conditions and that those that adapt best are most likely to survive. This theory was summarized by the catch phrase "survival of the fittest." Social Darwinism was the application of these doctrines to the human realm. Applied to the success or failure of individuals within society, it justified brutal competition. Similarly, applied to the rise and fall of nations, it focused on military and civil competition. In both cases, "the fittest" were those who came out on top and thereby contributed to human progress.

Social Darwinism, purporting to have a scientific basis, offered a persuasive explanation of the present yet held out hope for a different future. It explained why Japan had been unable to resist the Western powers but held out the promise that a nation did not have to accept permanent inferiority. Thus, it justified Japanese efforts to develop national strength by mastering the learning and techniques of the West. Unlike natural law with its moral rules, it turned strength itself into a moral criterion and justified not only resisting foreign aggression but also engaging in aggressive expansionism.

In the mid-1870s, Fukuzawa first became skeptical of natural law and then abandoned it. He lost confidence in international law and formed a new view of international relations as an arena in which nations struggle for survival. In 1876 Fukuzawa remarked, "a few cannons are worth more than a hundred volumes of international law."[4] By 1882 he was willing to accept even autocracy if it meant strengthening the nation. Furthermore, he favored imperialist expansion, both to assure Japan's safety and to bring the benefits of "civilization" to neighboring countries such as Korea. Thus, he welcomed the war when it came in 1894.

Fukuzawa found words of praise for some aspects of the Japanese tradition, including the samurai value of loyal service, but continued to look primarily to the West for his models and ideas. However, he avoided the extremes of Westernization. In early Meiji some thinkers allowed their enthusiasm to get the better of their judgment, and there were all kinds of extreme proposals for radical Westernization, including one to abolish the national language and another to intermarry with Europeans. However, not all supporters of Westernization were genuine enthusiasts. Many desired to impress Westerners to be accepted as equals and to speed treaty revision. This was the motive behind a variety of movements, ranging from a drive to reform public morals to the revision of the legal code. It also accounts for one of the symbols of the era, the Rokumeikan, a hall completed in 1883 to accommodate mixed foreign and Japanese social gatherings. Designed by an English architect in the elaborate manner of the European Renaissance, it provided the setting for dinners, card parties, and fancy dress balls.

# The Arts

In the arts, Western influence was both audible and visible. It affected the music taught in the schools and that performed in military bands. In literature, the 1870s and 1880s have been defined as "the age of translation,"[5] during which Japanese versions of European novels were published and read with great enthusiasm to be joined, in the mid-1880s, by the first modern Japanese novels, worthy forerunners of great achievements to come. In painting, we have already noted the work of Takahashi, but the presence of the West was also visible in more traditional genres. Sometimes called the last of the major *ukiyo-e* artists was Kobayashi Kiyochika (1847–1915). He introduced Western light and shading into *ukiyo-e,* using the principles of Western perspective yet retaining a traditional Japanese sense of color (see Figure 18.2).

Western styles of painting were advanced by foreign artists who taught in Japan and by Japanese who studied abroad, particularly in France, bringing back new styles and ways of looking at the world. Kuroda Seiki (1866–1924) studied in France from 1884 to 1893, and it was there that he painted *Morning Toilet* (see Figure 18.3), which caused a stir when exhibited in Tokyo in 1894 and unleashed a storm of controversy when shown in more conservative Kyoto the following year. Japan and East Asia had no tradition of painting the nude. There were protests that Kuroda's painting was pornography, not art. But Kuroda won the battle and went on to become one of Japan's most influential Western-style painters.

The initial enthusiasm for Western art led to the neglect of, and even disdain for, traditional art. This shocked the American Ernest Fenollosa (1853–1908) when he came to Japan in 1878 to teach at Tokyo University. Fenollosa did what

**FIGURE 18.2** *Train at Night*, Kobayashi Kiyochika. Woodcut. This was the great age of the railway, a force and a symbol of technological and economic transformation. With his unique techniques of light and shadow, the artist sets his train rushing through the night against a calm, seemingly eternal Japanese landscape. (© Arthur M. Sackler Gallery, Smithsonian Institution, Washington, D.C. Robert O. Muller Collection)

he could to make the new generation of Westernized Japanese aware of the greatness of their artistic heritage. He was an admirer of the last of the masters of the China-influenced Kanō school, Kanō Hogai (1828–1898) and, with the younger Okakura Tenshin (1862–1913), sparked a revived interest in traditional styles. Meanwhile, Japanese art fascinated such Western artists as Gaugin, van Gogh, and Whistler.

## Conservatism and Nationalism

The reaction against the enthusiasm of the early Meiji Westernizers was not limited to the arts. Starting in the late 1880s, there was a tide of conservative thought. Many were attracted by the old formula, "Eastern ethics and Western science," a concept earlier advanced by Sakuma Shōzan.

Some feared that acceptance of a foreign culture was a step toward national decline and sought ways to be both modern and Japanese, to adopt universalist aspects of Western culture yet retain what was of value in their own past. The edu-

**FIGURE 18.3** *Morning Toilet,* Kuroda Seiki. Kuroda learned an academic style under the French painter Louis-Joseph-Raphael Collin but also acquired an Impressionist vision that incorporated bright outdoor light. Oil, 1893, 38.6 in × 70.3 in. (© National Research Institute of Cultural Properties, Tokyo.)

cated and sensitive were especially troubled by the tensions inherent in a program of modernization under traditionalist auspices. Western scientific rationalism could, by questioning the founding myth, undermine the throne and polity. In 1892, a Tokyo University professor was forced to resign after he wrote that Shinto was a "survival of a primitive form of worship."[6] That was sacrilege. Similarly, Western individualism, fostered by the policy of modernization, clashed with the old family values that, Fukuzawa notwithstanding, continued strong and remained in official favor.

Drawing on German thought, new conservative voices affirmed Japanese uniqueness and their belief in national progress, arguing that change should come about gradually, growing organically out of past traditions, with emphasis not on the individual but on the state. There was talk about a national "essence," although little agreement on how it should be defined.

Akira Iriye has drawn attention to the weakness in Japan of the liberal elements that Western nationalism inherited from its origins, when it "had been part of the democratic revolution in which national identity was sought less in a country's ethnic and historical uniqueness than in the belief that it embodied certain universal values such as freedom and human rights." Such a nationalism "could often be transformed into internationalism because a nation could envision a world order that embodied some of the universalistic principles that it exemplified itself."[7] Japanese particularism often took a benign form but was also prone to lead to cultural exceptionalism and political chauvinism, even if Japanese nationalists were hardly unique in celebrating (and exaggerating) the uniqueness of their nation. Such views could easily lead to a sense of special national mission.

Some Japanese intellectuals, notably Okakura, soon went on to define a wider world role for Japan by emphasizing Japan's Asian roots. Thus, in a book bearing the revealing title, *The Ideals of the East* (1902), Okakura presented the nation's mission in terms of preserving an "Asian" cultural essence. Not only Japan's cultural place in the world but also its political mission remained key issues throughout modern times.

# Education

Japanese intellectual and political leaders were quick to realize the importance of education in fashioning a new Japan capable of competing with the West. In this, as in other areas, they showed great interest in the practices and institutions of European countries and of the United States. One member of the Iwakura mission paid special attention to education and wrote fifteen volumes on the subject after his return from abroad.

At the beginning of the Meiji Period, Japan sent many students overseas to obtain the advanced training it could not provide at home. One-eighth of the Ministry of Education's first budget (1873) was designated for this purpose, and 250 students were sent to the United States and Europe on government scholarships that year. Furthermore, many foreign instructors from the same countries were brought to Japan to teach in various specialized schools. However, these were temporary expedients to be used until Japan's own modern educational system was in operation. By the late 1880s, the number of foreign instructors was down, and only fifty to eighty students were being sent abroad by the government annually. A landmark in the history of higher education was the establishment of Tokyo University in 1877 with four faculties: physical science, law, literature, and medicine.

Considerable progress was made in building a complete educational system to replace the uncoordinated network of now-outdated academies and *han,* temple, and family schools. Yet actual accomplishments fell short of the ambitious plan drawn up in 1872 calling for 8 universities, 256 middle schools (equivalent to American high and junior high schools), and 53,760 elementary schools. Thirty years later, in 1902, there were only 2 universities, 222 middle schools, and 27,076 elementary schools. Similarly, the government had to retreat from its 1872 ordinance making four years of education compulsory for all children. Among the difficulties this program encountered were money problems (elementary education was locally financed), teacher shortages, and the reluctance of rural parents to send their children to school. However, by the time four years of compulsory education were reintroduced in 1900, most children who were supposed to be in school were in attendance, and in 1907 the government was able to increase the period to six years. By that time the teachers were predominantly graduates of Japanese Normal Schools (teacher training institutes), the first of which was established in Tokyo in 1872 with the assistance of Marion M. Scott, an American educator.

When the Ministry of Education was first established in 1871, the French system of highly centralized administration was adopted. Although local schools were locally financed, the ministry not only determined the general direction of education but also prescribed textbooks, supervised teacher training, and generally controlled the curriculum of schools throughout the country. Government educational policy therefore was decisive in determining what was taught.

There was wide agreement among political leaders that an essential function of the educational system was to provide the people with the skills necessary for modernization. They realized that not only factories and businesses but also armies and navies require a certain level of literacy and command of simple arithmetic among the rank and file, as well as higher education for managers and officers. Beyond that, the leaders recognized that schools foster values and looked to them to help mold the Japanese people into a nation. On the question of specific moral content, however, there were intense disagreements reflecting different visions of Japan's future. In the 1870s, when enthusiasm for the West ran high, even elementary readers and moral texts were frequently translated from English and French for use in Japanese schools. But there were also critics who insisted that the schools should preserve traditional Confucian/Japanese values. Another influential position was opposed to both Western liberal values and to traditionalist ideals but looked to the schools to indoctrinate the populace with modern nationalist values. An influential proponent of this last position was Mori Arinori (1847–1889), minister of education from 1885 until he was assassinated by a nationalist fanatic in 1889.

Although Mori had a strong hand in shaping the educational system, the most important Meiji pronouncement on the subject was drafted under the influence of Motoda Eifu (1818–1891), the emperor's lecturer on Chinese books, who for twenty years provided Confucian guidance and advice. This was the *Rescript on Education,* issued in 1890. For half a century it remained the basic statement of the purpose of education, memorized by generations of schoolchildren. It begins by attributing "the glory of the fundamental character of Our Empire" to the imperial ancestors who "deeply and firmly implanted virtue," calls on his majesty's subjects to observe the usual Confucian virtues beginning with filiality toward their parents, and enjoins them to "pursue learning and cultivate arts" for intellectual and moral development and "to advance public good and promote common interests." Furthermore, "should emergency arise, offer yourselves courageously to the State, and thus guard and maintain the prosperity of Our Imperial Throne coeval with heaven and earth."[8] In this document, Confucianism is identified with the throne (no mention is made of its foreign origins), and a premium is placed on patriotic service to the state and to the throne. These values were further drummed into schoolchildren in compulsory ethics classes. Education was intended to prepare Japan for the future in the name of the past.

# Modernizing the Economy

In the twenty years that followed consolidation of the Meiji regime, Japan laid the foundations for a modern industrial economy. The nation was still primarily agrarian, but Western experience had shown that capital accumulated through the sale of surplus agricultural production and labor obtained through the migration of surplus rural population to the cities were necessary conditions for industrial development. Both conditions existed in Meiji Japan.

Japanese agriculture had become more efficient because of the introduction of new seed strains, new fertilizers, and new methods of cultivation. New land for farming was being opened, especially in Hokkaido. New applications of science to agriculture were being tried at experimental stations and agricultural colleges. In consequence, during the fourteen years preceding the Sino-Japanese War, rice yields increased by 30 percent, and other crops showed comparable gains; per capita rice consumption increased. Agriculture was further stimulated by the development of a substantial export market for silk and tea and a growing domestic demand for cotton. Thus, trade also helped generate capital needed for investment in manufacturing.

Increased agricultural production did not result in major changes for the grower. Village government and the organization of village labor remained largely the same. Rents remained high: it was not unusual for a peasant's rent to equal half his rice crop. Profits resulting from the commercialization of agriculture went to the landlord, who handled the sale, rather than to the tenant. Even the creation of factory jobs did little to relieve population pressure on the land.

Much of the factory labor was performed by peasant girls sent to the city to supplement farm incomes for several years before they were married. Housed in company dormitories and strictly supervised, they were an inexpensive workforce. When times were bad and factory operations slowed, they could be laid off and returned to their villages. It was a system advantageous to both the landlord and the industrialist.

In Western countries, the industrial revolution was largely carried out by private enterprise. In Japan, however, where it was government policy to modernize so as to catch up with the West, the government took the initiative. The Meiji regime invested heavily in the economic infrastructure—those basic public services that must be in place before an industrial economy can grow: education, transportation, communication, and so forth. As previously mentioned, students were sent abroad at public expense to study Western technologies and techniques, and foreigners were brought to Japan to teach in their areas of expertise. A major effort went into railroads. The first line was completed in 1872, running between Tokyo and Yokohama. By the mid-1890s there were 2000 miles of track, much of it privately owned, because government initiative was followed by private investment once the feasibility, and especially the profitability, of railroads had been established. Transportation within cities began to quicken as Kyoto, in 1895, became the first Japanese city to have trolleys.

This sequence of state initiative followed by private development can also be observed in manufacturing. The government took the lead in establishing and operating cement works, plants manufacturing tiles, textile mills (silk and cotton), shipyards, mines, and munitions works. The government felt these industries were essential, but private interests were unwilling to risk their capital in untried ventures with little prospect of profits in the near term. Thus, if such ventures were to be started, the government had to start them and finance the initial period of operations.

# *The* Zaibatsu

The expenditure of capital required for this effort, the payment due to samurai on their bonds, the costs of the Satsuma Rebellion, and an adverse balance of trade combined to create a government financial crisis. Rising inflation damaged the government's purchasing power and hurt the samurai, whose income depended on the interest paid on their bonds. These problems came to a head in 1880. The government's response was mainly to cut back on expenditures, leading to a deflation generally seen as preparing the way for a period of economic growth sustained to the end of World War I.

As part of its economy move, the government decided, late in 1880, to sell at public auction all its enterprises with the exception of the munitions plants. Most buyers were men who were friendly with government leaders and who recognized the long-term advantages of buying the factories, which were selling at bargain prices. These enterprises did not become profitable immediately, but when they did, this small group of well-connected companies enjoyed a controlling position in the modern sector of the economy. These were the *zaibatsu,* huge financial and industrial combines.

The *zaibatsu* were usually organized by new entrepreneurs, because most of the old Tokugawa merchant houses were too set in their ways to make a successful transition into the new world of Meiji. The outstanding exception to this generalization was the house of Mitsui, originally established in Edo as a textile house and enriched by its banking activities. When it became apparent that government initiatives were creating new economic opportunities in commerce and industry, Mitsui brought new men into the company to take advantage of them. The new leadership was vigorous and capable, establishing first a bank and then a trading company. These institutions became important factors in Japan's foreign commerce; they also engaged in domestic transactions, profiting handsomely from handling army supply contracts during the Satsuma Rebellion. In 1881, Mitsui bought government coal mines, which ultimately contributed greatly to its wealth and power. By that time, the traditional drapery business had been relegated to a sideline and delegated to a subordinate house.

In contrast to Mitsui, the Mitsubishi *zaibatsu* was founded by a former samurai from Tosa, bold and ruthless in the wars of commerce. This was Iwasaki Yatarō

(1834–1885), who developed a strong shipping business by obtaining government contracts, government subsidies, and for a time, even government guarantee of its dividend payments. At one point the government lent the company ships, a loan that eventually became a gift. Mitsubishi also benefited greatly from doing government business during the Taiwan expedition of 1874 and again during the Satsuma Rebellion. The company grew strong enough to displace some of its foreign competitors, and around its shipping business it developed banking and insurance facilities and entered foreign trade. It also went into mining, and its acquisition of the government-established Nagasaki shipyard assured its future as the leader in shipbuilding and heavy industry, although Iwasaki did not live long enough to see the shipyard turn a profit. Iwasaki ruled the combine like a personal domain, but he also recruited an able managerial staff composed largely of graduates of Fukuzawa's Keiō University.

For Iwasaki, personal ambition and patriotism were fused. As he conceived it, his mission was to compete with the great foreign shipping companies, and he was convinced that whatever benefited his company was also good for the nation. Not everyone, however, agreed with this assessment. For a time Iwasaki had to face the competition of a rival company, one of whose organizers was Shibusawa Eiichi (1840–1931), one of the great Meiji entrepreneurs and bankers, founder of the Tokyo Chamber of Commerce and Bankers' Association, and a believer in joint-stock companies, in competition, and in business independence from government. Iwasaki won this battle, but Shibusawa remained enormously influential, not only because of his economic power but also because of his energetic advocacy of higher business standards and the view that business could contribute to public good by remaining independent of government.

The success of such men as Iwasaki and Shibusawa should not obscure the fact that new ventures continued to entail risk. Not all new ventures were successful. For example, the attempt to introduce sheep raising into Japan was a failure. Initial attempts at organizing insurance companies were similarly ill conceived because they used rates and tables appropriate for European rather than Japanese conditions. But insurance companies were finally established, and altogether successes outnumbered failures.

One reason for the success of the *zaibatsu* and other new companies was their ability to attract capable and dedicated executives. Formerly, many capable members of the samurai class had refused to enter the business world because concern with moneymaking was considered abhorrent. But this obstacle was largely overcome after the restoration, not merely because these were now ex-samurai families but also because commercial and industrial development was required for the good of the state. Those who helped build a strong bank, trading company, or manufacturing industry were seen as rendering a service to the emperor and to Japan. Indeed, the government's initial sponsorship of many enterprises lent them some of the prestige of government service. Many companies were created by men of samurai origins, helping make business socially acceptable.

The association of business with government also influenced business ideology in Japan. From the beginning, the ethos of modern Japan business focused on its contributions to the Japanese nation, not on the notions of economic liberalism that prevailed in the West. The company did not exist only, or even primarily, to make a profit for its shareholders. Likewise, provisions were made in the internal organization of the business to encourage group solidarity and mutual responsibility, to give participants in the venture a strong sense of company loyalty, and to keep workers in their place. The association of business and government also helped justify the government's influence on business and helped account for continued acceptance of policies that kept consumption low even as national income rose.

In somewhat similar fashion, in the 1890s the argument first appeared that Japanese factories were "exceptional sites of warm-hearted social relations,"[9] a contention that grew more insistent in the early twentieth century as movements for legislation concerning factory conditions, working hours, child labor, and so on gained momentum.

In describing the *zaibatsu* and other modern companies, it should not be supposed that large-scale trading, mining, and manufacturing represented the whole of Japanese business. On the contrary, many small-scale establishments continued to function well past the early Meiji era. But the new companies did represent major growth and change in economic activity, and they signaled a change in Japanese perceptions of Japan's role in international affairs. This was reflected in economic terms by efforts to preserve economic independence—for example, by protecting home markets, conserving foreign exchange, and avoiding dependence on foreign capital to assure Japanese ownership of railways and other large-scale enterprises. It was also reflected in Japanese foreign policy and especially in the modernization and deployment of the Japanese military.

# The Military

Japanese military forces engaged in three major operations in the twenty years following the restoration: the Taiwan expedition of 1874, the Satsuma Rebellion of 1877, and the Sino-Japanese War of 1894–1895. The first two operations were fought primarily for domestic purposes as the new Meiji government sought to consolidate its power. The Sino-Japanese War, on the other hand, was an outward-looking venture from the start, a test of strength with China on the Korean Peninsula. An even more striking difference was in the quality of Japanese military organization, armament, and tactical skill.

The Taiwan expedition of 1874 was far from brilliant. The landing was poorly executed, hygiene was so defective that disease took a great toll, and equipment had to be abandoned because it was unsuitable for use in a tropical climate. Similarly, the force that suppressed the Satsuma Rebellion did so because of its superiority in numbers and equipment rather than its military excellence.

To improve the quality of the army, Yamagata directed a major reorganization in 1878. He established a general staff along German lines, and Germany became the overall model for the army, which had previously been influenced by France. By strengthening the reserves, the military potential was greatly increased. During the ten or fifteen years before the Sino-Japanese War, generous military appropriations enabled the army to acquire modern equipment, mostly manufactured in Japanese arsenals and plants, and the creation of a staff college and improved training methods further strengthened the army and made it more modern. Like Yamagata, most leading generals were from Chōshū.

Naval modernization was similar to that of the army, except that England was the model and continued to be a source from which some larger vessels were purchased. In 1894 the navy possessed twenty-eight modern ships with a total displacement of 57,000 tons and twenty-four torpedo boats. Most importantly, Japan had the facilities to maintain, repair, and arm its fleet. From the start, most naval leadership came from Satsuma.

The military is a good example of the way in which the various facets of modernization were intertwined and supported each other, because the armed forces both benefited from and contributed to the process. Not only did they stimulate new industries, ranging from armaments to tin cans, but it was also in the army that the rural conscript was first exposed to a wider and more modern world. Indeed, when conscription was first introduced, many men from backward districts were bewildered by the accouterments of modern life. There are reports that some bowed in reverence to the stove in their barracks, taking it for some kind of god. For many men, the army provided the introduction to shoes. Before the spread of education, some men learned to read and write in the army. All were exposed to the new values of nationalism and loyalty to the emperor. Most also learned to smoke (cigarettes were first reported in 1877) and to drink native alcoholic beverages and excellent Japanese beer, first brewed in the 1870s. Most had their first experience with the modern city. Soldiers enjoyed a better diet, receiving more meat than the average Japanese. But discipline was harsh, and draft dodging was rampant. Nevertheless, the majority served.

In this and other ways life was changing for that majority, but compared with later times, it was changing slowly. There were changes in style, such as glass replacing paper inside the house or the use of Western umbrellas outside, but as Susan B. Hanley has shown, the essential consumption patterns and basic components of the material culture of the Japanese people remained traditional and stable.[10]

## Korea and the Sino-Japanese War of 1894–1895

Like Vietnam, Korea had adopted Chinese political institutions and ideology and maintained a tributary relationship with China yet guarded its political independence. Again, as in Vietnam, differences in size, social organization, and cultural tradition insured the development of a distinct Sino-Korean culture. In the nineteenth century, however, Korea was sorely troubled by internal problems and external pressures. The Yi dynasty (1392–1910), then in its fifth century, was in serious decline. Korea's peasantry suffered from "a skewered or concentrated pattern of landholding; small average per capita holdings; high rates of tenancy; a regressive tax structure; false registration of taxable land; extortion and illegal charges and gratuities at tax collection time; and usury, especially official usury in the management of the grain loan system."[11] There was a serious uprising in the North in 1811. In 1833 there were rice riots in Seoul. And in 1862 there were rebellions in the South.

From 1864 to 1873, there was a last attempt to save the situation through a traditional program of reform initiated by the regent, or Taewongun (Grand Prince, 1821–1898), who was the father of the king. The reform program proved strong enough to provoke a reaction but was not sufficiently drastic, even in conception, to transform Korea into a strong and viable state capable of dealing with the dangers of the modern world. That world was gradually closing in on Korea.

During the first two-thirds of the century, several incidents occurred involving Western ships and foreign demands. Korea's initial policy was to resist all attempts to "open" the country by referring those seeking to establish diplomatic relations back to Beijing. This policy was successful as long as it was directed at countries for which Korea was of peripheral concern, but this had never been the case for Japan. Japan, therefore, was the most insistent of the powers trying to pry Korea from the Chinese orbit. In 1876 Japan forced Korea to sign a treaty establishing diplomatic relations and providing for the opening of three ports to trade. The treaty also stipulated that Korea was now "independent," but this did not settle matters because China still considered Korea a tributary. Insurrections in Seoul in 1882 and 1884 led to increased Chinese and Japanese involvement in Korea, including military involvement, always on opposing sides. But outright war was averted by talks between Itō Hirobumi and Li Hongzhang, which led to a formal agreement between China and Japan to withdraw their forces and inform each other if either decided in the future that it was necessary to send in troops.

During the next years the Chinese Resident in Korea was Yuan Shikai (1859–1916), a protégé of Li, originally sent to Korea to train Korean troops. Yuan successfully executed Li's policy of vigorous assertion of Chinese control, dominating the court, effecting a partial union of Korean and Chinese commercial customs, and setting up a telegraph service and a merchant route between Korea and China.

Conflicting ambitions in Korea made war between China and Japan highly probable; the catalyst was the Tonghak Rebellion. Tonghak, literally "Eastern Learning," was an amalgam of Chinese, Buddhist, and native Korean religious

ideas and practices. As so often before in East Asian history, the religious organization took on a political dimension, serving as a vehicle for expressions of discontent with a regime in decay and for agitation against government corruption
and foreign encroachments. Finally outlawed, it was involved in considerable rioting in 1893, which turned to rebellion the following year when Korea was struck
by famine. When the Korean government requested Chinese assistance, Li responded by sending 1500 men and informing the Japanese, whose troops were already on the way. The rebellion was quickly suppressed, but it proved easier to
send than to remove the troops.

When Japanese soldiers entered Seoul, broke into the palace, and kidnapped
the king and queen, Li responded by sending more troops, and war was inevitable.
It was a war that everyone, except the Japanese, expected China to win, but all parties were stunned when Japan defeated China on sea and on land. Begun in July
1894, the war was over by March 1895. In retrospect, the reasons for the outcome
are easy to see: Japan was better equipped, better led, and more united than
China, a country hampered by internal division, corruption, and inadequate leadership in the field. Equipped with shells, some of which were filled with sawdust
rather than gunpowder, and commanded by an old general who lined up the fleet
as though he were still organizing a cavalry charge, it is no wonder that China lost
the war at sea. Furthermore, powerful governors-general considered it Li's war,
not theirs, and were slow in participating; the southern navy remained aloof.

# The Treaty of Shimonoseki (April 1895)

The war was terminated by the Treaty of Shimonoseki. China relinquished all
claims to a special role in Korea and recognized that country as an independent
state (although its troubles were far from over). In addition, China paid Japan an
indemnity and ceded it Taiwan and the Pescadores, thus starting the formation of
the Japanese Empire. A further indication that the Japanese had now joined the
ranks of the imperialist nations was the extension to Japan of most-favored-nation
status, along with the opening of seven additional Chinese ports. Japan was also to
receive the Liaodong Peninsula but, after diplomatic intervention by Russia,
Germany, and France, had to settle for an additional indemnity instead. The effects of the treaty on Korea, on domestic Chinese politics, and on international relations in the area are considered in the following chapters. Here, it should be
noted that the treaty marked an unprecedented shift in the East Asian balance of
power, a shift from China to Japan that was to continue until Japan's defeat in
World War II.

# *Notes*

1.  John W. Dower, "Sizing Up (and Breaking Down) Japan," in Helen Hardacre, ed., *The Postwar Development of Japanese Studies in the United States* (Leiden: Brill, 1998), p. 14.

2.  First article of the party platform as quoted by Kyu Hyun Kim, "Political Ideologies of the Early Meiji Parties," in Hardacre, *The Postwar Development of Japanese Studies in the United States,* p. 400.

3.  Quoted in Carmen Blacker, *The Japanese Enlightenment: A Study of Fukuzawa Yukichi* (London: Cambridge Univ. Press, 1964), p. 111.

4.  Quoted in Blacker, *The Japanese Enlightenment: A Study of Fukuzawa Yukichi,* p. 128.

5.  Donald Keene, "The Age of Translation," Chapter 3, in *Dawn to the West: Japanese Literature of the Modern Era—Fiction* (New York: Holt, Rinehart and Winston, 1984), pp. 55–75.

6.  Quoted in Kenneth B. Pyle, *The New Generation in Meiji Japan: Problems in Cultural Identity, 1885–1895* (Stanford: Stanford Univ. Press, 1969), p. 124.

7. Akira Iriye, in Marius Jansen, ed., *The Cambridge History of Japan, Vol. 5: The Nineteenth Century* (Cambridge: Cambridge Univ. Press, 1989), p. 754.

8. "Rescript on Education," in David John Lu, *Sources of Japanese History, Vol. 1* (New York: McGraw-Hill, 1974), pp. 70–71.

9. Andrew Gordon, "The Invention of Japanese-Style Labor Management," in Stephen Vlastos, *Mirror of Modernity: Invented Traditions of Modern Japan* (Berkeley: Univ. of California Press, 1998), p. 19.

10. Susan B. Hanley, "The Material Culture: Stability in Transition," in Marius Jansen and Gilbert Rozman, eds., *Japan in Transition: From Tokugawa to Meiji* (Princeton Univ. Press, 1986), pp. 467–69 sic passim.

11. James B. Palais, *Politics and Policy in Traditional Korea* (Cambridge: Harvard Univ. Press, 1975), p. 63.

# China: Endings and Beginnings, 1894–1927

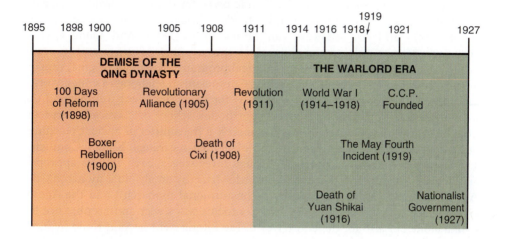

# The New Reformers

The shock of defeat allowed new voices to be heard. They differed from the proponents of self-strengthening both in the scope of the changes they advocated and in a willingness to reexamine basic assumptions. At the same time, the radicals of this generation still had received a Confucian education and had a command of traditional learning.

A major influence was Yan Fu, the one-time naval student at Greenwich, who voiced the bitter resentment of many:

> We thought that of all the human race none was nobler than we. And then one day from tens and thousands of miles away came island barbarians from beyond the pale, with bird-like language and beastly features, who floated in and pounded our gates requesting entrance and, when they did not get what they asked for, they attacked our coasts and took captive our officials and even burned our palaces and alarmed our Emperor. When this happened, the only reason we did not devour their flesh and sleep on their hides was that we had not the power.[1]

Emboldened by the more open atmosphere, Yan publicized his ideas, first in a series of essays and then in a number of extremely influential translations, notably Thomas Huxley's *Ethics and Evolution* (1898), Adam Smith's *Wealth of Nations*

(1900), and John Stuart Mill's *On Liberty* (1903). Yan argued that Western learning was needed to release Chinese energies and rejected much of Chinese tradition including even Confucius. He was especially attracted to Social Darwinism, with its dynamic view of history as evolutionary and progressive, and the hope it held out, on a supposedly modern scientific basis, for those who would struggle.

Yan Fu was no political activist, but others, notably Kang Youwei (1858–1927) and his followers Tan Sitong (1865–1898) and Liang Qichao (1873–1929), not only spread their ideas through their writings and in study groups but also tried to implement political programs. Kang, an original thinker deeply grounded in Buddhism as well as Confucianism, elaborated a highly original theory to construct a Confucian basis for ideas that went well beyond the Confucian tradition. Drawing on an unorthodox school of classical interpretation, he argued that Confucius was not merely a transmitter of ancient teachings but a prophet whose language was full of hidden meanings. Kang's Confucius saw history as a universal progress through three stages, each with its appropriate form of government: the Age of Disorder (rule by an absolute monarch), the Age of Approaching Peace (rule by a constitutional monarch), and the Age of Great Peace (rule by the people). His Confucius was a seer and prophet not for China alone but also for the entire world. Tan Sitong went beyond Kang to argue that the monarchy should be replaced by a republic and attacked the traditional Confucian family distinctions in the name of *ren,* the central Confucian virtue. Neo-Confucian thinkers had earlier given *ren* a cosmic dimension, but Tan drew on modern scientific concepts in identifying *ren* with ether. Kang Youwei, too, equated *ren* with ether and electricity.

In their political program, Kang and his followers sought to transform the government into a modern and modernizing constitutional monarchy along the lines of Meiji Japan. Thanks to a sympathetic governor, they were able to carry out some reforms in Hunan, but their greatest opportunity came during the "Hundred Days of Reform" (actually 103 days, June 11 to September 20), when Emperor Guangxu asserted his authority to issue a flood of edicts aimed at reforming the examination system, remodeling the bureaucracy, and promoting modernization. It was an ambitious program, but the edicts remained more significant as expressions of intent than as indicators of accomplishment, for most were never implemented.

The reforms were initiated by moderately experienced statesmen, but later accounts exaggerated the influence of Kang and his associates and the degree to which there was, from the start, a struggle between a progressive emperor and a supposedly reactionary Empress Dowager (see Figure 16.3). However, rumors of Kang's allegedly extremist influence on the emperor helped to solidify the opposition and pave the way for Cixi, backed by General Ronglu, to stage a coup. She placed Emperor Guangxu under house arrest and turned him into a figurehead for the remaining ten years of his life.

After the coup, Tan Sitong remained in China and achieved martyrdom. Kang Youwei and Liang Qichao managed to flee to Japan, where they continued to write and work for renewal and reform. Kang, elaborating on his utopia, dreamed of a future when the whole world would be united in love and harmony under a single popularly elected government, which would operate hospitals, schools, and nurseries, administering a society in which all divisive institutions would have disappeared, including even the family. Meanwhile, Liang continued to expand his horizons as well as those of his numerous readers. Like many of his contemporaries everywhere, he championed evolution and progress, processes which he conflated and, contrary to Darwin, saw as products of human will. But this will had to serve the group. Like most Chinese and Japanese thinkers, Liang was not an individualist.

The Empress Dowager's coup sent China's most advanced thinkers into exile but did not spell a wholesale reaction against reform. She approved moderate reforms, including military modernization and reforms in education and the monetary and fiscal systems. That little was accomplished was due to the weakness of the central government and the magnitude of the problems facing the dynasty. By no means the least of these came from abroad.

# The Scramble for Concessions

China's display of weakness in the war against Japan set in motion a scramble for special rights and privileges in which Russia, France, Britain, Germany, and Japan pursued their national interests and jockeyed for position in case China collapsed completely, as seemed quite likely at the time. The concessions extracted from China were economic and political. Loans were forced on the Qing, secured by tax revenues, such as maritime customs. Long-term leases of Chinese territory were granted, including the right to develop economic resources such as mines and railroads. Germany leased territory in Shandong; Russia leased Port Arthur in the southern Liaodong Peninsula; France held leases on land around Guangzhou Bay; and Britain obtained Weihaiwei and the New Territories, adjacent to the Kowloon area of Hong Kong. The powers frequently obtained the right to police the leased areas. Often they combined leaseholds, railroad rights, and commercial rights into a "sphere of interest," where they were the privileged foreign power, as, for example, Germany was in Shandong. Finally, there were "nonalienation" pacts in which China agreed not to cede a given area to any power other than the signatory: the Yangzi valley to Britain, the provinces bordering French Indochina to France, and Fujian to Japan. Russia received special rights in Manchuria.

Britain, as the prime trading nation in China, pursued an ambiguous policy, concerned to retain access to all of China but also to obtain a share of the concessions. The United States at this time was acquiring a Pacific empire. In 1898 it annexed Hawaii and, after war with Spain, the Philippines and Guam. At the urging of Britain, the United States then adopted an open-door policy enunciated in two diplomatic notes. The first of these (1899) merely demanded equality of commercial opportunity for all the powers in China, whereas the second (1900) also affirmed a desire to preserve the integrity of the Chinese state and Chinese territory. This was a declaration of principle, not backed by force; neither its altruism nor its effectiveness should be exaggerated.

# The Boxer Rising

The Boxers, members of the *Yihequan* (Righteous and Harmonious Fists), developed in response to harsh economic conditions. Popular anxieties were also fueled by antiforeignism, stemming from alarm over the spread of railways, which cut across the land regardless of the graves of ancestors or the requirements of geomancy, railways along which stood telephone poles carrying wires from which rust-filled rainwater dripped blood-red. As a counterforce, the Boxers relied on *qigong* (ritualized exercise), spells, and amulets to endow them with supernatural powers, including invulnerability to bullets. In 1898 flood and famine in Shandong, combined with the advance of the Germans in that province, led to the first Boxer rising there in May of that year; but it was drought in the spring and summer of 1900 that brought many new members and wide popular support.

Originally antidynastic, the Boxers changed direction when they received the support of high Qing officials prepared to use the movement against the foreign powers. Thus encouraged, the Boxers spread, venting their rage on Chinese and foreign Christians, especially Catholics. On June 13, 1900, they entered Beijing. Eight days later the court issued a declaration of war on all the treaty powers. The Boxers were officially placed under the command of imperial princes. There followed a dramatic two-month siege of the legation quarter in Beijing, where 451 guards defended 473 foreign civilians and some 3000 Chinese Christians who had fled there for protection. The ordeal of the besieged was grim, but they were spared the worst, for the Boxers and the Chinese troops were undisciplined, ill-organized, and uncoordinated. The city was full of looting and violence, but the legation quarter was still intact when an international relief expedition reached Beijing on August 15 and forced the court to flee the capital.

During these dangerous and dramatic events, southern governors-general ignored the court's declaration of war, claiming it was made under duress. The powers, nevertheless, demanded from the Qing court a very harsh settlement. It included a huge indemnity (450 million taels, or 67.5 million pounds sterling) to be paid from customs and salt revenues. Other provisions required the punishment of pro-Boxer officials and of certain cities, where the civil service examinations were suspended. The powers received the right to station permanent legation guards in the capital and to place troops between Beijing and the sea. The Boxer rising also provided Russia with an excuse to occupy Manchuria, where some Russians remained until Russia's defeat by Japan in the war of 1904–1905.

The Boxer rising became a source of literature focusing on one of its leading figures, Sai Jinhua (1874–1936), who was a courtesan, the concubine of a Chinese diplomat in Europe, and supposedly the mistress of the German field marshall who commanded the allied forces occupying Beijing. Depraved strumpet to some, selfless heroine to others, she fills both roles in *A Flower in a Sea of Sins* (*Niehai hua,* 1907) by Zeng Pu (1872–1935).

# Winds of Change

Between 1895 and 1911, the modern sector of the Chinese economy continued to grow, but it was dominated by foreign capital. Extensive railway concessions were granted to the treaty powers, and Chinese railroads, like that linking Beijing and Hankou, were financed by foreign capital. Foreigners also controlled much of China's mining and shipping and were a major factor in manufacturing, both for export (tea, silk, soybeans, and so on) and for the domestic market (textiles, tobacco, and so on). Modern banking was another area of foreign domination, prompting the Qing government in 1898 to approve the creation of the Commercial Bank of China as a "government operated merchant enterprise." Two more banks were formed in 1905 and 1907.

Except for railways and mines, foreign investments were concentrated in the treaty ports. It was also there that Chinese factories gradually developed, taking advantage of modern services and the security found in foreign concession areas. Chinese enterprises were particularly important in textile manufacturing. Most remained small (by 1912 only 750 employed more than 100 workers), but they were an important part of China's economic modernization. It was during this time that Shanghai became China's largest city.

In Shanghai and, to a lesser extent, in other treaty ports, changes in social structure occurred. During the last five years of the dynasty there emerged a bourgeoisie, "a group of modern or semi-modern entrepreneurs, tradesmen, financiers, industrial leaders, unified by material interests, common political aspirations, a sense of their collective destiny, a common mentality, and specific daily habits."[2] There were also the beginnings of an urban working class, who at times expressed their resentment over terrible working conditions by going on strike. In the city, too, the old family system lost some of its economic underpinnings, and an audience receptive to new ways of looking at things developed.

There were now 170 presses supplying 2 to 4 million readers for the "depravity," "chivalric/court case," "exposé," and "science fantasy" novels studied by David Der-wei Wang. More often than not they took a jaundiced view of those in power, although few were as blunt as the prostitute in the depravity novel *Nine-tailed Turtle* who tells her customer, "The whole of officialdom is just like a big whorehouse."[3] In *The New Story of the Stone* (1908), Wu Jianren (1866–1910) brings back the main protagonist of *The Dream of the Red Chamber,* and at one point has him arrested as a dissident, but also takes him to "The Civilized World," filled with technological wonders, a utopia (unlike Kang Youwei's) not to be taken as actually attainable.

Meanwhile, out in the real world a strong influence on provincial affairs was exercised by a semimodern urban elite composed of merchants and bankers (more or less traditional), military and professional men (among them journalists) trained in modern methods, and absentee landowners, an elite whose interests and even values often differed from those of the landed gentry on the one hand and from the central government on the other. The very definition of elite status was changed forever when the examination system was abolished in 1905, putting an end to a key institution that had linked government and society, thought and action, and the local and the central for well over a thousand years. The government took this radical step primarily in recognition of the need for more modern specialists, but also to secure the loyalty of graduates of new schools by reassuring them in their career expectations.

# Stirrings of Protest and Revolution

Some were caught off balance by the winds of change. Others trimmed their sails, but there were also those who looked to the future with hope and organized attempts to induce further changes. An early and notable example was the formation of the first anti-footbinding movement in 1894, which resulted in a law banning the practice in 1902. However, even in the cities the law was largely ignored. Footbinding persisted longest in rural areas, and old women with bound feet can still be seen in remote areas. Other expressions of public opinion included a flurry of criticism at what appeared to be a maneuver to depose the emperor (1900), protests at Russia's refusal to leave Manchuria (1903), a boycott against the United States protesting exclusionary immigration laws (1905), and a boycott against Japan (1908), as well as movements to regain railway rights.

Readers of the political press that emerged after 1895 were now exposed to articles and cartoons linking dissatisfaction with the government to resentment against foreign exactions (see Figure 19.1). Politically, the defeat of 1895 not only opened the way for radical reformism but also set Sun Yat-sen (1866–1925) on the path of revolution. Sun was born into a Guangdong peasant family, received a Christian education in Hawaii, and studied medicine in Hong Kong. He founded his first revolutionary organization in 1894. Throughout his life overseas, Chinese communities remained an important source of moral and financial support. Over the years he elaborated his "Three Principles of the People"—nationalism, democracy, and the people's livelihood. He called for the overthrow of the dynasty and the establishment of a republic, principles broad enough to attract the varied and loosely organized membership of Sun's Revolutionary Alliance (Tongmenghui), formed in Tokyo in 1905 by the merger of a number of revolutionary groups. His supporters now included students, many from elite families.

Many looked to political revolution to solve China's ills, but some more radical voices sought social revolution as well. One such was the pioneer feminist Qiu Jin, born in 1877 and executed as a revolutionary in 1907. In 1904, shortly after she had left not only the husband her family had selected for her but also a son and a daughter, she wrote the following poem:

**FIGURE 19.1** "A record of the situation in China." Cartoon in *Shibao*, August 26, 1907. The ladle in the center represents officials scooping from the jug of the people (on the right) and pouring their resources through a government funnel into the foreigners' teapot. (From *Print and Politics: "Shibao" and the Culture of Reform in Late Qing China*, by Joan Judge [Stanford: Stanford University Press, 1996], p. 184. Reprinted courtesy Stanford University Press.)

*Regrets: Lines Written en Route to Japan*

Sun and moon have no light left, earth is dark;
our women's world is sunk so deep, who can help us?
Jewelry sold to pay this trip across the seas,
Cut off from family I leave my native land.
Unbinding my feet I clear out a thousand years of poison,
With heated heart arouse all women's spirits.
Alas, this delicate kerchief here
Is half stained with blood, and half with tears.[4]

# Eleventh-Hour Reform

The abolition of the examination system was the most drastic of a series of reforms by which the Empress Dowager hoped to save the dynasty after the failure of the Boxers. Some, like the drive against opium, accomplished much, but the program as a whole failed to inspire officials to change their ways. The momentum was all downhill. In *Modern Times: A Brief History of Enlightenment* (*Wenming xiaoshi,* 1905) Li Boyuan (1867–1906), a widely read author of exposé novels, depicts officials whose venality is matched only by the ignorance and arrogance of purveyors of the new Western learning. According to David Der-wei Wang, "Li Boyuan saw in this campaign for reform and modernization less a promise of new economic and political structure than an omen of collective self-delusion, incompetence, and procrastination."[5]

Frequently, measures taken to save the Qing ended up undermining it. The educational reforms are an example. By 1911 even remote provinces boasted new schools, teaching new subjects and ideas. Students also studied abroad in record numbers, especially in Japan where, by 1906, there were at least 8000 Chinese students, many supported by their provincial governments. There, away from home, they enjoyed new personal and intellectual liberty. Even those who did not manage to complete their education drank in the heady wine of new ideas. From the writing of the highly influential Liang Qichao, many learned about the major events of world history and were introduced to Western social and political thought. The example of Japan was itself a powerful influence, as were books translated from Japanese. More books were translated into Chinese from Japanese than from any other language. Many Japanese loanwords entered the Chinese language, thus reversing the flow that had taken place more than a millennium earlier.

Chinese students thus learned about Western history, law, science, and logic, became convinced of the truths of Social Darwinism, and were inspired by the visions of nationalism. As non-Chinese, the Manchus were an obvious target. The Japanese example showed that nationalism was compatible with the preservation of elements of traditional culture, but a commitment to nationalism entailed a willingness to jettison those elements of tradition that failed to contribute to national development. Toward the end of the decade students became increasingly restive and revolutionary.

Manchu political reform included restructuring the government along modern lines and developing a constitution. After a study mission abroad (1905–1906) and subsequent deliberations, in 1908 the government announced a nine-year plan of constitutional reform, beginning with provincial assemblies in 1909. Although elected on a limited franchise, these assemblies, as well as the central legislative council convened in 1910, became centers of opposition rather than sources of popular support.

Nothing was more urgent than the creation of a modern military, but here too the reform program backfired. The new forces proved unreliable because they were either influenced by new, subversive ideas or were loyal to their commanders rather than to the throne. The main beneficiary of military modernization turned out to be Yuan Shikai, who, after his service in Korea (see p. 482), had advanced his career by siding with Cixi in her coup and by standing firm against the Boxers. He became commander of the New Army in 1895 and, as governor-general of Chihli (pinyin: Zhili) from 1901 to 1907, continued to build up the army with which he retained ties even after he was dismissed from the government in 1909.

The government had some foreign policy success, especially in reasserting sovereignty over Tibet, but failed to emerge as a plausible focus for nationalism. Not only was it handicapped by its non-Han ethnic origins, but also at this critical juncture, there was general confusion and disorganization after the Empress Dowager and Emperor Guangxu both died in 1908. Because the Emperor had seemed to be in good health, there were rumors that his death one day before that of the Empress Dowager was caused by poison. The rumors were never proven, but this was not a propitious way to start a new reign. The new emperor was an infant, and the regent was inept but bitterly resentful of Yuan Shikai, who was fortunate to be allowed to retire in 1909.

# The Revolution of 1911

In its program of modernization, the dynasty was handicapped by its financial weakness. This became painfully apparent in its handling of the railway issue. To regain foreign railway concessions, a railway recovery movement was organized by provincial landed and merchant elites, who created their own railway companies. The Qing government, however, wanted to centralize, and in 1911 decided to nationalize the major railway lines. Lacking the necessary financial resources, it was able to do so only by contracting foreign loans, inevitably with strings attached. The loans and the subsequent disbanding of provincial railway companies caused a furor, nowhere more so than in Sichuan, where the local investors felt cheated by the price the government was willing to pay for their shares. Provincial interests resented the threat to provincial autonomy. Nationalists were indignant over the foreign loans that financed the transaction. This was the prelude to revolt. The insurrection that set off the revolution took place in Wuchang on October 10 when a New Army regiment mutinied, led by men only very loosely connected with the Revolutionary Alliance, the main revolutionary organization in the land. Its leader, Sun Yat-sen, was traveling in the United States raising money, but rushed home when he heard the news.

After the October 10 incident, province after province broke with the dynasty. It turned for help to Yuan Shikai, who had served as Grand Councilor and Foreign Minister in 1907–1908 but had been dismissed after the death of his patron Cixi in 1908. Yuan was the obvious man to turn to, for he enjoyed foreign support as well as the loyalty of China's best army, and he had prestige as a reformer. However, he was not about to sacrifice himself for a losing cause, but he was not strong enough to impose his will on all of China. The revolutionaries had in the meantime formed a government at Nanjing with Sun Yat-sen as provisional president. A compromise between Yuan and the revolutionaries was clearly called for if China was to avoid prolonged civil war and the nightmare of direct foreign intervention. An agreement was reached. The Manchu child-emperor formally abdicated on February 2, 1912, bringing an end not only to a dynasty but also to a political system whose foundations had been laid in 221 B.C.E. China now became a republic.

# II. From Yuan Shikai to Chiang Kai-shek

## Yuan Shikai

After the Qing abdication, Sun Yat-sen stepped aside, and Yuan accepted the presidency of a republic with a two-chambered legislature. He also agreed to move the capital to Nanjing, but once in office he evaded this provision, and Beijing remained the capital of the Republic. In the absence of well-organized political parties or deep-rooted republican sentiment among the public, there was little to restrain Yuan from rapidly developing into a dictator. To be sure, elections were held in February 1913 with about 5 percent of China's population entitled to vote.

The Guomindang (GMD or Nationalist party), the successor to the Tongmenghui, was the largest party in the new parliament. Yuan, however, was not about to share power. He bullied the elected parliament, and in March 1913, Song Jiaoren (1882–1913), architect of the constitution and leader of the parliamentary GMD, was assassinated on Yuan's orders. That summer Yuan forced a showdown by ordering dismissal of pro-Nationalist southern military governors. When they revolted in what is sometimes known as the Second Revolution, Yuan crushed them easily. For the next two years, the other military governors remained loyal, but Yuan remained dependent on military authority.

Yuan basically sought to continue the late Qing program of centralization, but to do so he had to struggle against the forces of reformist provincialism as well as revolutionary nationalism. Often the two combined, because to finance a program regarded with suspicion by provincial interests, Yuan needed funds, and, in the absence of a radical social revolution, this meant obtaining foreign loans. But such loans antagonized nationalists because they came with foreign strings and "advisors." The *Shibao* cartoon rang truer than ever (see Figure 19.1).

In 1915, taking advantage of the great powers' preoccupation with World War I, Japan presented China with the notorious Twenty-One Demands, divided into five groups: (1) recognition of Japanese rights in Shandong; (2) extension of Japanese rights in Mongolia and Manchuria; (3) Sino-Japanese joint operation of China's largest iron and steel company; (4) agreement that China was not to cede or lease any coastal area to any power other than Japan; and (5) provisions that would have obliged the Chinese government to employ Japanese political, financial, and military advisors, to give the Japanese partial control over the police, and to purchase Japanese arms. Yuan managed to avoid the last and most onerous group of demands, which would have reduced China to a virtual Japanese satellite. However, with the other powers preoccupied in Europe, Yuan was forced to accept Japan's seizure of Germany's holdings in Shandong, grant Japan new rights in southern Manchuria and Inner Mongolia, and acknowledge her special interest in China's largest iron and steel works, which had previously served as security for Japanese loans. The domestic result was a wave of anti-Japanese nationalist outrage, which expressed itself in protests and boycotts.

Yuan made no attempt to harness nationalist feelings to his own cause but prepared for restoration of dynastic rule with himself as emperor. According to an American advisor to Yuan, China was not ready for a republic. Yuan probably was not off the mark in believing that bringing back the emperorship would follow the preferences and meet the expectations of the vast majority of China's population, but he did nothing to tap or mobilize mass support or to mollify the resentment of the educated. He just went ahead. The new regime was proclaimed in December 1915, to begin on New Year's Day. Hostility to the new dynasty was so overwhelming that in March 1916 Yuan gave way and officially abandoned his imperial ambitions. He never regained his old prestige and died in June of that year, a failure.

# The Warlord Era

After the fall of Yuan Shikai, the pattern of Chinese politics became exceedingly complex, as military men came to the fore. In 1917 there was even a two-week restoration of the Qing. In August of that year China, under the premier and warlord Duan Qirui (1865–1936), entered World War I by declaring war on Germany. During the next year the Chinese government received loans of some 145 million yen from Japan (the Nishihara loans), ostensibly to strengthen the Chinese ally, but actually siphoned off to support Duan's military and political plans.

Although a national government ruled in Beijing, actual power lay in the hands of regional strongmen (warlords) who came to dominate civil administration in the areas under their control largely through force of arms and who struggled with each other to enlarge or protect their holdings. They constantly made and unmade alliances with each other, while the foreign powers (especially Japan and the Soviet Union), fishing in these troubled waters, sought to play the warlords off against each other for their own benefit.

Some of the warlords, including Duan, had been generals under Yuan Shikai; others had begun their careers as bandits and more or less continued to behave as such. One of the most notorious was the "Dog-Meat General" of Shandong, with his entourage of White Russian guards and women. A huge brute of a man, greedy and cruel, he decorated his telegraph poles with the severed heads of secret society members. Other warlords showed a genuine interest in social welfare and education and tried to build up their areas economically, but they lacked the vision and organization to clear a way for the future. Conditions varied widely, but for many these were years of great insecurity and suffering.

Internationally, the 1920s were peaceful, but China's sovereignty was more impaired than ever. Its customs and salt revenues were committed to paying foreign obligations, and tariffs were kept artificially low. China's major cities were designated as treaty ports, some—most notably Shanghai—with foreign concession areas under foreign jurisdiction. In these enclaves foreigners led privileged lives. They also continued to enjoy extraterritoriality wherever they went. Although the foreigners' economic impact should not be exaggerated, both commercial travelers and missionaries used British steamers to travel inland on waterways, policed if necessary by foreign gunboats, to service churches and clinics. Foreigners were everywhere. Their presence was politically offensive and profoundly degrading.

Economically, the modern sector expanded during the global postwar boom so that 1917–1923 has been called "the golden age of Chinese capitalism."[6] The influence of the world economy on China expanded, with, for example, the sale of kerosene spreading into interior villages. Over all, these economic developments were insufficient to destabilize the economy enough to bring about either a fundamental breakdown or a breakthrough to growth. However, economic activity can never be separated from other aspects of life. We may speculate that with the state too weak to exert pressure, the examination system no longer in place to reward Confucian learning, and the old paternalistic ideology tarnished, there was increasingly little to prevent former gentry families from turning into landlords pure and simple. If so, this suggests fragmentation of the social fabric analogous to the political fragmentation produced by the warlords. Meanwhile, the shattering of the old world was most visible in the intellectual arena.

# Intellectual Ferment

It did not take the fall of the Qing to produce iconoclasm and protest. Revolutionary ideas had already been current among Chinese students in Tokyo and were discussed in magazines and schools in China itself. We have already noted the beginnings of feminism. In China, as in Japan, radicals were drawn to the teachings of anarchism—especially the ideas that the state is inherently oppressive and that natural human social tendencies can create a just society. The abolition of the examinations and the collapse of the Qing opened the floodgates to new ideas but destroyed neither the respect accorded scholars and intellectuals nor their commitment to society and their sense of their own importance.

A major landmark was the founding in 1915 of *New Youth,* the journal that came to stand at the core of the new intellectual tide. In the first issue, its founder, Chen Duxiu (1879–1942), issued an eloquent call for the rejuvenation of China, accompanied by an equally strong denunciation of tradition. The new intellectuals castigated Confucianism as being responsible for all that was found wanting in the old state and society, for stifling human creativity and suppressing women, and for standing in the way of freedom and progress. Few were convinced by Kang Youwei, who tried to cast Confucianism in a new role as the official state religion. Unsuccessful in his earlier attempt to construct a Confucian justification for modernization that would persuade scholars grounded in the classics, he now failed to make Confucianism acceptable to those whose primary loyalty was to the nation. He was not the only intellectual whom time passed by as ideas once considered radical appeared conservative in a changed world. Confucianism was not destroyed, but it was put very much on the defensive.

*New Youth* opposed not only the traditional teachings but also the language in which they were written. The journal opened its pages to Hu Shi (1891–1962), a former student of the American philosopher John Dewey and China's leading champion of the vernacular language (*baihua*). Hu Shi argued that people should write the spoken language, not the language of the classics, and that the vernacular should be taught in the schools. He praised the literary merits of the old novels written in the vernacular, which had long been widely read but had not been considered respectable. The campaign for the vernacular was a success, although classical expressions had a way of creeping into the vernacular, and newly borrowed terms stood in the way of easy comprehension. Nevertheless, the new language was both more accessible and more modern than the old. Introduced into the elementary schools in 1920, it was universally used in the schools by the end of the decade.

*New Youth* was also the first magazine to publish Lu Xun, pen name of Zhou Shuren (1881–1936), who became China's most acclaimed twentieth century writer. Although Lu Xun had gone to Japan to study medicine, he then decided to devote himself to combating not physical ailments, but China's spiritual ills. His bitter satire cut like a sharp scalpel, but a scalpel wielded by a humanist who hoped to cure, not kill. The protagonist in "A Madman's Diary" (*New Youth,* 1918) discovers the reality underneath the gloss of "virtue and morality" in the old histories: a history of man eating man. He ends with the plea, "Perhaps there are still children who have not eaten men? Save the children. . . ."[7]

Chen Duxiu and many other intellectual leaders taught at Beijing University. Their ideas found a ready following among the students at this and other universities. On May 4, 1919, some 3000 students staged a dramatic demonstration in

Beijing to protest the assignment at the Versailles Peace Conference of Germany's former possessions in Shandong to Japan, even though China, like Japan, had entered World War I on the allied side and sent labor battalions to France. The students were outraged. Their demonstrations became violent. The house of a pro-Japanese minister was burned and another minister was beaten badly. In clashes with the police one student died. There were arrests followed by more protest, a wave of strikes, and a show of merchant and labor support for the students. In the end the government had to retreat. Those arrested were released, and those who had ordered the arrests were forced to resign. China never signed the ill-fated Treaty of Versailles.

The May Fourth incident came to symbolize the currents of intellectual and cultural change first articulated in *New Youth* and gave rise to the broader term "May Fourth Movement" (c. 1915 to early 1920s). After the incident, there was a new sense of urgency. What had been a trickle of protest became a tide of attacks on just about every aspect of Chinese culture in a total rejection of the past—including basic institutions such as the family. Simultaneously, the movement introduced a host of new and radical ideas. New journals appeared, and there was much heady and excited talk, but also action, as young people spurned arranged marriage and engaged in increased social action, including organizing labor unions. The May Fourth movement had long-term revolutionary consequences, both in what it destroyed and in what it introduced. In the short term, although the current of nationalism ran deep and strong, there were intense disagreements over the future direction of Chinese culture, and a tremendous variety of ideas, theories, and styles swelled the eddies of intellectual and cultural life.

# Intellectual Alternatives

Europe's self-destruction in war and the failure of liberal principles at Versailles prompted Liang Qichao to turn back to the Chinese tradition in the hope of synthesizing the best of China and the West, with Chinese elements predominating. An important debate began in 1923 between the proponents of science and those of metaphysics, involving different evaluation of Chinese and Western cultures. Among the advocates of the latter were proponents of scientism, who believed that science holds the answers to all problems and that the scientific is the only method for arriving at truth. Their opponents argued that science is applicable only to a narrow field of study and that moral values have to be based on deeper metaphysical truths that by their very nature are beyond the reach of scientific methodology. Because similar problems agitated the West at this time, Chinese thinkers drew on the ideas of classic European philosophers such as Immanuel Kant and also on the thought of contemporaries with widely different methodologies and results. For example, some promoted the ideas of John Dewey (1859–1952), the American pragmatist who would replace "absolute truth" with truths that worked as solutions to problems; but others turned to Henri-Louis Bergson (1859–1941), the French exponent of vitalism, a doctrine centering on life as a force that cannot be explained in material terms.

Those who identified with the Chinese tradition further drew on the insights of Neo-Confucianism and Buddhism, particularly the former. One of the most noteworthy defenders of tradition was Liang Shuming (1893–1988), who put his Confucian principles into action by working on rural reconstruction. Another was Zhang Junmai (1887–1969), later the leader of a small political party opposed to both the Communists and the Nationalists. Other philosophers such as Feng Yulan (Fung Yu-lan, 1895–1990) and Xiong Shili (1885–1969) drew on Neo-Confucian thought, but the trend of the times was against them.

Among the champions of science and Western values were the scientist Ding Wenjiang (1887–1937) and the father of the vernacular language movement, Hu Shi. Hu Shi was a leading liberal who advocated a gradualist, piecemeal problem-solving approach to China's ills in the face of attacks both from the traditionalists on the right and from the left. His message increasingly fell on deaf ears, for his approach required time, and time was precisely what China lacked. More often than not, this included time to digest the heady dose of new intellectual imports or, for that matter, to study the old traditions in depth.

# Cultural Alternatives

Qi Baishi (1863–1957), probably the most beloved painter of the century, was singularly unaffected by the turmoil of the times. Qi began as a humble carpenter and did not turn to painting until his mid-twenties, but his industry and longevity more than made up for a late start. It is estimated that he produced more than 10,000 paintings. Qi was a great admirer of the seventeenth-century individualist Zhu Da, but followed his own inner vision. He was not given to theorizing but did express his attitude toward representation: "The excellence of a painting lies in its being like, yet unlike. Too much likeness flatters the vulgar taste; too much unlikeness deceives the world."[8] His works show, to quote a Chinese critic, "a loving sympathy for the little insects and crabs and flowers he draws" and have "an enlivening gaiety of manner" so that "his pictures are really all pictures of his own gentle humanism"[9] (see Figure 19.2).

There were other painters and calligraphers who remained uninfluenced by the West, but many felt that the new age required a new style. Among those who tried to combine elements of the Chinese and Western traditions were the followers of a school of painters established by Gao Lun (Gao Jianfu, 1879–1951). Gao sought to combine Western shading and perspective with Chinese brushwork and was also influenced by Japanese decorativeness. He sought to bring Chinese painting up to date by including in his works new subject matter, such as the airplanes in Figure 19.3.

In Shanghai, meanwhile, a small group of artists tried to transplant French style bohemianism into that international city. Xu Beihong (1895–1953), for ex-

**FIGURE 19.2** *Grasshopper and Orchid Leaves,* Qi Baishi (Qi Huang, 1863–1957). Although Qi also painted landscapes and portraits, he excelled in depicting the humble forms of life, such as rodents and insects, with a loving and gentle humor reminiscent of the haiku of Kobayashi Issa. Ink on paper, 12 in × 8.46 in, signed Baishi. (Courtesy Far East Fine Arts, Inc. San Francisco [http://www.fareastfinearts.com].)

ample, affected the long hair and general appearance popular in the artists' quarter of Paris. When he returned from that city in 1927, Xu also brought back a thorough mastery of the French academic style. Somewhat more advanced in his Western tastes was Liu Haisu (1896–1994), founder of the Shanghai Art School (1920), where he introduced the use of a nude model. This was also one of the first schools to offer a full course of instruction in Western music. Liu was inspired by French postimpressionists such as Matisse and Cezanne. Later, however, Liu returned to painting in a traditional manner, and Xu, too, abandoned his Western dress for a Chinese gown. Today Xu is perhaps most appreciated for his paintings of horses (see Figure 19.4).

Modern Chinese literature had its origins in the novels of the late Qing. A very popular but superficial genre was "butterfly" literature, named after poems inserted into a novel, comparing lovers to pairs of butterflies. Between 1910 and 1930, around 2215 such novels offered a literate but unlearned public amusement and escape. Also, going back to the late Qing there was a steady and swelling stream of translations. Lin Shu (1852–1924), the most famous and prolific early translator, rendered into classical Chinese the novels of Charles Dickens, Walter Scott, and others in an opus that grew to some 180 works. Thanks to the labors of Lin and other translators, soon examples of all the major European literary traditions as well as that of Japan were well represented in translation.

The May Fourth movement had a strong effect on literature. The intellectual revolution was accompanied by a literary revolution. This brought with it experiments, such as those of Xu Zhimo (1896–1931), who modeled his poetry on English verse, complete with rhyme. More widespread was a tendency toward romantic emotionalism, an outpouring of feelings released by the removal of Confucian restraints and encouraged by the example of European romanticism. One strain, as analyzed by Leo Ou-fan Lee, was the passive-sentimental, presided over by the hero of Goethe's *The Sorrows of Young Werther,* read in China and Japan as "a sentimental sob story." The

**FIGURE 19.3** *Flying in the Rain,* Gao Lun (Gao Jianfu), 1932. Chinese painters, like writers and intellectuals throughout East Asia, devised different ways to combine traditionalism and modernism in style and subject matter, but lyrical landscapes with airplanes bouncing through the sky are rare anywhere. Ink and color on paper. (© Art Museum, Chinese University of Hong Kong, China.)

subjectivism of these writers was not unlike that of the writers of "I novels" in Japan. Another strain was dynamic and heroic. Its ideal was Prometheus, who braved Zeus's wrath and stole fire for mankind. Holding a promise of release from alienation, it was compatible with a revolutionary political stance. For Guo Moruo (1892–1978), once an admirer of Goethe, Lenin became beyond all else a Promethean hero. Perhaps the strongest expression of Promethean martyrdom came from Lu Xun, "I have stolen fire from other countries, intending to cook my own flesh. I think that if the taste is good, the other chewers on their part may get something out of it, and I shall not sacrifice my body in vain."[10]

Controversies and rivalries stimulated the formation of literary and intellectual societies as like-minded men joined together to publish journals advocating

**FIGURE 19.4** *Standing Horse*, Xu Beihong, 1935. (© Kyoto National Museum.)

their causes and denouncing the opposition. Revolutionaries were not alone in arguing that literature should have a social purpose, but as the years passed without any improvement in Chinese conditions, the attractions of revolutionary creeds increased. Writers of revolutionary persuasion such as the Communist Mao Dun (Shen Yanbing, 1896–1981) depicted and analyzed the defects in the old society and portrayed the idealism of those who were out to change things. Such themes appeared not only in the work of Communist writers like Mao Dun, but also in the work of the anarchist Ba Jin (Li Feigang, 1905–), best known for his depiction of the disintegration of a large, eminent family in the novel appropriately entitled *Family* (1931), a part of his *Turbulent Stream* trilogy (1931–1940). Such works provide important material for the student of social as well as literary history.

# Marxism in China: The Early Years

Marxism was not unknown in China but had little appeal before the Russian Revolution. The few who were drawn to socialism were attracted more by its egalitarianism than by concepts of class warfare. The writings of Marx and Engels offered the vision of a perfect society, but their thesis that socialism could only be achieved after capitalism had run its course suggested that Marxism was inappropriate for a society only just entering "the capitalist stage of development."

The success of the Russian Revolution (1917) changed all that. Faced with a similar problem in applying Marxism to Russia, Lenin amended Marxist theory to fit the needs of his own country and thereby also made it more relevant to the Chinese. His theory that imperialism was the last stage of capitalism gave new importance to countries such as China, which were the objects of imperialist expansion and the places where capitalism was particularly vulnerable. Also most significant was Lenin's concept of the Communist party as the vanguard of revolution, for now party intellectuals could help make history even in a precapitalist state.

Furthermore, Marxism was modern and claimed "scientifically" valid doctrines. It shared the prestige accorded by Chinese intellectuals to Western and "advanced" ideas, even as its proponents opposed the dominant forms of economic and political organization in the West. A Western heresy to use against the West, it promised to undo China's humiliation, and its converts were persuaded that the doctrine of "dialectic materialism" assured that Communism was the wave of the future. Thus, China could once again be in the forefront of world history. The Russian Revolution demonstrated that it worked.

Li Dazhao (1888–1927), professor and librarian at Beijing University, was initially attracted by its promise as a vehicle for national revolution, whereas Chen Duxiu turned from science and democracy to Marxism as a more effective means of achieving modernization. Others were drawn to it for a mixture of reasons, high among them the promise it held for solving China's ills. By the spring of 1920, when Grigorii Voitinsky arrived in China as an agent of the Communist International (Comintern), a core group of Marxist intellectuals was available as potential leaders for the organization of the Chinese Communist Party (C.C.P.) that took place the following year.

At its first gathering in July 1921, the C.C.P. elected Chen Duxiu as its Secretary General. Despite considerable misgivings, the party submitted to a Comintern policy of maximum cooperation with the GMD. A formal agreement was reached in 1923, which allowed C.C.P. members into the GMD as individuals, subject to GMD party discipline. The C.C.P. leaders found it difficult to accept the Comintern's theoretical analysis of the GMD as a multiclass party, but submitted to Comintern discipline and the logic of the situation where the few hundred Communists were outnumbered by the thousands of GMD members and had little contact with the masses. This initial period of cooperation lasted until 1927. The C.C.P. grew, but the GMD remained the senior partner.

# The GMD and Sun Yat-sen (1913–1923)

After the failure of the "second revolution" of 1913, Sun Yat-sen was again forced into exile in Japan, where he tried to win Japanese support for his revolution. After the death of Yuan Shikai, Sun was able to return to China and establish a precarious foothold in Canton, where he depended on the good will of the local warlord. Denied foreign backing from Japan and elsewhere, Sun was also handicapped by the weakness of the GMD party organization, which was held together only loosely, largely through loyalty to Sun himself. The success of the Russian Revolution provided a striking contrast to the failure of Sun's revolution. Sun was also favorably disposed to the Soviet Union (U.S.S.R.) by its initial renunciation of Czarist rights in China. This corresponded to a new anti-imperialist emphasis in his own thought and rhetoric, after the end of Manchu rule had not led to a marked improvement in China's position in the world. Also, he was impressed by the mass nationalism of the May Fourth Movement.

Sun was therefore ready to work with the Communists and in 1923 concluded an agreement with the Comintern that concurred with Sun's view that China was not ready for socialism and that the immediate task ahead was the achievement of national unity and independence. Through this pact, Sun received valuable assistance and aid. Under the guidance of the Comintern agent Mikhail Borodin (originally named Grusenberg), the GMD was reorganized into a more structured and disciplined organization than ever before, while General Galen, alias Vassily Blyukher (or Blücher), performed the same service for the army. Sun made some minor ideological compromises but did not basically depart from his previous views.

# GMD and C.C.P. Cooperation (1923–1927)

For both sides this was a marriage of convenience. At first it worked. The GMD gained guidance and support. C.C.P. members rose to important positions in the GMD, and the party grew. A good example of a C.C.P. leader occupying an important GMD office is Zhou Enlai's (1898–1976) service as chief of the political department of the Whampoa Military Academy under Chiang Kai-shek (1887–1975). Here the cream of the GMD officer corps was trained and prepared to lead an army to reunify China and establish a national regime.

The C.C.P. devoted itself mainly to organizing the urban labor movement, which had already won its first victory in the Hong Kong Seamen's Strike of 1922. Shanghai and Canton were particularly fertile grounds for labor organizers, because in these cities the textile and other light industries continued their pre–World War I growth, assisted by the wartime lull in foreign competition. In around 1920, of some 2.7 million cotton spindles in China, 1.3 million were in Chinese-controlled factories, and 500,000 were owned by Japanese. In Chinese and foreign plants alike, wages were very low, working hours long (averaging nine and one-half hours in Shanghai and up to thirteen in the provinces), and all-around conditions remained very harsh. Under these circumstances, the C.C.P.'s work met with substantial success. It gained greatly by its leadership during and following the incident of May 30, 1925, when Chinese demonstrators were fired on by the police of the International Settlement in Shanghai, killing ten and wounding more than fifty. A general strike and boycott followed; in Hong Kong and Canton the movement held out for sixteen months. The strike did not achieve its goals, but C.C.P. party membership increased from around 1000 in early 1925 to an estimated 20,000 by the summer of 1926.

Sun Yat-sen did not live to witness the May 30 incident, for he died of cancer in March 1925. He was an energetic speaker and tireless visionary, glorified as the father of the revolution, but he left no clearly designated heir and an ambiguous ideological legacy. His last major statement, "Three Principles of the People" (1924), stressed the first principle, nationalism—now directed against foreign imperialism—and provided for self-determination for China's minorities. The second principle, democracy, contained proposals for popular elections, initiative, recall, and referendum, but full democracy was to come only after a preparatory period of political tutelage. He emphasized the need for a disciplined people and believed that the Chinese people had too much freedom, not too little. The state would be a republic with five branches of government: legislative, executive, and judicial (as in the West), plus an examination branch to test applicants for government posts and a censorial branch to monitor government officials and control corruption, as under the emperors.

Finally, the principle of the people's livelihood was aimed at both egalitarianism and economic development. It incorporated a proposal by the American reformer Henry George (1839–1897) to tax the unearned increment on land values to equalize holdings. An additional refinement was a land tax based on each landowner's assessment of the value of his land. To prevent underassessment, the state was to have the right to purchase the land at the declared value. Beyond that, Sun had a grandiose vision of "building the wealthiest, most powerful and happiest nation on earth,"[11] but his plan for Chinese industrialization was unrealistic. More realistic was a proposal for state ownership of major industries, but he remained critical of Marxist ideas of class struggle.

After Sun Yat-sen's death, Wang Jingwei (1883–1944) was well placed to succeed to the GMD leadership, for he had been associated with Sun in Japan and was considered a revolutionary hero for his attempt to assassinate the Manchu Prince Regent in 1910. But in 1926 it became apparent that he had a formidable challenger in Chiang Kai-shek. In 1923, Sun had sent Chiang to Moscow to study the Soviet military. On his return to China, Chiang became head of the Whampoa Military Academy, where he was highly successful, esteemed alike by the Soviet advisors and by the officer candidates.

While Wang Jingwei loosely presided over the GMD, the C.C.P. steadily gained influence in the party, much to the alarm of the GMD right and of Chiang Kai-shek. In March 1926, Chiang decided to act: he declared martial law, arrested Soviet advisors, and took steps to restrain the C.C.P. influence in the GMD, yet managed to retain the cooperation of both the C.C.P. and of its Soviet supporters, whose assistance he needed for the military unification of the country. This he began in the summer of 1926 by launching the Northern Expedition (see Figure 19.5), setting out with his army from Canton. Although there was some heavy fighting against warlord armies, the force made rapid headway on its march to the Yangzi, and some warlords decided to go over to the Nationalist side. In the fall of 1926, the Nationalist victories enabled them to shift the capital from Canton to more centrally located Wuhan. There, Wang Jingwei headed a civilian government but could not control Chiang and his army.

**FIGURE 19.5** China and the Northern Expedition, 1926–1928. 🌐

# The Break

On its march north to the Yangzi, the army was assisted by popular support, and nowhere was this support more enthusiastic than among the Communist-led workers of Shanghai, where the General Labor Union seized control even before the arrival of the troops. Elsewhere, too, there was an increase in labor activity. This alarmed Chinese bankers and industrialists, who, ready to support a national but not a social revolution, financed the increasingly anti-Communist Chiang Kai-shek. In April 1927, Chiang finally broke with the C.C.P. completely by initiating a bloody campaign of suppression in Shanghai, which then spread to other cities. Union and party headquarters were raided, those who resisted were killed, and suspected Communists were shot on sight. C.C.P. cells were destroyed, and unions were disbanded in a devastating sweep that left the urban C.C.P. shattered.

The C.C.P.'s emphasis on city factory workers was entirely consistent with Marxist theory, but the majority of the Chinese people continued to work the land. Marx, as a student of the French Revolution, despised the peasantry as "the class which represents barbarism within civilization."[12] But Lenin, operating in a primarily agrarian land, assigned the peasantry a supporting role in the Russian Revolution. The C.C.P., although it concentrated on cities, had not neglected the peasants. Beginning in 1923, China's first modern peasant movement was organized by Peng Pai (1896–1929), and by 1927 the C.C.P. was at work in a number of provinces, most notably Hunan, where the young Mao Zedong (1893–1976) wrote a famous report urging the party to concentrate on rural revolution and predicting, "In a very short time . . . several hundred million peasants will rise like a mighty storm, like a hurricane, a force so swift and violent that no power, however great, will be able to hold it back." In another famous passage in the same report, he defended the need for violence, saying, "A revolution is not a dinner party."[13]

In Hunan, as in other rice areas, tenancy rates were high, and the poorer peasants were sorely burdened by heavy rental payments and crushing debts. Tenants had few rights and faced the recurring specter of losing their leases. It was, as Mao saw, a volatile situation, fraught with revolutionary potential. But the Chinese party and its Soviet advisors remained urban-minded.

After Chiang's coup, the C.C.P. broke with him but continued to work with the government at Wuhan, which also broke with Chiang, but still depended for military support on armies officered largely by men of the landlord class, the prime object of peasant wrath. In this situation Comintern directives were wavering and contradictory, reflecting not Chinese realities but rather the exigencies of Stalin's intraparty maneuvers back in Moscow. The end result was that in June the C.C.P. was expelled from Wuhan. Borodin and other Soviet advisors were sent back to the U.S.S.R. The C.C.P. entered into a difficult period of regrouping and reorganization.

# Establishment of the Nationalist Government

After Chiang Kai-shek's coup in Shanghai, he established a government in Nanjing, which remained the capital until 1937. The Northern Expedition resumed in 1928, by which time the Wuhan leaders, bowing to the inevitable, had made their peace with Chiang, as had a number of warlords whose forces now assisted the Nationalist drive north and actually outnumbered Chiang's own troops. In June 1928, after a scant two months of fighting, Beijing fell. China again had a national government, but the often only nominal incorporation of warlord armies into the government forces meant that national unification was far from complete. Warlordism remained an essential feature of Chinese politics until the very end of the Republican period in 1949.

In 1927 anti-imperialist mobs attacked British concessions in two cities, and violence in Nanjing left six foreigners dead, a number wounded, and foreign businesses and homes raided. Such incidents were officially attributed to Chiang Kai-shek's leftist rivals. The powers concluded that he was the most acceptable leader, who would negotiate rather than expropriate their holdings. Chiang's victory re-assured all the powers except Japan, which had plans of its own for Manchuria and Inner Mongolia. Japan had restored its holdings in Shandong to Chinese sover-eignty in 1922 but now sent troops to Shandong, claiming they were needed to protect Japanese lives and property. In 1928 they clashed with Chinese soldiers. Still more ominous was the assassination that year of the warlord of Manchuria, Zhang Zuolin, by a group of Japanese army officers who acted on their own, hop-ing this would pave the way for seizure of Manchuria.

The Japanese officers did not get their way in 1928, but their act was to serve as a prelude to the Japanese militarism and expansionism that threatened China during the 1930s, even as the Nanjing government tried to cope with warlords and revolutionaries at home, in its attempt to achieve stable government.

# *Notes*

1.  Quoted in James Reeve Pusey, *China and Charles Darwin* (Cambridge: Harvard Univ. Press, 1983), p. 50.

2.  Marianne Bastid-Bruguiere, "Currents of Social Change," in John K. Fairbank and Kwang Ching Liu, eds., *The Cambridge History of China* (Cambridge: Cambridge Univ. Press, 1980), Vol. 2, pp. 558–59.

3.  David Der-wei Wang, *Fin-de-siecle Splendor: Repressed Modernities of Late Qing Fiction, 1849–1911* (Stanford: Stanford Univ. Press, 1997), p. 216.

4.  Quoted in Jonathan D. Spence, *The Gate of Heavenly Peace: The Chinese and Their Revolution, 1895–1980* (New York: Viking, 1981), p. 52. Reprinted with permission of Jonathan Spence.

5.  Wang, *Fin-de-siecle*, p. 223.

6.  Marie-Claire Bergere, in John K. Fairbank, ed., *The Cambridge History of China* (Cambridge: Cambridge Univ. Press, 1983), Vol. 12, pp. 745–51.

7.  Joseph S. M. Lau and Howard Goldblatt, *The Columbia Anthology of Modern Chinese Literature* (New York: Columbia Univ. Press, 1995), p. 15.

8.  See the biographical entry for Ch'i Pai-shih in Howard L. Boorman, ed., *Biographical Dictionary of Republican China* (New York: Columbia Univ. Press, 1967–71), Vol. 1, pp. 302–304. Qi's statement is quoted on p. 302.

9.  Michael Sullivan, *Chinese Art in the Twentieth Century* (Berkeley: Univ. of California Press, 1959), p. 42.

10. Quoted in Leo Ou-fan Lee, *The Romantic Generation of Modern Chinese Writers* (Cambridge: Harvard Univ. Press, 1973), p. 74.

11. Quoted in David Strand, "Calling the Chinese People to Order: Sun Yat-sen's Rhetoric of Development," in Kield Erik Brødsgaard and David Strand, eds., *Reconstructing Twentieth-Century China: State Control, Civil Society, and National Identity* (Oxford: Oxford Univ. Press, 1998), p. 155, citing Lu Fangshan, *Zhu Zhixin yu Zhongguo geming* (*Zhu Zhixin and the Chinese Revolution*) (Taibei: Sili dongwu daxue, 1978), p. 236.

12. Karl Marx, quoted in Lucien Bianco, *Origins of the Chinese Revolution, 1915–1949,* trans. Muriel Bell (Stanford: Stanford Univ. Press, 1971), p. 74.

13. Mao Tse-tung, "Report on an Investigation of the Peasant Movement in Hunan," in *Selected Works of Mao Tse-tung* (Peking: Foreign Language Press, 1967), Vol. 1, reprinted in Ranbir Vohra, *The Chinese Revolution: 1900–1950* (Boston: Houghton Mifflin, 1974), pp. 115–17.

# Imperial Japan: 1895–1931

## I. Late Meiji (1895–1912)

*Foreign Policy and Empire Building*

*Economic and Social Developments*

*Politics*

*Literature and the Arts*

## II. The Taishō Period (1912–1926) and the 1920s

*The Taishō Political Crisis (1912–1913)*

*Japan during World War I*

*Politics and Policies (1918–1924)*

*Party Government (1924–1931)*

*Popular Culture*

*Fine Arts*

Mingei

*Literature*

*Intellectual Trends*

| 1895 | | 1912 | | 1926 | 1931 |
|------|--|------|--|------|------|
| LATE MEIJI | | TAISHŌ | | EARLY SHOWA | |

Between the founding of the empire in 1895 and the advent of militarism in 1931, Japan increasingly participated in world history. It was in many respects a success story, but later history was to reveal the potential for disaster. The death of the Meiji Emperor in July 1912, although not as momentous as the abdication of China's last emperor earlier that year, marked something of a watershed and was experienced as such. People at the time felt that the passing of the emperor, who had presided over Japan's transformation for more than forty years, signified the end of an era, a judgment with which many later scholars have concurred. We have divided this chapter accordingly.

## Foreign Policy and Empire Building

From the beginning, Meiji foreign policy aimed to achieve national security and equality of national status. But how were these to be defined and attained? As Louise Young put it, "In an international order where the 'strong devour the weak,' Japanese concluded they could either join with the West as a 'guest at the table' or be served up with China and Korea as part of the feast."[1] Both the army's German adviser and Yamagata Aritomo, the hardheaded, realistic architect of Japan's modern army, held that Korea was the key to Japan's security and in 1890 propounded the thesis that Japan must defend its "line of sovereignty" and secure its "line of interest," which ran through Korea. The Japanese navy, heavily influenced by the ideas of Admiral Alfred T. Mahan (1840–1914), an American advocate of the importance of sea power, demanded Japanese naval domination of the surrounding seas. Colonies were desired as "the ultimate status symbol" and for strategic reasons. Economic and other considerations also played a part, but an authority on the subject concluded "no colonial empire of modern times was as clearly shaped by strategic considerations."[2]

Equality was as elusive a concept as security, but at a minimum it required the end of extraterritoriality and the restoration of tariff autonomy. In the 1870s work

513

began on revision of the law codes to bring them into line with Western practices so that the powers would no longer have reason to insist on maintaining jurisdiction over their own subjects. Even before the lengthy process of revising the codes had been completed, there was strong and vociferous public demand for an end to extraterritoriality. One result was that in 1886 the government was forced to back down from a compromise it had negotiated for mixed courts under Japanese and foreign judges. The intensity of public pressure also helped induce the British to agree in 1894, shortly before the start of the Sino-Japanese War, to give up extraterritoriality when the new legal codes came into effect (1889). Other countries followed suit. In return, foreign merchants were no longer limited to the treaty ports. These treaties also secured tariff autonomy, and in 1911 Japan regained full control over its customs duties.

By that time, Japan, under the most-favored-nation clause of the Treaty of Shimonoseki, was enjoying extraterritorial rights in China and benefiting from China's lack of tariff autonomy. As a result, Japan's exports to China increased both absolutely and in proportion of total exports, rising from less than 10 percent before 1894 to 25 percent by World War I. A commercial treaty negotiated with China in 1896 gave Japan and other nations enjoying most-favored-nations treatment the right to establish factories in the treaty ports, spurring investment in China but limiting China's ability to nurture its own industries.

The acquisition of Taiwan gratified the navy, but most of the public shared the army's disappointment and outrage when French, German, and Russian intervention forced Japan to give up the strategic Liaodong Peninsula. The government's response to this setback was to follow a prudent foreign policy but increase military spending. Accordingly, Japan exercised careful restraint during the Boxer Rebellion (1900) and earned respect for the disciplined behavior of its soldiers.

Japan's chief rival in northeast Asia was Russia, which had demonstrated its intent to become a major power in the area by constructing the Trans-Siberian Railway (1891–1903). In 1896 Russia had obtained permission to run tracks across northern Manchuria directly to Vladivostok, and in 1898 it obtained the lease of Port Arthur on the Liaodong Peninsula, thereby acquiring a much-needed warm-water port but further alienating the Japanese, who had so recently been denied the peninsula and were concerned to hold their own in the scramble to gain concessions from China.

Russia also interfered in Korea, allying itself with conservative opponents of Japanese-backed reformers. Agreements reached in 1896, 1897, and 1898 kept the Russo-Japanese rivalry from exploding into immediate war, but Russian use of the Boxer Rebellion to entrench its interests in Manchuria intensified Japanese apprehensions.

Japan was not alone in its concern over Russian expansion. Great Britain, which had not joined the intervention after the Sino-Japanese War, had long been alarmed over Russia's eastward expansion. In 1902 it abandoned its policy of "splendid isolation" to form an alliance with Japan. Great Britain recognized Japan's special interest in Korea, and each nation recognized the other's interests in China. Britain and Japan agreed that each would remain neutral in any war

**FIGURE 20.1** *Sea Battle near Port Arthur, March 10, 1904: A Sailor from the Sazanami Jumps to the Russian Ship and Kicks Its Captain into the Sea,* Migita Toshihide (1866–1905). Woodcut print triptych, ink and color on paper, 1904. (© Arthur M. Sackler Gallery of Art, Smithsonian Institution, Washington, D.C. Gift of Gregory and Patricia Krugla [S1999.131a-c])

fought by the other against a single enemy in East Asia and that each would assist the other if either were attacked by two powers at once. This meant that if Japan and Russia went to war, British forces would join Japan if France or Germany supported Russia. Japan would not have to face a European coalition alone. This alliance with the foremost world power gave Japan new prestige and confidence. But Russia remained determined to maintain and expand its position in East Asia.

These conflicting ambitions led to the Russo-Japanese War of 1904–1905, fought both on land (mostly in Manchuria, which was Chinese territory) and at sea. For both belligerents the cost was heavy, but victory went to Japan. Despite some hard fighting, Russian troops were driven back on land, and in two separate naval actions the Japanese destroyed virtually the entire Russian navy. The naval war was spectacular and much celebrated in Japan (see Figure 20.1). Japan attacked the Russian Pacific fleet at Port Arthur just before the declaration of war. Russia's Baltic fleet then embarked on an 18,000-mile trip, sailing around Africa because Britain refused passage through the Suez Canal. Its destination was Vladivostok, but it was demolished by the Japanese in a decisive battle in the Tsushima Straits, between Japan and Korea. Only four of the thirty-five Russian ships reached Vladivostok.

Not only in Japan but throughout Asia people were deeply impressed by this first victory of a non-Western nation over a European power. In Russia, these defeats had fateful consequences. The failed Revolution of 1905 was a precursor of the successful Revolution of 1917. Although victorious, the Japanese were exhausted. Thus, both sides were happy to accept the offer from the United States to mediate and to participate at a peace conference in Portsmouth, New Hampshire.

In the resulting Portsmouth Treaty, Japan gained recognition of its supremacy in Korea, the transfer of Russian interests in Manchuria (railways and leaseholds on the Liaodong Peninsula), and cession of the southern half of Sakhalin Island (north of Hokkaido). Japan had demanded all of Sakhalin and a war indemnity, but Russia successfully resisted these demands. This aroused the anger of the Japanese public, which, drunk on victory and uninformed of their country's inability to continue the war, had expected more. In Tokyo the treaty was greeted by three days of rioting.

Korea became a Japanese "protectorate" until annexed in 1910 after the 1909 assassination of Itō Hirobumi then serving as "resident general". In Manchuria, Japan's South Manchurian Railway Company was soon engaged in shipping, public utilities, and mining, as well as railroading. From the start, the Japanese government held half of the company's shares and appointed its officers. Although private Japanese companies also entered Manchuria, it has been calculated that in 1914, 79 percent of all Japanese investments in Manchuria were in the South Manchurian Railway. Furthermore, 69 percent of all Japanese investments in China before World War I were in Manchuria. Japan's economic reach stretched beyond its formal empire.

## Economic and Social Developments

Both the Sino-Japanese War and the Russo-Japanese War stimulated the Japanese economy. Both wars were followed by an outburst of nationalist sentiment that gave a strong boost to heavy industry (for example, Yawata Steel Works, established in 1897) and to armaments, including shipbuilding. After 1906, Japan produced ships comparable in size and quality to any in the world. Japanese technology continued to progress, with advances in new fields such as electrical engineering. Light industry, particularly textiles, continued to flourish and dominate the modern sector. The most important item of export, amounting to nearly half the total, was in partly finished goods, especially silk. (Because of superior quality control, Japanese silk exports overtook those of China.) Trade figures revealing an increasing emphasis on the import of raw materials and the export of manufactured goods are indicative of economic change, and in 1912 the industrial sector accounted for 36 percent of the gross national product (GNP). Other statistics indicate increases in labor productivity and in urbanization, widening the gulf between city and country. The government, guided by pragmatic conservative reformers, sponsored a program of rural cooperatives, which were established by an act of the Diet in 1899. Through the cooperatives—which helped with credit, marketing, and production—and through intense propaganda, the government hoped to avoid class conflict.

Not everyone in the industrial sector benefited from economic growth. Those working in the numerous small, traditional establishments experienced little change in their living conditions. Especially harsh were the working and living conditions of those who labored in the factories and shops. These were comparable to those in Western countries at a similar early stage of industrialization. During the first decade of the twentieth century, 60 percent of the workforce was still female. An act promulgated in 1900 outlawed strikes, but when conditions became too bad, male workers, for whom a factory job was not an interlude before marriage but a lifelong occupation, rebelled, sometimes violently. Thus, in 1909, three infantry companies were required to quell violence in the Ashio Copper Mines. Another labor action that made a deep impression was the 1912 Tokyo streetcar strike.

Conservative reformers, mindful of the social legislation of Bismarckian Germany, insisted early on that the government had the responsibility to ensure a balance between capital and labor, but the first factory laws were not passed until 1911. Efforts to improve the lot of women and children working in the factories also made headway only slowly. Not until 1916 did a law take effect that gave them some protection, such as limiting their working day to eleven hours.

The distress of the workers was much on the minds of radicals. Beginning in the early 1890s, there was a small group of radicals composed of Christian socialists and anarchists. They courageously opposed the war with Russia, holding antiwar rallies in the Tokyo YMCA even after the war began. However, barred by the government from forming a political party and facing government repression, they were unable to expand their influence beyond the world of intellectuals and college students. In 1911, twelve of their leaders were convicted, on mostly flimsy evidence, of plotting the death of the emperor and were executed.

Among the main beneficiaries of economic growth were the huge industrial–financial combines (*zaibatsu*), which retained close ties with government. The dominant political party during this period, the Seiyūkai (Association of Friends of Constitutional Government), also had a stake in economic development, because projects for railway and harbor development were a major means by which it won regional support and built local power.

# Politics

During the Sino-Japanese War, the oligarchs and the party-controlled Diet were united in pursuit of common national aims, but after the war, political struggles resumed. A handful of men, enjoying the prerogatives of elder statesmen (*genrō*), advised the emperor on all major matters. They tended to see themselves as guardians of the public good in contrast to the private interests represented by the parties and to stress the need for unity in face of a hostile world. As participants in fashioning the new state and architects of its major institutions, they enjoyed great prestige and the support of their protégés and associates. The party politicians, on the other hand, resented the perpetuation of the *genrō*'s power and their propensity to limit political decision making to a few handpicked insiders.

The politicians' main weapon against a prime minister who defied them was that under the constitution only the Diet could authorize increases in the budget.

Complicating the political situation were divisions within both the oligarchy and the party leadership. Among the former, Yamagata, a disciplined, rather austere military man, was committed to "transcendental government"—dedicated to emperor and nation and above political partisanship. His main *genrō* rival was Itō Hirobumi, the more flexible conservative who had supervised the writing of the constitution. Itō was more willing than Yamagata to compromise with the parties. Similarly, not all Diet members were adamantly opposed to collaborating with the *genrō*. Some lost their enthusiasm for opposing a government that could dissolve the Diet and thereby subject them to costly reelection campaigns. Also, the oligarchs could trade office for support. Accommodation had its appeal, but initially it was an uneasy accommodation; there were four dissolutions of the Diet between 1895 and 1900.

Another political factor was the influence of the military. As stipulated by the constitution, the chief of the general staff reported directly to the emperor concerning command matters, thus bypassing the minister of war and the Cabinet. In 1900 the military's power was further strengthened when Yamagata obtained imperial ordinances specifying that only officers on active duty could serve as minister of the army or minister of the navy. In effect, this gave the military veto power over any Cabinet, because it could break a Cabinet simply by ordering the army or navy minister to resign. Still, control over funds for army expansion remained in the hands of the lower house.

Up to 1901 the oligarchs themselves served as prime minister, but after that date Yamagata's protégé Katsura Tarō (1847–1913) and Itō's protégé Saionji Kimmochi (1849–1940) alternated as prime minister for the remainder of the Meiji Period. Katsura, like Yamagata, was a general from Chōshū; Saionji was a court noble with liberal views but little inclination to political leadership.

Katsura and Saionji were able to govern because they had the cooperation of the Seiyūkai, which Itō had founded in 1900 as a means to obtain assured support in the Diet. In 1903 Itō turned the presidency of the party over to Saionji, but the real organizing force within the party was Hara Kei (1856–1921), an ex-bureaucrat who became the leading party politician of his generation. Hara greatly strengthened the party by building support within the bureaucracy during his first term as home minister (1906–1908), and he used his power to appoint energetic partymen as prefectural governors. He linked the party to the provinces and freely resorted to the pork barrel to build constituencies among the local men of means who formed the limited electorate.

The business community, including the *zaibatsu*, was interested in maintaining a political atmosphere favorable to itself, and political leaders welcomed business support. Thus, Itō, when he organized the Seiyūkai, obtained the support of Shibusawa Eiichi and other prominent business leaders, although many remained aloof. The head of Mitsui was so intent on establishing his company's independence from government that he even discontinued the practice of extending loans to Itō without collateral. However, the trend was toward closer association between the *zaibatsu* and politics, as exemplified by the relationship between Mitsubishi and Katsura after 1908. During Katsura's second ministry (1908–1911), his chief economic adviser was the head of the Mitsubishi Bank.

The relative strength of the participants in the political process did not remain unchanged. The *genrō* enjoyed great influence as long as they remained active, but theirs was a personal, not an institutional, power. It tended to diminish with time. As the number of living participants in the restoration decreased, the power of the oligarchs to orchestrate politics declined. As prime minister, Katsura did not always follow Yamagata's advice. Furthermore, the *genrō* lost an important source of support when a new generation of bureaucrats came to the fore. These men did not owe their positions to *genrō* patronage because, after 1885, entrance to and promotion in the bureaucracy were determined by examinations. As servants of the emperor, bureaucrats enjoyed high prestige and considerable influence.

Political compromise eroded much of the idealism found in the early movement for people's rights, but the Seiyūkai prospered. Its strength in the Diet alarmed the parliamentary opposition, which was divided and diverse. It included not only men opposed in principle to the Seiyūkai's compromises but also small and shifting groups of independents and a series of "loyalist" parties that habitually supported the Cabinet. Decision making was complicated, because government policies were determined by the interaction of various power centers, none of which could rule alone. The arrangement functioned as long as funds were sufficient to finance both the military's and the Seiyūkai's highest priority projects and as long as none of the participants felt their essential interests threatened. When that ceased to be the case, it brought on the Taishō political crisis.

# Literature and the Arts

The beginnings of modern Japanese literature can be traced to Tsubouchi Shōyō (1859–1935), a translator and the author of *The Essence of the Novel* (1885), in which he opposed both didacticism and writing solely for entertainment and advocated Western realism, that is, the view that literature should portray actual life. From 1887 to 1889, Futabatei Shimei (1864–1909) followed with *Drifting Cloud,* a psychological study of an ordinary man told in a style more colloquial than usual.

Following the introduction of realism came Western romanticism with its emphasis on expression of feelings and of naturalism, which aimed at scientific detachment as advocated by the French writer Emile Zola. Although in Europe naturalism was hostile to romanticism, this was not necessarily the case in Japan, where Shimazaki Tōson (1873–1943) won fame for his romantic poetry and for *The Broken Commandment* (1906), a naturalistic account of a member of the pariah class (*burakumin*) who tries to keep his pledge to his father never to reveal that he was born into this group, which continued to suffer discrimination and contempt even though it was not subject to legal restrictions.

Two late Meiji writers, Mori Ōgai (1862–1922) and Natsume Sōseki (1867–1916), produced works of lasting literary merit. Ōgai identified with his family's samurai heritage, while Sōseki was a proud son of plebeian Edo. Their writings differed in substance and style, but both men, although deeply influenced by the West, achieved greatness by drawing on their Japanese heritage. Both spent time abroad. Ōgai was sent by the army to study medicine in Germany. After returning to Japan, he had a distinguished career as an army surgeon, rising in 1907 to the post of surgeon-general. He was both a modern intellectual profoundly influenced by his time in Europe and a samurai-style army officer, not an easy combination but one that stimulated major achievements. Admired for the masculine, restrained style of his original works, he was also a prolific and excellent translator. Among his finest translations are his renderings of Goethe, including the full *Faust,* and of Shakespeare, which he translated from the German. He also translated modern German poetry with the result that more modern German verse was available in Japanese translation than in English. Furthermore, he introduced German aesthetic philosophy to Japan and influenced the development of modern Japanese theater; the performance of his translation of an Ibsen play in 1908 was a major cultural event.

Mori Ōgai's first story, "Maihime" ("The Dancing Girl," 1890), recounts the doomed romance between a Japanese student sent by his government to Germany and a German girl named Alice. It became a precursor of the many "I novels," thinly disguised autobiographical works, which became one of the standard genres of modern Japanese fiction and owe something to the Heian tradition of literary diaries. After his initial romantic period, Ōgai went on to write works of increasing psychological insight and philosophical depth. He increasingly turned to Japanese themes, as in his novel *The Wild Goose.* Ōgai was greatly moved when his friend General Nogi (1849–1912), hero of the Russo-Japanese War, followed the Meiji Emperor into death by committing ritual suicide with his wife. Afterward, Ōgai published painstakingly researched accounts of samurai. A particularly acclaimed late work is his *Chibu Chūsai,* an account of a late Tokugawa physician with whom Ōgai identified.

Natsume Sōseki studied in England, where a meager government stipend forced him to live in poverty, and he had virtually no friends. Later he described himself as having been "as lonely as a stray dog in a pack of wolves."[3] Both this experience of loneliness and the extensive reading he did while in England were reflected in his subsequent work. Sōseki returned from Europe to teach English literature at Tokyo Imperial University before resigning this position to devote himself wholly to writing. He was acclaimed not only for his fiction but also for his poetry in Chinese, his haiku, and his literary criticism. He once described his mind as half Japanese and half Western, and his early novels reflect English influence, particularly that of George Meredith, but in his mature work the Japanese element predominates.

Sōseki's early novels, *I Am a Cat* (1905) and *Botchan* (1906), present slices of Meiji life with affectionate good humor. Also in 1906, in a mere week, he wrote the remarkable painterly and diary-like *The Grass Pillow,* also translated as *The Three-Cornered World* because "an artist is a person who lives in the triangle which remains after the angle which we may call common sense has been removed from this four-cornered world."[4] Travel in that world was by railway train:

It is an unsympathetic and heartless contraption which rumbles along, carrying hundreds of people crammed together in one box. . . . People are said to board and travel by train, but I call it being loaded and transported. Nothing shows greater contempt for the individual than the train. Modern civilization uses every possible means to develop individuality and then having done so, tries everything to stamp it out. It allots a few square yards to each person within that area. At the same time, it erects railings around him, and threatens him with all sorts of dire consequences if he should dare to take but one step beyond their compass.[5]

The main theme of Sōseki's mature works is human isolation, studied in characters given to deep introspection. Like Mori Ōgai, Natsume Sōseki was stricken by the death of the Meiji Emperor and General Nogi's suicide, which entered into *Kokoro* (1914), a novel concerning the relationship between a young man and his mentor, called "Sensei" (master or teacher). Sōseki links Sensei's personal tragedy and suicide to the deaths of the emperor and general and to the larger tragedy of the passing of a generation— and with it the loss of the old ethical values. Sensei perceives he has become an anachronism.

Painters, like writers, were grouped in several schools. The disciples of Okakura Tenshin, for example, continued to avoid the extremes of formalistic traditionalism and imitative modernism, seeking a middle ground that would be both modern and Japanese. One such was Yokoyama Taikan (1868–1958). His screen shown in Figure 20.2 depicts the Chinese poet Tao Qian (365–427), whose blend of regret and relief at withdrawal from public life continued to strike a responsive chord.

Among the artists working in European styles was Kuroda Seiki, whose nude had so shocked Kyoto in the 1890s. Kuroda continued to paint

**FIGURE 20.2** *Tao Qian* (Chinese poet, 365–427). Detail from one of a pair of six-fold screens, *Master Five Willows*, by Yokoyama Taikan. Taikan favored tradition, but his style resonates with his own time. Color on paper, 1912, 5.6 feet × 11.9 feet. (Tokyo National Museum. © Shokodo C. Ltd./APG-Japan 2002)

**FIGURE 20.3** *Concert Using Japanese and Western Instruments,* Sakaki Teitoku (1858–1925). Playing the violin while kneeling must have taken much practice—one can only hope the ensemble's music was as charming as the painting. Oil, 1910. (© Takakiyo Mitsui Collection)

in a Western manner, and he had many students. At the time of his death in 1924, he had come to be "the Grand Old Man of Western painting in Japan."[6] Some attempts at rendering Japanese themes in Western style produced paintings that are little more than historical curiosities, but in other cases there was a happier result. The painting by Sakaki Teitoku (1858–1925) shown in Figure 20.3 was executed in oil around 1910. While young men blow traditional bamboo flutes, two young women play violins.

Western influence on the visual arts was often direct and immediate, as it was for Umehara Ryūzaburō (1888–1986), who studied in France, met Renoir in 1909, and became his favorite pupil. The strongest influence on Japanese sculpture during this period was Rodin, who enjoyed a great vogue in Japan, especially after a major exhibition of his work in Tokyo in 1912.

Music also changed. The Meiji government early on sponsored Western military music, and in 1879 the Ministry of Education agreed to a proposal made by Izawa Shūji (1851–1917) to combine Japanese and Western music in the schools. Izawa had studied vocal physiology in the United States and persuaded the Ministry of Education to bring Luther Whiting Mason (1828–1896) from Boston to Japan to help develop songs for use in elementary schools. The first songbook (1881) consisted half of Western songs supplied with Japanese words ("Auld Lang Syne," for example, turned into a song about fireflies) and half of Japanese pieces harmonized in the Western manner.

Meiji popular music was more freely eclectic than that taught in schools. Beginning during the last decade of the nineteenth century, Japanese composers began working with sonatas, cantatas, and other Western forms, and, because of the Tokyo School of Music, good performers were available on the piano and violin, as well as on the koto and other traditional instruments taught at the school. However, performers made greater progress than composers. As suggested by William P. Malm, training in Western harmonics "created a series of mental blocks which shut out the special musical potentialities of traditional styles."[7] The rediscovery of the latter and their creative employment did not take place until after World War II.

# II. The Taishō Period (1912–1926) and the 1920s

*The Taishō Political Crisis (1912–1913)*

*Japan during World War I*

*Politics and Policies (1918–1924)*

*Party Government (1924–1931)*

*Popular Culture*

*Fine Arts*

Mingei

*Literature*

*Intellectual Trends*

## The Taishō Political Crisis (1912–1913)

The Taishō Period began with a political crisis, when financial conditions forced a cutback in government spending that made it impossible to fund both the Seiyūkai's domestic program and two new divisions for the army. Although the Seiyūkai won support at the polls, Prime Minister Saionji was forced out of office in December 1912 when the army ordered the minister of the army to resign. Although the *genrō* deliberated about a successor to Saionji, a number of politicians, journalists, and businessmen organized a movement "to protect constitutional government." The ensuing mass demonstrations were reminiscent of those protesting the Portsmouth Treaty in 1905.

Called on to form a government once more, Katsura, no longer willing to compromise with the Seiyūkai, attempted to organize a party strong enough to defeat it but failed. When the Seiyūkai threatened a vote of no confidence, Katsura tried to save the situation by obtaining an imperial order forcing the Seiyūkai to give up its planned no-confidence motion. This was a stratagem previously employed by embattled prime ministers, but this time it did not work: the Seiyūkai turned down the order. The crisis ended with Katsura's resignation. Such use of an imperial order was discredited and never tried again.

For the first time, a party majority in the Diet, backed by public opinion and a vociferous press, had overthrown a Cabinet. Katsura died in 1913, but the coalition he had created held together under the leadership of Katō Kōmei (Katō Takaaki, 1860–1926) whose background included graduation from Tokyo Imperial University, service in Mitsubishi, and a career in the Foreign Office capped by an appointment as foreign minister at the age of forty. He enjoyed a financial advantage from his marriage into the family that controlled Mitsubishi. A capable and determined man, he was personally reserved. But this was no handicap, because there was no need for party leaders like Katō or Hara to cultivate mass support. The power of a party leader depended on his strength within his party, although this was influenced by the party's showing at the polls.

The emergence of a strong second party meant that now the Seiyūkai faced a rival for control of the lower house. The parties represented a cross section of skills and resources needed to make participation in government viable. Arthur E. Tiedemann described it as follows:

> Each party had associated with it the three essential ingredients for achieving political power: professional politicians to do the nitty-gritty of day-to-day party management; former bureaucrats who had the administrative talents required to form a viable alternative government acceptable to the *genrō;* and businessmen who could supply the funds and influence essential to successful election campaigns.[8]

Although the Taishō political crisis confirmed the importance of the Diet and the parties, they were not the only power center. Again there were compromises: not until Hara became prime minister in 1918 did the top government post go to a man who had made his career as a party politician. Before Hara, there were three prime ministers: Admiral Yamamoto Gombei (1913–1914), a military bureaucrat from Satsuma whose government was brought down by a scandal in naval procurement; the septuagenarian Ōkuma Shigenobu (1914–1916), who was intent on destroying the Seiyūkai but failed; and Terauchi Masatake (1916–1918), a Yamagata-backed Chōshū general who had been governor-general of Korea. It was the Ōkuma and Terauchi governments that guided Japan during World War I.

# Japan during World War I

When the Western powers became immersed in war, new opportunities opened up for Japan. In August 1914 Japan declared war on Germany and within the next three months seized German holdings in Shandong and the German islands in the Pacific. In January 1915 the Ōkuma government presented the Twenty-One Demands to China. As we have seen, Japan obtained additional rights but at the cost of stirring up strong Chinese resentment. A prominent critic of this policy was the pro-German Yamagata, who wanted Japan to be on good terms with China to prepare for the war he anticipated against the West.

Much larger and more costly than the military effort against Germany during World War I was Japan's attempt to prevent the extension of Bolshevik power over territory that had belonged to the Russian Empire but had become a battleground after the Revolution of 1917. Russia and Japan had been wartime allies, but in March 1918 the Bolsheviks signed a separate peace with Germany (the Treaty of Brest-Litovsk). Complicating the situation in the East was the presence of Czech troops fighting their way out of Russia and determined to continue the war against Germany.

The Japanese intervened and by midsummer 1918 controlled the eastern Trans-Siberian Railway and Vladivostok. The United States then changed its earlier opposition to intervention, although President Woodrow Wilson envisioned only a limited military operation. The Japanese, however, sent 75,000 troops, triple the number sent by the Allies (United States, Britain, France, and Canada). Faced with Russian Communist victories and the absence of a viable alternative, the United States withdrew its forces in January 1919. The other Allies soon did likewise, leaving only the Japanese, who continued their efforts in the vain hope of at least keeping the Bolsheviks from controlling eastern Siberia. Although failure was apparent by 1920, the last Japanese troop did not withdraw until 1922.

Japan could pay for such a costly undertaking largely because its economy boomed during the war, which brought an unprecedented demand for its industrial products and the withdrawal of European competition. Old industries expanded, new ones grew up, and exports surged, turning Japan from a debtor into a creditor. But while some prospered, others suffered. The sudden economic expansion produced inflation, but workers' wages, as well as the income of those in fishing and other traditional occupations, failed to keep pace. The price of rice rose until people could no longer afford this most basic food. In August 1918, rice riots erupted in cities, towns, and villages all over Japan. Even as Japanese troops were setting off for Siberia, other soldiers were firing on hungry people rioting at home. The bitter irony was not lost on Japanese radicals. The immediate effect of the turbulence was to bring down the Terauchi government. When the *genrō* met to choose the next prime minister, they settled on Hara.

## Politics and Policies (1918–1924)

Hara Kei had spent his career building up the Seiyūkai in preparation for the day of party rule, but by 1918 he was too set in his ways to embark on significant new policies or initiate meaningful change. From then until his assassination by a demented fanatic in November 1921, he initiated only minor changes and remained partisan in his concerns. Democratic intellectuals, students, and leaders of labor and farmer unions were disillusioned when the government turned a deaf ear to their demands for universal suffrage and instead passed an election law that retained a tax qualification for voting and reconstructed local electoral districts to favor the Seiyūkai. Abuse of office, financial scandals, and narrow partisanship had damaged the public image of the parties for years, and the record of the first party prime minister did nothing to alter this. Liberals who had placed their hopes in parliamentary reform either became cynical or looked elsewhere, and the public was apathetic.

In foreign affairs, Hara's prime ministership began with the peace conference at Versailles, where Japan failed to obtain a declaration of universal racial equality but did gain acquiescence to its claims in China and the Pacific. His government then adopted a policy of cooperation with the United States, the only possible source for capital badly needed by Japanese industry facing difficult adjustments after peace brought an end to wartime prosperity. The first product of the new policy was the Washington Conference of 1921–1922, as a result of which Japan's alliance with Britain was replaced by a Four Power Pact signed by France, Great Britain, Japan, and the United States. The signatories also agreed to limit construction of capital ships (ships over 10,000 tons with guns over eight inches) to maintain the existing balance of naval power at a 3:5:5 ratio for Japan, the United States, and Britain, calculated in tonnage. In February 1922, Japan further agreed to a Nine Power Treaty, acceding to the American Open Door Policy. In October 1922, Japan agreed to withdraw from Siberia.

That October Japan also reached an agreement with China, where nationalist sentiment had turned bitterly anti-Japanese. At Versailles, Japan had agreed, in principle, to the restoration of Chinese sovereignty in Shandong provided that it retained economic rights there. This was now officially agreed upon. To secure and advance Japanese interests in Manchuria, Zhang Zuolin, the local warlord, was supported by the Japanese army. However, Shidehara Kijūrō followed a general policy of getting along with the United States and conciliating China during his tenure as foreign minister from 1924 to 1927 and again from 1929 to December 1931.

The purpose of this policy was to avert another anti-Japanese outburst and costly boycotts of Japanese goods, which would hinder continued Japanese economic expansion. After 1914, Japanese investments in China accelerated. By 1931 more than 80 percent of Japan's total foreign investments were in China, where they amounted to 35.1 percent of all foreign investments in that country.* In 1930, 63 percent of Japanese investments in China were in Manchuria and another 25 percent were in Shanghai, where Japanese engaged in trade, banking, and textile manufacturing. In 1930 Japanese owned 39.6 percent of the Chinese textile industry (calculated in number of spindles). They were also a major factor in China's iron industry, with interests in Hankou and Manchuria.

Hara was succeeded by his finance minister, but this man lacked political skills and lasted only until June 1922. Three nonparty prime ministers followed, two ad-

---

* Great Britain accounted for 36.7 percent of foreign investment in China, but this was only 5 to 6 percent of all British overseas investments. Three other countries each accounted for more than 5 percent of foreign investment in China: The Soviet Union for 8.4 percent, the United States for 6.1 percent, and France for 5.9 percent.

mirals and one bureaucrat who organized his Cabinet entirely from the House of Peers but resigned when faced by a three-party coalition in control of the Diet. The leader of the strongest of these parties, the Kenseikai (Constitutional Government Association, established 1916), was Katō, who had last served as foreign minister under Ōkuma during the war. He was now called upon to form a new government.

The most momentous event of the years between Hara and Katō was geological, not political: in September 1923 the Tokyo–Yokohama area was devastated by a severe earthquake followed by a conflagration, which came close to leveling the area. The red sky was visible all night from a distance of a hundred miles. Around 100,000 people lost their lives. As so often in a disaster, the earthquake and fires brought out the best and the worst in people. Although some courageously and selflessly helped their fellows, others joined hysterical racist mobs rampaging through the city killing Koreans. The police reacted to the emergency by rounding up socialists, anarchists, and Communists as a "security measure," and there were cases of police torture and killing.

# Party Government (1924–1931)

The increase in the power of the parties signified a shift in the balance of power rather than a systemic reordering of power centers. It was the power of the parties that induced Tanaka Giichi, a Chōshū general much favored by Yamagata, to accept the presidency of the Seiyūkai in 1925 when it was out of power. But the party's choice also confirmed the willingness of the parties to work within the existing parameters and highlighted the continued prestige and influence of the army, even during the peaceful 1920s.

The main accomplishments of party government came while Katō was prime minister (1924–1926). Foremost among them was passage of a "universal" suffrage act, which gave the vote to all males twenty-five and older. To still the fears of conservatives apprehensive over the possible spread of radical ideas, a Peace Preservation Law was also passed. This made it a crime to advocate change in the national political structure or to urge the abolition of private property. The Katō government never invoked the law, but it was available to later, less liberal regimes.

Katō also tried to reform the House of Peers (changing its composition and reducing its powers) but succeeded in making only minor changes. His government was more successful in introducing moderate social reforms, including legalizing labor unions, establishing standards for factory conditions, setting up procedures for mediating labor disputes, and provisioning health insurance for workers. There was, however, no similar program to alleviate the problems of the rural poor.

Katō soon became embroiled in difficult political negotiations with other parties and the House of Peers, among others. When Katō died in 1926, he had not transformed Japanese politics, but he did leave a record of accomplishment that might, under different circumstances, have served as a basis for building a strong system of party rule. That this did not happen is partly the result of the kinds of problems Japan had to face during the next five years, but it also reflects the weakness of the parties. Even the increased suffrage was a mixed blessing, because the larger electorate made election campaigns costlier and politicians more open to corruption.

From 1927 to 1929 the government was led by Tanaka. In foreign policy Tanaka departed from Shidehara's conciliatory approach. When, in 1927, Chiang Kai-shek resumed the military expedition to unify China, Tanaka, under political pressure at home, sent an army brigade to Shandong, where clashes with Chinese soldiers ensued. Still more ominous was the assassination, in June 1928, of Zhang Zuolin by a group of Japanese army officers who did not think him sufficiently pliant and hoped their action would pave the way for the seizure of Manchuria. This did not happen—at least not then. Instead, Manchuria was brought under the new Chinese government by Zhang's son, and Tanaka had to recognize the GMD regime in Nanjing as the government of China. Tanaka's government itself collapsed when he incurred the displeasure of the Showa emperor (r. 1925–1989) and court by failing to obtain from the army suitable punishment for Zhang's murderers. This episode was a harbinger of future unilateral army actions, but first, party government had one more chance.

In 1929, Hamaguchi Ōsachi became prime minister, and in 1930 his party, the Minseitō, won the election. Shidehara once again became foreign minister and resumed his policy of reconciliation with China. He cooperated with Britain and the United States in negotiating the London Naval Treaty of 1930, which provided for a 10:10:7 ratio for other than capital ships. The treaty was ratified only after heated debate and the forced resignation of the naval chief of staff. It generated bitterness among the military and members of patriotic societies, such as the young man who shot the prime minister in November 1930. Hamaguchi never recovered from his wound but hung on in office until April 1931. From then until December 1931, the Minseitō Cabinet continued under Wakatsuki Reijirō (1866–1949), who earlier had served as home minister under Katō and as prime minister from January 1926 to April 1927. He was an experienced politician, but during 1931 the government lost control over the army.

The restlessness of the military was not government's only problem. During most of the 1920s, Japan was beset by persistent economic difficulties, including an unfavorable balance of payments, failure of jobs to increase fast enough to keep up with population growth, and a sharp decline in the price of rice, which helped consumers but hurt farmers. The giant *zaibatsu* profited from new technology, the economics of scale, and the failure of weaker companies, but times were hard on small operators. In 1921 a dramatic dockyard strike in Kobe resulted in an eight-hour day, which was extended to other heavy industries, but the union movement progressed only slowly. This was also the case for unions of tenants, many of whom now worked for landlords who had moved to the city. Carol Gluck aptly summed up the situation when she characterized Japan as being in "a hiatus between a traditional agrarian paternalism that was disintegrating and a modern industrial paternalism that was still in its formative stages. The landlords were no longer offering succor to distressed tenants, and the companies were not yet acting in a paternalist role on any significant scale."[9]

To solve the balance-of-payments problem, there were calls for the government to cut expenses and retrench to reduce the cost of Japanese goods and improve their competitive position in international trade. This was the policy followed by Hamaguchi, who also strengthened the yen by returning to the gold standard. Unfortunately, he initiated this program just as the Great Depression was getting under way and persisted in it despite great economic dislocations and suffering. From 1925 to 1930 the real income of farmers declined about a third. The poorest were, as always, the hardest hit. As in earlier periods of famine, there were cases of peasants eating bark and digging for roots or maintaining life by selling daughters into brothels.

The government's economic failure undermined the credibility of the political parties, which even in normal times had little public esteem. No mass movement arose directed against them, but there was also little in their record to inspire people to do battle in their defense. Their enemies included those dissatisfied not only with their policies and politics but also with just about every facet of 1920s liberalism, internationalism, and "modernity."

## Popular Culture

During the 1920s a wave of Western influence affected lifestyles, diet, housing, and dress, particularly in Tokyo and other great cities, where there was a boom in bread consumption, Western dress became prevalent in public, and fashionable houses included at least one Western room. On the Ginza, the "modern boy" (*mobo*) and "modern girl" (*moga*), dressed and coiffured in the latest imported styles, might be on their way to listen to jazz or see a movie. Although there was always an audience for films filled with melodrama and swordplay, others dealt with the problems and joys of daily life.

Western sports gained ground, including baseball, although the first professional teams date from the 1930s. People began playing golf and tennis. Friends met in cafes, or a fellow could practice the latest steps with a taxi dancer at The Florida or another of Tokyo's dance halls. The old demimonde dominated by the geisha, a world fondly chronicled by Nagai Kafū (1879–1959), was on the decline, and modern mass culture was in the ascendancy.

Centered in the cities, the new popular culture was steadily diffused as even the remotest village became accessible by train and car, not to speak of the radio, introduced in 1925. Mass circulation magazines, some directed at a general audience and others written especially for women or young people, catered to the unquenchable thirst of the Japanese public for reading matter.

## Fine Arts

Internationalism was represented not only in politics but also in the arts. Tokyo was not far behind Paris or London in experimenting with the latest styles and techniques. Indeed, it sometimes led the other capitals, such as when in 1922 Frank Lloyd Wright built the Imperial Hotel in Tokyo, a break with Japan's own version of the European Art Nouveau. The American architect, influenced by the Japanese tradition, was not the only stimulating visitor from abroad during the Taishō and early Showa years. Japanese scientists, for example, could converse with Einstein on his visit to their country in 1919, and music lovers enjoyed concerts by eminent foreign performers: both Kreisler and Heifetz gave concerts in Tokyo in 1923. Bach, Mozart, and Beethoven were becoming as much a part of the musical life of Japan as of any other country, foreshadowing the time when, after World War II, the Japanese pioneered in teaching young children to play the violin and became the world's foremost manufacturers of pianos.

A grand piano dominates the four-panel screen (see Figure 20.4) painted in 1926 by Nakamura Daizaburō (1898–1947), which is representative of the followers of the Okakura school. Conversely, there were Japanese artists who, like Xu Beihong in China, depicted traditional subjects in Western style.

**FIGURE 20.4** *At the Piano*, Nakamura Daizaburō. Not only the traditional dress of the young woman playing by the light of an electric lamp but also the technique and aesthetics of the painting recall the earliest Japanese art rather than contemporary Western styles. Fourfold screen, color on silk, 1926, 9.9 feet × 5.4 feet. (© Kyoto Municipal Museum of Art)

A major influence for modernism was the *White Birch* (*Shirakaba*) journal (1910–1923), one of whose editors was Shiga Naoya (1883–1971). In contrast to the school of naturalism and the advocates of proletarian literature, the *White Birch* group was dedicated to the exploration of the inner self, the pursuit of deeper personal understanding and self-expression such as in the "I novel" or in individualistic art. Seeking to become "children of the world," they introduced many European writers and published articles on the work and theories of such artists as van Gogh—whose suicide for art's sake they praised as superior to that of General Nogi.

Much of the art produced during this period was imitative, but one artist who developed his own style was Umehara Ryūzaburō. A disciple of Renoir, Umehara also owes something to his childhood in Kyoto, where he became thoroughly familiar with the styles of Sōtatsu and Kōrin as still practiced in his family's silk kimono business (see Figures 14.4 and 14.5).

European pointillism, cubism, futurism, dadaism, and surrealism all affected the Japanese avant-garde, here represented by a painting dated 1926 (see Figure 20.5). Tōgō Seiji (1897–1978), in Europe at the time, was influenced by French and Italian futurism and dadaism but here shows an inclination toward cubism.

**FIGURE 20.5** *Saltimbanques*, Tōgō Seiji. The title of this cheerful, decorative picture is French for "traveling showmen," and it would take a keen eye, not to say considerable imagination, to detect a particularly Japanese element. Oil, 1926, 30 in. × 44.9 in. (© Togo Tamami. Courtesy Togo Tamami and the National Museum of Modern Art, Tokyo)

# Mingei

Many trends converged in the "folk craft" or "folk arts" movement promoted by Yanagi Muneyoshi (or Sōetsu, 1889–1961), who coined the term *mingei* in 1926. His deep belief in the creative genius of the people was in tune with Taishō democracy, while his rejection of machine mass production and his devotion to the strong, honest beauty created by anonymous craftsmen working together to create objects for daily use are reminiscent of John Ruskin (1819–1900) and William Morris (1834–1896), founder of the late Victorian Arts and Crafts Movement. Yanagi, like Morris, championed the dignity of the craftsman and linked the aesthetic beauty of folk art to the ethical qualities under which it was produced. His attempt to establish a commune for *mingei* artists failed, but he succeeded in inspiring a new appreciation for traditional woodcarving, housewares, woven and dyed cloth, and all kinds of articles made of bamboo, straw, handmade paper, wood (including furniture and traditional buildings), metal, and leather. The list goes on to include virtually all the products of traditional workmanship. Such works found a home in the museums, such as the Japan Folk Art Museum in Tokyo (1936), where they continue to be displayed, studied, enjoyed, and celebrated.

Yanagi's interest in folk culture was shared by Yanagida Kunio (1875–1962), Japan's foremost scholar of folklore. The massive survey he directed in the 1930s laid the foundations for a whole field of studies. Beyond preserving and studying the folk craft (his preferred translation of *mingei*) of the past, he strove to further the production of *mingei* as a living force. Foremost among his associates in the *mingei* movement were four potters: Tomimoto Kenkichi (1886–1963), the British potter Bernard Leach (1887–1979), Kawai Kanjirō (1890–1966), and Hamada Shōji (1894–1978). Others worked in textiles and other crafts. Among the woodcut artists influenced by Yanagida was Munakata Shikō (see pp. 650–651).

## Literature

Naturalism, symbolism, social realism, neoperceptionism—in literature as in the visual arts, a multitude of agendas had their proponents and special vocabulary, "pushing this or that 'ism,' this or that school and inflicting on the reader who wishes to comprehend the book's argument prior belief in this jargon." These words were written in 1930 by Kobayashi Hideo (1902–1983), Japan's foremost modern critic, who went on to say, "I don't trust the jargon. I believe that not trusting jargon is the mark of the critical spirit."[10]

Kobayashi admired Shiga Naoya, already mentioned as a member of the *White Birch* group, master of the autobiographical short story and "I novel" and of a concise, unaffected (although carefully crafted), sensitive style. Shiga was much admired and imitated, but he also had his detractors. Prominent among those who rejected the autobiographical mode were the advocates of proletarian literature exemplified by such novels as *The Cannery Boat* (1929) by Kobayashi Takiji (1903–1933), in which the workers revolt against a brutal captain. Although much of this literature was propagandistic, it did make the reader and writer more sensitive to social conditions.

A gifted writer who defies classification was Akutagawa Ryūnosuke (1892–1927), author of some 150 short stories between 1917 and 1927, many of them modern psychological reinterpretations of old tales. Because of the famous film of the same name released in 1950 by Kurosawa Akira, he is probably best known in the West for "Rashomon," which presents the story of a murder and rape as told from the viewpoint of three protagonists and a witness. In doing so, it raises questions about all our perceptions of historical truth. Akutagawa's stories are frequently eerie but are saved from being merely macabre by the keenness of his psychological portrayals. Pessimistic, given to self-doubt, and distressed at the changing world about him, he committed suicide in 1927, citing "a vague unease."

In poetry as in art, some dedicated themselves to new experiments and others continued working with the old forms. In the nineteenth century, Masaoka Shiki (1867–1902), known primarily as a haiku poet, contributed toward revitalizing traditional poetry, which continued to be written and published throughout the twentieth century. Others, however, looked to the West, and some even employed the Roman alphabet (*rōmaji*). Foreign influence did not necessarily produce timeless verse; one poet proclaimed, "My sorrow wears the thin garb of one-sided love."[11] The most admired master of free verse was Hagiwara Sakutarō (1886–1942), whose collection *Howling at the Moon* (1917) caused a sensation. Moving from the canine to the feline, he published *Blue Cat* in 1923—using "blue" in the sense of the blues. *Age of Ice* (1934), his last book of new free verse, includes a poem in which he identifies with a caged tiger.

A major prose writer was Tanizaki Junichirō (1886–1965), who began with a fascination with the West but turned increasingly to the Japanese tradition. The protagonist of *Some Prefer Nettles* (1917), unhappily married to a "stridently" modern wife, finds comfort in the arms of a Eurasian prostitute, symbolic of the West, but as the novel unfolds he is increasingly attracted to a traditional Kyoto beauty. Tanizaki himself moved to Kyoto following the great earthquake of 1923. Some of his best work still lay in the future, including his masterpiece, *The Makioka Sisters,* written during World War II. One theme in this long, panoramic novel is the contrast between two of the sisters, one traditional in appearance and mentality, the other modern. Tanizaki's devotion to tradition also led him to translate the *Tale of Genji* into modern Japanese.

A similar trajectory from avant-garde to tradition was followed by Kawabata Yasunari (1899–1972), whose main works and fame were still to come. A very different writer then also at the beginning of her career was Uno Chiyu (1897–1996), whose persona and writings were more in tune with the 1920s and the post-World War I years than with the 1930s, when she published her best-known novel, *Confessions of Love* (*Iro Zange,* 1935), based on the well-known failed love suicide attempted by Tōgō Seiji (see Figure 20.5) in 1929. Uno's interview with Tōgō a month later led that same night to a famous liaison that lasted five years.

# Intellectual Trends

Philosophers and political theorists, like artists and writers, were challenged by claims that modern Western ideas possessed universally valid principles and by their need to make sense of and find value in their own tradition. On the left, there was a revival of interest in anarchism and socialism, suppressed in 1911, and Marxism enjoyed new prestige after the Russian Revolution. Some were active in the labor movement, but the labor parties formed after passage of the universal suffrage act suffered from an excess of factionalism and a lack of mass participation. This was also true of the Japanese Communist party, which was dominated by intellectuals, some of great personal status. There was also a fledgling feminist movement, which campaigned for equality and women's rights, particularly the right to vote, because at the time women were legally minors and remained excluded from the political process.

Most widely read among liberal theorists were Minobe Tatsukichi (1873–1948) and Yoshino Sakuzō (1878–1933), both deeply versed in German thought. Minobe was a legal scholar who followed his teacher at Heidelberg, Georg Jellinek, in making a distinction between sovereignty, which belongs to the whole state, and the power to rule, which is supervised by the emperor. In this sense, the emperor becomes the "highest organ" of the state, limited by the other components of the state and by the constitution. The constitution, furthermore, in Japan as elsewhere (according to Minobe), allows, and indeed requires, continuing change in the direction of increasing rationality, responsible government, and popular participation. Minobe's work gained wide currency, and his book was the most frequently assigned text in courses on constitutional law. In 1932 he was appointed to the House of Peers, but his prominence was to cost him dearly later on.

Yoshino did not obtain such Establishment approval, but his many articles were widely read. A Christian populist and a democrat, he was a philosophical idealist who argued for democracy as an absolute rather than on utilitarian or pragmatic grounds. He also held an idealistic view of the nation and rejected any suggestion that democracy was incompatible with the Japanese tradition: "Those who argue that democracy is not compatible with the national spirit believe in the anachronistic and erroneous notion that the Emperor and people are mutually exclusive of each other."[12] Democracy would fulfill, not diminish, the emperor's role.

After World War I, Japanese intellectuals were attracted to Hegel, Kant, and Nietzsche; the phenomenalism of Husserl; the hermeneutics of Heidegger; and the vitalism of Bergson and Eucken. Outstanding among the philosophers who digested Western philosophy and assimilated it into their own original work was Nishida Kitarō (1870–1945), strongly steeped in Buddhism and best known for his philosophy of transcendent nothingness. Other theorists used Western philosophy to differentiate an authentic Japaneseness from the West and what they perceived as the diluted or hybrid culture that they disliked and dismissed. Nishida was not alone in refraining from discussing politics, but others defined Japanism in political terms and demanded political action.

Some ideologues, conscious of the hardships suffered by the countryside, condemned the life and values of the cities and called for a return to virtuous agrarianism. Among the most severe critics of the parties and *zaibatsu* was Kita Ikki (1883–1937), who combined advocacy of imperialistic assertiveness abroad with a call for egalitarianism at home to bring emperor and people together. Unhappy with Japan's political organization and its stance in the world, he did not look to the electorate or a mass popular movement for salvation but placed his faith in change from above enacted by a few dedicated men. Accordingly, his ideas found a friendly reception in small societies of superpatriots and among army officers who saw themselves as continuing in the tradition of the *rōnin,* who had selflessly terrorized Kyoto during the closing days of the Tokugawa. Kita also found more recent exemplars among the ex-samurai who, after Saigō's death, had formed the Genyōsha (Black Ocean Society, 1881) and the Kokuryūkai (Amur River Society, also translated Black Dragon Society, 1901). The former was dedicated to expansion in Korea; the latter concentrated on Manchuria. Both employed intimidation and assassination.

The story of the attempts made by these men to effect a "Showa Restoration" belongs in the 1930s, but Kita's most influential book was written in 1919. The rejection in the 1930s of party government and internationalism that had prevailed in the 1920s revealed that these had as yet shallow roots.

# *Notes*

1. Louise Young, *Japan's Total Empire: Manchuria and the Culture of Wartime Imperialism* (Berkeley: Univ. of California Press, 1998), p. 21.

2. Mark R. Peattie, in Ramon H. Myers and Mark R. Peattie, eds., *The Japanese Colonial Empire, 1895–1945* (Princeton: Princeton Univ. Press, 1984), p. 8. See p. 10 for colonies as "the ultimate status symbol."

3. Quoted in Natsume Soseki, *Ten Nights of Dream–Hearing Things: The Heredity of Taste,* Aiko Ito and Graeme Wilson, trans. (Rutland, Vt., and Tokyo: Charles E. Tuttle, 1974), p. 12.

4. Natsume Soseki, *The Three-Cornered World,* Alan Turney, trans. (Chicago: Henry Regnery, 1965), p. iii.

5. Natsume, *The Three-Cornered World,* p. 181.

6. Shuji Takashina and J. Thomas Rimer, with Gerald D. Bolas, *Paris in Japan: The Japanese Encounter with European Painting* (St. Louis: The Washington Univ. Press, 1987), p. 105.

7. William P. Malm, "The Modern Music of Meiji Japan," in Donald H. Shively, ed., *Tradition and Modernization in Japanese Culture* (Princeton: Princeton Univ. Press, 1971), p. 300.

8. Arthur E. Tiedemann, "Big Business and Politics in Prewar Japan," in James W. Morley, ed., *Dilemmas of Growth in Prewar Japan* (Princeton: Princeton Univ. Press, 1971), pp. 278–79.

9. Carol Gluck, *Japan's Modern Myths: Ideology in the Late Meiji Period* (Princeton: Princeton Univ. Press, 1985), p. 282.

10. Quoted in Paul Anderer, ed. and trans., *Literature of the Lost Home: Kobayashi Hideo—Literary Criticism, 1924–1939* (Stanford: Stanford Univ. Press, 1995), p. 108.

11. Quoted in Donald Keene, ed., *Modern Japanese Literature: An Anthology* (New York: Grove Press, 1956), p. 20.

12. Tetsuo Najita, "Some Reflections on Idealism in the Political Thought of Yoshino Sakuzō," in Bernard Silberman and Harry D. Harootunian, eds., *Japan in Crisis: Essays on Taisho Democracy* (Princeton: Princeton Univ. Press, 1974), p. 40.

# 21

# The 1930s and World War II

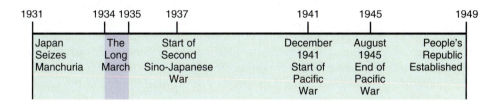

| 1931 | 1934 1935 | 1937 | 1941 | 1945 | 1949 |
|------|-----------|------|------|------|------|
| Japan Seizes Manchuria | The Long March | Start of Second Sino-Japanese War | December 1941 Start of Pacific War | August 1945 End of Pacific War | People's Republic Established |

The fate of Nationalist China and Imperial Japan became fatally intertwined when Japan seized Manchuria in 1931, entering into what in Japan is now called "a dark valley." These were dark years also in much of the rest of the world. In the wake of the Great Depression, people in many countries, desperate for vigorous action, accepted dictatorship of one kind or another as the most effective way of pulling through. The Soviet Union claimed to be on the road to Communist utopia, and it was not only in Italy and in Germany that many people viewed Fascism as the wave of the future. In Japan, militarists seized power from the political parties, and in China too the military gained in power and prestige.

During most of the 1930s the Western democracies were preoccupied with domestic problems, and the strongest, the United States, was committed to isolationism. International statesmanship was at a low ebb. The failure of the League of Nations to respond to Japanese aggression in Manchuria revealed the inability or unwillingness of any government to do more than pay lip service to the principles of collective security.

## The Manchurian Incident and Its Consequences

The Japanese government derived its legitimacy from the emperor, but the ruling political parties confronted charges that they were betraying their sacred trust. In the name of the emperor, the enemies of constitutional government criticized the political manipulations of the Diet leaders, their ties to business, and their policy of accommodating the West and conciliating China, exemplified by the Washington Conference of 1921–1922. Such sentiments animated the members of various patriotic organizations and prevailed in the army, chafing from the cuts made in its budgets and the restrictions imposed by civilian administrations. Military leaders' dissatisfaction with the political ethos and governmental policies fused with their sense of being charged with a separate mission for which they were responsible to the emperor alone. There were calls for a "Showa

Restoration," and much talk of the divinity of the emperor as the embodiment of the national polity (*kokutai*), a term that became an "incantatory symbol"[1] all the more powerful for being vague.

Among the most vehement critics of party government were radical egalitarians such as Kita Ikki, who favored nationalizing industry, and radical agrarians like Gondō Seikyo (1868–1937), who would abolish industry and return Japan to rural simplicity. Although their visions of the future differed, they agreed on two things: that the existing government obtruded on the imperial will and must be swept away and that Japan had a divine mission overseas. Such ideas formed the agenda for small societies of extremists given to direct action, such as the Cherry Society, which planned an unsuccessful military coup in Tokyo in March 1931. The membership of this society consisted entirely of army officers, none higher in rank than lieutenant colonel.

The assassination of the Manchurian warlord Zhang Zuolin in 1928 was the work of men such as these. They hoped that Zhang's murder would trigger a war in which this vast, strategic, and potentially wealthy area would be conquered for Japan. This did not happen, but another attempt to start a war appealed to the superpatriots, not only because it might gain Manchuria but also because it would strengthen their support in the army, increase the army's power and popularity at home, and undermine the government they so detested.

Emphasis on Manchuria was also consistent with the thought of more analytical army men, such as Ishiwara Kanji (Ishihara Kanji, 1886–1949), who worked out the plan of attack. He and other students of World War I wanted Japan to control the economic resources of Manchuria as a step toward attaining the economic independence required for waging total war. Many officers, concerned with the possibility of war with the Soviet Union, were also mindful of Manchuria's strategic value.

In the fall of 1931 the time seemed ripe, because China was hampered by floods in the Yangzi River valley and the Western powers were neutralized by the depression. The seizure was masterminded by Ishiwara and other officers serving with the Japanese Army on the Liaodong Peninsula. These officers, none higher than colonel, fabricated a supposed Chinese attempt to sabotage the South Manchuria Railway Company as an excuse for hostilities and then made sure that the fighting continued until the army controlled Manchuria. Although certain high army officials in Tokyo likely knew of the plot, it was carried out without the knowledge, let alone the authorization, of the civilian government in Tokyo, which, once informed, tried to halt the operations but found itself powerless to do so. An attempted military coup in Tokyo in October did not immediately topple the government, but it did intimidate civilian political leaders. The Wakatsuki government, divided and helpless, resigned in December. It was followed by a Seiyūkai government under Inukai Ki (Inukai Tsuyoshi, 1855–1932), which for another half year tried to maintain a semblance of party control.

Events moved swiftly on the continent and at home. In Manchuria, the army consolidated its hold and established a puppet state, which early in 1932 declared its independence from China. Manchukuo, as it was known, was placed under the titular rule of Puyi, who as an infant had been the last emperor of China—but it was actually controlled by the army. Meanwhile, the fighting had spread to China proper; for six strenuous weeks, Japanese and Chinese fought around Shanghai until a truce was arranged. However, Japanese efforts to reach a general settlement with China and obtain recognition of Manchukuo were rebuffed. Japan was condemned by the League of Nations and withdrew in March 1933. The failure of the League to do anything more than talk was not lost on Mussolini and Hitler.

After Japanese troops crossed the Great Wall in the spring of 1933, a truce was concluded in May 1933 that left Japanese troops in control of the area north of the Wall and provided for a demilitarized zone whose boundaries were marked by the railway line running between Beijing, Tianjin, and Tanggu—but it did not prevent the Japanese from setting up a puppet regime in that area or from exerting continuous pressure on North China. In December 1935, Japanese army officers failed in their plans to engineer a North Chinese puppet regime, and full-scale war broke out in the summer of 1937. In the meantime, in Manchuria and Korea, the Japanese concentrated on the development of heavy industry, building an industrial base on the continent under army control.

## Japanese Politics and the Road to War

At home, too, 1932 was an eventful year, as members of the patriotic societies continued to further their cause by assassinating prominent men, including the head of the house of Mitsui. On May 15 they raided the Tokyo power station, a bank, Seiyūkai headquarters, and the official residence of the prime minister. They assassinated Inukai in his home.

When the men responsible for the May 15 violence were brought to trial, they were treated with great respect. They were allowed to expound their doctrines for days at a time and were given a national podium from which to proclaim the selflessness of their patriotic motives. In this way they largely succeeded in portraying themselves as martyrs. The light sentences meted out at the conclusion of the lengthy trials further discouraged those who hoped for a return to civilian rule. Instead, power shifted from the political parties into the hands of civilian bureaucrats and especially the military.

In 1936 the leftist Social Mass Party managed to win half a million votes. The following year that party's total climbed to 900,000 votes, and it captured thirty-seven seats in the lower house of the Diet. In that same election, the Seiyūkai and Minseitō together polled some 7 million votes, giving them 354 out of 466 seats. But their showing in the polls was to little avail. The parties were too weak to control the military. Those who wished to preserve constitutional government chose to compromise with the military establishment in the hope of averting a complete overthrow of the existing order.

Efforts to achieve political stabilization through a national union government, in which all the power centers were represented, were fostered by Saionji, the last of the *genrō,* who hoped to protect the throne from involvement in politics. But these efforts met with only partial and temporary success. The next two Cabinets, in office from May 1932 to March 1936, included party men but were headed by admirals, who were considered more moderate than certain potential prime ministers from the army.

Prime sources of continued instability were the divisions within each of the power centers. Within the bureaucracies there was rivalry among ministries and disagreement between conservative officials and technocrats who envisioned radical restructuring of state and society.

The military, too, was divided. The army and navy frequently clashed, and the breakdown in discipline during the actions in Manchuria and the violence at home reflected disunity in the army. The lines of army factionalism were complex: for example, there was a division between those who had studied at the Central War College and those who had attended officers' training school. However, two main groups stood out. The more extreme faction, led by Generals Araki Sadao (1877–1966) and Mazaki Jinzaburō (1876–1956), was known as the Kōdōha, or "Imperial Way faction," because it emphasized the imperial mystique and advocated an ill-defined doctrine of direct imperial rule. Like the radical civilian theorists of the right, it opposed existing political and economic institutions and sought a moral and spiritual transformation that would assure a glorious future for both army and country. In contrast, the Tōseiha, or "Control faction," led by General Nagata Tetsuzan (1884–1935), the leading proponent of total war, and including Ishiwara and General Tōjō Hideki, gave priority to the long-range buildup of the economy and the transformation of Japan into a modern military state.

For a few years the advantage lay with the Imperial Way faction, but it suffered a setback in 1935 when General Mazaki was dismissed from his post as director-general of military education. A lieutenant colonel retaliated by assassinating General Nagata. The Control faction responded by arresting the officer and laying plans for the transfer of other firebrands to Manchuria. The lieutenant colonel's trial was still in progress when, on February 26, 1936, a group of junior Kōdōha officers, commanding more than 1000 men, seized the center of the capital and killed several prominent leaders, although some of their intended victims, including the prime minister, Admiral Okada Keisuke (1868–1952), managed to elude them. The young officers hoped that their action would bring down the old system and that Generals Araki and Mazaki would take the lead in restructuring the state, but these senior generals remained aloof. As in 1928, the emperor intervened, and the navy responded to the crisis with vigor. On the third day of the insurrection, the rebels surrendered. This time the leaders were tried rapidly and in secret. One of those who perished at the hands of a firing squad was Kita Ikki, who had not participated in the mutiny but was too closely associated with the young officers and their movement to escape punishment.

The elimination of the Imperial Way faction actually increased the army's political power because it could now threaten a second mutiny if it did not get its way. The army still had to consider the wishes of other components of the power elite, but it was able to secure a substantial increase in military spending. Japan now withdrew from the naval limitation agreement, opening the possibility that it might have to confront the combined might of the Western powers and the Soviet Union. The army's strategic planners thought primarily in terms of a war with the latter, thus providing a strong inducement for Japan to sign an anti-Comintern pact with Hitler's Germany in December 1936.

Domestically, there ensued an intensification of propaganda and indoctrination with a continuation of repression directed at the radical left and those whose ardor for emperor and *kokutai* was deemed insufficient. The most notorious case took place in 1935 when Minobe Tatsukichi, the distinguished legal theorist, was charged with demeaning the emperor by considering him merely "the highest organ of the state." Minobe defended himself with spirit but was forced to resign from the House of Peers. Even so, in 1936, while living in seclusion, the old man suffered an attempt on his life that left him wounded. By that time, his books had been banned. Censorship became more severe, and expressions of intense national chauvinism filled the media.

The abandonment of the gold standard and the military buildup stimulated the economy and enabled Japan to recover from the depth of the depression, but agriculture remained depressed, and small companies benefited much less than did the *zaibatsu*.

## China: The Nanjing Decade— An Uneasy Peace

From 1927 to 1937, the Nationalist government in Nanjing avoided war with Japan, but those were hardly peaceful years. Even after the completion of the Northern Expedition in 1928, the government controlled only the lower Yangzi River valley. Elsewhere it depended on the unreliable allegiance of local power holders. In 1930 the government secured its authority in the north after waging a costly campaign with heavy casualties against the combined armies of two warlords.

Nanjing was strengthened by this victory but still lacked the power to subdue the remaining warlords permanently. That some of these could claim to stand for national goals reinforced the Nationalists' strong tendency to give highest priority to building military strength, even before Japan's seizure of Manchuria and the threat of further Japanese aggression made such a policy imperative.

At home, the Nanjing regime had to deal with warlords and Communists. The government's policy toward the warlords was to temporize, to try to prevent the formation of antigovernment warlord coalitions, and to settle for expressions of allegiance until it could establish central control. Its power and prestige increased when it defeated a rebellion in Fujian in 1933 and 1934 and especially after it obtained control over Guangdong and the submission of Guangxi in 1936. Its campaigns against the Communists provided occasions for the dispatch of central government troops into warlord provinces, especially after the Communists began their Long March in 1934 (described later in this chapter); similarly, the Japanese threat proved useful in eventually bringing certain warlords into line. Thus, the trend favored Nanjing, but the balance between central and local power varied widely in different parts of China. The tenacity of the warlord phenomenon in certain regions is illustrated by Sichuan, in parts of which warlords remained powerful even after the Nationalists moved their wartime capital to that province. Similarly, Xinjiang, in the far west, remained virtually autonomous.

# China: The Nanjing Decade— Domestic Policies

The regime's military emphasis was reflected in government spending, with 60 to 80 percent of the annual outlay going to military expenses and debt service. The latter amounted to about one-third, reflecting heavy government borrowing, but military considerations were also paramount in such civil projects as road and railway construction. Taking the place of the ousted Soviet Union military advisers were a series of German military men who tried to introduce German military doctrines (including concepts of military organization not necessarily suitable to the Chinese situation) and helped arrange for the import of German arms and munitions. In 1935, at the height of their influence, there were seventy German advisers in China, but their number decreased after Germany and Japan signed the anti-Comintern pact in December 1936. The last were recalled in 1938.

Noteworthy within the army were the graduates of the Whampoa Military Academy, particularly those who completed the course during Chiang Kai-shek's tenure as director, because they enjoyed an especially close relationship with their supreme commander. During 1931, Whampoa graduates formed the Blue Shirts, a secret police group pledged to complete obedience to Chiang. They and the so-called CC clique (led by two Chen brothers trusted by Chiang) were influenced in ideology and organization by European Fascism. The Blue Shirts were greatly feared because of their spying and terrorist activities, including assassinations.

The CC clique, too, had considerable power but failed in its prime aim, which was to revitalize the GMD. After the split with the Communists in 1927, the GMD purged many of its own most dedicated revolutionaries. One result was that young activists, often from the modern schools that had earlier supplied recruits for the GMD, were drawn to the Communist party. Another result was the creation within the ruling party of an atmosphere attractive to careerists who, concentrating on their own personal advancement, were disinclined to rock the boat. Meanwhile, Chiang saw to it that the party remained just one of several centers of power.

The deterioration of the party was a particularly serious matter, because the Nanjing government suffered from factional politics, favoritism, and bureaucratic overorganization, which spawned departments with overlapping functions and countless committees grinding out lengthy reports and recommendations, detailing programs that consumed vast quantities of paper but were rarely implemented.

Coordination was poor. Sometimes, for example, government censors suppressed news items deliberately issued by the government. The conduct of official business lumbered along unless quickened by the personal intervention of Chiang, whose power was steadily increasing.

His power was based on the loyalty of the military, the Blue Shirts, and core partisans such as the CC clique; on the financial backing of bankers and businessmen (including the relatives of Chiang's wife); and on Chiang's manipulation of various political cliques and factions. The Soong family deserves special mention because it included not only Sun Yat-sen's widow, who was politically inactive during the 1930s, but also the decidedly active wife of Chiang, another sister who married the notoriously corrupt H. H. Kung, and T. V. Soong, a brother who was a reformist finance minister. Chiang was indispensable but lacked the charisma to inspire his officials, who feared rather than loved him. Nor did he have the gift of eloquence with which to rouse the people had he so desired. Negative sanctions, such as the executions sporadically ordered by Chiang when an exceptionally flagrant case of corruption was brought to his attention, were not enough: the regime lacked drive and direction.

The regime was also weak ideologically. Sun Yat-sen became the object of an official cult, but his ideas were not further refined or developed. Nor was political tutelage enacted. Instead, emphasis shifted toward a revival of Confucianism. In contrast to Sun's admiration for the Taiping, Chiang sought to emulate Zeng Guofan, who in his day had crushed the Taiping by revitalizing Confucian values.

Chiang's regard for Confucius and Zeng was apparent during his days at Whampoa, but it became even more obvious in 1934 when he launched an extensive program to foster traditional values known as the New Life Movement. He exhorted the populace to observe four vaguely defined Confucian virtues and spelled out the criteria for proper behavior in detailed instructions. The people were to sit and stand straight, eat quietly, refrain from indiscriminate spitting, and so forth, in the hope that they would thus acquire discipline. It did not work. Officials and commoners continued to act much as before. The government never did devise an ideology that could arouse the enthusiasm of its own personnel, command the respect of the people, or convince intellectuals. Censorship clearly was not the answer, although even foreign correspondents were subjected to it; some complained that China was worse than Japan.

Local government under the Nationalists was equally ineffective. They restructured county government; established four bureaus charged with education, construction, public security, and finance; and even attempted to reach below that level by assigning officials to the wards into which they divided the counties. But they failed to wrest control over taxes and local security from the entrenched local elite, who continued to wield actual power. Like its predecessors, the Nanjing regime failed to mobilize the financial or human resources of the village. With income from land taxes remaining in the provinces, the government was financed primarily from the modern sector.

Despite early links with the business community, the GMD tended to treat business as a source to be exploited for revenue rather than as an asset to be fostered as a component of national strength. During 1928 and 1929, China finally regained the tariff autonomy lost in the Opium War, but this was of little help to China's industries because exports were subjected to the same tariffs as imports and imported raw materials were taxed as heavily as finished goods.

In 1933, heavily in debt to the banks, the government took control of the banking system in a move that benefited the treasury but not the private sector. Overall, the modern sector grew during the first ten years of Nationalist rule, but only at roughly the same pace as during the years between the fall of the Qing and the establishment of the regime in Nanjing.

During the early 1930s, the traditional agrarian sector of the economy, which accounted for most of China's production and employed most of its people, was afflicted by severe weather conditions, the exactions of the tax collector piling on surtax after surtax (later changed to special assessments), and the decline in commodity prices brought on by the Great Depression. Not only climate but also taxation and exposure to international markets varied widely, making generalization risky. Even in provinces such as Jiangsu and Zhejiang, firmly controlled by the government, taxes paid by one district often far exceeded those paid by another.

When the international price of silk collapsed, peasants dependent on sericulture, such as those of Wuxi County in Jiangsu, were badly hurt. Parts of the north were no better off. Statistics for parts of northern China indicate that by 1934 and 1935 nearly half of the peasant households were farming less than ten mu (1 mu = 0.167 acres) when fifteen were needed for subsistence, reflecting a deepening agrarian crisis. Everywhere, because the government did nothing to change the status quo in the villages or on the land, the poorest and the weakest suffered most.

Like so much legislation promulgated during those years, a law passed in 1930 limiting rents to 37.5 percent of the harvest was not enforced. Payments of 50 percent were common, and those of 60 percent were not unusual. Programs for developing cooperatives and fostering rural reconstruction were organized, but their benefits rarely filtered down to the rural poor. In 1937 there was a price recovery, and harvests were good, but by that time millions had suffered bitter poverty and despair.

Chiang and his supporters wanted to unify the country and stabilize society. They wished to consolidate the revolution that had brought them into power, not expand it. Consequently, they put a premium on suppressing forces pushing for continued revolution and were intent on destroying the Communists, who maintained that the revolution was unfinished and proclaimed their determination to lead it to completion. To Chiang, nothing was more urgent than the elimination of his old enemies. For the C.C.P., too, these were crucial years.

# The Chinese Communists (1927–1934)

The Shanghai massacre and the subsequent suppression of the C.C.P. and its associated labor movement effectively eliminated the party as an urban force, altered its geographic distribution, and profoundly affected its strategy and leadership.

For some years it remained unclear just what direction it would take. Neither the Comintern in Moscow nor its Chinese followers were willing simply to write off the cities. Urban insurrection was tried but failed: the Canton Commune (December 1927) met with profound popular apathy and lasted only four days.

The use of armed force to capture cities such as Changsha in Hunan in 1930 also failed. Although no one was ready to say so, at least in public, Moscow clearly did not have the formula for success. Meanwhile, in China various groups and factions contended for power and the adoption of their policies.

One of these groups was the C.C.P. military force, reorganized in the mountains on the Hunan–Jiangxi border, where, in the spring of 1928, Zhu De (1886–1976) joined Mao Zedong, who had arrived the previous fall. In command of some 2000 troops, the two men laid the groundwork for the Red Army, with Zhu in military command and Mao in charge of political organization and indoctrination.

As Mao said in 1938, "Political power grows out of the barrel of a gun. Our principle is that the Party commands the gun; the gun shall never be allowed to command the Party."[2] Through indoctrination, the recruitment of soldiers into the party, and the formation of soldiers' committees, Mao secured the control of the party over the army. On the military side, Zhu and Mao emphasized guerrilla warfare, which put a premium on mobility and surprise, rapid retreats to avoid battle with superior enemy forces, lightning strikes to pick off small contingents of the enemy, and constant harassment to keep the enemy off balance.

Essential to this type of warfare is popular support to provide intelligence, supplies, recruits, and cover for guerrillas under enemy pursuit. Peasant participation and support were secured by redistributing land and furthering the revolution in the countryside.

This strategy focused on the development and expansion of rural C.C.P.-controlled bases. In the early 1930s there were several such areas with the largest in Jiangxi, where the founding of the Chinese Soviet Republic was proclaimed in December 1931. The basic agrarian policy was "land to the tiller," involving the confiscation of large holdings for reassignment to the poor with "middle peasants" left largely unaffected. But there was a good deal of disagreement over definitions and wide variations in the degree of local implementation of the program. In Jiangxi, Mao and Zhu were strong, but they had by no means won complete acceptance of either their program or their leadership, even after party headquarters were moved from Shanghai to Jiangxi in recognition of the new C.C.P. power center, a defeat for those oriented toward the Comintern in Moscow. Factionalism continued to threaten party unity, but the most severe challenge was external.

Chiang's first three "annihilation campaigns," from 1930 to 1931, helped strengthen rather than weaken the C.C.P. as the Red Army employed its tactics to good effect, capturing weapons, men, and land. The fourth campaign, from 1932 to 1933, again ended in defeat for the Nationalists. In the fifth campaign, begun late in 1933, Chiang, on German advice, changed his strategy. Deploying some 750,000 men supported by 150 airplanes, he surrounded the Jiangxi soviet and gradually tightened the circle of his blockade. When, in the fall of 1934, their situation became

**FIGURE 21.1** China, 1930–Spring 1944. The Long March. 🌐

untenable, the Communist forces abandoned their base, broke through a point in the blockade manned by former warlord armies, and began their Long March (see Figure 21.1).

## The Long March

When the Communists left Jiangxi, their first priority was survival and their destination was unclear. That was settled in January 1935 in an important conference held at Zunyi in Guizhou, where it was decided to proceed to Shaanxi, where a small soviet was already in place. In Shaanxi the C.C.P. would be out of easy reach of GMD armies. They would be able to act on their declaration of war against Japan and might even hope for some aid from the Soviet Union. At Zunyi, Mao gained a new prominence, although he did not control the party until the 1940s.

The march was a heroic vindication of Mao's belief in the power of human will and determination. In just over a year, the marchers covered some 6000 miles, traversing snow-covered mountain passes, where they froze in their thin clothes, and crossing treacherous bogs and marshes. To the hardships provided by nature was added the hostility of man, because there was rarely a day without some fighting. At one point they had no alternative but to cross a mountain torrent spanned by a thirteen-chain suspension bridge from which the enemy, armed and waiting on the other side, had removed the planks.

The six- or seven-day crossing of grasslands in the Chinese–Tibetan border region was a terrible ordeal. Here, heavy rainfall and poor drainage had created a waterlogged plain on which green grass grew on multiple layers of rotting grass beneath. First a vanguard was sent to chart the way; in the central grasslands they could find no place dry enough to sleep, so the marchers had to remain standing all night, leaning against each other. The rest of the army followed through the slippery, treacherous terrain, trudging on despite hunger and fatigue, trying to ward off rain and hail and to survive the unbearable cold of the nights. Because the men and women carried only a small amount of grain, they subsisted mostly on wild grasses and vegetables eaten raw because there was no firewood for cooking. Sometimes the vegetables turned out to be poisonous, and the stagnant water reportedly smelled of horse urine.

The marchers succeeded in overcoming this and other obstacles. Some women even gave birth. But many perished. Of about 100,000 who set out from Jiangxi, less than 10 percent completed the march. Some were left behind to work in various areas, but many more perished. The losses were only partially offset by new recruits who joined along the way. After completion of the march, Mao's headquarters in the caves of Yan'an controlled a force of about 20,000 including the newcomers as well as those already in Shaanxi.

The survivors of the march emerged toughened and filled with a sense of solidarity forged by shared hardships. There was also a heightened self-confidence—a conviction that the movement would surmount all obstacles. Something of this spirit is conveyed in a poem Mao wrote shortly before reaching Shaanxi:

> Lofty the sky
> and pale the clouds—
> We watch the wild geese
> south till they vanish.
> We count the thousand
> leagues already traveled.
> If we do not reach
> the Great Wall we are not true men.
> High on the crest
> of Liupan Mountain
> Our banners billow
> in the west wind.
> Today we hold
> a long rope in our hands.
> When shall we put bonds
> upon the grey dragon?[3]

The saga of the Long March remained a source of heroic inspiration for decades. The last veteran of the march did not leave the stage until the death of Deng Xiaoping in 1997.

# United Front and War

With the Communists in Shaanxi, Chiang remained as determined as ever to crush them, but their call for a united front against Japan had special appeal for the troops of Marshal Zhang Xueliang, who had been ordered to end resistance against the Japanese in Manchuria in 1931 and move south with his armies to Xian. Marshal Zhang's forces were less than enthusiastic in fighting the C.C.P. To breathe life into the anti-Communist campaign, Chiang flew to Xian in December 1936. But he had misjudged the situation. Instead of pledging themselves to renewed anti-Communist efforts, Marshal Zhang and some of his men seized Chiang and held him prisoner for two weeks while his fate was negotiated. Exactly what transpired is not clear, but the C.C.P., agreeing with Stalin's policy of forming a worldwide united front against Fascism, intervened.

Chiang was finally released after agreeing to terminate his campaign against Yan'an and lead a united front against Japan. He was at the time China's most distinguished military man, the leader of the government recognized as legitimate at home and abroad, and the heir to the mantle of Sun Yat-sen. Even his enemies saw him as the only man possessing the political, military, and ideological authority to lead China in an effort to stop the Japanese.

Following Chiang's 1936 success against Guangdong and Guangxi, the formation of the Chinese united front in 1937 dismayed Japanese army officers intent on dominating China. Since 1933 there had been a constant danger that an unplanned military incident might escalate into a major war. This is, in effect, what happened when the Chinese held firm and refused further concessions following a clash between Chinese and Japanese soldiers on the Marco Polo Bridge outside Beijing in July 1937. Thus began the second Sino-Japanese War that in 1941 merged into World War II, although this is not what Japan intended in 1937.

The conflict rapidly expanded into large-scale fighting. By the end of July, the Japanese were in possession of Beijing and Tianjin, and in August Japanese forces attacked Shanghai, the main source of Nationalist revenue. Here, Chiang used some of his best German-trained troops in three months of heroic and bloody fighting with heavy casualties. After Shanghai fell, the Chinese retreated in disarray and failed to take a stand at Wuxi as planned but poured into Nanjing, which fell in December.

The Nanjing Massacre followed. Japanese soldiers, backed by their superiors, went on a rampage, terrorizing, killing, raping, burning and looting for seven weeks. Sixty years later, the number of people who perished remains a matter of bitter contention—as though sheer numbers can measure the horror. The figure inscribed in the memorial erected in Nanjing (1985) is 300,000, but "whether 200,000 or 240,000 people were killed does not alter the dimension of the horror."[4] How and why it happened, and the lessons to be drawn therefrom, continue to generate intense controversy and stimulate reflection. The Japanese acquired a reputation for terrible cruelty, which stiffened the Chinese determination to resist and continued to cast a pall long after the war.

After Nanjing, the Japanese maintained and continued their offense, taking Canton in October and Wuhan in December; Chiang, refusing to submit, adopted a strategy of "trading space for time." Japan's prime minister at this time was

Prince Konoe Fumimaro (1891–1945), a descendant of the Fujiwaras and protégé of Saionji. He held office from June 1937 to January 1939 and again from July 1940 to July 1941. Japanese policy making continued to be a very complicated process. The general staff, for example, did not share the optimism of the armies in the field, yet the government continued to expand the war, encouraged by a string of victories. As the war escalated, so did the Japanese government's aims and rhetoric. What had begun as a search for a pro-Japanese North China turned into a holy crusade against the West and Communism.

In 1938, unable to obtain Chinese recognition of Manchukuo, the Konoe government declared Chiang's regime illegitimate and vowed to destroy it. In November Konoe proclaimed Japan's determination to establish a "new order in East Asia" that would include Japan, Manchukuo, and China in a political, economic, and cultural union, a bastion against (Western) imperialism and against Soviet Communism. Those who did not see the light were to be brought to their senses by force. Originally, in the summer of 1937, Japanese plans had called for a three-month campaign by three divisions, at a cost of 100 million yen, to destroy the main Chinese force and take possession of key areas while waiting for Chiang to ask for peace. But by the following spring they were preparing orders for twenty divisions and had appropriated more than 2.5 billion yen with promise of more to come and no end in sight.

The Nationalist government moved its wartime capital to Chongqing in Sichuan. Many refugees followed the government to the southwest (see Figure 21.2). Not only universities but also hundreds of factories were transported piecemeal to help the war effort in Chongqing, where Chiang held on gamely. Before the Japanese attack on Pearl Harbor (December 1941), China obtained financial assistance from the United States and the Soviet Union, and Stalin sent some pilots to be stationed in Gansu Province. From 1939 to 1941, Chongqing suffered repeated bombings. Not until August 1941 did help come in the form of the Flying Tigers, volunteer American pilots later incorporated into the Fourteenth U.S. Air Force, commanded by General Claire L. Chennault. However, the West's support remained primarily moral, and the Soviet Union alone sent some official assistance. Meanwhile, from 1939 to 1941, fighting on the ground was limited to skirmishes, with both sides working to consolidate their positions.

In 1940, when it became obvious that the Chinese would not bow to their demands, the Japanese established a puppet regime in Nanjing headed by Wang Jingwei, the erstwhile follower of Sun and leader of the left wing of the GMD. However, like a similar regime established earlier in Beijing, it was clear to the Chinese populace that the Japanese were pulling the strings.

## Expansion of the War into a Pacific War

A major Japanese foreign policy concern during the 1930s was relations with the Soviet Union. From 1937 to 1940 there were three military confrontations along the Soviet Union's frontier with Korea and, far more serious, along the Mongolian border with Manchukuo. These operations, which increased in scale, involved the deployment of armor, artillery, and aircraft. The Japanese fought well, but the

**FIGURE 21.2** *Refugees Crowding onto Trains Bound for Guilin,* Cai Dizhi. Chinese refugees escaping from Japanese-occupied territory followed the Chinese Nationalist government southwest to its temporary wartime capital in Chongqing. Scenes such as this were common in 1937 and 1938. Woodcut. (From *Woodcuts of Wartime China, 1937–1945,* Yonghua lingxin, ed. [Taiwan: L. Ming Cultural Enterprises, Dist.].)

Soviets proved more than a match. The last and most severe conflict cost Japan 180,000 men and resulted in an armistice.

Japan was caught off guard diplomatically when Germany, without warning, came to terms with the Soviet Union in August 1939. Japan was therefore neutral when World War II began in Europe shortly thereafter. However, the dramatic success of the German blitzkrieg strengthened the hands of those in Tokyo who favored a pro-German policy, and in September 1940, Konoe signed the Tripartite Pact, forming an alliance with Germany and Italy.

The Germans again surprised the Japanese in June 1941 when Hitler invaded the Soviet Union. Some army men wanted Japan to join the attack on the Soviet Union. As Alvin D. Coox pointed out, they saw this as a way out of the China impasse, "apparently convinced that the best way to climb out of a hole was to widen it."[5] However, the navy wanted to advance into the oil- and mineral-rich south. Officially, Japan claimed its mission to be the creation of a "greater East Asian co-prosperity sphere," but the underlying perception was that the resources of Southeast Asia were essential for Japan's economic security.

Konoe hoped that, armed with the Tripartite Pact, he would be able to reach his aims without going to war with the United States, but the American government was becoming increasingly alarmed over Japanese expansion. When in the summer of 1941 Japan moved troops into southern Vietnam, the United States, Britain, and Holland (then in control of the East Indies, modern Indonesia) retaliated by applying the economic sanctions they had withheld in 1931. An embargo on scrap iron was serious, but the crucial product cut off from Japan was oil.

America and Japan were on a collision course. Michael A. Barnhart put it as follows:

> The Japanese Empire was determined to retain the rights and privileges it considered necessary for its economic and political security. The United States thought these rights and privileges contrary to its own deeply held principles and to the survival of what were now in effect its allies in the struggle against global aggression.[6]

The United States was determined that Japan should withdraw from China and Indochina. For Japan, this would have meant a reversal of the policy pursued in China since 1931 and the relinquishment of the vision of primacy in East Asia. Dependent on oil and rubber from Southeast Asia, the Japanese were in no position to carry on protracted negotiations. They had to fight or retreat. It is a bitter irony that Japan now prepared to go to war to attain the self-sufficiency that its proponents of total war had once considered a precondition for war.

When it became clear to Konoe that the situation had reached an impasse, he resigned; he was followed by General Tōjō Hideki (1884–1948), prime minister from October 1941 to July 1944. When last-minute negotiations proved fruitless, the Japanese decided on war as the least unpalatable alternative. It began on December 7, 1941, with a surprise attack on Pearl Harbor, Hawaii, that destroyed seven American battleships and 120 aircraft and left 2400 dead. With the United States and Japan at war, Hitler, too, declared war against the United States, but German–Japanese cooperation during the war remained limited.

# The Course of the War

At first the war went spectacularly well for Japan. By the middle of 1942 Japan controlled the Philippines, Malaya, Burma, and the East Indies. Japan was also in charge in Indochina (officially under the jurisdiction of Vichy France) and enjoyed the cooperation of a friendly regime in Thailand. However, contrary to hopes in Tokyo, the United States, far from being ready to negotiate a quick peace, mobilized for full-scale war.

In June 1942 Japan suffered a major defeat when it was checked at the battle of Midway, 1200 miles northwest of Hawaii (see Figure 21.3). The Americans, taking advantage of advance knowledge of Japanese movements obtained from breaking the Japanese secret code, destroyed many Japanese planes and sank four

**FIGURE 21.3** The Pacific War. 🌸

Japanese aircraft carriers, losing only one of their own. Three more years of intense warfare, including bloody hand-to-hand combat, lay ahead, but the American use of aircraft carriers and the extensive deployment of submarines, which took a tremendous toll on vital Japanese shipping, were two factors contributing to Japan's ultimate defeat. Another was the island-hopping strategy, whereby the American forces seized islands selectively for use as bases for further advances, by-passing others with their forces intact but out of action. One consequence of this strategy was that although the Allies wanted Japan to remain bogged down in China, China itself was not a major war theater.

## China at War

The conviction that eventually the United States would enter the war sustained Chiang during the long years China faced Japan virtually alone. When, after Pearl Harbor, this happened, it buoyed the spirit of the Chinese, now allied to the one country powerful enough to crush Japan. More material forms of support were forthcoming, although there was never enough, because in 1942 Japan cut off Chongqing's last land route to its allies by seizing Burma and closing the Burma Road. Thereafter, supplies had to be flown from India to Yunnan over the Himalayas (the "hump"). In addition, China ranked low in the American war effort. The Allies decided first to concentrate on the defeat of Germany, and the island-hopping strategy adopted against Japan largely bypassed China, although the Allies appreciated that China tied down vast numbers of Japanese troops that otherwise might have been used elsewhere (see Figure 21.3).

The top American military man in China was General Joseph Stilwell, who in 1942 became concurrently Chiang's chief-of-staff and commander of American forces in the China–Burma–India theater. General Stilwell was a fine soldier, but General Chennault disregarded his warnings against building airbases unprotected by ground troops, bases from which, in early summer 1944, heavy bombers attacked industrial facilities in Kyushu and Manchukuo, airfields in Taiwan, and oil refineries in Sumatra. However, General Stilwell was proved right when later that summer Japan launched their Ichigo (Number One) campaign into Hunan and Guangxi and captured the airfields. A heavy blow for the GMD, it proved a hollow victory for the Japanese.

General Stilwell had high regard for the ordinary Chinese fighting man but scarcely concealed his irritation and impatience with the inefficiencies and corruption he encountered in Chongqing and his disgust at Chiang's policy of preparing for a postwar showdown with the C.C.P. rather than joining in a single-minded effort against the Japanese enemy. The relationship between the two men deteriorated until Chiang requested and received General Stilwell's recall in 1944.

General Stilwell was replaced by General Albert Wedemeyer, who was friendlier to Chiang but equally critical of conditions in the Chinese army, which were, by all accounts, horrendous. Induction was tantamount to a death sentence. Those who could afford to do so bribed the conscription officer. The remainder were marched off, bound to each other with ropes, to join their units, often many miles and days away. Underfed and exhausted, many never completed the trip. Those who did found that food was equally scarce at the front and that medical services were almost completely lacking.

Misery and corruption were not unique to the military. Even in times of famine (as in Henan during 1942 and 1943) peasants were sorely oppressed by the demands of the landlord and the tax collector, and the urban middle class suffered from mounting inflation, which had reached an annual rate of 40 to 50 percent between 1937 and 1939, climbed to 160 percent for 1939–1942, and rose to an average of 300 percent for 1942–1945. By 1943 the purchasing power of the salaries paid to bureaucrats was only one-tenth what it had been in 1937, and teachers were receiving 5 percent of their former earnings. The result was widespread demoralization of the military and civilian populations under Nationalist control. The secret police were unable to root out corruption. Government exhortations and the publication of Chiang's book, *China's Destiny* (1943), failed to reinvigorate ideological commitment to the government and party.

**FIGURE 21.4** Jiang Qing (left) and Mao Zedong in Yan'an, 1960. After the Long March and during the war, the Chinese Communist Party leaders lived and worked in the Yan'an caves. (© Revolutionary Workers Online.)

A major reason for the wartime deterioration of the GMD was Japan's seizure of the eastern seaboard and China's major cities, which deprived the Nationalists of the great business centers of eastern China (especially Shanghai). In Sichuan, they depended on the elements in society that were most resistant to change and reform. Moreover, Chiang, hoarding his strength for the coming showdown with the C.C.P., was unwilling to commit his troops to battle with the Japanese more than absolutely necessary. As a consequence, he missed whatever opportunity existed for building a modern Chinese force with American assistance and for translating anti-Japanese nationalism into support for his own regime.

The shortcomings of the Chongqing government were highlighted by the accomplishments of the Communists, headquartered in Yan'an (see Figure 21.4). From 1937 to 1945, the party expanded its membership from roughly 40,000 to more than 1 million, and its troop strength increased tenfold to an estimated 900,000, not counting guerrillas and militiamen.

Furthermore, the Communists enjoyed widespread peasant support in northern China, where they established themselves as the effective government in the countryside behind the Japanese lines. The Japanese, concentrated in the cities and guarding their lines of supply, did not have the manpower to patrol the rural areas constantly and effectively.

In the areas nominally under Japanese control, the Communists skillfully pursued policies to fuse national resistance and social revolution. The key to their ultimate success was mass mobilization of the peasantry, but the mix of policies and the pace of change varied according to local conditions. Carefully avoiding premature class warfare, they frequently began by organizing the peasants to wage guerrilla war, enlisting support from the village elites for the war effort, and manipulating them into going along with rent and interest reduction. Building their military power, they enlisted elite support even as they undermined elite power.

Crucial was the creation of new mass organizations led by poor peasant activists, who, freed from the exactions of landlords and given a voice in government, became enthusiastic supporters of the party and government. The peasant associations and local party branches took the lead in effecting changes in taxation and reducing rent and interest payments, thus destroying the economic foundations of the old system. Similarly, new energies were released by organizing women and young people in an attack on traditional family authority. Actual or potential rivals such as secret societies or bandits were attacked and eliminated. The twin lessons of nationalism and revolution were brought home to the people through indoctrination programs and a campaign to combat illiteracy, conveying new ideas to the peasantry even as they gained access to the written word, shattering the old monopoly on learning.

The Japanese patronized puppet armies and even tolerated trade with the GMD-controlled areas of China, but the Wang Jingwei regime was too obviously controlled by the Japanese ever to gain credibility. At best, life in occupied China went on as usual, but Japanese arrogance alienated many Chinese. Humane behavior on the part of some individuals was overshadowed by acts of cruelty that evoked Chinese hatred and resistance. An example is the notorious "kill all, burn all, destroy all" campaign carried out in 1941 and 1942 in parts of northern China in retaliation for a C.C.P. offensive. Implemented literally, the Japanese hurt the C.C.P. badly, but they also helped turn apolitical peasants into determined fighters.

The policies and record of the C.C.P. also helped attract urban intellectuals. To insure discipline and preserve the cohesion of the movement, swollen by new adherents, the party under Mao (now firmly established as leader) organized a rectification campaign to assure "correct" understanding of party ideology and to bring art and literature into line. Art for its own sake or for self-expression was condemned, and those guilty of being insufficiently mass oriented were induced to confess their faults. Many were sent to work in villages, factories, or battle zones to "learn from the masses."

From the war, the C.C.P. emerged stronger than it had ever been. The outcome of the civil war that followed was not obvious to observers, but it is one of the ironies of the war that the Japanese, who proclaimed that they were combating Communism in China, instead ended by contributing to its victory.

## Japan at War

Well before Pearl Harbor, the effects of the continued war in China were felt by the Japanese people as militarization and authoritarianism increased at home. The National General Mobilization Law of 1938 strengthened the prime minister at the expense of the Diet, and the government began to place the economy on a war basis, with rationing, economic controls, and resource allocations administered by a technological and bureaucratic elite drawn from the most prestigious universities. Getting the various centers of economic and political power to pull together remained a problem, but a precedent was set for government to direct the economy; institutions for this were founded, and Japan gained a cadre of economic and social bureaucrats.

The war entailed a greater role for government not only in industry and commerce but also in agriculture. The war years were hard on rural landlords, already hurt by the depression, whereas ordinary tenant farmers benefited from measures to control inflation, such as rent control (1939), and from government efforts to increase production by allocating fertilizer. In the last years of the war, the government paid much larger bonuses to farm operators than to noncultivating landlords, who emerged from the war much weakened. As Ann Waswo has shown, "in purely economic terms and in terms of local political influence, ordinary farmers made significant gains."[7] As ever, war proved a potent catalyst for change.

In October 1940, the political parties were merged into the Imperial Rule Assistance Association, which, however, did not become a mass popular party along the lines of European Fascism but served primarily as a vehicle for the dissemination of propaganda throughout Japan. Similarly, labor unions were combined into a single patriotic organization. Great pressures were exerted to bring educational institutions and the public communications media into line so that the whole of Japan would speak with one collective voice.

To effect the "spiritual mobilization" of the country, the government tried to purge Western influence from Japanese life. As one writer put it, "While the black ships that represent the material might of the West have left, a hundred years later the Black Ships of thought are still threatening us."[8] Prominent intellectuals insisted on Japanese uniqueness and exceptionalism and drew on German concepts of irony and angst, nostalgia for the past, and aesthetics of death, subjectivity, and poetry to attack the "modern" at home and abroad. Not only were foreign radical and liberal ideas banned from theoretical discourse, but popular culture was also purged. Permanent waves and jazz, so popular during the 1920s, were banned. Efforts were made to remove Western loanwords from the language, and the people were bombarded with exhortations to observe traditional values and revere the divine emperor. Heterodox religious sects with no ostensible political agenda were suppressed, and in a "triumph of religious stateism,"[9] all religions were subordinated to the imperial cult. To mobilize the public down to the ward level, the people were formed into small neighborhood organizations.

## Colonial East Asia during the War

Japan's attempt to win over the population of the conquered areas by encouraging their native religious traditions, exploiting their resentment against Western imperialism, and teaching them the Japanese language was more than offset by Japan's own imperialistic exploitation, the harshness of its rule, and the cruelty of its soldiers. The slogan "Asia for the Asians" did not disguise the realities of what Mark R. Peattie has characterized as a "mutant colonialism when the tightening demands on the energies, loyalties, and resources of Japan's colonial peoples by a nation at war with much of Asia and most of the West transmogrified an authoritarian but recognizably 'Western' colonial system into an empire of the lash, a totalitarian imperium, that dragged along its peoples as it staggered toward defeat."[10]

Conditions were particularly harsh in Korea, but in Taiwan, too, there was a campaign to assimilate the population and turn them into people who spoke Japanese, had Japanese names, and even worshiped at Shinto shrines. Although Taiwanese were regimented and controlled at home, Taiwanese entrepreneurs took advantage of new opportunities in Manchuria and elsewhere, and young people responded positively to efforts to recruit them into the Japanese military. The largest contingent served on Hainan island, where many perished. However, on the whole, people in Taiwan, as in Korea, welcomed Japan's defeat. When Nationalists forces arrived in October 1945, they were welcomed as liberators.

Japanese forces dominated Vietnam, although until the fall of Vichy France in March 1945, they left the Vichy French colonial administration in place. The Japanese conducted a cultural campaign claiming that they had come as liberators from all European colonialism and seeking support especially among Buddhists, in contrast to the French who encouraged and gave new freedoms to Catholics. Resisting both Japanese and French were the Viet Minh (short for Viet Nam Doc Lap Dong Minh, or League for the Independence of Vietnam), established in the northwest by Ho Chi Minh when he returned to Vietnam in 1941. Viet Minh policy was to postpone the Marxist revolutionary agenda to form a broad nationalist coalition and possibly to gain assistance from the Allies. Established in 1941, the policy resulted in Ho's cooperation with the American Office of Strategic Services in 1944. That the United States would support the reimposition of French colonialism was not yet apparent by war's end.

Elsewhere in Japan's bloated empire the colonial authorities were replaced by Japanese-controlled puppet regimes. The history of Southeast Asia is beyond the scope of our text, but we should note that although Japan won no friends, they shattered the myth along with the actuality of Western hegemony and paved the way for the end of colonialism—ultimately throughout the globe.

# The End of the War

The closer the American forces came to the Japanese homeland, the easier it was for them to bomb Japan itself. Such raids were aimed not only at military and industrial installations but also at economic targets and population centers. Incendiary bombs were dropped to sap the morale of the people, who by the last years of the war were suffering from scarcities of all kinds, including food and other daily necessities, many of which were available only on the black market.

In July 1944, after the fall of Saipan, largest of the Mariana Islands, General Tōjō was forced out of office, but there was no change either in the fortunes of war or in policy under his successor, General Koiso Kuniaki (1880–1950). General

Koiso remained in office until April 1945, when he was succeeded by Admiral Suzuki Kantarō (1867–1948). Some civilian leaders sent out peace feelers to the Allies, but their efforts were hampered by the noncooperation of the Soviet Union, anxious to have the war continue long enough to allow it to participate, and by the demand issued at Potsdam in July 1945, insisting on Japan's unconditional surrender.

This demand reflected the Allied belief that it had been a mistake to allow World War I to end in an armistice rather than in a full capitulation, permitting Hitler to claim that Germany had been "betrayed" into defeat, not beaten on the field of battle. Determined not to commit a similar mistake, the Allies now demanded an unconditional surrender, which stiffened the resistance of Japanese leaders concerned about the fate of the emperor.

The last year of the war was especially terrible; on one night in March 1945, some 100,000 people died as the result of a firebomb raid on Tokyo, and a similar raid in May devastated another large part of Japan's capital city. Meanwhile, bombers created an "iron-storm" over Okinawa, sending local people to seek refuge in caves, where some would perish after Japanese soldiers forced them into "compulsory group suicide."[11] Short of resources, and with its cities in ruins, during the last months of the war Japan was reduced to desperate measures, such as the use of flying bombs directed by suicide pilots, called "kamikaze" after the "divine wind" that once had saved the land from the Mongols.

Tokyo and other major cities had been practically leveled by conventional bombing, but on August 6 the United States dropped an atomic bomb on Hiroshima (see Figure 21.5)

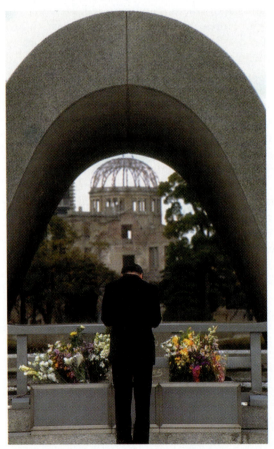

**FIGURE 21.5** *Hiroshima.* Through the vault over the Memorial Cenotaph for the Atomic Bomb Victims can be seen the Atomic Bomb Memorial Dome. The steel skeleton of the dome and the gutted building (formerly the city's Industrial Promotion Hall) have been left standing unaltered, in witness to the tragedy. (© John Van Hasselt/Corbis Sygma)

in southwestern Honshu, razing more than 80 percent of the buildings and leaving some 200,000 people dead or injured and countless others to continue their lives under the specter of radiation sickness. Two days later, on August 8, the Soviet Union entered the war, and the next day the United States dropped a second atomic bomb, this time on Nagasaki.

Recent scholarship shows that all along the emperor paid careful attention to the war without intervening in actual military operations. But now his throne was at stake, as Edward J. Drea explains:

> In the face of total defeat, he valued the imperial institution more than his people, his army, and his empire. . . . Perhaps more than fire raids, atomic bombs, the Soviet entry into the war against Japan, and the specter of invasion, it was the threat to his imperial ancestors, and therefore the survival of the imperial institution itself, that provided the steel otherwise missing from Hirohito's regal backbone.[12]

In any case, twice during these fateful days a government deadlock was broken by the personal intervention of the emperor, each time in favor of peace. Even after the final decision for peace, diehards tried to continue the war by a last resort to violence in the tradition of the terrorists who had first helped steer Japan toward militarism and war. They set fire to the homes of the prime minister and president of the Privy Council and invaded the imperial palace in search of the recording of the emperor's peace message, but they failed. When all was lost, several leaders, including the war minister, committed ritual suicide.

On August 15, the imperial recording was broadcast over the radio, and throughout Japan the people, for the first time, heard the voice of their emperor. In the formal language appropriate to his elevated status, he informed them that the war was lost. This is how Ōe Kenzaburō, the future winner of the Nobel Prize for literature, ten years old at the time, recollects the effect of the broadcast:

> The adults sat around their radios and cried. The children gathered outside in the dusty road and whispered their bewilderment. We were most confused and disappointed by the fact that the Emperor had spoken in a human voice, no different from any adult's. None of us understood what he was saying, but we had all heard his voice. One of my friends could even imitate it cleverly. Laughing, we surrounded him—a twelve-year-old in grimy shorts who spoke with the Emperor's voice. A minute later we felt afraid. We looked at one another; no one spoke. How could we believe that an august presence of such awful power had become an ordinary human voice on a designated summer day.[13]

# *Notes*

1. The term "incantatory symbol" comes from Masao Maruyama, in Ivan Morris, ed., *Thought and Behavior in Modern Japanese Politics,* expanded edition (New York: Oxford Univ. Press, 1969), p. 376.

2. Stuart R. Schram, *The Political Thought of Mao Tse-tung* (New York: Frederick A. Praeger, 1963), p. 209.

3. Jerome Ch'en, *Mao and the Chinese Revolution* (New York: Oxford Univ. Press, 1965), p. 337.

4. Joshua A. Fogel, "Introduction," in Joshua A. Fogel, ed., *The Nanjing Massacre in History and Historiography* (Berkeley: Univ. of California Press, 2000), p. 6.

5. Alvin D. Coox, in Peter Duus, ed., *The Cambridge History of Japan, Vol. 6: The Twentieth Century* (Cambridge: Cambridge Univ. Press, 1988), p. 324.

6. Michael A. Barnhart, *Japan Prepares for Total War: The Search for Economic Security, 1919–1941* (Ithaca: Cornell Univ. Press, 1987), p. 234.

7. Ann Waswo, in *The Cambridge History of Japan, Vol. 6,* p. 104.

8. Kamei Katsuichiro, quoted in Kevin Michael Doak, *Dreams of Difference: The Japan Romantic School and the Crisis of Modernity* (Berkeley: Univ. of California Press, 1994), p. 101.

9. Sheldon Garon, *Molding Japanese Minds: The State in Everyday Life* (Princeton: Princeton Univ. Press, 1997), pp. 84–87.

10. Mark R. Peattie, in *The Cambridge History, Vol. 6,* p. 269. For "mutant colonialism," see p. 234.

11. Norma Field, *In the Realm of a Dying Emperor: Japan at Century's End* (New York: Vintage Books, 1993), p. 61.

12. Edward J. Drea, *In the Service of the Emperor: Essays on the Imperial Japanese Army* (Lincoln: Univ. of Nebraska Press, 1998), p. 215.

13. Ōe Kenzaburō, *A Personal Matter,* John Nathan, trans. (New York: Grove Press, 1968), pp. vii–viii.

# Part Six

# East Asia since World War II

*T*hroughout East Asia, as across the globe, World War II was followed by a period of change unprecedented in its rapidity and scope, affecting the direction of civilization, economic systems, social structure, and the lives of millions of people. The war destroyed the Japanese Empire, confirmed the eclipse of the Western European powers begun by World War I, and hastened the end of the old colonialism. In Asia, the British Empire was dismantled as India and Burma attained independence (1947) followed by the Malay Peninsula (1957), leaving only Hong Kong as a Crown Colony—and it reverted as scheduled to Chinese rule in 1997. However, the Dutch in Indonesia and especially the French in Indochina resorted to military means in futile attempts to preserve their colonies.

The war left only two superpowers, the United States and the Soviet Union, with the capacity to exercise major influence over events in East Asia. By 1947 they had developed a bitter rivalry and a "cold" war. I. M. Roberts wrote the following:

> Even if the Cold War stopped short of actual armed conflict between the two principals, subversion, bribery, murder, espionage, propaganda and diplomatic quarrelling long gave fresh colour to the basic premise, that it was impossible for Communist and non-Communist societies to cooperate and relate to one another in the way civilized societies had once believed to be normal."[1]

The end of the Cold War in 1989 left only one superpower, the United States, but brought on new crises and challenges domestically and internationally, marked by Tiananmen in China and the death of the emperor in Japan.

The dynamics of yin and yang interacting, with a dash of each in the other, can represent numerous processes past and present. The image suggests cyclical change but also the generation of the new—birth and rebirth. It invites the viewer to reflect on just how it may apply to our own time, in China and Japan and at home.

# The Aftermath of the War and Unfinished Business

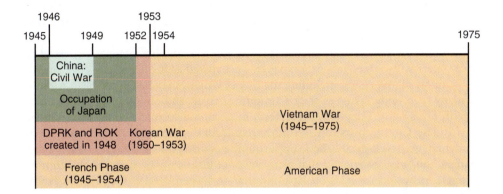

The effect of the war on Japan and China was profound. In both cases, the political and social system was transformed—although, at least initially, the changes appeared to cut much deeper in China than in Japan. Now, from the perspective of a new century, we can detect more continuities in both countries than were evident to the actors at the time. This may be a product of historical hindsight but should not obscure that the people who lived through these years experienced them as revolutionary.

Postwar change was immediate in Japan, but it took another four difficult years for the end of the war to establish a new order in China. Because for most people in China, the end of the war brought more of the same, we begin there and then describe a newly important Taiwan before considering Japan. In Korea and Vietnam, the aftermath of the war was long and bitter: for each, it took another war to determine their trajectories once they were freed from Japanese domination. They belong in our book because of their importance for China and Japan, for the broader history of the region during a period of hot and cold war, and for America's role in that history.

# China: Civil War and Communist Triumph (1946–1949)

When Japan surrendered, Chiang Kai-shek, with American concurrence, directed Japan's generals in China to submit only to Nationalist forces. To enable the GMD armies to accept the Japanese surrender, the United States transported them by water and by air to those parts of the country then occupied by Japan. However, they were not allowed into Manchuria until January 1946. Manchuria had been occupied by the Soviet Union during the last days of the war, and the Soviets, intent on harvesting the Japanese military and industrial assets there, did not completely withdraw their troops until May 1946. By that time, they had allowed the C.C.P. to gain substantial control of the Manchurian countryside. Chiang, determined to recover the territory in which the Japanese had begun their aggression in 1931, disregarded American warnings against overextending his forces and dispatched almost half a million of his best troops to Manchuria.

During the year or so immediately after the war, the Nationalists appeared to have superior resources, at least on paper. Recognized as the legitimate government of China by all the Allies, including the Soviet Union, they had three or four times as many men under arms as their Communist rivals and enjoyed a similar advantage in armament. They were, therefore, in no mood to make concessions to the C.C.P. The Communists, on the other hand, had come through the war battle-hardened, with well-established support in the countryside and high morale. Their leaders, too, were convinced that victory would ultimately be theirs in the coming struggle. It was against this background that, in December 1945, President Harry S. Truman sent General George C. Marshall to China to attempt to mediate between the two parties. Given their history of conflict, divergence of views, and confidence in their respective causes, the American initiative was probably doomed from the start. General Marshall's efforts were also undercut by American support of the Nanjing government, even though President Truman stipulated that large-scale aid to China was contingent on a settlement. As during Mao Zedong's visit to Chongqing from August through October (see Figure 22.1), there was a show of cordiality, but the Marshall mission produced only a brief breathing spell before fighting broke out in earnest in mid-1946.

Initially, until July 1947, the GMD armies enjoyed success, even capturing the wartime C.C.P. capital at Yan'an. However, these were hollow victories. Like the Japanese before them, in northern China and Manchuria the GMD controlled only the cities amid a hostile countryside. Moreover, the military efficacy of the armies was undermined by the rivalries among their commanders, by Chiang's penchant for personal decision making even when he was far from the scene, and by his abiding concern to prevent any possible rival from amassing too much power. Also much in evidence were the harshness and corruption that had sapped the soldiers' morale during the war against Japan; these were even more demoralizing now that they were supposed to fight fellow Chinese.

In other respects, too, far from stimulating reform, the defeat of Japan merely transferred to the rest of China the ills that had been incubating in wartime Chongqing. A nation badly in need of political, economic, and social reconstruction was subjected to a heavy dose of autocracy and to a galloping inflation. Liberal reformers, disillusioned by the corruption and alarmed at the prospect of civil war, tried to rally the opposition. One leader of this non-Communist opposition to the GMD was Wen Yiduo (1899–1946), a professor at Qinghua University on its wartime campus in Kunming who tried to encourage those who hoped for a rebirth of democracy and greater freedom to criticize the government. However, the GMD responded to these calls for reform by assassinating the critics. In 1946, GMD agents assassinated Wen just after he gave a fiery eulogy for one of his mur-

**FIGURE 22.1** Mao Zedong (left) and Chiang Kai-shek exchange toasts at Chongqing during a welcoming party for Mao Zedong. August–October 1945. (© Bettman/Corbis [BE046254].)

dered colleagues. Wen's death shocked China and exposed the depths to which the ruling group had sunk in its desperation to retain power.[2]

Intellectuals and students were not the only ones disenchanted with the regime; many suffered from the arrogance of the Nationalist soldiers and the rapacity of those with political connections. The situation was particularly bad in Taiwan, where carpetbaggers from the mainland enriched themselves at the expense of alleged Taiwanese "collaborators"—a convenient charge against any uncooperative Taiwanese who had done well during the preceding half-century of Japanese rule. When the Taiwanese rioted in protest in 1947, the Nationalist government responded with brutal and bloody repression. The exact number of casualties is unknown; however, Taiwanese leaders in exile claimed that more than 10,000 were killed.

The government, inefficient and autocratic, proved unable to halt rapidly accelerating inflation that threatened all whose incomes did not keep up with rising costs. Toward the end, people in the cities had to carry enormous bundles of paper money on their daily rounds of shopping for the necessities of life.

In the C.C.P. areas, in contrast, a disciplined and well-organized political and military leadership offered credible leadership. Unlike the GMD, which promised reform only after the fighting was finished, the C.C.P. implemented one change after another. A crucial and impressive demonstration of their expertise in mass

**FIGURE 22.2** *Seizing the Landlord and Transporting His Movable Property.* Dongbeizhibao, October 9, 1947. Energized by the Chinese Communist Party's campaign for land redistribution, local populations reversed the traditional power structures. (From *Anvil of Victory: The Communist Revolution in Manchuria, 1945–1948,* by Steven Levine. Courtesy Columbia University Press.)

mobilization took place in Manchuria, where they made the most of the window of opportunity granted them by the Soviet Union before it withdrew. Here, once their military presence was established, they were able in a mere eighteen months to transform indifferent, suspicious peasants into ardent participants in and supporters of the party and of the military campaigns directed by the brilliant general Lin Biao (1907–1971). Cooperation was secured by a mixture of hope and fear that varied with groups and individuals. Party cadres led a series of carefully orchestrated campaigns attacking and systematically displacing the old local elite that could no longer summon support from a provincial or regional elite undermined and compromised during the preceding fourteen years of Japanese rule. The campaigns culminated in land redistribution (see Figure 22.2), which revolutionized the local power structure.

The contrast between C.C.P. dynamism and GMD decay helps explain not only the outcome but also the unexpected rapidity of the course of events. The military turning point came in July 1947 when Communist armies attacked along several fronts in northern China. In Manchuria, Lin Biao commanded a campaign that put the GMD forces on the defensive and ended in October 1948 by completely routing them. During that same month and into November, the last great battle of the war was fought at the strategic city of Xuzhou on the Huai River where the Beijing-Nanjing Railway line joins the Longhai line that runs from Shaanxi to the sea. Around half a million men on each side were involved in this battle, generally known as the battle of Huai-Hai after the Huai River and the Longhai Railway. When it was over, the Nationalists, under Chiang's personal command, had lost 200,000 men and no longer had any way to supply their forces to the north. In January 1949, Nationalist generals surrendered Beijing and

Tianjin. Throughout the campaigns, the Communist army not only gained military advantages from its victories but also captured valuable military equipment and supplies and increased its manpower as Nationalist soldiers defected or surrendered and were incorporated into the People's Liberation Army.

During 1949 the Communists continued their advance. They crossed the Yangzi River in April, took Nanjing the same month, and were in control of Shanghai by the end of May. On October 1, Mao, in a great ceremony in Beijing, formally proclaimed the establishment of the People's Republic of China (P.R.C.). There was still some fighting in the south, but clearly the C.C.P. had won control of the Chinese mainland. Meanwhile, Chiang and the Nationalists took refuge on Taiwan and vowed continued resistance.

The triumph of the Communists in 1949 began a new chapter in China's long history. It was the result of a long revolutionary process that had started well before the founding of the C.C.P., but in terms of the party's programs and goals, the revolution had only just begun.

# Taiwan

Taiwan's history requires separate consideration because it differs from that of the mainland, because it continues to play a difficult and prominent role in the dynamics of the region, and because it forms part of the history of both China and Japan. Its story of modern transformation also merits study in its own right.

When Japan acquired Taiwan as its first colony in 1895, it did so with many of the objectives that subsequently prompted it to seize Korea, and the Japanese implemented many of the same policies in both colonies. Consequently, the inhabitants of the island shared many of the experiences of their fellow colonials, but in the final analysis the differences between Taiwan and Korea, then as now, loom at least as large as the similarities.

One difference was that in 1895 the people on Taiwan were given two years in which to decide whether to stay on as Japanese colonials or to move to the mainland as subjects of the Qing. The latter choice proved attractive to many local elite. This included men who had staked their future on the examination system, because by the time of the Japanese takeover the "gentrification"[3] of what had once been a frontier elite was well advanced. To serve their needs, between 1860 and 1893 fourteen academies had been established on the island, which only in 1885 had been elevated to provincial status.

The departure of 6400 people, about 2.3 percent of the population, no doubt removed some potential leaders of resistance, but as it was, the Japanese occupation began with five months of fighting. The Taiwanese, however, lacked coordination. The "Republic of Taiwan," declared by the last Qing governor, lasted only twelve days. Until 1902 the Japanese faced occasional scattered attacks. Even after Japanese authority had been firmly established over the Han (ethnic Chinese) population (2,890,455 according to the 1905 census), armed clashes continued with Taiwan's original inhabitants (estimated at 122,000 in 1909), who occupied the central highlands and continued to lose ground as they had under the Qing. It was their misfortune that their forest contained camphor trees. Camphor, turned into a government monopoly by Japan, was a prime export, in great demand for use in the manufacture of smokeless gunpowder.

As in Korea, in Taiwan the governor-general was the supreme administrative and judicial authority. Until 1919 he was a military man, but from 1898 to 1906 civil administration was in the hands of Gotō Shimpei (1857–1929), a medical man responsible for much of the basic framework of the Japanese colonial system. A major objective, accomplished by 1905, was for Taiwan to pay for itself despite continuing heavy government expenditures. To rationalize their administration, the Japanese conducted a land survey and a census. As they did later in Korea, the colonial authorities relied heavily on the police for a range of services, including tax collection, agricultural, hygiene, water supply, and sanitation services. But in Taiwan, unlike in Korea, the Japanese controlled these matters by cleverly adapting an old Chinese system of mutual responsibility (*baojia*), under which the population was organized into groups of (theoretically) 100 households, each composed of units of 10. In contrast to the ineffectiveness of this system on the mainland, in Taiwan the *hokō* system (pronouncing the term the Japanese way) became the instrument by which the state reached down into the villages to affect each individual, something beyond the ability of all Chinese mainland governments before 1949. Only the Han population was organized in this manner.

The *hokō*, together with earlier guard units composed of Han settlers and acculturated aborigines, supplied the manpower for a local militia that acted as police auxiliaries. They not only provided security and surveillance but also undertook road repair and even railroad maintenance, as well as contributing to various rural campaigns. They also constituted a heavy burden on the population, who, in addition to the regular taxes, were saddled with *hokō* dues and had to supply labor when needed. Although nominally the *hokō* leaders were elected by the households, the system was controlled by the police, which came to include 20 to 30 percent Taiwanese but remained firmly under Japanese command.

The Japanese developed the Taiwan economy but did so to meet their own needs and serve their own purposes. A central bank (The Bank of Taiwan, 1899) issued currency and sought to manage the economy. By the time Japan acquired Taiwan, it was an exporter of tea and sugar, as well as camphor, but the sugar industry was faltering. The Japanese changed that, turning Taiwan into a major producer of sugar able to fulfill their domestic needs and thus saving foreign exchange that otherwise would have gone for sugar imports. Along with tea, the Japanese fostered rice cultivation and initiated irrigation projects. They also did much to develop the network of roads and railways, and they improved the harbors for ocean shipping. Modern postal and telegraph systems were established. Beginning with Gotō, they were also active in public health. The death rate was reduced, and by 1945 the population almost doubled.

Consumer industries included food processing, logging, and textiles, but not until Japan began preparing for total war did heavy industry start. The completion of the Sun Moon Lake Electrical Generation Plan (1935) was a milestone. Aluminum, textiles, iron, cement, and chemical industries grew in what nevertheless remained an essentially agrarian economy.

As in Korea, there were local people of wealth and education who worked with the Japanese-dominated establishment. There was an ambivalence about education. True, schools were established, but initially there were only lower-level and inferior schools for the Taiwanese, in contrast to the higher levels of education available to Japanese who settled in Taiwan. In 1928, an imperial university was established in Taipei, but it had three times as many Japanese students as it did Taiwanese. In 1945 there was only one Taiwanese professor on its faculty.

As shown by the establishment of the university, there was a relaxation of control in the 1920s, followed by the severity of the 1930s. In the 1920s, Japanese liberals talked of eventual assimilation, and there was a temporary and limited loosening of the colonial reins, with greater tolerance for Taiwanese to express their own views at home and in Tokyo. In 1921 a Taiwanese intellectual even demanded the abolition of the *hokō* system. Although some changes were made, it was not abolished until two months before Japan surrendered in 1945. To follow Siomi Shunji's analysis, from 1895 to 1920 the police were the prime movers, but during the next quarter of a century they were a background force.[4]

Stimulated by developments in China and Japan, there was a quickening of intellectual life in Taiwan and among Taiwanese in Tokyo, with movements to forge a new and modern culture and to write in the vernacular about current concerns. The main character of the first novel written by Lai Ho (1894–1943), often considered the father of modern Taiwanese literature, was a Taiwanese vegetable seller whose small manual scale for weighing out his sales was broken in two by Japanese policemen. A central issue facing Lai and a new generation of younger writers trying to forge a Taiwanese identity was that of language, because classical Chinese was rapidly becoming obsolete and the new literary language that gained currency on the mainland after the May Fourth Movement was based on a vernacular incomprehensible to the people of Taiwan. Lai himself was really most at home in classical Chinese, which he had to translate into the local vernacular.

One solution was to write in Japanese. From the start, the Japanese had encouraged people to learn Japanese, and by the 1930s there was a substantial audience for writers such as Wu Cho-liu (1900–1976), whose *An Orphan of Asia* expressed a sense that Taiwan had been abandoned by its Chinese parents and never become a full-fledged member of the Japanese household in which it now found itself. The problem of defining Taiwan's place in the world was to persist long after the Japanese were gone.

As in Korea, during the 1930s and especially during the war there were campaigns to have Taiwanese adopt Japanese names and worship at Shinto shrines, but these did not make them first-class subjects of the emperor. Taiwanese men fought in the imperial army, and Taiwanese living on the China coast enjoyed status as Japanese subjects, forming an imperial vanguard much as Korean settlers did in Manchuria. However, many Taiwanese suffered under the heavy hand of Japanese rule. Like the people in Japan itself, they were surprised by the defeat of Japan but welcomed reversion to Chinese rule, even though they had not been consulted. We have already noted their bitter disappointment.

# Japan: The Occupation (1945–1952)

The war left Japan in ruins, its cities largely destroyed, the economy wrecked. About 40 percent of Japan's total urban area was wiped out, including 65 percent of residential housing in Tokyo, 57 percent in Osaka, and 89 percent in Nagoya, Japan's third largest city. At the time of the surrender there were 9 million homeless. There was hunger, despair, psychic shock, and fear. In preparation for the arrival of the victors, the Japanese evacuated many women to the countryside, and even the government ordered its female employees out of town. It is not difficult to imagine people's relief when such measures turned out to have been unnecessary.

## Means and Ends

Officially, the Occupation was under the authority of the Far Eastern Commission, which sat in Washington, D.C. Its members included representatives of all the countries that had fought Japan, but actual control was in American hands. The Japanese government continued to function, but it did so according to the directives and "suggestions" of the Occupation authorities, headed by General Douglas MacArthur, Supreme Commander for the Allied Powers (SCAP). Despite the "Allied Powers" in the title and the presence of some British and Commonwealth officials, the Occupation was essentially American. In General MacArthur it had a leader who won easy credibility—a commanding figure, a "blue-eyed shogun" convinced of his historic mission, and a military man who commanded respect, exuded confidence, and had a flair for drama. The process of policy formation was complex, involving Washington, the Occupation bureaucracy, and the Japanese and reflecting divisions within and among these groups. But General MacArthur had a strong hand in fashioning, interpreting, and administering policy.

The Occupation's mission to demilitarize Japan and turn the country into a peaceful and democratic state was accepted with enthusiasm by a staff composed partly of New Dealers and by General MacArthur, who regarded the Japanese as an immature people ready for and in need of tutelage. Despite or because of their lack of preparation, the Americans were convinced they had the answers, and their conviction of the righteousness of their values and policies remained firm, even after the onset of the Cold War induced them to change course.

At the outset, the Occupation faced the pressing tasks of disarming the Japanese military and providing enough relief to prevent famine. The widespread destruction of capital goods and industrial plants, a soil starved for lack of fertilizers, the loss of the natural resources from the former empire and of the entire merchant fleet, and the need to feed around 6 million Japanese expatriates and refugees from overseas threatened economic catastrophe. In this situation, suffering was unavoidable. By supplying food and medical supplies, the Occupation authorities helped avert the worst, but the alternative to the black market was starvation. It was not until 1947 that the United States became seriously concerned with rebuilding the Japanese economy. Even in 1948 a magazine editorial complained, "in today's Japan, the only people who are not living illegally are those in jail."[5]

Demilitarization entailed dismantling the military establishment and purging from positions of political and economic leadership those most closely associated with leading the country to war. Outside Japan—and excluding the Soviet Union and parts of China controlled by the C.C.P.—5700 individuals were tried by fifty military tribunals with the result that 984 were sentenced to death, among them 173 Taiwanese and 148 Koreans. Twenty-eight top leaders charged with responsibility for the war were tried in Tokyo by an international tribunal of eleven judges that sat in Tokyo from May 1946 to April 1948 and included a Chinese, a Filipino, and an Indian jurist but no Korean. When the sentences were handed down in November 1948, seven leaders were condemned to die, including Tōjō Hideki, the rather colorless general who had headed Japan's wartime government. His role during the war had been more like a chairman of the board than a dictator, but wartime propaganda had cast him as a Japanese Hitler. The lengthy judicial proceedings produced voluminous records but never attained the legal clarity or the moral authority achieved by the trial of Nazi leaders at Nuremberg.

In the end, around 200,000 persons were purged, about half of them from the military. However, most of these men were later reinstated, and some became prominent. The military elite lost the most, but the decision of the Occupation to operate through, rather than to replace, the existing government made for a high level of continuity within the bureaucracy. This contributed to the continuing importance of the bureaucracy even after a new constitution placed government on a new footing.

Although he had sanctioned a war fought in his name, the emperor was not charged with war crimes, nor was there a judicial inquiry into the part he had played. Instead, SCAP's policy was to use the emperor's authority yet demystify his person and throne. He was pressured to substitute a more open lifestyle (akin to that of the British monarch) for the secluded and ritualized existence traditionally led by Japanese emperors. An example of the demystification process was the emperor's unprecedented visit to General MacArthur at SCAP headquarters. The resulting photograph (see Figure 22.3), showing the stiffly formal emperor standing next to the open-shirted general, caused considerable shock and dismay throughout Japan. In his New Year's message of 1946, the emperor publicly denied his divinity, and under the new constitution he became a symbol of the nation. For the remainder of his life he never acknowledged any responsibility for the war, setting an example not lost on his subjects.

This constitution, which went into effect in May 1947, was drafted and practically dictated by the Occupation. It stipulated that sovereignty belongs to the people, placed the highest political authority in the hands of the Diet (to which the executive was now made responsible), and established an independent judiciary. Another noteworthy set of political changes were those decreasing the power of the central government, particularly the Home Ministry, and fostering local self-

**FIGURE 22.3** General Douglas MacArthur, Supreme Commander for the Allied Powers (SCAP) occupation forces, and Emperor Hirohito of Japan, soon to publicly deny his divinity. (© AP/Wide World Photos [APA5163982])

government. Accompanying these structural changes were provisions for universal suffrage and human rights, including the equality of women. A unique feature was the renunciation of war. Article IX stipulates, "The Japanese people forever renounce war as a sovereign right of the nation and the threat or use of force as a means of settling international disputes," and it goes on to say, "land, sea, and air forces, as well as other war potential, will never be maintained."[6] In this way, the authors of the constitution sought to incorporate peacefulness into the very framework of the new Japanese state.

## Social Policies

The authorities at SCAP headquarters knew that Japan could not be turned into a democracy simply by changing the political system. Consequently, they tried to change Japanese society. Because many American officials lacked previous study or experience in Japan, they tended to rely excessively on American prototypes without taking into sufficient account Japan's own experience and situation. Thus, they restructured the educational system to conform to the American sequence of elementary school, junior high school, high school, and college, and they forced the Japanese to eliminate their old technical schools and special higher schools, which previously covered the eleventh to thirteenth years of education and prepared students for university study. Under the old system, only the student elite had access to a university education, but under the new, all students were to be given equal educational opportunities through high school. In an effort to expand opportunities for higher education, many of the old technical and higher schools were upgraded to become universities. But these new universities were not of a quality comparable to the old, established schools, such as Tokyo University. Competition for admission to this and other prestigious universities remained brutal. Students found themselves embroiled in a veritable "examination hell."

To reform the content of education, the Occupation abolished the old ethics courses and purged textbooks fostering militaristic and authoritarian values. Its attack on these old values was rather successful, especially because they had already been largely discredited by defeat. Similarly, language reform found ready acceptance: the list of standard characters, many of them simplified, issued by the Cabinet in 1946 (1850 *tōyō kanji*) required only minor modifications and additions when revised in 1981 (the current system of 1945 *jōyō kanji*).

The Occupation was less successful in its attempts to create a positive sense of individual civic responsibility and citizenship. Social change entails a transformation of values, and thus naturally takes longer than institutional change, but changes in the legal system can encourage social change. Among the Occupation's notable efforts in this direction were measures to enhance the status of women and to limit the powers and privileges of the family's male head. The new constitution stated explicitly in Article XXIV, "Marriage shall be based upon the mutual consent of both sexes, and it shall be maintained through mutual cooperation, with equal rights of husband and wife as a basis." The presence of thousands of Americans in their country also gave the Japanese an unusual opportunity to observe foreign mores. It may have encouraged them to become somewhat more relaxed toward authority, and it stimulated a measure of cosmopolitanism.

## Economic Policy

It was generally recognized that the desired political and social changes demanded an economic foundation, and the authorities set about restructuring the Japanese economy. Most successful in this respect was the program of land reform. This prohibited absentee landlordism and restricted the amount of land a resident landowner could hold to a maximum of seven acres to work himself and another two acres to rent out (except in Hokkaido, where the average farm was twelve acres, because the climate precludes intensive rice cultivation). Anything in excess had to be sold to the government, which resold it to former tenants. There was provision for compensation for the landlords, but inflation made this meaningless. The old inequity in the countryside was eliminated. In terms of productivity, too, the land policy was a success, because the agrarian sector was the first to recover.

In the urban industrial sector, the Occupation began by trying to eliminate, or at least reduce, the concentrations of economic power, which Americans viewed as a major component of Japanese authoritarianism. One policy was to foster labor unions. The constitution guaranteed the right of workers to organize and to bargain and act collectively. As intended, a vigorous union movement developed, but contrary to American wishes, the Japanese unions did not, like the American Federation of Labor and Congress of Industrial Organizations, limit themselves to economic demands. Much like European unions, they were political in orientation, developing into labor arms of the Socialist and Communist parties. In February 1947, the Occupation banned a planned general strike and thereafter was less friendly toward the unions. Laws prohibiting public employees from striking followed.

On the management and ownership side, the Occupation did break up the old holding companies and purged the old *zaibatsu* families from positions of economic leadership. Contrary to initial expectations, however, this did not lead to genuine decentralization. Where old systems were broken up, new and equally pervasive patterns of trade and finance developed, bearing a marked resemblance to the old. Furthermore, a plan to break up operating companies petered out: of 1200 companies initially considered, only 28 were, in the end, split apart. Economic power and decision making remained concentrated. The reasons for this are instructive for understanding the accomplishments and failures of the Occupation as a whole, because they include both a Japanese and an American component.

On the Japanese side, strong support for land reform contrasted with a marked lack of enthusiasm for American-style trust busting. Few shared the American faith in the ultimate benefits of maximum competition. Instead, the feeling was that Japanese companies needed to be large to compete in the international market. Radicals and conservatives disagreed about ownership and control, not about the structure of industry and commerce.

Decentralization of the economy also faltered because it was abandoned with a shift in American policy already signaled by the ban on the 1947 general strike. In an atmosphere of mounting Cold War tension and in line with what is frequently called the "reverse course," economic and strategic considerations prevailed. Increasingly, the United States saw Japan, called by the secretary of state "the workshop of Asia," as a potentially valuable and much-needed ally after the victory of the Chinese Communists in 1949. On the advice of Joseph Dodge, a Detroit banker sent out by Washington in 1949, in April of that year the value of the yen was set at 360 to the dollar—low even then—to encourage exports by making Japanese goods inexpensive abroad and to promote frugality at home. In May, the Ministry of International Trade and Industry (MITI) was formed by merging the Ministry of Commerce and Industry and the Board of Trade, "constituting a greater centralization of economic authority than had been achieved at the peak of Japan's mobilization for war."[7] Meanwhile, the Ministry of Finance exercised paramount sway over budgets and monetary policy. Both would continue playing these roles long after the Occupation ended.

More than labor and economic policies were affected by the policy shift. Communists were purged (1949–1950), and others who had been purged earlier were allowed to reemerge in public life. Because an armed ally, capable at least of self-defense, would be more valuable than an unarmed one, the United States had second thoughts about Japan's renunciation of military force.

Dodge's deflationary policies led to economic decline until the outbreak of the Korean War in June 1950 brought a flood of orders for equipment and supplies, a procurement boom that gave an enormous boost to the faltering economy. Even after the war, orders to supply American troops and bases continued to benefit the Japanese economy. Under American encouragement, Japan also created a paramilitary force of 75,000.

## The End of the Occupation

The end of the Occupation, a subject broached by General MacArthur as early as 1947, was delayed largely because of Soviet opposition. Although the Occupation continued, by the time General MacArthur took command in Korea in July 1950, its work was practically complete. Dismissed by President Truman, he departed from East Asia for good in April 1951. Although in his subsequent testimony to Congress he spoke glowingly of the Japanese, they were distressed to hear him compare them with children.

Under the Occupation, electoral politics was reintroduced, and political parties representing a broad range of ideas and a variety of interests battled for votes. The Diet again became the central arena for national politics. The leading political personality to emerge during the Occupation was Yoshida Shigeru (1878–1967), a former diplomat who had opposed the military leadership in Japan during the 1930s. Yoshida dominated Japanese politics for the better part of a decade, serving as prime minister in 1946 and 1947 and again from 1948 to 1954. A coalition of conservatives and socialists of various shades of radicalism held power briefly in 1947 and 1948 but was unable to create a viable government, partly because of divisions within its ranks and partly because of Occupation hostility toward socialism. Upon reassuming the prime ministership, Yoshida called a new election. Held in 1949, it provided his Liberal party with an absolute majority.

It was Yoshida who signed the peace treaty in San Francisco in September 1951, which was ratified the following April and accompanied by a defense treaty that provided for American bases in Japan and continued occupation of Okinawa. At the insistence of the U.S. Senate, Japan signed a parallel treaty with the Chinese nationalists on Taiwan and agreed to follow the American policy of nonrecognition and containment of the P.R.C. The Soviet Union was not a party to the San Francisco treaty. Formal diplomatic relations were established in 1956, but Moscow and Tokyo could not agree on the disposition of four small islands and entered the twenty-first century without ever signing a peace treaty to conclude World War II.

Assessments of the Occupation must naturally take into account later history because so many institutions and practices of contemporary Japan are rooted in this period. What came to be known as the Japanese model of bureaucratic capitalism has been dubbed the "SCAPanese model."[8] Some people think the reforms went too far and too fast, and others deplore the "reverse course" taken in response to the Cold War and the persistence of certain traditional institutions and patterns. These include the treatment and retention of the emperor, the role of the bureaucracy, the relationship between government and business, and the failure to adhere strictly to Article IX.

What seems clear is that the Occupation brought about major changes, but it was most successful in areas in which there were Japanese precedents and substantial support. This was true of much of the political program, the land reform, and the advocacy of liberal values. Representative institutions, after all, went back to the nineteenth century, and demands for land reform, calls for equality, and opposition to authoritarianism all predate the rise of militarism. The movement for women's rights had begun in the 1910s. Despite misconceptions and mistakes, and despite the contradiction inherent in a plan to foster democracy by command, much of what the Occupation attempted took hold.

The Occupation also had unplanned side effects, including the influx of foreign culture. Intellectuals who were eager to catch up with the recent Western developments devoured translations of Western books. Many turned to Marxism, but the whole spectrum of ideas found translators and readers. Popular culture was more open than ever to foreign influence. In some respects, the scene resembled that after World War I. It did not take the Occupation to introduce the Japanese to baseball and jazz. However, this time change went deeper, and there was to be no radical turning away such as took place in the 1930s. If anything, the doors and windows opened by defeat and occupation are even more widely open today.

# II. Unfinished Business: Korea and Vietnam

*The Korean War*

*International Relations After the Korean War*

*Vietnam*

*The Vietnam War (1946–1975) and Its Aftermath*

Korea's last decade under Japanese rule was a bitter one. The Japanese relentlessly stamped out Korean nationalism, sending its leaders into prison, exile, or underground activities. In the late 1930s the Japanese expanded their suppression of political nationalism into an attack on Korean cultural identity. In line with a policy of total forced cultural assimilation, they stopped Korean language instruction in all secondary schools in 1938, and soon elementary schools followed suit. No longer could Korean children learn their own language in school; the use of Japanese was mandatory. In 1940 the Korean press was closed down. The Japanese made strong efforts to propagate state Shinto as the official state religion of Korea. To help the war effort, they first launched a movement of voluntary conscription. Then, in 1943, military service became compulsory. The Koreans had to bear the hardships and deprivations of war.

During World War II, the United States and the Soviet Union agreed on the thirty-eighth parallel as a dividing line: north of this line the Japanese forces would surrender to Soviet troops; south of the parallel they would submit to the United States. Perhaps the thirty-eighth parallel was selected by Pentagon officers to assure the inclusion of Seoul in the American zone. In any case, when the Soviet army entered the peninsula three weeks before the Americans, they abided by the agreement. What was not clear at the time was that this was to become a semi-permanent dividing line.

In the north the Soviet army backed the creation of a Communist state under Kim Il-sung (1912–1994), a former leader of Korean guerrilla fighters in Manchuria who had spent some time in the Soviet Union and now entered Korea as a major in the Soviet army. Gradually, Kim overcame factionalism among Korean revolutionaries and fashioned a party and government along Soviet lines. Officials and policemen who had served the Japanese were purged. Industry was nationalized with minimal opposition because it had mostly been owned by Japanese. Land reform followed, and a start was made in economic planning. A military force also was created.

In the south, the American army did not arrive until three weeks after the end of the war. The American military government then refused to recognize an existing interim government, suspecting it of pro-Communist or pro-Japanese leanings. The initial American policy was to await the outcome of negotiations for unification, and there seemed hope that these would reach an early settlement when the United States and the Soviet Union agreed on a joint commission to supervise a five-year period of transition to independence of a unified Korea. This plan, however, ran into the vociferous opposition of a group of Korean nationalists who demanded immediate unification, and when the Soviet Union wanted to bar such men from participating in scheduled elections, Soviet–American cooperation came to an end.

The United States then initiated moves to give South Korea a representative government and in the meantime allowed the economic status quo to persist. Because the Japanese had effectively suppressed organized political activity, there was at the end of the war something of a political vacuum. The victor in the battle over who was to fill that vacuum was Syngman Rhee (Yi Sung-man, 1875–1965), a longtime Christian nationalist who had suffered seven years imprisonment as a young man. Forced to leave Korea in 1911, he had lived in exile (mostly in Hawaii) before returning to his native land after Japan's defeat. A strong advocate of immediate unification, Rhee was an eloquent speaker and a capable organizer. He was also strongly antileftist. In August 1948, the septuagenarian Rhee became president of the Republic of Korea, and the American military government came to an end. Thus, Korea was divided into two mutually hostile parts.

# The Korean War

Increasing international tensions between the United States and the Soviet Union and bitter antagonism between the governments of the two Koreas reduced the chances for unification by negotiation. Both the Communist state in the north and the anti-Communist government in the south harbored the ambition to rule the entire country. These ambitions erupted into war in June 1950 when North Korea attacked South Korea.

The period of intense fighting can be divided into three main phases, each with its own subdivisions. First, from June to September 1950, the North Koreans were on the offensive, pushing the South Korean and American forces back until they established a defense perimeter around Pusan from which they could not be dislodged. The second phase began with General MacArthur's amphibious landing at Inchon in September, which led to the recapture of Seoul and then to an offensive intended to unify Korea by force. Then, in November, the Chinese, alarmed by the American advance to the Yalu River and having had their warnings ignored, sent massive "volunteer" armies into Korea. These succeeded in regaining the North but were unable to win control over the South. This became clear in late May 1951, and in July of that year truce talks began. Earlier, in April, President Truman had dismissed General MacArthur, thereby making it clear that America would not extend the war beyond Korea. His dismissal of the eminent and popular general also demonstrated the American system of civil control over the military, a demonstration that had a considerable effect on Japan.

Casualties in this war were heavy on both sides. They included more than 800,000 Koreans (approximately 520,000 North Koreans and 300,000 South Koreans) and probably as many or more Chinese soldiers. The southern forces were sanctioned by the United Nations and fought under a United Nations command, but approximately half of the ground troops and most of the air and naval forces were supplied by the United States, which suffered 142,000 casualties. South Korea supplied two-fifths of the remaining United Nations troops, and thirteen other countries combined to make up the remainder. The truce talks dragged on for two years until an armistice was signed in July 1953. Although marred by incidents, this armistice remains in effect today.

# International Relations after the Korean War

The Korean War did not alter the international configuration of power in East Asia, but it did considerably embitter Sino-American relations. Both sides were now more convinced than ever of the enmity of the other. In the United States, proponents of a moderate China policy were removed from influence and subjected to slander. The American commitment to the Nationalist regime was confirmed.

Taiwan was given economic and military assistance, and in 1954 the United States signed a mutual defense treaty with the GMD government. Meanwhile, American troops remained in Korea and on their bases in Japan and Okinawa. The Chinese, alarmed by these developments, were confirmed of the wisdom of allying themselves with the Soviet Union, with whom they had signed a treaty of friendship and alliance in February 1950, directed at preventing a revival of Japanese aggression. Whereas the Chinese viewed America as an imperialist aggressor, throughout the 1950s many people in the United States, even those in high places, considered the P.R.C. to be little more than a Soviet satellite.

If the Korean War merely solidified alliances already in the making and froze the participants into their Cold War postures, it also enhanced China's international status by demonstrating the ability of its peasant army, a bare year after the triumph of the revolution, to resist the formidable armed might of the United States. Among those impressed with the caliber of the Chinese military were the authors of the official U.S. Marine Corps history, who found much to admire in the Chinese style of semi-guerrilla warfare, with its emphasis on infiltration, deception, and surprise. Within China, the Korean War helped the government to mobilize the people under the banner of national resistance, and it created its share of national heroes. Above all, it meant that the revolution had been tested in foreign and domestic war.

For Japan, the war brought profitable orders for equipment and supplies, a procurement boom that gave a substantial boost to a still faltering economy. Even after the war, orders to supply American troops and bases continued to benefit the Japanese economy. Under American encouragement, Japan also created a paramilitary force of 75,000, a first step toward limited rearmament. A basic pattern of internal economic growth and dependence on the United States for ultimate military protection was set. For decades, Japan continued to take its foreign policy cues from the United States.

During the years after the Korean War, both China and Japan were able to concentrate on domestic development, although this always took place within the parameters of the Cold War. The two leading countries of East Asia remained keenly aware of each other, but they had little to do with each other. Kept apart by Japan's alliance with the United States, oriented toward contrasting models of social and economic development, and influenced by different ideologies, they interacted only sporadically and then in a limited way.

# *Vietnam*

Comparison of Vietnamese history with that of Korean reveals significant similarities and major differences that may help put their postwar histories into perspective. In both countries the traditional rulers and elite looked to China as a model of organization and a source of high culture, but in both cases political independence from China was jealously guarded and cultural identity was maintained. In modern times, both Korea and Vietnam, after unsuccessful Chinese intervention, experienced a period of colonial rule (under the Japanese and the French) that strained and distorted traditional society and failed to prepare the countries for independence. Then, after World War II, both suffered division into two mutually hostile states, each supported by rival international power blocks. In both cases, bitter warfare between north and south ensued, and in each case, massive American participation in aid of the south was a major factor.

On the other hand, Korea and Vietnam differ in climate, terrain, and internal geographic configuration, as well as in their wider cultural and regional settings. Korea's neighbors are China, Japan, and the Soviet Union, whereas Vietnam is a major power in Southeast Asia. Furthermore, there were differences in their experiences under colonialism. For one thing, the Japanese were much closer to the Koreans culturally, geographically, and even in physical appearance than the French were to the Vietnamese. And Japan and France were countries with different histories and traditions. The present situation of the two lands is also different: Korea remains divided, whereas Vietnam is now a unified nation.

French policy in Vietnam was not consistent over the years, and it differed in the north and the south, but in neither area did it provide a viable fusion of either the modern and traditional or the foreign and native. In the center (Annam) and the north (Tonkin), the French maintained "protectorates" with parallel French and Vietnamese systems of administration, although the French had superior authority. Under this arrangement, the French maintained the Nguyen emperor in Hue, with the result that the throne failed to become a symbol of Vietnamese nationalism. Even the examination system, modeled on that of China, was retained until 1919 by what Alexander Woodside has aptly termed "the embalming agency of colonialism."[9] The south (Cochin China), in contrast, was governed as a full colony on French lines by French and French-oriented officials.

The difference between north and south extended to economic organization. In the south, plantations (rice and rubber) developed, creating great economic inequities and dependence on the vagaries of the international market. The northern lowlands were an area of small, fragmented holdings, but here too life became hard as population growth created great and increasing pressures on the land.

In the beginning, resistance to the French came from members of the traditional elite, and it is noteworthy that men of mandarin (elite) background continued to figure prominently in the leadership of Vietnam's national and social revolutions. An important nationalist leader who shared this background was Phan Boi Chao (1867–1940), who studied with Liang Qichao in Japan and hoped to transform Vietnam into a modern state along the lines of Meiji Japan. Japan was also admired by the founders of the Free School of Tonkin, in Hanoi, modeled on Keio University. Here, a Romanized script was used in place of Chinese characters, the examination system was attacked, and modern political and social ideas were disseminated. Opened in 1907, it lasted less than a year before it was forcibly closed by the French.

The French could repress radical ideas, suppress insurrections, and arrest, imprison, or execute their enemies, but they could not breathe life into moribund social and political structures. Nor could they restrict the import of Western ideas to Catholicism: Paris itself was, after all, a major center of Western radicalism. During World War I, 100,000 Vietnamese served in France as soldiers and laborers. Many returned to their native land ready to question the continued legitimacy of colonial rule. The most famous Vietnamese to be influenced by a stay in France was Ho Chi Minh (Nguyen That Thanh, 1890–1969). Ho was already a nationalist before he arrived in France, but it was in Paris that he complemented his nationalism by fusing it with Marxism.

Ho's status in the Vietnamese Revolution is comparable to that of Mao in China, but the Vietnamese leader differed from the Chinese not only in having extensive overseas experience but also in coming from an impoverished but nonetheless distinctly scholar-official family. His father eventually became a district magistrate. In 1911 Ho left Vietnam as a seaman and after a period of travel spent a crucial six years (1917–1923) in France, supporting himself as a gardener, sweeper, waiter, photograph retoucher, and oven stoker. He also became a convinced Marxist and assisted in the founding of the French Communist Party. Subsequently, he went to Moscow and was then sent by the Comintern to assist Borodin in Canton. However, Ho's interest always remained focused on his native Vietnam. In 1930 he succeeded in fusing various groups into the Communist Party of Vietnam (soon changed to Indochina).

Strong ideological foundations, powerful international models, and especially dedication to organizing grass-roots support in the villages were some of the factors that gave the Communists an advantage in their competition for leadership of Vietnam's national revolution. However, in the south, highly organized syncretic religious movements such as the Cao Dai and Hoa Hao sects supplied many of the same social, organizational, and psychological needs. Furthermore, on the eve of World War II in the Pacific, the Communists were beset by factionalism.

But this changed after 1941 when Ho organized a broad anticolonial movement known as the Viet Minh (more formally, the League for the Independence of Vietnam). The purpose of this organization, established with Nationalist Chinese support, was to resist both the Japanese who occupied Vietnam in 1941 and the French (adherents to the puppet regime established by the Germans at Vichy), whom the Japanese kept in office until March 1945.

From a base along the Chinese border, the Viet Minh expanded their military and political influence to the Red Delta and beyond. They built an effective military force under the command of General Vo Nguyen Giap (1912–), who had studied guerrilla warfare techniques in Yan'an. During the war, the demands of Vietnam's new masters created increased economic hardships. In Tonkin, in 1940, between 400,000 and 2 million people starved to death, having been deprived of the rice reserves necessary to combat famine.

When Japan surrendered in August 1945, the Viet Minh were the most effective force in the land. On August 26, Ho proclaimed an independent Vietnam in Hanoi. The French, however, had other ideas, and Ho lacked the resources to prevent them from reestablishing their presence in Vietnam.

# The Vietnam War (1946–1975) and Its Aftermath

The Vietnam War can be divided into two wars: one fought against the French (1946–1954) and a second in which the United States became a principal party.

The first war began in 1946, after negotiations had revealed the gulf separating the Viet Minh, dedicated to achieving national independence, and the French, seeking to recover former glory and adamant in their refusal to relinquish their empire. As the fighting continued, the Cold War developed and the Communist character of the Viet Minh came more to the fore. The French tried to attract non-Communist nationalist support by sponsoring a regime under the former emperor Bao Dai. This, however, won little support from the Vietnamese people. Furthermore, the French made little military headway against an enemy who knew the terrain and had the support of the civilian population. They committed 420,000 troops to Vietnam, not counting another 200,000 in the Vietnamese army, but the end came in spring 1954 when General Giap, with the aid of artillery laboriously transported over the mountains, vanquished the French at the famous battle of Dien Bien Phu.

Negotiations at Geneva led to the partition of Vietnam at the seventeenth parallel into a Communist-dominated state with its capital at Hanoi and a southern state ruled from Saigon. Nationwide elections were agreed upon for 1956. The elections, however, were never held because they were blocked with American support by the head of the Saigon government. This was Ngo Diehm Diem (1901–1963), a Catholic nationalist whose government lacked popular roots and administrative efficacy. In 1963 his government was overthrown and Diem★ was killed in the coup. By that time, the United States had 17,000 troops in Vietnam to assist in what the American government viewed as the containment of world communism.

The removal of the unpopular and aloof Diem and his corrupt family did not result in any marked improvements in government, which beginning in 1965 was in military hands. The Saigon government remained autocratic, ineffective, and corrupt, and the insurgents gained ground. Leadership of the southern revolutionaries was now exercised by the National Liberation Front (NLF), organized in December 1960.† The NLF was supported by the North Vietnamese, and there was logistical aid from the Soviet Union and China.

The Chinese continued to give moral and material support to their Vietnamese allies but, unlike the United States, did not send troops. American in-

---

★ Like Chinese, Japanese, and Korean names, Vietnamese names are written with the surname first. However, probably because certain surnames are extremely frequent, it is customary to refer to people by their personal names. An exception is made for Ho Chi Minh, actually a pseudonym.

† In the United States, both the NLF and its supporters were known as "Vietcong," an abbreviation of "Vietnamese Communism" or "Vietnamese Communist."

volvement, meanwhile, increased. Leading American policymakers justified this by drawing historical analogies from the appeasement of Germany and Japan in the 1930s, when they might better have drawn lessons from the Japanese experience in China or the fall of Chiang. An elaboration of this approach was the "domino theory," which held that if Vietnam fell to Communism the other countries of Southeast Asia would follow suit, toppling one by one like a row of dominoes. Furthermore, the United States government treated the war not as a civil war but as a case of combating "northern aggression." After gaining U.S. Senate support in the Tonkin Gulf Resolution (1964), President Lyndon Johnson ordered the bombing of North Vietnam (February 1965). By July 1965, there were 70,000 American troops in Vietnam. The number continued to increase until early in 1968, when there were 510,000. In addition, Vietnam underwent the most massive bombing in history. As American involvement in Vietnam increased, the horrors of the war were brought home to the American people by casualty lists and by the sight of gruesome destruction of Vietnamese people and villages, which they witnessed daily on their television screens. The American government was increasingly unable to justify the war to its own people, and the bombings and destruction reinforced the will of Vietnamese revolutionaries on both sides to persist in their struggle.

In February 1968 it became apparent that the American effort, despite its great destructiveness, had destroyed neither the will nor the ability of the revolutionaries to continue to fight. That month they launched an offensive in which they attacked more than 100 cities. This show of strength prompted a reexamination of American policy, and the United States began to withdraw its troops from Vietnam. However, apparently in an attempt to bolster the Saigon regime, President Nixon in 1970 widened the war to include Cambodia and Laos. It was not easy for an American president to withdraw without "victory," but strong domestic pressures and the situation in Vietnam left him little choice. Finally, an agreement was reached in Paris, and the last American military personnel left Vietnam in March 1973.

The war continued another two years, but the outcome was a foregone conclusion to anyone who calculated military strength, not in terms of official statistics and armaments but in terms of such factors as the participants' will to fight, the political credibility of the leadership, and the attitude of the people. Saigon fell in April 1975. In 1976 the establishment of the Socialist Republic of Vietnam, with its capital in Hanoi, was proclaimed. Saigon was renamed Ho Chi Minh City.

The victory of the Vietnamese revolution did not bring peace to the region. In December 1978, Vietnam invaded Cambodia, where the brutal Khmer Rouge regime, established in 1975, enjoyed Chinese support. In 1979, Vietnam beat back a Chinese invasion in a seventeen-day war and installed a client regime in Phom Penh. Vietnamese forces remained in Cambodia and Laos until 1989.

During the first decade of the new regime, relations with China remained tense, and there were border skirmishes in 1985. Economically and diplomatically, Vietnam relied on the Soviet Union, which was granted a valuable military base in

Southeast Asia. Domestically, the government in 1975 faced an enormous task of unification and economic restoration. The first few years were particularly hard on numerous city dwellers, many of them ethnic Chinese, who fled the country when faced with the prospect of transfer to the countryside. Although recovery was accomplished, the Vietnamese economy continued to falter.

At the Sixth Party Congress held in December 1986 and in the subsequent elections of April 1987, a major change of directions and leadership occurred. Nguyen Van Linh (1915–) became the first secretary general of the Communist Party of Vietnam from outside Ho's inner circle. Committed to raising Vietnam from "the quicksand of bureaucratic centralism and subsidization," the new leadership adopted a policy of reducing central control, allowing greater play to the profit motive and to market forces. The authority of individual factory managers was increased, and the door was opened to the creation of joint ventures with foreign companies.

During the 1990s, tensions with China and the United States eased. The lifting of the American trade embargo in 1994 was followed by diplomatic recognition in 1995, a visit by President Bill Clinton in 2000, and an agreement normalizing trade relations signed into law by President George W. Bush in 2001. Meanwhile, Vietnam had joined the Association of Southeast Asian Nations (1995) and pursued a policy of "guarded friendship" with a China in the midst of its own vast changes.[10]

# Notes

1. I. M. Roberts, *Twentieth Century: The History of the World, 1901–2000* (New York: Viking, 1999), p. 462.

2. For the eulogy in which Wen Yiduo attacked Chiang Kai-shek personally and predicted that the GMD leaders would meet the same fate as Mussolini and Hitler, see Pei-kai Cheng and Michael Lestz with Jonathan D. Spence, *The Search for Modern China: A Documentary Collection* (New York: W. W. Norton, 1999), pp. 337–38.

3. Robert Gardella, in Murray A. Rubinstein, ed., *Taiwan: A New History* (Armonk, N.Y.: M. E., Sharpe, 1999), p. 180.

4. Hui-yu Caroline Ts'ai, *One Kind of Control: The Hoko System in Taiwan Under Japanese Rule, 1895–1945* (Ph.D. Dissertation, Columbia Univ., 1990), pp. 494–95, citing Siomi Shunji's essay as translated into Chinese by Chou Hsien-wen in *T'ai-wan yin-hang chi-kan,* comp. T'ai-wan Yinhang Ching-chi Yen-chiu-shih, Vol. 5, No. 4 (Taipei: Bank of Taiwan, 1953), pp. 267–68.

5. Quoted in John W. Dower, *Embracing Defeat: Japan in the Wake of World War II* (New York: W. W. Norton, 1999), p. 97.

6. Article IX of the constitution. A convenient source is David John Lu, *Sources of Japanese History, Vol. 2* (New York: McGraw-Hill, 1975), pp. 193–97.

7. Dower, *Embracing Defeat,* p. 544.

8. Dower, *Embracing Defeat,* p. 558.

9. Alexander B. Woodside, *Community and Revolution in Modern Vietnam* (Boston: Houghton Mifflin, 1976), p. 3.

10. Robert Templar, *Shadows and Wind: A View of Modern Vietnam* (New York: Penguin Books, 1998), p. 298.

# *China under Mao*

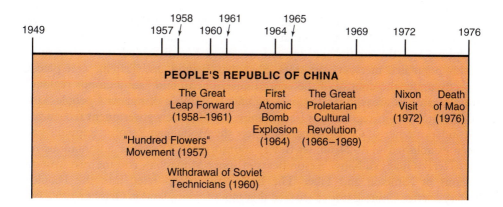

| 1949 | 1957 | 1958 | 1960 | 1961 | 1964 | 1965 | 1969 | 1972 | 1976 |

**PEOPLE'S REPUBLIC OF CHINA**

The Great
Leap Forward
(1958–1961)

First
Atomic
Bomb
Explosion
(1964)

The Great
Proletarian
Cultural
Revolution
(1966–1969)

Nixon
Visit
(1972)

Death
of Mao
(1976)

"Hundred Flowers"
Movement (1957)

Withdrawal of Soviet
Technicians (1960)

When Mao Zedong proclaimed the establishment of the People's Republic on October 1, 1949, it marked a watershed in the history of modern China. After a century of internal disintegration and foreign aggression, China made a new beginning under leaders deeply committed to the revolutionary transformation of the nation. Mao and his associates were determined to create an egalitarian society and make China strong and prosperous.

In taking control of the entire country and then restructuring Chinese society, the new leaders faced problems as immense as China itself. They were dedicated Marxists, and in their march to power had brilliantly adapted the foreign ideology to Chinese conditions. The challenge that now awaited them of transforming China in the spirit of that ideology proved a formidable one, and the course they took was anything but smooth.

The People's Republic of China (P.R.C.) began with an initial period (1949–1952), during which the regime consolidated its rule and forged the basic framework of a new sociopolitical order. This was followed by a period of Socialist Construction (1953–1958), initiated by the first Soviet-style five-year plan—begun in 1953, but not published until 1955.

## Government and Politics

Following the example of the Soviet Union (U.S.S.R.), the Chinese formed parallel government and party structures with high party officials appointed to top government posts. Thus, Mao headed the party as Chairman of the Chinese Communist

Party (C.C.P.) Central Committee and, until 1959, was also officially head of state. High party members also held positions of leadership in various quasi-official organizations such as trade unions; and, as earlier, party members served as political commissars in the army, which reported to the Military Affairs Commission headed by Mao.

Administratively, China was divided into provinces, which remained the primary political subdivisions after an additional governmental level between the provinces and the central government was tried but discarded. The three most highly populated metropolitan areas, Shanghai, Beijing, and Tianjin, were placed directly under the control of the central government, and "autonomous regions" were created in areas inhabited by a significant number of minority people. One such "autonomous region" was Inner Mongolia. (The new government recognized the independence of Outer Mongolia, where the Mongolian People's Republic had been established in 1924, under Soviet sponsorship.) The other autonomous regions were Guangxi, Ningxia (southeast of Inner Mongolia), and the vast western regions of Xinjiang and Tibet. The latter was incorporated into the People's Republic after Chinese troops entered that mountainous land in October 1950, but Tibet did not receive autonomous region status until 1965. Aside from their strategic importance, the Inner Asian territories were significant because the government had to deal with the interests and sensitivities of their ethnic minorities.

A major step toward realization of the egalitarian aims of the revolution was taken in 1950 with the promulgation of a marriage law that gave women political and economic equality as well as equal rights to divorce. Women were free to participate in the workforce and pursue careers, although, in practice, this did not release them from their traditional household responsibilities.

An important factor in making the new system work was the cohesiveness of the Party leadership forged during years of struggling side by side. The only political conflict to erupt openly was an attack on Gao Gang, the C.C.P. leader in Manchuria who was accused of separatist ambitions. Additional factors were Gao's ties with the Soviet Union and the issue of Soviet influence in Manchuria. Gao's suicide was reported in 1955. At this juncture Rao Shushi, who was based in Shanghai, was also purged. Both leaders, in charge of prime industrial centers, were accused of "operating independent kingdoms" and of forming a political alliance.

To achieve its goals, the leadership launched massive national campaigns in what became a pattern. Thus, during 1951–1952 there was a "three antis" campaign against waste, corruption, and bureaucratism, aimed at disciplining the greatly enlarged C.C.P. membership, and a "five antis" campaign against bribery, tax evasion, fraud, the stealing of state property, and the theft of economic secrets. As a result, many wealthy men had to pay heavy fines. In line with Mao's *On the New Democracy* (1940), members of the "national bourgeoisie" were initially tolerated, and only capitalists with Guomindang or foreign ties were labeled enemies of the revolution. Gradually, however, private companies were turned over to the state, although their former owners often remained as managers.

Not all drives were directed against human evildoers; there was also a concerted attack on the "Four Pests": a war against rats, sparrows, flies, and mosquitoes. Although the inclusion of sparrows was misconceived, it was partly by such campaigns that the P.R.C. achieved enormous improvements in public health. Furthermore, by involving all the people in these campaigns, the leadership not only made use of China's greatest asset (manpower) but also gave the people a sense of participation and pride in the resulting accomplishments.

## Foreign Relations and the Korean War

The Communist victory was hailed with enthusiasm in Moscow and bitterly deplored in Washington. Partly for ideological reasons and partly in response to continued, even if unenthusiastic, American support for the Nationalists, the C.C.P. adopted a policy of "leaning to one side," formally aligning itself with the U.S.S.R. in a treaty in February 1950, a product of Mao's first visit to Moscow and, in fact, his first trip outside China. However, relations between the two allies were not easy, for Stalin drove a hard bargain and was slow to relinquish special interests in Manchuria and Xinjiang. Still, the relationship with the U.S.S.R. was very important to China because the Soviet Union provided a model for economic and political development as well as moral, political, and economic support.

On the American side, although some observers had taken the measure of Chiang Kai-shek, large sectors of the American public continued to view him as China's savior, a view fostered by wartime propaganda and the efforts of ex-missionaries, politicians, and other supporters, including those who claimed he would have triumphed had he received adequate American aid. Regardless of their appraisal of the GM, many in and out of government considered Communism a monolithic threat and failed to appreciate the fact that the C.C.P. were Nationalists as well as Communists. All this stood in the way of easing tensions between Washington and Beijing, but it is clear that "both Chinese and American leaders were interested in and groping uneasily toward accommodation."[1] However, time ran out with the beginning of the war in Korea in June 1950.

As we saw in the previous chapter, The Korean War deepened the enmity between China and the United States and solidified the Cold War alignment on the Korean Peninsula and throughout East Asia. Beijing's representatives played an important role in the Geneva Conference on Indochina (1954) and at the conference of Asian-African states held at Bandung (Indonesia) in 1955. However, the Nationalists retained the China seat at the United Nations, and the United States prevailed on most of its allies to join it in withholding recognition of the P.R.C. The buildup of Nationalist strength on Taiwan rankled Beijing, but with the U.S. Seventh Fleet patrolling the Taiwan Strait, actual fighting was limited to sporadic shelling of the two Nationalist-held islands off the coast of the Fujian Province.

## Economic Policies

Economic matters were of central concern to the new government right from the start. It had inherited a land ravaged by war and floods, with both agricultural and industrial output badly decreased from prewar levels and the monetary system wrecked by inflation. In addition, the underlying economy had serious structural weakness. In the agrarian sector, the prevalence of small, uneconomical, scattered landholdings and uneven land ownership helped to perpetuate traditional farming techniques and discouraged investment and capital formation. The industrial sector, on the other hand, consisted primarily of light industry concentrated around Shanghai and heavy industry in Manchuria. The latter had been developed to meet the requirements of foreign capital rather than the needs of China and its people.

Any government would have had to restore and strengthen the economy, but as Marxists, China's new leaders were also committed to the transfer of the means of production from private to public ownership and the creation of an egalitarian system of distribution. Their aim was to create a socialist state with a strong proletarian (working-class) base. The necessary precondition for this was vigorous industrialization, and because this was also required for the attainment of national strength, economic ideology and patriotism pointed to the same end.

By 1952, despite the strains of the Korean War, the economy had been restored to prewar levels. Factories had been put back into operation, railway lines had been repaired, and inflation had been brought under control. In the cities, the private sector was temporarily retained and even encouraged, but control over materials and marketing, as well as wages, prices, and working conditions, was in the hands of the state. Meanwhile, in the countryside, land redistribution was carried out not by government decree but by mobilizing the suppressed fury of the rural poor.

Landlords were denounced and humiliated in public trials and at mass "speak bitterness" meetings. The more fortunate ones were allowed to retain enough land to support themselves, but many lost their lives. The campaign became associated with a general suppression of potential counterrevolutionaries during the Korean War. The end result was not only a more equitable distribution of land but also a change of village leadership, now drawn from the poor peasantry.

The achievements of the first three years of the People's Republic were viewed as merely a preamble for further socialization and economic development. A planning organization was established, as was a statistical bureau, and in 1953 China took its first modern census, showing a total population of 582,600,000 on the mainland. Although its accuracy has been questioned, this figure is accepted as a general indication of the size of China's population at the time.

China's First Five-Year Plan followed the U.S.S.R. model of economic development in stressing heavy industry, with some 85 percent of total investments going into this sector. The Soviet Union supplied technical assistance (plans, blueprints, and so forth), helped train Chinese technicians (28,000 Chinese technicians and skilled workers went to the U.S.S.R. for training during the 1950s), and sent about 11,000 of its own experts to work in China. Development was accelerated by importing entire plants from the Soviet Union. Most of what was left of the private sector was now eliminated. Control over the plants was given to professional managers and technocrats, whose prime responsibility was to carry out government economic directives. To enable them to do this, they were placed firmly in charge of their factories.

Because loans advanced by the Soviet Union amounted to only 3 percent of China's total state investments, the financing of this industrialization effort was predominantly Chinese. These funds came out of the government's budget. The government, in turn, derived much of its revenue from taxes and from the income of state enterprises. Ultimately, a considerable portion of investment capital came from agriculture, which remained the heart of the Chinese economy.

To increase output and channel agricultural surplus more effectively into capital formation, the government in 1953 began a program of more radical transformation of the pattern of land management. To replace the existing system of small fields, individually owned and worked, the government planned to collectivize agriculture by pooling land, labor, and other resources. The change was not to be accomplished all at once. First, "mutual-aid" teams, which shared labor, tools, and work animals, were organized. The next stage was to create village producers' cooperatives in which land also was pooled.

Initially, agricultural collectivization was planned as a gradual program, because the Chinese leadership wanted to avoid the terrible bloodshed and suffering that had accompanied Stalin's rapid collectivization in the U.S.S.R. Mao, however, in a major speech delivered in July 1955, drew on the experience of the Chinese as distinct from that of the Russian Revolution and reaffirmed his faith in the revolutionary spirit of the Chinese peasantry. Just as the peasantry had been in the vanguard of the revolution that gave birth to the People's Republic, it would now lead the nation to socialism. In Mao's view it was the party, not the people, that was dragging its feet. The immediate effect of Mao's speech was an acceleration in the agricultural collectivization program, so much so that it was largely accomplished within a single year (1955–1956), and the timetable for full collectivization was set ahead. This speech marked the emergence of a radical Maoist strategy of economic development. In 1957 the process of collectivization was completed.

At the end of the First Five-Year Plan, the Chinese viewed the results with considerable satisfaction. The government was now firmly in control of the industrial sector: agriculture had been reorganized; iron, coal, and steel production targets had been exceeded; industrial output doubled from 1953 to 1957; and, altogether, remarkable progress had been made on the road to industrialization. There were problems, to be sure. One was the widening gap between city and country, a problem that has plagued all industrializing countries but was of special concern in China, where the peasantry remained the majority and where the party leaders identified with it. Another problem was the reemergence of bureaucracy and the transformation of a revolutionary party into the mainstay of the establishment.

# Thought Reform and Intellectuals

The leaders of the People's Republic were convinced not only of the scientific correctness of their doctrine but also of its moral rightness, and they believed that virtually everyone could be brought to share their vision and act accordingly. They were optimistic not only about the course of history but also about human nature. In keeping with tradition, they had faith that everyone could attain moral perfection, now redefined in terms of an ideal socialist person. It was their belief that given the proper environment and correct guidance, people would become selflessly devoted to revolution and community.

Naturally, the most promising were the young, uncontaminated by the old society, and the government saw to it that they were educated in the new values. Special attention was paid to the political awareness of Communist Party members and cadres, who were relied on to set examples of personal conduct and lead the people. To further the thought reform and moral transformation of even the most unpromising individuals, the authorities devised techniques of group discussion, self-criticism, and public confession. By using the individual's own feeling of moral inadequacy and guilt and by applying external pressures, the authorities induced people to renounce old values and prepared them for conversion to the new faith. Perhaps the most famous example of such a change of heart, accomplished in the controlled environment of a correctional institute, was provided by Puyi. As an infant he had been the last occupant of the Qing throne, and more recently he had served the Japanese as puppet ruler of Manchukuo. After undergoing thought reform, he reemerged as a citizen in good standing.

Not only prominent personages but also ordinary people now spent much time in small discussion groups, analyzing their lives as well as problems or incidents at their places of work. In this way the new ideology was transmitted to the people, and they were taught to use it in analyzing everyday problems. At the same time, social pressures were applied to everyone to conform to generally accepted standards of behavior.

The thought reform of intellectuals, already a target of Mao's wartime rectification campaign (see Chapter 21), remained difficult. Highly trained and educated people were a rare and precious resource for a nation bent on industrialization and modernization. Yet few came from peasant or worker backgrounds. More serious than their class background was the persistence of traditional elitist attitudes among intellectuals, as well as their critical habits of mind. They tended to resent taking directions from party cadres less well educated than themselves. Their special knowledge and skills were needed, but could they be trusted?

With education and the media under tight party control, the arts too were meant to serve the revolution. Whereas Western style artists were taught "Socialist Realism," a style intended to inspire, not to mirror, life (see Figures 23.1 and 23.4), artists working in traditional styles (*guohua*) were accepted as furthering national glory but urged to incorporate modern subjects in their work (see Figure 23.2).

**FIGURE 23.1** *Chairman Mao Standing with People of Asia, Africa, and Latin America*, Wu Biduan (b. 1926) and Jin Shangyi (b. 1934). Notice the new artistic style of Socialist Realism. Oil on canvas, 56.29 in × 61.42 in. (Collection National Art Gallery of China, Beijing. © Jinn Shangyi. Used by permission.)

The integration of artists and intellectuals into the new society remained problematic. When, in May 1956, Mao invited writers and thinkers to "let a hundred flowers bloom; let a hundred schools contend," there was little response from intellectuals, wary of exposing themselves to attack. But in February 1957, Mao said in a speech, "On the Correct Handling of Contradictions Among the People," that nonantagonistic contradictions should be resolved by persuasion rather than force. After some further reassurance, the floodgates of criticism were opened.

Criticism was directed not only against the behavior of individual party functionaries and at specific party policies but also at the C.C.P. itself for seeking "to bring about the monolithic structure of a one-family empire."[2] Intellectuals and writers asked for independence from the party's ideological control. Academic problems should be left for professors to solve: "Perhaps Mao has not had time to solve these problems for us,"[3] one history professor suggested.

Mao had intended the campaign to rectify the party, but the criticism was more than he had bargained for. Weeds grew where he had invited flowers. A full-fledged anti-Rightist campaign developed, beginning in June 1957. Not only did prominent intellectual, literary, and artistic figures disappear into labor camps, but also so did more than 400,000 others, with the government announcing a target of 5 percent per organization and the campaign quickening to include a massive purge of party members and cadres. Under these pressures some saved themselves by denouncing their friends. The upshot was that people with negative entries in their files had their lives ruined. Many of the victims were not fully rehabilitated until after Mao's death. By 1958 few were left to dare object when Mao launched his Great Leap Forward.

An underlying issue was how to balance the demands for ideological purity and revolutionary fervor with the professional competence required to operate a modern state and build an industrial system. Without the former, a new elite of experts, technocrats, and managers would pursue its own aims, and the revolution would be jeopardized. Mao believed that progress toward Communist egalitarianism and the building of national strength went hand in hand, but he put his faith in Redness, often at the expense of expertise.

# II.  The Revolution Continued, 1958–1976

*The Great Leap Forward*

*The Sino-Soviet Split*

*Domestic Politics, 1961–1965*

*The Great Proletarian Cultural Revolution: The Radical Phase, 1966–1969*

*The Winding Down, 1969–1976*

By the end of the First Five-Year Plan there were indications that following the Soviet model was not producing the desired economic or social results, but there was no agreement on what should be done. Although the party establishment saw a need for only relatively minor adjustments, Mao advocated a far more radical line. In the subsequent complicated, often turbulent, years, he did not always get his way, but he did prevent the revolution from settling down into comfortable routines.

## *The Great Leap Forward*

The Great Leap Forward was initiated in January 1958, but lost momentum the following year. After 1959 it continued, but without vigor, until it was terminated in January 1961. On Mao's initiative, the gradualism of Soviet-style central planning was abandoned in favor of reliance on the energies of the masses imbued with revolutionary consciousness. Mao believed that ideology was a force that could motivate people to heroic accomplishments. History was not confined to a series of well-defined objective stages of economic and sociopolitical development, but could be turned into a process of "permanent revolution" driven by the subjective will transforming the objective world. The P.R.C. had made use of massive manpower in labor-intensive projects all along, projects such as the building of water-ways, roads, and other giant construction works. Now the glorification of labor became more intense:

> Labor is joy; how joyful is it?
> Bathed in sweat and two hands full of mud,
> Like sweet rain my sweat waters the land
> And the land issues scent, better than milk.
> Labor is joy; how joyful is it?
> Home from a night attack, hoe in hand,
> The hoe's handle is still warm,
> But in bed, the warrior is already snoring.[4]

The author of these lines, written in 1958, was Yuan Kejia (1921–), who had once been an admirer of T. S. Eliot.

All of China's human resources were to be focused in a giant leap. Through Redness and revolutionary fervor, Mao hoped to accelerate China's economic development and speed the advance toward socialism. The spirit of the people was to be the driving force for continued economic growth and social transformation. Through the catharsis of intense participation, the Great Leap Forward mobilized the emotional involvement of many people in the creation of a new order. They were made to feel that building a strong China was not something to be left to experts and technocrats; it was to be done by, as well as for, the people.

As the prime vehicle for this effort, rural communes were formed by combining the already existing cooperatives. By the end of 1958 there were 26,000 rural communes in which 98 percent of China's rural population lived. Each averaged about 25,000 people. The communes were divided into production brigades, each corresponding roughly to the traditional village, and these, in turn, were divided into production teams. The communes were intended to function as China's basic political as well as economic and social units, integrating all aspects of life. As economic units they supervised agricultural production and distribution, provided banking services, and ran small factories and machine shops, which were operated at the commune- or production-brigade level, depending on the size and degree of specialization of the plant. The communes were further responsible for police functions, and they ran schools and hospitals, provided day-care facilities and mess halls, took care of the aged, and staged plays and other entertainment. They represented an ambitious attempt to create new, large-scale communities. But they turned out to be too large, and the cadres who ran them were too far removed from the realities of farming. Their size was therefore reduced, so that by the end of the Great Leap Forward the original number of communes had almost tripled to 74,000, with a corresponding decrease in the size of their memberships. Later the communes lost many of their functions to the smaller production brigades and peasants were given greater discretion.

There was also a movement to establish communes in the cities by combining or transforming earlier street associations that included the inhabitants of one street (or of several small streets, or of a section of a large street) originally organized for security and welfare. They were now given additional responsibilities for economic enterprises as well as for educational and medical facilities. In general, the formation of urban communes involved the transfer of authority over factories from central and provincial ministries to the local party committee that controlled the communes. Some of the communes consisted of workers in one large factory, others included the residents of one part of a city, and still others, located on the outskirts of cities, included some farmland along with an urban sector. Whatever the form of urban organization, an effort was made to release women for work by establishing mess halls, nurseries, homes for the aged, and service facilities such as laundries.

To enlist popular enthusiasm and encourage local initiative, local authorities were granted substantial leeway in deciding how to implement government directives. The central government still set general economic policy and retained control over the largest heavy industrial plants, but 80 percent of all enterprises were decentralized. No longer was there to be reliance on experts in far-off Beijing making all the decisions and operating with a centralized bureaucracy as in the U.S.S.R.

As far as possible, literature and the visual arts were to be not only for but also by the people. Teams were sent out to collect the people's literature and to encourage peasants to compose poetry and otherwise participate in the creation of art. In Shanghai alone some 200,000 people participated in producing 5 million poems. Many thousands undoubtedly were exhilarated at achieving recognition in a field previously reserved for an exclusive elite.

High social as well as economic expectations were raised by the creation of the communes. According to Communist theory, the achievement of a truly communist society entails a change from paying people according to their productivity to paying "each according to his needs." In line with this, experiments were conducted in paying people approximately 70 percent of their wages in kind (produce to satisfy their needs) and the rest in cash according to their productivity. Meanwhile, impressive production targets were announced, including the goal of catching up with British industrial production in fifteen years. To the Chinese leaders, the social and economic goals seemed entirely compatible.

If the Great Leap Forward achieved some of its political and psychological goals, it also produced an economic disaster. This did not become apparent for some time; the initial statistics of production were impressive, but they turned out to have been grossly inflated. An unanticipated consequence of the Great Leap Forward was a breakdown in China's statistical services, and serious mistakes were made because the government accepted the exaggerated figures forwarded by overenthusiastic local authorities. Some projects originally pursued with enthusiasm later had to be abandoned as unworkable. Perhaps the best known was the campaign to use local villagers and materials to build and operate backyard furnaces for making iron and steel. Because this fitted in well with the policy of decentralization and relying on the masses, the plan was vigorously implemented. All over China small furnaces were set up and utensils were melted down, but the furnaces proved incapable of turning out iron of acceptable quality, let alone steel.

The most serious failure of the Great Leap Forward was in agriculture. Misconceived irrigation projects leached nutrients from the soil and mass mobilization for work projects exhausted and demoralized the people. Here, too, the government worked with misleading statistics, as local units vied with each other in reporting productivity gains. The harvest of 1958 was seriously exaggerated. Relying on faulty expectations and inflated reports, the government took so much grain that in many areas practically nothing was left for the peasants. Massive famine resulted. The number who perished is difficult to determine, but 16–27 million is a conservative estimate. The Great Leap ended in a stupendous crash.

# The Sino-Soviet Split

From the beginning of the People's Republic there were areas of tension and potential conflict between China and the Soviet Union. As we have seen, the C.C.P. came to power only after going its own way, independent of Moscow. Furthermore, the Chinese leadership was as determinedly nationalistic as the Soviets, who, under Stalin, operated on the principle that what was good for the Soviet Union was good for world Communism. This equation had some plausibility as long as there was only one great Communist state in the world, but it was a thesis that the Chinese, sooner or later, were bound to challenge.

Initially, the forces holding the alliance together were stronger than those pulling it apart. These included not only ideological ties but also shared Cold War enemies. However, around the mid-1950s serious cracks in the alliance began to appear. One cause of friction was territorial. The Chinese reluctantly accepted the independence of Outer Mongolia, whose historical status resembled that of Tibet, but they were very unhappy about their northern and western boundaries with the Soviet Union. These borders had been drawn in the nineteenth century and thus formed part of the history of imperialism that China's new government was pledged to undo. As early as 1954 Chinese publications indicated the country's refusal to accept vast regions of Central and Northeast Asia as permanently belonging to the U.S.S.R.

Another source of trouble was the Chinese desire for recognition as leaders of world Communism, as suggested in Figure 23.1. After the death of Stalin in 1953, they expected that Mao would be honored as the leading living contributor to Marxist ideology and the architect of strategies to advance the cause in the Third World. Instead, Khrushchev went his own way by denouncing Stalin in a famous speech in 1956 that implied the illegitimacy of all "personality cults," including that forming around Mao. Figure 23.1 shows Mao as a world figure. Stylistically, it exemplifies a turning away from Soviet models and "the nationalization of oil painting," a term applied to "any means of imbuing oil painting with recognizably Chinese aesthetics." As illustrated here, one way of doing so was by forgoing the effects of light and shadow and favoring "flat patches of unmodulated color rather than painterly textures."[5]

Khrushchev's theory of peaceful coexistence and the U.S.S.R.'s new international stance further irritated the Chinese. Even Mao's opponents within the C.C.P. felt insulted that Chinese leaders had not been consulted before these major shifts in Soviet policy were announced. For their part, the Soviet leaders could hardly be expected to welcome Chinese claims, made during the Great Leap Forward, that their communes represented a higher stage on the road to the ideal society than anything achieved in the Soviet Union after forty years of Communist rule.

Despite efforts toward reconciliation, such as Chinese support for the Soviet suppression of the Hungarian uprising in 1956, Mao's visit to Moscow in 1957, and Khrushchev's to Beijing in 1958 and 1959, the strains in the alliance continued to mount. Contributing to this was the U.S.S.R.'s unwillingness to exploit its temporary supremacy in rocketry to support a possible Chinese attack on Taiwan, an attack that would have had no hope for success unless the United States were neutralized by Soviet threats. Khrushchev's relatively unbelligerent stance toward the United States seemed to the Chinese like a cowardly betrayal, whereas Mao's belittling of the dangers of nuclear warfare made him appear to the Soviets as a dangerous adventurer gambling with the lives of millions. No wonder the Soviets were hesitant about sharing nuclear secrets with the Chinese.

The split became unbreachable in the summer of 1960, when the Soviets withdrew their technicians from China. They even took their blueprints with them. After that, despite limited cooperation during the Vietnam War, relations remained bitter, as China and the U.S.S.R. denounced each other's policies and challenged the Marxist legitimacy of each other's revolutions. Whereas the Chinese charged that the Soviets had deviated from the true revolutionary path, Russian and East European ideologists depicted Chinese aberrations as arising from their lack of a firm proletarian base as well as an inadequate understanding of Marxism.

An aspect of this situation was the Soviet Union's support of India in its disputes with China. Relations between China and India became tense in 1959, after the Chinese, asserting their rights under international law, imposed their rule on Tibet and used their soldiers to suppress Tibetan resistance. India's welcome of Tibetan refugees, including the Dalai Lama, the spiritual and sometime secular leader of Tibet, was resented in Beijing. As it was, China and India, the world's two most populous nations, were natural rivals for Asian leadership. The resulting tensions would not have led to outright hostility, however, had it not been for a border dispute over a remote area through which China had built a road linking Xinjiang with Tibet. The result was a short border war in 1962 in which the Chinese quickly humiliated the Indian troops. The Soviet Union continued its policy of friendship with India, and China cultivated good relations with India's arch rival, Pakistan. Meanwhile, within the Communist world, China defended and allied itself with the bitterly anti-Soviet regime of Albania.

Militarily, the Soviet Union remained much the stronger of the two powers, but the People's Republic was also developing its armed strength. A milestone was reached in 1964 when it exploded its first atomic bomb. Although, as indicated by its title, the painting reproduced as Figure 23.2 was understood as celebratory, it may have been an ironic response to relentless pressures on Wu Hufan (1894–1970) to produce art that would serve the revolution and the state, for Wu was a highly sophisticated and sensitive traditional-style painter and a careful student of the paintings of the Four Wangs, who had delighted the court of Kangxi (see Chapter 15). To quote Julia F. Andrews, "As incongruous as it seems, this painting of the mushroom cloud is one of the most beautiful demonstrations of brushwork to be found during the period." She goes on to cite its "casual lively strokes and subtly varied ink tones."[6]

The bomb did not soften relations between the two Communist giants. Numerous border clashes endangered the peace between them, and both feared that the situation might escalate into full-fledged war. Beijing built an extensive system of underground shelters for use in case of an attack by air. The hostility of the Soviet Union was one of the principal factors that led to a gradual rapprochement between China and the United States during the 1970s.

**FIGURE 23.2** *Celebrate the Success of Our Atomic Bomb Explosion*, Wu Hufan. Hanging scroll, ink and color on paper, 1965. (Shanghai Institute of Chinese Painting. © Wu Hufan. Used by permission.)

## Domestic Politics, 1961–1965

The failure of the Great Leap Forward led to retrenchment in domestic policies, a willingness to accept, at least for a while, more modest interim social and economic goals. It was a serious setback for Mao's personal authority as well as plans.

He remained party chairman, but in December 1958 had to resign as head of the government. That post was filled by Liu Shaoqi (1898–1969), a hard-working organization man long associated with Mao. Liu had supporters in high party and government positions, but the supervision of the state's administrative machinery, including the various ministries, remained under the direction of the head of the State Administrative Council, who had the title of premier. This position had been held since 1949 by another trusted party veteran, Zhou Enlai. Zhou also served as foreign minister until 1959 and continued even after he left that post to act as China's main spokesman in foreign affairs. By all accounts, Zhou was one of the most capable and versatile of all the C.C.P. leaders, a superb political and military strategist and a truly gifted administrator and negotiator.

Another important government position was that of minister of defense. In 1959 Peng Dehuai (1898–1974), a veteran general, was ousted from this post for going too far in criticizing Mao and the Great Leap Forward. He was further accused of pro-Soviet tendencies and held responsible for overemphasizing professionalism and failing to imbue the troops with sufficient ideological spirit. His successor as minister of defense was another distinguished general, Lin Biao (1907–1971), who was favored by Mao.

Under the direction of Liu Shaoqi, the government relaxed the tempo of social change. There was now greater appreciation of expertise and less reliance on the revolutionary enthusiasm of the masses. There was an increased use of economic rather than ideological incentives: in the communes the more productive workers could earn extra work points, and in the factories there were wage increases, bonuses, and promotions to be earned, measures later castigated as "economism." Peasants, although still under the obligation to produce a fixed amount of grain for the state, were allowed small private plots and permitted to sell on the free market whatever they could grow on them.

No longer able to rely on the U.S.S.R. in the international arena, China in 1964 channeled investments into creating a "Third Front," described as "a crash program to build heavy industry in inland provinces away from the militarily vulnerable coastal and northeast areas."[7] Despite political turmoil, this effort continued until 1971, augmenting the damage already inflicted on the environment by misguided dam building and other abuses during the Great Leap Forward. From the beginning, as in the campaign against sparrows, Mao and his followers advocated and pursued the conquest of nature.

After the great exertions and the disappointments of the Great Leap Forward, there was a natural slackening not only of the pace of change but also of revolutionary fervor. This alarmed Mao, who sought to combat this trend by initiating a socialist education movement in 1962 without, however, much effect. Furthermore, there now appeared in print thinly veiled attacks on Mao himself. Among them was the historical play, *Hai Rui Dismissed from Office*, written by the deputy mayor of Beijing. In this play the sixteenth-century official (see Chapter 10) was portrayed sympathetically as an honest minister who stood up for the peasants and was dismissed by a foolish and autocratic emperor. What was implied was a critique of Mao's own dismissal, in 1959, of Minister of Defense Peng

Dehuai. In November 1965 an article was published in the Shanghai press denouncing this play. Thus began the Cultural Revolution.

# The Great Proletarian Cultural Revolution: The Radical Phase, 1966–1969

The Cultural Revolution was profoundly ideological and strongly political. It was cultural in the broadest sense, for it sought to remold the entire society and to change the consciousness of the Chinese people. Utopian in its aims, its results were disastrous. Its moving force was Mao himself, who was determined not to allow the revolution to drift into Soviet-style revisionism. Thus, he resolved to combat the reemergence of old patterns of bureaucratic arrogance and careerism, convinced that drastic measures were necessary to prevent the entrenchment of new vested interests in state and party and hungry to resume personal control. Now an old man, Mao was unwilling to rest on his laurels as the father of the revolution. He actively involved himself in the Cultural Revolution and dramatically displayed his physical vigor by publicly swimming some ten miles across the Yangzi River five months before he turned 74 in 1966.

The obstacles to the Cultural Revolution were formidable, because it affected the interests of a majority of party functionaries both at the center and in the provinces. But among Mao's assets were not only his unequaled prestige but also the support of the People's Liberation Army, which, under Lin Biao, emphasized guerrilla-style revolutionary spirit and fostered solidarity among officers and men by deemphasizing rank. In the summer of 1965, insignia of rank were abolished and uniforms in no way differentiated officers and men. Mao and other leaders hoped similarly to reduce or, if possible, to eliminate the distinctions and privileges of rank in society at large.

To accomplish this required the destruction of the Establishment. To carry on the battle, the country was inundated with copies of *Quotations from Chairman Mao,* the omnipresent Little Red Book cited on all occasions as the ultimate source of authority. Mao himself was glorified as never before. His sayings and pictures were everywhere; his writings were placed on family altars, his name filled the air; some villages began meetings by people holding hands and dancing to the tune of "Sailing the Seas Depends on the Helmsman, Making Revolution Depends on Mao Zedong's Thought."

The vanguard and shocktroops of the Cultural Revolution were the Red Guards, young people mostly born since the founding of the People's Republic. Mao hoped that their youthful spirit would revitalize the revolution and rescue it from sinking into comfortable revisionism. In his view it was not enough for these young people merely to read theoretical and historical works and to sing revolutionary songs. They must actually live and make revolution, so that they would be molded by direct personal revolutionary experience. As Mao had said, "a revolution is not a dinner party" (see p. 509). Going on their own "long marches" was not enough. The Red Guards were responsible for many excesses as they organized public humiliations of prominent people; administered beatings and took captives; ransacked houses; and destroyed books, art, and anything old or foreign. Many people were beaten to death or committed suicide and countless others were imprisoned or sent to labor on the land. Among the most enthusiastic participants were urban youths of questionable class background, proving to others and themselves their revolutionary purity.

Opposition to the Red Guard and the Cultural Revolution was considerable. In many places the local authorities were able to draw on popular support. There was rioting, and pitched battles were fought between rival groups, each claiming to represent the thought of Mao. Much of the information on these struggles comes from numerous posters written in large characters. Mao himself, in August 1966, wrote such a poster, "Let Us Bombard the Headquarters."

Many party headquarters were attacked, and the party was crippled. Leaders of the government, from Liu Shaoqi down, were made to confess their sins in public and then were removed from public view. Universities were closed, scientific and scholarly journals ceased publication (although nuclear development went on apace), intellectual and cultural life was disrupted, and there was turmoil in the cities. However, Zhou Enlai managed to keep the basic machinery of government working and was able to protect some from attack. Meanwhile, Mao's wife, Jiang Qing (c. 1914–1991), and Mao's secretary, Chen Boda (1904–1989), emerged as leaders of the Cultural Revolution group.

Writers and artists were prominent among the victims of the Cultural Revolution, and a narrow orthodoxy was also enforced in the other arts. Jiang Qing, herself once an actress, championed revolutionary operas. In place of traditional Chinese opera, audiences were now treated to dances on the theme, "We Are So Happy Because We Are Delivering Grain to the State," or expressing joy at the completion of an electric power plant.

The Cultural Revolution reached its most radical phase in early 1967. At the beginning of that year a dramatic series of events in Shanghai led to the triumph of a workers' movement that was able to overthrow the local party apparatus by overcoming factional divisions. In February the workers formed a People's Commune, which lasted only nineteen days, because Mao, thinking it too radical, did not endorse it. He preferred the formation of "revolutionary committees" in which the army played a leading role. With the party out of commission and the country badly divided, the army grew in importance as the single organized and disciplined institution capable of forceful action on a national scale. However, the revolution developed a new "ultraleft" intensity before the army was called in to calm things down. In the summer of 1967, hundreds of thousands demonstrated in Beijing against Liu Shaoqi and Zhou Enlai. Radicals even occupied the foreign ministry for two weeks. Outside of the capital the army killed countless numbers in clashes with opponents. The most dramatic events took place in July, when the army intervened to suppress insurgents in Wuhan. Further violence ensued elsewhere. Finally, in September, Mao and the leadership turned toward the army to restore order. The Red Guards were disbanded in July 1968.

Military men were prominent on the various revolutionary committees set up to administer provinces, factories, and communes as the Cultural Revolution continued, increasingly under army auspices. The revolution came to an end in 1969. In April of that year, a party congress officially confirmed the new prominence of the army by adopting a new constitution designating Lin Biao as Mao's successor. An important official criterion for party membership was class background. "Bad elements," such as the descendants of landlords, rich peasants, capitalists, and "rightists," continued to face obstacles in career advancement.

Earlier, party cadres and intellectuals had been "sent down" to work the land among the peasants, and now thousands of Red Guards were similarly removed from the cities for a stint of labor in the fields. This was not only a practical measure for restoring order but also had a theoretical basis in the "mass line," which embodied Mao's conviction that the people were the source of valuable ideas and that the function of leaders was to obtain these ideas from the masses, to concentrate and systematize them, and then take them back to the masses. The function of leaders was to learn humbly from the masses and also to teach them. The idea was that leaders would identify with the common people, but the actuality was that for ten years most of China's best and brightest had to suffer physical hardship and mental anguish and despair. Some were never to make it back to the cities, and numerous others would never be able to make up for years lost in education and training. China as a whole was to pay a heavy price for the loss of ten years of educational, intellectual, and technological advances.

The Cultural Revolution saw the resumption of Great Leap Forward trends that had been discarded during the early 1960s. A policy of economic decentralization and provincial self-sufficiency was emphasized as consistent with the Third Front program as well as with Maoist ideology. Again, Redness was emphasized over expertise and private economic incentives, and, again, the focus was on the rural sector, which benefited from programs that extended medical care and education. Plants were built in rural areas to manufacture and repair farm machinery, produce fertilizer, or process local products, thereby diminishing the distinction between city and country. There were experiments in calculating work points for farm work on the basis of political criteria rather than in terms of an individual's productivity. Similarly, in urban factories there were provisions for greater worker participation in factory management and programs to lessen the distinction between workers and managers and between mental and manual labor.

# The Winding Down, 1969–1976

Although the Cultural Revolution was officially ended in 1969, Jiang Qing and her associates retained control over the media and cultural affairs. During the next seven years radical Maoists remained influential in national politics and had some victories. Nevertheless, there was a gradual turn to moderation. The party was rebuilt, and moderate leaders reappeared. Mao himself wanted to curb the power of the military and turned against Lin Biao, whose downfall came in the autumn of 1971. Allegedly, Lin tried to save himself by staging a coup, and, when that failed, he attempted to flee in an airplane that crashed in Mongolia.

The fate of Liu Shaoqi and Lin Biao demonstrated the hazardous position of those marked for the succession, but Zhou Enlai, as usual, was on the winning side. Zhou continued as premier, and, with Mao's aging, he was more influential than ever. Army influence decreased and more moderate economic policies were adopted. There was a general relaxation of emphasis on revolutionary fervor. For example, when universities were first reopened in 1970, after a four-year hiatus, admission was based on recommendations from comrades in the candidate's work unit and the approval of the appropriate revolutionary committee, but in 1972 academic criteria for admission were reintroduced. Also in that year, the first scientific periodicals reappeared but with an emphasis on applied science. Public exaltation of Mao was toned down. There were even attacks on the Little Red Book; C.C.P. members were now urged to pursue a thorough study of Marxist writings.

During 1973–1974, Lin Biao, although dead, was further denounced in a campaign linking him with Confucius. Both men were portrayed as "political swindlers" and sinister reactionaries. Confucius was depicted as representing a declining slave-owner class, whereas Lin Biao was charged with wanting to restore capitalism, each man exerting himself to reinstate an outdated system. The campaign against Confucius and Lin Biao was a sign of the continuing influence of the Cultural Revolution leaders' attack on the past, but the ancient philosopher and modern general made a strange pair, and very likely Confucius was actually a surrogate for Zhou Enlai. The politics and ethos of the time are illustrated in Figure 23.3. The slogan spanning and dominating the entrance reads, "Workers, Peasants, and Soldiers Are the Main Force Criticizing Lin and Criticizing Confucius." Parking their bicycles and small tractors outside the gate, people have entered the compound to peruse wall posters spelling out the case against the two villains while loudspeakers, high on their poles like their counterparts everywhere, blare out announcements, slogans, and revolutionary music.

Most peasant paintings do not serve overt political campaigns but celebrate rural life and work. Their urban counterparts were paintings showing people working in factories. Many show women at work, for China was determined that women were to become fully equal with men (see Figure 23.4). In China, as in the Soviet Union, the challenges and triumphs of a socialist society were the main topics of art and literature, depicted in a style usually designated "socialist realism," although intended to inspire, not to mirror life.

Peasant and "social realist" paintings represent a break with old styles of painting, but other artists painted new subjects in a traditional way (see Figure 23.2) or placed modern subjects in an essentially traditional setting rendered in a traditional manner, as in Qian Songyan's *Ode to Yan'an* paying homage to the place

**FIGURE 23.3** *Repudiating Lin Biao and Confucius,* Yang Zhixian. Like many peasant paintings, this one employs bright colors. Peasant painting exhibited in Beijing in 1973. (From *Peasant Paintings from Huhsien County.* Compiled by the Fine Arts Collection Section of the Cultural Groups under the State Council of the People's Republic of China [Peking, 1974].)

where the victory of the Chinese Communist Party was forged and the revolutionary Yan'an spirit supposedly held sway (see Figure 23.5).

During the 1960s and 1970s, workers and peasants continued to be encouraged to participate in the creation of art. There were efforts to produce collective writing and painting. Another arrangement was for part-time authors to get a day

**FIGURE 23.4** *Wo shi haiyan (I am a Seagull)*, Pan Jianjun (designer/artist), c. 1973. Chinese poster showing a strong, exuberant woman defying the elements to bring modernity to the countryside. (Photograph © Stefan R. Landsberger. [Chinese Propaganda Poster Pages, online exhibit, http://www.iisg.nl/~landsberger.])

off from their factory jobs to write. Professional writers were periodically "sent down" to a factory or commune so that they would not lose touch with the people. As a matter of routine, they invited popular criticism of their work and responded to suggestions for changes. For example, before *The Golden Road* (1972) was published, 200 copies were sent to communes and factories for criticism. This novel by Hao Ran (Liang Jinguang, 1932–), 4 million copies of which were sold, dealt with the change from individual farming to the formation of mutual aid teams. In all the arts, the same themes occur over and over: the ideals and struggles of the revolution, the wisdom of Mao, the heroism of soldiers, the triumph of socialist virtue over selfishness, and the glory of work.

During and after the Cultural Revolution, Chinese relations with the Soviet Union remained tense, even though both powers supported North Vietnam in its war against the Saigon regime and the United States. Concern over Soviet intentions was heightened to alarm when the U.S.S.R. invaded Czechoslovakia in 1968 and Party Secretary Leonid Brezhnev announced that the U.S.S.R. had the right to intervene in socialist countries, which he accorded only "limited sovereignty."

Fears of a Soviet nuclear strike, actual troop deployments along the lengthy Sino-Soviet frontier, and armed clashes in Manchuria induced China to seek broader diplomatic contacts with the United States. Although Chinese personnel did assist the North Vietnamese, there was no repetition of Korea. Chinese terrain was not threatened and no massive intervention by Chinese troops took place. Meanwhile, a channel of communication was maintained with the United States through periodic meetings of the ambassadors of the two countries, held first in Geneva and later in Warsaw. The fall of Lin Biao and the emergence of Zhou Enlai increased the prospect for improved Sino-American relations.

A contributing factor on the American side was the intention of President Nixon, elected in 1968, to withdraw the United States from the war in Vietnam. As long as

China and the United States were committed to the opposing sides of a war that was raging at full force and threatening to escalate still further, substantial improvement in Sino-American relations remained highly unlikely.

Nevertheless, a high-level Sino-American dialogue was not dependent on the actual end of the war—a shift in direction toward peace was enough. By 1971 both sides were ready to talk. A new approach to China was deemed a logical corollary of the Kissinger-Nixon concept of international balance-of-power politics. The Chinese were receptive. The Sino-American rapprochement began informally with the Chinese invitation of an American ping-pong team, whose members were personally greeted by Zhou Enlai. Then came President Nixon's visit to Beijing in February 1972 and the Shanghai

**FIGURE 23.5** *Ode to Yan'an*, Qian Songyan (1898–1985). A pagoda and a transmission station face each other across a space defined, as in traditional landscapes, by mist and clouds rendering just barely visible the entrances to Yan'an's famous caves. (Schirokauer Collection. Photograph © Lore Schirokauer.)

Communiqué, which provided for partial normalization and paved the way for the resumption of full formal diplomatic relations in 1979. In 1971, even before the Nixon visit, the United Nations had voted to admit the People's Republic in place of the Nationalists, and the new American stance now removed the last obstacle to recognition by most countries.

Two deaths dominated the news in 1976. When Zhou died in January of that year, his enemies banned public mourning but were unable to prevent a massive gathering at the Martyrs' Memorial in Beijing's great Tiananmen Square on China's Day of Mourning in April. This expression of reverence for the late premier was tantamount to a rejection of the Cultural Revolution. Mao, aged and ailing, still had sufficient authority to designate Hua Guofeng (1920–) as Zhou's successor.

Hua was soon called upon to demonstrate his administrative talents, for in July China's worst earthquake in four centuries devastated Tangshan, an industrial and mining city 100 miles from Beijing. In old China, people would have interpreted this as a signal of further shocks to come—and they would have been right, for on September 9 Mao died. Architect of the triumph of the C.C.P., Mao presided over the successes of the revolution, but he was also responsible for its failures and for needless suffering, hardship, and dying. His passing marked the end of an era.

# Notes

1. Warren I. Cohen, ed., *New Frontiers in American-East Asian Relations* (New York: Columbia Univ. Press, 1983), p. 144.

2. Quoted in Merle Goldman, *Literary Dissent in Communist China* (Cambridge: Harvard Univ. Press, 1967), p. 192.

3. Quoted in Goldman, p. 193.

4. Hsu Kai-yu, *The Chinese Literary Scene— A Writer's Visit to the People's Republic* (New York: Vintage Books, Random House, 1975), p. 227.

5. Julia F. Andrews, "The Victory of Socialist Realism: Oil Painting and the New Guohua," in Julia F. Andrews and Kuyi Shen, eds., *A Century in Crisis: Modernity and Tradition in the Art of Twentieth-Century China* (New York: Guggenheim Museum, 1998), p. 230.

6. Julia F. Andrews, *Painters and Politics in the People's Republic of China, 1949–1979* (Berkeley: Univ. of California Press, 1994), p. 303.

7. William A. Joseph, Christine P.W. Wong, and David Zweig, *New Perspectives on the Cultural Revolution* (Cambridge: The Council on East Asian Studies/Harvard University, 1991), Introduction, p. 2.

# 24

# The Chinese World since Mao

| 1976 | 1978 | | 1989 | 1992 | | 1997 | | 2002 |

Death of Mao (1976)

Four Modernizations (1978)

Tiananmen (1989)

Death of Deng (1997)

Recovery of Hong Kong (1997)

**Era of Deng Xiaoping**

**Jiang Zemin 1992–2002**

After the death of Mao Zedong, China embarked on a profound change of course. Many of the policies of the previous quarter century were reversed, and new measures were adopted that bore scant resemblance to either those of Mao or of his more conventional opponents. The economy changed dramatically, and by 2000 China was the fastest growing country in the world, creating new problems and opportunities including well over 100 million migrant workers—assets to employers but potential liabilities to state and society as well. Many unemployed laborers returned to their villages, and two thirds of China's people continue to live in the countryside, but an estimated 150 million have moved to cities and towns in what shows every sign of a continuing pattern.

All spheres of life were affected by change, but in different ways and at different speeds. Artistic and intellectual change was most intense; changes in politics and its institutions lagged.

China's relationships to the external world, both in East Asia and beyond, also changed. One factor initially spurring China's leaders to adopt new policies was the recognition that economically and technologically it had fallen behind the impressive achievements of the rest of East Asia. That included not only Japan and Korea but also Hong Kong (returned to China in 1997) and especially Taiwan, whose twentieth century continued to be so different from that of the mainland as to call for separate treatment.

## Deng Xiaoping and the Four Modernizations

After a period of adversity (1977–1978), it became clear that Mao's true successor was not Hua Guofeng, as he had intended, but Deng Xiaoping (1904–1997). Deng was a party veteran who, during the Cultural Revolution, had been removed from office and denounced as second only to Liu Shaoqi in "taking the capitalist road," but more recently Deng had enjoyed the backing of Zhou Enlai. In July 1977, Deng became first deputy premier and from 1978 on was clearly China's most powerful political figure. Blamed for all the ills of the Cultural Revolution were the "Gang of Four," led by Jiang Qing, Mao's widow, who insisted, in vain, that she had simply been carrying out Mao's directives. By November 1980 the new leadership under Deng felt sufficiently secure to put the Gang of Four on trial and have the trial televised. In January 1981 Jiang Qing and another leader were given suspended death sentences, later commuted to life imprisonment. Hua Guofeng was soon shunted into political obscurity.

Deng's program was epitomized by the slogan "The Four Modernizations," first introduced by Zhou Enlai in 1975. Directed at agriculture, industry, science, and defense, the aim was to turn China into a modern industrial state. The years since 1952 had seen considerable economic progress, but China remained an underdeveloped country. Furthermore, the Cultural Revolution had taken a heavy toll in lost educational and technological progress. Now, under Deng, merit, not revolutionary virtue, was rewarded. Professionalism and individual initiative were encouraged, and market forces were allowed greater play.

There were drastic changes in the countryside as agriculture was decollectivized. In 1982 communes lost their social and political authority, and their economic power was also curtailed. Under the "responsibility system," peasants were assigned land on contracts to produce a certain amount of grain and increasingly won the right to decide on just how to do this and to dispose of any surplus produce on the open market. The amount of land to be assigned was to depend on the number of people in each family, an arrangement that seemed new but actually resembled both the 1951 Land Reform and the "equal-field system" enacted in 486 and discarded in the eighth century! Gradually, restrictions on commercial activities were eased, and enterprising peasants did notably well.

Similar changes took place in light industry and commerce, but at a slower pace. Official enterprises were expected to justify their existence by making a profit, government regulation was decreased, and individuals were allowed to open restaurants and workshops. Under a new open door policy welcoming foreign companies, special economic zones were established, where foreign investment was encouraged. At the same time, the skylines of first Beijing, then Shanghai, and more recently even cities in the interior, were being transformed by high-rise buildings, among them international luxury hotels where the affluent traveler could savor China in luxury and at an antiseptic distance.

Mao Zedong had once seen China's large population as an asset, but even before his death it became clear that China's future would be dim if the population continued to grow without restraint. In the early 1970s, China adopted a vigorous birth-control program. Even so, the population continued to increase, topping 1 billion in 1982. In the cities, the birth rate had fallen even before severe pressures ensured virtually full compliance with the one-child-per-couple law. But this was not the case in the countryside, where children, in the absence of a public safety net, continued, with good reason, to be regarded as an asset to a family.

Industrialization and population growth put additional strains on China's already hard-pressed environment. We will return to them in our discussion of the 1990s, but note here that air and water pollution were on the rise and that land erosion had already turned the Yangzi River into a second Yellow River. In the mid-1980s topsoil loss of more than 5 billion tons annually deprived China of more soil nutrition than that produced by its entire synthetic fertilizer industry. Major programs of reforestation were one positive response, but in general the environmental degradation accelerated. The state's obligation to protect the environment did find its way into the 1982 constitution, and a body of law ensued, but environmentalism did not figure in the Four Modernizations.

From early on some, mostly elderly, party leaders objected to the pace of change, but there were also voices at the opposite end of the political spectrum calling for more rapid liberalization. They found expression in postings on Beijing's "Democracy Wall," where, for a time, people could freely state their views. Especially notable was a poster put up in December 1978 by Wei Jingsheng (1949–), a young man who worked as an electrician and had four years of army service under his belt. In his poster Wei called for democracy as a Fifth Modernization absolutely necessary for the attainment of the other four.

This was too much for Deng and the political leadership. The wall was abolished. In May 1979 Wei was arrested. Subsequently, he received a fifteen-year sentence. Instead of a fifth modernization, Deng, in March 1979, proclaimed "four cardinal principles" as guides for the future.

# The Four Cardinal Principles

The four principles consisted of "the socialist road," "the dictatorship of the proletariat," "the leadership of the Chinese Communist Party (C.C.P.)," and "Marxism-Leninism and Mao Zedong Thought." In practice, as in theory, all four were vague at best. In 1981 "socialism with Chinese characteristics" was adopted as the official policy, but clearly the attainment of utopian egalitarianism receded into the distant future. The "socialist road" was to be a long one, with China deemed to be only in the "initial stage of socialism," as General Secretary Zhao Ziyang (1919–2005) put it at the Thirteenth Party Congress in 1987. That same year the mayor of Shenyang was quoted as saying, "When used to promote the development of China's socialist economy, bankruptcy, leasing, shareholding and these sorts of things are no longer capitalist."[1]

Of the other cardinal principles, the leaders took "the leadership of the C.C.P." most seriously and brooked no challenge to the political dominance of their party, which they equated with "the dictatorship of the proletariat," the orthodox Marxist label for the stage between revolution and the withering away of the state that would usher in true communism.

The status of "Marxism-Leninism and Mao Zedong Thought" was more problematic. Nineteenth-century self-strengtheners had once firmly believed in the Confucian ends they meant to serve with novel and foreign means, but China's new leaders conveyed no similar depth of conviction. To many it seemed that the official ideology commanded little more than lip service, whereas acquiring and enjoying personal wealth became the order of the day. China took on a new look as revolutionary posters and slogans gave way to commercial advertisements on billboards and in the media, clumsy at first but then "gradually transmogrified into slavish imitations of Hong Kong, Taiwanese and Japanese models." Geremie R. Barmé goes on to point out, "The world presented in such advertising was one nearly entirely divided from the ideological landscape constructed by the party." Referring to the vision projected by international consumerism and playing off Marx's denunciation of religion, he concludes, "During the early 1990's, this vision of the consumer's paradise, rather than the state religion of Marxism-Leninism and Mao Thought, became the true opiate of the masses."[2]

# Intellectual Life and the Arts in the 1980s

It was a heady time, stimulated by a deluge of new ideas, forms, and styles. The period began with the "literature and art of the wounded," as artists and writers gave expression to their suffering during the Cultural Revolution. This was followed by a "search for roots," expressed not only in literature but also in films, such as *Yellow Earth,* directed by Chen Kaige (1952–), who, along with his fellow "fifth generation" director, Zhang Yimou (1952–), won international acclaim for Chinese film. One of the many writers expressing similar sentiments was Mo Yan (Guan Moye, 1956–) whose *Garlic Ballads* depicts, with great human sympathy, the bitter life of peasants suffering at the hands of arrogant party cadres. He also wrote *Red Sorghum,* in which the villains are the Japanese military in China during World War II. Made into a movie directed by Zhang Yimou, it shocked the Chinese audience but won the best picture award at the Berlin Festival in 1988.

Some writers turned more to psychological themes or to the interplay of human feelings and engaged in stylistic experiments such as the flow of consciousness technique used by Wang Meng (1934–), Minister of Culture from 1987 to 1989. Others favored the magic realism of Gabriel García Marquéz. Meanwhile, Chinese intellectuals in all fields rejoined the international intellectual community and undertook a reexamination and reevaluation of their own past. Foreign scholars too were welcomed, as at conferences on Confucius and Zhu Xi (1987) held in the philosophers' home provinces (Shandong and Fujian, respectively). Temples and monuments were restored, as were mosques and churches. Jiang Qing's revolutionary operas disappeared from the stage, and Arthur Miller was invited to help prepare a Chinese performance of *Death of a Salesman* (1985).

Now, too, the Chinese public had its first look at modern artists ranging from Picasso to Jackson Pollock. While members of the Obscure School of Poetry expressed their alienation in verse, avant-garde painters depicted faceless figures set in endless, barren space. Some determined nonconformists, such as the Dada

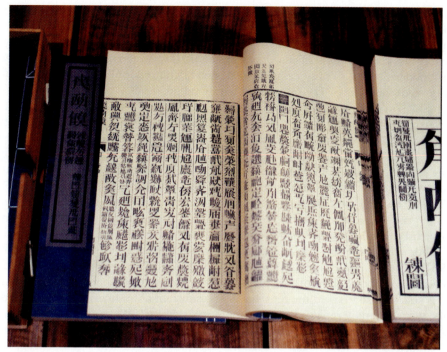

**FIGURE 24.1** Detail view of the nonsense characters on the printed pages of the books from *Book from the Sky* (1987–1991) by Xu Bing. Mixed media installation: hand-printed books, ceiling, and wall scrolls form intentionally false letter blocks. At first glance, the writing looks like Chinese, for the characters are composed of elements found in traditional writing. They are, however, nonsense characters invented by the artist. (© 1991 Xu Bing. Used by permission of the artist.)

group of Xiamen, Fujian's largest city, sought to smash all frames. Like the original proponents of Dada in post–World War I Europe, they mocked all art. Proclaiming the end of art, they ended their 1986 exhibit by burning all the works on display, frames and all. A kindred spirit was Xu Bing (1955–), who devoted three years of hard work to compose his *Book from the Sky* that no one can read, thus challenging the viewer to reflect on the nature of writing, language, art, and life in a postmodern world (see Figure 24.1).

The spirit of iconoclasm and revolt was not limited to the highbrows. Many aspects of Western popular culture found a following in China, where Japanese and Taiwanese pop tunes were widely enjoyed and rock and roll gained an ardent audience. In the mid-1980s Beijing's own Cui Jian (1961–), "the John Lennon of China,"[3] formed a rock group whose records were best-sellers, much to the puzzled dismay of the establishment.

Although raucous music and critical writings continued to find a ready hearing among students and intellectuals, the regime, guided by Deng, was concerned that matters might get out of hand, but for some ten years refrained from strong-arm measures that could alienate the intellectuals whose cooperation was needed for modernization. Thus, campaigns against "cultural pollution" (1983) and "bourgeois liberalism" (1987) were relatively mild.

Still, pressure for change mounted. An outspoken advocate of openness in government, free speech, and political pluralism was the astrophysicist, party member, and university vice president Fang Lizhi (1936–1986), who encouraged his students to campaign for genuine local elections in Anhui, where his university was located. The movement spread from Anhui. In December, some 30,000 students demonstrated in Shanghai, and there were further demonstrations in Tianjin, Nanjing, and Beijing. In response, the government removed Fang from his job and expelled him from the C.C.P. More than 1 million students were sent to spend the following summer recess in the countryside.

For some ten years Deng successfully orchestrated the pace of change, and in 1987 he had the satisfaction of seeing the Thirteenth Party Congress affirm the general directions of his policies, including the primacy of economic development. This session also marked the retirement of a substantial number of the old guard, who were generally replaced by men more inclined to "seek truth from facts," an expression found in the *History of the Han (Han Shu,* first century C.E.), taken up by Mao, and used as a slogan by Deng. Deng now felt sufficiently confident to resign as deputy premier although, significantly, he retained his chairmanship of the Military Commission for two more years.

## Tiananmen

The policy of mild repression of demands for democracy and human rights failed to deter student activism or dampen student demands for greater freedom of speech and of the press, an end to favoritism and government corruption, the right to form their own organizations, and the right for the people to have a greater say in government. In the spring of 1989 the government was caught off guard when students demonstrated, boycotted classes, held sit-ins, and occupied Beijing's huge Tiananmen Square in their determination to be heard.

With the approach of the seventieth anniversary of the May Fourth Movement, students and officials alike were aware of the historical significance of the occasion, as was the press, now including international television as well as print media. Marches and demonstrations on May 4 quickened the movement, but did not settle anything. On May 13, two days before the state visit of Premier Mikhail Gorbachev, more than two hundred students began a hunger strike supported by thousands of Beijing residents. When Gorbachev arrived, the government had to change the program and avoid Tiananmen. By May 16, the number of hunger strikers had mounted to more than 3000. Meanwhile, as the movement gathered steam,

**FIGURE 24.2** *Goddess of Democracy,* Tiananmen Square, Beijing, May 30, 1989. Radical students erected the statue to democracy, and tanks and soldiers destroyed it six days later in their violent assault on Tiananmen Square. (© Peter Turnley/Corbis [TL009252].)

students in many other cities demonstrated in support. Most alarming to the government, ordinary people, including factory workers, increasingly became involved.

Opposition within the government prevented even a mild compromise with the students, who were not well organized and did not speak with a single voice. When Deng Xiaoping asserted his leadership, the government moderates, including General Secretary Zhao, lost out. On May 20 martial law was declared, and 250,000 soldiers were brought into Beijing, where they were greeted by roadblocks and demonstrations. On May 29, in a show of determination, radical students erected a large statue of the Goddess of Democracy holding high the torch of freedom to serve as the symbol of their movement (see Figure 24.2). Cui Jian's "Long March Rock" was their unofficial anthem.

The end came early on June 4 when, shortly after midnight, columns of tanks and armored cars charged into the city and on to Tiananmen, crushing barriers and shooting anyone in the way. After the soldiers destroyed the student encampments and the statue on the square, the violence escalated. Many students and civilians were shot, and some soldiers died too. Victims of the carnage overwhelmed Beijing's hospitals, many of which were forbidden to treat civilian casualties. Nor could they or anyone else compile statistics on the numbers of dead and wounded.

Military suppression was followed by the arrest, and in some cases execution, of student leaders in the capital and elsewhere. Others found their way into exile in the

West, where some continued as leaders of a nonunified and contentious political/intellectual community. Fang Lizhi, too, found freedom abroad. In 1997, after a second imprisonment, Wei Jingsheng also found sanctuary abroad. After 1989 Chinese voices in many parts of the world presented alternatives to the ideology and policies proclaimed by Beijing. In the 1980s use of the telephone, photocopier, and fax helped undermine the government monopoly on information, which proved even more difficult to sustain with the spread of email, cell phones, and the Internet toward the end of the century. The leadership's credibility now depended not on the old ideology but on its performance, especially its economic performance.

## State, Economy, and Society in the 1990s and into the New Century

An immediate result of Tiananmen was that Deng's leading protégé, General Secretary Zhao Ziyang, was forced out of office and placed under house arrest. His place was taken by Jiang Zemin (1926–). In 1992 the octogenarian Deng made a dramatic tour of the south, proclaiming his determination to continue the pragmatic economic policy. After this trip, Deng, although still considered China's paramount leader, faded into the background, allowing Jiang to establish himself and ensure a smooth transition when Deng died in 1997.

Essentially, Jiang continued Deng's policies of economic liberalization without relaxing C.C.P. control over politics and public discourse. Economic liberalism without relaxation of political control became the hallmark of Jiang's leadership and legacy. Indicative of this dual policy was his speech of July 1, 2001, declaring that capitalists should be welcomed into the Communist Party and the government's subsequent shutting down of a publication named *The Pursuit of Truth* for criticizing this extraordinary departure from Marxist practice. Jiang redefined the role of the party as representing "advanced productive forces, advanced Chinese culture, and the fundamental interests of the majority."[4]

These "Three Representations" were billed as major theoretical contributions and were seen as a bid by Jiang to gain status as a thinker before he relinquished his post as General Secretary of the C.C.P. in November 2002. He did, however, retain his position as chairman of the Military Commission without any public indication that he would relinquish that important post in the fall of 2004. Furthermore, the appointments to positions of leadership of many of Jiang's protégés suggested a wish to remain the country's paramount leader as had Deng Xaioping after his "retirement." Meanwhile, the record of the new General Secretary, Hu Jintao (1942–), included some grounds to encourage both hard-liners and reformers, and a *New York Times* headline announced, "China's New Leader Promises Not to Sever Tether to Jiang."[5] In the fall of 2004, China had effected a smooth political transition and continuity in its basic policies.

Whatever it represented, the C.C.P. still controlled the state, but, with the state no longer "commanding" the economy, the relationship between state, economy, and society had changed. The direction of economic change remained much the same as before, although there were times of pause and hesitation. Under the direction of Premier Zhu Rongji (1928–), like Jiang an engineer by background, and a former mayor of Shanghai, the economy weathered bouts of inflation, peaking in 1988 and 1995, and the government continued to encourage foreign investment and trade, negotiating its way into the World Trade Organization in 2001.

Whereas previously people had depended on their work unit to supply everything from housing to entertainment, these functions were now privatized, with the result that in Shanghai and other eastern cities a hundred stores blossomed, a thousand restaurants contended, and advertisements urged, "buy a house and become a boss."[6] The private sector prospered and new boom towns appeared, but not everyone could become a boss.

During the early years of the new century the economic boom reached new proportions. Abroad it turned China into a major factor in determining global commodity prices, while at home there was some success in implementing banking and other policies meant to provide for a smooth landing to avert a traumatic bust.

Throughout the Jiang-Hu Period, the government reduced the scope of the state-run sector and announced its determination to continue doing so, because these enterprises were inefficient, frequently lost money, drained funds, and weakened the state banks on which they depended. However, the government had to proceed gradually because of the threat of social unrest posed by workers deprived of the security of their "iron rice-bowls." The labor market was already swollen by about 60 million peasants who were annually leaving their villages in search of better pay. The urban and rural unemployed formed a "floating population" that appeared in China's major cities looking for a day's work.

In the countryside, peasants received longer leases on their land but continued to be required to sell a quota of grain to the state, which was anxious to maintain grain self-sufficiency. At the same time, many peasants now engaged in rural industries, which came to account for 60 percent of China's industrial output but did not solve the problem of rural poverty. Like authorities of other governments at the time, those of the P.R.C. accepted a widening income gap as the price of economic growth.

Similarly in line with global trends, China moved in the direction of market economics, but the government often gave mixed political and economic signals. Heavy taxes, land requisitions, autocratic and corrupt officials, and/or severe water pollution elicited peasant petitions (70,000 in 1995) and demonstrations, some large and violent. One response was the provision for village elections "as a safety valve to let the peasantry vent their dissatisfaction." Jean C. Oi goes on to point out that different constituencies and different agendas left China "a country riddled with policy contradictions."[7]

That the new relationship between state and society is unstable and difficult to define is reflected in the proliferation of labels proffered by Western academics, including, but by no means limited to, *capitalism with Chinese characteristics, capital socialism, state-socialist corporatism, symbiotic clientism, Confucian Leninism,* and *bureaupreneurialism.* The proliferation of terms reflects the inadequacy of traditional categories as well as the blurring of the line between state and society. It also reflects the variety of relationships between state and society to be found in China. One reason is that the initiative to a considerable degree passed to local, especially county, levels. Following the penchant for fours favored in the post-Mao years, Richard Baum and Alexei Shevchenko have characterized local governments as "Entrepreneurs, Patrons, Predators, and Developers." One of their major conclusions is that the situation "augurs neither the continued potency of the central party state nor the emergence of a pluralistic civil society but the proliferation of quasi-autonomous (and potentially corrupt) local economic empires."[8]

The potential for corruption was fully realized in what Lionel M. Jensen has aptly termed a "hybrid political economy" and in "the moral confusion wrought by a contradictory ideology."[9] The country was riddled with corruption, and crime was on the increase. Nor was malfeasance by any means purely local. In August 1999 China's auditor-general reported that one-fifth of China's annual revenue had been "misappropriated," that all eighteen provincial governments were guilty, and that the Ministry of Water Resources was building luxury office buildings rather than much-needed dams and dikes.

## The Environment

Industrialization and the efforts to meet the needs and some of the aspirations of a population reported to be 1.248 billion in 1998 placed great strains on the environment. Quality of both air and water posed health threats. China's major cities were shrouded in a permanent haze, and people breathed polluted air not only outside but also even indoors, where it especially threatened women cooking over stoves burning raw coal. Most coal remained untreated, and most women, although theoretically the equals of men, remained unliberated from the stove. China was well on the way to replacing the United States as the planet's foremost producer of greenhouse gases.

Water, too, can be lethal in China. All too often "the river runs black."[10] Irrigation water is often contaminated by discharge. In the case of a village in Gansu inhabited by descendants of Confucius, the village leaders were able to obtain some redress only after challenging managers of a fertilizer plant to drink some water from a stream they had poisoned. Whether a farmer near Beijing whose geese all died after imbibing poisonous water will obtain legal redress is not yet known, but at least the courts have agreed to hear his case.

Pollution is not the only water problem. In the north water tables have sunk alarmingly and water shortages are severe. The diversion of Yellow River water for irrigation has reduced the transport of silt to the sea. Instead it is deposited on the riverbed, raising it above the surrounding countryside and posing a threat of devastating floods as of old. Meanwhile, recurrent floods inundated southern regions. Not until 1999 did the government officially acknowledge that chopping down trees in the headlands of the Yangzi had something to do with this. There have been people in and out of government who were aware of the problem, but environmental policies formulated in Beijing were often ignored locally, especially when the problem mostly affected people downriver or far away.

However, the government too contributed to the destruction of the environment. In 1992 it approved a major project to dam the Three Gorges of the Yangzi River to address China's need for clean energy and flood control and to open Sichuan, China's most populous province, to oceangoing vessels. The waters of the river were diverted in 1997, and the dam is scheduled for completion in 2009. It is to be 170 meters high and run for 2 kilometers, comparable to a four-story building a mile wide, and will cost much more than the $25 billion of the very optimistic official estimate. It will displace well over 1 million people and inundate priceless cultural sites. The government discounted warnings about the potential disasters posed by the buildup of silt behind the dam, unpredictable geologic effects, the dangers of forming a lake even more polluted than the present river, and possible adverse effects downstream. Nor was it impressed by the turning of world opinion against megadams. Although energy generation and water control could be achieved more cheaply and less dangerously by a series of small dams, these would not provide maritime access to Sichuan, where Chongqing is growing into a huge metropolis.

In April 2004 Wen Jiaobao (1942–), who had succeeded Zhu Rongji as Prime Minister in 2002, surprised Chinese and foreign observes by ordering a major review and at least a temporary halt of a huge dam project on the Nu river in Western Yunnan province that would displace 50,000 people and threaten the ecology and beauty of a region selected as a World Heritage Site. Whether and to what degree increased awareness and laws can avert the worst environmental destruction remains to be seen. The example of what the wealthy nations do will be a factor. Meanwhile, in some places local gods have sometimes been enlisted to defend the local environment.

# The Revival of Religion

One response to the loosening of central government reins was the reemergence of religion, condemned not only by Cultural Revolution enthusiasts but also denounced by Karl Marx himself as the "opiate of the people." Village temples to local and lineage deities were rebuilt, traditional burial practices resumed, and traditional beliefs and practices such as geomancy (*fengshui*) resurfaced. These cults and practices were still denounced as "superstition" by the political and intellectual establishment, which distinguished them from "legitimate" religions such as Buddhism, Daoism, Islam, and Christianity. As Stephen Feuchtwang attests, partly on the basis of personal observation, "In some places new religious buildings were tolerated, in others the Public Security forces periodically destroy them."[11] Much depended on local authorities and circumstances. For example, at Black Dragon Pool in northern Shaanxi the head of the officially sanctioned Cultural Management Institute also heads the temple association, and the Institute is responsible for the upkeep of the Black

Dragon god's temple and the conduct of its main annual festival, featuring a tour by the god around the dry land to bring rain.

During the Cultural Revolution there was a tendency to elevate Mao to a status far beyond that of an ordinary human, and now tens of thousands of pilgrims have visited a monastery in Hunan, Mao's native province, where:

> some pray for the safety and harmony of family members while others ask Mao to cure chronic diseases. [Members of] the latter group are given a glass of "holy water" after their prayers. Those who feel Mao has listened to their prayers thank him for the kindness received.[12]

Some mosques and churches, converted to factories during the Cultural Revolution, were returned to their congregations and became once again places of worship sanctioned and supervised by the state. Chinese Catholics remained separated from Rome, as the government refused to let them obey the pope, and neither Catholic nor Protestant missionaries were permitted into the country. Unsupervised worship in private houses was also prohibited. But the loss of credibility of official materialism provided fertile ground for those seeking something beyond the quest for wealth and the passing satisfactions of consumerism.

The state remained suspicious of religion as an alternate source of authority and potential nucleus of resistance and was particularly wary of Vajrayana Buddhism in Tibet and Islam in Xinjiang and Qinghai. But the government's concerns were not limited to peripheral minorities such as these. They were taken aback, and the security apparatus was caught by surprise, when 10,000 followers of *Falungong* quietly assembled in Beijing to protest the outlawing of their sect. Led from New York by its exiled founder, the sect, estimated by the government to have 70 million adherents, offered spiritual and physical health through dance-like *qigong* exercises and mental concentration. Its leader insisted from the start that it was nonpolitical, but the authorities were alarmed at its abilities to mobilize thousands and troubled that its followers were largely middle-aged and well-integrated members of the community, some even belonging to the C.C.P. It was outlawed, and periodic arrests and trials followed.

The suppression of religious expression and the arrest of political dissidents continued in the face of international concern over human rights. Although avoiding a second international outrage like Tiananmen, the regime continued to try to stamp out any sparks of separatism it feared might catch fire in Tibet or elsewhere. In international relations, particularly with the United States, the human rights issue continued to smolder, only to be doused by geopolitical and geoeconomic considerations. This was all the more the case when, after September 2001, China gave its support to the American war on terror.

# Foreign Relations and Hong Kong

Foreign relations during the late 1970s and 1980s remained within the pattern set earlier, and China remained at peace except that conflicting ambitions in Cambodia prompted an unsuccessful invasion of Vietnam in 1979. Sino-Vietnamese relations remained tense for some time. There were border clashes in 1985, but relations improved in the late 1990s. China did not engage in any further military combat but concentrated on modernizing its military.

China's relations with the Soviet Union became more cordial, especially after the U.S.S.R. withdrew from Afghanistan in 1988, whereas the fall of Communism in Eastern Europe and the disintegration of the Soviet Union were taken by China's rulers as warnings of what could befall them and their country.

Full diplomatic relations with the United States were established on January 1, 1979. Although Chinese wariness of the only remaining superpower was balanced by American unease over an emergent giant, relations remained generally cordial while trade grew and Americans entered into joint ventures with Chinese partners. With its business community enthralled by the old Western dream of an unlimited Chinese market, the United States tolerated widening trade deficits, and in the first year of the new century agreed to forgo annual reviews of China's generally unsatisfactory human rights situation. As already noted, the next year China was admitted to the World Trade Organization.

A notable diplomatic success was the agreement signed in 1984 with Great Britain to return Hong Kong to Chinese sovereignty in 1997. China in turn guaranteed that for the next fifty years Hong Kong would retain its own laws and institutions. The People's Republic thus acknowledged the economic importance of Hong Kong, which, by the mid-1980s, had developed into a major world financial and trade center with a thriving manufacturing sector. Symbolizing the future, China's Central Bank erected the city's tallest skyscrapers (1982–1990), designed by I. M. Pei (Ieho Ming Pei, 1917–), the Chinese-born American architect who in 1983 had received architecture's highest award, the Pritzker Prize. Much younger, and not nearly as famous, was Yuen Kwok-chung (1964–), whose *Triptych* (see Figure 24.3), which was exhibited at the 1994 Hong Kong Contemporary Art Biennial Exhibition, invites the viewer to see the barcode as the true flag of Hong Kong and infers that commercial consumerism (mediated through Hong Kong?) is what links the United States and the P.R.C. The Chinese title, "study hard and make progress every day," would make a splendid slogan for a textbook, but here heightens the sardonic effect. Fortuitously, in the exhibition catalog *Triptych* is preceded by a painting titled *Perplexity* and followed by *Coiling Incense Smoke.*

Although *Triptych* represents the money-making spirit of Hong Kong and of would-be Hong Kongs further up the China coast, the city also provided a haven for the likes of the noted philosopher of "New Confucianism," Mou Zongsan (1909–1995), and highly original painters such as Irene Chou from Shanghai (see Afterword Figure A.2) and Liu Guosong from Taiwan (see Figure 24.5).

With the erosion of its old ideological base, the government of the P.R.C. could seek legitimacy from its economic performance—the success of "managed consumerism," as Richard Kraus has termed it. Or it could emphasize "orchestrated nationalism"[13]—orchestrated lest it get out of hand in demonstrations that could interfere with the conduct of foreign policy and might even threaten the established order. During the 1990s it pursued both consumerist and nationalist aims. With Hong Kong safely in the fold, the de facto independence of Taiwan remained a major irritant.

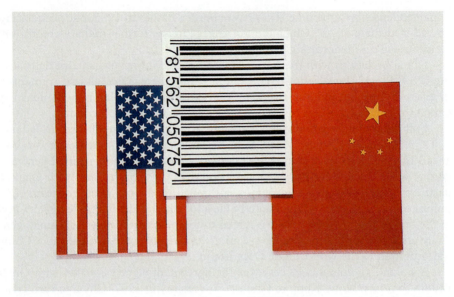

**FIGURE 24.3** *Triptych 1994*, Yuen Kwok-chung (1962–). Most people in the People's Republic at this time would probably recognize the American flag as well as their own but had never seen a barcode. That, however, was a familiar symbol in Hong Kong. Acrylic on canvas, 114.17 in × 72.44 in. (© Yuen Kwok-chung. Used by permission of the artist.)

Although chafing over foreign criticism of its suppression of human rights in Tibet and elsewhere, the government of the P.R.C. was particularly troubled by Taiwan's failure to be persuaded of the benefits of its "one country–two system policy." On the eve of Taiwan's first direct presidential elections in 1996, the P.R.C. fired missiles and conducted naval maneuvers in a show of force. As the new century began, the future of P.R.C.-Taiwan relations remained very much in doubt.

# Intellectuals and Artists in the 1990s and into the New Century

The P.R.C. continued to jail dissidents and did not tolerate political opposition. They allowed people to choose their own jobs but no longer guaranteed them a job. In general, the government gave people more latitude in the conduct of their lives to enjoy their electric appliances and other new possessions. People were allowed freedom of movement. The arts continued much in the spirit of the 1980s, producing a profusion of styles and agendas as well as a renewed appreciation of

**FIGURE 24.4** Shanghai Museum (1996), architect Xing Tonghe. The circular building placed on top of a square recalls the tradition that heaven is round and the earth is square, and the arches on the roof resemble the handles on ancient bronzes. (© Lore Schirokauer.)

tradition, including Confucianism. An unusually satisfactory marriage of new and old was the Shanghai Museum (see Figure 24.4), by the Shanghai architect Xing Tonghe, completed in 1996 to house the city's treasures, including China's foremost collection of bronze vessels from the first dynasties. Two years later it was joined by the Shanghai Grand Theater designed by Jean-Marie Charpentier, a French architect. Paul Andreu, another French architect, designed a new airport for Shanghai, and the city's postmodernist flavor will be further strengthened if and when the new art museum to be built in collaboration with New York's Guggenheim Museum sees the light of day.

Many of those prominent in the 1980s remained productive. Wang Meng fought off his critics and advocated cultural pluralism with the market as judge. In 1992 he founded *Green Leaves,* a journal on the environment. Mo Yan published *Wine Republic.* Characterized by David Der-wei Wang as a "Swiftian satire and Kafkaesque fable," it follows a detective sent to a country where people eat children. Wang comments:

> In a world where the high and the low, the fragrant and the putrid, mingle, nobody has clean hands; the protagonist is fittingly murdered by being drowned in a manure pit at the end of the novel. Eschatology and scatology turn out to be two readings of the same reality.[14]

In 1995 Chen Kaige directed *Farewell My Concubine,* which found a warm reception overseas. The work of some of the most experimental artists was confined to their apartments, whereas the audience of others, like the computer artist Feng Mengbo, was primarily overseas. Feng, a resident of Beijing, explained the thought behind his series of paintings *Taxi! Taxi!—Mao Zedong I–III* as follows:

> In 1990, when I was still at the academy, I suddenly realized that the way Mao Zedong waved his hand at the army [of Red Guards] gathered in Tiananmen Square during the Cultural Revolution was very similar to the way people wave to hail a taxi. So I copied the image of Mao waving and put a common yellow taxicab in front of him—the kind you see everywhere in Beijing today.[15]

Mao had been taken off his pedestal and made to hail a cab! Once inside he was likely to encounter a Mao traffic safety charm. To recover from the shock would he have taken a swig of "The East is Red" health drink, thirsting for the days when this had been the anthem of the revolution?

Cui Jian, the rock star, had his ups and downs, but mostly was tolerated by the authorities and allowed to perform at home and abroad. David Fricke, critic for *Rolling Stone,* heard him in concert in 1995 and wrote:

> But just as he challenges the arthritic authority of his country's leaders, Cui tolerates no laws or limits to his music. The rumble of Chinese barrel drum fattened the surge of angular guitar grooves. Beastie-style beats, fierily Jamaican ska and the roadhouse rattle of early Springsteen collided in such anthemic fireballs as "The Other Shore," "Together we confront the same reality—Together we sing a song loudly."[16]

Listeners will need to judge the results for themselves as postmodern Chinese intellectuals engage "in a new search for a real 'hybridization' or 'hybridity' based on a dialectical synthesis beyond the old dichotomies between the traditional and the modern, the particular and the universal."[17]

One dichotomy that was breaking down was that between the thought and symbolic world of artists and writers living in the P.R.C. and those living elsewhere in a Chinese or semi-Chinese world. Whereas critics worried about the hybrid culture, the mixing of elements from different traditions continued to the point that when a joint exhibit was held in New York in 1999, it was often difficult to distinguish the works of those in the P.R.C. from the works of those outside. Mainland exiles in America, Europe, Australia, and New Zealand as well as artists and writers from Taiwan contributed to "a China defined not by geopolitical boundaries and ideological closures but by overlapping cultural and shared imaginative resources."[18]

In 2004 Xu Bing exhibited *Where Does the Dust Itself Collect,* an installation in Wales and Berlin employing dust from Ground Zero in New York to represent the dust in the poem of the Sixth Patriarch (see p. 121) to make a Zen statement. Also in 2004 the reaction of people at the Shanghai Biennal suggested that at least in that increasingly cosmopolitan city the most determinedly avant garde art had just about lost its ability to shock.

## Taiwan

**TAIWAN**

| 1945 | 1947 | 1949 | | 1975 | 1988 | 2000 |

**REPUBLIC OF CHINA**

Return to China (1945)

Feb. 28 Uprising (1947)

Loss of the Mainland (1949)

**Chiang Kai-shek** — **Chiang Ching-kuo** — **Lee Denghui**

Chen Shuibian 2000–

As noted earlier, Taiwan's first two years under the Guomindang-controlled Republic of China were so oppressive as to provoke the violence of 1947. One result of Guomindang actions was that the Taiwanese elite was decimated. Ironically, this removed not only resistance to the political dominance of the Nationalists but also a potential source of opposition to land redistribution and other economic reforms undertaken during the 1950s with American backing, pressure, and advice. As in postwar Japan, the end of landlordism had profound economic and social effects.

During the Japanese years, Taiwan had acquired much of the necessary infrastructure for industrialization, and many of the approximately 2 million civilian refugees who fled from the mainland also brought training and skills that contributed to the development of light industry and commerce. Capital came in part from the great sums of money the Nationalists brought over with them. Until terminated in 1966, American economic aid also helped, and once the Japanese economy had recovered, Japanese companies invested heavily. The government generally supervised and advanced development, first building up infrastructure and then fostering exports. In 1965 it created special Export Processing Zones where companies enjoyed tax incentives and were free of import taxes as long as they exported whatever they made or assembled.

Culturally, the government saw its mission as preservation of old Chinese traditions. Taiwan became the home for institutes of higher learning. The use of the local Taiwanese language was suppressed and, as in the P.R.C., instruction was in Mandarin. A museum was built to house the priceless Palace Collection the Nationalists brought with them from the mainland.

At a time when mainland artists were caught in the political storms, artists in Taiwan and elsewhere were free to explore new ways to draw on their tradition to create forms of expression suitable for the twentieth century. One of the most gifted of these was Liu Guosong (Liu Kuo-sung, 1932–), who was born in Shandong, was educated in Taiwan, established himself as a painter there, taught many years in Hong Kong, and returned to Taiwan, where he now lives.

As Liu explained, "We are no longer ancient Chinese nor modern Westerners. We do not live in the Song or Yuan society, nor in the modern European or American environment. If it is false for us to copy old Chinese paintings, isn't it the same to copy modern Western painting?"[19] Not satisfied with working in either Chinese or Western styles, Liu asserted, "'Chinese' and 'modern' are the two blades of the sword, which will slash the Westernized and the traditionalist schools alike."[20]

Liu is deeply conversant with both traditions. Chu-tsing Li describes the collage in Liu's *Metaphysics of Rocks* (see Figure 24.5) as follows:

> In the lower middle part are two pieces of collage, one large and the other small, both suggesting rock shapes. The paper is in color, but combined with some textures printed with wrinkled paper. Thus there seem to be several kinds of rocks, done with different techniques and brushwork. Yet none of them is realistic enough to resemble real rocks. But each gives us an idea of some quality of rocks, such as jutting up, having interesting textures, or showing watery surfaces.[21]

Liu went on to paint a distinctive series on the sun and moon and continued to experiment with textures and techniques and paint abstractions that suggested the metaphysics of mountains.

Under the Guomindang, the Republic of China remained ideologically committed to the reunification of China and to Sun Yat-sen's Three Principles of the People. Until ousted from the United Nations in 1971, its claim to speak for China was widely accepted abroad. At home, although the Guomindang was reformed, it remained dictatorial, refusing to share substantive power with the Taiwanese, that is, people of Chinese stock who had settled on the island before 1945. Although the native Taiwanese did win elections to local governments, real control remained in the hands of the central government. Prosperity and repression kept dissent to a minimum. Among those imprisoned on Green Island was Bo Yang (1920–), given ten years for translating an English language comic deemed insulting to Chiang Kai-shek. His acerbic critique of Chinese ways won him a wide readership on the mainland.

When Chiang Kai-shek died in 1975, there was an easy and smooth passing of power to his son Chiang Ching-kuo (in *pinyin*, Jiang Jingguo, 1910–1988). Progress was sufficient for the economy to come through both the oil crisis and the diplomatic defeats of the 1970s in good shape. As in Japan, there was a turn to more advanced technology such as computers. In 1980 the state established a science-oriented industrial park and an electronics industry.

By that time Taiwan had attained a level of per capita income second in Asia only to that in Japan. In many ways, it became a modern country. By 1979 more

**FIGURE 24.5** *The Metaphysics of Rocks*, Liu Guosong. The artist uses calligraphy, brushwork, and collage. Ink and acrylic with collage on paper, 1968, 26.49 in × 27.01 in. (© Liu Kuo-sung. Used with permission of the artist.)

than one-half of the people owned a color television set and 90 percent had refrigerators. During the 1980s air conditioners became common, and cars largely captured the road dominated previously by motorbikes.

The normalization of U.S. relations with the P.R.C. meant that relations with Taiwan were formally downgraded. Semiformal relations were maintained, but the Guomindang's claim to the rulership of all of China was weakened, and those born in Taiwan who coupled demands for democratization with calls for a Republic of Taiwan found their case strengthened. Chiang Kai-shek's response had been repression, but his son alternated between jailing leaders of the opposition and instigating reform. The latter was predominant during his last two years, when martial law was revoked, press restrictions were eased, and the prohibition against opposition parties relaxed.

These reforms allowed the Democratic Progressive Party (D.P.P.) to field candidates in the election of December 1986. Inhabitants of Taiwan were, for the first time in thirty-eight years, allowed to visit relatives on the mainland. The government was confident that they would return with an appreciation for the higher standard of living they enjoyed on Taiwan. In practice, even the post-1945 newcomers came to see themselves as different from mainlanders and as having much in common with their fellow Taiwanese.

When Chiang Ching-kuo died in January 1988, he was succeeded by Lee Teng-hui (Li Denghui, 1923–), a Taiwanese with a Ph.D. in agricultural economics from Cornell who brought more Taiwanese into the top party and government posts and included fourteen holders of American doctorates in his cabinet. The emergence of a strong middle class, strong advances in education, and continuing affluence provided fertile ground for continued movement in the direction of greater democracy, whereas the ultimate nature of a Taiwanese identity remained in dispute. The GMD won the election of 1989, but the D.P.P. gained ground. Despite the P.R.C.'s show of force, Lee was victorious in Taiwan's first direct popular presidential election in 1996. However, he had to face not only D.P.P. opposition but also divisiveness within his own party that led to a major defection in 2000. In the election of that year, Chen Shui-bian (also written Chen Shui-bien or Chen Shuibian) (1951–) of the D.P.P., with 39.3 percent of the vote, defeated two rival candidates to become the Republic of China's youngest and first non-GMD president. His vice president, the women's rights advocate Lu Hsiu-lien (Lu Xiulian, Annette Lu, 1944–), was the first woman elected to that high office. Elected on a promise to put an end to widespread corruption, Chen, on assuming office, played down his Taiwanese nationalism and gave priority to domestic house-cleaning. Beijing, which had issued threatening statements before the election and had made it clear that it would not rule out the use of force if Taiwan declared independence, was quieted for the time being, but the example of a party losing an election to an opposition running on an anticorruption platform must have been distasteful, not to say unnerving, to those too deeply implicated in the mainland status quo.

The broad picture was little changed after March 2004 when Chen and Lu were reelected by less than 30,000 of 13 million votes, although 300,000 protested the election results in a demonstration that ended in violence.

# *Notes*

1. Christopher R. Wren, "Comparing Two Communist Paths to 'Reform,'" *The New York Times,* Sept. 6, 1987, Section 4, p. 2.

2. Geremie R. Barmé, *In The Red: On Contemporary Chinese Culture* (New York: Columbia Univ. Press, 1999), p. 123.

3. Shen Tong, *Almost a Revolution* (Boston: Houghton Mifflin, 1990), p. 310, as

quoted in Andrew E. Jones, *Like a Knife: Ideology in Contemporary Chinese Popular Music* (Ithaca: East Asia Program, Cornell Univ., 1992), p. 95.

4. *The New York Times,* August 16, 2001, p. A13.

5. *The New York Times,* November 21, 2002, p. A16.

6. *Xinmin wanbao (New People's Evening News),* Shanghai, May 11, 1994, as

quoted by Deborah S. Davis in her introduction to *The Consumer Revolution in Urban China* (Berkeley: Univ. of California Press, 2000), p. 9.

7.  Jean C. Oi, "Two Decades of Rural Reform in China: An Overview and Assessment," *The China Quarterly,* No. 159 (Sept. 1999), p. 627.

8.  Richard Baum and Alexei Shevchenko, "The State of the State," in Merle Goldman and Roderick MacFarquhar, eds., *The Paradox of China's Post-Mao Reforms* (Cambridge: Harvard Univ. Press, 1999), pp. 345, 349. The list of labels at the beginning of this paragraph is taken from the same source, where each label is documented.

9.  Lionel M. Jensen, "Everyone's a Player, but the Nation's a Loser: Corruption in Contemporary China," in Timothy B. Weston and Lionel M. Jensen, eds., *China Beyond the Headlines* (Latham, Md.: Rowman and Littlefield, 2000), p. 42.

10. Elizabeth C. Economy, *The River Runs Black* (Ithaca: Cornell Univ. Press, 2004.)

11. Stephen Feuchtwang, "Religious Resistance," in Elizabeth J. Perry and Mark Selden, eds., *Chinese Society: Change, Conflict and Resistance* (London: Routledge, 2000), p. 171.

12. *Eastern Express,* October 5, 1955, p. 39, as quoted in Elizabeth J. Perry, "Crime, Corruption, and Contention" in Goldman and MacFarquhar, *The Paradox of China's Post-Mao Reforms,* p. 323.

13. Richard Kraus, "Public Monuments and Private Pleasures in the Parks of Nanjing: A Tango in the Ruins of the Ming Emperor's Palace," in Deborah S. Davis, ed., *The Consumer Revolution in Urban China,* p. 306.

14. David Der-wei Wang, *Fin-de-siecle Splendor: Repressed Modernities of Late Qing Fiction, 1849–1911* (Stanford: Stanford Univ. Press, 1997), p. 332.

15. Quoted in Barmé, *In the Red: On Contemporary Chinese Culture,* p. 231.

16. David Fricke, "Cui Jian: New York, The Bottom Line, Aug. 31, 1995," *The Rolling Stone,* Nov. 2, 1995.

17. Min Lin with Maria Galikowski, *The Search for Modernity: Chinese Intellectual and Cultural Discourse in the Post-Mao Era* (New York: St. Martin's Press, 1999), p. 197.

18. David Der-wei Wang, "Chinese Fiction for the Nineties," in David Der-wei Wang and Jeanne Tai, eds., *Running Wild: New Chinese Writers* (New York: Columbia Univ. Press, 1994), p. 238.

19. Quoted in Chu-tsing Li, *Liu Kuo-sung— The Growth of a Modern Chinese Artist* (Taipei: The National Gallery of Art and Museum of History, 1969), p. 32.

20. Preface to *The Way Forward for Modern Chinese Painting* (Taipei: Literary Star, 1965), pp. 3–4, quoted in program for the Hong Kong Museum of Art Exhibit "Liu Guosong, a Universe of His Own," curated by Christina Chu (Hong Kong: The Leisure and Cultural Service Department, 2004).

21. *The Way Forward for Modern Chinese Painting,* p. 53.

# The New Japan

## I. The New Japan (1952–1989)

The Economy

Government and Politics

The 1970s and 1980s

## II. Society, Thought, and the Arts

Social Change
and Quality of Life

Film

Intellectual Life and Literature

The Visual Arts

## III. From 1989 into the New Century

## Key Dates

| | |
|---|---|
| **1952** | Termination of the Occupation |
| **1954** | Resignation of Prime Minister Yoshida Shigeru |
| **1955** | Formation of the Liberal Democratic Party (L.D.P.) |
| **1956** | Admission of Japan into the United Nations |
| **1960** | Demonstrations against Continuation of the U.S.–Japan Mutual Security Treaty |
| **1968** | Awarding of the Nobel Prize to Kawabata Yasunari |
| **1971** | Floating of the Dollar |
| **1972** | Visit of Prime Minister Tanaka Kakuei to Beijing |
| **1976** | Lockheed Scandal |
| **1980** | Automobile Production Exceeds That of the United States |
| **1989** | Death of Showa Emperor<br>Recruit Scandal |
| **1990** | Stock Market Plunge |
| **1991** | Beginning of a Decade of Weak Economy |
| **1993** | L.D.P. Crisis |
| **1994** | Awarding of the Nobel Prize to Oe Kenzaburo |

After regaining independence in 1952, Japan went on to achieve such phenomenal economic growth that by the 1970s it had become one of the world's industrial giants. By the 1980s, people in the United States and Britain were turning to Japan for lessons in industrial management. Despite a setback in the last decade of the century, Japan remained an economic power second only to the United States.

Japan's economic growth was part of a broader transformation that affected every aspect of life. The pace of change was steadier than in China, but that did not make it less extensive or profound. The absence of the drastic shifts in direction that punctuated Chinese history enables us to describe the new Japan in a single chapter—but makes it harder to divide into periods. We have chosen to break our story at 1989, when a new emperor ascended the throne, primarily because the end of the Cold War coincided with the end of the economic exuberance of the 1980s.

# I. The New Japan (1952–1989)

## The Economy

In Japan as elsewhere, economic and political history are deeply intertwined. As we have seen, the Japanese economy was greatly stimulated by the Korean War. Thereafter, Japan continued to profit from access to foreign raw materials, technology, and markets, including those of the United States. Because of popular sentiment, constitutional constraints, and the country's reliance on the American "nuclear umbrella," Japan was freed from the burden of supporting a large and costly military establishment, releasing funds and energies for economic development. At the same time, business benefited from a probusiness political system.

Politically, the period began with Yoshida in power and his Liberal party in control of the Diet. He remained in office until 1954, when he was forced to resign in the wake of a scandal involving the shipping industry. In the elections of 1955, the Democratic party, a rival conservative party, won a plurality but not the majority required to govern. It therefore entered into negotiations with the Liberal party that led to the formation of the Liberal Democratic Party (L.D.P.) which dominated Japanese politics until 1993.

By 1953, economic production had practically returned to prewar levels, although the volume of trade was still only half of what it had been previously. After 1954, the economic surge continued, transforming recovery into growth at an average of 10 percent a year from 1955 to 1974 (including more than 11 percent during the 1960s). During the 1950s, with government support, great strides were made in heavy industry—even though Japan lacks raw materials and is poor in energy resources. By building manufacturing plants in port cities, which provided the advantage of low-cost ocean transport, and through the sophisticated application of modern technologies, Japan was able to become the world's leading shipbuilder and the third largest producer of iron and steel (after the United States and the Soviet Union). By 1974 its steel production had reached 89 percent of that of the United States. There were investments in chemicals, textiles, and consumer products. The washing machine, vacuum cleaner, and refrigerator of the 1950s were soon joined by the television set and the air conditioner, with the video recorder, microwave, and computer following in the 1980s. Car production reached 10 million in 1966, dubbed "year one of the My-Car Era" by the media. Cameras, watches, and even pianos—it is difficult to think of a major consumer technology in which Japan failed to excel.

Some of these products were built by new companies, such as Sony or Honda, founded by entrepreneurs who took advantage of the opportunities offered by postwar economic dislocation to build new enterprises from scratch. Other ambitious men (in what remained a man's world) reorganized or rejuvenated older companies, often importing technology by buying rights to foreign patents. In the dominant position in the economy, however, familiar old names reappeared, including Mitsui, the world's oldest major company, as well as Mitsubishi, Sumitomo, and others.

The names were old, but they now designated a new kind of enterprise grouping consisting of affiliated companies (*keiretsu*) rather than the family-centered *zaibatsu* of the prewar period. Each group included a bank, likely an insurance company, a real estate firm, and a cluster of companies engaged in every conceivable line of business, where its main competitor was most frequently a member of a rival group. The activities of the various member firms of each group were coordinated in periodic meetings of their presidents in presidents' clubs. Interlocking directorships, mutual stock holdings, and internal financing further held the organizations together, although more loosely than in the old *zaibatsu*. The *keiretsu* grew in size and strength until in the mid-1970s a study by Japan's Fair Trade Commission found that the six major groupings, composed of 175 core companies, held 21.9 percent of all the capital in Japan and had a controlling interest in another 3095 corporations that held 26.1 percent of the nation's capital. In addition, they had substantial investments in other companies that they influenced without controlling.

Among the member firms of these enterprise groupings, the most spectacular were trading companies (*shōsha*) that conducted their business not only at home but all over the world. These were exporting and importing, transporting and storing, and financing and organizing a host of multifarious projects—an airport in Kenya, a large commercial farm on Sumatra, a petrochemical industry for Iran, or copper mining in Zaire, linked by communications networks that, for a time, were unparalleled. Furthermore, Mitsui, Mitsubishi, and the others built their own research organizations, analyzing information, charting future trends, and drawing up plans to provide for future project recommendations. Their experts engaged in city planning, energy research, and research into the world's oceans.

Japanese companies provided varied services and facilities for their employees, including company dormitories for the unmarried. There were company athletic teams and a host of recreational activities, such as organized outings to mountain retreats. These were intended not only to foster the health and well-being of the employees but also to strengthen feelings of group solidarity and identification with the sponsoring company, which used them to convey an image of paternalistic solicitude. At Toyota, Japan's leading automobile manufacturer, white-collar men received an entire year of training, including a month in a company camp. Recruitment patterns that centered on certain universities, encouraging ties among men entering a company in the same year; an emphasis on longevity in promotions; the practice of extensive consultation; and a strong preference for decision by consensus all helped foster management solidarity.

Japanese companies, especially the large modern concerns, mostly retained the loyalty of their employees, who were made to feel that what was best for the company was also best for Japan. This business ideology gained credence from management's practice of plowing earnings back into the company so that it could continue to grow and hopefully surpass its rivals. At the same time, the efficacy of persuasion should not be exaggerated, because company extras increasingly became matters not of paternalism but of contractual rights subject to collective bargaining, like fringe benefits in other countries. However, management was able to get workers to agree to moderate wage increases and fringe benefits. The threat of foreign competition was also used effectively, and for years Japanese companies enjoyed a lower labor bill and more labor peace than many of their competitors in Europe and America. The quest for economic growth gave Japan a sense of national purpose even as it promised an improved standard of living for the people.

Japan's concentration on economic development was epitomized in the income-doubling policy of Ikeda Hayato (1899–1965, prime minister 1960–1964) that provided for the doubling of per capita production in ten years. The government fostered growth by establishing a political climate favorable to economic expansion, by investing in infrastructure, by adopting appropriate fiscal and monetary policies, and by setting production targets, assigning priorities, and generally orchestrating the economy. It sponsored the bullet train, which in 1964 reduced what had been a major overnight journey between Kyoto and Tokyo to a trip of three hours and ten minutes. The government built roads and dams, and it financed the reclamation of coastal lands.

Although the Construction Ministry controlled the bulk of infrastructure spending, the Finance Ministry and the Ministry of International Trade and Industry (MITI) coordinated economic growth. The importance of the MITI reflected the crucial role of foreign trade in Japan's economy and the determination of the government to oversee the country's economic and political relations with other countries. By deploying foreign exchange allocations, manipulating quotas, and establishing barriers protecting native capital from foreign competition, the government channeled the flow of investment funds. It could also extend or deny tax privileges. It thus had at its disposal a variety of weapons to bring recalcitrant companies into line if persuasion, pressures, or both failed. Generally, it preferred to rely on discussion and to act as much as possible on the basis of a shared government–business consensus. Businesses competed with each other within a more tightly defined arena than in most other capitalist nations.

Consensus was possible not only because of the shared aims and interests of government and business but also because of ties between the government and the business community. Often these ties were personal, because the men at the top in the private sector and those heading the influential and prestigious government ministries tended to share similar backgrounds (both included a high proportion of Tokyo University graduates). Some ties were ideological, because Japan was ruled during these years by conservatives. And some ties were financial, because elections were costly and business constituted a major source of funds for conservative politicians.

## Government and Politics

After 1955, the L.D.P. was opposed by the two Socialist parties (the Japan Socialist Party and the Democratic Socialist Party), by the Clean Government Party (formed in 1964, it first ran candidates for the lower house in 1967), by the Communist party, and by independent politicians. This opposition was too divided to constitute a serious alternative to conservative rule, but it was sufficient to prevent the L.D.P. from gaining the two-thirds majority in the Diet needed for revising the constitution. Some conservatives, concerned about Japan's security, favored the revocation of Article IX to enable Japan to acquire its own military power. In view of a dangerous world and in response to American urgings, the Self-Defense Forces were expanded to include well-equipped naval and air arms, and the defense budget continued to increase. However, Japan persisted in foregoing offensive weapons or capabilities, and total defense expenditures remained limited to 1 percent of GNP until 1987.

About a quarter of L.D.P. Diet members were former bureaucrats, as were Prime Minister Ikeda; his immediate predecessor, Kishi Nobosuke (1957–1960); and his successor, Satō Eisaku (1964–1972). Subsequently, only Nakasone Yasuhiro (1982–1987) occupied that position for more than two years. Throughout the period, the well-educated, capable, and prestigious higher bureaucracy wielded great influence not only on executing government policies but also on policy making.

Dominating the internal dynamics of the L.D.P., and thus determining the composition of Japan's government, was the interplay of political factions. After 1972, all prime ministers came from five factions—formal, recognized political groupings built around a leader, usually a potential prime minister. From his faction a member derived political and financial support in his election campaigns and backing in his attempts to gain high government or party office. In return, he owed his faction leader political support, especially during the complex maneuvering that determined the party presidency and the prime ministership. What counted was skill in assembling political combinations and seniority, not popular appeal.

The L.D.P.'s origin as an association of independently based politicians helps account for the strength of the factions. Another factor was a system of multimember election districts in which there were frequently more conservative candidates than could reasonably expect to win election. Thus, in a five-member district, there might be four L.D.P. candidates with only three likely to win. In such cases, they would be backed by rival factions within the L.D.P.

The power of the factions set limits on the prime minister's authority and weakened the party at the grass-roots level, where each politician cultivated his (or in rare cases her) own local support organization composed of various groups within his constituency. The politician maintained his following by supporting various community activities and offering personal assistance to constituents. He kept his political machine oiled by maintaining a "pipeline to the center" so that he could take credit for obtaining public works and other special-interest legislation. In seeking to fulfill these expectations, politicians depended on the political clout of their faction and a purse kept full by friendly interests. Although the most successful politicians were solidly entrenched, there were enough shifts in political fortunes on both the local and the national levels to provide for political interest. More importantly, the system retained the flexibility to adjust policies to changing circumstances.

For the opposition parties of the left, these were years of frustration. The two Socialist parties were closely associated with labor, each linked to one of the labor confederations. They depended on organized labor for votes, and labor leaders figured prominently in their leadership. Many of their Diet members also came from a labor background. Ideologically, the Socialists ran the gamut from Maoist radicals calling for revolution to moderate reformists. During the 1950s the Communist party was weak, but it picked up strength in the late 1960s after adopting pragmatic policies. However, even had they been able to unite, the three leftist parties lacked the strength to topple the L.D.P. regime.

Domestically, the opposition parties viewed with special alarm L.D.P. measures that looked suspiciously like a retreat from Occupation reforms and a return to the past—for example, measures to recentralize the police and education functions and to give Tokyo greater control over local government. Socialist fears were fortified by the prominence in the conservative leadership of men who had held Cabinet offices in the 1930s and had been purged from politics by the Occupation authorities. The left was adamantly opposed to government moves to recreate a military establishment and did what it could to block or at least delay the expansion of the Self-Defense Forces.

The left also objected to the government's pro-American foreign policy, protested against the continued presence of American bases, and argued against American nuclear weapons and tests. Unrestrained by expectations of forming a government themselves, they engaged in bitter struggles, including boycotts of the Diet and physical disruption, prompting police intervention. The L.D.P. did not refrain from using its majority to ram legislation through the Diet with little regard for the niceties of parliamentary procedure. This is what Prime Minister Kishi did in 1960 to gain renewal of the Security Treaty with the United States, first signed in 1952 together with the peace treaty. The renewal of this treaty prompted demonstrations sufficiently strong to prompt the cancellation of President Dwight Eisenhower's planned visit to Japan.

Political animosity now reached its greatest intensity. Opponents felt that instead of providing for Japanese security, the treaty endangered Japan, threatening to involve it in American wars. The specter of nuclear war was particularly terrifying to a people who had experienced Hiroshima and Nagasaki. The Socialists mustered impressive support for their opposition to the renegotiated treaty. Union workers, housewives, students, professors, and members of diverse organizations took to the streets in mass demonstrations in which millions of people participated. There was also a one-day general strike. All this did not block ratification or enactment of the treaty, but Kishi did resign.

After the 1960 confrontation, politics simmered down to less violent exchanges as the success of Japan's economic development became apparent. Ikeda's ten-year plan to double per capital GNP was achieved in only seven years. Although there were student protests against the Vietnam War, the Security Treaty was renewed in 1970 with little trouble.

In 1964 the political scene was complicated by the appearance of the Clean Government Party, formed by the Sōka Gakkai (Value Creation Society), a religious sect. As implied by its name, the party program opposed corruption, but it was vague on other issues. After obtaining 10.9 percent of the vote in the 1969 election, it declined to 8.5 percent in 1972 but remained a presence for the rest of the century. Meanwhile, the L.D.P. aroused little enthusiasm and was particularly weak in the cities. Before 1967 its candidates had received over half of the vote, but in the election of that year it declined to 48.8 percent and continued slowly downward until it bottomed in 1976 at 41.8 percent. Even then it remained by far the largest vote getter and benefited from an electoral system that favored rural areas.

# The 1970s and 1980s

In the 1970s, Japanese resilience was tested by a series of short-term economic and political shocks. The first came in 1971, when the United States, Japan's largest trading partner, placed a 10 percent surcharge on imports and abandoned a fixed rate of exchange. Instead, it was left to the international monetary market to determine the value of the yen, with the result that it rose, making Japanese goods more expensive overseas but also making imports cheaper. Both these American actions were aimed at reducing, if not eliminating, a mounting U.S. trade-and-payment deficit with Japan, but they proved ineffective, and the problem persisted.

A political blow followed these economic acts when, still in the same year, Washington announced the impending visit of President Nixon to China, an act on which Japan was not consulted and one that undercut Prime Minister Satō, who, primarily to please Washington, had been following the unpopular policy of maintaining the fiction that the Nationalist regime on Taiwan was the government of China. In 1972, after Tanaka Kakuei (prime minister, 1972–1974), became the first Japanese prime minister to visit Beijing, Japan recognized the P.R.C.

The next shock came in 1973 when the Arab oil boycott reminded Japan of its dependence on imported energy and was followed by a quadrupling of the price of this vital import. As a result, from 1974 to 1976 Japan suffered a severe recession. However, the system demonstrated remarkable resilience. An outstanding example was the rescue of the Japanese automaker Mazda, saved from collapse through the cooperation of government-backed financial interests, management, workers, dealers, suppliers, and the local community. This "lesson in managing interdependence" led two American experts to conclude, "Relatively low interest rates, MITI bureaucrats, trade barriers, and the like are, no doubt, important factors in a comparative history of economic growth, but only managers and workers build cars and other products. And their capacity to pull together in a crisis is a crucial measure of a society's strength."[1]

In the later 1970s and 1980s, Japan's emphasis on high technology led to a decrease in dependence on imported raw materials. By 1984, Japan had reduced its use of imported raw material per unit of manufacture to 60 percent less than it had been twenty years earlier. This change also positioned Japan to compete with the emerging economies of such neighbors as Korea and Taiwan. Encouragement was given to electronics, telecommunications, biochemicals, and machine tools. In these ways, the economy continued to sustain a population that by 1985 had reached 121 million, up from 65 million in 1930 and about four times the number of inhabitants of Japan at the time of the Meiji Restoration.

As elsewhere, the move away from "smoke-stack industries" hurt the labor movement by reducing the number of its members. Furthermore, most people considered themselves middle class. Growth of GNP declined to the level of other fully developed countries, but Japan's trade imbalance, especially with the United States, posed a continuing problem. Expectations to the contrary, it was not solved by the rising value of the yen, which did, however, facilitate Japanese investment in the United States.

One business response to new conditions was the transformation of Japanese companies into multinationals. Increasingly, Japanese concerns, in addition to trading in world markets, became involved in manufacturing overseas. These operations were generally successful on the factory floor, but it proved more difficult to internationalize management or "localize" the "transplants." In many cases, Japanese companies were resented for reserving the best jobs for those at home, for building factories far from the troubled and job-hungry cities, for favoring their *keiretsu* partners, and for generally taking advantage of opportunities abroad denied to foreign companies at home.

In politics as in economics, the system proved vulnerable but resilient. Early in 1976, the Lockheed scandal ("Japan's Watergate") shook the political world when it was revealed that millions of dollars of the American company's funds had been used to corrupt the highest Japanese government officials. Although prosecutors lacked the independence and tools to be truly effective, they were able to indict the former Prime Minister Tanaka Kakuei, who was found guilty in a 1983 decision upheld in 1987.

Predictions that the L.D.P. would decline to the point of losing its ability to form a government proved false. It reached a low of 41.8 percent of the popular vote in 1976 but made a strong comeback in 1980. In 1986 it won 49.6 percent of the vote, entitling it to 300 seats, the highest number of the party's history. Not only the party but also its internal factional structure remained essentially the same. Despite the Lockheed scandal, Tanaka continued to control his faction until he suffered a stroke in 1985.

The leading political figure in the 1980s was Nakasone Yasuhiro (1918–), who, as prime minister from 1982 to 1987, brought an unusually vigorous style of leadership and national assertiveness into the office. Prosperity, self-confidence, and American pressure combined to induce the government in 1986 to exceed the previous 1 percent of GNP cap in the military budget for the next year. Although the increase was modest, it had symbolic significance. At the same time, the Socialist party dropped its long-standing opposition to the Self-Defense Forces based on Article IX of the constitution. It now held that the Self-Defense Forces were "unconstitutional but legal." Ten years earlier the Supreme Court had ruled that the constitutionality of the forces was for the legislature to decide and had left it up to the legislature to rectify an electoral system that was unconstitutional in discriminating against urban voters.

Nakasone cooperated with the United States to reduce the trade surplus by emphasizing domestic spending, cooperating on monetary policy, and trying to open Japanese markets to more imported goods. The last of these, however, was difficult in face of powerful, deeply entrenched domestic interests and business patterns. Farmers and construction companies were just two examples of major domestic constituencies on which many L.D.P. leaders had long depended. For the rest of the 1980s, the trade imbalance was more acute than ever. Japan developed expertise in industrial ceramics, robotics, and biotechnology.

The yen remained strong, propelled by a hot economy that sent the stock market soaring and raised land prices to astronomical levels. Japan became a major exporter of capital—building factories and buying foreign debt, prestigious hotels, and trophy real estate such as New York's Rockefeller Center, acquired by a Mitsui affiliate in 1989. Nevertheless, the balance of payments remained in Japan's favor.

In keeping with a general trend in the capitalist world, Japan divested itself of the government railway in 1987 and sold its shares in the National Telegraph and Telephone Company and in Japan Air Lines. By that time, Nakasone had been succeeded by Takeshita Noboru (1924–2000), who headed the Tanaka faction after 1985 but lasted less than two full years (November 1987–June 1989). He was forced to resign under a cloud arising out of revelations that the head of the Recruit group of companies had attempted to buy influence by giving large amounts in shares and money to leading politicians and bureaucrats. The next prime minister, who lied about giving hush money to a mistress, lasted two months. His successor, too, was a weak leader. The L.D.P.–dominated system was coming unglued, and now the financial bubble burst. Between January and October 1990 the stock market plunged 48 percent, and in 1991 recession set in.

# II. Society, Thought, and the Arts
## Social Change and Quality of Life

Economic growth brought unprecedented affluence. The very physiognomy of the Japanese people changed as an improved diet produced a new generation taller and healthier than their parents. By 1990 the Japanese people had the world's highest rate of life expectancy, and this was still the case in 2000, when it reached 74.5 years.

People now ate more fish and meat. Dairy products became daily staples, and wheat consumption rose steadily. Japan became a nation of coffee, as well as tea, drinkers. During the 1970s the arch of McDonald's hamburgers spread from Tokyo's Ginza to the provinces, where it was soon joined by the figure of Colonel Sanders inviting passersby to partake of Kentucky Fried Chicken. Mr. Donut and Dairy Queen did their part to propagate fast-food culture American style.

Changes in dress were equally dramatic. In the 1980s blue jeans became the universal dress of the young, and pants were worn in public by women of all ages. Conversely, the kimono was reserved for special occasions, but wealthy sophisticates now could prance about in the latest fashions by Japan's world-renowned designers.

Consumerism reigned as old crafts declined, and traditional elegance gave way to modern practicality—except that the modern was not always practical; during the 1980s so many realized their dream of owning an automobile that the roads were choked and the savvy driver had to learn how to "diagnose traffic paralysis."[2] Fortunately, public transportation within and between cities was excellent, although in Tokyo's rush hour ("crush hour" would be more appropriate) "pushers" had to cram the people quickly into the overflowing subways.

There was a shift of population from the country into cities. Nevertheless, because mechanization reduced the need for farm labor, agricultural production increased. Thanks to the L.D.P., the government purchased rice at several times the international price. The prewar gulf between urban wealth and rural poverty disappeared, and the spread of television accelerated the process, begun by radio, of diminishing the cultural gap. However, despite the omnipresence of the television set, the Japanese remained the world's most avid consumers of newspapers, magazines, and comic books.

Public transportation, communication, and security were excellent early on, but the environment suffered. Japan's industrial zone, running along the Pacific coast from Tokyo to northern Kyushu, developed into a "polluters' paradise":

> Polluted air choked urban residents with respiratory difficulties, which were fatal in some areas. Water pollution wiped out coastal fishing along the industrial belt. In the cities exhaust from automobiles mixed with pollutants from smokestacks and produced toxic photochemical smog during the day.[3]

Only after Tokyo became enshrouded in a semiperpetual screen of smog did the government take action. In the Mie prefecture, asthma was linked to pollution, and in Toyama a river caused cadmium poisoning. Most notorious was the Minamata disease (1953) caused by people eating fish contaminated by methyl mercury discharged by a fertilizer plant in Kyushu. Because of obstruction by the company and government connivance, the victims had to wait until 1968 for official acknowledgment that mercury was the cause. In 1973 a group of Minamata plaintiffs prevailed in court and won the largest tort award in Japanese history. In 1978 a National Institute for Minamata Disease was established. The name Minamata still conjures up both the deadly threat of environmental pollution and the people's determination to fight back.

Government measures taken in the 1970s ameliorated the problem, but the quality of air and water remained a matter of concern, and excessive dam construction boded ill for the future of Japan's rivers. Visual pollution was all too apparent as Japan's industrial area became one of the ugliest anywhere. Although the Japanese people continued to cherish nature in miniature, lovingly tending tiny gardens on the most unlikely bits of land, Japan's business and political leaders, in their rush to modernize, sacrificed much of the natural beauty that had once been Japan's cherished heritage.

In the 1980s, preserving the environment was widely accepted as a public good, so much so that in 1990 the Ministry of Construction sponsored an International Flower and Greenery Exposition even as it was planning an airport that would kill the last healthy coral reef in Okinawa. By the end of the 1980s, environmentalists not only were expressing concern over the situation at home but also were calling attention to the destruction Japanese companies were inflicting on the tropical forests of Borneo and other lands. If the aims of Japanese environmentalists were similar to those elsewhere, the same was even more true of the power of the forces arrayed against them.

Even before the land boom of the 1980s, the escalating price of land and housing in Japan's large cities forced young married couples to live with their parents and in-laws because they could not afford separate establishments or to crowd into tiny apartments in drab and monotonous buildings made of reinforced concrete. Raising a family in such confined quarters was no easy task. Although the small apartments reduced women's household chores, releasing time for other activities, the residents of such buildings were slow to develop a sense of community because they regarded these quarters as temporary, marking a stage of their lives and careers soon to be surmounted.

The absence of grandparents in the new housing was but one of the factors making for discontinuity between the generations. Such discontinuity was not unique to Japan; in other countries, too, rapid changes during the postwar years created a "generation gap." However, in Japan the gap was particularly severe. Not only did the younger people grow up in a society that had suddenly become very different from that of their parents, but a whole generation of wartime leaders also had been thoroughly discredited and the old values had been blamed for leading the nation to catastrophe. Included were many values that had strengthened the cohesiveness of Japanese society.

New lifestyles and values appeared in the factories as young workers preferred to spend their leisure time manipulating pachinko (vertical pinball) machines, playing video games, or listening to rock music rather than going on company outings. They valued skill more than length of service and tended to regard the factory not as a second home but merely as a place to work. The number of hours they would have to spend there was also decreasing, and a survey conducted in 1990 revealed that workers were more interested in obtaining more leisure than in obtaining higher pay.

Those fortunate enough to survive a brutal entrance examination system gained admission to universities oriented largely to research and graduate work. Ostensibly paternalistic, the universities demonstrated their supposed concern for the youngest members of the academic community by virtually guaranteeing graduation to all matriculants. Neglected after having worked so hard for university entrance, the students expressed their discontent in radical political activities. Their dissatisfaction helped fuel widespread demonstrations and disruptions in the late 1960s, directed against both national and university policies. In this again, Japanese young people were not alone, and, as elsewhere, the pendulum swung back to greater conservatism in the 1970s and 1980s.

The general loosening of traditional patterns and values presented contemporary Japanese with a range of choices but within what remained overall a closely knit society. For example, young people increasingly insisted on making their own selection of a spouse, and they were now always consulted before a marriage was arranged by their parents. Nevertheless, even in love marriages, most young people still asked their employer or teacher to serve as official matchmaker. A surprisingly large number continued to leave the initiative to their parents. Under the postwar legal system, wives and husbands could now initiate divorce proceedings; the divorce rate grew but remained low.

Women now had more options. Many remained content with their traditional roles, which gave them a predominant influence over their children and firmly established the home as their field of authority. Although submissive to their husbands in public, most wives controlled the family budget, ran the household, and often treated their husbands as they would an older, somewhat difficult, and rather special child. They accepted their exclusion from much of their husbands' social lives, which the husbands spent largely in the company of their fellow workers. Such couples, like their Tokugawa predecessors, led separate social lives. These wives did not share in their husband's nightlife. However, as time went on, an increasing number of women chose a career and either a companionate marriage or a single life. They made progress in the professions and, more slowly, in business, where they often had to choose between temporary employment followed by marriage or the more regular male-oriented career path. The passage of the Equal Opportunity Act in 1985, making sex discrimination illegal, reflected a new consciousness, but the law lacked teeth.

As in all periods of social change, there were some who suffered because change was too rapid and others for whom it was too slow. Among the former were the elderly, bewildered and distressed by the whirl about them. One of the strengths of the old society had been the dignity and security afforded to the aged, but now cramped quarters and new ideas ate away at old values and threatened traditional comforts. These were people who found that the social rules had changed just when their turn came to reap the rewards the system offered those who played by the rules. Although the erosion of respect for the aged diminished the traditional attractions of longevity, forced retirement at an early age (usually fifty-five) and the devaluation of savings because of continual inflation deprived the old of a sense of economic security. Most families managed to take care of the elderly one way or another. Most old people were not shunted off into nursing homes or set up in special retirement communities, but the social arrangements made for the elderly by their children were often grudging and poisoned by resentment.

At the other end of the spectrum were those who felt that change was too slow. They felt stifled rather than supported by a social system that still expected the individual to be subordinate to the group, whether it be family or company. They also balked at conforming to a social hierarchy that had lost much of its theoretical support. The discontented were a disparate group. They included career women frustrated by roadblocks and ceilings, those constrained to maintain and live with parents, and people seeking to fill the vacuum left by the passing of the old values with something more solid than consumerism and the race to elevate the economic standing of their country. Their discontent was frequently shared by students and by radicals impatient for a more egalitarian society. Some young men without prospects for university study joined motorcycle gangs. However, most worked out a modus vivendi for themselves, and many of the young gradually came to terms with society.

Most of the population, however, neither mourned the passing of the old nor were impatient for the arrival of the new. Appreciative of the increase in material wealth, they were nevertheless unsure of the future. Many turned to religion, maintaining home altars, visiting temples and shrines, and going on pilgrimages. Shrines and temples had always offered prayers and amulets protecting against disease, assurance of safe childbirth, and the like. Adjusting to new conditions, many now offered traffic-safety charms; a temple in Tokyo added air safety. Shrines and temples offering examination success were popular with young people. The elderly were serviced by temples offering prayers and amulets to quiet their fears of senility. This had excellent prospects of becoming a growth industry, because, as a byproduct of longevity, Japan counted half a million senile people by 1994, and the average age of the population was on the rise.

New religious sects arose seeking to satisfy the spiritual hunger and alleviate the mental malaise brought on by loss of community. As they moved from traditional village to modern city, people sought "a religious frame of meaning relevant to contemporary life."[4] Attracting the largest membership was Sōka Gakkai, the sponsor of the Clean Government Party. Doctrinally based on Nichiren Buddhism, it denounced all other faiths and insisted that its members proselytize relentlessly and go on a pilgrimage to the head temple at the foot of Mount Fuji, where an average of 10,000 people a day came to pay their homage. By passing a series of examinations, the faithful could rise in an academic-like hierarchy of ranks. For the devoted members, the sect provided not only spiritual community but also a sense of personal worth and of belonging to a large, integrated, pur-

**FIGURE 25.1** Darumas greet the visitor everywhere in the Hōrinji Temple, Kyoto, founded in 1718 but frequently rebuilt. Commonly known as the Daruma Temple, it houses around 8000 daruma figurines. (© Lore Schirokauer)

poseful group. Others found it more difficult to find new certainties, however, because the world offered a bewildering range of choices.

Not all the choices were solemn. Everyone, not only the devout, then as now, flocked to temples and shrines on festival days when the lanes leading to their gates were lined with stands offering various trinkets, souvenirs, and good things to eat—everything from octopus snacks to chocolate-covered bananas. This combination of piety and fun also accounts for the continued popularity of roly-poly darumas, popular doll-like figures named after Bodhidharma, the monk who was thought to have brought Zen to China and lost his legs after nine years uninterrupted wall contemplation. Even the skeptical made sure to paint in an eye and make a silent wish, hoping they would be able to paint in the other eye once their wish was granted. Although ubiquitous, daruma also had his special temples (see Figure 25.1).

## Film

If, as is often said, film was the characteristic art form of the twentieth century, then the worldwide acclaim accorded Japanese films is but one more indication of Japan's full participation in that century's culture. By no means were all Japanese films masterpieces: Japanese companies were second to none in turning out ephemeral entertainments—samurai movies that were the artistic equivalents of American westerns, unbearably sentimental tear-jerkers, horror and monster films, and, in the 1970s and 1980s, a wave of erotica with little artistic or social value but plenty of sexual action. Such films, reflecting social stereotypes and people's day-dreams, are of considerable interest to psychologists and social scientists, but it is important to remember that the stereotypes they contain—the self-sacrificing but self-centered mother, the wife finding herself, daughters in various degrees of revolt—are never simple mirror images of society. The more ambitious and truly fine films reflected the times and the society but rose above them. The major films were the creations of fine actors, sensitive cameramen, and, above all, great direc-tors who were able to use the medium to create their own personal styles, con-veying their own personal visions. If they had anything in common, it was a superb visual sense employed to create an atmosphere. Some may be said to have used the camera to paint their vision on the screen.

Exercising classic restraint in his insistence on a strict economy of means (empty spaces, simple objects, and minimal plot) and avoiding anything superfi-cial or artificially clever was Ozu Yasujiō (1903–1963), whose traditionalism also extended to his subject matter because he was the filmmaker par excellence of the Japanese family. Other directors, like their Chinese counterparts, were highly crit-ical of their country's traditions and values. For example, in *Harakiri* (*Seppuku*, 1962), directed by Kobayashi Masaki, the hero sets out to avenge his son, who had been forced to commit an unimaginably painful *seppuku* (ritual suicide) using a sword with a bamboo blade, but in the end the whole system is revealed to be founded on hypocrisy. Or there is *Night Drum* (*Yoru no Tsuzumi*, also known as *The Adulteress*, 1958), directed by Imai Tadashi, in which a samurai kills the wife he loves. By doing what society demands, he deprives his own life of meaning. Such vivid and moving historical films were among the triumphs of the postwar cinema, a part of a continuing and sometimes bitter dialogue with a still-living past.

An outstanding director was Kurosawa Akira (1910–1998). His world-famous *Rashomon* (1950) suggests the relativity of all truth through a demonstration of the power of human subjectivity and self-interest. *Ikiru* (1952) takes the viewer through a Faust-like quest for meaning in life. The main character, a petty bu-reaucrat dying of cancer, in the end finds fulfillment in one meaningful social act: surmounting endless red tape and bureaucratic obstructionism, he gets a small park built. Kurosawa's mastery of large scenes with vast casts and his versatility and creative vigor was apparent in *Ran* (1985), an imaginative metamorphosis of King Lear into sixteenth-century Japan. Like his earlier *Seven Samurai* (1954), it is one of those rare films in which powerful and sensitive acting, beautiful visual composition and realistic detail, story line and structure, friction and harmony, vi-olence and stillness blend into a major artistic statement.

In the 1980s, Japanese studios increasingly churned out films of violence and pornography. Refreshing exceptions were films of Itami Juzo (Ikeuchi Yoshihiro, 1933–1997), who poked fun at the Japanese way of burial in *The Funeral* (1984), noodle mania in *Tampopo* (1986), and tax collection methods in *A Taxing Woman I* and *II* (1987, 1988). His satire on the Japanese mob, *Minbo no Onna—The Gentle*

*Art of Extortion* (1994), provoked the Yakuza (organized crime) to a physical attack on his person. Itami survived this but later committed suicide, leaving a note explaining this act as proving the untruth of rumors that he was having an affair with a much younger woman.

## Intellectual Life and Literature

After the war Japan rejoined the international intellectual community, participated in scientific and scholarly meetings at home and abroad, and increasingly contributed to specialized disciplines in important ways. Many scholars became conversant with a foreign language, usually English, and all had access to a broad and steady stream of translations.

Writings addressing broader human or philosophical issues, published in journals of opinion and in books, have attracted less attention abroad than have the works of the filmmaker or novelist. One reason, no doubt, is the language barrier. Another may be that much was derivative. Also, many Japanese intellectuals, like their American counterparts, applied their energies to studying their own society and to addressing their own countrymen. Notably fascinating but problematic has been the literature of exceptionalism (*Nihonjinron*) that burgeoned in the 1970s and continued thereafter to fuel a sense of self-confidence and assertiveness. This literature, which focused on Japanese uniqueness, included the highly respected and stimulating work of such scholars as the psychiatrist Doi Takeo and the sociologist Nakane Chie. Lesser scholars, however, expounded on and frequently took pride in the uniqueness of just about every aspect of Japanese behavior, institutions, and climatic and racial characteristics. Increasing cosmopolitanism did not prevent the persistence of insularity.

What it meant to be Japanese was also one of the themes explored in postwar fiction. After the war, older novelists published manuscripts they could not release during the war, and new writers sounded new themes. An outstanding example of the former is the long novel by Tanizaki translated as *The Makioka Sisters*.

In 1947 Kawabata Yasunari published the last installment of *Snow Country*. Previous segments of the novel had been published in various journals over the preceding twelve years, as though each part were a stanza in a *renga* (linked verse) rather than a building block for a novel. In this and later works, Kawabata explored "the ceaseless attempt of his male heroes to free themselves from their alienation and egotism to achieve a kind of monastic state of grace by a purifying contact with a pure, virginal girl."[5]

Kawabata's novels sacrifice structure and plot for naturalness and poetry. *A Thousand Cranes* (1948) and *The Sound of the Mountain* (1951) followed, each imbued with the author's visual sensibility and with his concern for beauty and sadness, inseparable as ever in Japanese literature and evoking what one critic termed a "vibrant silence."[6] The essential Japaneseness of Kawabata's method and vision was clearly demonstrated in his Nobel Prize acceptance speech (1968). Translated as *Japan, the Beautiful, and Myself*, it is an evocation of the Japanese tradition, a string of poems and images held together by a perception of beauty and truth.

Japan's literary classics were written by women, but most eminent writers during the Tokugawa Period and in the first years of Meiji were men. Women writers reappeared toward the turn of the century but really came into their own after the war. As Donald Keene pointed out, "At no time since the Heian Period had women figured so prominently in the literary world."[7] Appropriately, one of the most distinguished among them, Enchi Fumiko (1905–1986), translated the *Tale of Genji* into modern Japanese (1972–1973). She also wrote realistic novels such as *Waiting Years* (1957) and the subtle and imaginative *Masks* (1958).

A brilliant and versatile but uneven writer was Mishima Yukio (1925–1970), who, in a series of well-constructed novels, developed his ideas on such themes as the nature of beauty and the relationships between art and life and between warrior and poet. One of his most compelling novels is *The Temple of the Golden Pavilion* (1956). Based on an actual act of arson in postwar Kyoto, it includes powerful psychological and philosophical explorations. A dramatist and critic, as well as novelist, Mishima was prolific, self-contradictory, and even self-parodying. He tried to mold his life and his body as he did his art. Wishing to be both athlete and artist, he took up body building and developed a strong torso—but on spindly legs. Seeking to achieve a unity of knowledge and action, as in the philosophy of Wang Yangming, whom he admired, Mishima's culminating act was a dramatic public *seppuku* committed in 1970 after the completion of his final work, a tetralogy titled *The Sea of Fertility*. He was joined in death by a member of his small, private, rightwing army. Mishima exhorted the Self-Defense Forces to rise up before performing his ritual suicide at their headquarters. Regarded by the public as irrelevant and bizarre, Mishima intended this act to be a fulfillment of his life's work.

A productive writer who was well-known abroad was Endō Shūsaku (1923–1996), who, in a series of brilliant novels, grappled with the tensions between his Catholic faith and his Japanese heritage. Just as Endō contributed to both modern Christian and Japanese literature, Abe Kobō (1924–1993) earned an international reputation as an existentialist. He is perhaps best known for his novel *Woman in the Dunes* (1962), subsequently made into a film. In this work and later novels such as *Face of Another* (1964), *The Boxman* (1973), and *The Ark Sakura* (1984), and in such plays as *Friends* (1967), Abe explored themes and predicaments besetting the contemporary human condition, including the search for identity.

The search for identity and roots also infuses the work of Ōe Kenzaburō (1935–), two of whose novels, *A Personal Matter* (1964) and *The Silent Cry* (1967), were widely read in Japanese and in translation. Insight into psychological complexities of modern people—including the sources of violence, a concern for social morality, and a strong personal symbolism—and his grappling with basic problems of existence in the second half of the twentieth century mark him as a major writer who speaks to the central problems of his age.

Working a different vein was Inoue Yasushi (1907–1991), many of whose novels were set in China, including his last, *Confucius* (1989), in which the sage, seen through the eyes of a disciple, is treated with great respect. Less well-known abroad is Maruya Saiichi (1925–), an entertaining writer, serious but funny, whose *Singular Rebellion* (1972) provides a delightful, comic window into the times.

# The Visual Arts

Like filmmakers and novelists, Japanese painters, potters, and architects won international recognition. As earlier, some artists found their inspiration in, and took their cues from, the latest trends so that Japan had its practitioners of abstract expressionism, action painting, pop art, and the various other international art movements, which, at their best, represented the search for a style appropriate to a bewildering age and, at their worst, degenerated into fads.

More traditional was the work of artists who strove to create beauty without attempting to convey a symbolic message. Japanese potters, innovators and traditionalists, continued to blend shapes, textures, and colors to create works worthy of the tradition.

An old genre in new form was the woodcut. Unlike the earlier *ukiyo-e* artists, their twentieth-century successors took responsibility for the entire process of printmaking. They did their own cutting and printing, although they might have students assist them in the more routine aspects of the process. Among the finest was Munakata Shikō (1903–1975), also a gifted painter, whose style was influenced by traditional Japanese folk art but who also developed new techniques. One was to apply color on the back of the print and let it seep through the paper to create gentle, diffused coloring. This helped Munakata create a general decorative effect, as in his rendition of the clothing in *Lady in Chinese Costume* (see Figure 25.2). In subject matter his work ranged from the religious to the sensuous and the whimsical (for example, a nude with the artist's eyeglasses resting on her belly). In tone his art is positive—there is no echo here of the agony of the century.

Perhaps no art is as revealing of society as architecture. Although many opportunities were missed in the rush of postwar reconstruction, and Japan's industrial centers are among the ugliest cities in the world, there were also buildings of great distinction. The achievements of Tange Kenzo (1913–2005), designer of the Hall Dedicated to Peace at Hiroshima, were recognized internationally when he received the Pritzker Prize in 1987. The swimming pool and sports center he designed for the 1964 Tokyo Olympics won wide acclaim. Thirty years later, he designed the Tokyo City Hall Complex (1995). His buildings can also be seen in Singapore, Europe, North Africa, the Middle East, and Minnesota (the arts complex in Minneapolis, 1970–1974). In addition to designing superb buildings, Tange involved himself deeply in urban planning.

One of Tange's most creative students was Isozaki Arata (1931–). Postmodernist in seeking a "shifting, revolving, flickering style" rather than a "lucid, coherent institutional style" for his Tsukuba Science Center, Isozaki is also an internationalist who could write, "the Katsura Palace, the Parthenon, the Capitoline piazza, and so on all

**FIGURE 25.2** *Lady in Chinese Costume,* woodcut, Munakata Shikō, 1946, 21 in × 15 in. There are strong hints of Persia and India in Munakata's work. But in the vigor of his lines, his gentle eroticism, and the decorative qualities of his art, he resembles Matisse, and his coloring is reminiscent of Chagall. (© "Tornado" from the series "In Praise of Shokie" by Munakata Shikō, Munakata Museum in Kamakura)

live in a time and place equidistant from us. Anything occurring in the history of architecture even the history of the world—is open to quotation."[8] Such quotation yields new and complex meaning. But often Isozaki does not quote, and some of his most successful buildings employ solid geometric forms, as in his Museum of Contemporary Art in Los Angeles. Illustrated here (see Figure 25.3) is the tower for his arts center in Mito, which, although located in a place once famous for historiography, does not refer to anything except itself.

The diversity of modern Japanese architecture is far too great for any single building possibly to be representative, but architecture can, among other things, be

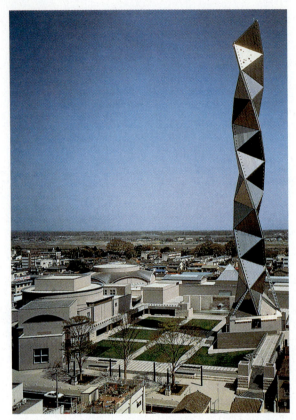

**FIGURE 25.3** Art Tower Mito, 328 feet high. Mito Ibaraki, 1986–1990. Although as a postmodernist Isozaki delights in playing with references to buildings of the past, he also likes to give his imagination free play, as in this tower. (© Mita Arts Foundation)

fun. The example of Japanese "pop architecture" in Figure 25.4 was built to house an exhibit on coffee for an exposition celebrating the completion of an artificial island in Kobe. Later, it was turned into a permanent coffee museum and given a more dignified but conventional exterior. Perhaps the cup ranneth over and the joke wore off—humor may be as ephemeral as beauty. Still, it is a splendid museum, housing exhibits on the history, the preparation, and the consumption of coffee and providing facilities for study and a "training room" for coffee makers. It is a striking reminder that Japan, which had perfected the tea ceremony, became a world leader in coffee appreciation, famed for its many and varied coffee houses serving the choicest South American beans. A serious beverage befitting hard workers and diligent students, coffee had found a home in Japan.

**FIGURE 25.4** Coffee Pavilion, 82 feet high, c. 72 feet in diameter. Port-pia Exposition, Kobe, 1981. Takenaka Construction Firm. Although the era of pop architecture has passed and the coffee museum has changed the face it shows the world, coffee has found a permanent home in Japan. (© Arata Isozaki & Associates, Photo by Yasuhiro Ishimoto)

# III. From 1989 into the New Century

The death of the emperor in January 1989 had little immediate political effect. Most Japanese were happy with the personality of the new, more accessible emperor, the first to have married a commoner. However, the performance of Shinto funeral and enthronement rites as official ceremonies troubled those committed to a secular state. And the focus on the monarchy drew renewed attention to the past role of the throne in leading Japan into the dark valley of authoritarianism and war. The tendency of high government officials to minimize wartime atrocities, government reluctance to compensate Korean "comfort women" forced into sexual slavery during the war, claims that the Pacific War had been righteous, and the widespread view of the Japanese exclusively as history's innocent victims combined to disturb people, at home and abroad, who knew otherwise.

For progressives, Japan had paid far too high a price for development. They saw the system as "a kind of state capitalism brokered by the elites that held the masses in thrall and precluded the emergence of a genuine democratic polity . . . a capitalism brokered by conservative elites in order to achieve nationalist goals."[9] A strong voice for a more positive appraisal was that of Murakami Yasusuke (1931–1993), professor of economics at Tokyo University and author of *An Anticlassical Political–Economic Analysis* (1992). Murakami blamed Japanese imperialism on the West and historical circumstances, and he emphasized the positive achievements of Japanese-style developmentalism. A nuanced thinker, he was not uncritical and sharply warned against Japanese particularism, but, convinced that there was more than one road to success, he maintained that Japan, with its "capacity to nurture a community of cultural systems,"[10] had achieved a viable way that could serve as a model for late developing nations and enable Japan to be a leader in the post–Cold War world.

The message that there is more than one road to development was a timely one for a world in which only one superpower remained and triumphalism was in the air, but it seemed increasingly less likely that Japan would serve as an economic, let alone political, exemplar. Essentially, the country muddled through the decade but did not shine.

As already noted, recession took hold in earnest in 1991. That same year Japan contributed $13 billion to the war effort in the Persian Gulf but did not send troops. Two years later, however, despite Article IX of the constitution, it sent a token noncombatant force to support United Nations peacekeeping in Cambodia. Yet talk of Japanese membership in an expanded Security Council remained talk, and a new, more prominent international role eluded the nation with the world's second-largest economy. If the Persian Gulf War again highlighted Japan's dependence on foreign oil, the conference on global warming held in Kyoto in 1997 was a reminder that we all live on the same planet.

During the 1990s the economy sputtered along, each small spurt followed by a stall so that it neither advanced into sustained recovery nor sank into the depths of depression. The excesses of spending abroad were liquidated—Rockefeller Center went bankrupt in 1995. Japan was not as badly hit by the Asian Crisis of 1998 as Korea but nevertheless suffered serious losses. At the end of the decade there was an uptick, but all too soon it was clear that the banking system remained unsound and that Japan had not yet found a way back to economic health.

Although earlier the Japanese economic system had been widely admired, the pressures now were toward opening its markets to American-style entrepreneurs and to foreign companies and goods. By the end of the decade, the *keiretsu* were dissolving as banks sold stocks and companies became more dependent on equity financing. American financial institutions became a major presence. Among the companies taken over by international firms based elsewhere was Mazda, the erstwhile survivor of the oil shock, which became a Ford subsidiary. Movement toward more efficient marketing and even discounting accelerated. In 2004 Wal-Mart opened its first supercenter in Japan.

Several factors kept the economy afloat. A vital one was Japan's sheer wealth. This enabled the government to finance substantial deficit spending on public works, to underwrite housing projects and small business loans, and to prime the economy in general. In 1994 it completed the scintillating Kansai Airport. Designed by the Italian architect Renzo Piano (Pritzker, 1999), it was built off-shore in fifty-nine feet of water on soft foundations that keep subsiding, running the cost up to the enormous figure of roughly 5 trillion yen with no end yet in sight. In addition to stimulating the economy with construction money, this project gave easy international access to the Osaka area.

There were numerous smaller projects nourishing the politically and economically important construction industry. In 1995 these included 400 dams either under construction or planned. By that time, postwar Japan had already built 1000 dams, many of which were already clogged by more than 1 billion tons of silt. Writing in 1996, Gavan McCormack described the situation as "an ecological nightmare to which Japan is only beginning to wake."[11] Economic recovery remained Japan's top priority, and the national debts continued to mount until it reached 130 percent of gross domestic product in 2002.

Another way the government sought to stimulate the economy was by lowering interest rates, which at one point reached zero. Even so, the yen did not sink precipitously. The balance of payments with the United States remained in Japan's favor, although by 2000 China had replaced Japan as the country with the largest U.S. trade deficit. Trade with a booming China was a major factor in revitalizing the Japanese economy during 2003 and 2004, creating a mood of optimism despite the possibility that this could be one more false start.

An element of strength was Japan's continued technological excellence. People everywhere eagerly bought Japanese cars, laptop computers, and electronics. Robotics not only led to triumphs in manufacturing but also gave birth to toys that delighted children throughout the world. It is too early to know whether robotic cats and dogs will eventually catch on. Somewhere between a tool and a toy were the cellular email telephones ubiquitous among Japanese teenagers, who found a space of their own in cyberspace.

Companies cut back but tried to limit layoffs. People did not prosper, but most continued to work. The authorities worried less about present or future unemployment than about the aging of the population and a declining birthrate that reached 1.34 per 1000 in 1999. An increase to 1.35 per 1000 in 2000 was thought to be temporary, a product of a belief that this was an especially propitious year ("the millennial factor"). Further decline was expected as women sought more fulfilling roles than that of the traditional mother. At home, as abroad, the spending boom was over. Although there was an increase in poverty, most people were able to maintain a satisfactory lifestyle.

People had little faith in government, but there was not a sense of urgency sufficiently strong to stir up an effective public demand for a radical change in political direction or leadership. That all was not well with government was dramatically revealed by its failure to prepare for or deal adequately with the earthquake that shook the Kobe area in 1995, officially designated not earthquake-prone. More than 6000 people died, and the heart of one of Japan's most modern and international cities was destroyed, along with a brand new highway, revealing shoddy construction made possible by corruption. Government failure to assure adequate standards was matched by the slowness and inadequacy of its response. In contrast, organized crime stepped in to provide help and relief. The government was effective in suppressing the apocalyptic Aun Shinrikyō sect after it used sarin in 1995 in a subway attack that shocked people in Tokyo and, even before the September 11, 2001, attack in the United States, demonstrated just how menacing modern terrorism could be. In 2003, after a lengthy trial, the leader of the sect was condemned to death. However, faced with a nuclear mishap in 1999, the government's response was again slow and inept.

On the political stage, the L.D.P. finally came apart in 1993 when there was a major factional exodus, but the first non-L.D.P. prime minister, Hosokawa Morihito, lasted less than a year (August 1993–April 1994) before he was undone by involvement in yet another scandal. In 1989, under the leadership of Doi Takako (1928–), the first woman to become a major force in Japanese politics, it looked as if the Socialists might grow into a viable second party, but this did not happen. Instead, badly divided and compromised by ill-advised political alliances, they declined. Although the women's vote was important and two women served in the Cabinet for a short time, at century's end more than 95 percent of the Diet members were men. With men also in control of the bureaucracy, government and politics remained male domains.

Coalition governments between 1993 and 1996 were hampered by internal rivalry and conflict. One thing accomplished in 1994 was a major change in the electoral system, abolishing multimember districts and providing a total of 500 seats, 300 from small, single-member districts and 200 filled by proportional representation. In 1996 the first election under the new law was held, with the result that a weakened and divided L.D.P. regained power.

Prime Minister Hashimoto Ryutarō (1996–1998) was succeeded by Obuchi Keizo (1937–2000), who died suddenly and unexpectedly in May 2000. His successor, Mori Yoshirō (1937–), lost no time causing widespread consternation by calling Japan "a divine nation with the emperor at its core," saying out loud what more circumspect rightist politicians kept to themselves. New elections were held in June with the result that the opposition gained strength, but Mori managed to remain in office until April 2001, when he was succeeded by Koizumi Junichirō (1942–), who owed his position to a landslide victory in provincial party elections rather than through the usual political horse trading by faction leaders.

Koizumi, an unconventional politician noted for an outspoken and frank manner, with an easy sense of humor and something of a bad-boy image, came in with a broad but vague program of financial reforms, which he warned would cause short-term economic pain but long-term recovery. He also called for constitutional change to legalize the military and pleased nationalists by visiting the Yasukuni Shrine paying homage to Japan's fallen soldiers, including those condemned as war criminals. Koizumi took a bold step in appointing an outspoken woman as Japan's first female foreign minister. She was Tanaka Makiko (1944–), the eldest daughter of former Prime Minister Tanaka Kakuei.

In July, Koizumi, Japan's most popular prime minister since World War II, was able to lead the L.D.P. to an electoral victory. This was a personal triumph, but there was much opposition, especially in his own party, to his plans to remake the banking system, halt public works projects, and get the L.D.P. to change its ways. Many were disillusioned after he gave in to Foreign Ministry pressure and forced Tanaka out of the Cabinet at the end of January 2002.

Lower house elections in 2003, followed by those for the upper house in 2004, left both Koizumi and his L.D.P.–led coalition weakened but still in charge. At home, progress was made in restructuring the banking system; abroad, the Koizumi government supported the United States in its war on terrorism and sent a small contingent of troops to help rebuild Iraq. At home and abroad, the government showed little inclination for the kind of bold innovation once associated with Koizumi's name.

An ardent critic of Establishment thinking was Ōe Kenzaburō, who in 1994 became only the second Japanese—or, for that matter, East Asian—to receive the Nobel Prize for literature. In conscious contrast to Kawabata, he titled his acceptance speech "Japan, the Ambiguous and Myself" and not long after shocked the public by refusing the Imperial Order of Culture. In 1995 he completed his trilogy *The Burning Green Tree* (*Moegaru midori no ki*, 1992–1995), its title derived from "Vacillation," a poem by William Butler Yeats (1865–1939). *Burning Green Tree* remains untranslated but not so *Somersault* (1999), which revisits many of the themes that animate Ōe's earlier novels but does so in a post-Aun Shinrikyō age. This long, complex novel is not his most accessible, but it moved Fredric Jameson to praise Oe as an author who does honor to the Nobel Prize rather than being honored by it.[12] Ōe's trilogy, like Mishima's tetralogy, ends with a death, but, to quote Susan J. Napier:

> Unlike Mishima whose dead protagonists leave the living with only a feeling of betrayal and emptiness, or Abe whose characters survive in misery, and above all unlike Murakami whose protagonists commit a sort of suicide to the outside world, Ōe gives us a vision of the outside world revitalized by the sacrifice of a body.[13]

As we have seen, Mishima and Abe belonged to the recent past, but Murakami Haruki (1949–), a prominent writer of the 1980s and 1990s, represented a generational shift that Ōe deplored:

> In contrast to much postwar writing which fictionalized the actual experience of writers and readers, who, as twenty- and thirty-year-olds, had known war, Murakami and Yoshimoto convey the experience of a youth politically uninvolved or disaffected content to exist within a late adolescent or postadolescent subculture.[14]

Yoshimoto is Yoshimoto Banana (Yochimoto Mahoko, 1964–), who had adopted "banana" as her pen name. Both writers are easy to read and prolific. Both were attuned to the market, enjoyed sensational sales, and were found lacking in gravitas by their elders. Bananas are, after all, delicious but not taken that seriously. Both were steeped in popular culture, probably read too many comic books, and have been taken to represent a postmodern comodification of literature. Especially Yoshimoto, beginning with *Kitchen* (1987), is treated as much a cultural as a literary phenomenon. Her novels often depict alternate lifestyles in deadpan, commonplace language. They signal the disintegration of the traditional family but are bright and cheerful. Murakami, who once ran a jazz bar, wrote long novels filled with the music of his youth, interesting situations, and characters not given to reflection. Pico Iyer had this to say about *The Wind-up Bird* (*Nejimaki-dori kuronikuru*, 1994–1995):

> It does not require much reflection that almost every image in the book's 600 pages—a dry well, a haunted house, a faceless man, a dead-end street—stands in some way for a hollowed out Japan, whose motto might be, "I don't think, therefore I am." Again and again, characters say, "I was like a walking corpse" or "I was now in a vacant house" or "I felt as if I had turned into a bowl of cold porridge." Murakami's storytelling ease and the pellucid, uncluttered backdrop he lays down allow moments to flare up memorably. Yet the overall effect of his grand but somewhat abstract novel is to give us X ray after X ray into the benumbed soul of a wannabe Prozac Nation.[15]

In the 1990s, the director Kurosawa, then in his eighties, drew on his earlier films to produce works new in content and technique. An example of the latter, described by Stephen Prince, is his use of axial cutting, and the dreams in *Dreams* (1990) represent an old theme given new meaning. Once he had seen dreams as being in tension with social commitment, but now Kurosawa cherished them as "the fruit of pure and human desire" and went on to say, "A human is a genius while dreaming."[16] Be that as it may, it takes a great artist to convey a dream to others. One who was able to do so was Miyazaki Hayao (1941–), who, in a series of works, raised film animation to new heights. His *Princess Mononoke* (1997) won widespread popular and critical acclaim. Similarly, *Spirited Away* (2001) broke all box-office records in Japan.

Japanese architects, too, continued to dream. One who did so with great imagination was Ando Tadao (1941–; Pritzker, 1995), a self-taught master who, early in his career, built a lovely, small Christian church in Osaka. Among his most notable subsequent works were an underground temple entered though stairs in a lotus pond (1991) and, on Naoshima, an island in the Inland Sea, a museum/hotel for contemporary art (1992). The art, mostly non-Japanese, is not confined to the inside but continues outdoors and includes an enormous pumpkin and a Chinese stone garden. In 1997 I. M. Pei completed his masterpiece, the Miho Museum at Shigaraki. Like Ando's temple and museum/hotel, it is mostly underground, and it blends in with and makes the most of the natural beauty of the landscape.

In the Pulitzer Foundation for the Arts in St. Louis (2001) and Modern Art Museum in Fort Worth (2002), Ando brought his feeling for the possibilities of concrete to the United States. Meanwhile, as earlier, Japanese artists participated in all the international styles and movements of the day. Some of them spent considerable time overseas. Performance and installations remained popular, conveying the sense that art, like all things, was not forever. A sculptor obsessed with time was Miyajima Tatsuo (1957–), whose *Running Time* (1994) consisted of battery-powered "U-cars," each with a colored, single-number light emitting diode counter on its roof and with sensors front and back so that the cars changed direction as they randomly bumped each other. The effect has been likened to "glowing numerical fireflies," and the artist explained that the "U" refers to the "uncertainty principle," as in the physics of Heisenberg.[17]

*Running Time,* like the writings of Yoshimoto and Murakami, is a work in a modern idiom with its own aesthetic appeal. It says something in a new way without reference to what others in the long tradition have said on the subject. Like traditional works of art, it leaves interpretation to the viewer, but, unlike them, it does not demand the cultivation of connoisseurship to unlock the message.

# Notes

1. Richard Pascale and Thomas P. Roblen, "The Mazda Turnaround," *Journal of Japanese Studies* 9.2 (Dec. 1983): 263.

2. David Plath, "My-Car-isma: Motorizing the Showa Self," in Carol Gluck and Stephen R. Graubard, eds., *Showa: The Japan of Hirohito* (New York: W. W. Norton, 1992), p. 239.

4. Koji Taira, "Dialectics of Economic Growth, National Power, and Distributive Struggles," in Andrew Gordon, ed., *Postwar Japan as History* (Berkeley: Univ. of California Press), p. 171.

5. Roy Starrs, *Soundings in Time: The Fictive Art of Kawabata Yasunari* (London: Curzon Press, 1998), p. 218.

6. Masao Miyoshi, *Accomplices of Silence: The Modern Japanese Novel* (Berkeley: Univ. of California Press, 1974), p. 120.

7. Donald Keene, *Dawn to the West: Japanese Literature in the Modern Era* (New York: Holt, Rinehart, and Winston, 1984), p. 1162.

8. Isozaki Arata, in Masao Miyoshi and Harry D. Harootunian, eds., *Postmodernism and Japan* (Durham: Duke Univ. Press, 1989), pp. 57 and 59.

9. Kenneth B. Pyle, "The World Historical Significance of Japan," in Kozo Yamamura, ed., *A Vision of a New Liberalism? Critical Essays on Murakami's Anticlassical Analysis* (Stanford: Stanford Univ. Press, 1997), pp. 233 and 237.

10. Pyle, in Kozo Yamamura, ed., *A Vision of a New Liberalism?* p. 127.

11. Gavan McCormack, *The Emptiness of Japanese Affluence* (Armonk, N.Y.: M. E. Sharpe, 1996), p. 46.

12. Fredric Jameson, "Pseudo-Couples," *The London Review of Books* (20 November 2003): 21.

13. Susan J. Napier, "Oe Kenzaburo and the Search for the Sublime at the End of the Twentieth Century," in Stephen Snyder and Philip Gabriel, eds., *Oe and Beyond: Fiction in Contemporary Japan* (Honolulu: Univ. of Hawaii Press, 1999), pp. 32–33.

14. Quoted in Snyder and Gabriel, *Oe and Beyond,* p. 2 of introduction.

15. Pico Iyer, "Tales of the Living Dead," *Time* 150.8 (Nov. 3, 1997), available at http://www.time.com/time/archive/preview/0,10987,987303,00.html.

16. Kurosawa Akira, as quoted in Stephen Prince, *The Warrior's Camera: The Cinema of Akira Kurosawa,* revised and enlarged edition (Princeton: Princeton Univ. Press, 1999), p. 303.

17. Michael Auping, org., *Tatsuo Miyajima (1957) BIG TIME,* exhibition catalog (Fort Worth: Modern Art Museum of Fort Worth and Hayward Gallery London, June 19–Aug. 17, 1997), pp. 25–26.

# Afterword

A major theme of modern history is the interaction of regional civilizations and cultures, each with its own dynamic, in an accelerating process that links us all, in varying degrees, and, for better or worse, in a multitude of ways—some obvious, others less apparent. The roots of contemporary globalization extend deeply into the past, but the process has reached new dimensions in our time as history becomes increasingly world history and no country, no matter how large or how powerful, has the luxury of withdrawal.

Around the globe, the modern era saw the growth in power of the nation-state to a degree unprecedented by that of any institution in human history, even as economic links were formed that became the precursor of the contemporary global economy. At the start of the twenty-first century, in China and Japan as elsewhere, the state's role in managing the economy was diminishing in the face of a global economic and financial system grown beyond the power of even the strongest state to control. Nevertheless, the nation-state remained the dominant military and political institution. After the events of September 11, 2001, national governments strengthened the state in its battle against terrorist enemies with radical religious and antiglobalization agendas but needed and sought greater international cooperation.

Both globalization and nationalism held promise of a brighter future, but both also entailed dangers. It remains to be seen whether sovereign states can solve global problems while focusing on local issues and while national rivalries continue to generate international dangers.

## International Tensions

One source of tension remains a divided Korea, especially the plans of the impoverished but nuclear North. This is a particular cause of concern for Japan, where it intensified calls to build up the military, calls that alarm a China ever wary of Japanese ambitions.

Further south, despite differences in scale and relative size, Taiwan and the P.R.C. are similar in that they reject each other's political and economic systems and tell different versions of China's modern story. One side—Taiwan—has achieved much greater wealth than the other. Like Hong Kong, Taiwan is an element of "Greater China," with a standard of living dramatically higher than that of the P.R.C. There is every sign that the flow of capital, knowledge, goods, and people between Taiwan and the mainland will continue to accelerate, creating common ground and enhancing each side's stakes in a peaceful reintegration of the Chinese nation.

Although economic reintegration of China is taking place, political reintegration remains a difficult problem. The P.R.C. insists that it wants peaceful reunification with Taiwan—but on its own terms. Meanwhile, it is willing to wait for changes to occur that will permit political reintegration, whatever those changes might be. However, it will *not* permit overt secession and the establishment of an independent republic on Taiwan that rejects the principle of Taiwan's belonging to "one China." The P.R.C. has made it clear that in that circumstance, it would intervene militarily to enforce its claim to Taiwan's "belonging" to China.

Under this threat from the mainland, the Republic of China on Taiwan continues to proceed cautiously in asserting its intention to move toward independence. Although its president, Chen Shui-bian, was elected on an independence platform, in December 2004 the Nationalist Party gained seats in parliament, making it unlikely that President Chen will get his way and change the constitution despite Beijing's strong opposition.

Other countries, meanwhile, remain nervous about the potential for conflict between the two governments. The United States, which has committed itself to defending Taiwan from encroachment or invasion from the mainland, sometimes aggravates tensions in the Taiwan Straits by selling weapons to Taiwan and implying that Taiwan is a country. This raises hackles in Beijing and reminds the P.R.C. that the United States is a main reason that what the P.R.C. sees as a purely domestic issue remains unsolved after more than half a century. The development of American bases in Central Asia is another potentially disquieting development. However, concern about terrorism and North Korean nuclear policy, as well as economic ties, have encouraged Beijing and Washington to cooperate and keep the Taiwan issue off the center stage.

Japan is only indirectly involved in the future of Taiwan, but a potentially dangerous point of friction are the tiny Sentaku/Diaoyu (or Diayu/Sentaku) islands in the China Sea, claimed by Japan, China, and Taiwan, that could provide a focus of conflict. Furthermore, anti-Japanese nationalism remains strong among a Chinese populace unconvinced of the depth and sincerity of Japanese contrition, their misgivings confirmed by Koizumi's annual visits to the Yasukuni Shrine.

Strong and strengthening economic ties and a common interest in the stability of the region, particularly the Korean peninsula, continue to foster friendly relations between Japan and China. However, international tensions are potentially dangerous now that the credibility of China's government depends on its performance in the economic and nationalist arenas. In that sense, all of China's neighbors have a major stake in the continued success of its economy.

# Economic Globalization

A momentous development emerged in 2004 when the growth of the economy made China a major player in global trade and finance. Japan remains the world's second largest economy, but China has become Japan's major customer and the country with which the United States has the largest trade deficit. Chinese demand for crucial commodities such as oil and iron became a decisive factor in setting world prices. China became more dependent on the global economy, but the global economy and Japan depend more on China. In the long run, the growth of the Chinese economy provides a splendid market for Japanese companies but also a challenge to avoid overdependence on that potentially unstable market.

Globalization has benefited some but harmed others. In China, it has brought unprecedented prosperity to those in a position to take advantage of new opportunities but reduced the unfortunates to dire poverty. In both China and Japan, it has created new customers abroad and reduced the prices of imports at home, but in Japan small mom-and-pop shops struggle to survive competition by chains, which benefit from more effective and ruthless distribution. In China, as in the United States, the gap between winners and losers has widened. Even as luxury car dealerships are being established in Beijing, Shanghai, and Guangzhou to cater to the rich, there are people who live by foraging in garbage dumps.

In East Asia, as elsewhere, cities are the nodes of the global system, and Chinese cities are transforming at a dizzying pace. "This is a country where everything is changing before your eyes, and a visitor can return after a year's absence and be surprised at the transformation. It has a kind of frontier character,"[1] writes John R. Logan, who has contributed to making Chinese urbanization a "research frontier." The transformation continues, but by now sleepy provincial capitals such as Changsha (Hunan) have acquired skylines and boast theme parks, whereas Beijing looks and feels like any world capital dominated by high-rise buildings and choked with traffic. Gone are the bicycles that used to crowd Shanghai's Nanjing Road; that city now competes with Hong Kong in trade, manufacturing, and international panache. In their appearance, too, the major cities are becoming global, as prominent European architects are commissioned to design buildings in the latest styles and museum visitors greet even the most outrageously avant-garde art with sophisticated nonchalance.

Meanwhile, Tokyo continues to glitter, enlivened by buildings of startling architecture, designed by leading foreign and Japanese architects, and as up to date as any city in the world. Earthquake danger precludes Tokyo from entering the competition for the world's tallest building (first place is held by Taipei), but no other city can boast of anything equal in dimensions and ambitions to the huge Roppongi Hills complex that opened in 2003, boasting some 700 shops and boutiques, a Grand Hyatt Hotel, elegant apartments, Tokyo's largest movie hall, some 68,000 plants and trees, and a museum as global in the provenance of its displays as it is indiscriminate in its tastes. Setting the tone for the architecture is Louise Bourgeois's giant spider, which spent the 2001 season at Rockefeller Center but has reportedly found a permanent home—although real-life spiders, after staying still for a long period, are prone to sudden, unexpected moves (see Figure A.1). Roppongi Hills is, among

**FIGURE A.1** Spider by Louise Bourgeois (1911–). A spider by a Franco-American sculptor has found a fitting home in a global Tokyo, where people go about their business underneath with only an occasional passerby taking note. (© Photograph by Lore Schirokauer.)

other things, an expression of optimism in the future, when the challenges to Japan's technological edge and economic well-being are sure to increase.

Cities are important but are fed by the countryside, and everyone depends on air and water. Economic growth increases demands on the environment but also opens opportunities for more efficient use of resources. The situation is particularly acute in China. After a distinguished career of research on the Chinese environment, Vaclav Smil concludes by emphasizing "contending trends" at work "in every instance of securing China's energy and food while maintaining an acceptable quality of environment."[2] In the light (and heat) of global warming, we should bear in mind that China is a major factor in world ecology, as well as economy.

## Contending Trends

Contending trends can be found in almost every dimension of human life, including the political, the economic, and the relationship between politics and economics. On the one hand, globalization has entailed a strengthening of markets and has asserted pressure for financial and commercial restructuring; on the other, the establishment continues to hold great power in Japan and China. Globalization affects political structures and the relationship between state and society, as well as just about everything, but despite the dreams of some and the nightmares of others, it does not equal Americanization.

In China, globalization has entailed a strengthening of the rule of law, but political change has lagged behind economic change, and stability continues to have higher priority than political liberalization. Although some commentators predict democratization, Hu Jintao announced that China does not need more than one party. Human rights advocates and other dissenters face arrest, but it is difficult for the government to control the flow of information in an age of cheap and easy global communication.

From Sun Yat-sen through Mao Zedong and Deng Xiaoping to the present, China has sought its own "Chinese" way of building a strong, modern state and society, and the same holds for Japan. The imperatives of twenty-first-century globalization may set certain limits but leave ample room for variation, and again, contending trends including the meaning of what it means to be Chinese or Japanese, an examination of national identity that is itself a global trend.

In Japan, the L.D.P. and Koizumi's reform movement have lost much of their dynamism. Consciousness of the larger world, political and economic, is strong, but people are groping for a new definition of the role Japan should play in what some conjecture may end up as "China's Century." They may or may not be on the mark, but there is little prospect of the century being Japan's. For Japanese, unlike Germans and their neighbors, there is no East Asian political or cultural identity comparable in depth and strength to the one that has broadened the vision of many Europeans.

In the absence of a broader regional identity, some Japanese affirm their Japaneseness, others are determined internationalists, but most try to combine the two. This strategy is made considerably easier by the strong presence of Japanese designs, products, and a hybrid, transnational culture at home all over the globe, and, conversely, the presence in Japan of works by leading transnational, non-Japanese artists—represented in Figure A.1 by an artist who was born French but became American.

For those in the know and those who listen to her words, Louise Bourgeois's signature spider represents motherliness, but, as with all effective contemporary sculpture, everyone is invited to let their imagination roam. Is she a symbol of creativity, persistence, and (although shown here without a web) interconnectedness, a symbol of female strength with a hint of potential menace?

# Cultural Globalization

Parallel to economic globalization, we can write of cultural globalization, in terms both of a youth culture with shared taste in music and dress and of a global "transcultural" avant-garde of literary and visual artists in which China and Japan are well represented. If these people have found inadequate representation in our text, we make amends by including an illustration from one of the earliest of their number, Irene Chou (Zhou Luyun, 1924– ), who left Shanghai for Hong Kong in 1949 but now resides in Australia. In an eloquent style very much her own, she continues to present a vision that soars beyond our normal perceptions of space and time (see Figure A.2).

**FIGURE A.2** *Satin Painting II,* Irene Chou, 1998. Ink and color on satin, 22.8 in × 48.4 in. The title leaves viewers free to explore and understand the painting on their own. (Used by permission of artist and Helina Chan, iPreciation, http://www.ipreciation.com.)

Among the younger generation we could cite Ha Jin (1956–), winner of the 1999 National Book Award, who once served in the People's Liberation Army but owes his reputation to novels written in English, and Gao Xingjian (1940–), China's first Nobel Prize winner (2000), who moved to Paris in 1989. But Chinese globalization has its limits; neither Ha Jin nor Gao Xingjian can be published in his native land.

However, the transformation of film and song, of popular and "high" culture, continues apace. As Beijing prepares to host the summer Olympics in 2008, its leaders are using the occasion to liven up the city's modern architecture and its people have become passionately involved in international sports. Meanwhile, the range of the effect of Japanese aesthetics is suggested by, on the one hand, Taniguchi Yoshio (1937–) whose revitalization of the Museum of Modern Art in New York (2004) is universally acclaimed and, on the other hand, the plans of Murakami Takahashi's (1962–) trilogy of "Superflat" exhibits (Los Angeles 2001, Paris 2002, New York 2005), featuring paintings, films, placards, and installations melding various veins of Japanese pop art, the fantastic, and the grotesque—inspiring the *New York Times* headline "Where Hello Kitty Meets Godzilla."[3]

# *Notes*

1. John R. Logan, ed., *The New Chinese City: Globalization and Market Reform* (Oxford: Blackwell Publishers, 2002), p. 21.

2. Vaclav Smil, *China's Past, China's Future: Energy, Food, Environment* (New York: RoutledgeCurzon, 2004), p. 214.

3. Carol Vogel, "Inside Art," *New York Times* (Dec. 17, 2004): E40.

# Appendix: Suggestions for Further Study

The literature in English on the history and civilizations of China and Japan is so extensive that careful selection is imperative for student and researcher alike. The effort here has been to suggest books that are broad enough in scope to serve as introductions to their topics, that incorporate sound and recent scholarship, that make for good reading, and that in their totality reflect a variety of approaches. This listing gives special attention to sources with well-researched bibliographies. When such sources are up-to-date and readily available, additional readings are generally not given. Please also note that the length of individual subsections depends in part on the availability of a good recent source for further readings—not on the intrinsic importance of a topic nor on the current state of research. Therefore, there may be fewer items given for a well-researched topic on which there is a recent bibliographical essay or other source of readings than for a topic on which less work has been done but for which there exists no good bibliography. Textbooks and collections of classroom readings are not included. Years given are dates of first publication. For the most part, we have not listed here books already cited in the individual chapters.

## General

The website of the Association for Asian Studies (www.aasianst.org) maintains a list of the numerous websites dealing with China and Japan. It also publishes the *Annual Bibliography of Asian Studies* online that is available in many libraries. Endymion Wilkinson, *Chinese History: A Manual* (1998), is the place to begin researching any topic through Qing. Keith Schoppa, *The Columbia Guide of Modern Chinese History* (2000), is the best place to begin further study of topics in modern Chinese history. The various volumes of the *Cambridge History of China* and the *Cambridge History of Japan* are a major resource. *China Review International* is a journal that reviews books on China in all periods and disciplines.

Surveys of early East Asian history and archaeology are provided by Charles Holcombe, *The Genesis of East Asia 221 B.C.–A.D. 907* (2001), and Gina L. Barnes, *The Rise of Civilization in East Asia: The Archaeology of China, Korea, and Japan* (1999). The nature and meaning of borders during the long period ecompassing most of human history prior to the modern nation state is something that requires and repays careful thought. Bruce Batten, *To the Ends of Japan: Premodern Frontiers, Boundaries, and Interactions* (2003), is an ambitious examination of Japan's premodern history viewed in terms of its borders.

Sherman E. Lee, *A History of Far Eastern Art,* 5th ed. (1994), includes a consideration of Indian art that is helpful for understanding the Buddhist art of East Asia. It is a well-written, insightful, and perceptive, but also a demanding book. European knowledge of Asia in early modern times and European reactions to Asian cultures and peoples is the subject of a detailed study by Donald Lach, *Asia in the Making of Europe,* 3 vols. (1965).

A number of books concern intellectual and religion developments common to China and Japan. *East Asian Civilizations: A Dialogue in Five Stages* (1988), by Wm. Theodore de Bary, is a masterful brief interpretative overview of the mainstream of Chinese and Japanese intellectual history. For more recent perspectives, see *Rethinking Confucianism: Past and Present in China, Japan, Korea, and Vietnam,* edited by Benjamin A. Elman, John B. Duncan, and Herman Ooms (2002). Gilbert Rozman, ed., *The East Asian Region: Confucian Heritage and Its Modern Adaptation* (1991), contains stimulating essays treating Japanese Confucian tradition in comparative perspective. Also recommended is *Women and Confucian Cultures in Premodern China, Korea, and Japan,* edited by Dorothy Ko, JaHyun Kim Haboush, and Joan R. Piggott (2003). Mary Evelyn Tucker and John Berthrong, *Confucianism and Ecology: The Interrelation of Heaven, Earth, and Humans* (1998) is a very timely book.

The literature on Buddhism in English is rich and varied. Heinz Bechert and Richard Gombrich, *The World of Buddhism: Monks and Nuns in Society and Culture* (1984), is a well-illustrated introduction. Donald S. Lopez, Jr., *The Story of Buddhism: A Concise Guide to Its History and Teachings* (2001), is a more recent introduction. Two well-regarded books on Buddhist thought are Paul Williams, *Mahayana Buddhism: The Doctrinal Foundations* (1989), and Roger J. Corless, *The Vision of Buddhism: The Space Under the Tree* (1989). Donald W. Mitchell, *Buddhism: Introducing the Buddhist Experience* (2002), focuses on the history of Buddhist ideas and religious practice. There are good up-to-date entries on many topics in Mircea Eliade, ed., *The Encyclopedia of Religion,* 16 vols. (1987, 2nd ed. forthcoming). Additional books on Buddhism are listed under the China and Japan sections.

# China
## General Overviews and Interpretations

A book stimulating to neophyte and expert alike is *Cultural Atlas of China* (1983, 1998), by Caroline Blunden and Mark Elvin. For anthropological perspectives on Chinese society and religion, Arthur Wolf, ed., *Religion and Ritual in Chinese Society* (1974), is still worth consulting but should be read in conjunction with Hymes,

*Way and Byway,* cited in our discussion of the Song dynasty. For an overview on the burgeoning field of women's history, in addition to the already cited *Women and Confucian Cultures in Premodern China, Korea, and Japan,* see Susan Mann and Yu-Yin Chen, eds., *Under Confucian Eyes: Writings on Gender in Chinese History* (2001).

Thomas J. Barfield, *The Perilous Frontier: Nomadic Empires and China, 221 B.C. to A.D. 1757* (1989), is a thoughtful and well-informed study of a major theme in Chinese history, but for the early period it should be read in conjunction with Nicola Di Cosmo, *Ancient China and Its Enemies* (2001). Kang Chao, *Man and Land in Chinese History* (1986), is an ambitious interpretation of China's premodern economic history. *The Rice Economies: Technology and Development in Asian Societies,* by Francesca Bray (1986), is an excellent introduction to rice agriculture, whereas K. C. Chang, ed., *Food in Chinese Culture: Anthropological and Historical Perspectives* (1977), deals with an important (and delicious) subject. Another book that provides much food for thought, *The Retreat of the Elephants: An Environmental History of China* (2004), by Marek Elvin, concerns premodern China. Language provides a key to any civilization: John de Francis, *The Chinese Language: Fact and Fantasy* (1984), and S. Robert Ramsey, *The Languages of China* (1987), are recommended.

## The Arts and Literature

Michael Sullivan, *The Arts of China,* 4th ed. (1999), is a good survey. Also see *Three Thousand Years of Chinese Painting* by Richard M. Barnhart (1997). *Theories of the Arts in China* (1983), edited by Susan Bush and Christian Murck, is a stimulating collection of essays on a variety of important topics.

The best brief general survey of Chinese literature remains Liu Wu-chi, *An Introduction to Chinese Literature* (1966). For more detailed studies, see Victor H. Mair, ed., *Columbia History of Chinese Literature* (2001). For a concise introduction, also see J. Y. Liu, *Essentials of Chinese Literary Art* (1979). *The Indiana Companion to Traditional Chinese Literature* (1985), William H. Nienhauser, Jr., et al., eds., is indispensable but uneven (see review in *Journal of the American Oriental Society* 107 [1987] 1: 293–304). Also see Wilt Idema and Lloyd Haft, *A Guide to Chinese Literature* (1997). For a sensitive reading of Chinese poetry, see Stephen Owen, *Traditional Chinese Poetry and Poetics: Omens of the World* (1985). Tao-Ching Hsu, *The Chinese Concept of Theater* (1985), is multifaceted and highly informative. *The Confucian Progress: Autobiographical Writings in Traditional China* (1990), by Wu Pei-yi, offers unusually thoughtful and well-formulated insights into literary and intellectual/psychological history.

When, in 1954, Joseph Needham published the first volume of his monumental series *Science and Civilization in China,* he began a project that continues after his death to produce well-researched, reliable, and stimlating studies of a wide range of sciences and technology. The most recent volume (1999), by Peter Golas, deals with mining. Two noteworthy contributions by Nathan Sivin, today's leading senior student of Chinese science, are *Medicine, Philosophy and Religion in Ancient China: Researches and Reflections* (1995), and *Way and the Word: Science and Medicine in Early China and Greece* (2002).

## Thought and Religion

In addition to the works on East Asian thought already cited above or in the text we recommend Thomas A. Wilson, ed., *On Sacred Ground: Culture, Society, Politics, and the Formation of the Cult of Confucius* (2002). A basic resource for the student of Chinese philosophy is Wing-tsit Chan, *A Source Book in Chinese Philosophy* (1963), which covers all periods. The journal *Philosophy East and West* publishes articles on Chinese philosophy.

Donald S. Lopez, Jr., ed, *Religions in China in Practice* (1996), offers an important entry into a tradition that has been characterized as emphasizing orthopraxis rather than orthodoxy. Introductory surveys of Chinese religion are provided by Daniel L. Overmyer, *Religions of China* (1986), and Christian Jochim, *Chinese Religions* (1986). Anthony S. Cua, *Encyclopedia of Chinese Philosophy* (2003), Xinzhong Yao, ed., *RoutledgeCurzon Encyclopedia of Confucianism* (2003), and Livia Kohn, ed., *Handbook of Daoism* (2000), are valuable resources, and there are also good discussions on many Chinese topics in Mircea Eliade, ed., *The Encyclopedia of Religion,* in 16 volumes (1987, 2nd ed., forthcoming).

# Part One: The Classical Civilization of China (Through the Han)

*Early China* is the leading scholarly journal focusing on this period. The essays in Michael Loewe and Edward Shaughnessy, eds., *Cambridge History of Ancient China: From the Origins of Civilization to 221 B.C.* (1999), reflect the sometimes but not always different perspectives of leading scholars summarizing research in a variety of disciplines. For Shaughnessy's own views, see *Before Confucius: Studies in the Creation of the Chinese Classics* (1997). All of David N. Keightley's writings merit serious study. His *Time, Space, and Community in Late Shang China, ca. 1200–1045 B.C.* (2000), is highly recommended.

Poo Mu-chou, *In Search of Personal Welfare: A View of Ancient Chinese Religion* (1998), is an oustanding study, as is Donald J. Harper, *Early Chinese Medical Literature: The Mawangdui Medical Manuscripts* (1998). Both are highly recommended for those interested in early Chinese religion.

Mark Lewis, *Sanctioned Violence in Early China* (1990), is an important book on a most important topic. A. C. Graham, *Disputers of the Tao: Philosophical Argument in Ancient China* (1989), is a masterly interpretative survey of early Chinese thought. Michael Puett, *The Ambivalence of Creation: Debates Concerning Innovation and Artifice in Early China* (2001), is itself highly innovative. Michael Nylan, *The Five "Confucian" Classics* (2001), is a superb introduction to some of the world's most influential texts. Also see Robin D. S. Yates, *Five Lost Classics: Tao, HuangLao, and Yin-yang in Han China* (1997). *Knowing Words: Wisdom and Cunning in the Classical Traditions of China and Greece* (1992), by Lisa Raphals, is a fascinating comparative study. Benjamin Schwartz, *The World of Thought in Ancient China* (1985), has been described by A. C. Graham as "a lucid, accurate, agreebly written and comprehensive survey" written from the point of view of those who prefer to think of the Chinese as like ourselves" (*Times Literary Supplement,* July 18, 1986, p. 795).

For the Qin, see Martin Kern, *The Stele Inscriptions of Ch'in Shih-hwang: Text and Ritual in Early Chinese Imperial Representation* (2002). On Qin law, see A. F. P. Hulsewe, *Remnants of Ch'in Law: An Annotated Translation of the Ch'in Legal and Administrative Rules of the 3rd Century B.C., Discovered in Yün-meng Prefecture, Hupei Province, in 1975* (1985), and Robin Yates and Katrina McLeod, *Forms of Ch'in Law: An Annotated Translation of the Feng-chen Shih* (1981).

Important perspectives on the Han are provided by Martin Powers, *Art and Political Expression in Early China* (1991), and Wu Hung, *Wu Liang Shrine: The Ideolology of Early Chinese Pictorial Art* (1989). For the history of women, see Lisa Raphal, *Sharing the Light: Representations of Women and Virtue in Early China* (1998); Michael Nylan, "Golden Spindles and Axes: Elite Women in the Achaemenid and Han Empires," in *The Sage and the Second Sex, Essays on Classicism, Confucian Learning, and Feminism,* edited by Li Chenyang (2000, pp. 199–222); and Miranda Brown, "Mothers and Sons in Warring States and Han China, 453 B.C.–A.D. 220," in *Nan Nü: Men, Women and Gender in Early and Imperial China* (5.2 [2003]).

For the period's (and China's) own greatest historian, there is Burton Watson's *Ssu-ma Ch'ien: Grand Historian of China* (1958); Watson's very readable translation, *Records of the Historian: Chapters from the Shih Chi of Ssu-ma Ch'ien,* 2 vols. (1961); and Michael Nylan's, "Sima Qian: A True Historian" in *Early China* (23–24 [1998–99], pp. 203–246). Roger T. Ames, *The Art of Rulership: A Study in Ancient Chinese Political Thought* (1983), is a translation of a major Han text by a scholar who in collaboration with the philosopher David L. Hall went on to publish a number of studies of Chinese thought in comparative perspective. For life and poetry, also see Anne Birrell, *Popular Songs and Ballads of Han China* (1988).

# Part Two: China in a Buddhist Age
## Buddhism in China

The literature on Buddhism in English is rich and varied. Heinz Bechert and Richard Gombrich, *The World of Buddhism: Monks and Nuns in Society and Culture* (1984), is a well-illustrated introduction.

Donald S. Lopez, Jr., *The Story of Buddhism: A Concise Guide to Its History and Teachings* (2001), is a more recent introduction. Two well-regarded books on Buddhist thought are Paul Williams, *Mahayana Buddhism: The Doctrinal Foundations* (1989), and Roger J. Corless, *The Vision of Buddhism: The Space Under the Tree* (1989). Donald W. Mitchell, *Buddhism: Introducing the Buddhist Experience* (2002), focuses on the history of Buddhist ideas and religious practice.

For a brief account of Buddhism in China viewed as a rich and complex historical process of interaction between China and the Indian religion, see Arthur F. Wright, *Buddhism in Chinese History* (1959). Of all the sects of East Asian Buddhism, Chan has attracted the most attention in the West. The most scholarly translation of a key text is Philip P. Yampolsky, *The Platform Sutra of the Sixth Patriarch: The Text of the Tunhuang Manuscript* (1967). The relationship between Chan (Zen) and the arts remains as difficult to define as the religion itself, but the arts, especially painting, testify to the power of Zen even as they offer an approach to understanding. Enthusiastically recommended is Jan Fontain and Money L. Hickman, *Zen Painting and Calligraphy* (1970), a catalog of an exhibition of both Chinese and Japanese works.

Robert Ford Campany, *To Live as Long as Heaven and Earth, a Translation and Study of Ge Hong's Tradition of Divine Transcendents* (2002), is a major recent contribution to the study of Daoism during the period of disunity with a good bibliography.

## Secular Developments

Studies in Chinese secular culture during the period of division include Robert Van Gulik, *Hsi K'ang and His Poetic Essay on the Lute* (1940). Richard B. Mather has translated the *Shishuo Xinyu* under the title *A New Account of Tales of the World* (1976). This very learned and meticulous translation makes available in English a major source for the study of the period's sophisticates. Three out of a projected eight volumes have been published to date of David Knechtges' monumental translation of China's oldest surviving literary anthology, *Wen Xuan or Selections of Refined Literature*, by Xiao Tong (1982, 1987, 1996).

# Sui and Tang

*The Cambridge History of China*, Volume 3, *Sui and T'ang, 580–906, Part 1* (1979), edited by Denis Twitchett, is a major resource. Arthur F. Wright, *The Sui Dynasty* (1978), remains authoritative. Charles Hartman, *Han Yü and the T'ang Search for Unity* (1986), deals with political as well as literary and intellectual history. David McMullen, *State and Scholars in T'ang China* (1988), is a major work of scholarship that, however, may be tough going to a beginner. Peter Bol, *This Culture of Ours—Intellectual Transitions in T'ang and Sung China* (1992), is demanding and essential reading.

Tang poetry is well represented in anthologies as well as in studies of individual poets. Selecting from a number of titles is in part a matter of taste, but it is generally recognized that one of the best books by a master translator is Arthur Waley, *The Life and Times of Po Chü-i* (1949). Although not as fully biographical as Waley's book, the following studies also provide windows on Tang life: Arthur Cooper, *Li Po and Tu Fu* (1973); David R. McCraw, *Du Fu's Laments from the South* (1992); A. R. Davis, *Tu Fu* (1971); and three books by Stephen Owen—*The*

*Poetry of Meng Chiao and Han Yü* (1975), *The Poetry of the Early T'ang* (1977), and *The Great Age of Chinese Poetry: The High T'ang* (1981). For late Tang poetry, see A. C. Graham, *Poems of the Late T'ang* (1965), and James J. Y. Liu, *The Poetry of Li Shang-yin* (1969). A leading student of Tang culture is Edward H. Schafer. Two of his finest books are *The Golden Peaches of Samarkand: A Study of Tang Exotics* (1963) and *The Vermillion Bird: Tang Images of the South* (1967). For a fascinating view of Tang China as seen through the eyes of a visiting Japanese monk, see Edwin O. Reischauer, *Ennin's Travels in T'ang China* (1955).

# Part Three: Late Imperial/Early Modern

Much of the general literature considers late imperial and/or early modern as beginning in the Ming and focuses on that period; works are mostly listed there although they have implications also for Song/Yuan. One such that we think does belong here is Theodore Huters and Bin Wong, eds. *Culture and State in Chinese History: Conventions, Accommodations, and Critiques* (1997). For insights into the transformation of the environment, see *Sediments of Time: Environment and Society in Chinese History,* edited by Mark Elvin and Liu Ts'ui-jung (1998). The individual contributions are of high quality, although some are more demanding than others. Nicholas K. Menzies, *Forest and Land Management in Imperial China* (1994), is similarly broad in scope. R. Keith Schoppa, *Xiang Lake—Song Full of Tears: Nine Centuries of Chinese Life at Xiang Lake* (2002), is highly recommended, as are the books by Marks and Perdue cited in our text.

A book on economic history and thought rare in its broad chronological coverage is Richard Von Glahn, *Fountain of Fortune: Money and Monetary Policy in China 1000–1700* (1990). *Kinship Organization in Late Imperial China 1000–1400,* edited by Patricia B. Buckley and James J Watson (1986), is an influential volume, which, like James L. Watson and Evelyn S. Rawski, eds., *Death Ritual in Late Imperial and Modern China* (1988), exemplifies fruitful collaboration of anthropology and history.

## Song China

For current scholarship, see the *Journal of Song-Yuan Studies.* Robert P. Hymes, *Statesmen and Gentlemen: The Elite of Fu-Chou, Chiang Hsi in Northern and Southern Sung* (1986), is essential reading for social history, as is John W. Chaffee, *The Thorny Gates of Learning in Sung China: A Social History of Examinations* (2nd ed., 1995). Another major contribution to the relationship between state and society is *Powerful Relations: Kinship Status and The State in Sung China (960–1279),* by Beverly J. Bossler (1998). Recommended as another major study is Thomas H. C. Lee, *Government Education and Examinations in Sung China* (1985). Village structure is analyzed in Brian E. McKnight, *Village and Bureaucracy in Southern Sung China* (1971), who is also the leading authority on Song law. Among his more recent contributions is *The Enlightened Judgments: Ch'ing-ming Chi: The Sung Dynasty*

*Collection* (1999), translated by Brian E McKnight and James T. C. Liu. Liu's *China Turning Inward: Intellectual and Political Changes in the Early Twelfth Century* (1988), remains an important and influential study.

A stimulating discussion of the Song economy in the light of world history is provided in the first chapter of William H. McNeill, *The Pursuit of Power: Technology, Armed Force, and Society since A.D. 1000* (1982). For insights into the vital world of maritime trade, see Angela Schottenhammer, ed., *The Emporium of the World: Maritime Quanzhou, 1000–1400* (2001). Also see Billy K. L. So, *Prosperity, Regions, and Institutions in Maritime China: The South Fukien Pattern, 946–1368* (2000).

*Family and Property in Sung China: Yuan Ts'ai's Precepts for Social Life* (1984), Patricia B. Ebrey, trans., is a fascinating and important contribution to social history, as is her book, *The Inner Quarters: Marriage and the Lives of Chinese Women in the Sung Period* (1993). Richard von Glahn, *The Country of Streams and Grottoes: Expansion, Settlement, and the Civilizing of the Sichuan Frontier in Song Times* (1987), deals with a major theme in a sophisticated manner.

Ronald C. Egan, *The Literary Works of Ou-yang Hsiu (1007–72)* (1984), examines a key literary and intellectual figure. Michal A. Fuller, *The Road to East Slope: The Development of Su Shi's Poetic Voice* (1990), is a study of the dynasty's major poet and literatus. For the study of Song poetry, James J. Y. Liu, *Major Lyricists of the Northern Sung* (1974), has the great merit of including for each poem the Chinese text, a word for word rendition, and a polished translation. A thoughtful and highly commendable book is Jonathan Chaves, *Mei Yao-ch'en and the Development of Early Sung Poetry* (1976). Chaves is also the author of the excellent and delightful, *Heaven My Blanket, Earth My Pillow—Poems from the Sung Dynasty by Yang Wan-li* (1975). Also see Julie Landau, *Beyond Spring: Tz'u Poems of the Sung Dynasty* (1994). There are a number of other worthy books on Song poetry that cannot be listed here, but we should mention a study of China's foremost woman poet: *Li Ch'ing-chao*, by P'in-ch'ing Hu (1966). For readers interested in the history of music, there is Rulan Chao Pian, *Song Dynasty Musical Sources and Their Interpretation* (1967). Also recommended is Peter C. Sturman, *Mi Fu and the Art of Calligraphy in Northern Song China* (1997).

A prime source for the study of Neo-Confucian thought is Wing-tsit Chan, trans., *Reflections on Things at Hand: The Neo-Confucian Anthology Compiled by Chu Hsi and Lu Tsu-ch'ien* (1967). Among the many other contributions by Wingtsit Chan to the study of Neo-Confucianism are his translation of *Neo-Confucian Terms Explained (The Pei-hsi tzu-i) by Ch'en Ch'un, 1159–1223* (1986) and his editing of *Chu Hsi and Neo-Confucianism* (1986), a wide-ranging volume of essays by East Asian as well as Western scholars. A fine study of one of the alternatives to Zhu Xi is Hoyt C. Tillman, *Utilitarian Confucianism: Ch'en Liang's Challenge to Chu Hsi* (1982). Tillman is also author of *Confucian Discourse and Chu His's Ascendancy* (1992), an important book that views Zhu Xi in the perspective of the intellectual life of his time. See also Bol's book cited under earlier under "Sui and Tang."

# The Yuan

Volume 6 of the Cambridge History, *Alien Regimes and Border States 907–1368* (1994), includes chapters by the major scholars in the field as well as useful bibliographic essays. For those who would like to explore Yuan culture, there are two books that are authoritative and sensitive: Chungwen Shih, *The Golden Age of Chinese Drama* (1976), and Hok-lam Chan and Wm. Theodore de Bary, eds., *Yuan Thought* (1982), which remains the best book on its subject.

The study of Marco Polo is a field all to itself. http://www.silk-road.com/artl/marcopolo.shtml is a useful and attractive website; also see http://www.usnews.com/usnews/doubleissue/mysteries/marco.htm. A learned and delightful older study is Leonardo Olschki, *Marco Polo's Asia: An Introduction to His "Description of the World" Called "il Milione"* (1960). For other travel accounts, see Christopher Dawson, ed., *Mission to Asia: Narratives and Letters of the Franciscan Missionaries in Mongolia and China in the Thirteenth and Fourteenth Centuries* (1955). Also see Jeannette Mirsky, ed., *The Great Chinese Travelers* (1964), which includes three accounts falling into this period. For a traveler in the opposite direction, see Morris Rossabi, *Voyager from Xanadu: Raban Sauma and the First Journey from China to the West* (1992).

# Ming/Qing

Before turning to the last two dynasties individually, it behooves us to mention a few books on Late Imperial China that are useful for students of either or both periods. These include the influential and still very useful collection of essays edited by G. William Skinner, *The City in Late Imperial China* (1977). Randall A. Dorgen, *Controlling the Dragon: Confucian Engineers and the Yellow River in Late Imperial China* (2001), studies an important topic. Philip C. C. Huang, *The Peasant Family and Rural Development in the Yangzi Delta, 1350–1988* (1990), and its counterpart, *The Peasant Economy and Social Change in North China* (1985), are both rich in stimulating interpretations. Francesca Bray, *Technology and Gender: Fabrics of Power in Late Imperial China* (1997), is superb.

On intellectual history, see Kwang-Ching Liu, ed., *Orthodoxy in Late Imperial China* (1990), and its companion volume, which includes important work on religious history, *Heterodoxy in Late Imperial China* (2004), edited by Liu and Richard Shek. Also see Richard Smith, *Cosmology, Ontology, and Human Efficacy* (1993). Benjamin A Elman is a leading scholar interested in the history of thought and institutions. See his *From Philosophy to Philology: Intellectual and Social Aspects of Change in Late Imperial China* (1984) and *A Cultural History of Civil Examinations in Late Imperial China* (2000), as well as *Education and Society in Late Imperial China, 1600–1900,* edited by Elman and Alexander Woodside (1994).

Robert E. Hegel, *Reading Illustrated Fiction in Late Imperial China* (1998), discusses the physical appearance of books and the expectations of those who read them. Also see Hegel, *The Novel in Seventeenth Century China* (1981).

## *Ming*

The Cambridge History of China, Volume 7, Part 1, *The Ming Dynasty, 1368–1644* (1988), Frederick W. Mote and Denis Twitchett, eds., is a detailed narrative history of the dynasty, and Part 2 (1998) consists of topical essays. A number of studies on social and economic history begin with the Ming but also include later history. A still useful survey of major topics complete with excellent suggestions for further reading is Lloyd E. Eastman, *Family, Fields, and Ancestors* (1988). An authoritative study of an important subject is Ray Huang, *Taxation and Government Finance in 16th Century Ming China* (1974). A real treasure house of information is the monumental *Dictionary of Ming Biography 1368–1644,* 2 vols. (1976), edited by L. Carrington Goodrich and Chaoying Fang.

Wm. Theodore de Bary, *Neo-Confucian Orthodoxy and the Learning of the Mind-and-Heart* (1981), takes Neo-Confucianism from the Song to the Ming and beyond. Also see Wm. Theodore de Bary, et al., *Self and Society in Ming Thought* (1970). On Wang Yangming, there are two complementary studies: Julia Ching, *To Acquire Wisdom: The Way of Wang Yangming* (1976), and Tu Wei-ming, *Neo-Confucian Thought in Action: Wang Yangming's Youth (1472–1509)* (1976). On late Ming thought, see Wm. Theodore de Bary, et al., *The Unfolding of Neo-Confucianism* (1975), Edward Ch'ien, *Chiao Hung and the Restructuring of Neo-Confucian Thought in the Late Ming* (1985), and Irene Bloom, ed. and trans., *Knowledge Painfully Acquired: The K'un-chih chi by Lo Ch'in-shu* (1987).

Craig Clunas, *Pictures and Visuality in Early Modern China* (1997), and his *Fruitful Sites: Garden Culture in Ming Dynasty China* (1996), are stimulating and informative. Music as well as art was central to the culture. For music, we are fortunate to have Joseph S. C. Lam, *State Sacrifices and Music in Ming China: Orthodoxy, Creativity, and Expressiveness* (1998). Literature provides fascinating vignettes of Ming life as well as insights into Ming sensibilities. For translations, see the *Indiana Companion to Chinese Literature* (see earlier under "General Works"). Andrew H. Plaks, *The Four Masterworks of the Ming Novel* (1987), is superb. For painting, see James Cahill, *Parting at the Shore: Chinese Painting of the Early and Middle Ming Dynasty, 1368–1580* (1978), and his *The Distant Mountains: Chinese Painting of the Late Ming Dynasty 1570–1644* (1982), as well as Anne De Coursey Clapp, *The Painting of T'ang Yin* (1991), which also provides insights into the social life of Ming Suzhou.

## *First Encounters*

David E. Mungello, *The Great Encounter of China and the West, 1500–1800* (1999), is a short and highly recommended account complete with bibliography. Other books on China's relations with the rest of the world are the following: Philip Snow, *The Star Raft; China's Encounter with Africa* (New York: Weidenfeld & Nicolson, 1988); Jacques Gernet, *China and the Christian Impact: A Conflict of Cultures* (New York: Cambridge University Press and Paris: Editions de la Maison des sciences de l'homme, 1982), trans. Janet Lloyd, deserves a close reading. Also see L. J. Gallagher, trans., *China in the Sixteenth Century: The Journals of Matteo*

*Ricci* (1953). Jonathan D. Spence, *The Memory Palace of Matteo Ricci* (1984), is a fascinating exercise in comparative history. For the later history of Christianity, see Daniel H Bays, *Christianity in China from the Eighteenth Century to the Present* (1996). For the arts, see Michael Sullivan, *Meeting of Eastern and Western Art* (1973, 1989).

## Qing

The recent publication of *The Cambridge History,* Volume 9: Part 1, *The Ch'ing Empire to 1800,* edited by Willard J. Peterson (2003), reduces the number of studies that we need to list separately here. Readers should, however, be aware of the very recent work edited by Lynn A. Struve, *The Qing Formation in World Historical Time* (2004), a thoughtful collection of essays viewing Qing in terms of world history, which adopts a global perspective. Evelyn Rawski, *The Last Emperors: A Social History of Qing Imperial Institutions* (1998), is an excellent account of the Qing as a multiethnic dynasty. Pamela K. Crossley, a leading scholar of Manchu studies, has published *Orphan Warriors—Three Manchu Generations and the End of the Qing World* (1990), a general survey titled *The Manchus* (1996), and *A Translucent Mirror: History and Identity in Qing Imperial Ideology* (1999). Also see Mark Elliott, *The Manchu Way: The Eight Banners and Ethnic Identity in Late Imperial China* (2001), and Edward J. M. Rhoades, *Manchu and Han Ethnic Relations and Political Power in Late Qing China, 1861–1928* (2000).

For demographic information, see *One Quarter of Humanity: Malthusian Mythology and Chinese Realities, 1700–2000,* by James Z. Lee and Wang Feng (1999). For the eighteenth century, see Susan Naquin and Evelyn S. Rawski, *Chinese Society in the Eighteenth Century* (1987), an ambitious synthesis and excellent source for additional references on government as well as other topics. William T. Rowe, *Saving the World: Chen Hongmou and Elite Consciousness in Eighteenth-Century China* (2001), is a major study of political thought and action. R. Kent Guy, *The Emperor's Four Treasures: Scholars and the State in the Late Ch'ien-lung Era* (1987), is illuminating on both scholars and state. Jonathan D. Spence, *Treason by the Book* (2001), and Philip A. Kuhn, *Soulstealers: The Chinese Sorcery Scare of 1768* (1990), are sophisticated, well-written accounts rich in insights on Qing political culture. Harold L. Kahn, *Monarchy in the Emperor's Eyes: Image and Reality in the Ch'ien-lung Reign* (1971), has fun showing how elusive the reality behind the image truly is.

Arthur Waley, *Yuan Mei: Eighteenth Century Chinese Poet* (1956), is a sensitively drawn portrait. Research and interpretation of the century's and China's most acclaimed novel has grown into a major industry known as "Red Studies." Two outstanding studies are Andrew H. Plaks, *Archetype and Allegory in the Dream of the Red Chamber* (1976), and Anthony Yu, *Rereading the Stone: Desire and the Making of Fiction in Dream of the Red Chamber* (1997). Also see Shang Wei, *Rulin Waishi and Cultural Transformation in Later Imperial China* (2003). Kai-wing Chow, *The Rise of Ritualism in Late Imperial China: Ethics, Classics, and Lineage Discourse* (1994), is a major contribution to intellectual history for which also see the books by Benjamin Elman listed above.

The texture of ordinary life is brilliantly conveyed by Jonathan Spence in *Death of Woman Wang* (1979). More elite women are studied by Susan Mann, as quoted in our text. Also see *Under Confucian Eyes: Writings on Gender in Chinese History*, Susan Mann and Yu-Yin Chen, eds. (2001). See http://www.pem.org/yinyutang/, the Peabody Essex Museum website for a Qing merchant house.

# Part Four: China in the Modern World

Paul A. Cohen, *Discovering History in China: American Historical Writing on the Recent Chinese Past* (1984), is a thoughtful account of some of the constructs and concerns underlying American Chinese studies. Also see his more recent *China Unbound: Evolving Perspectives on the Chinese Past* (2003).

# The Long Nineteenth Century (to 1911)

*The Cambridge History of China*, Volume 11, Part II, *Late Ch'ing, 1800–1911,* edited by John K. Fairbank and Kwang-Ching Liu (1980), remains a valuable reference with useful bibliographical essays.

Jane Kate Leonard, *Controlling from Afar: the Daoguang Emperor's Management of the Grand Canal Crisis, 1824–1826* (1996), is a study of China's internal crisis. For subsequent internal politics, see the study by James M. Polachek cited in the text. For an important perspective on early Sino-Western relations, see Jane K. Leonard, *Wei Yuan and China's Rediscovery of the Maritime World* (1984). Some of the denizens of the maritime world are studied in Dian H. Murray, *Pirates of the South China Coast, 1796–1889* (1984). For a different, comparative, and less maritime-oriented perspective, see James L. Hevia, *Cherishing Men from Afar: Qing Ritual and the Macartney Embassy of 1793* (1995). Also see the same author's review article, "Opium, Empire, and Modern History," *China Review International* (10, No. 2 [Fall 2003] pp. 307–326).

*Hankow: Commerce and Society in a Chinese City, 1796–1889* and *Hankow: Conflict and Community in a Chinese City, 1786–1895* (1984, 1989), both by William T. Rowe, summarized much research even as they broke new ground. Yen-p'ing Hao, *The Commercial Revolution in Nineteenth Century China* (1986), is an authoritative account of the modern sector.

On Christianity, see the book by Daniel H. Bays cited above; and for the Taiping Rebellion, the book by Jonathan Spence quoted in the text is an excellent narrative account. Historians have increasingly turned to local history in their search for answers to major questions of social and political history. A fine example of the genre is Mary B. Rankin, *Elite Activism and Political Transformation in China: Zhejiang Province, 1865–1911* (1986).

The study of modern Chinese intellectual history has been deeply influenced by the brilliant writings of Joseph R. Levenson, especially his *Confucian China and Its Modern-Fate*, 3 vols. (1972, 1958–1965). Also see Maurice Meisner and Rhoads Murphy, eds., *The Mozartian Historian: Essays on the Works of Joseph R. Levenson* (1976). A different approach is taken by Chang Hao in his *Chinese Intellectuals in Crisis: Search for Order and Meaning, 1890–1911* (1987). An excellent example of what can be accomplished by a master in the field of intellectual biography is Benjamin Schwartz, *In Search of Wealth and Power: Yen Fu and the West* (1964). *An Intellectual History of Modern China,* by Merle Goldman and Leo Ou-fan Lee (2002), provides a useful survey. Also see Kirk A. Denton, ed., *Modern Chinese Literary Thought: Writings on Literature, 1893–1945* (1996).

Two of the leading figures during the last decade of the Qing are examined in Daniel H. Bays, *China Enters the Twentieth Century: Chang Chih-tung and the Issues of a New Age, 1895–1909* (1978), and Stephen R. MacKinnon, *Power and Politics in Late Imperial China: Yuan Shi-kai in Beijing and Tianjin, 1901–1908* (1980). Also see Joan Judge, *Print and Politics: "Shibao" and the Culture of Reform in Late Qing China* (1996).

Luke S. K. Kwong, *A Mosaic of the Hundred Days* (1984), lays some myths to rest. For newer research and analysis, see Rebecca E. Karl and Peter Zarrow, ed., *Rethinking the 1898 Reform Period: Political and Cultural Change in Late Qing China* (2002). Paul A. Cohen, *History in Three Keys: The Boxers as Event, Experience and Myth* (1987), is a good place to begin reading about the Boxer Rebellion.

## From Revolution to Revolution: 1911–1949

Periodizations differ, reflecting different purposes. A case in point is *Remaking the Chinese City: Modernity and National Identity, 1900–1950* (2000), edited by Joseph Esherick, a social historian whose other books are also recommended.

Bonnie S. McDougall and Kam Louie, *The Literature of China in the Twentieth Century* (1997), is one of the few books that treats the twentieth century as a whole. James R. Pusey, *China and Charles Darwin* (1983), is very informative on Liang Qiqao, but it may turn out that a certain Social Darwinism continued throughout the century.

Republican China is the subject of Volumes 11 and 12 of *The Cambridge History.* The discussions found there should be read in conjunction with *Reappraising Republican China* (2000), a collection of essays edited by Frederick Wakeman, Jr., and Richard L. Edmonds, which to some extent cast a more favorable light on the period.

The bitter rejection of tradition by the leaders of the May Fourth Movement continues to generate much controversy, and it may be too early for a general history. For a study of the post-Imperial city, see David Strand, *Rickshaw Beijing: City People and Politics in the 1920s* (1989), a masterful account of its multifaceted subject. Among the rich literature on Shanghai is Leo Ou-fan Lee, *Shanghai Modern: The Flowering of a New Urban Culture in China, 1930–45* (1999).

Thomas G. Rawski, *Economic Growth in Prewar China* (1989), is highly informative. His contention that China's economy grew from 1912 to 1937 is a valuable contribution to economic history and discourse. For business history, see Sherman Cochran, *Encountering Chinese Networks: Western, Japanese, and Chinese Corporations in China, 1880–1937* (2001). Frank Dikötter, *Crime, Punishment and the Prison in Modern China* (2002), analyzes prison policies in the pre-Communist period.

The warlord period is particularly complex. Edward A. McCord, *The Power of the Gun: The Emergence of Modern Chinese Warlordism* (1993), includes an analysis of interpretative approaches as well as a detailed study focusing on Hubei and Hunan. Prasenjet Duara, *Culture, Power, and the State: Rural China, 1900–1942* (1988), is a major influential interpretative study.

Arif Dirlik, *The Origins of Chinese Communism* (1989), is thoughtful and complex. Philip Short, *Mao: A Life* (2000), is the most comprehensive study of Mao available in English.

Jeffrey C. Kinkley, *Chinese Justice, the Fiction: Law and Literature in Modern China* (2000), is far reaching and outstanding. Also see Kinkley's *The Odyssey of Shen Congwen* (1987). Leo Ou-fan Lee, *The Romantic Generation of Modern Chinese Writers* (1981), and the same author's *Voices from the Iron House: A Study of Lu Xun* (1987), as well as the conference volume he edited, *Lu Xun and His Legacy* (1985). Ralph Crozier, *Art and Revolution in Modern China: The Lingnan (Cantonese) School of Painting, 1906–1951* (1988), explores the relationship between art and politics and that between nation and province.

## The People's Republic of China

An excellent account of the various approaches scholars have used in their attempts to analyze the Chinese revolution is provided by the introduction to Kathleen Hartford and Steven M. Goldstein, eds., *Single Sparks: China's Rural Revolutions* (1989). Volume 14 of *The Cambridge History* (1987), edited by Roderick MacFarquar and John K. Fairbank, deals with the People's Republic from 1949 to 1965 and contains discussions of bibliography.

A leading student of ideological developments in China is Maurice Meisner, whose *Marxism, Maoism, and Utopianism: Eight Essays* (1982) is recommended. A major topic is examined in James L. Watson, ed., *Class and Social Stratification in Post-Revolution China* (1984). *Popular Chinese Literature and Performing Arts in the People's Republic of China, 1949–79* (1984), edited by Bonnie S. McDougall, is another valuable collection of essays.

Two important and very useful studies of China under Mao are John Wilson Lewis and Xue Litai, *China Builds the Bomb* (1998), and Judith Shapiro, *Mao's War Against Nature* (2001). A book that belongs on everyone's list is Richard P. Madsen, *Morality and Power in a Chinese Village* (1984). Its empirical basis is an outstanding village study by Anita Chan, Richard Madsen, and Jonathan Unger, *Chen Village: The Recent History of a Peasant Community* (1984). Its sequel, Chan and Unger, *Chen Village under Mao and Deng* (1984 and 1992), is also highly recommended. Zhang Xinxin and Sang Ye, *Chinese Lives: An Oral History of Contemporary China* (1987), edited by W. J. E. Jenner and Delia Davin, is a collection of personal vignettes—windows into life in China.

For the cultural revolution, see Roderick MacFarquar, *The Origins of the Cultural Revolution* (1974); Elizabeth Perry, *Proletarian Power: Shanghai in the Cultural Revolution* (1997); Barbara Barnouin. *Ten Years of Turbulence: The Chinese Cultural Revolution* (1993); and Heng Liang, *Son of the Revolution*, translated by Judith Shapiro (1993). The fallout of the Cultural Revolution years can be sampled in *Mao's Harvest: Voices from China's New Generation* (1983), edited by Helen F. Siu and Zelda Stern. Also see Yue Daiyun and Carolyn Wakeman, *To the Storm: The Odyssey of a Revolutionary Chinese Woman* (1985), a gripping personal account.

Orville Schell, *Mandate of Heaven: A New Generation of Entrepreneurs, Dissidents, Bohemians, and Technocrats Lay Claims to China's Future* (1994), is an account of Tiananmen and its aftermath by an experienced China observer. Tony Saich, ed., *The Chinese People's Movement: Perspectives on Spring 1989* (1990), provides analyses and includes a chronology.

A good way to keep up with current developments is in the pages of *The China Quarterly*. Economic development had first priority in Deng Xiaoping's China so *The Political Economy of Reform in Post-Mao China* (1985), edited by Elizabeth J. Perry and Christine Wong, deserves special attention. For the countryside, also see Ashwani Saith, *The Re-emergence of the Chinese Peasantry: Aspects of Rural Decollectivisation* (1987). John P. Burns and Stanley Rosen, eds., *Policy Conflicts in Post-Mao China: A Documentary Survey with Analysis* (1986), is very useful. Energy policy is the focus of a fine study of how Chinese politics operate: Kenneth Lieberthal and Michael Oksenberg, *Policy Making in China: Leaders, Structures, and Process* (1988).

One of the distinguished contributors to Jonathan Ungar ed., *The Nature of Chinese Politics* (2002), is Andrew J. Nathan., an authority on contemporary China and author of *China's Crisis: Dilemmas of Reforms and Prospects for Democracy* (1990) and other studies. Also see *The Paradox of China's Post-Mao Reforms* (1999), edited by Merle Goldman and R. MacFarquar. Doug Guthrie, *Dragon in a Three-Piece Suit: The Emergence of Capitalism in China* (1999), is right on track. Jun Jing, *The Temple of Memories: History, Power, and Morality in a Chinese Village* (1996), is a superb study of a branch of the Kong clan, which claims descent from Confucius, and how they revived their tradition and built a temple to the sage. Vaclav Svil, an outstanding student of the Chinese environment, has recently published a collection from his previous writings along with his latest reflections in *China's Past, China's Future: Energy, Food, Environment* (2004). Also see Lester Ross, *Environmental Policy in China* (1988).

The arts are worth studying for their own sake as well as for what they reveal about the people who produce and support them. Julia F. Andrews, author of *Between the Thunder and the Rain: Chinese Painting from the Opium War to the Cultural Revolution, 1840–1979* (2000), and *Painters and Politics in the People's Republic of China 1949–79* (1994), is an art historian well grounded in history. Also see Andrews and Kuiyi Shen, *Century in Crisis: Modernity and Tradition in the Art of Twentieth-Century China* (1998), Ellen J. Laing, *The Winking Owl: Art in the*

*People's Republic of China* (1988), and Joan L. Cohen, *The New Chinese Painting, 1949–1986* (1987).

Richard C. Kraus, a political scientist with a keen eye and ear has written *Brushes with Power: Modern Politics and the Chinese Art of Calligraphy* (1991), and *Pianos and Politics in China: Middle-Class Ambitions and the Struggle over Western Music* (1989). Yingjih Zhang, *Encyclopedia of Chinese Film* (1999), is a useful reference work. Also see Cyrus Berry, ed., *Perspectives on Chinese Cinema* (1991), and Linda C. Ehrlich and David Desser, eds., *Cinematic Landscapes: Observations on the Visual Arts and Cinema of China and Japan* (1994).

Jeffrey C. Kinkley, *After Mao: Chinese Literature and Society, 1978–81* (1985), is an analysis of the post-Mao literary world by a leading authority on contemporary literature and intellectuals. Another thoughtful and authoritative book is Perry Link, *The Uses of Literature: Life in the Socialist Chinese Literary System* (2000). For popular culture, see Michael Dutton, *Streetlife in China* (1998).

Wu Hung, *Chinese Art at the Crossroads* (2002), makes for rewarding reading, like his other books and essays such as his contribution to *Inside Out* (1998), the catalog to a notable exhibition of the works of artists who live on the mainland, Taiwan, and elsewhere. Similarly, Chinese writers from all over are included in *Running Wild: New Chinese Writers,* edited by David Der-Wei Wang with Jeanne Tai (1994). Also see *Chinese Literature in the Second Half of a Modern Century: A Critical Survey* (2000), edited by Pang-Yuan Chi and Wang, who stress here as elsewhere commonalities in Chinese writing wherever performed.

Travel accounts generally reveal as much about the traveler as they do about China, and it would be interesting to compare systematically the reports of recent visitors with those of foreigners who visited China in earlier times. Among the most engaging of the contemporary books are those by professional writers (Simon de Beauvoir, Alberto Moravia, and Colin Thubron), those by journalists with Chinese experience (Edgar Snow and Seymour Topping), and those by specialists in Chinese studies (Ross Terrill, Simon Leys, and Orville Schell). Especially noteworthy are books by those who have resided in China for a time as university teachers (Tani E. Barlow and Donald M. Lowe), journalists (Fox Butterfield and David Bonavia), or embassy officials (Robert Garside).

## Tibet, Taiwan, and Hong Kong

John Powers, *History as Propaganda: Tibetan Exiles versus the People's Republic of China* (2004), is an even-handed account of two starkly different views of Tibetan history and a useful guide through the literature. *The Cambridge History* volume does not include Taiwan (which will be discussed in Volume 15). Murray A. Rubinstein, *Taiwan: A New History* (1999), is a good place to begin reading about the history of Taiwan. Important books that have appeared subsequent to publication of Rubinstein's history include Jay Taylor, *The Generalissimo's Son: Chiang Ching-kuo and the Revolutions in China and Taiwan* (2000), and Stephane Corcuff, *Memories of the Future: National Identity Issues and the Search for a New Taiwan* (2002). Among older studies expecially worth consulting, see Thomas B. Gold,

*State and Society in the Taiwan Miracle* (1986), and, for earlier social history, Johanna M. Meskill, *A Chinese Pioneer Family: The Lins of Wu-feng, Taiwan, 1729–1895* (1979).

Issues of identity are also foremost in the minds of Hong Kong artists and intellectuals. See *Hong Kong Becoming Chinese,* a series published in Armonk, New York, by M. E. Sharp under the editorship of Ming K.Chan and Gerald A Postiglioe.

## The Sociology/Anthropology of Knowledge

Postmodernism has given new urgency to the need for students be fully aware of the human context of the work in their discipline. Archeology is no exception to this rule, but archeologists occupy a special place in China as intellectuals who work with their hands as well as minds and do so thoughout a country that continues to prize history. That at least is the argument advanced by Erika E. S. Evasdortir in *Obedient Authority: Chinese Intellectuals and Their Achievement of Orderly Life* (2004), a brilliant anthropological examination of the lives and careers of archeologists in China today. Published just as we complete our work, it is a completely contemporary book that takes us back to the beginnings.

# Japan
## General

Please also see the resources listed under "General" at the beginning of our "Suggestions," all of which pertain to Japan in addition to China. "The Bibliography of Japanese History to 1912" at http://www.oriental.cam.ac.uk/jbib/bibtitle.html covers a range of subjects. Less up to date but still valuable is John W. Dower and Timothy George, *Japanese History and Culture from Ancient to Modern Times: Seven Basic Bibliographies* (revised 2nd ed., 1995). Gary D. Allinson, *The Columbia Guide to Modern Japanese History* (1999), includes a resource guide. Helen Hardacre, *The Postwar Development of Japanese Studies in the United States* (1998), provides assessments, with bibliography, of the current state of American-Japanese studies on history, foreign relations, art, religion, literature, anthropology, political analysis, and law that prove excellent points of departure for further study. *The Cambridge History of Japan* is a major resource. Although outdated in varying degrees, the essays in these volumes offer reliable accounts of the field and provide bibliography for further study. However, inevitably there is some unevenness. The *Journal for Japanese Studies* is interdisciplinary and well edited, and *Monumenta Nipponica* includes articles on history, culture, and religion of consistently high quality. The *Kodansha Encyclopedia of Japan,* online or in its more extensive although less up-to-date print version, is a useful reference work. For a readable historical survey with edifying maps and extensive illustrations, see Martin Collcutt, Marius Jansen, and Isao Kumakura, *Cultural Atlas of Japan* (Facts on File, 1988).

Considering the explosion of knowledge, the age of monumental, all-inclusive syntheses seems past (and only teachers of survey courses and textbook writers are left to dare a general overview). It therefore seems unlikely that anyone soon will emulate George Sansom's *A History of Japan,* three vols. (1958–1963). Although out of date, it can still be read with profit and pleasure.

## General Works on Culture, Literature, the Arts, Thought, and Religion

On the visual arts, see Penelope Mason, *History of Japanese Art* (2005). A still-valuable survey is Robert Treat Paine and Alexander Soper, *The Art and Architecture of Japan* (1955). Other fine books on art include the volumes in the *Heibonsha Survey of Japanese Art* (1972–1975) and *The Japanese Arts Library* (1976–). For the visual arts, see "Studies of Japanese Art by Period" at http://www.asiasociety. org/arts/japan_guide/index.html. William Howard Coaldrake, *Architecture and Authority in Japan* (1996), is a readable and wide-ranging survey.

For an introduction to literature, see J. Thomas Rimer, *A Reader's Guide to Japanese Literature* (1988). Donald Keene, *The Pleasures of Japanese Literature* (1988), is itself a pleasure, as are his collections, *Anthology of Japanese Literature* (1955) and *Modern Japanese Literature* (1956). Other important anthologies include Helen Craig McCullough, *Classical Japanese Prose: An Anthology* (1990); Steven Carter, *Traditional Japanese Poetry: An Anthology* (1991), Haruo Shirane, *Early Modern Japanese Literature: An Anthology, 1600–1900* (2002), and Theodore W. Goossen, *The Oxford Book of Japanese Short Stories* (1997). For an extensive and readable literary history, see Donald Keene's four volumes: *Seeds in the Heart: Japanese Literature from Earliest Times to the Late Sixteenth Century* (1993), *World within Walls: Japanese Literature of the Pre-Modern Era 1600–1867* (1976), and *Dawn to the West: Japanese Literature of the Modern Era* (two vols., 1984). A large and up-to-date listing of translations of premodern works can be found at "Classical Japanese Texts and Translations," http://www. meijigakuin.ac.jp/~pmjs/trans/trans.html.

On drama, see Karen Brazell, *Traditional Japanese Theater: An Anthology of Plays* (1998), and Benito Ortolani, *The Japanese Theater: From Shamanistic Ritual to Contemporary Pluralism* (1990).

H. Byron Earhart, *Japanese Religion: Unity and Diversity* (1974), is an excellent introduction, and Joseph M. Kitagawa, *Religion in Japanese History* (1966), is more extensive. See also George Tanabe, *Religions of Japan in Practice* (1999), and John Breen and Mark Teeuwen, eds., *Shinto in History: Ways of the Kami* (2000). Hitomi Tonomura et al., *Women and Class in Japanese History* (1999), includes essays covering all periods of Japanese history. Roy Andrew Miller, *The Japanese Language* (1967), is still of great interest, although a more recent survey is provided by Masayoshi Shibatani, *The Languages of Japan* (1990). Finally, fascinating accounts of two important areas of cultural and intellectual history can be found in Masayoshi Sugimoto and David Swain, *Science and Culture in Traditional Japan* (1989), and Peter Kornicki, *The Book in Japan: A Cultural History from the Beginning to the Nineteenth Century* (1998).

# Beginnings and Foundations

The best introduction to prehistory can be found in Keiji Imamura, *Prehistoric Japan: New Perspectives on Insular East Asia* (1996). Richard Pearson, *Ancient Japan* (1992), is a lavishly illustrated and clearly written exhibition catalog. Junko Habu, *Ancient Jōmon* of Japan (2004), is demanding but up to date and informative, and Mark Hudson, *Ruins of Identity: Ethnogenesis in the Japanese Islands* (1999), is a clear survey of the onset of the Yayoi Period and subsequent developments. William Wayne Farris, *Sacred Texts and Buried Treasures: Issues in the Historical Archaeology of Ancient Japan* (1998), is thorough and accessible. For a ground-breaking account of the early state, see Joan Piggott, *The Emergence of Japanese Kingship* (1997). The eighth-century histories are available as Donald L. Philippi, *Kojiki* (1968), and William G. Aston, *Nihongi: Chronicles of Japan from the Earliest Times to A.D. 697* (1896, with multiple reprints). For translations of poems from these texts, the *Man'yōshū*, and other early sources, see Edwin Cranston, *A Waka Anthology, Vol. 1: The Gem-Glistening Cup* (1993).

# Aristocrats, Monks, and Samurai

Institutional history from the Heian Period to the mid-sixteenth century is well represented in *The Cambridge History of Japan, Vol. 3,* edited by Kozo Yamamura (1990). It can be supplemented by the numerous books written and edited by John W. Hall and Jeffrey P. Mass. On politics, also see G. Cameron Hurst, III, *Insei: Abdicated Sovereigns in the Politics of Early Heian Japan* (1976). William Wayne Farris, *Population, Disease and Land in Early Japan, 645–900* (1985), presents findings and ideas that merit the attention of all students of early Japan. Robert Borgen, *Sugawara no Michizane and the Early Heian Court* (1986), is important for both political and cultural history. A recent treatment of Late Heian and early medieval history is Mikael Adolphson, *The Gates of Power: Monks, Courtiers and Warriors in Premodern Japan* (2000).

For more on the religion of the Heian Period, see Paul Groner, *Saichō: The Establishment of the Japanese Tendai School* (1984); Ryūichi Abé, *The Weaving of Mantra: Kūkai and the Construction of Esoteric Buddhist Discourse* (1999); and Allan G. Grapard, *The Protocol of the Gods: A Study of the Kasuga Cult in Japanese History* (1992).

Heian literature is well represented in translation (see the "Classical Japanese Texts and Translations" website), and there is a growing literature on the *Tale of Genji* in English. A useful introduction to Japan's greatest novel is Richard Bowring, *Murasaki Shikibu: The Tale of Genji* (1988). Critical studies include Norma Field, *Splendor of Longing in the Tale of Genji* (1987), and Haruo Shirane, *Bridge of Dreams: A Poetics of the Tale of Genji* (1987). A delightful although outdated description of Heian elite lifestyles is Ivan Morris, *The World of the Shining*

*Prince: Court Life in Ancient Japan* (1964). In addition to the general anthologies cited previously, Joshua Mostow, *At the House of Gathered Leaves: Shorter Biographical and Autobiographical Narratives from Japanese Court Literature* (2004), provides a new perspective on Heian narrative. For an introduction to traditional poetry, see Koji Kawamoto, *The Poetics of Japanese Verse: Imagery, Structure, Meter* (2000).

An engaging survey of history from the Late Heian Period through the mid-sixteenth century is Pierre François Souyri, *The World Turned Upside Down: Medieval Japanese Society* (2001). The leading Western authority on Kamakura institutional history was Jeffrey P. Mass, who wrote and edited several books. Good places to start are *The Bakufu in Japanese History* (1985), edited with William B. Hauser and concerning later periods, and *Yoritomo and the Founding of the First Bakufu: The Origins of Dual Government in Japan* (1999). Also see Karl F. Friday, *Samurai, Warfare, and the State in Early Medieval Japan* (2004). Andrew Goble, *Kenmu: Go-Daigo's Revolution* (1997), is a superb study of the attempt at imperial restoration during the Kamakura–Ashikaga transition. Two books by H. Paul Varley are recommended for the political history of the fourteenth and fifteenth centuries: *Imperial Restoration in Medieval Japan* (1971) and *The Onin War* (1967).

Suzanne Gay, *The Moneylenders of Late Medieval Kyoto* (2001), shows how things actually worked. The history of Kyoto is further explored in Mary Elizabeth Berry, *The Culture of Civil War in Kyoto* (1994), already cited in our text. We also recommend Thomas Conlan, *State of War: The Violent Order of Fourteenth Century Japan* (2003).

William R. LaFleur, *The Karma of Words: Buddhism and the Literary Arts in Medieval Japan* (1983), includes an excellent description of Buddhism, literary analysis, and a provocative thesis. Daigan and Alicia Matsunaga, *Foundations of Japanese Buddhism* (two vols., 1976), provides a detailed account of Japanese Buddhism. James Dobbins, *Jodo Shinshu: Shin Buddhism in Medieval Japan* (1989), deals with a subject central to Kamakura religious history.

There is a vast literature on Zen. The standard work on its history remains Heinrich Doumoulin, *Zen Buddhism: A History: Japan,* 2nd ed. (1989). For an excellent philosophical study, see T. P. Kasulis, *Zen Action–Zen Person* (1981). On the monasteries and their role in society, see Martin Collcutt, *Five Mountains: The Rinzai Zen Monastic Institution in Medieval Japan* (1981). Recommended with enthusiasm is Jan Fontein and Money L. Hickman, *Zen Painting and Calligraphy* (1970), a catalog of an exhibition of both Chinese and Japanese works. For other works on the arts, see the appropriate volumes in *The Japanese Arts Library* (1976–) and *Heibonsha Survey of Japanese Art* (1972–1975) series. Paul Varley and Kumakura Isao, eds., *Tea in Japan: Essays on the History of Chanoyu* (1989), is recommended on this subject.

The heroes of an age reveal much about its values: See Helen Craig McCullough, trans., *Yoshitsune: A Fifteenth-Century Japanese Chronicle* (1971). Among McCullough's numerous contributions to our understanding of traditional Japanese literature is her translation of *The Tale of the Heike* (1988), which includes a description of this work as literature. Other aspects of the period's literature are apparent in Donald Keene's translation of the *Essays in Idleness* (1967), and Thomas B. Hare, *Zeami's Style: The Noh Plays of Zeami Motokiyo* (1986). *Japan in the Muromachi Age* (1977), John W. Hall and Toyoda Takeshi, eds., includes essays on cultural and social–political topics.

# Modern General

James L. McClain, *Japan: A Modern History* (2002), a masterful survey begins with the Tokugawa Period. The following recent surveys are also worthy of consideration: Andrew Gordon, *A Modern History of Japan from Tokugawa to the Present* (2003), and Elise K. Tipton, *Modern Japan: A Social and Political History* (2003). Also see *The Making of Modern Japan* (2000) by Marius Jansen, author of many thoughtful and well-researched books. Conrad Totman, *Early Modern Japan* (1993), is particularly strong on the history of the environment. Helen Hardacre, *The Postwar Development of Japanese Studies in the United States* (1998), mentioned previously, provides assessments with bibliography of the current state of American-Japanese studies on history, foreign relations, art, religion, literature, anthropology, political analysis, and law that prove excellent points of departure for further study.

Volumes 5 and 6 of the *Cambridge History of Japan,* edited by Marius Jansen and Peter Duus, respectively, deal with the nineteenth and twentieth centuries. Akira Iriye, *Japan and the Wider World: From the Mid-Nineteenth Century to the Present* (1997), is a survey by a senior authority. Andrew Gordon, ed., *Postwar Japan as History* (1993), contains essays on social, cultural, political, and economic history by the foremost contemporary scholars.

Tessa Morris-Suzuki, *A History of Japanese Economic Thought* (1989), provides a clear and balanced brief survey of its topic from the Tokugawa to the present. Also see the same author's *The Technological Transformation of Japan: From the Seventeenth to the Twenty-First Century* (1994). Similarly broad in scope are the essays of Thomas C. Smith collected under the title, *Japanese Industrialization, 1750–1920* (1988). For a more recent masterly and geographically informed study of the same period, see Karen Wigen, *The Making of a Japanese Periphery, 1750–1920* (1995).

A. J. H. Lathan and Heira Kawakatsu, *Japanese Industrialization and the Asian Economy* (1994), is an important, and in places somewhat technical, contribution to economic history. Albert Craig and Donald H. Shively, eds., *Personality in Japanese History* (1971), spans the last two centuries.

Donald Keene, *Dawn to the West: Japanese Literature of the Modern Era* (two vols., 1998–1999), is a comprehensive and authoritative account of modern Japanese literature from the Meiji Period until the present with an extensive bibliography. A fine book that approaches modern Japanese literature through its historical roots is J. Thomas Rimer, *Modern Japanese Fiction and its Traditions: An Introduction* (1978). On poetry, see Makoto Ueda, *Modern Japanese Poets and the Nature of Literature* (1983). William Howard Coaldrake, *Architecture and Authority in Japan* (1996), begins with the Ise Shrine and ends with contemporary Japan. Donald Richie, *A Hundred Years of Japanese Film* (2001), is highly recommended as the work of a distinguished, perceptive, and erudite critic.

# Tokugawa and Its Immediate Background

For the Tokugawa political system and its background, see Harold Bolitho, *Treasures among Men: The Fudai Daimyo in Tokugawa Japan* (1974). Many aspects of the Tokugawa system go back to Hideyoshi; see Mary Elizabeth Berry, *Hideyoshi* (1984). Hideyoshi also appears as a major player in George Elison, *Deus Destroyed: The Image of Christianity in Early Modern Japan* (1973). Another well-written, informative account is C. R. Boxer, *The Christian Century in Japan* (1951). Also see Michael Cooper, *They Came to Japan: An Anthology of European Reports on Japan, 1543–1640* (1965, 1974).

For foreign relations under the Tokugawa, see Ronald P. Toby, *State and Diplomacy in Early Modern Japan: Asia in the Development of the Tokugawa Bakufu* (1984). Tokugawa was the age of the samurai; see *The Taming of the Samurai: Honorific Individualism and the Making of Modern Japan* by Eiko Ikegame (1995). For insight into what it meant to be a woman in a late Tokugawa samurai family, see Edwin McClellan, *Woman in the Crested Kimono: The Life of Shibue Io and Her Family Drawn from Mori Ogai's "Shibue Chusai"* (1985), and *Women of the Mito Domain: Recollections of Samurai Family Life* by Yamakawa Kikue, Kate Wildman Nakai, trans. (2001). *Tokugawa Japan: The Social and Economic Antecedents of Modern Japan,* edited by Chie Nakane and Shinzaburō Ōishi and translated by Conrad Totman (1990), presents the views of Japanese scholars, including those of the influential Chie Nakane.

The variety of Tokugawa thought and of scholars' approach to it is illustrated by Herman Ooms, *Tokugawa Ideology: Early Constructs, 1570–1680* (1985), and Mary Evelyn Tucker, *Moral and Spiritual Cultivation in Japanese Neo-Confucianism: The Life and Thought of Kaibara Ekken (1630–1714)* (1989). For the intellectual history of the merchant class, see the important book by Tetsuo Najita, *Visions of Virtue in Tokugawa Japan: The Kaitokudo Merchant Academy of Osaka* (1987). Najita's *Readings in Tokugawa Thought* (1998) provides translations of twenty-four Japanese articles. James McMullen, *Idealism, Protest, and the Tale of Genji: The Confucianism of Kumazawa Banzan (1619–1691)* (1999), is highly recommended. A good place to begin studying nativism is Peter Nosco, *Remembering Paradise: Nativism and Nostalgia in Eighteenth-Century Japan* (1990). A delightful book on Dutch Learning is Donald Keene, *The Japanese Discovery of Europe, 1720–1830* (1969). Keene is also author of the masterful survey *World within Walls: Japanese Literature of the Pre-Modern Era, 1600–1867* (1976). Benito Ortolani, *The Japanese Theatre: From Shamanistic Ritual to Contemporary Pluralism,* revised ed. (1995), is a valuable resource. Ronald P. Dore, *Education in Tokugawa Japan* (1965), is a major study of a major topic.

The lively culture of the Tokugawa is depicted in several books. Howard Hibbett, *The Floating World in Japanese Fiction* (1959), remains a good place to begin, as does Richard Lane, *Images from The Floating World: The Japanese Print*

(1978). On Japan's master of haiku, see Haruo Shirane, *Traces of Dreams: Landscape, Culture, Memory, and the Poetry of Basho* (1997). For individual artists, see the volumes in the *Masterworks of Ukiyo-e* series published by Kodansha (1968–). Other worthy books on Tokugawa art include *Hokusai: One Hundred Views of Mt. Fuji,* introduction and commentaries by Henry D. Smith, II (1988), and the same author's *Ando Hiroshige 1797–1858: One Hundred Famous Views of Edo* (1999, 1981). Elise Grilli's superb *The Art of the Japanese Screen* (1970) is a beautiful book, a feast for mind and eye.

Local history has proved a particular fertile field of research with far-reaching implications. Notable recent studies include Philip C. Brown, *Central Authority and Local Autonomy in the Formation of Early Modern Japan: The Case of Kaga Domain* (1993); Herman Ooms, *Tokugawa Village Practice: Class, Status, Power, Law* (1996); and Luke S. Roberts, *Mercantilism in a Japanese Domain: The Merchant Origins of Economic Nationalism in 18th-Century Tosa* (1998). Two studies that include solid research on the Tokugawa Period, even as they take the story beyond the Meiji Restoration, are Karen Wigen, *The Making of a Japanese Periphery, 1750–1920* (1995), and David L. Howell, *Capitalism from Within: Economy, Society, and the State in a Japanese Fishery* (1995). The rewards of comparative urban studies are illustrated by *Edo and Paris: Urban Life and the State in the Early Modern Era,* edited by James L. McClain, John M. Merriman, and Kaoru Ugawa (1994). Also see Nishiyama Matsunosuke and Gerald Groemer, trans., *Edo Culture: Daily Life in Urban Japan, 1600–1868* (1997), and Susan B. Hanley, *Everyday Things in Premodern Japan: The Hidden Legacy of Material Culture* (1997).

The investigation of traditionally neglected topics continues to enliven the study of Tokugawa history. Although different in all but the solidity of their scholarship, the following three books are essential reading in major aspects of Tokugawa history: Ann B. Jannetta, *Epidemics and Mortality in Early Modern Japan* (1987); Gregory M. Pflugfelder, *The Cartography of Desire: Male–Male Sexuality in Japanese Discourse, 1600–1950* (1999); and Conrad Totman, *The Origins of Japan's Modern Forests* (1985), which analyzes and documents a case of successful reforestation and poses a basic question: "What level of human disaster must overtake a society before it is moved to confront its problems?" (p. 58).

# *Meiji*

Meiji was the formative period of modern capitalism. For underlying ideas and attitudes, see Byron K. Marshall, *Capitalism and Nationalism in Prewar Japan: The Ideology of the Business Elite, 1868–1941* (1967), and Earl Kinmonth, *The Self-Made Man in Meiji Japanese Thought* (1981). Mikiso Hane, *Peasants, Rebels, and Outcastes: The Underside of Modern Japan* (1982), calls attention to those who did not benefit from "modernization." See also E. Patricia Tsurumi, *Factory Girls: Women in the Thread Mills of Meiji Japan* (1990); Andrew Gordon, *The Evolution of Labor Relations in Japanese Heavy Industry, 1853–1955* (1985); the same author's *Labor and Imperial Democracy in Prewar Japan* (1991); and Sheldon Garon, *The*

*State and Labor in Modern Japan* (1987). On agriculture, see Penelope Francks, *Technology and Agriculture Development in Pre-War Japan* (1984) and *Agriculture and Economic Development in East Asia: From Growth to Protectionism in Japan, Korea, and Taiwan* (1999). Michael A. Barnhart, *Japan and the World since 1868* (1995), provides a concise account.

Donald Keene, *Emperor of Japan: Meiji and His World, 1885–1912* (2002), is a masterful account of the Meiji Emperor. For Meiji political history, the following are still useful: George Akita, *Foundations of Constitutional Government in Modern Japan* (1967); Nobutaka Ike, *The Beginnings of Political Democracy in Japan* (1950); and Joseph Pittau, *Political Thought in Early Meiji Japan, 1868–1889* (1967). A study of a major Meiji statesman is provided in Roger F. Hackett, *Yamagata Aritomo in the Rise of Modern Japan, 1838–1922* (1971). An important institutional development is examined in Robert M. Spaulding, Jr., *Imperial Japan's Higher Civil Service Examinations* (1967). Also see Mark E. Lincicome, *Principle, Praxis, and the Politics of Educational Reform in Meiji Japan* (1997).

A good way to begin studying Meiji intellectual history is by examining the life and ideas of Fukuzawa Yukichi. His *An Encouragement of Learning*, David A. Dilworth and Umeyo Hirano, trans. (1969), is a collection of essays written in the 1870s. Also worth reading is *The Autobiography of Fukuzawa Yukichi*, Eiichi Kiyooka, trans. (1934). Important secondary studies are Carmen Blacker, *The Japanese Enlightenment: A Study of the Writings of Fukuzawa Yukichi* (1964), and an article by Albert Craig in *Political Development in Modern Japan*, Robert E. Ward, ed. (1973, 1968). Also see James L. Huffmann, *Creating a Public: People and Press in Meiji Japan* (1998), and William R. Braisted, trans. and ed., *Meiroku Zasshi: Journal of the Japanese Enlightenment* (1976). Two other valuable books on intellectual history are Kenneth B. Pyle, *The New Generation in Meiji Japan: Problems of Cultural Identity, 1885–1895* (1969), and Irwin Scheiner, *Christian Converts and Social Protest in Meiji Japan* (1970). For intellectual and social history from a different perspective, see Sharon Sievers, *Flowers in Salt: The Beginnings of Feminism in Modern Japan* (1983). This might be read with Gail L. Bernstein, ed., *Recreating Japanese Women, 1600–1945* (1991).

For Meiji art, see Frederick Baekeland's *Imperial Japan: The Art of the Meiji Era, 1868–1912* (1980) and Julia Meech-Pekarik, *The World of the Meiji Print: Impressions of a New Civilization* (1986). For literature, see Donald Keene's *Dawn to the West: Japanese Literature of the Modern Era* (two vols., 1998–1999). A good selection of the period's foremost poet is contained in *Masaoka Shiki: Selected Poems,* Burton Watson, trans. (1998); Robert A. Rosenstone, *Mirror in the Shrine: American Encounters with Meiji Japan* (1988), is subtle and sensitive.

## Late Meiji and Imperial Japan

Late Meiji saw the beginnings of imperial Japan. Carol Gluck, *Japan's Modern Myths: Ideology in the Late Meiji Period* (1985), is a brilliant, nuanced study that considers a range of sources. *Japan's Competing Modernities: Issues in Culture and*

*Democracy,* Sharon A. Minichiello, ed. (1998), is a collection of essays on important issues.

L. W. G. Beasley, *Japanese Imperialism, 1894–1945* (1987), is a thoughtful synthesis. For a major recent study, see Louise Young, *Japan's Total Empire: Manchuria and the Culture of Wartime Imperialism* (1998). *The Japanese Empire, 1895–1945,* Ramon H. Myers and Mark R. Peattie, ed. (1984); *Japan's Informal Empire in China, 1895–1937,* Peter Duus, Myers, and Peattie, ed. (1989); and *The Japanese Wartime Empire,* Duus, Myers, Peattie, and Zhou Wanyao, ed. (1996), all published by Princeton University Press, are all recommended. Please also see the relevant readings listed under Korea.

Late Meiji politics are analyzed by Tetsuo Najita in *Hara Kei in the Politics of Compromise, 1905–1915* (1967). For the political system as it developed during the next decade, see Peter Duus, *Party Rivalry and Political Change in Taishō Japan* (1968). For the 1930s, see Gordon M. Berger, *Parties out of Power in Japan: 1931–1941* (1977), and Michael A. Barnhart, *Japan Prepares for Total War: The Search for Economic Security, 1919–1941* (1987).

The increasing reach of the state is the topic of Sheldon Garon, *Molding Japanese Minds: The State in Everyday Life* (1997). Also see Helen Hardacre, *Shinto and the State. 1868–1988* (1989). J. Thomas Rimer, ed., *Culture and Identity: Japanese Intellectuals during the Interwar Years* (1990), is wide ranging. Gail L. Bernstein, *Japanese Marxist: A Portrait of Kawakami Hajime (1879–1946)* (1976, 1990), is indispensable for the study of Japanese Marxism. Kevin Michael Doak, *Dreams of Difference: The Japan Romantic School and the Crisis of Modernity* (1994), is a closely argued study that excels in placing 1930s Japanese discourse in an international perspective. *Overcome by Modernity: History, Culture, and Community in Interwar Japan* by Harry D. Harootunian (2000) is brilliant and difficult. Also see Harootunian, *History's Disquiet: Modernity, Cultural Practice, and the Question of Everyday Life* (2000).

Most major writers are available in excellent translations too numerous to list here, and there is a growing corpus of secondary studies. See http://library.kcc.hawaii.edu/asdp/biblio/lit/easian/japan/jplitbib.htm. For Japan's own critics, we suggest two books by Paul Anderer, *Arishima Takeo and the Bounds of Modern Fiction* (1983) and *Literature of the Lost Home: Kobayashi Hideo—Literary Criticism, 1924–1939* (1995). Also see Karatani Kōjin, *Origins of Modern Japanese Literature,* Brett de Bary, trans. (1993), and Maeda Ai, *Text and the City: Essays on Japanese Modernity,* edited with an introduction by James A. Fujii (2004).

On a different facet of cultural history see J. Victor Koschmann, Keibo Oiwa, and Shinji Yamashita, *International Perspectives on Yanagita Kunio and Japanese Folklore Studies* (1985).

A great deal has been written about the Pacific War. Barbara J. Brooks, *Japan's Imperial Diplomacy: Consuls, Treaty Ports, and War in China 1895–1938* (2000), provides a fresh look at the Foreign Ministry officials involved in China policy. Edward J. Drea, *In the Service of the Emperor: Essays on the Imperial Japanese Army* (1998), is a good place to begin reading on the Japanese army. For the navy, see Paul S. Dull, *A Battle History of the Japanese Navy* (1978). Additional perspectives are provided by Akira Iriye, *Power and Culture: The Japanese–American War, 1941–1945* (1981), and John W. Dower, *War without Mercy: Race and Power in the Pacific War* (1986). Saburo Ienaga, *The Pacific War 1931–1945: A Critical Perspective on Japan's Role in World War II* (1978), is an unflinching account of the "dark valley."

The Pacific War began with Pearl Harbor and ended with the atomic bomb. Both events have been written about extensively and remain controversial. On Pearl Harbor, see Gordon Prange, *Pearl Harbor: The Verdict of History* (1985), and *Pearl Harbor Reexamined: Prologue to the Pacific War,* Hilary Conroy and Harry Wray, ed. (1990). The emperor's role before and during the war is examined in depth in *Hirohito and the Making of Modern Japan* by Herbert Bix (2000). For a bibliography on the atomic bomb, see http://www.doug-long.com/bibliog.htm. For a study of how the war is remembered in different places and by different peoples, see *Perilous Memories: The Asia–Pacific War,* T. Fujitani, Geoffrey M. White, and Lisa Yoneyama, eds. (2001).

# Postwar and Contemporary

The basic book on the occupation of Japan is John W. Dower, *Embracing Defeat: Japan in the Wake of World War II* (1999). Also see Dower's *Japan in War and Peace: Selected Essays* (1993).

Nathan Thayer, *How the Conservatives Rule Japan* (1969), is a cogent analysis of the system of local support organizations. Also see Gerald L. Curtis, *The Japanese Way of Politics* (1988). For a blow-by-blow analysis of the L.D.P.'s response to various challenges until the 1980s, see Kent E. Calder, *Crisis and Compensation: Public Policy and Political Stability in Japan, 1949–1986* (1988). One of the more interesting and informative analyses of Japanese politics remains Karel Van Wolferen, *The Enigma of Japanese Power* (1989).

The end of the Showa Period (1926–1989) with the death of the emperor drew new attention to his role during the war and stimulated some to look at the Showa Period as a whole. One happy result was the publication of *Showa: The Japan of Hirohito* edited by Carol Gluck and Stephen R. Graubard (1992). Norma Field, *In the Realm of the Dying Emperor: Japan at Century's End* (1991), is eloquent and vivid.

Theodore C. Bestor, *Neighborhood Tokyo* (1989), is a worthy sequel to Ronald P. Dore's fascinating and thoughtful *City Life in Japan: A Study of a Tokyo Ward* (1958). A book with implications beyond Japan is David Plath, *Long Engagements: Maturity in Modern Japan* (1980). Plath is also the editor of *Work and Life Course in Japan* (1983).

Studies of the changing role of women include Jane Hunter, ed., *Japanese Women Working* (1993); Mary C. Brinton, *Women and the Economic Miracle: Gender and Work in Postwar Japan* (1993); and Anne E. Imamura, *Re-Imagining Japanese Women* (1996). Also see Vera C. Mackle, *Fighting Women: A History of Feminism in Modern Japan* (1997).

A great deal has been written on the postwar Japanese economy. Ezra Vogel's influential *Japan as Number One: Lessons for America* (1985) exemplifies the views of its time. A valuable perspective is provided by Hugh T. Patrick in his *The Development of Studies of the Japanese Economy in the United States: A Personal Odyssey* (1988). His many other works are recommended, including *Crisis and Change in the Japanese Financial System* (2000). Gavan McCormack, *The Emptiness of Japanese Affluence* (1996), is a trenchant indictment of environmental abuse, political irresponsibility, and unmitigated developmentalism. See William J. Holstein, *The Japanese Power Game: What it Means for America* (1990), for a picture of the business–bureaucrats–politician nexus in the 1980s.

Shunsuke Tsurumi, *A Cultural History of Postwar Japan 1945–1980* (1987), is unsystematic but contains worthwhile information on popular culture. Also see Ross Mover and Yoshio Sugimoto, *Images of Japanese Society: A Study of the Structure of Social Reality* (1986), and John Whittier Treat, ed., *Contemporary Japan and Popular Culture* (1996). Peter N. Dale, *The Myth of Japanese Uniqueness* (1986), pulls no punches.

*A Hundred Years of Japanese Film* is by Donald Richie (2001), the foremost foreign critic and student of Japanese film. The serious student of films will also want to consult Beverly B. Bueher, *Japanese Films: A Filmography and Commentary, 1921–1990* (1990). Fortunately for those interested in fiction, the works of the writers described in the text are available in good translations, and the number of works available in English continues to increase. The Japanese enthusiasm for reading extends also to comic books; see Sharon Kinsella, *Adult Manga: Culture and Power in Contemporary Japanese Society* (1998). D. P. Martinez, *The Worlds of Japanese Popular Culture: Gender, Shifting Boundaries and Global Cultures* (1998), includes descriptions of sumo, soccer, and other sports; karaoke and soap operas; woman's magazines and morning television dramas.

Ian Reader, *Religion in Contemporary Japan* (1991), is based on intimate knowledge gained from fieldwork and from reading. The same holds for the book he coauthored with George J. Tanabe, *Practically Religious: World Benefits and the Common History of Japan* (1998). Another outstanding book on Japanese religion is Karen A. Smyers, *The Fox and the Jewel: Symbolizing Shared and Private Meaning in Japanese Inari Worship* (1998).

Botond Bogner, *The New Japanese Architecture* (1990), is a valuable study. Katsukiyo Matsuba, *Ando, Architect* (1998), examines a leading contemporary Japanese architect (and a Schirokauer favorite). The Japanese tradition of woodworking is evoked by the American master craftsman George Nakashima in his *The Soul of a Tree: A Woodworker's Reflections* (1988).

# Photo Credits

This page constitutes an extension of the copyright page. We have made every effort to trace the ownership of all copyrighted material and to secure permission from copyright holders. In the event of any question arising as to the use of any material, we will be pleased to make the necessary corrections in future printings. Thanks are due to the following authors, publishers, and agents for permission to use the material indicated.

**A.1:** © Lore Schirokauer **A.2:** © Irene Chou. Used by the permission of artist and Mandy Lee, IPreciation Gallery. (http://www.ipreciation.com) **PO.1:** © Bridgeman Art Library, London/New York/Zhang Shui Cheng **PO.2:** From *Return of the Buddha: The Qingzhou Discoveries,* by the Royal Academy of the Arts (London, 2002) **PO.3:** © Sakamoto Photo Research Laboratory/CORBIS **PO.3:** © Sir Percival David Foundation of Chinese Art, University of London. **PO.4:** © Lore Schirokauer **PO.5:** Schirokauer Collection

**Chapter 1. 1.01:** © National Museum of China **1.03:** © C.V. Starr East Asian Library, Columbia University **1.04:** Drawn by Dr. Léon L.Y. Chang **1.05:** © Berkeley, Society for the Study of Early China, 1997 **1.06:** © Cultural Relics Publishing House **1.07:** © C.V. Starr East Asian Library, Columbia University **1.08:** From Michael Loewe, Edward L. Shaughnessy, *The Cambridge History of Ancient China* (Cambridge University Press, 1999) **1.09:** © HIP/Art Resource, NY **1.10:** © Metropolitan Museum of Art, Munsey Fund (24.72.1–14). Altar Set © 1986 The Metropolitan Museum of Art **1.11:** From William Willets, *Chinese Art,* vol. 1 (Hamondworth, England, 1958) by permission Penguin Books Ltd. and courtesy of William Willets **1.12:** © Asian Art & Archaeology, Inc./CORBIS **1.13:** © Cultural Relics Publishing House

**Chapter 2. 2.02:** © Cultural Relics Publishing House **2.03:** From Xiaoneng Yang, *The Golden Age of Archaeology* (New Haven: Yale University Press, 1999) **2.04:** © National Museum of China **2.05:** © National Museum of China

**Chapter 3. 3.01:** © Bridgeman Art Library **3.03:** © Giraudon/Bridgeman Art Library **3.04:** © A.M.S. Foundation for the Arts, Sciences and Humanities. Photograph courtesy of the Arthur M. Sackler Gallery, Smithsonian Institution, Washington, D.C.: MLS1802. **3.05:** From Feng Yunpeng and Feng Yunyuan ca. 1821. *Jin shisuo.* Reprinted: Shanghai: Shangwu Press, 1934 3.18–19 **3.06:** © Cultural Relics Bureau of Sichuan **3.07:** © National Museum of China **3.08:** © Cultural Relics of Sichuan Province **3.09:** © National Museum of China **3.10:** © Cultural Relics Bureau of Sichuan Province

**Chapter 4. 4.02:** © Lore Schirokauer **4.03:** Photograph © 2005 Museum of Fine Arts, Boston **4.04:** Calligraphy by Dr. Léon L.Y. Chang **4.05:** © National Palace Museum, Taipei, Taiwan, Republic of China **4.06:** © The Trustees of The British Museum **4.07:** © Askaen

**Chapter 5. 5.02:** © University of Pennsylvania, Negative No. T4171 **5.03:** © Lore Schirokauer **5.04:** Courtesy of Karen Schlansky, www.rosecourtasianantiques.com **5.05:** © Schirokauer Collection **5.06:** Drawing by Jean-Paul Tramblay **5.07:** © Seattle Art Museum, Eugene Fuller Memorial Collection, 38.6. Photo by Paul Macapia **5.08:** © Freer Gallery of Art, Smithsonian Institution, Washington, D.C.: Gift of Charles Lang Freer, F1909.98 **5.09:** © National Palace Museum, Taiwan, Republic of China **5.10:** Adapted from Robert M. Somers, "The Collapse of the T'ang Order," Ph.D. dissertation, Yale University, 1975, pp. 204–205. Reprinted with permission of Robert M. Somers.

**Chapter 6. 6.02:** © The Cleveland Museum of Art, John L. Severance Fund, 1984.68 **6.03:** © Scala/Art Resource, NY **6.04:** © Tohoku University Archeology Laboratory stored **6.05:** © Tomb of Emperor Nintoku, Mozu, Sakai City Osaka **6.06:** © TNM Image Archives, http://TNMArchives.jp **6.08:** © Askaen **6.09:** © Chris Lisle/CORBIS **6.10:** © Chris Lisle/CORBIS **6.11:** © Lore Schirokauer **6.12:** © Askaen **6.13:** © Archivo Iconografico, S.A./CORBIS **6.14a:** From Robert Treat Paine & Alexander Soper, *The Art and Architecture of Japan: Pelican History of Art,* 2nd revised ed. (Penguin Books, 1974), p. 186. Reprinted with permission. **6.14b:** © Lore Schirokauer **6.15:** Schirokauer Collection

**Chapter 7. 7.01:** © Lore Schirokauer **7.02:** Calligraphy by Dr. Léon L.Y. Chang **7.03:** © Lore Schirokauer **7.04:** © Muroji Publishers **7.05:** © Sakamoto Photo Research Laboratory/CORBIS **7.06:** © "Red Fudo, Myooin, Koyasan, Wakayama **7.07:** © The Tokugawa Art Museum **7.08:** © Kozanji, Kyoto **7.09:** © Sakamoto Research Laboratory/CORBIS **7.10:** © Lore Schirokauer

**Chapter 8. 8.02:** Photograph © 2005 Museum of Fine Arts, Boston **8.03:** © Collection of the Palace Museum, Bejing, China **8.04:** © TNM Image Archives, http://TnmArchives.jp/ **8.05:** © National Palace Museum, Taiwan, Republic of China **8.06:** © National Palace Museum, Taiwan, Republic of China **8.07:** © National Palace Museum, Taiwan, Republic of China **8.08:** © National Palace Museum, Taiwan, Republic of China **8.09:** © Michael Sullivan & Domenique Dabois

**Chapter 9. 9.02:** © Abe Collection, Osaka Municipal Museum of Fine Arts **9.03:** © National Palace Museum, Taiwan, Republic of China **9.04:** © National Palace Museum, Taiwan, Republic of China **9.05:** © National Palace Museum, Taiwan, Republic of China

**694**

**Chapter 10. 10.02:** © The Asian Society, Mr. & Mrs. J.D. Rockefeller, 3rd Collection, photograph by Lynton Gardiner **10.03:** © Honolulu Academy of Arts, Gift of Mrs. Carter Galt, 1952 (1666.1) **10.04:** © Cleveland Museum of Art, 2003. Leonard C. Hanna, Jr., Bequest, 1980.10 **10.05:** © Asian Art Museum of San Francisco, Gift of the Avery Brundage Collection Symposium Fund and the M.H. de Young Memorial Museum Trust Fund, B69D17. Used by permission

**Chapter 11. 11.02:** © Rokuhara Mutsuji, Kyoto/M. Asanuma **11.03:** © Michael S. Yamashita/CORBIS **11.04:** Photo by Mark Schumacher, www.onmarkproductions.com **11.05:** © Royalty-Free/CORBIS **11.06a:** © Lore Schirokauer **11.06b:** © Lore Schirokauer **11.07a and b:** From Robert Treat Paine and Alexander Soper, *The Art and Architecture of Japan* (Pelican History of Art, 2nd rev. ed., 1974). Reprinted with permission of Penguin Books Ltd.

**Chapter 12. 12.01:** © *Six Persimmons,* by Muqi, Daitokuji, Kyoto **12.02:** © *Patriarchs of the Three Creeds,* by Josetsu, Ryosokuin, Kyoto **12.03:** © Tokyo National Museum **12.04:** © Lore Schirokauer **12.05:** © Lore Schirokauer **12.06:** © 1988 Kyoto National Museum

**Chapter 13. 13.02:** © Freer Gallery of Art, Smithsonian Institution, Washington, D.C.: Purchase, F1965.22 **13.03:** © Rijksmuseum voor Volkenkunde Leiden **13.04:** © Collection of the Palace Museum, Bejing, China **13.05:** Courtesy of the Peabody Essex Museum

**Chapter 14. 14.01:** © Lore Schirokauer **14.02:** © Sakamoto Photo Research Laboratory/CORBIS **14.03:** © Tokyo National Museum **14.04:** © Kyoto National Museum **14.05:** © Sakamoto Photo Research Laboratory/CORBIS **14.06:** © Allen Memorial Art Museum, Oberlin College, Ohio. Mary A. Ainsworth Bequest, 1950.202 **14.07:** © Fine Arts Museum of San Francisco, Achenbach Foundation for Graphic Arts Purchase (A057901 1970.25.14) **14.08:** Museum Purchase made possible by the Margaret Watson Parker Art Collection Fund 1968/2.22 **14.09:** © Mr. & Mrs. John D. Rockefeller, 3rd Collection of Asian Art 1979.219. Asia Society, New York: Photograph by Lynton Gardiner **14.10:** © Spencer Collection (SOR579: Hokusai), New York Public Library, Astor, Lennox, and Tilden Foundations.

**Chapter 15. 15.02:** © Honolulu Academy of Arts, Gift of Wilhelmina Tenney Memorial Collection, 1955 (2045.1) **15.03:** © Cleveland Museum of Art, John L. Severance Fund, 1953.247 **15.04:** © Asian Art Museum of San Francisco. Gift of the Tang Foundation presented by Nadine, Martin, and Leslie Tang to the Asian Art Museum in celebration of Jack C.C. Tang's sixtieth birthday, B87D8. Used by permission **15.05:** © Rijks Museum, Amsterdam, AK-RK-1991-10 **15.06:** © Lore Schirokauer.

**Chapter 16. 16.01:** © Time Life Pictures/Mansell/Time Life Pictures/Getty Images **16.02:** © Hulton-Deutsch Collection/CORBIS **16.03:** © Cixi, Empress Dowager of China, 1835–1908 Photographs. Freer Gallery of Art and Arthur M. Sackler Gallery Archives. Smithsonian Institution, Washington, D.C., Purchase. Photographer: Xunling, SC-GR 256 **16.04:** © Lore Schirokauer **16.05:** Reproduced from The Cause of the Riots in the Yangtse Valley: a 'Complete Picture Gallery', Hankow 1891. Courtesy Houghton Library, Harvard University

**Chapter 17. 17.02:** Courtesy of the Peabody Essex Museum **17.03:** Courtesy of the Peabody Essex Museum **17.04:** "The Ginza" Taisei Corporation

**Chapter 18. 18.01:** © Imperial Household, Tokyo, Japan **18.02:** © Arthur M. Sackler Gallery, Smithsonian Institution, Washington, D.C.: Robert O. Muller Collection, S2003.8.1179 **18.03:** © "Morning Toilet" by Kuroda Seiki

**Chapter 19. 19.01:** Courtesy Stanford University Press. **19.02:** Courtesy Far East Fine Arts, inc. San Francisco. (http://www.fareastfinearts.com) **19.03:** © Art Museum, Chinese University of Hong Kong, China **19.04:** © Kyoto National Museum

**Chapter 20. 20.01:** © Arthur M. Sackler Gallery of Art, Smithsonian Institution, Washington, DC: Gift of Gregory and Patricia Kruglak, S1999.131. **20.02:** © TNM Image Archives, http://TnmArchives.jp/ **20.03:** © Takakiyo Mitsui Collection **20.04:** © Kyoto Municipal Museum of Art **20.05:** Collection of The National Museum of Modern Art, Tokyo. © Togo Tamami. Used by permission

**Chapter 21. 21.02:** From Woodcuts of Wartime China, 1937–1945, Yonghua lingxin, ed. (Taiwan: Li Ming Cultural Enterprises, Dist.) **21.04:** © Revolutionary Workers Online **21.05:** © John Van Hasselt/CORBIS SYGMA

**Chapter 22. 22.01:** © Bettman/CORBIS **22.02:** From *Anvil of Victory: The Communist Revolution in Manchuria, 1945–1948,* by Steven Levine. Courtesy Columbia University Press **22.03:** © AP/Wide World Photos (APA5163982)

**Chapter 23. 23.01:** © National Art Gallery of China, Beijing. Used with permission **23.02:** Shanghai Institute of Chinese Painting. © Wu Hufan. Used by permission **23.03:** From Peasant Paintings from Huhsien County. Compiled by the Fine Arts Collection Section of the Cultural Groups Under the State Council of the People's Republic of China (Peking, 1974) **23.04:** From the Stefan R. Landsberger Collection (Chinese Propaganda Poster Pages, Online Exhibit, http://www.IISG.NL/~Landsberger) **23.05:** Collection Conrad Schirokauer. Photograph © Lore Schirokauer

**Chapter 24. 24.01:** © 1991 Xu Bing. Used by permission of the artist **24.02:** © Peter Turnley/CORBIS **24.03:** © Yen Kwok-Chung. Used by permission of the artist. **24.04:** © Lore Schirokauer **24.05:** © Liu Kuo-Sung. Used by permission of the artist

**Chapter 25. 25.01:** © Lore Schirokauer **25.02:** © "Tornado" from the series "In Praise of Shokei" by Munakata Shiko, Munakata Museum in Kamakura **25.03:** © Mita Arts Foundation **25.04:** © Arata Isozaki & Associates, Photo by Yasuhiro Ishimoto

# Text Credits

**Chapter 1. Figure 1.2, p. 5:** After Michael Loewe and Edward Shaughnessy, eds., *The Cambridge History of Ancient China: From the Origins of Civilization to 221 B.C.* (Cambridge: Cambridge University Press, 1999), p. 49. Reprinted with permission of Cambridge University Press. **14 lines of poetry, p. 16:** From Edward Shaughnessy, "Western Zhou History," in Michael Loewe and Edward Shaughnessy, eds., *Cambridge History of Ancient China: From the Origins of Civilization to 221 B.C.* (Cambridge: Cambridge University Press, 1999), pp. 309–310. Reprinted with permission of Edward Shaughnessy. **8 lines of poetry, pp. 20–21:** From *The Book of Songs,* translated by Arthur Waley (New York: Grove Press, 1996), pp. 88–89. Copyright © 1937 by Arthur Waley. Used by permission of Grove/Atlantic, Inc. **8 lines of poetry, p. 21:** From *The Book of Songs,* translated by Arthur Waley (New York: Grove Press, 1996), p. 140. Copyright © 1937 by Arthur Waley. Used by permission of Grove/Atlantic, Inc. **11 lines of poetry, p. 21:** From *The Book of Songs,* translated by Arthur Waley (New York: Grove Press, 1996), p. 271. Copyright © 1937 by Arthur Waley. Used by permission of Grove/Atlantic, Inc. **11 lines of poetry, pp. 21–22:** From *The Book of Songs,* translated by Arthur Waley (New York: Grove Press, 1996), p. 114. Copyright © 1937 by Arthur Waley. Used by permission of Grove/Atlantic, Inc. **9 lines of poetry, p. 22:** From *The Book of Songs,* translated by Arthur Waley (New York: Grove Press, 1996), p. 114. Copyright © 1937 by Arthur Waley. Used by permission of Grove/Atlantic, Inc. **3 lines of poetry, p. 22:** From James Legge, *The Chinese Classics, IV: The She King* (Hong Kong: Hong Kong University Press, 1960), p. 216. Reprinted with permission of Hong Kong University Press.

**Chapter 2. 8 lines of poetry, p. 29:** From *The Songs of the South: An Ancient Chinese Anthology of Poems by Qu Yuan and Other Poets,* translated by David Hawkes (Penguin Classics, 1985). Copyright © David Hawkes, 1985. Reproduced by permission of Penguin Books Ltd.

**Chapter 3. 18 lines of poetry, p. 53:** From Martin Kern, *The Stele Inscriptions of Ch'in Shih-huang: Text and Ritual in Early Chinese Imperial Representation* (New Haven, CT: American Oriental Society, 2000), p. 17. Reprinted by permission of the American Oriental Society. Translation slightly modified. **Table 3.1, p. 64:** From *Sources of Chinese Tradition,* Volume I, edited by Wm. Theodore de Bary, Wing-tsit Chan, and Burton Watson. Copyright © 1960 Columbia University Press. Reprinted with permission of the publisher. **46 lines of poetry, pp. 66–67:** From Burton Watson, *Chinese Rhyme-Prose* (New York: Columbia University Press, 1971), pp. 38–39. **21 lines of poetry, pp. 69–70:** From Miranda Brown, "Sons and Mothers in Warring States and Han China, 453 B.C.E.–220 C.E.," *Nan Nü* vol. 5, no. 2 (2003): 156. Reprinted with permission from Brill Academic Publishers.

**Chapter 4. 10 lines of poetry, p. 99:** From Liu Wu-chi, *An Introduction to Chinese Literature* (Bloomington: Indiana University Press, 1966) p. 64. Reprinted by permission of Indiana University Press. **2 lines of poetry, p. 99:** From Eric Sackheim, *The Silent Zero in Search of Sound: An Anthology of Chinese Poetry from the Beginning through the Sixth Century* (New York: Grossman Publishers, 1968) p. ii. Reprinted with permission.

**Chapter 5. 8 lines of poetry, p. 119:** From Burton Watson, *Chinese Lyricism: Shih Poetry from the Second to the Twelfth Century,* (New York: Columbia University Press, 1971), p. 175. **12 lines of poetry, p. 121:** From *Sources of Chinese Tradition,* Volume 1, 2nd ed., edited by Wm. Theodore de Bary and Irene Bloom. Copyright © 1999 Columbia University Press. Reprinted with permission of the publisher. **14 lines of poetry, pp. 125–126:** From Liu Wu-chi and Irving Yucheng Lo, eds., *Sunflower Splendor* (Garden City, NY: Anchor Press/ Doubleday, 1975), p. 109. Reprinted by permission of Indiana University Press. **2 lines of poetry, p. 126:** From A. R. Davis, *Tu Fu* (New York: Twayne Publishers, 1971), p. 46. Reprinted with permission of The Gale Group. **8 lines of poetry, p. 127:** From *Poems of the Late T'ang,* translated with an introduction by A. C. Graham (Penguin Classics, 1965). Copyright © A. C. Graham, 1965. Reproduced by permission of Penguin Books Ltd. **20 lines of poetry, pp. 128–129:** From Liu Wu-chi and Irving Yucheng Lo, eds., *Sunflower Splendor* (Garden City, NY: Anchor Press/Doubleday, 1975) pp. 206–207. Reprinted with permission of Eugene Eoyang. **10 lines of poetry, pp. 129–130:** From James J.Y. Liu, *The Poetry of Li Shang-yin—Ninth Century Baroque Chinese Poet* (Chicago: The University of Chicago Press, 1969), p. 78. Reprinted with permission of the University of Chicago Press. **4 lines of poetry, p. 132:** From Robert M. Somers, "The Collapse of the T'ang Order," Ph.D. dissertation, Yale University, 1975, p. 145. Reprinted with permission of Robert M. Somers.

**Chapter 6. 5 lines of poetry, p. 158:** From Edwin Cranston, *A Waka Anthology, Volume 1: The Gem-Glistening Cup.* Copyright © 1993 by the Board of Trustees of the Leland Stanford Jr. University. All rights reserved. Used with permission of Stanford University Press, www.sup.org. **19 lines of poetry, pp. 165–166:** From Edwin Cranston, *A Waka Anthology, Volume 1: The Gem-Glistening Cup.* Copyright © 1993 by the Board of Trustees of the Leland Stanford Jr. University. All rights reserved. Used with permission of Stanford University Press, www.sup.org. **17 lines of poetry, p. 166:** From Edwin Cranston, *A Waka Anthology, Volume 1: The Gem-Glistening Cup.* Copyright © 1993 by the Board of Trustees of the Leland Stanford Jr. University. All rights reserved. Used with permission of Stanford University Press, www.sup.org. **Figure 6.14(a), p. 169:** From Robert Treat Paine and Alexander Soper, *The Art and Architecture of Japan: Pelican History of Art,* 2nd revised ed. (Penguin Books, 1974), p. 186. Reprinted by permission.

**Chapter 7. 4 lines of poetry, p. 176:** From Burton Watson, trans., *Japanese Literature in Chinese,* Volume I (New York: Columbia University Press, 1975), p. 122. **Figure 7.2, p. 186:** From G. B. Sansom, *Japan: A Short Cultural History.* Copyright © 1931, 1943, 1952 by the Board of Trustees of the Leland Stanford Jr. University. All rights reserved. Used with permission of Stanford University Press, www.sup.org. Calligraphy by Dr. Léon L.Y. Chang. **5 lines of poetry, p. 189:** From Steven Carter, *Traditional Japanese Poetry: An Anthology.* Copyright © 1991 by the Board of Trustees of the Leland Stanford Jr. University. All rights reserved. Used with permission of Stanford University Press, www.sup.org. **5 lines of poetry, p. 189:** From Helen McCullough, *Kokin Wakashu: The First Imperial Anthology of Japanese Poetry.* Copyright © 1985 by the Board of Trustees of the Leland Stanford Jr. University. All rights reserved. Used with permission of Stanford University Press, www.sup.org. **6 lines of poetry, pp. 189–190:** From Helen McCullough, *Classical Japanese Prose: An Anthology.* Copyright © 1990 by the Board of Trustees of the Leland Stanford Jr. University. All rights reserved. Used with permission of Stanford University Press, www.sup.org.

# Index